Readings in
Macroeconomics

ECONOMIC SERIES
Under the Editorship of
Clark W. Reynolds
Stanford University

Readings in Microeconomics, second edition
edited by William Breit, *University of Virginia*
and Harold M. Hochman, *The Urban Institute, Washington, D.C.*

Readings in Labor Market Analysis
edited by John F. Burton, Jr., Lee K. Benham, William M. Vaughn, III,
and Robert J. Flanagan, *All of the University of Chicago*

Modern Political Arithmetic
Bruce F. Davie and Bruce F. Duncombe
Georgetown University

Readings in Macroeconomics, second edition
edited by M. G. Mueller
University of Glasgow

Economic Analysis and Industrial Structure
Douglas Needham
State University of New York, Brockport

Readings in the Economics of Industrial Organization
edited by Douglas Needham
State University of New York, Brockport

Readings in the History of Economic Theory
edited by Ingrid H. Rima
Temple University

Readings in Macroeconomics

Second Edition

Edited by
M. G. Mueller, Ph.D.
University of Glasgow

HOLT, RINEHART AND WINSTON

London   New York   Sydney   Toronto

A/330.1

Preface to the First Edition

Macroeconomics has become an integral part of basic economics, and the recent mushrooming of textbooks in this particular field attests to its growing importance in university curricula. While a number of useful readings are available, each concentrating on some specialized topic—such as money and banking, fiscal policy, business cycles, income distribution, and economic growth—none of the existing volumes is directed primarily towards supplementing the material that is currently covered in the intermediate and more advanced college courses in macroeconomics. The purpose of this collection is to fill this void and to make available in one volume diverse and significant contributions that can conveniently be used with any of the standard macroeconomics texts. To this end, a judicious balance has been sought between theory, empirical verification, and policy considerations.

Papers were selected for inclusion in this volume because their interpretative skill, seminal ideas, or empirical contributions greatly enhance understanding and stimulate interest. They have been arranged by topics, as shown in the Table of Contents, but each makes its own contribution and, as such, can be read in any sequence. Their relevance is discussed in the Introduction. Professor Hagen's paper on "The Classical Theory of the Level of Output and Employment" (Selection 1) appears in print for the first time; all the other selections have previously been published, originally in the professional journals or in collections of essays; subsequently, many of them have been reproduced wholly or in part in a variety of publications. They are reprinted here, as originally published, with only minor editorial corrections and amplifications, except for Dr. White's "Interest Inelasticity of Investment Demand—The Case from Business Attitude Surveys Reexamined" (*American Economic Review*, 1956), which the author has revised and brought up-to-date with this reprinting, and Professor Patinkin's "Price Flexibility and Full Employment" (*American Economic Review*, 1948), which is reproduced in its revised version, as published in the American Economic Association's *Readings in Monetary Theory* (1951).

In the preparation of this book, I received help from numerous people. I am especially indebted to Professor Lawrence S. Ritter for his detailed comments on a preliminary list of selections, which in a substantial measure influenced the final outcome. Many other colleagues were consulted and generously gave their advice, including Professors W. R. Allen, K. Brunner, B. O. Campbell, M. DePrano, W. L. Hansen, H. Kisch, J. LaPittus, A. P. Lerner, T. Mayer, J. P. McKenna, H. L. Miller, H. M. Somers, and W. P. Strassmann. In addition, I am of course most grateful to the various authors and publishers who so readily permitted their material to be reprinted in this collection. Specific acknowledgment and complete identification of source are to be found at the beginning of each selection; in those cases where the author's present institutional location is different from that at the time when his publication first appeared in print, his former affiliation is also indicated.

Tot homines, quot sententiæ.

M. G. Mueller

LOS ANGELES, CALIFORNIA
MAY 1965

Preface to the Second Edition

The warm reception which the first edition of this book received in many quarters has encouraged me to reissue all the papers in that volume, together with a new section on "Income Stabilization and Forecasting" (Part VIII). Following my previous procedure, the added papers are reprinted in their entirety, except for Professor Hagen's "The Role of Economic Forecasting in Income Stabilization" (from *Income Stabilization for a Developing Democracy* (1953)), which has been revised and updated to make it more relevant to our problems today.

I have taken this opportunity to correct some printing and other errors in the first edition, to bring up-to-date the present institutional affiliation of the authors, and to add three postscripts—*viz.*, a bibliographical note by Professor Friedman on recent developments in the monetary field (Selection 11), a reaffirmation of the stagnation thesis by Professor Hansen (Selection 19), and a comment by Professor Meade on the current situation concerning the international monetary mechanism (Selection 28).

My thanks go to the authors and publishers for their additional cooperation which has made this expanded volume possible.

M.G.M.

GLASGOW, SCOTLAND
JULY 1970

Introduction

The study of macroeconomics received great impetus from the publication of John Maynard Keynes's *The General Theory of Employment, Interest and Money* in 1936. Though the book was primarily concerned with the short-run static analysis of the determination of the level of employment in a closed industrialized society of the Western world, the tools that it fashioned and the many *obiter dicta* scattered throughout its pages had a catalytic effect upon a wide range of topics. Various "Keynesian" theories, though in many cases not found in the *General Theory*, have developed out of it. The problems with which macroeconomics is concerned, such as aggregate output, employment, and the general level of prices were not newly discovered in 1936, and yet few would deny that the foundations of current macroeconomics are deeply rooted in the *General Theory*. That the content of macroeconomics today goes far beyond that seminal book accords with Keynes's earlier stated belief, expressed in his celebrated Introduction to the Cambridge Economic Handbooks series, that "The Theory of Economics does not furnish a body of settled conclusions immediately applicable to policy. It is a method rather than a doctrine, an apparatus of the mind, a technique of thinking, which helps its possessor to draw correct conclusions." Few books in any discipline, and perhaps only Adam Smith's *Wealth of Nations* in economics, have had such a profound influence upon thought and policy as the *General Theory* has had over the past three decades.

The thirty-two papers collected in this volume seek neither to verify nor to disprove the wisdom of either the *General Theory* or Keynes's other writings. Though individual papers may do that, this book as a whole is concerned with furthering our understanding of macroeconomics—be it a part of, or apart from, the insights of the late Lord Keynes.

Part I, "Determinants of the Level of Aggregate Income," contains four papers, of which the first two are introductory and the other two are summaries of more advanced work. Hagen's analysis of the classical macroeconomic theory, based upon the writings of Ricardo, Mill, and Marshall, points out some of the more serious inadequacies of that theory in explaining the depression conditions of the 1930s. Hansen's reassessment of Keynes's *General Theory*, written eleven years after the publication of that book, provides a penetrating introduction to that work. Going beyond the confines of the *General Theory*, Samuelson's algebraic treatment and Smith's geometrical presentation incorporate more recent contributions to the aggregate theory of income determination.

The three papers on "Consumption," Part II, are largely empirical in nature. Lubell's statistical inquiry into the quantitative effects of a redistribution of income on consumption expenditures suggests, contrary to prevalent intuition, that they would probably be quite small. Duesenberry's essay, subsequently slightly revised in his *Income, Saving, and the Theory of Consumer Behavior* (1949), attempts to explain and reconcile the cyclical and secular movements of saving. The shift from income flows to capital and stock concepts is reflected in the new theories of consumer behavior that were developed in the 1950s by Friedman, Modigliani, and Brumberg, and are dealt with in the paper by Farrell.

Part III, "Investment," includes two papers. Questioning the skepticism about the effectiveness of interest rate changes on the volume of investment, White examines the shortcomings of various surveys upon which this pessimism is based. Knox's review article on the acceleration principle is a useful starting point for the study of business cycles and economic growth.

The five papers in Part IV, "Money, Interest, and Income," cover a wide range of great current interest. Hicks's interpretation of the classical and Keynesian models has become a standard reference, popularized by Hansen's *Monetary Theory and Fiscal Policy* (1949) in terms of the IS-LM curves. The modern quantity theory of money, as restated by Friedman, is primarily a theory of the demand for money and not, as in the classical version, a theory of the level of prices; no longer is money merely a "veil" without any permanent influence on the real sector. A critical review of the reformulated quantity theory of money is presented in Ritter's broad examination of the significance of money in Keynesian economics. Tobin's liquidity preference paper represents a major theoretical advance by introducing risk-avoiding behavior, and hence portfolio diversification, into his analysis. Liquidity functions are empirically derived for the American economy by Bronfenbrenner and Mayer who find no evidence of any "liquidity trap."

Part V, "Wage Rates, the Price Level, and Employment," consists of three articles. The pre-Keynesian and Keynesian analyses of the effects of a change in money wage rates on the aggregate level of employment are examined by Tobin. Patinkin's article concerns itself largely with the "Pigou effect," more generally referred to nowadays as the "real-balance effect," which denies the theoretical possibility of underemployment equilibrium in the classical model, with flexible wage and price levels, though as a policy matter it is not suggested that wage rate reductions would be a practical method, via their effect on the real value of cash balances, for achieving full employment (Pigou himself, in his Preface to *Lapses from Full Employment* (1945), explicitly stated that "Professor Dennis Robertson, who has very kindly read my proofs, has warned me that the form of the book may suggest that I am in favour of attacking the problem of unemployment by manipulating wages rather than by manipulating demand. I wish, therefore, to say clearly that this is not so."). Phillips' study explores the statistical evidence pertaining to unemployment and the rate of change of money wage rates in the United Kingdom during the period 1861–1957. The negative relation revealed in his diagrams was the basis of what has become known as the "Phillips curve," which has figured so prominently in recent discussions on the possible conflict between full employment and price stability.

The six papers in Part VI, "Fluctuations and Growth," represent contributions in a rapidly expanding area of macroeconomics. Samuelson's paper on the interactions between the multiplier and accelerator has become basic reading in dynamic analysis, especially in cycle theories. The stagnation thesis, as formulated by Hansen, envisages the possibility of a deflationary gap over the long run. Less visionary, Domar concerns himself with stipulating more rigorously the conditions that are required to maintain full employment in a growing economy, given the deflationary consequences of productive investment. Harrod, whose pioneering work in growth economics predates that of Domar, elaborates on his own contribution and on Domar's close affinity to it. Kaldor and Mirrlees' paper advances the latest revised version of a growth model, put forward originally by Kaldor, in which the "technical progress function" plays a crucial part. Solow's courageous attempt to estimate, by means of an aggregate production function, the relative shares attributable to capital and technical change in furthering economic progress reveals a surprisingly low figure for capital—probably much too low, since no allowance is made for the important fact that technical change often needs to be embodied in new capital equipment in order to become effective.

Five papers are included on "Policy Issues," Part VII. Friedman's proposal against discretionary action and Lerner's functional finance are two opposing and strong views on matters of domestic policy. The inadequacies of functional finance in preventing a cost-induced inflation is taken up in Lerner's second paper where the phenomenon of sellers' inflation and the author's solution for it are set forth. Inflation is further, and more generally, analyzed by Samuelson and Solow who apply the "Phillips curve" technique to American data. Meade's article on international monetary questions deals with issues that have continued to be of great concern to policy makers, addressing itself to the twin problems of adjustment and liquidity on international account. Although the recent introduction of the Special Drawing Rights facility within the International Monetary Fund has tackled the liquidity problem, the more crucial task of providing an orderly framework for exchange rate adjustments has yet to be accomplished.

The added section on "Income Stabilization and Forecasting," Part VIII, includes four contributions. Okun's study seeks to measure the gap between actual and potential output in America and finds that a change in the unemployment rate, within a certain range, produces about a threefold inverse change in the rate of real output. This approximate relation between unemployment and the resulting loss in output, sometimes called "Okun's Law," has had a profound influence on domestic policy considerations. But how to reach and maintain the economy's potential is another, and more disputed, matter. Here, Chow gives some statistical content to the IS-LM curves in order to determine empirically for the American economy the predictive power of different variables on economic activity. His

conclusion about the importance of the multiplier and accelerator in income determination is only one of several conflicting findings underlying the current debate
on the relative effectiveness of monetary and fiscal policy. Some of the inherent
difficulties of both monetary and fiscal policy in achieving economic stability are
discussed in Phillips' paper, and Hagen assesses more specifically the role and
limitations of short-term forecasting as a guide to policy action.

Contents

Part III   Investment

Part IV   Money, Interest, and Income

Part V   Wage Rates, the Price Level, and Employment

Part VI   Fluctuations and Growth

Part VII   Policy Issues

Part VIII   Income Stabilization and Forecasting

Part I

DETERMINANTS
OF THE LEVEL
OF AGGREGATE
INCOME

1

The Classical Theory of the Level of Output and Employment

EVERETT E. HAGEN

During the century and a half following the publication of Adam Smith's *Wealth of Nations* (1776), a body of economic theory was developed step by step which has become known as the classical theory. Its main architects were David Ricardo, John Stuart Mill, and Alfred Marshall.[1] It did not concern itself primarily with the problem of employment. In the main, it took full employment for granted, and discussed the forces which determine what goods would be produced, what the relative value of different types of goods and of different types of resources would be, and how the income from production would be distributed among the productive factors.

The classical economists took full employment (without inflation) for granted because they accepted an underlying theory of employment. This classical

✳ ✳

This is a slightly revised version of Chapter 4 in Everett E. Hagen, *Six Chapters on the Theory of Output, Income, and the Price Level* (mimeographed, 1949). Published by permission of the author.

Everett E. Hagen teaches at the Massachusetts Institute of Technology; he was formerly at the University of Illinois.

[1] A. C. Pigou modified somewhat the superstructure of the system.

theory of employment leads to the conclusion that forces operate in the economic system which tend to maintain full employment, and hence tend to maintain output at the level which can be produced under conditions of full employment.

Full employment of course does not imply that there are no unemployed. Even at "full employment" there will be frictional or transitional unemployment—temporary unemployment between jobs or on entry into the labor force while searching for a job, unemployment due to lack of knowledge of available job opportunities, etc. Involuntary unemployment above this level, the classical theory of employment concludes, can occur only as a result of unusual disturbances. The term "involuntary unemployment" may be used, without rigorous definition, in the common sense meaning of a state of being unemployed in spite of willingness to work at the going wage rate.

If involuntary unemployment occurs, the theory states, natural economic forces will tend to eliminate it and to restore full employment. Depressions can therefore be expected to be only infrequent, and when they occur, short lived.

This conclusion may puzzle a reader who knows of the severe and prolonged depressions of the 1930's, the 1880's, the 1870's, and other periods. Nevertheless, this conclusion of the classical school of economists rested upon careful reasoning and deserves serious study.

A. SAY'S LAW OF MARKETS

The central pillar of the classical theory of employment is commonly known as "Say's law," because it was first clearly and definitely stated by the early nineteenth century French economist Jean B. Say. Persons not versed in classical economic theory had asserted in Say's day, just as they assert in our day, that depressions are caused by "general overproduction," the production of more goods than people can afford to buy. Say said that this is impossible, because when any unit of goods is produced, that act increases the supply of goods and the demand for goods by equal amounts, so that aggregate demand always equals aggregate supply.

**Say's Law of Markets
in a Barter Economy**

In expounding this principle, Say "tore aside the monetary veil," to "get at the realities behind it," in the belief that this would permit a sounder analysis of economic truths. That is, he analyzed the economic system as it would operate if there were no money and all exchange of goods was by barter. Like almost all of the classical economists, he believed that money facilitates exchange and thus increases the efficiency of production but causes no essential change in the operation of the economic system.

It is easy to see that in a barter economy, Say's law of markets is correct. When a seller offers an item for barter, he increases the supply of goods, but since he is seeking other goods in exchange for his, he increases the demand for other goods correspond-ingly. Aggregate supply is always not only equal to, but identical with, aggregate demand. If there is an "oversupply" of one type of goods, this means that the supplier of that good cannot find suppliers of other goods who are willing to offer him enough of their goods in exchange for his to justify his continuing to produce so much. From his point of view, there is a scarcity of other goods. These are not available in sufficient quantity to meet the demand. The lack of demand for the good he is producing may cause him to curtail production of that good, but it cannot cause involuntary unemployment (except transitionally), for the same situation which motivates him to curtail production of the good which is in relative oversupply will motivate him (or his employees) to shift to production of the goods whose supply is inadequate to meet the demand for them.

If there is increased production of all goods, all suppliers will have more to offer. This however constitutes an increase in aggregate demand as well as in aggregate supply. Human wants being insatiable, persons with goods to offer will gladly accept in exchange more of some other things. Their increased demand will probably not be for additional quantities of the types of goods they have obtained previously, in the same proportions, but if not, it will be for these goods in different proportions or for different types of goods to whose production the added demand will cause a shift of productive efforts. Thus, an increase in total output can never cause general unemployment, but at worst only transitional or frictional unemployment.

**Say's Law in a Money Economy: (a) The
Equality between the Aggregate Cost of
Production and Aggregate Money Income**

Whether Say's law holds true in an economic system in which exchanges are typically made by the use of money is a more complex question. Only the most recent of the classical school of economists have specifically discussed this question, since the earlier members of the school, who were firmly convinced of the general principle that the use of money does not alter the principles of economic analysis, made no special analysis of a money economy.

The validity of Say's law in a money economy depends upon the correctness of two principles. The first is that the production of goods and services creates, in the aggregate, an amount of money income equal to the cost of production of the goods and services produced. The second is that aggregate spending will be equal to aggregate income. The term spending is used here to include investment as well as spending by consumers and government. These two principles will be considered in turn.

The cost of production of any given volume of output, as the term is used by economists, includes all costs which must be covered if producers, in competitive conditions, are to be motivated to continue production of that volume of output. The term includes, therefore, not only costs in the sense in which the accountant uses that term, but also a certain amount of profits, in the accounting sense—a sufficient rate of profits so that, in the absence of monopoly, producers just find it worth while to continue production at the given rate. The economist includes this rate of profits in costs, and says that there are no "pure profits" unless profits, as the accountant measures them, exceed that rate.

Most types of income are paid out in the process of production. Profits, however, are not paid out "in the process of production"; rather, they are realized only at the time the productive process is brought to an end by the sale of the products. Therefore, it has been argued that the income created in the process of production falls short of the cost of production by the margin of necessary profits.

This argument contains a small grain of truth, as will be seen. However, if we consider the process of production-and-sale, in a going economy, we realize that profits are continually being realized, and either paid out as dividends or held within business enterprises. These profits which are continually being realized are income to the economic unit receiving them. If we consider the profits being realized during any given time period, plus the incomes of other sorts being created in the process of production, we realize that a constant flow of income is being created which is in excess of the accounting cost of production of the current output, since it includes in addition a flow of profits. Suppose that production is going on at a level rate (that is, is neither rising nor declining), with "satisfactory" profits; that is, profits sufficient to cover the cost of production of the goods which have just been sold. It follows that these profits, plus other incomes from current production, together constitute aggregate income large enough, if all respent, to cover the cost of production of the goods which are about to appear on the market in the immediate future. The profits from the sales in the immediate future, plus other current incomes from production, will in turn be enough to cover cost of production in the next period, and so on.

If this reasoning is not entirely clear, it may be made clearer by visualizing production as going forward in overlapping "layers." While one layer of goods, whose production is complete, is being sold, another layer of goods is approaching completion, production of another layer is more than half complete, production of another layer is in mid-process, production of another layer has recently been started, and so on. The income produced during the current time period includes profits from the sale of the layer of goods whose production is complete, and also incomes from the continuing production of each of the other layers. So long as production is continuing at a constant rate, if the layer whose production is just complete is sold at a satisfactory profit, then the total income from production (part contributed by the continuing production of each of the layers) is just equal to the cost of production of the layer which is just appearing on the market.

Thus, once the economic system is operating in such an equilibrium, incomes are being created equal to the full cost of production. The first of the two principles on which Say's law depends is true in a money economy, under these circumstances.

Suppose, however, that output rises, because of a growing labor force, or an increase in productivity. As the added output appears on the market, will current income be equal to its aggregate cost of production (assuming no change in the price level)?

Before this question is discussed, it is necessary to draw a distinction between income actually paid out and income accrued. Income accrues to a wage-earner (for example) from day to day as production goes forward. It is paid to him periodically—say every two weeks. Even if accrued income during the process of production is equal to the cost of production, it is possible that income actually received by the factors to whom it is due may not be. At this point, consider whether, when output increases, the income which accrues during the process of production is equal to the cost of production.

Assume that there is being produced an additional increment of output whose cost of production, including profit margin, is $10,000. That is, this output must yield revenues of $10,000 when sold if the increased level of production is to be continued. Suppose that the product has passed through several intermediate stages, and is in the hands of the business firm

which does the last stage of processing and puts the final product on the market; and that the costs up to this point total $9,500. These costs, of course, include the profit margins of firms which produced the intermediate products which enter into the final product. The sum of the gross values added up to this point total $9,500, and it is clear that incomes equal to this amount have accrued.

At this point, however, the grain of truth in the argument that production does not create income equal to the cost of production becomes evident. If the accounts of the business firm which does the last stage of processing and puts the final product on the market are kept in the usual manner, profit will not accrue in advance of sale, for a firm cannot accrue profits on its books in advance of the sale which may yield those profits. Therefore, at the time of sale, the income which has accrued is less than the cost of production by the amount of this final profit margin. Since income actually paid to factors will lag behind income accrued, it may be below the cost of production by some additional margin. Thus, it is correct that at a time of increasing output, neither income actually received by factors, nor income accrued in the process of production, will be equal to the cost of production of the output.[2]

However, it would be erroneous to regard this failure of income to equal cost of production under certain circumstances as necessarily leading to deficiency of demand. An example may make clear that demand need not be deficient. Suppose that during the period in which the goods in the example above are placed on the market, investment totalling $500, financed by an expansion of bank credit,

[2] It is also true that if the cost of production of the existing volume of output rises, without prior increase in demand, income actually received by factors may lag below the cost of production during the transitional period of rising costs.

has been made. The income from the production of the $500 worth of capital goods will be received by someone, and this income will equal the difference between cost of production and income accrued from production of the $10,000 of goods referred to previously. A small amount of added investment could also make up the difference between income accrued and income actually received by factors. Thus, circumstances can easily be thought of in which the failure of income to equal cost of production when output or cost of production is rising will be counterbalanced by the creation of income from other sources.

Nevertheless, this analysis shows that under conditions of rising output, the first principle which is necessary to the validity of Say's law does not hold good. This should be regarded as a minor rather than a major deficiency in Say's law.[3]

Whether Say's law holds true, except for this qualification, remains to be discussed. For if Say's law is to be valid except for this qualification, it must be shown that the second principle involved is sound; namely, that demand will equal total income.

Say's Law in a Money Economy: (b) Will Demand Equal Total Income?

The classical economists' thesis that production creates income sufficient to purchase all the output at prices high enough to cover both the accounting costs and a profit margin has been seen to be correct, with certain qualifications in the case of an economy with expanding value of output. The fact that this is true is

[3] Two American economists, William T. Foster and Waddill Catchings, have written extensively about the failure, as they saw it, of productive activity to create income sufficient to cover profit margins under certain circumstances. They call this phenomenon "the flaw in our price system" and regard it as the basic cause of unemployment. While their writings are involved, and sometimes confused, the germ of truth in their analysis is the phenomenon referred to above.

not, however, sufficient to prove that Say's law is true in a money economy, even at a constant level of output. For Say's law states that aggregate *demand* is always equal to the value of aggregate output. All that has been shown above is that aggregate *income* is equal to the value of aggregate output. If total demand (by consumers, government, and for planned or intended investment) is less than total current income, then aggregate demand will be less than aggregate income; and aggregate demand will therefore be less than the value of total output. Some output will be left on the hands of producers who had produced it for sale; there will be either an unintended increase in inventories or sales at a loss.

At this point the reader must be careful to avoid confusion in terminology. Total spending is always equal to the value of total output, in one sense, since if someone had not paid or contracted to pay to have the output produced, it would not have been produced. But if a business enterprise produces goods for sale and then has them on its hands because there are no buyers at a price equal to the cost of production, *demand* for its goods cannot be said to be equal to the cost of production. The enterpriser who invests in inventories because he cannot get rid of them at profitable prices is, so to speak, an unintentional buyer. Aggregate *demand* in the economic system is equal to the cost of production (including profits) of output, only if aggregate spending by *intentional* buyers is equal to the cost of production. That is, personal consumption expenditures plus government purchases of goods and services plus *planned* investment must equal the aggregate cost of production of output. To show that this will be true at any level of output, it is necessary to show that savings will equal *planned* investment at any level of output.

This equality between demand and the cost of production of course does not mean that every individual producer will receive the cost of production of his total output, but only that producers in the aggregate will do so. Some producers may be facing inadequate demand, so that they are curtailing output, while others are facing more than sufficient demand and are induced to expand.

The belief that aggregate demand will equal aggregate income, *i.e.*, that all saving will find investment outlets, no matter how great the volume of output and income, was held almost universally by economists from the time when classical economic theory was first expounded in full form by John Stuart Mill, down through the time of Alfred Marshall and his followers to very recent years. A few theorists, most notably Malthus, dissented, but until Keynes wrote the *General Theory* they were unable to formulate a full-blown theory expressing the theoretical basis for their dissent, and their voices were lost in the general chorus of agreement. The basis for this belief is a theory that interest rates will behave so as to bring saving and investment into equality, at any level of income and of saving. This theory of the equilibrating action of interest rates is summarized in the paragraphs which follow.

Consumers and business enterprises find it convenient to hold on hand a certain amount of money. The term money is used here to include demand deposits as well as currency and coin. The amount of money held will be the amount required for the current operations of the business, or in the case of consumers to make disbursements between pay periods; to meet emergencies which may arise; and for related purposes. The amount held will be a determinate amount, related in the case of a consumer to the size of his income and to his spending habits, and in the case of a business enterprise to the size and nature of the business operations.

If a consumer saves part of current income, he will not accumulate any part of the savings in the form of increasing money balances—unless his income and expenditures are rising, so that he desires larger cash balances for purposes such as those mentioned above. Similarly, an enterprise will not accumulate any part of its revenues in the form of increasing money balances, unless its volume of activity is expanding. For to do so would be to sacrifice the income which could be earned by lending the money out at interest. Typically, therefore—so the classical theory runs—current savings will be put to work earning interest; for example, they may be used to buy bonds or stocks, or may be placed on deposit in savings banks, building and loan associations, or other institutions which pay interest on deposits.[4]

Government may of course decide to hoard any surplus of revenues above expenditures—that is, simply to hold funds idle. But in a period of stable full employment without inflation, such as would normally exist if the classical theory is correct, there would be no occasion for this. It may therefore be assumed that if any government had a surplus of revenues, it would use them to retire outstanding debt, so as to save the interest outlay. This debt retirement would place government savings in the hands of the bondholders, and presumably the funds would thereafter be handled like any private savings. If the government had no debt it could be expected to reduce taxes, thus eliminating its saving.

Thus, all current savings, the classical theory argued, can be expected to be placed on the market as funds available for loan. The financial institutions entrusted with them will of course not hold them idle, thus losing the potential income from them, but will lend them out. These loans will be made at the going rate of

---

[4] If money balances are increased, an increment of investment or other expenditure, financed by credit creation, will be necessary to prevent unemployment or a fall in prices.

interest, if possible. But if there are not enough borrowers at the going rate, rather than hold loan funds idle the institutions will offer them for loan at a lower rate—thus reducing the going rate to a lower level. Can it be expected that enough borrowers will appear to take all of the funds and put them to use?

Since the great bulk of all borrowing is done by business enterprises, the discussion will be confined to them; for simplicity, borrowing by consumers will be ignored. Business enterprises borrow in order to invest the funds. At any given time, various investments—new enterprises, or expansion of existing enterprises—will be expected to yield various rates of return. To the persons considering them, some projects may seem to offer the prospect of a 6% return, others $5\frac{1}{2}$%, 5%, and so on, down to some conceivable investments which do not offer the prospect of yielding any return on the money invested and, hence, would not be undertaken under any circumstances.

If funds can be borrowed at an interest rate below the expected rate of return on any given investment, it will pay to borrow money and make the investment. (If funds can be borrowed at an interest rate exactly equal to the expected rate of return, there will be neither a gain nor a loss in undertaking the investment, and it is a marginal question whether or not the enterpriser will decide to undertake it.) At any given going rate of interest, it may be presumed that all investment projects promising rates of return down to that rate are being undertaken. That is, current investment at any time consists of all projects which offer prospects of a rate of return over cost equal to, or greater than, the going rate of interest.

Under these circumstances, any reduction in the rate of interest may be expected, the classical theorists argued, to induce an expansion of the current flow of investment. Further, on both empirical and theoretical grounds, many classical economists argued that a large amount of added investment would be induced by each small reduction in the rate of interest.

This chain of reasoning ignores some of the complexities of real life, but these were believed by classical economists not to impair the applicability of the theory to the real world. One of these complexities is that there is not one but many rates of interest on different types of loans. This was dealt with by noting that whenever "the rate of interest" is mentioned for simplicity, what is referred to is the entire complex of rates of interest, which in general move up and down together. Usually, a rate of interest on "riskless" loans was conceived of as the basic rate, and the excesses of other rates above it as margins for risk.

Another complexity is that in real life no one rate of return on an investment project is anticipated with certainty. There is always a greater or less degree of uncertainty concerning the future. While the enterpriser considering the project may view some rates of return as more probable than some others, uncertainty is a prominent characteristic of his anticipations. Classical theorists recognized this fact, but argued that it may be assumed for simplicity of discussion that the enterpriser behaves, as a result of the various possible rates of return which face him, just as he would if some one rate of return—sort of an average of the probable rates—faced him.

Assume that the economy is in a period of full employment. This implies that the full employment flow of saving is being invested, so that aggregate demand equals the cost of production, including profit margins, of aggregate output. Now assume that because of some change in conditions, the flow of saving becomes for the moment greater than the flow of investment. This may become true because investment declines. Or, consumers may become stocked up with consumer durable goods, and may reduce their consumption expenditures and increase their saving. In either case, the flow of loan funds will not be able to find takers at the going rate of interest. According to the classical theory, what would happen?

Because they had funds available for loan for which there were no takers, the institutions holding these funds would reduce the interest rate at which they offered loans. This would probably reduce the flow of saving. (Present day economists are not so sure that if the interest rate were reduced, consumers would find saving less attractive and would consume a larger proportion of their income.) But, regardless of its effect on saving, the reduction in interest rate would increase the number of investment projects regarded as profitable, and would increase investment activity. Inability to find borrowers would induce financial institutions to lower the rate of interest to the rate at which investment demand was equal to the flow of savings, so that all loan funds found takers. Thus, at any level of income and of saving, the interest rate mechanism can be expected to equilibrate the flows of saving and investment, and by doing so to insure that there will be demand for the aggregate output of the economic system, no matter how large.

This theory can be illustrated diagrammatically. In the following diagram, curve *SS* is the schedule of aggregate saving at full employment in an economic system. It has been drawn so as to indicate that the flow of saving per time period (measured along the horizontal axis) will be slightly higher at higher interest rates (which are measured along the vertical axis). If it were assumed that saving remained the same at any rate of interest, so that *SS* were vertical, the analysis would not be altered in any significant way. The investment curve (*II*) indicates that the flow of investment per time period (also measured along the horizontal axis) will be greater, the lower the interest rate.

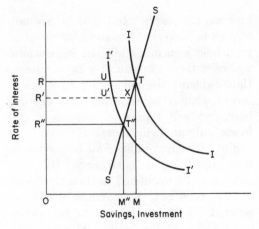

INTEREST RATE AS THE EQUILIBRATOR OF SAVING AND INVESTMENT.

Interest rates are at the level *OR* (or *MT*), and savings and investment per time period are each at the level *RT* (or *OM*).

Now assume that the investment curve moves to the left, to the position represented by curve *I'I'*. This means that at any given rate of interest the flow of investment will be smaller than before. Will output and income decline? Not according to the classical theory. In the new situation, investment at the previous interest rate will be only *RU*, while saving will continue at *RT*. This will cause the supply of loan funds to be greater than the demand for them. If institutions lower the interest rate to *OR'*, investment will increase to *R'U'*, and saving will decrease slightly, to *R'X*. Since the supply of loanable funds will still be in excess of the demand, interest rates will be reduced further. At an interest rate of *OR''*, investment will increase to *R''T''* (=*OM''*), saving will decrease to the same amount, and all saving made at the full employment level of income will flow into investment.

The reader may object that output and income may decline during the transitional period, and may not rise again to full employment. The classical economists thought that it would. Their reasons are summarized in Section B.

The analysis stated above is the classical economic analysis which leads to the conclusion expressed in Say's law, namely, that any level of output creates demand equal to the cost of production of that output. With interest as the equilibrating force, any flow of saving will find an outlet in investment, and demand for any level of output is assured. Since the classical economists ordinarily "pierced the veil of money" and discussed things in real terms, as if money did not exist, the terminology in which the theory of employment is expressed in the writings of classical economists is more abstract than the language used above; but the discussion above presents the essence of the reasoning of the classical economists.

The classical doctrine is clearly expressed in the works of two of the master architects of classical theory. In his *Principles of Political Economy*, John Stuart Mill states:

> What constitutes the means of payment for commodities is simply commodities. Each person's means of paying for the productions of other people consist of those which he himself possesses. All sellers are inevitably, and by the meaning of the word, buyers. Could we suddenly double the productive powers of the country, we should double the supply of commodities in every market; but we should, by the same stroke, double the purchasing power. Everybody would bring a double demand as well as supply; everybody would be able to buy twice as much, because every one would have twice as much to offer in exchange.[5]

And in his early work, the *Pure Theory of Domestic Values*, Alfred Marshall wrote:

> The whole of a man's income is expended in the purchase of services and of commodities. It is indeed commonly said that a man spends some portion of his income and saves another. But it is a familiar economic axiom that a man purchases labour and commodities with that portion of his income which he saves just as much as he does with that he is said to spend. He is said to spend when he seeks to obtain present enjoyment from the services and commodities which he purchases. He is said to save when he causes the labour and the commodities which he purchases to be devoted to the production of wealth from which he expects to derive the means of enjoyment in the future.[6]

Though the classical economists of the twentieth century had begun to doubt these doctrines thus boldly stated, they still adhered to conclusions which depended on these premises for their validity. As J. M. Keynes stated in 1936:

> The doctrine is never stated to-day in this crude form. Nevertheless it still underlies the whole classical theory, which would collapse without it. Contemporary economists, who might hesitate to agree with Mill, do not hesitate to accept conclusions which require Mill's doctrine as their premiss. The conviction, which runs, for example, through almost all Professor Pigou's work, that money makes no real difference except frictionally and that the theory of production and employment can be worked out (like Mill's) as being based on "real" exchanges with money introduced perfunctorily in a later chapter, is the modern version of the classical tradition. Contemporary thought is still deeply steeped in the notion that if people do not spend their money in one way they will spend it in another.[7]

B. THE TENDENCY TOWARD FULL EMPLOYMENT WITHOUT INFLATION

Say's law does not of itself give reason for believing that full employment will be the normal state of affairs. Say's law asserts that a low level of output will finance itself; or that a high level of output will do so; but it does not suggest the existence of any set of forces which will cause the economic system to move from either level to the other.

There is, however, another section of classical economic theory which does sug-

[5] Book III, chap. XIV, section 2. Quoted by J. M. Keynes, *The General Theory of Employment, Interest and Money* (1936), p. 18.

[6] P. 34. Quoted by Keynes, *op. cit.*, p. 19.

[7] Keynes, *op. cit.*, pp. 19–20.

gest the existence of such a set of forces. This suggestion is contained within one branch of marginal productivity theory, namely, the branch dealing with the effect of the price of any factor of production upon the quantity of that factor which will be used in production. In explaining this theory, for simplicity the functions performed by government and by the factor enterprise (whose reward is profits) will be ignored. Attention will be concentrated upon the decisions of enterprisers concerning how much to employ of each of the three other traditional factors of production—land, labor, and capital (each of which, for simplicity, is assumed to be homogeneous).

In combining these three factors in production, each enterpriser will be guided by the technological facts which are summarized in the principle of diminishing returns. This principle relates to the use of the factors of production in varying proportions. It states that as successive equal added amounts of one factor are used in combination with fixed amounts of the other factors, beyond some point the added output obtained by use of each successive addition of the varied factor, or the marginal product of that factor, will be less and less.[8]

If only a small quantity of one of the three factors is available, it will pay enterprisers to pay a high price per unit for its use, since its marginal product is high. The larger the relative amount available, the less the price which will be paid per unit, for it will not pay any enterpriser to offer more for the "last" unit available than the value of the marginal product. If the price of one of the factors (say labor) was initially too high, not all laborers would be offered employment,

but if the unemployed laborers competed with the employed to obtain work, their competition would reduce wages to equality with the marginal product of labor when all available labor was employed. If the initial wage was too low, when all labor was employed, wages would still be below the marginal product of labor, and since it would pay each employer to use more labor, competition among employers to obtain labor would cause wages to rise to equality with the marginal product of labor.

This analysis was initially advanced to explain the relative level of wage rates, land rent, and the rate of return on capital, and the price per unit of a factor referred to in the analysis was its price relative to that of the other two factors. The argument *assumed* full employment of all three factors,[9] and assumed also that the types of capital equipment which had been constructed and the uses to which land and labor were put had been adjusted to the relative supply of the three factors. It was not concerned with, for example, variation in the amount of labor used in a given plant as that plant is operated at varying percentages of full capacity.

However, when questions of explaining the prolonged unemployment of labor arose, some neo-classical economists thought that the analysis was pertinent. There can be continuing unemployment of labor, they said, only if through collusion, stubborn insistence on what laborers think of as a "proper" wage, or for some other such reason, laborers are asking wages higher than the value of their marginal product. If they were not, employers would hire more labor, until unemploy-

---

[8] Strictly, the term marginal product is not applicable unless the added quantity of the factor being considered is infinitesimal in size; *i.e.*, the marginal product, in mathematical terms, is the partial derivative.

[9] What is full employment of each factor will depend in turn on its relative price, for at a higher price more of the factor may be offered. Moreover, if we assume varying grades of each factor, at high wages it may pay to employ labor of too low quality to be employed otherwise, and similarly for land. Since capital becomes used up and must be replaced, the effect in the case of capital is not parallel to that in the cases of the other two factors.

ment vanished. There is therefore no such thing as involuntary unemployment (aside from frictional unemployment). Any worker who is unemployed, other than temporarily and transitionally, must be unemployed because he is asking a price for his services higher than anyone can profitably pay him. In preference to accepting an economic wage, he chooses to remain idle. His idleness is voluntary.

Parallel to this doctrine that competition will maintain full employment is the thesis that the normal operations of competition will never cause inflation. While the competition among employers to hire added workers, so long as wages are at a level which makes it profitable, will prevent wages from falling below the level consistent with full employment, there will be no inducement for employers to bid wages above this level. Hence there is no reason to expect "cost inflation." Further, there is nothing in competitive processes to create an inflationary level of demand, for production will not create money demand in excess of the amount required to purchase the full employment level of output at going prices. The full employment level of output will create that level of demand, but only that level, not a higher one.

Suppose that aggregate demand changes because of some development not related to current production. Can this cause an excessive level of aggregate demand? Suppose, for example, that new inventions make an increase in the flow of investment profitable. Will this increase aggregate demand and bring inflation? Not at all. For, unless the money supply is increased by the banking system, this added demand for savings will merely cause the interest rate to rise. This will have the dual effect of increasing the flow of savings, and of making unprofitable the investment projects which were barely profitable at the old interest rate. The projects resulting from the new invention may be profitable

at the higher interest rate; in that case, they will be undertaken, and some old projects will be squeezed out. This screening or rationing effect of the interest rate will continue until the rate reaches a level at which the demand for investment funds is no greater than the flow of saving, so that, as before, aggregate demand is just equal to the aggregate cost of production of output, and there is no inflationary pressure.

If consumer demand increases, this too will not increase aggregate demand. For an increase in consumer expenditures involves a decrease in consumer saving. This decrease in the flow of saving will make it inadequate to finance the current flow of investment. The interest rate mechanism will then operate just as described above, so as to cut down the flow of investment and thus to prevent aggregate demand from increasing. Thus the interest rate mechanism, the classical economists thought, prevents an increase in any type of demand from becoming an increase in aggregate demand which would cause inflation, just as it insures that all income will be consumed or invested, and thus no deficiency of aggregate demand will arise.

What, then, causes inflation, in the classical view? Inflation is caused by the injection of added money into the economic system, in greater amount than is needed to care for the expanding output of an economy.

Unemployment, on the other hand, is not caused (or cured) by a reduction (or increase) in the quantity of money in the economic system, for if the system is really competitive, this, in the classical view, will merely cause a fall (or rise) in the price level; *i.e.*, in accordance with the classical quantity theory of money, variations in the supply of money would affect only the absolute level of prices and not relative prices.

Depressions have often occurred without any sharp rise in the wage rates asked by labor (which might make it possible to argue that labor was pricing itself out of the market). When asked what, then, was the cause of such depressions, the classical economists could only reply that their onset was due to some unusual shock to the economic system—a banking crisis, bursting of a speculative bubble, or a sharp major shift in demand, such as a sudden large drop in the rate of investment, for example at the end of a construction boom. But failure to recover from the temporary maladjustment could be due only to the stubborn refusal of laborers to accept wage cuts.[10] The onset and prolongation of the depression of the 1930's, neo-classical economists of the time asserted, were due in part to various shocks and maladjustments, most of them resulting directly or indirectly from World War I, and to unwise governmental policies. But a basic associated cause of the prolongation of the depression was the deep-rooted attitude of workers that it is wrong to undercut other workers by underbidding the going wage rate, an attitude strongly reinforced during this period in the United States by government-encouraged growth in the strength of labor unions. The neo-classical economists would no doubt have agreed that a stubborn refusal of banks to reduce interest rates would also have deterred the revival of investment, but that stubborn refusal, they would have noted, did not occur.

[10] Pigou, in his later writings, suggested that a fall in wages would increase employment for a reason quite unrelated to the marginal productivity argument. If wages fell in a money economy, prices would also fall, and this rise in the purchasing power of money would reduce the amount which individuals and business firms felt it desirable to hold in their pockets, bank accounts, tills, etc. Consequently, spending would increase, and there obviously was a level of wages and prices at which spending would be enough to restore full employment. The same would result from an increase in the quantity of money, provided that workers were willing to accept a fall in real wages; this, however, would not occur if workers insisted on wage increases proportionate to price increases.

Neither, in fact, did wages stay entirely rigid. They did fall during the depression, but not, the neo-classical economists argued, enough.

In the early 1930's, many economists, though they had no theoretical weapons with which to challenge the classical theory of unemployment, felt uneasy about it—some perhaps because their social sympathies made them reluctant to accept doctrines which led to the advocacy of wage-cutting, others because of a more purely intellectual failure to find the classical analysis acceptable. The theory of shocks and disturbances was typically an *ad hoc* argument, advanced after the event. But if one picked any year at random during prosperity periods, one could likewise select shocks or disturbances or maladjustments which could plausibly have been advanced as causes of a downturn, if only a downturn had happened to occur then. Why did the adjustment apparatus of the interest rate seem able to cope with shocks at some times and then at others fail miserably?

Nor did the absence of perfect competition seem an adequate explanation of the failure of the adjustment mechanism to function successfully. For if the imperfections of competition did not prevent successful adjustment for a considerable period of years—say during the 1920's—why did they suddenly prevent it at some other time?

Further, as for the "too high wages" argument: Why were wages, which were much below those which for years previously had been consistent with high employment, now in depression "too high"?

Perhaps more basic than any of the other objections, if wages were too high there should have occurred, according to classical theory, a shift of demand from labor to capital and land. Admittedly, such a shift might not cause full employment of land and capital immediately, for some time is required to make the shifts in land use to those best adapted to high labor costs, and to devise and construct new capital which economizes on labor to a greater degree than did the old. But at least there should have been eager bidding for land and even for the old imperfectly adjusted capital. Instead, the situation was one of low demand for all three factors, while money was idle, a situation quite incredible within the scope of classical theory.

These objections do not imply that the classical theory is illogical on its own assumptions, or even that it did not have important and correct policy implications of some sorts of the empirical situation. They do imply, however, that if classical theory was not wrong, it was inadequate—that there are some important characteristics of the depression which it was quite unable to explain.

2

The General Theory

ALVIN H. HANSEN

I.

It would be a mistake, I think, to make too sharp a dividing line between pre-Keynesian and Keynesian economics. That some line has to be drawn I do not believe will be denied by anyone who will examine the economic literature before and after 1936. But every contributor to any field of knowledge stands on the shoulders of his predecessors. Specialists in any field of knowledge know that no one man ever single-handed invented anything. In a sense there are no "revolutionary" discoveries. Nevertheless, in the progress of man's thinking new plateaus are from time to time cast up not unlike a geological upheaval. And these *are* revolutionary developments even though the constituent elements composing the structure can be found elsewhere and have long been well known.

If a stranger from Mars should undertake to read the literature of economics from, say, 1700 to the present day, he would be struck, I believe, particularly

* *

Copyright 1947 by Alfred A. Knopf, Inc. Reprinted from *The New Economics*, edited by Seymour E. Harris, pp. 133–144, by permission of the publisher and author.

Alvin H. Hansen is Professor Emeritus at Harvard University.

by the new direction and outlook injected by the publication of (a) *Wealth of Nations*, (b) the works of Jevons, the Austrians, and Walras, and (c) Keynes' *General Theory*. Scarcely has any issue of an economic journal or any serious volume since 1936 appeared which has not been influenced by, or primarily concerned with, the concepts and thinking of Keynes.

The record will also verify, I think, that friend and foe alike have experienced a considerable enrichment of their "mental furniture" by reason of the Keynesian contribution. This indeed is nothing new. Alfred Marshall's *Principles of Economics* was profoundly influenced by Jevons and the Austrians, though he was far from sympathetic when this "attack" on the classicals first appeared. There are plenty of parallels today.

While it is not possible now to assess the ultimate place of Keynes in the history of economic thought, it is safe to say that no book in economics has ever made such a stir within the first ten years of its publication as has the *General Theory*. And this interest continues unabated. It is further true, I believe, that economic research has tackled new problems and is better equipped with tools of analysis by reason of the work of Keynes. Moreover, a correct appraisal of Keynes' work cannot be made by confining attention to the contents of the *General Theory*. The

Keynesian "revolution" is far from having been completed, and it is, accordingly, not possible this early accurately to appraise the importance of his work in relation to the great peaks of intellectual achievement which have gone before.

Keynes proved to be quite right when he predicted in his Preface to the *General Theory* that many economists would fluctuate between a belief that he was quite wrong and a belief that he was saying nothing new. This conundrum, it appears, still torments some economists; but many more, during the process of criticizing Keynes, have acquired as a by-product the new analytical apparatus. Keynes himself felt he was "treading along unfamiliar paths," and that the composition of the *General Theory* had been a long "struggle of escape from habitual modes of thought and expression." In the literature of the last ten years, one cannot fail to be impressed with the change that has occurred in the "habitual modes of thought and expression" of Keynes' critics, also.

II.

David McCord Wright, in a recent article on the "Future of Keynesian Economics"[1] put his finger quite accurately on the basic change in *outlook* effected by the "Keynesian Revolution." We cannot follow, he says, the main lines of Keynes' argument and say that the capitalist system, left to itself, will automatically bring forth sufficient effective demand. Keynes' ideas "derive much of their unpopularity because they form the most widely known arguments for intervention even though such intervention may be quite capitalist in nature." It is the analysis of the problem of *aggregate demand*, together with the implications of this analysis for practical policy, which challenges the old orthodoxy.

[1] AER, June, 1945.

In this connection an illuminating passage appears in the Preface to Pigou's recent pamphlet, *Lapses from Full Employment*, as follows:

> Professor Dennis Robertson ... has warned me that the form of the book may suggest that I am in favour of attacking the problem of unemployment by manipulating wages rather than by manipulating demand. I wish, therefore, to say clearly that this is not so.

This sentence would not likely have been written prior to the *General Theory*.

III.

It has been my conviction for many years[2] that the great contribution of Keynes' *General Theory* was the clear and specific formulation of the consumption function. This is an epoch-making contribution to the tools of economic analysis, analogous to, but even more important than, Marshall's discovery of the demand function.[3] Just as Marshall's predecessors were fumbling around in the dark because they never grasped the concept of a demand *schedule*, so business-cycle and other theorists from Malthus to Wicksell, Spiethoff, and Aftalion, never could quite "reach port" because they did not have at hand this powerful tool. It is illuminating to re-read business-cycle and depression theories in general prior to 1936 and to see how many things settle neatly into place when one applies the consumption function analysis—things that were dark and obscure and confused without it. The consumption function is by far the most powerful instrument which has been added to the economist's kit of tools in our generation. It is perfectly true that embryonic suggestions (as also

[2] See my *Fiscal Policy and Business Cycles*, Chapter XI.

[3] Not until Marshall did the demand function play a significant rôle in economic analysis. Yet Cournot (and perhaps others) had formulated the principle before.

with the demand function) appear in earlier literature, but the consumption function was never fashioned into a workmanlike instrument until the *General Theory*. This, I repeat, is Keynes' greatest contribution. And in more general terms, the effect of variations in income upon all manner of economic variables has, since Keynes, become an important field for research and analysis. Income analysis at long last occupies a place equally as important as price analysis. This part of the Keynesian contribution will remain, regardless of what happens to that which relates to policy.

Time and again when I thought I had discovered this or that error in the Keynesian analysis, either on my own or at the suggestion of a critic, I have been surprised to find how often, upon examination, the point had already been anticipated and covered in the *General Theory*. I regret that I have not kept a list of these points, but only recently I came upon another interesting example which relates to the consumption function. In my *Fiscal Policy and Business Cycles* I had pointed out (p. 233 *et. seq.*) that, on grounds of general reasoning and such facts as are available (Kuznets' long-run data) we may assume an upward *secular* drift in the consumption function. Later, this was elaborated more fully by Paul Samuelson.[4] This upward secular drift is often (but erroneously) cited as proof that the consumption function analysis is not valid. Until recently, I had supposed that Keynes had overlooked the secular aspect of the problem, and it was therefore of great interest for me to discover that his particular formulation does in fact (possibly inadvertently) cover the matter in a fairly satisfactory manner. The consumption function of two periods, widely separated in time, can be made comparable by correcting for changes in prices, per

capita productivity, and population increase.[5] This would correct for the secular drift, and, if the corrected functions were found to be similar, we could say that the consumption function was stable over time. Now Keynes achieves a fairly satisfactory result by casting his consumption function in terms of wage-units. When the consumption-income schedules of two different periods are cast in terms of wage units, the effect is to correct for price and productivity changes. Thus the schedules become quite comparable over time,[6] and we are accordingly in a position to determine whether or not a shift has in fact occurred in the consumption function.

Not only is consumption a function of income in the short run, but also in the long run. The secular upward shift in the consumption function[6a] could not occur except *as a result of* the prior rise in income. It is sometimes argued that the fact that the historical data reveal an upward secular drift in the consumption function itself proves that consumption is autonomously determined so far as the *long-run* relationship is concerned. But this is, I believe, wrong. The upward shift in the consumption function is a result of the secular rise in income. For example, the statistical evidence points to the conclusion that the *secular* upward shift in the consumption function did not occur from 1929 to 1940. In other words, the consumption schedule, measured in terms of a "full employment" income, had fallen from 1929 to 1940. Thus, at corresponding income levels (measured as ratios of a full

---

[4] See Chapter II, in *Postwar Economic Problems* (edited by Seymour E. Harris, New York, 1943).

[5] This would amount to much the same thing as calculating each schedule as ratios of a full-employment income in each period. Thus the consumption function could be said to be stable over time if the schedules so constructed had the same relation to a full-employment income in each period.

[6] This, at any rate, is true if the schedules are reduced to a per capita basis.

[6a] See my *Fiscal Policy and Business Cycles*, p. 233; and Paul Samuelson in Harris' *Postwar Economic Problems*.

employment income in each period), individuals saved a higher per cent in 1940 than in 1929.[7] Had a full employment income been reached, however, in the late thirties, the higher income would have "educated" the public to higher consumption standards so that the per cent saved of the higher income might have been no higher than in 1929. The point is that it is necessary first to *achieve* the higher potential income level which progress makes possible, in order to induce people to live at a higher standard. The rising standard follows from the rising income, not the other way around.

The rôle and significance of the consumption function can be illustrated by a comparison of the *Treatise* with the *General Theory.* In the *Treatise* $\pi o = E + (I - S)$, where πo is the current income, E the normal (full employment) income, and S is the current saving which *would* be made from a normal full-employment income. Thus the current realized income is, according to the *Treatise,* less than the normal or full-employment income by the amount that current investment falls below the potential saving at full employment.   But this, of course, is wrong, since it leaves out the multiplier. The missing link is supplied by the consumption function.   This in a nutshell reveals one of the great advances of the *General Theory* over the *Treatise.*

In this connection it is interesting to compare Robertson's

$$Y_1 = Y_0 + (I_1 - S_1)$$

with Keynes' $\pi o = E + (I - S)$ in the *Treatise.* They bear a superficial resemblance.   An important difference is that Robertson's is a period analysis which

does not pretend to explain the *level* of Y_1 but only its relation to Y_0, while Keynes' (*Treatise*) equation pretends to explain the *level* of πo.   By combining Robertson's formulation with the consumption function analysis (as I have done in Chapter XII in *Fiscal Policy and Business Cycles*), one can solve by the period analysis the problem attacked by Keynes in the *Treatise.* Keynes, however, chose in the *General Theory* to implement the consumption function analysis in terms of a logical or mathematical formulation[8] involving no time-lags.   Thus if the consumption function is given, the level of income is uniquely determined (time-lags assumed away) by the volume of investment.

IV.

With respect to the determinants of investment—the marginal efficiency of capital and the rate of interest—Keynes' contribution relates chiefly to the latter. The real factors, in a dynamic society, which determine the marginal efficiency of capital are largely taken for granted. The psychological and institutional aspects are indeed at points well treated, but the "real" or "objective" aspects—the dynamics of technical progress—are passed by almost unnoticed. Keynes, however, contributed greatly to the theory of the rate of interest. As a result of his analysis we now place less emphasis than formerly on the rate of interest as a means of increasing the volume of investment. The rate of interest

[7] See Louis Bean's estimates in RES, Nov., 1946. Bean, however, appears mistakenly to conclude that his data point to the conclusion that the consumption function may be expected to remain low, relative to 1929, even though we achieve a full employment income.

[8] It is not correct, as is often done, to identify the Keynesian *logical* formulation with the "ex post" or "statistical" formulation.   Nevertheless, Keynes was realistic enough to recognize that time-lags do occur, and so the *actual* marginal propensity to consume may, for a time, until the adjustment is made, fall below the *normal* marginal propensity to consume.   Thus the "statistical" formulation and the Keynesian realistic formulation (involving time-lags) are alike in that saving and investment are both equal to *current* income minus *current* consumption.   See *General Theory*, pp. 122–4.

is indeed enormously important in the effective implementation of fiscal policy (debt management, lending and guaranteeing operations in such areas as housing, etc.), but as a means of increasing purely private investment it could *only* be of great importance as a determinant of income and employment if the marginal efficiency schedule were very highly elastic. And even so, once a minimum low rate of interest had been reached (Keynes' liquidity preference), nothing more could be accomplished by means of monetary policy. In so far as anything can be achieved (and something can within limits be done) by reducing as far as possible the rate of interest, this method obviously, from the long-run standpoint, is non-recurring and quickly runs out. The movement *along* the marginal efficiency curve would be a "once for all" movement were it not for the *upward shift* of the curve, due to growth and technical progress. It is the upward shift of the marginal efficiency schedule that provides the outlet for a *continuing* flow of investment.

The volume of investment during the last century can be accounted for mainly by growth and technical progress. "Growth" has provided vast outlets for investment of the "widening" type; technical progress has provided outlets of the "deepening" type (greater capital intensity per worker). In addition, some "deepening of capital" has been achieved through some secular decline in the rate of interest.[9] This is important in the sense that we have in consequence more nearly approached the condition of "full investment"—a fuller realization of the potentialities of technical progress. But the contribution which the secular fall in the rate of interest has made to *annual* investment over the last century

is surely negligible compared with the contribution to annual investment made by population growth and technical progress.

It is not necessary to argue that the marginal efficiency schedule is highly inelastic. The movement *down* the curve cannot be of great importance for *continuing* income and employment creation. What is needed in order to develop a considerable flow of investment is a continuing upward shift of the marginal efficiency schedule such as may be caused by technological improvements, the discovery of new resources, the growth of population, or public policy of a character which opens up new investment outlets. The effect of *lowering* the rate of interest would quickly wear off in the absence of an upward shift in the marginal efficiency schedule. Thus, little can be expected for *continuing* investment from progressively lowering the rate of interest, even though this were feasible. A low rate of interest is desirable, nevertheless, because this permits an approach to "full investment" which would mean higher productivity per worker. But in the absence of dynamic growth and innovation, a constant level of the rate of interest, no matter how low, would ultimately result in zero net investment.

V.

The liquidity preference analysis is important as an explanation of the enormous volume of liquid assets which it is possible for an advanced and rich industrial society to hold without inflationary consequences. And while the growth of liquid assets beyond a certain point may have little effect on the rate of interest, it may nevertheless affect income and employment by raising the consumption function. How important this may or may not be depends upon certain circumstances to which I refer below. Mere *volume* alone is not the controlling factor.

---

[9] I am aware that secular upswings and downswings in the rate of interest have occurred; these have been associated particularly with the so-called "long waves." Moreover, the rate of interest reached a low level, roughly comparable to that of the present period, in the eighteen-nineties.

Thus under-employment equilibrium may be reached, given a fairly low consumption function, not merely because of an elastic liquidity preference schedule, but mainly because of limited investment opportunities (technical progress, etc.) combined with a marginal efficiency schedule which is not very highly elastic. Keynes, however, rests his case heavily on the liquidity preference analysis, from which it follows that the economy does not tend toward full employment merely through the automatic adjustment of the rate of interest.

VI.

Wage reduction, as a means of increasing employment via the fall in the interest rate (Pigou), is thus, along with other policies designed to lower the interest rate, relatively ineffective.[10] And with respect to the effect of increased liquid assets (whether in terms of an *absolute* increase in the quantity of money or a *relative* increase caused by wage reductions) on the consumption function, that all depends upon who it is that holds the liquid assets. If the liquid assets are largely in the possession of the rich, the consumption function can rise very little unless, indeed, the accumulation of such assets in the hands of a concentrated few is pushed far beyond the limits of tolerance in a democratic society.

[10] Professor Haberler's quotation from Keynes (p. 17, *General Theory*), that an "increase in employment can only occur to the accompaniment of a decline in the rate of real wages," fails to include the very important conditions which must be assumed to make this statement true, namely, no change in "organization, equipment and technique"; in other words, no change in productivity. Moreover, Keynes (March, 1939, EJ) explicitly repudiated the notion that employment must increase *by or through* a lowering of real wages and a movement *along* a declining so-called general demand curve for labor. In his view, employment is increased by raising effective demand, thereby causing an upward *shift* in the demand curve for labor. For Professor Haberler's article see Chapter XIV [in *The New Economics*].

VII.

It is therefore important *how* the liquid assets came into being and who it is that holds them. The method of *relative* increase in liquid assets (via wage reductions) is clearly not a realistic method of increasing the consumption function for the general population. And with respect to the method of *absolute* increase brought about by the action of the monetary authorities, it makes considerable difference whether the monetary expansion merely came about through monetizing assets held by investors and wealthy individuals, or whether the new money was created as part of an expansionist's fiscal program of subsidization of mass consumption—school lunches, housing and household equipment for low-income groups, family allowances, etc.—or for public construction projects which directly increase the income of workers and start a round of expenditures (multiplier effect) throughout the economy. There is no assurance that a mere increase in liquid assets (whether absolute or relative) will raise the consumption function appreciably. That depends. Thus it is that monetary policy may be relatively ineffective unless combined with appropriate fiscal policy.[11] And it is considerations

[11] Professor Haberler, in his contribution to the RES symposium, argues that under-employment equilibrium with flexible wages and prices is impossible since wages and prices will under these conditions fall continually. But considerations of this kind have been fully and effectively discussed and answered by Keynes himself in Chapter 19 of the *General Theory*. (The reader who may feel confused in consequence of recent discussions about the rôle of wage rigidity in the Keynesian system should carefully study this chapter. See also my Chapter, "Keynes on Economic Policy," below [*i.e.*, Chapter XVI in *The New Economics*].) Completely flexible wages and prices would indeed give us a system so unstable as to be unworkable.

But this is not the question. The question is rather whether an orderly reduction of wages and prices which are *relatively* rigid could promote an increase in employment. And it was presumably

such as these here under discussion that reveal the essential differences between pure monetary policy and pure fiscal policy.

VIII.

After ten years of criticism, the Keynesian analytical apparatus remains as essential equipment if one pretends to work on the determinants of income and employment. The consumption function has become and will remain the pivotal point of departure for any attack on the problem of aggregate demand. Moreover, with respect to policy, little reliance in the future will be placed on the notion that it matters little what the consumption function may be, since, whatever its level, a volume of investment adequate to fill the "gap" will always automatically tend to develop if only wage and monetary adjustments are made. Special models set up to show how wage flexibility under certain conditions might so operate are notoriously unrealistic and unworkable in the practical world and so fail to come to grips with economic reality. Finally, a mere increase in the quantity of money, apart from the manner in which it is created and put into circulation, and apart from its distribution among the members of society, is not capable *per se* of raising the consumption function to a level

adequate to insure full employment. On the other hand, Keynesian economics has itself been the means of showing the important rôle of monetary expansion in conjunction with fiscal policy in the creation of adequate aggregate demand. Monetary policy is an essential instrument for an effective full-employment program. The volume of liquid assets and the rate of interest are indeed important, though if applied alone relatively ineffective.

These, then, are the essentials of the Keynesian system and these are the considerations with which we must grapple in appraising its continuing effectiveness for analysis and policy. Under-employment equilibrium is not dependent upon wage rigidity (properly defined). The fundamental explanation is to be found in (a) the consumption function, (b) investment outlets, and (c) the liquidity preference analysis.[12] There are no automatic processes that will produce under all circumstances adequate aggregate demand. Private consumption and private investment outlays will not automatically produce this result. And no other explanation for this has so far been offered that is as satisfactory as that presented by Keynes.

IX.

It is evident that a new outlook was injected into economics, both with respect to theory and policy, by the publication of the *General Theory*. That it was not just "old stuff" is evidenced by the terrific effort it required for economists to readjust their thinking and, indeed, the

---

such a policy which Professor Haberler had in mind when he discussed the *relative* increase of liquid assets (via wage reductions) and the effect of this on the interest rate or on the consumption function. Whether or not this is effective depends, as I have noted above, on circumstances. You cannot cure unemployment *merely* by expanding the money supply (absolutely or relatively) without regard to how this increase is brought about or who holds the money. The position of Modigliani, Polanyi, and others is, I think, a modern recrudescence of an excessive preoccupation with the mere *quantity* of money—a preoccupation no less indefensible than the old. I say this despite the fact that I myself place great stress upon the importance of adequate (but not excessive) monetary expansion as a part of fiscal policy.

[12] Professor Haberler's criticism of the elasticity of the liquidity preference schedule seems to me to require cautious interpretation. It relates to factors affecting a *shift* in the schedule rather than to *elasticities* along a given schedule. To be sure, a long-run schedule can sometimes be traced out by determinate shifts of short-run schedules; but Haberler's theory seems to be a special one, which denies, among other things, that as the rate of interest gets nearer and nearer to zero, the difficulties of lowering it further begin to increase.

difficulty they had in understanding what it was all about. Witness, for example, the first reviews (including my own) and the endless controversial articles on concepts which, in retrospect, are rarely a credit to the profession.[13]   More and more, even those who professed to see little in Keynes that was new or valid began to reveal that they had experienced a rebirth despite their protestations to the contrary.   Add to this the fact that the

[13] A recent example disclosing a number of elementary misconceptions is the pamphlet by Arthur F. Burns, on *Economic Research and the Keynesian Thinking of Our Times* (NBER, 1946). However, the pamphlet does strikingly reveal (perhaps inadvertently) how economic theory— whether Ricardian or Keynesian—serves the highly useful purpose of pointing up what factual data are relevant to a useful investigation. See my article, "Dr. Burns on Keynesian Economics," RES, Nov., 1947.

influence of Keynes permeates all official international gatherings grappling with economic problems and is present wherever internal economic problems are under consideration (witness postwar governmental pronouncements). It is difficult to avoid the conclusion that nothing like it has happened in the whole history of economics. It is too early to say, but it does not now appear an extravagant statement, that Keynes may in the end rival Adam Smith in his influence on the economic thinking and governmental policy of his time and age. Both lived at profound turning points in the evolution of the economic order. Both were products of their times. Yet both were also powerful agents in giving direction to the unfolding process of institutional change.

3

The Simple Mathematics of Income Determination

PAUL A. SAMUELSON

I. INTRODUCTION

Thanks in large measure to Professor Hansen and his associates, advanced students in business cycle theory have become proficient in calculating a large variety of different "income multipliers." In fact the subject has become something of a black art. Black because, to the uninitiated, the jargon must necessarily appear mysterious if not vicious; and an art because even the most adept are hard put to it to remember all the complex terms required for any particular multiplier formula.

Once we drop the most simplifying assumptions concerning income determination, and once we begin to seek the answer to a number of different policy or factual questions, most of this complexity is intrinsic. But by no means all. A large part of the difficulty of the subject—looked at from the standpoint of teacher or pupil—results from the practice of

✻ ✻

Reprinted from *Income, Employment and Public Policy*, Essays in Honor of Alvin H. Hansen, pp. 133–155, by permission of W. W. Norton & Company, Inc., and the author. Copyright 1948 by W. W. Norton & Company, Inc.

Paul A. Samuelson teaches at the Massachusetts Institute of Technology.

working with "multipliers," rather than concentrating on the equilibrium conditions which give rise to these expressions. The relations determining income are logically prior to those describing the way the equilibrium income changes. They are also easier to remember, easier to handle without making over-narrow straight-line assumptions, and they easily yield the appropriate multiplier formula for any particular problem.

The present discussion is purely expositional, dealing as it does with problems that have been thoroughly thrashed out in the advanced literature. It attempts to show, with the use of the simplest mathematical language, (1) the simplest Keynesian model by which "saving and investment" determine income; (2) how government expenditure and taxes enter into this picture; (3) the role of international trade; and (4) how the corporation and its savings are to be handled.

II. THE HEART OF INCOME ANALYSIS

By definition, *national income* (at market prices), Y, can initially be set equal to the sum of consumption expenditure, C, and *net investment*, I:

$$Y = C + I$$

If Keynes had stopped with this identity, we should be left with an indeterminate system. In his simplest model of income determination, he added the following two hypotheses: (a) consumption is a function of income, and (b) investment may provisionally be taken, at any one time, as a constant. Mathematically, these relations may be written

$$C = C(Y) \quad \text{and} \quad I = \bar{I}$$

When we substitute these into our first identity, we come up with the simplest Keynesian income system:

$$Y = C(Y) + \bar{I} \tag{1}$$

This is a determinate system, being one equation to determine one unknown variable. While much of the anti-Keynesian and Keynesian world was still arguing over the tautological character of the Keynesian concepts, Professor Hansen had quickly cut through the non-essentials to isolate the critically important role of the propensity-to-consume schedule, as embodied in this fundamental equation.

Equation (1) is crucially important for the history of economic thought. It is the nucleus of the Keynesian reasoning. If it *in no way* gives insight into the analysis of employment, then the Keynesian system is sterile and misleading. In its over-simplification, this relation must be compared with two other seminal single equations which contain by implication much of the remainder of economic theory: namely the equating of supply and demand to determine market price,

$$D(p) - S(p) = 0;$$

and the determination of a firm's best output, q (or anything else) by the condition that its profits, π, be at a maximum through the balancing of the effect of any decision on *total revenue*, R, and *total cost*, C,

$$\frac{d\pi}{dq} = \frac{dR(q)}{dq} - \frac{dC(q)}{dq} = 0$$

Geometrical Representation

Graphically, the simplest Keynesian equilibrium can be shown on a by now familiar 45° line diagram.[1] On the vertical axis the consumption function, $C(Y)$, is plotted against income. Investment is then superimposed onto consumption. The two together constitute the right-hand side of equation (1). The left-hand side, Y, is simply income itself plotted against income, or in short a 45° line. The intersection of $C(Y) + \bar{I}$ with the 45° line gives us our simplest "Keynesian-cross," which logically is exactly like a "Marshallian-cross" of supply and demand.

As an alternative to this geometrical presentation, we may let the intersection of a saving schedule with investment depict the determination of income. This amounts simply to transposing the consumption term in equation (1) over to the left-hand side, which now gives us the difference between income and consumption, or what may be called the *propensity-to-save* schedule, $S(Y)$. In its new version (1) reads,

$$Y - C(Y) = \bar{I} \quad \text{or} \quad S(Y) = \bar{I} \tag{2}$$

As before, income is plotted on the horizontal axis; but now on the vertical axis we must allow for both positive and negative amounts of saving or investment. The amount of investment is plotted as a horizontal schedule. The saving schedule will intersect it from below to yield the same equilibrium income as is shown in the 45° line diagram.

[1] See, for example, the contribution of Robert L. Bishop, p. 319 [in *Income, Employment and Public Policy*].

How does the fundamental income equation yield us the usual multiplier? Very simply, when we ask for the change in income which results from a change in the parameter investment, $\bar{I}$.[2] From (1) it follows that $d\bar{I}/dY = 1 - C'(Y)$; or the multiplier formula becomes

$$\left[\frac{dY}{d\bar{I}}\right] = \frac{1}{1 - C'(Y)} \qquad (3)$$

where C' is the familiar marginal propensity to consume at each different income level. Of the two equations, (1) and (3), the former is the more fundamental. By it we can appraise the effect of a large as well as a small change in investment, and without making the usual linear approximation to the consumption function.[3]

---

[2] The only mathematical technique used in this paper is the simple one of determining the derivative of one variable, Y, with respect to another variable or parameter, a, to which Y is related by an implicit equation. Thus, if Y depends on a as determined by $F(Y, a) = 0$, so that

$$dF = \frac{\partial F(Y, a)}{\partial Y} dY + \frac{\partial F(Y, a)}{\partial a} da = 0,$$

then necessarily

$$\frac{dY}{da} = -\frac{\dfrac{\partial F}{\partial a}}{\dfrac{\partial F}{\partial Y}}$$

where the symbol ∂ refers always to partial differentiation with "all other variables being held constant." An expression like $C'(Y)$ or C' always means $dC(Y)/dY$.

[3] If $C = a + bY$, a linear function on income, then the reader can show that

$$Y = \frac{1}{1-b}(a + \bar{I}) \quad \text{and} \quad \Delta Y = \frac{1}{1-b}\Delta\bar{I}$$

If C is curvilinear, then

$$\Delta Y = \frac{1}{1 - \bar{C}'}\Delta\bar{I}$$

where now the $\bar{C}'$ will be some marginal propensity to consume intermediate between the old and new income situations, and which can only be evaluated with perfect exactitude by Equation (1).

Autonomous Consumption Shifts and Induced Investment

Before leaving the simplest Keynesian system, we may briefly mention that an autonomous upward shift of the consumption schedule will have exactly the same multiplier effects upon income as will an increase in investment. Thus, we may rewrite the consumption schedule to include a new element, a, of autonomous consumption—or $C = a + C(Y)$. The reader may easily verify that in the new Equation (1), the a term can be grouped with $\bar{I}$ with exactly the same quantitative effects upon income. "Investment dollars are high-powered dollars." Consumption dollars are, too.

The problem of "induced" investment introduces no formal difficulties. From a long-run economic viewpoint, it is doubtful that net investment can be related to a stationary income level in the way that consumption can. But in the short run, when the stock of capital is more or less constant, and when each different level of income can be thought of as a *change* in income as compared to previous periods, then it may be legitimate to write investment as a rising function of income, $I(Y)$. This *propensity-to-invest schedule* will intersect (from above) the *propensity-to-save schedule* of (2) to give the equilibrium level of income.

If we now wish to calculate a "multiplier" coefficient, the problem is more complicated. Exactly what question do we really wish to ask? What "multiplicand" are we changing in order to appraise its effect on income? The reader should verify for himself that once induced investment enters the picture, the appropriate multiplier to show the effect on Y of an *autonomous* shift, a, in either the investment or consumption schedule is given by[4]

$$\left[\frac{dY}{da}\right] = \frac{1}{1 - C'(Y) - I'(Y)}$$

$$= \frac{1}{S'(Y) - I'(Y)} \qquad (4)$$

III. TREATMENT OF GOVERNMENT IN INCOME ANALYSIS

So far we have been ignoring the presence of government expenditure on goods and services, G, and of net algebraic tax collections or withdrawals, W (positive when people pay taxes, negative when they receive transfer payments such as old-age pensions, veterans' allowances, etc.). Actually, Net National Product at market prices consists of three components

$$Y = C + I + G$$

To make our four-variable system determinate we must be willing to commit ourselves to some additional hypotheses. As before, we may provisionally make investment a constant. Since government expenditure is primarily a matter of policy (particularly, since we are excluding from G, relief and other transfer items which vary with income), we may provisionally set it equal to a constant. But now the dependence of consumption upon national income becomes more complicated. If we abstract from changes in the distribution of income—and empirical studies suggest that the *marginal* propensities to consume of different income classes do not differ enough to make this a disastrous oversimplification—then as a first

---

[4] More generally, a may be an autonomous factor which shifts the I or C schedules (either or both) in a *non-parallel* fashion. Our multiplier then becomes

$$\left[\frac{dY}{da}\right] = \frac{1}{\left(1 - \frac{\partial C}{\partial Y} - \frac{\partial I}{\partial Y}\right)} \frac{\partial(C + I)}{\partial a}$$

approximation we can make consumption a function of "disposable income *after* net algebraic taxes or withdrawals," $Y - W$. By adding W as a variable, we must now demand that an additional hypothesis be made about its behavior. The simplest assumption is that net taxes or withdrawals are equal to some constant, set by policy. (We shall see in the next section that this is a rather misleading assumption.)

In symbols, our hypotheses are as follows

$$I = \overline{I}, \; G = \overline{G}, \; W = \overline{W}$$
$$C = C(Y - \overline{W})$$

which when substituted in the first definitional equation of this section, gives us a determinate equation for income

$$Y = C(Y - \overline{W}) + \overline{I} + \overline{G} \qquad (5)$$

The 45° line diagram is well designed to illustrate this equilibrium; our only change is to add government expenditure (whether on capital or current goods) to private investment, and to shift the consumption function rightward (and downward) in a parallel fashion by a distance equal to net tax withdrawals, $\overline{W}$.

The saving-investment diagram is now not quite so convenient to interpret, and a number of alternative re-groupings of terms can be imagined. The method which is most closely akin to the definition of saving of the Department of Commerce would be as follows

$$Y - C(Y - \overline{W}) - \overline{W} = \overline{I} + (\overline{G} - \overline{W}) \; (6)$$

Consumption has been transposed to the left-hand side and $\overline{W}$ has been subtracted from both sides. The left-hand side, saving, is equated to private investment plus the deficit (whether financed by borrowing or printing of money).

An alternative possibility, which is perhaps nearer in formulation to the National

Bureau definitions, would be to treat the deficit as negative government saving, and transpose it to the left-hand side, so that investment is equated to private and public saving. The only advantage to this second formulation is that it makes more plausible to beginning students such a statement as, "A reduction of taxes will raise income by reducing the community's saving." Intuitively, the student feels that a reduction of taxes will increase consumption, (private) saving, and income. Of course, either formulation is identical to Equation (5).

Now that income is a determinate function of $\overline{I}$, $\overline{G}$, and $\overline{W}$, it is simple to determine the appropriate multipliers for a unit change in each of these quantities. Using the technique described in the second footnote of this paper, it is easy to show that

$$\left[\frac{dY}{d\overline{G}}\right] = \left[\frac{dY}{d\overline{I}}\right] = \frac{1}{1 - C'(Y - \overline{W})}$$

$$\left[\frac{dY}{d(-\overline{W})}\right] = \frac{C'(Y - \overline{W})}{1 - C'(Y - \overline{W})}$$

$$= \left[\frac{dY}{d\overline{G}}\right] - 1 \qquad (7)$$

In words, government expenditure has the same favorable effect on income as does private investment, both effects being equal to the reciprocal of the marginal propensity to save out of disposable income. Tax reduction will also increase income, but dollar for dollar its effects are always less than those of increasing expenditure. *In fact a dollar of expenditure always increases income by exactly one dollar more than does a dollar reduction of taxes.*

The "Balanced-Budget Theorem"

This is the basis for the significant "balanced-budget theorem."[5] According to

this theorem, a deficit is not at all necessary for an expansionary fiscal policy. A balanced increase in expenditure and taxes— assuming no shift in the functional relationship of consumption to disposable income and no change in private investment— will result in an exactly equivalent increase in net national product.[6]

The explanations given for this paradoxical result are numerous:

(1) Mr. Salant pointed out that taxes do not enter directly into the net national product on the very first round, so that the two multiplier chains resulting from G and $-W$ are respectively

$$1 + C' + (C')^2 + (C')^3 + \ldots\ldots,$$
$$-C' - (C')^2 - (C')^3 - \ldots\ldots$$

---

[5] This theorem has been developed by several writers; see A. H. Hansen and H. S. Perloff, *State and Local Finance in the National Economy* (New York, 1944), pp. 245–246; T. Haavelmo, "Multiplier Effects of a Balanced Budget," *Econometrica*, Vol. XIII (1945), pp. 311–318; and the further comments by G. Haberler, R. M. Goodwin, E. E. Hagen, and T. Haavelmo, *Econometrica* Vol. XIV (1946), pp. 148–158; H. C. Wallich, "Income-generating Effects of a Balanced Budget," *Quarterly Journal of Economics*, Vol. LIX (1944), pp. 78–91; N. Kaldor's Appendix C to W. H. Beveridge, *Full Employment in a Free Society* (New York, 1945), pp. 346–347; P. A. Samuelson, "Full Employment after the War," in *Postwar Economic Problems*, edited by S. E. Harris (New York, 1943), p. 44. W. A. Salant's privately circulated memorandum was held up in publication by his war service. See also the early paper with similar notions developed from a different point of view by H. Somers, "The Impact of Fiscal Policy on National Income," *Canadian Journal of Economics and Political Science*, Vol. VIII (1942), pp. 364–385.

[6] If private investment is a rising function of total NNP, then the resulting increase in income and employment will be even larger; if, on the other hand, the net effects upon private investment are adverse, the increase in income will be smaller. Also it is quite possible that some changes in the distribution of disposable income might result, so that the saving and consumption schedules would shift in relationship to total disposable income. Consequently, the total income effects may differ, depending upon the type of taxes and the type of expenditures in question. For a development of this point, see R. A. Musgrave, "Alternative Budget Policies for Full Employment," *American Economic Review*, Vol. XXXV, No. 3, June, 1945, pp. 387–400.

with the difference being 1 regardless of the magnitude of C'.

(2) Another mode of explanation is to say that to some degree taxes must "come out of saving as well as consumption." Haavelmo has, with some justification, objected to this explanation on the ground that it erroneously suggests that the expansionary effect of a balanced budget is proportional to the quantitative size of the marginal propensity-to-save coefficient—which it is not.[7]

(3) A similar explanation follows the line that when the government's tax-financed expenditure is expanded, this amounts to adding an element in the system with a propensity to consume of unity. Increasing the weight of such an element must pull up the weighted-average propensity to consume of the community as a whole.

(4) The last explanation, which Hansen himself emphasized, stresses that tax-financed government expenditure constitutes a part of the "circular flow" of society's self-sustaining income. If the concept of net national product at market price had been adhered to from the beginning in our national income statistics, we should have more quickly emancipated ourselves from the Grover Cleveland notion of government expenditure as a *subtraction* from private national product.

To realize that government expenditure on goods and services is itself part of national product is almost, but not quite, enough to demonstrate the validity of the balanced-budget theorem. Just one further step of reasoning is necessary for a logically rigorous proof: It must be shown that private disposable income will actually remain constant when tax-financed government expenditure is superimposed upon it.

[7] But he perhaps stretches his case too far when he argues that the same result is achieved when the marginal propensity to consume is exactly unity. For in that limiting case, our system becomes indeterminate and its multiplier 0/0 so long as $G \equiv W$. If $W \neq G$, the system is inconsistent.

That private disposable income will remain constant is easily seen from Equation (5) or (6). Rearranging terms and designating *disposable income* as y and the deficit as D, $(= G - W)$, we now have

$$Y - \overline{W} = C(Y - \overline{W}) + \overline{I} + (\overline{G} - \overline{W})$$

or

$$y = C(y) + \overline{I} + \overline{D} \qquad (8)$$

Obviously, with $\overline{G}$ and $\overline{W}$ increased equally, with $\overline{D}$ and $\overline{I}$ unchanged, this equation determines y as a constant, $\overline{y}$. Hence, total Y must increase one for one with the superimposed amount of $\overline{G}$ or $\overline{W}$ added onto the fixed base of private disposable income, $\overline{y}$. Thus, the balanced-budget expenditure has a multiplier of exactly one; without recognizing this quantitative fact, we miss the kernel of the theorem.

A few concluding observations may be made: (1) The above analysis shows that there is, strictly speaking, no true unique multiplier to be associated with a deficit; i.e., $dY/d(G - W)$ is undefined until we know how the deficit is brought about in terms of the relative weights going to G and W. Such a "pseudo-multiplier" can be made to vary between minus and plus infinity. (2) Government transfer expenditure, as distinct from "exhaustive" expenditure on goods and services, tends to have a relatively weak multiplier exactly like that of taxes. In fact, raising taxes and transfer expenditure simultaneously will (apart from redistribution between income classes and indirect tax-distortion effects) have no effect on $\overline{W}$ or income. (3) The old Currie-Villard concept of "net income creating expenditure" of the government is seen to be slightly misleading. With no deficit, income may be created. It would be a little more appropriate to call this concept the "net disposable-income creating expenditure" of the government. This is because a unit increase in deficit has the same effect on disposable income as a unit increase in investment (or government expenditure) has on total net national product, as the reader may verify.

Collections from a Given Tax Structure versus Changing Rates

Realistically, it is misleading to treat net tax withdrawals, W, as a direct policy parameter. Congress legislates government expenditure, $\bar{G}$; but it can never legislate tax receipts. All it can do is legislate tax *rates* which determine the government's net take at each different level (and composition) of national income. Any change in rates will necessarily change income, so that the legislators can never quite know what tax collections will be—without estimating the solution to the simultaneous equations of income determination.

Instead of assuming W constant, therefore, we shall assume that it is a given function of income for each set of Congressional decisions concerning different tax rates and transfer expenditures. For simplicity, we may assume that the complex of rates can be summarized in a single parameter, $\bar{r}$, which shifts the whole tax schedule up or down at each income level. Hence[8]

$$W = \bar{r} + W(Y)$$

where $W'(Y) = \partial W/\partial Y$ is the marginal propensity to tax, a quantity which increases progressively with income. Our equation of income determination now gives us Y in terms of $\bar{G}$, $\bar{I}$, and $\bar{r}$:

$$Y = C[Y - \bar{r} - W(Y)] + \bar{I} + \bar{G} \quad (9)$$

[8] It would be more general to permit $\bar{r}$ also to "twist" the tax schedule as well as raise or lower it. This will produce only higher-order curvature effects on income which will be negligible for small changes in tax rates. In the general case, $W = W(Y, \bar{r})$ and $\partial W/\partial r$ depends upon the level of income.

Nevertheless, $(dY/dr)/(\partial W/\partial r)$ will be independent of any twist effect imparted by the term $\partial^2 W/\partial Y \partial r$.

If we wish to illustrate the equilibrium graphically, we can easily do so as long as net tax rates, $\bar{r}$, are constant. This being so, disposable income, $y = Y - \bar{r} - W(Y)$, becomes a determinate function of net national product, Y. Therefore, consumption itself becomes indirectly a function of Y, but now with a slope which is less than the marginal propensity to consume out of disposable income—perhaps by about a quarter. For fixed $\bar{r}$, we plot

$$C = C[Y - \bar{r} - W(Y)] = C(Y, \bar{r})$$

where

$$\frac{\partial C(Y, \bar{r})}{\partial Y} = C'(y)[1 - W'(Y)]$$

As we decrease $\bar{r}$, the consumption schedule is shifted leftward (and upward), but now by an amount greater than the reduction of taxes, and to an increasing degree as income increases.

Equation (9) will yield us an income multiplier with respect to $\bar{G}$ or $\bar{I}$, and also one with respect to $\bar{r}$. These three are the only basic multipliers possible. But when any given combination of these three parameters has been changed, it is always possible to relate the resulting change in income to the resulting change in any other variable of the system. Such a ratio can be called a multiplier if one pleases, but really it is a *mutatis mutandis* concept and had better be recognized as a chameleon creature whose numerical value can be changed at will by specifying different combinations of variation in the basic parameters, $\bar{r}$, $\bar{G}$, and $\bar{I}$. Examples of such a pseudo-multiplier will be provided later.

From Equation (9), we get the following two identical multipliers when we change only $\bar{G}$ or $\bar{I}$:

$$\left[\frac{dY}{d\bar{I}}\right] = \left[\frac{dY}{d\bar{G}}\right] = \frac{1}{1 - \dfrac{\partial C(Y, \bar{r})}{\partial Y}}$$

$$= \frac{1}{1 - C'(y)[1 - W'(Y)]} \quad (10)$$

Because the marginal propensity to tax, W', is about one-fourth, the marginal propensity to consume out of national income will be only three-fourths as large as that out of disposable income. Consequently, our new multiplier will be much smaller, its weakness being due to the superimposition of "tax leakages" on top of "savings leakages." Even if people consume all their disposable income, the tax leakages would be a heavy drag—in either direction—on the system's movement.

For a change in $\overline{G}$, we could easily calculate a pseudo deficit multiplier:

$$\left[\frac{dY}{dD}\right] = \frac{\dfrac{dY}{d\overline{G}}}{\dfrac{d(\overline{G} - W)}{d\overline{G}}} = \frac{1}{1 - \dfrac{\partial C}{\partial Y} - W'}$$

$$= \frac{1}{(1 - C')(1 - W')} \qquad (11)$$

This may be very large indeed, because an increase in expenditure—after it has had a multiplied effect upon income—may be accompanied by a substantial increase in taxes, with the result that a sizable change in income is associated with a small change in deficit. For a change in $\overline{I}$ only, the deficit goes down and income goes up, yielding a negative pseudo deficit multiplier, whose exact value the reader can easily verify to be the reciprocal of the marginal propensity to tax.

Our last basic multiplier will be that giving the change in income resulting from a unit autonomous downward shift of the tax schedule:

$$\left[\frac{dY}{d(-\overline{r})}\right] = \frac{C'(y)}{1 - C'(y)[1 - W'(Y)]} \qquad (12)$$

This results from differentiating Equation (9) with respect to $\overline{r}$ according to the stated rule of implicit functions. Note again, that (given the assumption of constant investment) tax reduction is less

powerful than expenditure. Beardsley Ruml does not have quite the leverage of Harry Hopkins.

Three Paths to Full Employment

Professor Bishop, in another paper [in *Income, Employment and Public Policy*, p. 317], has elaborated upon the three fiscal paths to full employment: (1) deficit spending (a change in $\overline{G}$ only, in our notation); (2) spending without deficit (an equal change in $\overline{G}$ and $\overline{W}$); (3) a deficit without spending (a reduction in net taxes, W, brought about by reducing rates, $\overline{r}$, in $W[Y, \overline{r}]$). Any two of the three cases can be combined to produce the third. Bishop prefers to regard (2) and (3) as "pure" cases, the former involving only expansion of the government component of net national product, and the latter involving only a change in the private sector. His first case is then simply a blending of these two.

From the standpoint of policy manipulation, it might be preferable to regard (1) and (3) as pure cases, the former involving a simple change in $\overline{G}$, and the latter a simple change in $\overline{r}$ or $\overline{W}$. The balanced-budget case (2) would then represent an equal blending of the two pure cases. Either viewpoint is equally admissible.

However, one thing is clear: Financial orthodoxy aimed at minimizing deficits turns out to be really most radical from the standpoint of maximizing free, private enterprise and minimizing the role of government. To a *laissez-faire* economist, route (3), which is the least orthodox, is the best path to follow when income is to be expanded.

IV. INTERNATIONAL TRADE AND INCOME DETERMINATION

Very briefly, the treatment of international trade, neglecting the government and corporations, may be indicated. Net national product is now the sum of home-produced consumption goods, c, home-produced investment goods, I, and home-produced goods for export, X. In exports are included such invisible service items as shipping and (net) interest and dividends from abroad. Then

$$Y = c + I + X$$

If for simplicity we assume that imports, M, are all consumption goods, we may subtract and add M and rewrite this equation as

$$Y = (c + M) + I + (X - M)$$
= total consumption goods + investment + foreign balance on current account

The Department of Commerce includes the foreign balance in private net capital formation.

As far as a single country is concerned, *exports* may often be taken as an autonomous factor, independent of income, without too great error. However, this is not strictly true with respect to some components of dividends payable to foreigners; also there will be some small reflex influence of our income on our own exports via the effect of our imports on income and imports of foreigners. These effects I disregard. Our demand for domestic consumption goods may be taken as a function of our national income, $c(Y)$, exchange rates and relative prices being given. With domestic investment, $\overline{I}$, being given, our income equation becomes

$$Y = c(Y) + \overline{I} + \overline{X} \qquad (13)$$

and our multipliers become

$$\left[\frac{dY}{d\overline{I}}\right] = \left[\frac{dY}{d\overline{X}}\right] = \frac{1}{1 - c'(Y)}$$

$$= \frac{1}{S'(Y) + M'(Y)} \qquad (14)$$

where the marginal propensity to consume, $c'(Y)$, falls short of unity by the

marginal propensity to import, M', plus the marginal propensity to save, S'. The increase in imports and the pseudo balance of trade multiplier can be shown to be given respectively by

$$\frac{dM}{d\overline{X}} = \frac{M'}{M' + S'} \qquad (15)$$

and

$$\frac{dY}{d(\overline{X} - M)} = \frac{1}{1 - c' - M'} \qquad (16)$$

These formulae, and indeed the whole analytical problem of exports versus balance of trade as multiplicand, are formally analogous to the problem of government expenditure versus deficit. [9]

An autonomous shift in imports would, other things being equal, have no effect on domestic income, except possibly through indirect effects which are excluded in this discussion. But most things which affect the propensity to import, such as tariffs, exchange rates, and relative prices, would also affect the domestic propensity to consume in the opposite direction. Therefore, I shall not present a formal multiplier for a shift in imports.

Are there not circumstances under which the balance of payments, $(X - M)$, rather than X is the appropriate autonomous variable or multiplicand? If so, and if $C = c + M$ is a determinate function of income, $C(Y) = c(Y) + M(Y)$, then the appropriate income equation becomes

$$Y = C(Y) + \overline{I} + (\overline{X - M}) \qquad (17)$$

and

$$\frac{dY}{d(\overline{X - M})} = \frac{1}{1 - C'(Y)}$$

$$= \frac{1}{1 - c'(Y) - M'(Y)} \qquad (18)$$

the same result as given just above. But

[9] See D. H. Robertson, "Mr. Clark and the Foreign Trade Multiplier," *Economic Journal*, Vol. XLIX (1939), pp. 354–356, for the classical treatment of this problem.

now the pseudo-multiplier has become the genuine article; and through our change of hypothesis, the basic multiplier has become a chameleon.

A few concluding observations may be made concerning international trade: (1) It is true that price changes, such as result from gold flows or exchange rates, find themselves supplemented by income effects. Nevertheless, when a country's exports increase, the resulting induced change in imports brought about by the income multiplier will always fall short of restoring equilibrium by an amount which depends on the relative strength of the marginal propensity to save and the marginal propensity to import. See Equation (15).

(2) When relative price changes are introduced into the picture, it becomes even more possible that domestic employment may be improved by a change in conditions which simultaneously expands exports and contracts the trade balance. This cannot be elaborated upon here.

(3) The cases in which the trade balance can be treated as an autonomous element are necessarily those in which— through the action of exchange control, exchange depreciation, or lender-borrower psychology—capital movements prove to be the bottleneck to which trade movements adjust themselves. The post-World War II world, where the availability of dollars calls the tune, may be such an example. In many if not most of such cases, imports are adjusted to exports so as to realize the preassigned balance of trade (for the foreign country at any rate) and the assumed relations between home-consumption goods, imports, and income cannot be assumed to hold, so that Equation (17) must be used with caution.

(4) Throughout part of this discussion, I have been following the customary loose practice of treating the foreign trade multiplier as if it were concerned only with the balance of trade and not with the more inclusive balance on current account. Usually, this does not matter since everyone realizes that shipping is just like exports, and tourist expenditure just like imports.

But confusion almost always arises in connection with interest and dividend payments. Very often one encounters the following type of statement: "Foreign lending for a while creates domestic employment. But finally, when interest payments become larger than new lending, the balance of trade will become unfavorable—*with necessary adverse effects upon domestic employment.*" The italicized passage is absolutely wrong.

Interest received from abroad, *per se*, increases domestic employment through its favorable secondary effects on consumption spending. To some (small) degree it increases our imports and thus tends to solve its own "transfer problem." But, alas, this effect is necessarily an incomplete one, so that exchange depreciation may be necessary for the paying country; the unfavorable employment effect of this must be compared with the favorable effect previously mentioned. Strangely enough, from the standpoint of modern income analysis, the Ohlin position of "conservation of purchasing power" becomes something of an archaic throwback to the classical Say's Law; and the orthodox economists (including Keynes), through bumbling reasoning, seem to have approached the correct position.

(5) A simultaneous increase in exports via reciprocal lowering of trade barriers will improve the efficiency of the international division of labor. But ordinarily its favorable effects upon employment are likely to be unimportant—except to the quite limited degree that the release of exchange controls can be expected to diminish thriftiness. This follows from Equation (17) and the earlier remarks concerning an autonomous shift in the import schedule.

Throughout the remainder of this paper, I shall follow the convention of including the foreign balance in *private net capital formation*, *I*, and shall not attempt to isolate that part of each component of net national product which can be imputed to home-owned factors. Therefore, international trade will be implicitly, rather than explicitly, in the income system.

V. THE BUSINESS CORPORATION AND INCOME DETERMINATION

The public's disposable income, *y*, falls short of net national product, *Y*, by more than taxes or net withdrawals once we admit the corporation into the picture. Taxes may now be split into business and personal, although the dividing line becomes rather arbitrary. But more important, corporate earnings (after corporate income taxes) may not all be paid out in dividends; undistributed profits may be ploughed back into the business, or in very bad times dividends may be maintained in excess of stated earnings. In short, algebraic net business saving, *B*, must be subtracted from net national product, along with taxes, before we get the disposable income of consumers.

If initially we ignore the role of government, our simplest income equation now becomes

$$Y = C(Y - \bar{B}) + \bar{I} \qquad (19)$$

An increase in investment will increase income; an increase in net business saving will, by itself, reduce disposable income, consumption, and income. The reader should be able to compute the appropriate multipliers $[dY/d\bar{I}]$ and $[dY/d\bar{B}]$. But first compare this last equation with our earlier treatment of government in Equation (5). It is easy to see that $\bar{I}$ and $\bar{B}$ are— in their relation to income and each other— playing exactly the same roles as did $\bar{G}$ and $\bar{W}$ respectively. This tells us im-

mediately that a reduction in corporate saving is not quite so stimulating as an increase in investment.

The Income Stimulus of Corporations

It also casts light on the way to measure the stimulating influence of business enterprise. Among income analysts, the notion is thoroughly discredited that corporations are flooding the community with purchasing power whenever they pay out more in dividends than they receive in earnings. Fortunately, this is so because in most years, net business savings are positive rather than negative, and a logical application of the discredited viewpoint would have led to the anomalous conclusion that business enterprise is normally *deflating* the community. At the other extreme are those who seem to argue that any real corporate investments made out of ploughed back profits, are fully income creating so that when corporate taxes take away funds that would be added to surplus, employment is being greatly reduced.[10]

Probably most income analysts will prefer a third magnitude to measure the income stimulus emanating from corporations—namely, the difference between net business investment and net business saving (or what is the same thing, the difference between these gross magnitudes). Even this third measure, however, turns out to be not quite correct. Just as a balanced budget increases income with a multiplier of one, so will a balanced increase in business investment and business saving increase employment and income. But, and this the reader can verify by treating Equation (19) the way (5) was treated, there will be no secondary multiplier effects.

[10] This would be nearly true if stockholders treated undistributed profits as part of their disposable income for consumption purposes. This is not realistic because capital gains are not actually, or believed to be, equal to additions to book surplus.

The Corporate Propensity to Save

It would be more realistic to modify (19) by making net business saving some function of net national product or $B = B(Y)$. This would give us

$$Y = C[Y - B(Y)] + \overline{I} = C(Y) + \overline{I}$$

$$(20)$$

and

$$\left[\frac{dY}{d\overline{I}}\right] = \frac{1}{1 - C'(Y)}$$

$$= \frac{1}{1 - C'(Y - B)[1 - B'(Y)]} \quad (21)$$

Between the wars, the marginal propensity of corporations to save appeared much more important than that of families. This may, however, be a short-run cyclical phenomenon which would not be true of the secular growth of high and stable levels of income. Much more statistical study of corporate behavior is needed, especially since there is no reason to expect the invariance of any unique simple hypothesis.[11]

VI. SYNTHESIS

One of the great advantages of quantitative econometric model building is the fact that the writer is pinned down by the concreteness of the arithmetical figures to making specific hypotheses about all the relevant magnitudes. We may summarize, therefore, all the special cases considered up until now by considering the simplest complete income model which takes account of all components of national product.

As always, net national product is the sum of consumption, C, investment, I (including the net foreign balance), and government expenditure on goods and services, G:

$$Y = C + I + G$$

[11] For example in (19) B may be made a function of I rather than Y giving a multiplier of $[1 - C'(\partial B/\partial I)] \div [1 - C']$.

For simplicity, G and I may perhaps still be taken as autonomous factors, although the reader may easily modify this assumption. But if consumption is to depend upon disposable income, a long list of assumptions must be made concerning the numerous subtractions which first have to be made from net national product before we get disposable income. These subtractions are:

(a) *Business taxes, BT*, which we may assume are a function of income.

(b) *Net corporate saving, B*, which is the difference between corporate earnings (after taxes), E, and dividends, D, not to be confused with the deficit referred to earlier. Earnings may, for simplicity, be assumed equal to a function of income; although a good argument could be made for the alternative assumption that earnings before taxes are an invariant function of Y regardless of tax policy. Dividends may most simply be made a function of earnings, although their simple correlation coefficient has not been very high in the past.

(c) *Net personal taxes or withdrawals, PW*, where transfer payments have been treated as negative items. (Obviously, $PW + BT = W$.) This term PW might be made a function of "income paid out," but for simplicity in grouping it with business taxes, we shall make it a function of total net national product, or $PW(Y)$.

Mathematically our hypotheses are

$$C = C(Y - BT - B - PW)$$
$$= C(Y - W - B) = C(Y)$$
$$W = BT(Y) + PW(Y) = W(Y)$$
$$B = E - D = E(Y) - D[E(Y)]$$
$$= B(Y)$$
$$I = \overline{I}, G = \overline{G}$$

Our simple income equation finally becomes

$$Y = C[Y - W(Y) - B(Y)] + \overline{G} + \overline{I}$$

$$(22)$$

The interested reader may depict this equilibrium graphically, and introduce policy parameters—such as tax rates, $\bar{r}$, or corporate "thriftiness"—into various places in this equation and work out the appropriate responses.[12]   He may also introduce in-

---

[12] The response to a change in $\bar{G}$ or $\bar{I}$ can be verified to be given by

$$\left[\frac{dY}{d\bar{G}}\right] = \left[\frac{dY}{d\bar{I}}\right]$$

$$= \frac{1}{1 - C'(Y)[1 - W'(Y) - B'(Y)]}$$

where $B'(Y) = E'(Y) \ [1 - D'(E)]$.   This is placed in a footnote to emphasize that the parent

duced investment if he pleases, or otherwise vary the hypotheses.

In all essentials, our final equation epitomizes the important previous equations, which are respectively (1), (5) or (9), (13) or (17), and (19) or (20).

In conclusion, I would not be doing justice to the pragmatic realism of Professor Hansen, if I did not emphasize the violence done to complex reality by the simplified statical abstractions of this paper.

---

income equations are more important than their multiplier offspring.

4

A Graphical Exposition of the Complete Keynesian System*

WARREN L. SMITH

The purpose of this paper is chiefly expository. A simple graphical technique is employed to exhibit the working of several variants of the Keynesian model. Many of the issues discussed have been dealt with elsewhere,[1] but it is hoped that the analysis presented here will clarify some of the issues and be useful for pedagogical purposes.

* *

Reprinted from *The Southern Economic Journal*, vol. 23 (October 1956), pp. 115–125, by permission of the publisher and author.

Warren L. Smith teaches at the University of Michigan; he was formerly at Ohio State University.

* The development of the technique employed in this paper is a result of discussions with many persons, particularly Professor Daniel B. Suits of the University of Michigan, to whom the writer wishes to express his thanks.

[1] See particularly L. R. Klein, "Theories of Effective Demand and Employment," *Journal of Political Economy*, April 1947, LV, pp. 108–131, reprinted in R. V. Clemence (ed.), *Readings in Economic Analysis*, Vol. I (Cambridge, Mass.: Addison-Wesley Press, 1950), pp. 260–283, and *The Keynesian Revolution* (New York: Macmillan Co., 1950), esp. Technical Appendix; F. Modigliani, "Liquidity Preference and the Theory of Interest and Money," *Econometrica*, Jan. 1944, XII, pp. 45–88, reprinted in F. A. Lutz and L. W. Mints (eds.), *Readings in Monetary Theory* (Philadelphia: Blakiston, 1951), pp. 186–239; also V. Lutz, "Real and Monetary Factors in the Determination of Employment Levels," *Quarterly Journal of Economics*, May 1952, LXVI, pp. 251–272; L. Hough, "The Price Level in Macroeconomic Models," *American Economic Review*, June 1954, LXIV, pp. 269–286.

I. THE KEYNESIAN SYSTEM WITH FLEXIBLE WAGES

This system can be represented symbolically by the following five equations:

$$y = c(y, r) + i(y, r) \qquad (1)$$

$$\frac{M}{p} = L(y, r) \qquad (2)$$

$$y = f(N) \qquad (3)$$

$$\frac{w}{p} = f'(N) \qquad (4)$$

$$N = \varphi\left(\frac{w}{p}\right) \qquad (5)$$

Here y = real *GNP* (at constant prices), r = an index of interest rates, M = money supply (in current dollars), p = index of the price level applicable to GNP, N = the volume of employment (in equivalent full-time workers), w = the money wage. The model represents a theory of short-run income determination with capital stock fixed and labor the only variable factor of production.

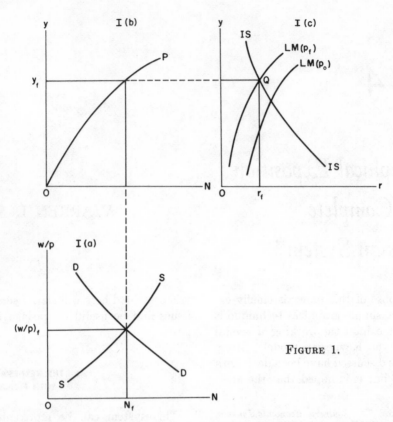

FIGURE 1.

The working of this model is illustrated in Figure 1. Figure 1 should be studied in clockwise fashion, beginning with Chart I (a) in the lower lefthand corner. In I (a), DD represents the demand for labor [equation (4)], and SS represents the supply of labor [equation (5)]. The level of employment and the real wage are determined at the full employment levels, N_f and $(w/p)_f$. Proceeding to I (b), the curve OP represents the aggregate production function [equation (3)], its shape reflecting diminishing returns.[2] With employment

[2] According to the mathematical formulation of our model in equations (1)–(5), the curve DD in I (a) is the derivative of curve OP in I (b), the relation reflecting the operation of the marginal productivity law under competitive conditions. This precise condition is not important, however, and we shall make no attempt to draw the curves in such a way as to fulfill it. For one thing, the presence of monopoly in the economy or failure of entrepreneurs to seek maximum profits would destroy the precision of the equations, but relations of the type depicted in Figure 1 would in all probability continue to hold.

of N_f, y would be at the level y_f, indicated in I (b).

Chart I (c) is the type of diagram developed by Hicks and utilized by others to depict the condition of monetary equilibrium in the Keynesian system.[3] The IS curve in I (c) depicts equation (1) and indicates for each possible level of the interest rate (r) the equilibrium level of income (y) which would prevail after the multiplier had worked itself out fully.[4] We treat the

[3] For a detailed discussion of this diagram, see J. R. Hicks, "Mr. Keynes and the 'Classics'; A Suggested Interpretation," *Econometrica*, April 1937, V, pp. 147–159 [reprinted in this volume, Selection 10]; also A. H. Hansen, *Monetary Theory and Fiscal Policy* (New York: McGraw-Hill, 1949), Chap. 5. The reader's attention is directed to the fact that we have reversed the axes of the Hicks diagram; we measure the interest rate on the horizontal axis and income on the vertical axis.

[4] It should be noted that the formal analysis in this paper falls entirely in the category of comparative statics, that is, it refers to conditions of equilibrium and changes in the equilibrium

stock of money as an exogenous variable determined by the monetary authority. Given M, the LM curves in I (c), of which there would be one for each possible price level (p) which might prevail, represent equation (2) in our model. For example, if the price level were held constant at p_0, the curve $LM(p_0)$ depicts the different interest rates that would be required to preserve equilibrium in the money market at different income levels. The fact that rising income levels are associated with higher interest rates reflects the presumption that as income rises, transactions cash requirements are larger, leaving less of the fixed (in real terms) quantity of money to satisfy demands for idle balances, thus pushing up the interest rate.

If prices and wages are flexible and the situation is as depicted in Figure 1, full employment will automatically be maintained, since the price level will adjust to the level p_f, establishing the LM curve in the position $LM(p_f)$ where it will intersect the IS curve at point Q which corresponds to the full employment level of income (y_f). If, for example, the real wage is initially above $(w/p)_f$, money wages will fall due to the excess supply of labor. This will reduce costs, resulting in increased output and employment and lower prices. Falling prices shift the LM curve upward by increasing the real value of cash balances (M/p), thus lowering the interest rate and expanding aggregate demand to the point where the market will absorb the output corresponding to full employment.[5]

Two important and related propositions can be set down concerning interest and money in the above model:

1. The rate of interest is determined solely by saving and investment and is independent of the quantity of money and liquidity preference.
2. The quantity theory of money holds for this model—that is, a change in the quantity of money will bring about an equal proportional change in the price level and will have no effect on real income or employment.

In other words the quantity of money and liquidity preference serve not to determine the interest rate, as alleged by Keynes, but the price level. As can readily be seen from Figure 1, income is established at the full employment level [I (a) and I (b)], the interest rate adjusts to equate saving and investment [on the IS curve in I (c)] at this income level, and the price level adjusts so as to satisfy liquidity requirements at this interest rate [establishing the LM curve at the appropriate position in I (c)].

It is a comparatively simple matter to modify the analysis of Figure 1 to take account of the possible effect of changes in the real value of liquid assets on consumption (the Pigou effect).[6] The real value of the stock of liquid assets would be included in equation (1), and falling prices would then shift the IS curve to the right, thus strengthening the tendency toward full employment equilibrium. This suggests the question: Does the introduction of the Pigou effect give the quantity of money the power to change the rate of interest when prices and wages are flexible? The answer to this question cannot be

---

values of the variables brought about by changes in data or exogenous variables and does not pretend to describe the *paths* followed by the variables as they move from one equilibrium position to another.

[5] We abstract from the possibility of dynamic instability which may arise due to falling prices if the public has elastic expectations. See D. Patinkin, "Price Flexibility and Full Employment," *American Economic Review*, Sept. 1948, XXXVII, pp. 543–564, reprinted with slight modification in Lutz and Mints, *op. cit.*, pp. 252–283 [also reprinted in this volume, Selection 16].

[6] On the Pigou effect, see A. C. Pigou, "Economic Progress in a Stable Environment," *Economica*, New Series, August, 1947, XIV, pp. 180–188, reprinted in Lutz and Mints, *op. cit.*, pp. 241–251; Patinkin, *op. cit.*; G. Ackley, "The Wealth-Saving Relationship," *Journal of Political Economy*, April 1951, LIX, pp. 154–161; M. Cohen, "Liquid Assets and the Consumption Function," *Review of Economics and Statistics*, May 1954, XXXVI, pp. 202–211; and bibliography in the latter two articles.

deduced from the curves of Figure 1, but it is not difficult to find the answer with aid of the following simple model:

$$\bar{y} = c(\bar{y}, r, a) + i(\bar{y}, r)$$

$$\frac{M}{p} = L(\bar{y}, r)$$

$$a = \frac{A}{p}$$

Here a = the real value of liquid assets which is included in the consumption function and A = their money value. The last three equations of our original model are assumed to determine the real wage, employment, and real income. These equations are dropped and y is treated as a constant (having value $\bar{y}$) determined by those equations. We can now treat M and A as parameters and r, a, and p as variables, differentiate these three equations with respect to M, and solve for dr/dM. This gives the following expression:

$$\frac{dr}{dM} = \frac{\dfrac{c_a}{i_r} \dfrac{A}{M} (1 - \eta_{AM})}{p\left(1 + \dfrac{c_r}{i_r} + \dfrac{A}{M} \dfrac{L_r c_a}{i_r}\right)} \qquad (6)$$

In this expression, the subscripts refer to partial derivatives, e.g., $c_a = \partial c/\partial a$. Normally, the following conditions would be satisfied: $c_a > 0$, $i_r < 0$, $L_r < 0$. We cannot be sure about the sign of c_r, but it is likely to be small in any case. The coefficient η_{AM} has the following meaning:

$$\eta_{AM} = \frac{M}{A} \frac{dA}{dM} = \frac{\dfrac{dA}{A}}{\dfrac{dM}{M}}$$

For example, if a change in M is brought about in such a way as to produce an exactly proportionate change in A, η_{AM} will be unity. Or if the change in M is not accompanied by any change in A, η_{AM} will be zero. It is apparent from the above expression that a change in the quantity of

money will not affect the rate of interest if $\eta_{AM} = 1$, while an increase (decrease) in the quantity of money will lower (raise) the rate of interest if $\eta_{AM} < 1$.[7] Thus, the way in which changes in the quantity of money affect the rate of interest depends upon what asset concept is included in the consumption function (i.e., what is included in A) and how the volume of these assets is affected by monetary change. If M itself is the appropriate asset concept to include in the consumption function (i.e., if $A = M$), changes in M will not affect the interest rate, since in this case η_{AM} is equal to unity. However, the consensus of opinion seems to be that some other aggregate, such as currency, deposits, and government securities held by the non-bank public minus the public's indebtedness to the banks, is more appropriate.[8] If this concept is employed, most of the usual methods of increasing the money supply will ordinarily either leave A unchanged ($\eta_{AM} = 0$) or cause it to increase less than in proportion to the increase in M ($0 < \eta_{AM} < 1$).[9] We may conclude that the Pigou effect gives monetary changes power to influence the rate of interest, even if

[7] We assume that $c_r \le 0$, or if $c_r > 0$, $1 + \dfrac{A}{M} \dfrac{L_r c_a}{i_r} > \left|\dfrac{c_r}{i_r}\right|$, so that the denominator of (6) is positive.

[8] The question of what asset concept is appropriate is discussed in Patinkin, *op. cit.*, Cohen, *op. cit.*, and J. Tobin, "Asset Holdings and Spending Decisions," *American Economic Review Papers and Proceedings*, May 1952, XLII, pp. 109–123.

[9] Open market purchases of government securities by the central bank from the non-bank public will leave A unchanged, since the initial purchase transaction will result in a decline in the public's security holdings and an equal increase in M, while any induced expansion of loans and investments by the banks will result in an increase in M offset by an equal increase in the public's indebtedness to the banks. On the other hand if the Treasury prints currency and gives it to the public, A will be increased by the same absolute amount as M but the increase in A will be proportionally smaller than the increase in M (provided the public's holdings of government securities exceed its indebtedness to the banks so that $A > M$).

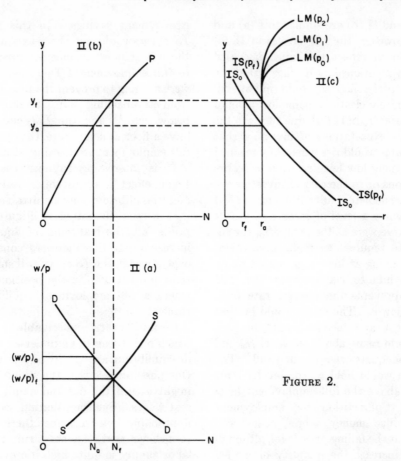

FIGURE 2.

wages and prices are fully flexible. An increase (decrease) in the quantity of money will ordinarily lower (raise) the rate of interest and also increase (decrease) investment and decrease (increase) consumption, but will not change income and employment which are determined by real forces (the last three equations of our complete model).[10, 11]

[10] The fact that the existence of a wealth effect on savings may confer upon the quantity of money the power to affect the rate of interest even with flexible wages is demonstrated in L. A. Metzler, "Wealth, Saving, and the Rate of Interest," *Journal of Political Economy*, April 1951, LIX, pp. 93–116. Metzler's conclusions, which differ from those given here, can be attributed to assumptions that he makes, particularly the assumption that the only assets are money and common stock.

[11] If the supply of labor is affected by the real value of wealth held by workers, changes in the quantity of money may affect output and employ-

II. POSSIBILITIES OF UNDEREMPLOYMENT DISEQUILIBRIUM

There are several possible circumstances arising from the shapes of the various schedules which might produce a situation in which, even though the relations in the above model held true, it might be impossible, at least temporarily, for equilibrium (full employment or otherwise) to be reached. The most widely discussed of these possibilities is depicted in Figure 2.

ment by shifting the *SS* curve in Figure 1 (a). Also, even though monetary change does not affect the *current* level of income and employment, if, due to the operation of the Pigou effect, it changes the interest rate and thereby investment, it may affect the *future* level of employment, since the change in capital stock will ordinarily shift the demand for labor [*DD* curve in Figure 1 (a)] at a future date. Both these points are mentioned in V. Lutz, *op. cit.*

II (a) and II (b) are similar to I (a) and I (b). However, the *LM* curves in II (c) are drawn to reflect the much-discussed possibility mentioned by Keynes[12] that the liquidity preference schedule might become infinitely elastic at some low level of interest rates [r_a in II (c)], due either to the unanimous expectations of investors that interest rates would rise when they reached this extremely low level relative to future expectations or to the cost of investments. In the case depictèd, full employment (N_f) would involve a level of income of y_f. If the *IS* curve were at the level IS_0, the interest rate required to make investment equal to saving at income y_f would be r_f. But the infinite elasticity of the *LM* schedule prevents the interest rate from falling below r_a. The result would be that employment and income would be prevented from rising above the level N_a and y_a by inadequate effective demand. The real wage would hold at the level $(w/p)_a$ which is above the full employment level $(w/p)_f$. Competition for employment would reduce money wages, costs, and prices. But the falling price level, although it would increase the quantity of money in real terms, would not affect the interest rate, hence would not increase investment. As prices fell, the *LM* curve would take successive positions, such as $LM(p_0)$, $LM(p_1)$, $LM(p_2)$, etc., leaving the interest rate unaffected.[13]

A special case of the situation depicted in Figure 2 may arise if a negative interest rate is required to equate investment to full employment savings. In this case, the *IS* curve would cut the *y*-axis and lie to the left of it at an income corresponding to full employment. Then, even if there were nothing to prevent the rate of interest from approaching zero, it could not go below zero,[14] and the *LM* curve would have a floor at a zero rate, thus preventing full employment from being attained.

It is interesting to note that if the Pigou effect is operative, a full employment equilibrium may be attainable even in the case illustrated in Figure 2. As prices fall, the real value of liquid assets increases. If this increases consumption expenditures, the *IS* curve will shift to the right until it attains the position $IS(p_f)$, where a full employment equilibrium is reached.

Certain other conceivable situations which might lead to an under-employment disequilibrium are worthy of brief mention. One possibility is that the supply of labor might exceed the demand at all levels of real wages. Such a situation seems very improbable, however, since there is reason to believe that the short-run aggregate labor supply is quite inelastic over a considerable range of wage rates and declines when wage rates become very low.[15]

Disequilibrium situations could also arise if (a) the demand curve for labor had a steeper slope than the supply curve at their point of intersection, or (b) the *IS* curve cut the *LM* curve in such a way that *IS* lay to the right of *LM* above their

---

[12] J. M. Keynes, *General Theory of Employment, Interest, and Money* (New York: Harcourt, Brace and Co., 1936), pp. 201–204.

[13] Equations (1)–(5) above apply to the situations covered in both Figure 1 and Figure 2. In the latter case, however, the equations are mathematically inconsistent and do not possess a solution. Mathematics does not tell us what will happen in this case (although the additional conditions necessary to describe the results could be expressed mathematically). The statements made above concerning the results (i.e., that income will be y_a, prices and wages will fall together, etc.) are propositions in economics.

[14] Since the money rate of interest cannot be negative, as long as it costs nothing to hold money. In fact, a zero rate of interest would be impossible, since in this case property values would be infinite; however, the rate might *approach* zero. The *real* rate of interest, *ex post*, may be negative due to inflation, but this is not relevant to our problem. On this, see I. Fisher, *The Theory of Interest* (New York: Macmillan Co., 1930), Chaps. II, XIX, and pp. 282–286.

[15] On the probable shape of the short-run aggregative supply of labor, see G. F. Bloom and H. R. Northrup, *Economics of Labor Relations* (Homewood, Ill.: Richard D. Irwin, 1954), pp. 250–253.

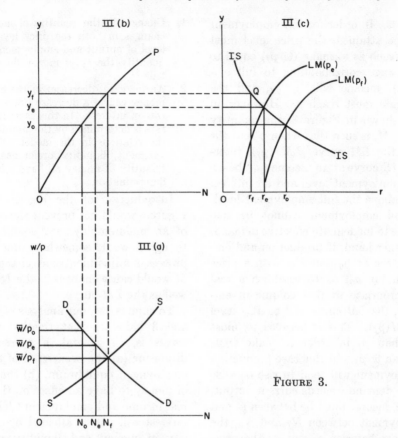

FIGURE 3.

intersection and to the left of *LM* below their intersection in Figure 1 (c) or 2 (c). Actually, these are situations of unstable equilibrium rather than of disequilibrium. However, in these cases, a slight departure from equilibrium would produce a cumulative movement away from it, and the effect would be similar to a situation of disequilibrium.

III. UNDEREMPLOYMENT EQUILIBRIUM DUE TO WAGE RIGIDITY

Next we may consider the case in which the supply of and demand for labor are essentially the same as in Figures 1 and 2, but for institutional or other reasons the money wage does not fall when there is an excess supply of labor.[16] This rigidity of

[16] We will assume that this rigidity does not prevail in an upward direction—i.e., money wages will rise when there is an excess demand for labor.

money wages may be due to various factors, including (a) powerful trade unions which are able to prevent money wages from falling, at least temporarily, (b) statutory provisions, such as minimum wage laws, (c) failure of employers to reduce wages due to a desire to retain loyal and experienced employees and to maintain morale,[17] or (d) unwillingness of unemployed workers to accept reduced money wages even though they would be willing to work at lower real wages brought about by a rise in prices.[18]

A situation of this kind is depicted in Figure 3. The fixed money wage is desig-

[17] See A. Rees, "Wage Determination and Involuntary Unemployment," *Journal of Political Economy*, April 1951, LIX, pp. 143–153.

[18] Keynes, *op. cit.*, Chap. 2; J. Tobin, "Money Wage Rates and Employment," in S. E. Harris (ed.), *The New Economics* (New York: Knopf, 1947), pp. 572–587 [reprinted in this volume, Selection 15].

nated by $\overline{w}$. In order for full employment (N_f) to be attained, the price level must be at p_f (such as to make $(\overline{w}/p_f)$ equal to the real wage corresponding to full employment), income will be y_f, and the interest rate must reach r_f. However, in the case shown in Figure 3, the quantity of money, M, is such that when p is at the level p_f, the LM curve $[LM\ (p_f)]$ intersects the IS curve at an income (y_0) below the full employment level and an interest rate (r_0) above the full employment level. Hence full employment cannot be sustained due to inadequate effective demand. On the other hand, if production and employment are at y_0 and N_0, with a price level such (at p_0) as to establish a real wage appropriate to this volume of employment, the LM curve will be at a level above $LM(p_f)$. This is because p_0 must be less than p_f in order to make $\overline{w}/p_0$ higher than $\overline{w}/p_f$. In this case production and employment will tend to rise because aggregate demand exceeds current output. Therefore, income must be between y_f and y_0, employment between N_f and N_0, the interest rate between r_f and r_0, the price level between p_f and p_0. An equilibrium will be reached somewhere between these limits, say at N_e, y_e, p_e, and r_e.[19]

This is a case of underemployment equilibrium. It should be noted that full employment can be attained by an increase in the quantity of money (M) sufficient to shift the $LM(p_f)$ curve to the position where it will intersect the IS curve at point Q. Two propositions can be set down here to be contrasted with the two stated in connection with Figure 1.[20]

1. Changes in the quantity of money cause changes in both the price level and the level of output and employment, and the quantity theory of money does not hold true.[21]
2. An increase (decrease) in the quantity of money causes a decrease (increase) in the rate of interest. In this case, the interest rate is determined by the interaction of all the relations in the model. Saving, investment, liquidity preference, and the quantity of money all have a hand in its determination.

Introduction of the Pigou effect into Figure 3 would not prevent the occurrence of an underemployment equilibrium, although it would somewhat complicate the process of adjustment since changes in p or M would cause changes in the IS curve as well as the LM curve.

To summarize, our analysis of Figures 1 and 3 indicates that rigidity of money wages is, in general, a necessary condition for (a) the occurrence of an underemployment equilibrium, (b) the quantity of money to have an effect on the level of real income and employment. The rate of interest will not be affected by the quantity of money and liquidity preference unless (a) there is rigidity of money wages or (b) the Pigou effect is operative with $\eta_{A \cdot M} \neq 1$. Monetary theories of the rate of interest, whether of the loanable funds or liquidity preference variety, ordinarily assume rigidity (or at least stickiness) in the structure of money wages.[22]

IV. CONCLUDING COMMENTS

In conclusion, we would like to call the reader's attention to further uses to which

---

[19] In the case depicted in Figure 3, an additional equation $w = \overline{w}$ is added to equations (1)–(5) above. This gives six equations and only five unknowns $(y, N, p, w,$ and $r)$. Such a system of equations is *overdetermined* and does not in general, possess a solution. If the quantity of money is treated as a variable which is adjusted so as to maintain full employment, we have six equations and six unknowns and there will be a solution (unless the equations are inconsistent).

[20] See p. 39, *supra*.

[21] In the limiting case in which the DD curve has a horizontal stage which includes the current level of employment, the entire effect of an increase in M is on y, with no change in p. A considerable part of Keynes' *General Theory* (prior to the discussion of wages and prices in Book V) has reference primarily to this situation.

[22] The relative merits of loanable funds and liquidity preference types of monetary interest theories we do not consider, except to say that when appropriately formulated, the two are equivalent.

our graphical technique can be put. With appropriate modifications to suit the occasion, it can be used to analyze other variations of the Keynesian model.[23] Additional factors affecting the income, employment, and price levels, such as those

suggested by Hough[24] and by Lutz[25] can be quite easily introduced into the analysis through appropriate shifts in the schedules shown in our system of graphs. Fiscal policy and its relation to monetary policy can be dealt with, since fiscal policy influences the level and shape of the *IS* curve. Finally, it provides a useful starting point for the study of economic growth. Factors affecting the rate of growth, such as capital accumulation, population growth, technological change, etc., can be brought in by allowing for their effects on the various schedules.

[23] For example, the models with which Modigliani begins his analysis (*op. cit.*, pp. 46–48 in original, pp. 187–190 in *Readings in Monetary Theory*). Analysis of these models requires some alteration in the graphical technique, since he assumes that consumption, investment, and the demand for money, all in current dollars, depend upon money income and the rate of interest, thus introducing "money illusions" into his scheme at several points.

[24] *Op. cit.*   [25] *Op. cit.*

Part II

CONSUMPTION

5

Effects of Redistribution of Income on Consumers' Expenditures[1]

HAROLD LUBELL

Introduction and Summary

It is a commonly held view among economists that underemployment is the result of the excess of intended saving over investment. There are two ways of reducing this excess, either by increasing investment or by increasing current expenditures so that current savings are reduced. This paper is an attempt to make use of

Reprinted from *The American Economic Review*, vol. 37 (March 1947), pp. 157–170, by permission of the publisher and author.

Harold Lubell is affiliated with the U.S. Agency for International Development Mission to India; he was formerly with the Board of Governors of the Federal Reserve System.

[1] This study was begun under the direction of Everett E. Hagen and completed under that of Richard A. Musgrave at the Board of Governors of the Federal Reserve System, Washington, D.C. The writer wishes to acknowledge his indebtedness to Mr. Hagen and Mr. Musgrave, and to other members of the research staff of the Board of Governors, who made valuable suggestions. He also wishes to express his appreciation to the Bureau of Labor Statistics and the Bureau of Old Age and Survivors Insurance, both of whom made available unpublished data.

available data in order to examine one of the means often suggested for increasing consumers' expenditures—the redistribution of current income.

Since the resulting estimates of the increase in consumer expenditures resulting from income redistribution are small, the conclusion is drawn that if the present data are correct, too much emphasis should not be placed on income redistribution for the solution of the savings-investment problem. However, the data are inadequate to arrive at a definite conclusion. A method is suggested for testing the data by linking survey estimates of income with social security data on incomes. Such linking has been done in the case of one small sample. The results suggest that reporting errors in available data may tend to cause understatement of the effects of redistribution. It is recommended that a similar test of survey data be made on a national scale. Whether redistribution of income will materially increase consumption is such an important socio-economic question that every effort should be made to improve our knowledge concerning it.

REDUCING SAVINGS
BY INCOME REDISTRIBUTION

Past income studies have shown that people in the upper income brackets save a larger fraction of their income than do people in lower income brackets. The substantial difference between the fractions of total income saved in different income brackets has led many to believe that transferring income from upper bracket consumers to lower bracket consumers would greatly increase aggregate consumer expenditures out of a given total income, and correspondingly reduce savings.

However, considering only the differences between fractions of total income spent for consumption by various brackets overestimates the results. Actually, the effect of redistribution depends on the marginal rather than the average propensity to consume at various levels of income. This principle, by now fairly familiar to econometricians, is illustrated by Chart 1, which presents two hypothetical sets of average expenditures by levels of income. Line AA, with constant slope, shows a situation where the marginal propensity to consume is the same at any level of income, even though the fraction of total income spent for consumption declines steadily as income increases. In such a case, redistribution of income from higher to lower income brackets will make for no change whatever in aggregate expenditures.[2] Each dollar of income transferred will reduce expenditures in the upper brackets by exactly the same amount by which it increases expenditures in the lower brackets. Line BB, convex from above, shows a situation where the marginal propensity to consume is greater in the low than in the high brackets. In such a case, redistribution will increase aggregate expenditures, since each increment of income transferred (ΔY) will increase expenditures in the low brackets ($\Delta C'$) by a greater amount than it will reduce expenditures in the high brackets (ΔC). Clearly, the greater the difference between the marginal propensities to consume at high and low income levels, the greater will be the change in expenditures brought about by income redistribution.

Many economists and political leaders who believe that income redistribution will increase consumer expenditures apparently base their belief upon the common observation that low-income families spend a greater share of their incomes than high-income families. Chart 1 demonstrates that this conclusion is a *non sequitur.* If the income-expenditure behavior of United States consumers resembles that portrayed by the curve AA, rather than the curve BB, a basic tenet of the current political philosophy of many liberals must be modi-

[2] For the lowest part of the income range, the curve shows dissavings, that is, expenditures in excess of income. There is no difference in principle between transfer to saving or dissaving groups. The result in each case will depend upon the amount of additional expenditures out of the increase in income, whether accompanied by increased saving or by reduced dissaving. An increase in income for dissaving groups will, in the case illustrated by the line AA, tend to be accompanied by a reduction in dissaving. Expenditures by consumers who dissave will, therefore, tend to increase by only a fraction of the additional income.

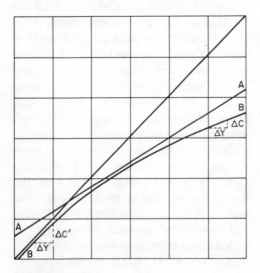

CHART 1.

fied. Hence the available data merit careful analysis.

Expenditure Lags

In any actual situation, redistribution of income may well be accompanied by a lag in adjusting expenditures and savings. This possibility is here ignored. It is assumed that there is no lag. That is, we assume that a man whose income rises from say $500 to $1,000 will immediately spend out of his new income the same amount as a man who had an income of $1,000 to begin with. Likewise, a man whose income falls from $4,000 to $3,000 will spend the same amount as a man whose income was $3,000 to begin with. Moreover, this analysis is limited to short-run aspects of redistribution. It measures changes in the percentage of income saved due to redistribution of a *given* income total, but does not attempt to analyze subsequent changes in total income which may result, or their later effects upon income distribution and savings. Further, no allowance is made for the fact that, with redistribution of income, saving habits might be materially altered. It is believed that these restrictions of the analysis do not destroy the validity of the conclusions drawn.

The study likewise ignores the effects upon total expenditures of any change in investment resulting directly or indirectly from income redistribution. Such effects must be allowed for in estimating the total effect of redistribution.

Basic Data

Two large-scale sample studies of spending and saving habits have been made in recent years. The first of these was the consumer expenditures study of 1935–36 by the National Resources Committee.[3] The second survey was the consumer spending and saving study of 1941 by the Bureau

[3] U.S. National Resources Committee, *Consumer Expenditures in the United States: Estimates for 1935–36* (Washington, 1939).

of Labor Statistics of the United States Department of Labor,[4] and the Bureau of Home Economics of the United States Department of Agriculture. One of the improvements of the 1941 survey over the 1935–36 study is in the 1941 personal tax data which are sufficiently inclusive to use with confidence to obtain "disposable income" or income after taxes.

The 1941 consumers' spending and saving study was a sample survey designed to reveal the national distribution of income and the patterns of expenditure and income of the country. The survey covered single individuals and families of two or more in urban, rural non-farm, and farm areas. For theoretical as well as practical reasons, it seemed advisable for our purposes to leave out all single individuals and all farm families and to include only urban and rural non-farm families of two or more.[5] In estimating a combined distribution, the sample data for urban and rural non-farm groups were given weights based in part upon unpublished Office of Price Administration data.[6] This distribution is shown in Table 1 which gives average income, expenditures after tax, and savings for each income bracket. Chart 2 illustrates these data by showing average expenditures by level of income. The shape of the income-expenditures curve indicates that income redistribution will cause some increase in expenditures.

Statistical Techniques of Redistribution

Our technique for redistributing income is to adjust the average income for each

[4] U.S. Bureau of Labor Statistics Bull. No. 723, *Spending and Saving of the Nation's Families in Wartime* (Washington, 1942).

Another study, *Survey of Prices Paid by Consumers in 1944*, was made in 1944 by the Bureau of Labor Statistics. It is not included here for the following reasons: (1) it covers only urban communities; (2) saving-spending habits were distorted by rationing and the non-availability of consumers' goods.

[5] See Appendix A.

[6] See Appendix A.

TABLE 1

AVERAGE INCOME AFTER DIRECT TAXES, AVERAGE EXPENDITURES AND AVERAGE SAVIGNS
BY INCOME BRACKET: ALL NON-FARM FAMILIES, 1941

(all data in dollars)

Income bracket	Average income	Average expenditures	Average savings
0– 500	321.1	408.5	−87.4
500– 1000	740.6	797.1	−56.5
1000– 1500	1252.0	1286.0	−34.0
1500– 2000	1751.2	1697.5	53.7
2000– 3000	2458.7	2400.9	57.8
3000– 5000	3693.5	3370.1	323.4
5000–10,000	6101.7	4925.8	1175.9
10,000–over	13,561.1	9580.0	3981.1

bracket by moving it closer to some inter-mediate income figure—for example, the mean of the entire distribution. Each bracket average is raised or lowered by a given percentage of the difference between it and the mean. Redistribution by this method leaves aggregate income unchanged.

In order to cover a wide range of possibilities, three percentage adjustments are used, a 10 percent movement toward the mean, as a moderate redistribution, 50 percent as a severe redistribution, and 100

percent, which makes all incomes equal, as the maximum redistribution. For example, the average income of the $0–500 bracket in Table 1 is $321 and the average for the entire distribution is $2,163. The difference between the two figures is thus $1,842, and the 50 percent redistribution raises the average of the $0–500 bracket by $921, so that the new average income for that bracket becomes $1,242. For the $5,000–10,000 bracket with a mean income of $6,102, $1,969 is subtracted so that the new average income for the bracket is $4,133.[7]

Some evaluation of the severity of the various degrees of redistribution is necessary. In terms of tax burden, the 50 percent redistribution case amounts to an added tax levied in addition to 1941 per-

[7] An alternative to our technique of redistributing income toward the mean was suggested by the fact that Chart 2 shows a fairly sharp change in the slope of the income-expenditures line at the $2,000–3,000 bracket. This would seem to indicate that the greatest effectiveness would be obtained by redistribution toward the average income for that bracket, since the differences between the marginal propensities are greatest above and below that point. However, the results upon aggregate expenditures of such redistribution are little different from our previous redistributions, principally because the average income for the $2,000–3,000 bracket ($2,459) is fairly close to the general average ($2,163). Data for this alternative procedure are, therefore, not presented.

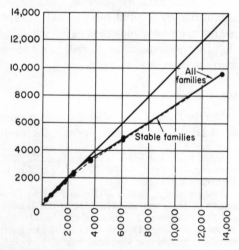

CHART 2. AVERAGE EXPENDITURES BY LEVEL OF DISPOSABLE INCOME (ALL FAMILIES AND FAMILIES WITH STABLE INCOME).

TABLE 2

PERCENTAGE OF NON-FARM FAMILIES BY INCOME BRACKET (1941),
BEFORE AND AFTER REDISTRIBUTION

Bracket	Percent movement toward mean			
	0	10	50	100
0– 1000	22.3	19.0	3.0	0
1000– 2000	32.9	35.0	47.0	0
2000– 3000	26.6	28.0	40.0	100
3000– 5000	13.6	14.0	8.0	0
5000–10,000	3.4	3.0	1.7	0
10,000–over	1.2	1.0	.3	0

sonal taxes. The new tax would be a 50 percent rate without exemptions on income above $2,163 remaining after paying 1941 income taxes. For income brackets above this level, it would thus be a far heavier tax than the heaviest federal income tax ever enacted in the United States, that in effect in 1943–45. For disposable incomes well below $2,163, redistribution by a 50 percent movement toward the mean would be equivalent to remission of all direct taxes in effect in 1941 and contribution of sizeable cash payments in addition. The 10 percent redistribution would imply taxes lighter on all income groups than during 1943–45. However, it would reduce 1941 taxes on groups below the mean while raising them on higher groups. Even this change would involve greater redistribution than that of the wartime federal income tax.[8] As a further measure of severity, changes in the approximate distribution of families by disposable income brackets which might be brought about by our redistributions are shown in Table 2.

Effects of Redistribution

Three new distributions are obtained by the 10, 50 and 100 percent movements to-

[8] These comments use the concept of distribution of income in a very loose sense. No attempt has been made to define the degree of reduction in inequality of income in the more rigorous sense in which the term inequality is used by Gini.

ward equality. For these distributions total income is broken down between consumer expenditures and savings by applying for each average income the income-savings relationship of the basis distribution. Table 3 shows the percentage changes in total expenditures and savings which result. These changes are shown as percentages since the absolute figures depend upon the size of the sample and have no general significance. Since aggregate savings are much smaller than aggregate expenditures, a small error in estimated change in savings will make a large percentage difference. The percentage change in expenditures, the more reliable figure, is therefore used as our measure of the effectiveness of redistributing income.

Strictly speaking, the percentages apply only to the 1941 savings-expenditure situation, or to a distribution of disposable in-

TABLE 3

EFFECTS ON EXPENDITURES AND SAVINGS OF
INCOME REDISTRIBUTION: ALL FAMILIES

Extent of redistribution	Percent increase in expenditures	Percent decrease in savings
100% toward equality	4.1	59.4
50% toward equality	2.4	34.7
10% toward equality	.5	7.2

come identical with that in 1941, in which the average and marginal rates of expenditures are the same for each family at a given position on the Lorenz curve as for the comparable family in 1941. However, the percentages of change in expenditures may be taken as a rough measure—but not too rough for our purpose—of the effect of redistribution in any recent or probable near-future United States income distribution.

The conclusion to be drawn from our data at this point is evident: no redistribution of any feasible severity will bring about a large enough change in aggregate expenditures to offer a major contribution to the problem of increasing total demand. If this conclusion is valid, it is of great social and economic importance since income redistribution is one of the basic methods by which many liberal economists believe the economic system can be made to work. Our data seem to demonstrate that income redistribution by itself would not make a major change in the magnitude of the problem.

Before such a conclusion may be drawn categorically, however, the data must be examined further.

Low Income Dissaving

The small increase in aggregate expenditures is due in great part to the phenomenon of average dissavings below an income of about $1,300. The tendency to dissave in the lower brackets shows up clearly in Table 1. As explained before, it means that an increase in income going to low-bracket consumers will only partly be reflected in increased expenditures, the rest being reflected in a reduction of dissaving.

The phenomenon of continued low-income dissaving requires some explanation. At first glance it is difficult to see how families are able to live from year to year increasing their debts continually (although it is just as difficult to see how they can live on such small incomes at all!). Except for some retired people,

families with low incomes are not in possession of large savings, particularly if they continue to dissave. And presumably there must be some limit to the amount of credit the corner grocery store will give. Two possible explanations present themselves. One might be that the low-income brackets do not include the same people at all times, that the individual families in the brackets vary from year to year. The other might be that reported income in the low-income brackets is understated.

If it were true that the low-income groups include a large portion of families which remain in these brackets only temporarily, the excess of expenditures over income might conceivably be explained by a tendency of expenditures to lag behind when income falls. Dissaving for any individual family would be just temporary while its income declines, although for the average of all families in each bracket dissaving might be continuous. However, to obtain dissavings for the bracket average, it must be assumed that there are more people whose incomes fall than there are whose incomes rise or that there is a greater lag when incomes fall than when incomes rise. The first assumption is obviously correct for the lowest income group, if shifts in income are large. There is no certain proof for either proposition. Since the 1941 income study was made during a period of generally rising income when most families moved to higher rather than lower levels of income, a downward expenditure lag seems questionable as a general explanation for the dissavings phenomenon.

Data for Families with Stable Income

However, in order to eliminate any possible distortion of the data by unstable families, our experiments were applied to families with relatively stable income, defining a relatively stable income as one which changed by less than 5 percent from the preceding year.

TABLE 4

AVERAGE INCOME AFTER DIRECT TAXES, AVERAGE EXPENDITURES AND AVERAGE
SAVINGS BY INCOME BRACKET: FAMILIES WITH STABLE INCOME

Income bracket	Average income	Average expenditures	Average savings
0– 500	328.7	361.2	−32.5
500– 1000	736.9	783.5	−46.6
1000– 1500	1253.3	1245.6	7.7
1500– 2000	1722.6	1625.3	97.3
2000– 3000	2399.9	2252.2	147.7
3000– 5000	3683.3	3218.4	464.9
5000–10,000	6018.7	4792.4	1226.3
10,000–over	11,079.2	7950.2[a]	3129.0

[a] Expenditures adjusted downward.

The 1941 survey, apart from detailed data for 1941, also obtained from each respondee a rough estimate of his 1940 income. These estimates were probably not very accurate, but are all that are available. Since no estimates of total taxes for 1940 were included, to obtain disposable income it was necessary to make an estimate of direct taxes in 1940, based on adjustment of the 1941 taxes. Those families whose disposable incomes had changed by more than 5 percent were then dropped out and the distribution in Table 1 was reconstructed including stable families only.[9] The new distribution is presented in Table 4.

Comparison of the income-expenditure pattern of the all families and stable families distributions shows that the marginal propensities to consume at various income levels are similar for the two groups. It is interesting in particular that this also holds for the lowest income brackets since dissaving is present for the stable families as well. When the three redistribution cases are applied to the stable income distribu-

[9] Average expenditures in the $10,000 and over income bracket were adjusted downward, since the sample for the top bracket was extremely small and the resulting average expenditure looked suspiciously high.

tion,[10] the similarity between the two groups of families is clearly shown. The results are summarized in Table 5.

The percentage increases in expenditures brought about by transferring income from high to low brackets in the "stable income" distribution are slightly smaller, not larger, than those for the all families distribution. The percentage decreases in savings for the stable families, however, are much smaller since the estimated reduction in dollar savings is about similar for both cases, while aggregate savings before redistribution are much larger for stable families.

It must be cautioned that the data used for the stable family estimates are very poor. Nevertheless, comparison of the two estimates seems to indicate that expenditure lags are not very important in ex-

[10] For the purposes of redistribution, the average income and expenditures for stable families as shown in Table 4 are used but the same family distribution by numbers is retained as applied to the all family case. Otherwise the results would not have been comparable. Since the income in each bracket is slightly lower for families with stable income than for all families, aggregate income in the revised distribution is somewhat reduced and the new mean income for the entire distribution is $2,104. Aggregate savings, on the other hand, are larger in the revised distribution because of the greater reduction in aggregate expenditures than in aggregate income.

TABLE 5

Effects on Expenditure and Savings of Income Redistribution, by
Type of Redistribution: Families with Stable Income

Type of redistribution	Percent increase in expenditures	Percent decrease in savings	Percent increase in expenditures, all families, from Table 2
100% toward equality ($2104)	3.3	33.5	4.1
50% toward equality	2.2	22.1	2.4
10% toward equality	.5	5.3	.5

plaining dissavings in the lower income groups.

Reliability of the Data

The second possible reason to question the tentative conclusion is that basic data obtained in the 1941 survey may be incorrect. The data for the individual respondees was checked as carefully as possible by the survey enumerators with data on changes in net worth of the respondees at the end of the year. Changes in net worth were obtained from a table of items entering into changes in assets and liabilities during the year and the enumerators were careful to see that the sum of expenditures and net changes in assets came within 5 percent of the total reported income. Nevertheless, a strong possibility of reporting errors in incomes and changes in net worth is inherent in the way the schedules were devised. The interview schedule was set up to get a much more detailed picture for expenditures than for income and for net changes in assets and liabilities. The figures for income by source and for net worth were obtained for the entire past year while expenditures were obtained by shorter time periods, by numbers of items, expense of each item, and so on. Summation of these details, item by item, makes the expenditures estimate fairly accurate. Estimates based upon memory of total income gained by intermittent employment during the year leave

a much greater margin for error, especially in the low-income groups where employment is most discontinuous.

When a reconciliation of income and net worth figures is made by considering one as a residual of the other, even if done by the respondee but at the behest of the interviewer, there is some danger of merely rationalizing an error in the first estimate. There are a number of items in the list of the components of net worth where faulty memory is perhaps as likely as in estimating income. Accurate figures on such items as money on hand, amounts due on various kinds of debts, payments and balances on installment purchases, and perhaps even bank accounts are difficult to remember. Thus even if the expenditures estimates are reliable, an important check on the respondees' estimates of their incomes for the past year is open to the same sort of errors as are the income estimates.

However, income reported by employers to the Social Security Board may be used as a further check on the estimates of income recorded by interviewers. Since the coverage of consumers by social security is wide, although far from complete, it is possible to make use of social security records to compare incomes reported by employees with those shown by employers' records. Particularly for low-income consumers with casual incomes, the presumably accurate records of the Social Security Board can be used as a check on incomes reported by consumers to the extent that income is earned in covered employment.

Evidence from Old Age and Survivors' Insurance Records

A comparison has been made by the Social Security Board of data obtained from a 1939 census study and from records of the Bureau of Old Age and Survivors' Insurance. This comparison presents an important clew. It suggests that the excess of expenditures over income in the lower brackets reported in income surveys may be due to progressively greater understatement of income by consumers, the lower their average income.

The OASI study compares data on taxable wages and total wage incomes reported in a trial census of population of two Indiana counties for 1939 with corresponding data for the same individuals from the old age and survivors' insurance records. If both reports were accurate, on the average incomes reported to the census would be higher than the recorded incomes in the old age and survivors' insurance files, since presumably not all the work done by employees would have been done in jobs covered by government insurance. This was expected to be most pronounced in the low-income groups where employment is highly irregular. The comparison showed, however, that incomes reported by individuals in the lower-income groups were *below* the incomes recorded for them in the old age and survivors' insurance records. In other words, low-income individuals on the whole understated their income and, interestingly enough, the degree of understatement increased the lower the income bracket.

Table 6 shows the ratios by income bracket of income understatement obtained in the Social Security Board comparison of census and old age and survivors' insurance reports. The ratio of understatement is defined as taxable income recorded by employers divided by the income reported to the census interviewers. These ratios are conservative estimates of underreporting which actually occurred, since some income will have been earned in jobs not covered by the old age and survivors insurance.

If this tendency toward understatement of income by low-income groups is general, it may also apply to the BLS survey. Hence, it will be of interest to test the extent to which this may affect our preceding estimates. If income for the low-income families was progressively more underreported, at decreasing levels of income, appropriate correction of the data would change the income-expenditure relation in such a way that in the lower-income brackets a greater increase in expenditures would accompany each increase in income. Graphically, the income-expenditure curve would become more concave downward. Redistribution of income then would result in larger increases in consumption expenditures.

For purposes of experiment it may be useful to apply the measures of income understatement of Table 6 to the 1941 study and observe the resulting effect on redistribution. Presumably the 1941 study was conducted with greater precision than the trial survey in 1939, so that the data obtained were more nearly accurate. Ap-

TABLE 6

RATIO OF OASI TAXABLE INCOME TO REPORTED INCOME, BY INCOME BRACKET

Income bracket	Ratio of OASI taxable income to reported income
$ 0– 500	121.4%
500–1000	116.4
1000–1500	111.1
1500–2000	102.7

TABLE 7

AVERAGE INCOME AFTER DIRECT TAXES, AVERAGE EXPENDITURES, AND AVERAGE
SAVINGS BY BRACKET: INCOME AND SAVINGS ADJUSTED FOR UNDERREPORTING[a]

Income bracket	Average income	Average expenditures	Average savings
$ 0– 500	389.8	408.5	−18.7
500– 1000	862.1	797.1	65.0
1000– 1500	1391.0	1286.0	105.0
1500– 2000	1798.5	1697.5	101.0
2000– 3000	2458.7	2400.9	57.8
3000– 5000	3693.5	3370.1	323.4
5000–10,000	6101.7	4925.8	1175.9
10,000–over	13,561.1	9580.0	3981.1

[a] Incomes and savings in the four brackets between $0 and $2000 adjusted by understatement ratios of old age and survivors' insurance. Expenditures unadjusted.

TABLE 8

EFFECTS ON EXPENDITURES AND SAVINGS OF INCOME REDISTRIBUTION, BY
TYPES OF REDISTRIBUTION: ALL FAMILIES, ADJUSTED FOR
UNDERREPORTING OF INCOME

Type of redistribution	Percent increase in expenditures	Percent decrease in savings	Increase in expenditures ($ billions)
100% toward equality	6.7	70.5	9
50% toward equality	4.7	50.0	6
10% toward equality	2.9	30.5	4

plication of the understatement ratios to the 1941 survey income figures may, therefore, be regarded as the extreme upper limit for correction of errors on the part of the respondees.

Redistribution of Incomes Adjusted by Old Age and Survivors' Insurance Ratios

Accordingly, average incomes in Table 1 were adjusted by the ratios in Table 6 while average expenditures in Table 1 were left unadjusted. This process, of course, raised both aggregate income and aggregate savings. A new savings figure for each bracket was derived by deducting the reported expenditures figure from the raised income figure, thereby changing the income-savings relationship considerably

and greatly reducing the amount of dissavings. Table 7 presents the distribution in Table 1 after this adjustment.

The three redistribution cases were again applied to Table 7 and the results are summarized in Table 8. The resulting percentage increases in expenditures are now considerably greater than in the preceding experiments. The relatively mild redistribution exemplified by the 10 percent shift results in a 2.9 percent increase in expenditures, as compared with .5 percent in Table 3. Moving all incomes 50 percent toward equality results in an increase in expenditures twice as great as before.

Using the assumption of a gross national product of 200 billion dollars, disposable income of 150 billions, and consumer expenditures of 135 billions, figures for aggregate changes in expenditures are included in Table 8.

The 10 percent redistribution might mean an increase in total expenditures of 4 billions, compared with an estimated increase of one billion on the basis of our original data which included heavy dissaving. The magnitudes are still not spectacular, but are certainly significant.

Conclusion

The data from the 1941 study of consumers' income and expenditures seem to caution against placing too much faith in the theory that income redistribution will greatly decrease the volume of savings in the economy. These data are the best we have to date, and until better data are available the conclusion drawn from them cannot be disregarded. However, two things should be kept in mind.

Available data on which estimates of this kind can be based are thoroughly inadequate for any definite judgment. Application of the old age and survivors' correction ratios shows that even fairly slight errors in reporting may affect the results considerably. Future income surveys should make use of the data available from the old age and survivors' insurance records as a check on the accuracy of the survey data. Furthermore, the case for and against income redistribution depends not only upon the considerations included here. Other aspects, such as the welfare effects of a more equal income distribution must also be considered.

APPENDIX A

The Sample

The Bureau of Labor Statistics-Bureau of Home Economics sample consisted of 1,007 urban families and 871 rural non-farm families. Of these, 211 urban and 464 non-farm had incomes which changed less than 5 percent from the preceding

year. Since the number of rural non-farm families was not in the same ratio to the number of urban families in the sample as in the actual population as estimated by the Office of Price Administration, the number of urban families in each bracket was multiplied by the appropriate factor, 2.595, in order to get the same ratio of rural non-farm to urban families in the sample as in the estimate of the total population.

The decision to include only non-farm families was taken for several reasons. In the first place, the sample of single individuals seemed too small for any further breakdowns which might have been necessary. Far more important, farmers and single individuals were left out in order to redistribute the incomes of a relatively homogeneous group. Farmers and single individuals differ greatly from non-farm families, with respect to both income distribution and expenditure patterns. Both farmers and single individuals in general have lower money incomes than non-farm families. Combining all the groups would weight the lower brackets heavily with the expenditure pattern of farmers and single individuals, who in general save a greater portion of their incomes than non-farm families.

Ideally, our study should show what change would take place in spending by each family and each individual in the country if no change took place in his socio-economic status, other than the change in his income caused by redistribution. We want to isolate the effect of income redistribution. But if all groups were combined in the sample used, redistribution of income would have the effect of causing many single persons and farm families to assume the spending characteristics of non-farm families, thus exaggerating the increase in expenditures. We would be testing the combined effect on expenditures of income redistribution, marriage, and farm-non-farm migration. To avoid this statistical aberration, only non-farm families were used. A complete study would of course redistribute income within each type of consumer units, and combine the results. The procedure used- seemed the most desirable simpler alternative.*

* [In a subsequent note on "Effects of Income Redistribution on Consumers' Expenditures: A Correction," *The American Economic Review*, vol. 37 (December 1947), p. 930, Mr. Lubell wrote:

Professor J. M. Clark has pointed out to me in correspondence that there is an error in Table 8 of my communication on the above topic in the March, 1947 number of this *Review*. Table 8 [see p. 58] purposes to estimate the increase in consumers' expenditures as a result of redistributing income after adjusting the lower income groups for possible understatement of income. The published figures, however, are too high. Professor Clark points out that the results shown in the published table could be correct only if the net difference between the marginal rates of consumption of persons losing and persons gaining by redistribution were greater than unity, *i.e.*, that the increase in expenditures shown was greater than the amount of income redistributed. The cause of the difficulty was a mechanical error which was made in computing the original table. The table should read [as given in the next column].

Thus the increase in expenditures is only slightly larger than that estimated originally for all families without adjustment for understatement of income. The first and pessimistic conclusion

EFFECTS ON EXPENDITURES AND SAVINGS OF INCOME REDISTRIBUTION, BY TYPES OF REDISTRIBUTION: ALL FAMILIES, ADJUSTED FOR UNDERREPORTING OF INCOME

Type of redistribution	Percent increase in expenditures	Percent decrease in savings	Increase in expenditures ($ billions)
100% toward equality	5.82	61.5	8.7
50% toward equality	2.87	30.5	4.4
10% toward equality	.52	5.5	.8

of the March communication is therefore further substantiated: that too much emphasis should not be placed on income redistribution for the solution of the problem of oversaving. Reporting errors in available data, in addition to being of interest in themselves, may tend to cause some understatement of the effects of redistribution but not of significant magnitude when moderate methods of redistribution are considered. Small changes in the shape of the consumption-income relationship apparently do not affect significantly the size of the effects of redistribution computed by our methods. Limitations of the amount of income to be shifted and the relative constancy of marginal rates of spending throughout the income scale seem to be the dominating factors.—*Ed.*]

6

Income-Consumption Relations and Their Implications

JAMES S. DUESENBERRY

Of all the new ideas introduced by Keynes in *The General Theory*, the concept of the "consumption function" was the easiest to accept. Few wished to deny that consumption expenditures are primarily determined by income; Keynes' arguments for the stability of the relationship were cogent enough to convince a great number of economists. The opportunities for empirical work opened up by the introduction of the new concept were at once apparent. Here, for once, was a theoretical relationship which involved magnitudes which could be measured not merely theoretically but practically. Econometricians went to work with a will and their efforts were amply rewarded. They were not only able to find a relationship between income and consumption, but they found that virtually all of the variation in consumer expenditures was explained by variations in income.

Yet, in spite of these empirical successes, the consumption function is a more controversial subject today than it was ten years ago. For empirical investigation has yielded not one consumption function but many, and each of them explains all the variations in consumption.

Like most economic magnitudes the literature on the consumption function seems to grow according to the compound-interest law. This would be easy to understand if the literature appeared as the result of the discovery of new data. But no fundamental changes in our knowledge of the facts about income and consumption have occurred in the past five years.

Most of the articles on the consumption function present hypotheses about the relation between consumption, income, and some other variable such as time, the price level, or the degree of unemployment. The hypothesis is presented in the form of an equation which makes consumption a func-

* *

Reprinted from *Income, Employment, and Public Policy*, Essays in Honor of Alvin H. Hansen, pp. 54–81, by permission of W. W. Norton & Company, Inc., and the author. Copyright 1948 by W. W. Norton & Company, Inc.

James S. Duesenberry teaches at Harvard University.

tion of the other variables. The appropriate regression is fitted to the data, and the correlation between the observed and calculated values of consumption or saving is computed. The correlation is invariably high, and most writers seem to be satisfied that a high correlation coefficient provides an adequate test of their hypothesis. But a test which is passed by so many different hypotheses is not a very satisfactory one. Before any more consumption functions are introduced it seems desirable to give some consideration to our methods of testing hypotheses.

In Section I it is shown that aggregate hypotheses cannot be adequately tested by the use of correlation analysis. The general principles on which appropriate testing methods can be developed are then discussed. Section II is devoted to a consideration of the possibility that the relation between saving and income is different at different points of the trade cycle. A test based on the principles developed in Section I shows that we must reject the hypothesis that the saving-income relation is invariant with respect to measures of position in the trade cycle.

In Section III hypotheses which explain both cyclical and secular movements of savings are developed. It is shown that these hypotheses are consistent with: (1) the long-run data on income and consumption given by Kuznets, (2) the annual data on income and consumption in the period 1923–1940, (3) the budget study data collected in 1935–1936 and 1941. These hypotheses lead to the conclusion that aggregate saving out of disposable income can be estimated by the equation $s_t/y_t =$ .165(y_t/y_0) − .066, where $s_t =$ current savings, $y_t =$ current disposable income, $y_0 =$ highest disposable income ever attained, with all variables corrected for population and price changes.[1]

[1] Part of this paper was presented at the meeting of the Econometric Society in January, 1947. At the same meeting Prof. Franco Modigliani presented a paper containing an almost identical income-saving relation.

I. TESTS OF AGGREGATE HYPOTHESIS

When we deal with a problem in aggregate economics we usually seek for relationships which are, in some sense, invariant. By invariance we do not mean a historical invariance like the Pareto law. Rather, we mean that the relationship between a certain set of variables is unaffected by changes in some other variables. The concept of an invariant relationship is therefore a relative one; a relation may be invariant with respect to one set of variables, but not with respect to some others. Indeed it might be said that hardly any economic relationship can be regarded as completely invariant. For no economic relation is likely to continue to hold good both before and after a fundamental change in social organization. In fact, one of the objects of economic policy is the modification of social organization in such a way as to produce relations of a desirable type among economic variables.

Our idea of invariance is somewhat as follows: We conceive that at any one moment certain variables within the control of households or firms are related in a definite way to certain other variables not within their control. For example, we suppose that the consumption expenditure of families depends on their income. The form of these relations is governed by the behavior characteristics of individuals and by institutional factors such as laws or customs. The relations we seek are invariant with respect to all variables except these psychological or institutional factors. A relation which satisfies that criterion may be said to be more or less stable according as these factors are more or less constant. We can make satisfactory predictions if we can find invariant relations of this type which are highly stable.[2]

[2] Finding invariant relations of this sort actually helps in only one kind of policy problem. We may conceive of the "structure" of the economy as being described by a certain set of invariant relations. Then one kind of policy consists in

If an invariant relation of this type holds for the variables associated with individual households or firms, then a corresponding invariant relation must hold among some functions (not necessarily sums) of all the household or firm variables of the same kind. If we can write $y_i = f_i(x_i)$ for every household (when x_i and y_i are variables applying to the ith household), then we can write $\emptyset(x_1, x_2 \ldots x_n, y_1, y_2, \ldots y_n) = 0$. The invariance of the second relation will depend on the constancy of the behavior characteristics and institutional elements which determine the invariance of the original relations, and in some cases on the constancy of the distribution of the x's. Aggregate relations which can be deduced from household or firm relations, I shall call fundamental aggregate relations. (There are of course some additional fundamental aggregate rela-

tions which are definitional and need not be deduced from anything.)

Now consider a pair of such fundamental aggregate relations:

$$\emptyset_1(x_1 x_2 \ldots x_n) = \psi_1(y_1 y_2 \ldots y_n) \quad (1)$$
$$\emptyset_2(x_1 x_2 \ldots x_n) = \psi_2(z_1 z_2 \ldots z_n) \quad (2)$$

where the x's are exogenous variables.

It is clear that a further relation (3) $x_1(y_1 y_2 \ldots y_n) = x_2(z_1 z_2 \ldots z_n)$ may be derived from the first two. Further, this relation will be invariant so long as (1) and (2) are invariant. This type of relation I shall call a derived aggregate relation.[3]

Now suppose that we observe the historical invariance of the relation (3) and conclude that it is a fundamental relation. We might then conclude that by changing the z's we could manipulate the y's. But we might find instead that we had merely invalidated the relation (2) without having any effect at all on the y's or x's. Derived relations like (3) may break down either as a consequence of policy changes or of structural changes in the economy. In addition there is an important class of derived relations which are likely to hold good only during the course of a single trade cycle. For example, a certain variable z may be partly dependent on the level of unemployment. Within the course of a single trade cycle, income is very closely associated with the level of unemployment. If we have data covering only a single trade cycle, we might conclude from the empirical evidence that z is determined by income. Actually we have a derived relation between z and income, which is bound to break up because the upward trend in income will ultimately change the association between income and unemployment. It is clear from these considerations that many of the relations observed empirically may be only derived relations which will break down because of a struc-

---

fixing the values of certain of the variables which enter into these equations without otherwise disturbing any of the relations. Fixing an interest rate or tax rate is a policy of this sort. If we know all the invariant relations necessary to describe the structure, we can predict the effect of this sort of policy (at least in the sense that we can assign a probability to any values of any economic variable at each point in the future).

On the other hand, many of the most important policies involve changes in the structure. If a law is changed which has never been changed before, then we may know that certain structural equations will be changed, but we may not be able to foretell exactly what the new equations will be like. Or, to take a simple example, if the Treasury undertakes a campaign to get people to save more, it will be difficult to know what its effect will be. For this is an attempt to induce changes in behavior patterns, and we have comparatively little experience with this kind of change. The kind of data with which economists deal is not likely to reveal anything about the possible effects of the Treasury's campaign. On the other hand, a sufficiently general theory of behavior ought to make a prediction possible, but this would be entirely a question of social psychology.

As a matter of fact, it seems probable that most of the economic policies of really fundamental importance involve structural changes of this sort. To the extent that this is true, economists can be regarded as competent to judge the effect of these policies only by default on the part of the social psychologists.

[3] Cf. T. Haavelmo, "The Probability Approach to Econometrics," *Econometrica*, July, 1944, Supplement.

tural change in one of the fundamental relations on which they are based. This is
particularly true of relations whose existence has been tested against the data of
only a single trade cycle. Whether we are
concerned with policy or with prediction,
we shall often make errors if we treat
derived relations as though they were
fundamental ones. The difficulty of distinguishing between these two kinds of
relations is one of the fundamental difficulties in testing economic hypotheses.

Let us now return to a consideration of
the adequacy of correlation methods of
hypothesis testing. Suppose we have a
hypothesis which asserts that total consumer expenditure is dependent on disposable income. We can fit a regression to
the data for income and consumption and
compute the correlation coefficient. When
we find a significant correlation, what,
exactly, have we found? We have not
shown that the "data are consistent with
the hypothesis." We have merely disproved the null hypothesis. That is, we
have shown that the association between
income and consumption was too strong to
allow us to ascribe it to chance. Then we
should be reasonably confident in asserting
that we have found either (a) a fundamental relation between income and consumption, or (b) a derived relation between
them. We might exploit our results a little
further. If it could be shown that the
lower confidence limit on the correlation
was (say) .95, we could assert that during
the period income was linearly related to
all the variables fundamentally related to
consumption. But this is about as far as
we can safely go. It can be argued, of
course, that a derived relation will tend to
produce lower correlations than a fundamental relation. But, when our data cover
only short periods, the connections between
economic variables may be so close that
the differences in correlations between the
two sorts of relations may be too small to
be statistically significant. Moreover, if the

variables in a derived relation have a lower
observational error than those in the
fundamental relations, the correlation in
the derived relation may be the higher one.

A very simple example of a derived relation is that which appears to have existed
between consumer expenditures in dollars
and disposable income in dollars during
the period 1929–1940. Just as good a correlation is obtained by using undeflated as
deflated data. This can be true only because the price level was related to income
during the period. If real consumption is
fundamentally related to real income, the
money relationship is a derived one and
will break down in the postwar period.
Conversely, if money consumption is fundamentally related to money income the
relation between the real variables is a
derived one and will break down. Now it is
obviously of vital importance to know
which is the fundamental relation, but the
correlation test is not very helpful.

The difficulties we have just been discussing arise because of the existence of
derived relations among aggregate variables. But, ordinarily, such derived relations will not hold for individual firms or
households. This suggests that in testing
hypotheses we ought to operate on the
following principles. First, every hypothesis ought to be stated in terms of the behavior of individual firms or households,
even when we are only interested in aggregate results. This does not, of course,
prevent us from considering interactions
among individuals, any more than the use
of the theory of the firm in analysis of
monopolistic competition prevents us from
dealing with interactions among firms.
Second, in so far as it is possible, we ought
to test our hypotheses against data which
indicate the behavior of individual households or firms. This does not mean that
we ought to abandon statistical procedures.
Nearly every hypothesis has to allow for
random elements in behavior so that in
making tests we have to measure the

average behavior of groups. But by dealing with relatively small groups we may escape the net of interrelations which makes it impossible to test aggregate hypotheses.

Suppose we are faced with the following situation: One hypothesis asserts that saving varies with income and the price level, another asserts that saving depends on income alone. Aggregate income and the price level are related in the period for which data are available. Then, if one of these hypotheses is true, it will be impossible to disprove the other by means of aggregate data alone. But, while movements of aggregate income may have been correlated with those of the price level, there are certainly some individuals whose incomes moved in a different way. By studying the behavior of those individuals it will be possible to disprove one of the hypotheses. When this has been done the parameters in the chosen relation may be fitted by the use of aggregate data (though in some cases this may still be difficult because of multicollinearity).

Of course it will not always be possible to find the data necessary to test every hypothesis. But there is a great deal of micro-economic data, which has never been properly exploited because of the tendency of econometricians to emphasize parameter fitting rather than hypothesis testing. Actually it is much more important to work with a true hypothesis than to make extremely precise estimates of parameters.

II. CHANGES IN INCOME AND THE RATE OF SAVING

In this section we shall apply the method just suggested to some questions about the consumption function. In the view of a number of writers, notably Smithies and Mosak,[4] consumer expenditures are essentially dependent on the prevailing level of disposable income. The effect on con-

sumption of an increase in income is supposed to be the same whether the increase comes about through a rise of employment during recovery from a depression or through a rise in productivity in a period of sustained full employment like that of the twenties. Professor Hansen[5] and Professor Samuelson[6] have maintained for some time that the relation between income and consumption varies through the trade cycle. Mr. Woytinsky[7] and Mr. Bean[8] have made similar statements and have tried to test them empirically. They obtained correlations just as good as the others but no better, and certainly cannot claim to have disproved the alternative hypothesis. There is, however, some evidence which proves nearly conclusively that the consumption function is cyclically variable though not quite in the ways suggested by Bean or Woytinsky.

This evidence is provided by the budget studies made in 1935–36[9] and 1941.[10] One of the remarkable results of the Study of Consumer Purchases of 1935–36 was that a great number of families reported expenditures in excess of income for the year. The average deficit of the under $500 a year group amounted to 50 percent of income, while the average deficit of the $500–$1000 group was 10 percent of income.[11]

---

[4] "Forecasting Postwar Demand, I, III," *Econometrica*, January, 1945.

[5] *Business Cycles and Fiscal Policy*, New York, W. W. Norton & Company, 1941, pp. 225–249.

[6] "Full Employment after the War," in *Postwar Economic Problems*, edited by S. E. Harris, New York, McGraw-Hill, 1943.

[7] "Relationship between Consumer's Expenditure, Savings and Disposable Income," *Review of Economic Statistics*, January, 1946.

[8] "Relationship of Disposable Income and the Business Cycle to Expenditure," *Review of Economic Statistics*, November, 1946.

[9] Summarized by the National Resources Committee in *Consumer Expenditures in the United States*, Washington, 1938; *Consumer Incomes in the United States*, Washington, 1939; *Family Expenditures in the United States*, Washington, 1941.

[10] Bureau of Labor Statistics, Bulletins 723 and 724.

[11] *Family Expenditures in the United States*, p. 1.

TABLE 1

WHITE URBAN AND RURAL NON-FARM FAMILIES WITH INCOMES
UNDER $1000 IN 1935–1936

	Relief	Non-relief
Retired	600,000	600,000
Independent business and professional	100,000	600,000
Partially or fully unemployed	2,100,000	1,900,000
Fully employed	—	2,400,000
Total	2,800,000	5,500,000

The results of the 1935–36 study are not above criticism, of course, but the fact that deficits were reported in every city and every area, together with the independent evidence of studies like those of Gilboy, Clague, and Powell, makes it clear that very substantial deficits did occur during the depression.[12]

The total deficits of urban and rural non-farm families (who were white and not on relief) alone amounted to 593 million dollars for 1935–36. Since total net savings of consumers during the twenties and thirties varied from $7.6 to $2.0 billion, an explanation of the deficits can contribute a good deal to our understanding of variations in saving.

But the real significance of the deficits does not lie in their magnitude but in what they reveal about the relations between income and saving. We shall first show that the deficits arose largely because families whose income fell in the depression tried to preserve their pre-depression living standards. Families in the higher income groups did the same thing but accomplished it by reducing their rate of saving rather than by dissaving. The analysis of the deficits is important chiefly because it helps us to analyze variations in the positive savings of higher income groups.

Let us first consider what kind of people were in the low income groups in 1935–36. While there is little direct information about the low income families in 1935–36, a rough estimate of their composition can be made from the data on income and employment in 1939 contained in the Census of 1940. Table 1 shows the result of this estimate.[13]

In the nature of the case this estimate can be only a rough one since it has to be based on a number of unverified assumptions. Yet there does not seem to be much doubt that the non-relief low-income families included a high proportion of families whose incomes were low because of unemployment and whose incomes were much higher in periods of full employment. Moreover, some of the families in the independent business and professional group would have higher incomes in more prosperous periods. Finally, some of the fully employed wage and salary workers were downgraded from higher wage jobs so that their normal incomes were higher than the incomes reported in 1935–36.

(1) Keeping these considerations in mind, let us now ask what is the signif-

[12] Elizabeth Gilboy, *Applicants for Work Relief*, Cambridge, Harvard University Press, 1940. E. Clague and W. Powell, *Ten Thousand Out of Work*, Philadelphia, University of Pennsylvania, 1933.

[13] This estimate was obtained by reconciling the data given by the National Resources Committee on numbers of families with incomes under $1000 in 1935–36 with the data in the Census of 1940 on the family wage and salary income and employment in 1939. See *Family Expenditures in the United States*, pp. 123, 127, 130 and Census of 1940, *The Labor Force (Sample Statistics)*, *Wage or Salary Income in 1939* and *Family Wage or Salary Income in 1939*.

icance of the deficits for the theory of saving. A supporter of the view that saving depends on real income would say, presumably, that $c/y = f(y)$ and that c/y exceeds 1 for some positive value of y (where y is in constant prices). When that value of y is reached, those who have assets or credit will have deficits; the others will have to be content with spending all of their income.

In its simple form this position is untenable, for the break-even point (the income at which consumption just equals income) stood at about $800 in 1917 and $1500 in 1935–36, using 1941 prices in both cases.[14] If consumption were merely a function of current income the break-even level of income should have remained the same. To this the sophisticated Keynesian will reply by introducing a trend factor. Consumption at a given level of income can be changed by the introduction of new goods (this is about the only factor likely to cause a trend in the consumption of urban families, and these are the families included in the budget studies in question). For the sake of the argument let us agree that introduction of new goods in itself increases consumption at a given level of income. We know too that families in the low income groups were driving automobiles and using various recently introduced household appliances. This does not advance the argument much, however, for the families in question were for the most part using these things rather than buying them. We can turn to other new goods, movies and silk stockings (say), which were also consumed by the low-income groups in the thirties. Let us grant that a family with an $800 income did not buy these things in 1917 and did in 1935. Then it follows that at least part of the deficits in the thirties were due to the fact

that low income families bought new goods which did not exist in the earlier period. But this is not the whole story. We can say on the one hand that families at an $800 income level in the thirties spent more than families with that income in 1917 because they had become used to a high standard of living (including silk stockings and movies) in the twenties and found it difficult to give up. Or we can say that even if income had remained constant from 1917 to 1935 the attraction of these new goods was so irresistible that they incurred deficits to get them (or at least that they would have done so if they had had the necessary assets or credit). The latter position seems to be a somewhat untenable one. But, if we argue that consumption depends on current real income and trend, that is the position which must be maintained in order to explain the facts. For, if we write $c/y = f(y, t)$, nothing has been said about the influence of past living standards on current consumption.

This does not disprove the proposition that consumption at a given moment is dependent on real income alone; but it does require the supporters of that proposition to subscribe to some very strong propositions about the influence of new products and similar trend factors.

(2) We can make a further test if we compare the deficits reported in 1935–36 with those reported in 1941. Deficits at given levels of income were much smaller in 1941 than in 1935–36. At every level deficits were less than one half as great in 1941 as in 1935–36. How is this shift to be explained? Suppose the deficits, in both cases, were due to the fact that families whose incomes had fallen as a result of unemployment found it hard to reduce their living standards. Then the explanation is easy. The low income group consists primarily of two subgroups: families whose earners are normally fully employed at low wages, and families whose incomes

[14] See G. Cornfield, W. D. Evans, and M. Hoffenberg, "Full Employment Patterns in 1950, Part I," *Monthly Labor Review*, February, 1947, p. 181.

have been reduced by unemployment. The second group will run deficits to protect the high living standard attained when they were fully employed. The first group balances its budget. Suppose now that we have complete data on families in the $1000 income group in two periods. Suppose that the situation is as follows:

	Number	Deficit
Fully employed families (with normal incomes)	5000	0
Partially employed families	5000	$300
Average		$150

Suppose that in a second period we obtain reports from the same group but that half of the families in the $1000 group have increased their incomes. The situation in the $1000 group now is as follows:

	Number	Deficit
Fully employed families	5000	0
Partially employed families	2500	$300
Average		$100

Now suppose that instead of subdividing the families in this way our report had shown only the average deficit of the $1000 income families. We would have observed a reduction in the average deficit from $150 to $100 per family without knowing why. The differences in the 1935–36 and 1941 studies seem to correspond very clearly to the examples just given. In 1935–36 there were about 8 million unemployed, in 1941 there were only 3 million. In 1935–36 a much higher proportion of families in the low income groups were there because of unemployment than in 1941. If, therefore, we accept the proposition that the deficits were due to unemployment, or to incomes low by comparison with previous ones, the difference between the two studies is easily explained.

If we try to support the view that consumption depends on absolute income, how shall we explain the difference? The trend explanation cannot be used in this case.

For the break-even point moves in the wrong direction.

We can suppose that the families left in the low income groups would like to have run deficits but were unable to do so because they lacked the necessary assets or credit. But we have argued that a higher proportion of the low income group in 1941 were permanent members of that group than in 1935–36. It follows that the higher deficits in 1935–36 must have been incurred by the group whose incomes had fallen. For those permanently in the low income group were in more or less the same position in both years. Then we have to explain the differences in the reactions of the two groups. There are three possible explanations. (1) The families with temporarily low incomes were technically in a better position to have deficits. That is, they were not more willing to run deficits, but more able to get the resources to do so. (2) The families with temporarily low incomes had expectations of reëmployment and higher income in the future. (3) These families had had higher living standards in the past and were therefore more willing to have deficits to protect their living standards.

If either of the last two factors is influential, then consumption must depend on past income (since this governs the expected level of income at full employment) as well as on current income. In this case a general rise in income to levels above the

1929 peak followed by a fall would bring about a recurrence of the deficits, for the standard of living and expectations of income would be based on the new peak. If income declined from this peak by the same percentage as 1935 income had declined from the 1929 peak, deficits of a relative magnitude as large as those of 1935 would occur. This would be true even if the absolute level of income were as high as the 1929 level. On the other hand if the break-even point is independent of past levels of income no deficits would occur unless income were absolutely low.

The budget study data do not tell us anything directly about which of the three factors just mentioned are actually relevant. We must leave the question open for the moment. However, it should be noted that the hypothesis that consumption depends on past as well as on current income is consistent with all the data discussed so far. The alternative hypothesis that consumption depends only on current income can be made consistent with the data only if we are willing to accept some rather doubtful subsidiary propositions.

(3) One further piece of evidence is available for testing these two hypotheses. The 1941 budget study reported income for the first quarter of 1942 as well as for 1941. Families at each income level were classified by the changes in their income.

Savings for the first quarter of 1942 were separately reported for those whose incomes had changed less than 5 percent, for those whose incomes had increased more than 5 percent, and those whose incomes had decreased more than 5 percent from the 1941 level. The results are shown in Table 2. Families whose incomes rose had about the same savings or deficits as those whose incomes stayed the same. On the other hand, families whose incomes fell had much smaller savings or larger deficits than those whose incomes stayed constant. Now these facts can be interpreted in two ways. On the one hand we can say that they show that a rate of change factor is important in the determination of saving. That is, we write $c/y = f(y, y')$ where y' is the rate of change of income. On the other hand we can say that saving is low when income is low relative to past income. The two explanations are not the same. In a year when income is declining, either explanation would lead to the same result. But suppose that income declines and then remains at a (more or less constant) low level. After the decline has stopped, the rate of change is zero but income is still low relative to its pre-depression level.

It is fairly easy to tell which of the two hypotheses is correct. If the rate of change of income is an important factor it should

TABLE 2

AVERAGE YEARLY SAVINGS IN 1942 FOR CITY FAMILIES BY INCOME
CHANGE FROM 1941 TO 1942

Money income class in 1942	Consumers whose incomes in 1942		
	decreased over 5 percent	changed less than 5 percent	increased over 5 percent
0 to $1000	−337	−35	−15
$1000 to $1500	−181	−34	62
$1500 to $2000	− 81	126	157
$2000 to $3000	0	242	290
$3000 and over	143	1228	1059

Annual rate for 1942 based on first quarter.
Based on B.L.S. Bulletin 724.

show up in regressions of aggregate data. But it is well known that when the equation $c = f(y, t, y')$ is fitted to aggregate data for the twenties and thirties the addition of the factor y' contributes very little to the correlation. In the face of the budget study data this is difficult to explain unless we accept relative income instead of rate of change as the explanation of the differences in saving at the same level of income.

The asymmetry in the results is also important. If we take the view that rate of change of income is a determinant of saving, then there are strong reasons for supposing that the adjustment lag works in both directions. On the other hand, if we argue that people whose incomes are low relative to their past incomes reduce saving to protect their living standard, the asymmetry is easy to understand. Those whose incomes rose were for the most part getting back to levels of incomes which they had previously experienced. In these circumstances they merely returned to the expenditure patterns of the past and no adjustment lag is involved.

The data just discussed seem to show fairly conclusively that consumption at a given level of income does depend on past income. This hypothesis is consistent with the existence of deficits in 1935–36 and 1941, with the changes in deficits (at given levels of income) from 1935–36 to 1941, with the upward movement of the break-even point from 1917 to 1935–36 and 1941, and with the differences in saving among families whose incomes had changed in different ways. It is difficult to explain all of these facts on any other hypothesis.

Psychological Foundation

So far our argument has been a strictly empirical one. But it must be clear that it also has a strong psychological foundation. The fundamental psychological postulate underlying our argument is that it is harder for a family to reduce its expenditures from a high level than for a family

to refrain from making high expenditures in the first place. Consider two families who have incomes of $1000 per year at a particular time. Now suppose one of these families has an income of $1000 per year for ten years thereafter. Suppose the other family gets an increase in income from $1000 to $1500, retains this position for nine years, and then has its income reduced to $1000 so that in the last year it is in the same position as the other family. Initially both families might have exactly balanced their budgets at $1000, and the first family might continue in this way for the whole ten-year period. But when the second family had its income increased it would increase its consumption by (say) $400 and its saving by $100. When the reduction in income occurred it would certainly find it difficult to cut its consumption to the $1000 level. The first family had only to refrain from increasing its consumption expenditures to balance its budget. The second family had actually to give up consumption of $400 per year to achieve the same result. It would be surprising if a family in these circumstances succeeded in reducing its consumption sufficiently to balance its budget after the loss in income. Since all of the data are consistent with the view that this does happen, there does not seem to be much doubt that past income has an influence on current consumption and saving.

The argument so far has been devoted to explaining the deficits reported in the budget studies. But the significant result of this argument is not the conclusion that deficits will occur when income falls below previously attained levels but the more general proposition that families are willing to sacrifice saving in order to protect their living standard. This proposition applies to all income groups who have suffered losses in income. We can argue in the following way. If a family has a certain income y_0 and this income is higher than any previously attained, it will save some amount. This amount will be a function of income $s_0 = f(y_0)$. If its income increases the same function will hold. But if after an increase income falls to the original level its saving will be less than $f(y_0)$. If the family's income and saving are low throughout, it will have a deficit after the fall in income. If the family is in a higher bracket it will simply save less after the fall in income than it did before the increase. This view is checked by the fact that savings in the last five years of the twenties averaged 10.2 percent of disposable income while from 1936 to 1940 they averaged only 9.0 percent. Real disposable income per capita was almost the same in the two periods.

A Base Year for Downward Adjustments of Consumption

We have now shown that consumption is dependent on current income relative to past income as well as on the absolute level of current income. The problem now is to find just which past incomes are relevant. In view of the argument just given we appear to be safe in supposing that past incomes lower than the current one are not very relevant. This is pretty well demonstrated by the 1941–42 budget figures cited above. Families whose incomes rose to a given level saved about the same amount as those whose incomes had been at that level in the previous year. At first glance then it would seem reasonable to suppose that current consumption depends on the ratio of current income to some weighted average of past higher incomes, with weights decreasing as the time interval involved grows longer. There are, however, some fairly strong arguments against this position. The declines in income which occur in the depression are not uniformly distributed even though the size distribution of income remains more or less unchanged.

Income losses will be of three kinds: (1) reductions in property incomes, (2) reductions in wage rates, (3) losses due to underemployment. Since real wage rates do not decline very much in the depression (and were even higher in the late years of the depression than in the twenties), losses of income are mostly of types (1) and (3). (A fourth class results from downgrading of workers either within or between industries, but for our purposes this can be regarded as underemployment.)

Let us first consider the effect of losses of income in the upper income groups. It is not important here whether the losses are due to reductions in property incomes or to salary reductions. It can be assumed, however, that unemployment among the upper income groups is not important. The upper 10 percent of the income distribution produces almost all of the positive saving for the whole economy. Moreover, families in this group save a high proportion of their income. This means that they have a good deal of leeway in maintaining consumption standards without running into deficits; also they have more free (non-contractual) saving. When high income families suffer a loss in income, therefore, they continue to live in the same kind of neighborhoods and maintain their contacts with others of the same socio-economic status. In general they maintain the way of life which was established before the onset of the depression. They will, of course, cut expenditures on some lines, particularly on durable goods. But in view of the high rate of savings maintained in prosperity they can absorb a considerable reduction of income by reducing saving without cutting consumption too deeply. Moreover, there is no reason why they should not continue in this position for several years. Suppose now that income falls sharply from a cyclical peak and then remains constant for several years. The peak year's consumption sets the standard from which cuts are made (provided the peak did not represent a mere spurt in income). The higher the peak consumption, the more difficult it will be to reduce consumption to any given level. After the initial reductions are made the situation becomes static. The peak year does not lose its influence because the consumption of the following years depends on the peak consumption. Of course, if income began to fall again further consumption cuts would take place, and the intermediate level of income would be important in determining the extent of the cuts as well as the previous peak income. But if the depression consists in a fall of income lasting only a couple of years followed by a rise or a low plateau, the consumption of the peak year is likely to have very heavy weight in determining consumption in the depression. The influence of the peak consumption will not "fade away" unless income continues to fall steadily.

All of the above argument applies only to the upper income groups. Those who were in the lower 90 percent of the distribution in prosperity are in a different situation. For this group, reductions in individual income are usually associated with unemployment. These people probably save very little even in prosperous times. In a depression they can only influence saving by having deficits. A considerable number of families in this group go nearly unscathed by the depression. Their real wages do not fall and they never have serious losses of employment. These we may leave out of account since their savings are simply zero throughout. The remaining families suffer serious loss of employment at some point during the depression. These may also be divided into two groups. Some will remain employed up to a certain point, then lose their jobs and never get steady employment again until a high level of prosperity is reached. These families will presumably run substantial deficits immediately after they become unemployed, but as their assets become smaller they will have to adjust to the new situation and presumably balance budgets in which relief is the principal source of income. They may continue to have defi-

cits for a long time, but in any case the influence of the prosperity living standard will certainly "fade away" as time passes. However, it should be noted that not all of the persons who will eventually constitute the "hard core" of unemployment get there at once. The result is that a certain number of families are going through the initial stages of long-term unemployment at any time during the depression. Presumably, however, there are rather more families in this position during the downturn in the early years than later on. We should expect, therefore, to find somewhat greater deficits and lower aggregate savings at a given income in the downturn than in the upturn. However, the total number of families in this group was not very large in the thirties, and the differences in the numbers entering cannot have been great enough to cause numerically important reductions in aggregate savings.

The remainder of the unemployment is widely spread so that a large number of workers "take turns" being unemployed. Families lose income through unemployment and accordingly cut consumption; they also run a deficit. When they get reëmployed they may return to something very close to the prosperity consumption standard. Sometime later unemployment may reoccur and the process repeats. Those families who are very frequently in and out of employment will presumably gradually reduce consumption (even when employed) because of the decrease in their assets and the accumulation of debt. The influence of the peak standard will therefore gradually lose its effect. But a great part of the total unemployment can be accounted for by families who have only one or two stretches of prolonged unemployment during the depression. For these families the influence of the peak consumption standard will not fade away because it renews itself with each stretch of full employment.

We can conclude then that the income or consumption of the last cyclical peak will carry a special and very heavy weight in determining consumption at a given (lower) level of income during a depression. In principle a weighted average of all the incomes from the peak year to the current year ought to be used. But with only a few observations it would be impossible to estimate the weights. In what follows we shall consider the relation of current consumption to the ratio (current income/highest previously attained income) but the results are to be taken as an approximation to the true relation.

If the argument just given is correct, then there is a cyclical component in the explanation of saving. Savings at a given level of income, when income is the highest ever attained, as in the late twenties, will be higher than savings at a similar income level reached in a decline from a still higher level. I conclude, therefore, that in a general way at least the propositions of those who have argued that saving varies with the trade cycle as well as with income are supported by the evidence of the budget studies.

III.   AGGREGATE INCOME-SAVING RELATIONSHIPS

So far it has been shown that saving depends on the level of current incomes relative to higher incomes in previous years. But saving also depends on the absolute level of income. We may write then, $s_t = f(y_t, y_t/y_0)$ where y_0 is the highest income attained previous to the year t. Then

$$\frac{ds_t}{dy_t} = \frac{df}{dy_t} + \frac{df}{d(y_t/y_0)} \cdot \frac{d(y_t/y_0)}{dy_t}$$

If we plot out the long period relation of saving and income considering only periods of approximately full employment, the term $(dy_t/y_0)/dy_t$ will be 0 so that

$$ds_t/dy_t = df/dy_t.$$

But, with data covering a trade cycle, $(dy_t/y_0)/dy_t$ will have a positive value, and, if we use cyclical data to estimate the secular marginal propensity to consume, our estimates will be too high.

If data covering a number of cycles were available, we could take the regression of saving on y_t/y_0 and y_t and estimate simultaneously the secular and cyclical components in saving. Unfortunately the period 1923–1940 covers only one major cycle, so that we are forced to estimate the influence of the two factors separately. First, it should be noted that there are strong grounds for supposing that (in the absence of cyclical fluctuations) aggregate saving remains a constant proportion of aggregate income.

This position can be best understood by a consideration of the apparent contradictions in the relations between saving and income. On the one hand, we have the Keynesian dictum that

apart from short period changes in the level of income, it is also obvious that a higher absolute income will tend to widen the gap between income and consumption. For the satisfaction of the immediate primary needs of a man and his family is usually a stronger motive than the motives toward accumulation, which only acquire effective sway after a margin of comfort has been attained. These reasons will lead as a rule to a greater proportion of income being saved as income increases.[15]

This argument which, at first glance at any rate, appears very plausible, has had wide acceptance. Moreover, it seems to be supported by important empirical evidence. Every budget study supports the view that families with high incomes save a greater proportion of income than those with low incomes. It is also known that, in the period 1923–1940, saving fluctuated more than in proportion to income. On the

[15] J. M. Keynes, *The General Theory of Employment, Interest, and Money,* New York, Harcourt, Brace and Co., 1936, p. 97. Reprinted by permission.

other hand, the data given by Kuznets indicate that aggregate saving has been an approximately constant proportion of income for a long time.[16]

From a psychological viewpoint, Keynes' argument about the relative importance of saving and accumulation at different income levels does not throw much light on the situation to which it is supposed to apply. It is no doubt true that a family will not save when its income is so low that it cannot satisfy its immediate primary needs. But in the United States, at least, the problem of getting an income high enough to maintain physical existence has hardly existed (for families whose workers are employed) for many years. The problem is not one of saving vs. consuming enough to maintain existence. It is one of choosing between an immediate comfort and security. Any psychological theory of saving must give an explanation of the resolution of the conflict between the desire for security and the desire for comfort. When the problem is put in this way the conclusion that saving rises more than in proportion to income is not at all obvious. Moreover, in view of the paucity and ambiguity of the empirical evidence a psychological basis is necessary if an adequate theory of saving is to be constructed.

Such a theory already exists in the form of marginal utility and "indifference map" analysis, but it is hardly adequate for our purposes. The whole structure of preference analysis is based on the assumption that one individual's preferences are independent of the actual consumption patterns of another individual's. It is this assumption which permits us to add up the demand functions of individuals to get a market-demand function.

Yet consumption preferences can hardly

be regarded as innate characteristics of individuals. Nor can they be regarded, in a society as dynamic as ours, as being determined by tradition. There is a great deal of evidence to show that consumer tastes are socially determined. This does not mean that consumer tastes are governed by considerations of conspicuous consumption. Rather, it means that any individual's desire to increase his expenditure is governed by the extent to which the goods consumed by others are demonstrably superior to the ones which he consumes. If we can assume that the degree of superiority of one set of goods over another is highly correlated with the relative costs of obtaining these goods, we are led to the following proposition. The strength of any individual's desire to increase his consumption expenditure is a function of the ratio of his expenditure to some weighted average of the expenditures of others with whom he comes in contact. The weights are determined by the social character of these contacts. If the distribution of income is constant (in the Lorenz curve sense) this weighted average can be regarded as a function of an individual's percentile position in the income distribution. The proportion of income saved is set by balancing the desire to increase current consumption against the desire to increase assets relative to current consumption (that is, to have a greater assurance of continued maintenance of the existing standard). We may therefore conclude that if the strength of the desire to increase consumption is a function of percentile position in the income distribution, the proportion of income saved will be a function of the same variable. It is also easy to see that it will be a rising function.[17]

---

[16] Simon Kuznets, *Uses of National Income in Peace and War*, New York, National Bureau of Economic Research, 1942, p. 30.

[17] In a paper of this length it is impossible to go too deeply into the theory of consumer behavior underlying the above propositions. This theory together with some empirical tests of its adequacy will be developed more fully in a forthcoming paper.

This hypothesis leads to the following conclusions:

1. At any one moment the proportion of income saved will be higher for the higher income groups than for low income groups.
2. If income increases, while the proportional distribution remains constant, the ratio of aggregate saving to aggregate income will be constant.

Both of these conclusions are in accord with known facts.

If we accept the hypothesis just given, then secularly consumer saving will be a constant proportion of disposable income.

This hypothesis, together with the cyclical relation, considered in Section II, should give a complete explanation of variations in saving.

If the secular relation between savings and income makes for a constant income-saving ratio, the *proportion* of income saved will depend only on cyclical factors.[18] Then we may write $s_t/y_t = F(y_t/y_0)$. There is not much basis for selecting any particular functional form for $F(y_t/y_0)$. However, a linear approximation, which fits the data well, is always satisfactory, provided that we do not have to make predictions involving values of the variable outside the range of the data used in fitting the approximation. In the period 1923–1940 values of y_t/y_0 ranged from about 1.1 to .5. It seems unlikely that income will ever decline to less than 50 percent of full employment levels, so that we can be safe in using a linear form for $F(y_t/y_0)$ for prediction. When the relation $s_t/y_t = a(y_t/y_0) + b$ is fitted to the data

[18] If we accept the proposition that the high marginal propensity to consume indicated by linear income consumption relationships is largely due to cyclical factors, there is no *evidence* of the existence of any powerful trend in consumption. Various factors which might have caused either an upward or a downward trend can be cited. But when we have a hypothesis which explains all the data there is no point in introducing a trend unless some evidence of its operation can be given.

for the period 1923–1940, we obtain $a = .165$, $b = .066$.[19] The correlation is .9, which is as good as that usually obtained for relations between savings and income.

However, the correlation is not the test of the adequacy of the relation. The test is based on the fact that the secular average propensity to consume is predicted by the relation just given. In a period when income is slowly rising with only minor cyclical fluctuations, each year's income should be slightly above that of the preceding year. y_t/y_0 should be about 1.02 in each year. If we put $y_t/y_0 = 1.02$ in the relation $s_t/y_t = .165 \, y_t/y_0 - .066$ we obtain $s_t/y_t = .102$ which is very close to Kuznets' estimate of the (stable) savings ratio in the period 1879–1919. Since the regression was based on the period 1923–1940 we may say that the regression "predicted" the Kuznets' results.

All three major sources of data about income and consumption are consistent with the two hypotheses, (1) that secularly an individual's propensity to consume is a function of his position in the income distribution (which implies that aggregate saving tends in the long run to be a constant proportion of income) and (2) that, cyclically, the aggregate propensity to consume depends on the ratio of current income to the highest income previously achieved. They are also consistent with the internal evidence of the budget studies and with the results of intertemporal comparisons of budget studies. So far as I am aware there are no data about saving and income which are inconsistent with these hypotheses.

There is, however, another important class of hypotheses which has not been considered here. These are the hypotheses

[19] The data used are those given by E. G. Bennion, "The Consumption Function Cyclically Variable," *Review of Economic Statistics*, November, 1946. Disposable income and savings are both corrected for price and population changes.

which introduce variables other than income into the consumption function. In
particular it has been suggested that saving
may vary with the price level (when the
price level is considered as a separate
variable and not as a mere deflator) and
with the value of assets. There is, of
course, no real conflict between these
hypotheses and the ones presented here.
The two variables just mentioned are
highly correlated with income, so that it is
quite possible that they may be important
contributors to the variance of saving,
even though a high correlation can be obtained without considering them. These
hypotheses will have to be tested by
methods similar to those used in Section II
of this paper.

The implications of the hypotheses developed here are fairly obvious. We may
expect that, when the transition period is
completed, consumer savings will fall to
around 10 percent of disposable income.
This may be compared with the estimate of
14 percent given by Smithies for consumer
savings out of a disposable income of
158.2 billion dollars in 1943 prices.[20] The
volume of offsets to savings required to
maintain full employment is therefore considerably smaller than would be expected
from estimates based on simple income-
consumption regressions.

[20] *Vide* A. Smithies, "Forecasting Postwar
Demand," *Econometrica*, January, 1945.

The relation $s_t/y_t = .166(y_t/y_0) - .066$
has the property that the marginal propensity to save out of disposable income is
fairly high with respect to cyclical movements of income, but the average propensity to save is much lower and does not
tend to rise with secular increases in income. During the trough of a cycle (from
the time income falls below the peak value
for one cycle until it rises above that value
in the next cycle) y_t/y_0 is dependent entirely on y_t (since y_0 is constant). We have
then $s_t = (.166/y_0)y_t^2 - .066y_t$; then
$ds_t/dy_t = .332(y_t/y_0) - .066$. The marginal propensity to save with respect to
decreases in income is therefore about .26
at the peak of a cycle. As income declines
ds_t/dy_t falls until it reaches zero at an
income equal to one-fifth that of the last
cyclical peak.

On the other hand, the average propensity to save does not rise as income rises
secularly. For in the upswing of a cycle
after full employment is reached, y_0 and
y_t move together. If income increases
steadily at an annual rate of 3 percent,
y_t/y_0 is constant at a value of 1.03. The
long-run savings function is therefore $s_t =
.166(1.03)\ y_t - .066y_t$ or simply $s_t =
.102\ y_t$. Thus the cyclical marginal pro-
pensity to save is (in the relevant range)
higher than the long-run propensity to
save, and the use of cyclical data to
estimate the long-period relationship leads
to invalid conclusions.

7

The New Theories
of the Consumption
Function

M. J. FARRELL

I. INTRODUCTION

There have recently been put forward—notably by Friedman (1957a) and Modigliani and Brumberg (1953 and 1954)[1]—new theories of the consumption function which have startling implications for a wide range of economic problems. It is my belief that the acceptance of these theories has been prejudiced, primarily by the conjunction of valuable and highly controversial hypotheses, and secondarily by

✳ ✳

Reprinted from *The Economic Journal*, vol. 69 (December 1959), pp. 678–696, by permission of the publisher and author.

M. J. Farrell teaches at Gonville and Caius College, Cambridge.

[1] The dates are misleading, as the theories were circulated in mimeograph and widely discussed as early as 1953. They had been partly anticipated by Harrod (1948) and Vickrey (1947), but these writers were interested primarily in other problems. The present paper owes a great deal to all three writers, and particularly to personal discussions with them during 1953–54. It has also benefited from the criticisms of Mr. J. S. Cramer and Dr. M. R. Fisher.

certain flaws in exposition. I have, therefore, attempted an exposition of the essentials of these theories which, I hope, avoids these disadvantages.[2]

I distinguish sharply the different hypotheses involved, and consider separately the evidence for, and implications of, each of them. I must apologise to the reader for introducing a new terminology into a subject already overburdened with jargon. My excuse is that I felt it was essential.

II. NOTES ON DEFINITIONS

Initial assets are the individual's net worth at the beginning of the year. A point of minor interest is that, since this includes his holdings of consumer's dur-

[2] The main ways in which my exposition differs from the original theories are as follows. First, I omit the utility theory, which is straightforward mathematics, and not really very illuminating, since uncertainty has to be introduced *after* the results have been derived. Secondly, I avoid Friedman's concept of "permanent income," which, although in some ways very attractive, involves considerable and unnecessary difficulties. In their treatment of the aggregate consumption function the New Theorists diverge sharply, and here I follow Modigliani and Brumberg.

ables, we are imputing to the individual as income the interest cost of these holdings (except during the current year).

Current income is the total of the individual's receipts (net of tax) during the year—including "earnings" in our sense and the interest yield of assets. The important point here is that contributions by employer or state to schemes for superannuation, health or unemployment insurance are clearly a part of the individual's income and must be included in computations of it.

Earnings differ from income in that (to avoid double-counting) they exclude the interest yield of assets.

Consumption would be perfectly straightforward were it not for the existence of consumers' durables. It has long been recognised (Hicks (1939), p. 176) in economic theory that purchases of consumers' durables are of the nature of capital expenditure, whereas the consumption of durables is the appropriate current cost—that is, depreciation plus interest costs. In the early work on the consumption function this was regarded (if at all) as a theoretical nicety, inappropriate to empirical work, and a great deal of the available empirical evidence is based on the assumption that purchases and consumption are equivalent, but in recent years the importance of the distinction has become quite widely appreciated, and not merely among the New Theorists.[3]

Savings are simply the accounting difference between current income and consumption. It should be noted that, as a result of their status as a residual, savings are particularly sensitive to any inaccuracies in the measurement of either income or consumption. In particular, any failure to impute employers' and state contributions to the individual's income is

[3] For example, Morgan (1951), Goldsmith (1951), Boulding (1950).

likely to produce a spectacular underestimate of his saving.

We may perhaps add that in *defining* savings as a residual we are not implying anything at all about the motives which lead a consumer to save.

III. THE NORMAL INCOME HYPOTHESIS

The basis of the new theories is the recognition that, if an individual plans rationally to maximise his utility over his lifetime, his consumption in any given year will depend, not on his income in that year, but on the resources of which he disposes during his lifetime. This is plausible but vague; we must first dispel the vagueness.

If an individual knows with certainty his future stream of earnings,[4] and faces a perfect capital market with a given rate of interest, it is possible to represent "the resources of which he disposes . . ." by the current value v of his current assets plus his expected future earnings, discounted at the rate of interest. The theory could be fully developed in terms of v, but it will assist the exposition if we convert v into an equivalent income stream. Consider a constant annual Y for the remainder of the individual's life-span; if Y is such that the current value of this income-stream is just equal to v, we shall call Y the individual's *normal income*.[5]

[4] "Earnings" is slightly misleading, as we define it to include all receipts except the interest yield of assets. But the obvious alternatives—"income" or "receipts"—would be at least equally misleading.

We must also note that in point of pure theory, earnings are determined by the individual in his maximising calculations, and what is known is the function relating earnings to work done. But this point is not important in the present context.

[5] It should be noted that, given the rate of interest and the life-span, normal income is uniquely determined by v. In this (as well as other ways) it differs from Friedman's "permanent income," which seems a rather flexible concept. We shall argue later that the relevant life-span is not the actuarial expectation of life, but a

It is easy to show that if such an individual also knows his future tastes and the future course of prices, and plans his consumption so as to maximise his satisfaction over his lifetime, his planned consumption in each year will be uniquely determined by his normal income Y.

There is not, in practice, a perfect capital market, and this raises a number of theoretical difficulties—notably that it is not clear at what rate to discount future earnings. But these are complications that can easily be dealt with—the main practical difficulty lies in the penal interest rates attached to borrowing that reduces the individual's net worth below a certain level. This means that the above conclusion could not be expected to hold for income-and-consumption patterns that lead temporarily to excessive indebtedness: that is, for income streams that are, in relation to the optimal consumption pattern, unduly deferred. This qualification would probably not be very important, were it not for the problem of durable consumption goods, to which we shall return later.

The fact that we live in an uncertain world is a source of much greater difficulties. Rational behaviour in the face of uncertainty is a problem that has not yet been solved even in simple cases—it would be foolish to suppose that our simple theorem held precisely for so vast a problem as the individual's lifetime consumption plan. But in fact we need only a much more limited result, and one which is quite defensible. Let us now state

The Normal Income Hypothesis: in any given period, an individual's current income y affects his consumption c only through its effect on his normal income Y. We may write $c = \beta(Y)$, where β is independent of current income and assets.

We are only concerned with consumption in the initial period (say, one year) of

slightly longer period, not directly measurable. This introduces a (relatively very small) element of flexibility into our concept.

the plan, and it is reasonable to suppose that the individual's expectations remain stable long enough for him to carry out that part of the plan. Uncertainty about the future will undoubtedly affect his planned consumption in many and complex ways, but we must now consider whether it is likely to give current income any direct influence on current consumption.

One way in which this might happen is that uncertainty about the future might lead people to spend every penny they could lay hands on. Some people probably do this, but not those who have positive savings or assets. This effect seems to be confined to a small minority, and to be unimportant in the community as a whole.

A second possibility is that people's expectations of future earnings should be directly and stably related to their current earnings. This again may be true for a minority, but seems unlikely to be important in the aggregate. More likely is it that, although such a relationship does not hold for individuals, it does hold in the aggregate as a result of averaging out of deviations. This seems quite possible in any particular case, but one would doubt very much the *stability* of such a relationship.

The most important possibility is that uncertainty may lead people to abandon maximising calculations in favour of conventional rules of the Mrs. Beeton type. This is not unlikely—such rules are important in business behaviour and might be expected to be at least as popular with private individuals. Moreover, they are not necessarily inconsistent with rational behaviour; detailed planning may itself have a disutility, and a conventional rule that approximated the optimal spending pattern might well be most satisfactory to the individual. But just as the businessman adheres to his conventional prices only so long as they are roughly optimal, so we might expect consumers to stick to their conventional saving rule only so long as it gave roughly the right answer. For example, we might expect to find many of those with stable incomes following conventional rules, but we would be surprised if people with very variable incomes did so.

To sum up, for people with variable incomes, the *Normal Income Hypothesis* is roughly equivalent to postulating rational behaviour; but people habituated to stable incomes could quite rationally follow some such rule as "always save $1/n$th of your income"—which would quite invalidate the hypothesis.

IV. THE PROPORTIONALITY HYPOTHESIS

The second hypothesis of the new theories concerns the shape of the function β. They postulate that it shall be a straight line passing through the origin. Formally, this is

The Proportionality Hypothesis: for any individual, the relationship between his consumption and his normal income is one of proportionality.

This was, I think, originally regarded by the New Theorists as purely a working hypothesis, but they may have given the impression that it is an integral part of their theories. At any rate, the attacks on the new theories have centred on this hypothesis.[6] I shall argue, first, that it is unnecessary, and secondly, that it is of doubtful validity.

It is unnecessary because, first and patently, the *Normal Income Hypothesis* is independent of it. More important, we shall see later that the *evidence* for the *Normal Income Hypothesis* is independent of the validity of the *Proportionality Hypothesis*.

I think it is a fair comment on the *a priori* arguments put forward by the New

Theorists[7] for the *Proportionality Hypothesis* that they were never designed to do more than establish its plausibility as a working hypothesis; and certainly that they do no more than this. It is also, I think, fair to say (and I shall in part substantiate this comment in a later section) that neither Friedman (1957a) nor Fisher (1956) found any good evidence for the hypothesis. In contrast, Friend and Kravis (1957a) produce a cogent *a priori* argument as to why the proportional relationship should not hold exactly, although it might be argued that the deviations in question affect only the very rich, and are therefore negligible in the aggregate. They also produce (in Table I) the only piece of (more or less) direct evidence that I have yet found. It concerns a sample of families who had had approximately the same income in the previous year and expected much the same income in the subsequent year. The regression of consumption on current income appears to be roughly

$$c = 900 + 0.68y$$

There are four qualifications to be made. First, consumption is defined to include purchases of durables; but a similar relation holds for nondurable consumption, and there seems no reason why the case should be different for consumption correctly defined. Secondly, income is defined to exclude the value of employers' and state contributions to schemes for superannuation, health and unemployment insurance. The inclusion of these items would undoubtedly make the results more favourable to the *Proportionality Hypothesis;* but they would have to amount to over $1,300 per family to remove the whole discrepancy. Thirdly, the constancy of current income over three years does not imply logically that normal income must,

[6] For example, Friend and Kravis (1957a), Klein and Liviatan (1957).

[7] Modigliani and Brumberg (1954), Part I, Friedman (1957a), Chapter II.

in the sample, vary proportionately with current income; but I can think of no convincing reason why there should be a substantial and systematic deviation in the requisite direction, except for the possibility that the lower-income groups contain a higher proportion of retired people. Here we must rely on a remark by Friend and Kravis (p. 544) that "when the self-employed and not gainfully employed are eliminated . . . the results are only moderately improved from the viewpoint of the permanent income theories." Fourthly, it is possible that each individual's consumption varies proportionately with his income, but that the factor of proportionality is correlated, within the sample, with income. For instance, intelligent and responsible people might tend to have both higher propensities to save and higher incomes than the rest of the population. Such a correlation would, however, make the Proportionality Hypothesis useless for analysing cross-section data.

In the circumstances, and particularly in view of the hostility provoked by the *Proportionality Hypothesis*, it seems wise to keep an open mind about the shape of the function β.

V. THE SHORT-PERIOD MARGINAL PROPENSITY TO CONSUME

On the *Normal Income Hypothesis* the individual's consumption function is $\beta(Y)$ and his marginal propensity to consume out of normal income simply the slope β' at the appropriate point. We cannot, of course, say anything *a priori* about the magnitude of any individual β', but on the average we would expect β' to be equal to, or as little less than, unity.[8] But if we

[8] If all saving is consumption-spreading and the rate of interest is zero, the individual will plan to spend at some time or other any increment in his normal income. Hence the β''s will average to unity over his life-plan, and thus, too, they will average to unity if the averaging is performed over a "representative" group of individuals. The fact that individuals usually die before the completion

wish to calculate the marginal propensity to consume out of current income, we have also to analyse the response of normal income to a change in current income. Formally,

$$\frac{dc}{dy} = \beta' \frac{dY}{dy}$$

We must now separate the direct and indirect effects on Y of a change in y. The direct effect of an increment Δy in y can be shown to be an increment in Y of the order of $(2/N)\,\Delta y$, where N is the life-span used in the individual's plan.[9] The indirect effect depends on his expectations. Suppose an increase Δy in current income leads him to expect an increase $\mu\,\Delta y$ in his earnings for n years; then it will produce an increase in normal income of approximately $(n/N)\mu\,\Delta y$.

Thus, adding the two effects,

$$\frac{dc}{dy} \simeq \beta' \left(\frac{2}{N} + \frac{n}{N}\,\mu \right)$$

$$\simeq \frac{2}{N} + \frac{n}{N}\,\mu$$

Except for those nearing the retiring age, the first term will be small compared with the second, and the individual's marginal propensity to consume out of current income will be dominated by his elasticity of expectations. Table 1 gives a few illus-

of their life-plan (see footnote[9] below) will tend to lower β'.

Saving-for-its-own-sake would tend to lower β', but probably not very much in the aggregate; the effects of a positive rate of interest are difficult to determine (see Graaff (1951)), but are likely to be relatively small.

[9] Consider an income stream ΔY for N years. Its present value, discounted at 5% per annum, falls from $6\Delta Y$ at $N = 10$ to $10\Delta Y$ at $N = 40$, so that $\Delta y \simeq 1/2N\Delta Y$.

Since he is uncertain about how long he will live, and since great disutility attaches to exhausting one's assets before one's death, the individual will probably "play safe" by basing his plans on a life-span N considerably greater than his actual expectation of life.

TABLE 1

Age ＼ μ	0	1	2
25	0.03	0.70	1.37
35	0.04	0.64	1.24
45	0.05	0.55	1.05
55	0.07	0.40	0.73

trative examples, assuming that the individual bases his plans on retiring at 65 and living to 85.

The short-period aggregate marginal propensity to consume is simply a weighted average of all the individual marginal propensities in the community—weighted, of course, by the increments of income received. The individual marginal propensities will vary not only with age, as shown in the table, but also with family responsibilities, social class, and so on. But speaking very roughly, and ignoring possible correlations between these factors and the elasticity of expectations, we may regard the aggregate marginal propensity as proportional to the weighted average of individual elasticities of expectations, the factor of proportionality being of the order of 0.5 or 0.6.

This short-period aggregate marginal propensity to consume is, of course, a relationship between hypothetical variations in income and the consequent changes in consumption, for a given group of people in a given year. It is not strictly applicable to year-to-year changes in income and consumption, as both the composition of the community and the individual β's will, in general, change from year to year. However, in the relatively short period the composition of the community will remain fairly constant and the changes in the β's may be assumed roughly to average out. Another complication is that the level of assets varies in time-series observations, but this can be neglected in the present rough calculations.

(The marginal propensity to consume out of assets is of the order of $2/N$—roughly 0.1, allowing for weighting the individual marginal propensities by asset ownership, which is positively correlated with age.)

As the elasticity of expectations is not directly measurable, observations of the cyclical marginal propensity cannot be expected to provide any very satisfactory evidence for or against the hypothesis. However, the readily available data seem to imply an *average* (over time and the community) elasticity of about unity.[10] This cuts both ways. In so far as unity is a plausible value, the data are consistent with the *Normal Income Hypothesis*; but unit elasticity of expectations also suggests the possibility of a simple relationship between y and c, which would make the hypothesis redundant.

It should be emphasised that this section relates only to the *marginal* propensity to consume. The average propensity involves the complicating factors discussed in the next section.

VI. THE LONG-PERIOD CONSUMPTION FUNCTION

It is very tempting to argue that the long-period aggregate marginal propensity to consume is derived from the individual marginal propensities in the same way as the short-period one, save that in the long-period the elasticity of expectations will be greater, thus giving a greater marginal propensity. This is indeed the essence of much of Friedman's treatment of the time-series evidence (Friedman (1957a), Chapter V), but it is, unfortunately, illegitimate. The difficulty is that the composition of the community cannot be assumed constant in the long period; and further, that

[10] Friedman (1957a), Table 12. Only lines 6–14 are based on a correct treatment of consumers' durables, and of these only lines 6–9 are for reasonably short periods. These give marginal propensities of 0.72, 0.65, 0.60 and 0.45.

the changes in composition found in real life have a considerable effect on the consumption function.

If all saving is for the purpose of consumption-spreading, and if there is no uncertainty, each individual will, over his lifetime, exactly consume his total income —that is, his savings would sum to zero over his lifetime. In a community which was in all relevant respects stationary, this would imply that individual savings summed over the community would be zero in any year. On these assumptions, positive savings in an economy would be evidence that it was *not* stationary. If dis-saving is principally done after retirement, there are two obvious forms of change that can lead to positive aggregate savings.

First, a growing population will, in general, mean a disproportionately small number of retired people, and hence of dis-savers. Secondly, a rising level of real income per head will mean that the savers will, on the average, have larger lifetime incomes than the dis-savers. Modigliani and Brumberg (1953), in a most striking piece of research, investigated these effects in detail. They found that, on a number of simplifying assumptions, for rates of growth up to 5 percent per annum, each 1 percent per annum of growth in either real income per head or population would lead to 3–4 percent of aggregate income being saved. Thus the saving-ratio is proportional to the rate-of-growth of aggregate real income, and is independent of how this growth is compounded of changes in population and in real income per head (so long as both change steadily). This suggests

The Rate-of-growth Hypothesis: In long-run equilibrium, aggregate saving is determined by changes in population structure and in real income per head. If these factors change steadily, the fraction of aggregate income saved is proportional to the rate of growth of aggregate real income.

The simplifying assumptions include a zero rate of interest, consumption spread evenly over the life-span and no bequests. There seems to be no reason why the calculations should be very sensitive to a positive rate of interest, or to plausible variations in the consumption pattern— so long as lifetime consumption equals lifetime income. But the assumption of no bequests seems crucial—and palpably false.

However, the hypothesis would still be valid if heirs planned to dis-save (the bulk of) their inheritances over their lifetime. They would do this on the *Normal Income Hypothesis* provided that saving-for-its-own-sake or for posterity was small; but they would also do so if they were "improvident," *i.e.*, deviated from the life-plan in the direction of shorter-run maximisation of utility. They would fail to dis-save adequately if for some reason they wished to maintain or increase their assets, or if they adopted some conventional rule (such as "never spend out of capital") which led them to do so. Such behaviour we may call "thrifty." The building-up of family fortunes over several generations is evidence of thrift, but the nineteenth-century saying, "From clogs to clogs in three generations," shows that even in the golden age of thrift, dis-saving by heirs was not uncommon.

It is obviously important to find out whether thrift generates a significant volume of saving, and Goldsmith (1955) gives estimates[11] of asset holdings by different age-groups which permit us to make a rough test. If the population is assumed to decline linearly after the age of 65 and if individuals are supposed to plan a linear running down of their assets over the same number of years, it is easy to show that average assets in the over-65 age-group will be $\frac{2}{3}$ of those at 65, assuming a history of stationary prices and incomes.

[11] Vol. I, pp. 214–25; Vol. III, pp. 102–35 and 284–381.

Goldsmith's Table XLII, Col. 1, shows observed net worth by age-groups, and estimating the 65 value by extrapolation, we get a ratio of 0.73. Goldsmith suggests (Vol. I, p. 217 n.) that this figure is too high, owing to the oldest age-group's having had a particularly favourable history of capital gains. In Col. 3 of the same table, Goldsmith gives estimates of accumulated life saving which yield a ratio of 0.52. (He regards these estimates as giving "the least distorted picture of life saving curves that can be fashioned out of the rough over-all data now available.") Unfortunately, the asset figures underlying both estimates exclude consumers' durables other than motor cars, and so probably give a downward bias; but this should not be large.

These calculations suggest that the population as a whole is not thrifty.[12] However, figures based on estate-tax data (Vol. III, Table E-29) give ratios of approximately unity, which are presumably underestimates, as no allowance is made for gifts *inter vivos*. Thus, thrift is important among those subject to estate tax, and its absence from the aggregate results is due to the cancelling out of thrift among the wealthy and improvidence among the poor.

The direct evidence of Modigliani and Brumberg's calculations leads to much the same conclusion. Saving 12 percent of aggregate income would, on the *Rate-of-growth Hypothesis*, correspond to aggregate real income growing at 3–4 percent per annum. Thus the saving that would be generated by growth on the hypothesis is of approximately the same amount as that observed; but this could easily conceal substantial cancelling of errors, and in

particular the balancing of thrift among the wealthy against improvidence among the poor.

We may conclude that the *Rate-of-growth Hypothesis* gives a good explanation of the long-period consumption function of the United States, but that this success depends partly on a balance of thrift and improvidence in different normal income groups. In applying the hypothesis to other economies, we must be prepared for the possibility that the balance will not hold there so that actual saving will differ from that predicted by the hypothesis. But however much thrift or improvidence may distort the picture, the rate of growth will remain the basic determinant of the aggregate savings/income ratio in the long run.

It is perhaps worth noting that the evidence considered in this section is quite unrelated to the *Normal Income Hypothesis*. Nor do Modigliani and Brumberg's calculations throw any light on the *Proportionality Hypothesis*—it is virtually impossible to make inferences from the observed long-run aggregate consumption function about the shape of the individual consumption functions. On the other hand, Goldsmith's data constitute some evidence against the *Proportionality Hypothesis*.

VII.   THE FRIEDMAN EFFECT

If consumption depends on normal income, the interpretation of a sample survey which gives observations of consumption and current income must depend on the relationship in that sample between current and normal income. Friedman (1957a, Chapter III) and Modigliani and Brumberg (1954, Part II) give *a priori* arguments that there will usually be a particular relationship between these quantities. We shall now attempt a brief summary of this argument. The brevity is achieved by sacrificing some detail and rigour, and also (I regret to say) by introducing a new notation.

[12] The data are approximate, and the theoretical figure of $\frac{2}{3}$ depends on linearity assumptions that may well not hold exactly. We must therefore allow for sizeable possible errors. Comparing an observed 0.52 with a theoretical 0.67, it seems reasonable to rule out the possibility that the observed value is really greater than the theoretical, but it would be risky to make any more precise inference.

Suppose that for a sample of families the elasticity of consumption with respect to normal income is E, and that the apparent elasticity with respect to current income, computed from survey data, is G. Suppose, too, that we can measure the relationship between normal income Y and current income y by the elasticity F of Y with respect to y. Then we can see at the intuitive level that $G = EF$, so that, for instance, if Y increases proportionately with y (that is, if $F = 1$) G is an estimate of E.

It is argued by the New Theorists that F is usually less than unity. Suppose that for the families in question year-to-year fluctuations in current income *which do not affect normal income* are important. Suppose further that in the particular period to which the survey refers the magnitude and direction of these fluctuations is not correlated with normal income. (This would clearly be true if we were considering the average over a number of years, but any particular year might, for example, be a good one for the rich and a bad one for the poor.) Then, abstracting from possible complications through the correlation of normal income with age, the magnitude and direction of the temporary fluctuations will be positively correlated with current income. In other words, in the higher current income groups a larger proportion will be enjoying a "good year." This implies that Y increases less than proportionately with y, and thus that $F < 1$.

We shall find it convenient to call this phenomenon, of $F < 1$, the "Friedman Effect," and to speak of a smaller value of F as a larger Friedman Effect. The argument for the Friedman Effect is plausible, but equally it is clear that it may apply to some societies or social groups and not to

TABLE 2

	A	B	C
Professional	1–5	61	60
	6–8	52	70
	9–10	69	53
Self-employed or managerial	1–5	23	35
	6–8	38	51
	9–10	50	50
Clerical and sales	1–3	65	68
	4–5	60	59
	6–8	62	58
	9–10	61	63
Skilled or semi-skilled	1–3	40	50
	4–5	48	49
	6–8	63	54
	9–10	68	63
Unskilled	1–3	38	47
	4–5	43	53
	6–10	55	68
Farm operator	1–3	26	40
	4–5	47	48
	6–10	58	53

A. Income group.
B. Percentage of those in that income group for 1947 who had an (appreciably) larger income than in 1946.
C. Percentage of those in that income group for 1948 who had an (appreciably) larger income than in 1947.
Data abstracted from Katona and Fisher (1951), Table 8.

others. As normal income is not directly measurable, we can make no direct tests, but there is a certain amount of indirect evidence.

Table 2, for example, shows for various American occupation groups the percentage of families in each current income group who were better off than they had been in the previous year. Where the Friedman Effect is present, this percentage will increase with income. Such a tendency is well marked among farm operators, manual workers and the self-employed and managerial groups. There is clearly no such effect in the "clerical and sales" group, while the professional group shows unsystematic movements.

Some similar figures for Dutch families are given in Table 3. The occupation groups are *handarbeiders* (manual workers) and *hoofdarbeiders* (roughly, clerical workers). For each occupation the average current income of each current-income group is compared with its average income over the previous four years. If the latter is taken as a measure of normal income the manual workers display the Friedman Effect while the clerical workers do not.

This evidence, limited though it is, is enough to confirm our impression that the Friedman Effect may well be present in samples from some occupation groups—such as farmers, business-men and manual workers—and missing from other samples, such as professional men and salaried workers.

VIII. THE EVIDENCE FROM THE FRIEDMAN EFFECT

Friedman's analysis of the cross-section evidence for his theory (Friedman (1957a), Chapters IV, VI and VII) is a most brilliant and fascinating economic argument, and occupies 132 pages. The present short discussion cannot do justice to the rich detail of his analysis, but it will, I hope, serve to indicate both the strengths and the weaknesses of his arguments.

His analysis of the survey data is based on three assumptions:

(a) that $F < 1$, *i.e.*, that the Friedman Effect is present;
(b) the *Normal Income Hypothesis;*
(c) that $E = 1$, *i.e.*, the *Proportionality Hypothesis.*

TABLE 3

Income group fl. per annum	Handarbeiders			Hoofdarbeiders		
	No. of families	Average current income	Average previous income	No. of families	Average current income	Average previous income
<1600	72	1144	1183	34	1336	1110
1600–2000	33	1740	1623	21	1745	1672
2000–2600	18	2215	2073	36	2287	2151
2600–3400	8	2950	2460	31	2983	2739
3400–4500	1	4140	3855	22	3847	3503
4500–6700	1	4832	4111	12	5094	5034
>6700	—	—	—	21	22,489	26,485

Taken from: "Resultaten von een inventarisonderzoeh in de Gemeente Rotterdam, ingesteld door de Schade Enquête Commissie aldaar, in 1941" in *Statistische en Econometrische Ondetzoekingen*, Maandschrift van het Centraal Bureau v.d. Statistiek 1943, nr. 4.

Mr. J. S. Cramer comments: "Not a very good sample, 'selected' by asking firms to ask for volunteers from among their employees." He quotes, "In several cases the current income could be ascertained with more accuracy than the 5 year average."

He finds almost all the evidence he considers consistent with this set of assumptions. Unfortunately, since direct measurement of F is impossible, it is impossible to estimate accurately the value of F for any particular sample, so that this "consistency" does not go very far towards confirming the hypotheses.

But although the absolute magnitude of F is difficult to estimate, there may be good grounds for believing that F will be smaller in one group than another, and this will provide a test of the *Normal Income Hypothesis*. For suppose we have reason to believe that F is smaller in group A than in group B, and no reason to expect a significant difference in the values of E. Then we must expect to find a smaller G in group A on the *Normal Income Hypothesis*, and not otherwise. (Once again, the test is independent of the *Proportionality Hypothesis*.)

Friedman quotes a number of pieces of evidence of this type. In Table 1, for example, he gives the values of G computed from a number of surveys in the United States, Britain and Sweden. One would expect that, of these three countries, year-to-year fluctuations would be most important in the United States and least so in Sweden. This accords with the values of G, which are systematically larger in Sweden than in the United States, with Britain in an intermediate position.

It is a commonplace of economics that farm incomes are particularly subject to year-to-year fluctuations, and much the same is true of the business community. Friedman shows (Tables 1, 3 and 4) that United States farm families exhibit smaller values of G than the rest of the community. In Table 5 he gives the results of a survey in which families are classified as "independent business," "farmers" and "others." The two former groups show values of G that are almost equal and much smaller than that of the "other." On the other hand, in Table 6 the G for independent business-men is higher than for most other occupations; but Friedman attributes this to a faulty definition.

Fisher (1956) gives similar evidence from a British survey. He gives values of G (the figures called P_γ in columns (b) of Table 2.5) for four occupation groups—manual, clerical and sales, managerial and self-employed—broken down by age. If all ages are taken together, the self-employed have the lowest G, but this does not hold for all the individual age-groups. The number of observations in some of the cells is quite small, but even so, this unsystematic result may be a sign of the importance of factors that vary with age.

Perhaps a more important aspect of Fisher's results is that the manual workers have an unusually high G. In view of the low value of F in Table 2 above, this must suggest a breakdown of the *Normal Income Hypothesis*. Of course, the figures in Table 2 were for American workers, and their British counterparts may well have a much higher F; but, as we shall see later, this in itself suggests a limitation of the hypothesis.

Friedman bases a further test on the argument that classifying a group of families according to the difference between their current income and that of the previous (or subsequent) year will increase F. The results he quotes in Tables 10 (farm families) and 11 (mainly urban) appear to show that such classification produces a definite increase in G.

In those rare surveys that record the family's income for two consecutive years, it is possible to make rather more direct tests. Friedman develops a method of estimating F for a group of families from the regression of their current on their previous year's income (or vice versa). I am not convinced that F is more closely related to these estimates than to the correlation coefficient of the two years' incomes, but it is clear that all four quantities are likely to be fairly highly correlated.

In Table 20 Friedman gives these statistical measures and values of G for three occupational groups—independent non-farm business, farm operators, and clerical and sales. Although one should not attach undue significance to a correlation based on three observations, it is noteworthy that the values of G (line 4) are virtually identical with those of the correlation coefficient (line 5).

A more substantial piece of evidence of the same sort is quoted by Friedman from an unpublished paper by Margaret Reid. In Fig. 15, Panel 1, he shows estimates of F, similar to those discussed in the previous paragraph, plotted against values of G for 27 groups of families. The correlation is most impressive, although it must be said that all the groups but one are farm families, and that it is not clear whether all the points plotted represent different groups, as opposed to the same group at different times. There is also the possibility that these account-keeping families might be unusually sophisticated in their economic thinking, and perhaps therefore obey the *Normal Income Hypothesis* where others would not.

In any test where one uses the previous year's income as a proxy for normal income, it is always possible that the effects one attributes to the *Normal Income Hypothesis* are really due to a simple lag in the adjustment of consumption to income. This is, of course, not so where the *subsequent* year's income is the proxy, but it is fortunate that Friedman provides a further piece of evidence on this point. In Fig. 15, Panel 2, he again plots estimates of F against G, but here the estimates use the *penultimate* year's income as a proxy. Most forms of adjustment lag would imply a substantially lower correlation for Panel 2 than Panel 1, while the *Normal Income Hypothesis* suggests a roughly equal correlation. On inspection there appears to be a slight reduction, which may be partly explained by the fact that these calcu-

lations were possible for only some of the groups in Panel 1.

Individually, each of the pieces of evidence described above lacks the conclusiveness of a direct test. But together, I feel, they constitute a fairly strong confirmation that the effects predicted by the *Normal Income Hypothesis* occur in real life. However, we must be careful not to overstate the case, for the fact that some people behave in a certain way does not mean that all do. In fact, if we look at the data with a view to determining what sort of people have gone into our tests, we find that the tests fall into three groups:

(a) tests based solely on figures for farmers and/or business-men;

(b) tests based on contrasting the behaviour of farmers and business-men with that of the rest of the community; and

(c) tests based on samples for the whole community, in which farmers and/or businessmen may be sufficiently important to account for the results we found.

Thus the evidence shows only that farmers and business-men behave according to the *Normal Income Hypothesis*—it says nothing about the behaviour of the rest of the community. Now these two groups are those for whom year-to-year fluctuations in income are particularly important, and for whom therefore conventional saving rules are most obviously irrational. For a man with a secure job at a steady salary, on the other hand, a conventional rule might work very well. We must therefore be prepared to find that those with steady incomes do not obey the *Normal Income Hypothesis*.

We are not, then, surprised to find a negative result in the case of the British manual worker, habituated to over-full employment. The same might turn out to be true of clerical workers, who do not display the Friedman Effect either in Holland or the United States, but, on the other hand, American manual workers, a large group who show a substantial Friedman Effect, might prove to obey the hypothesis. However, this is conjecture. The fact is that there is strong evidence that the hypothesis holds for farmers and business-men, and little or no evidence on the rest of the community.

We may note finally that since all the tests depend on relative magnitudes of F, their validity is independent of the *Proportionality Hypothesis;* and in so far as we have not felt able to provide estimates of the absolute magnitude of F, we have been unable to test the *Proportionality Hypothesis.*

IX. SOME FURTHER CONSIDERATIONS

Mr. H. W. Watts (1958, pp. 126–32) has recently produced evidence of a rather different sort for the *Normal Income Hypothesis.* He argues that a measure of the expected future income of a young man is given by the "cross-section income profile" of men with the same occupation, education and so on. (The "profile" is obtained by plotting average income against age for suitably qualified members of a cross-section survey.) He compares groups of men with different educational backgrounds, but otherwise similar, and finds that, for a given current income, the better educated have higher expected incomes and higher current spending.

The possible effects of education on spending behaviour are complex. Watts argues that it would promote rational rather than improvident behaviour, and thus lead, *ceteris paribus*, to higher saving; but it would also promote rational rather than thrifty behaviour. In addition, it might be argued that education develops a taste for the good things of life—books, foreign travel, winter sports, wine and food, and so on—and that this is only partly offset by the gambling and the television sets of the uneducated. However, Mr. Watts' results, so far as they go, favour the *Normal Income Hypothesis.*

"Contractual saving"[13]—for example, saving in the form of life-assurance premiums or annuity or mortgage payments— is a common phenomenon nowadays and is likely to work against the *Normal Income Hypothesis.* It is likely to make it more difficult for a man to reduce his net saving as much as would be rational during a temporary fall in income. However, one suspects that its popularity is largely confined to people with stable incomes—those with variable incomes are likely to have any contractual saving well-cushioned with liquid assets.

We have said little about saving for posterity. My own belief is that, while many parents give generously to their children during their own lifetime (and while the children are relatively young), few would deliberately reduce their own consumption in order to make a *post-mortem* gift to children who would by then be middle-aged. Bequests are certainly made, but these would be due to uncertainty as to the life-span, or to the need to maintain an equity in utility-yielding assets. However, it is possible that some people save in order to leave money to their children, and we must ask how this would affect our various hypotheses.

The phenomenon can best be represented by making the functions $\beta(Y)$ lower and less steep, on the average over a man's life, than they would otherwise have been. This will not affect the *Normal Income Hypothesis,* but will constitute an additional reason for doubting the *Proportionality Hypothesis.* So far as the *Rate-of-growth Hypothesis* is concerned, it will be just another factor making for thriftiness.

I am indebted to Mr. N. Kaldor for pointing out that, whereas capital gains are assumed by the New Theories to be included in current income, they are not so included in most of the data we have used. The cross-section data are the most important, and it is easy to show that here

[13] See, for example, Klein (1954).

the exclusion of capital gains leads to over-estimates of both the marginal and average propensities to consume. However, we have worked in terms of the income-elasticity of consumption, and the effect here depends on the relative magnitude of these two biases. In fact, if in any sample capital gains, on the average, increase more than proportionately with income—as I think we would expect—then the income-elasticity of consumption will be over-estimated. This tends to strengthen the evidence against the *Proportionality Hypothesis*, but its implications for the *Normal Income Hypothesis* are less clear. Our evidence there consisted in compari-sons of income-elasticities for different groups, and would therefore be affected only by differential bias between groups—a subject on which *a priori* argument is rather hazardous, though one would ex-pect such differential effects to be relatively small.

The omission of capital gains from aggre-gate time-series of personal disposable in-come will lead to an over-estimate of the short-period marginal propensity to con-sume if, as seems likely, capital gains are positively correlated with income. This means that the implied values for the elasticity of expectations, towards the end of Section V, will be somewhat too high; but it is doubtful whether this will make an appreciable difference to such rough calculations.

X. CONCLUSIONS

We have broken the New Theories down into three independent hypotheses. Of these, we have left on one side the *Pro-portionality Hypothesis;* it is unnecessary to the theories, and such evidence as we have found is against rather than for it. On the other hand, we found the *Rate-of-growth Hypothesis* to be substantially valid. Certainly, in the long-run the level of aggregate net saving is determined by balancing gross saving against dis-saving,

and is therefore sensitive to changes in the structure of the economy that affect this balance. But it is also determined by the balancing of thrift and improvidence, and although in the United States these fac-tors roughly cancel each other out, in other economies the balance might be different, with a consequent difference in the savings function.

It is thus an over-simplification to assert that, in the long-run, the proportion of aggregate income saved is proportional to the rate of growth of aggregate income; but it is much nearer the truth than the linear consumption functions so often postulated. It would be interesting to see the effect on the many "theories of economic growth" of substituting in them the *Rate-of-growth Hypothesis* for their present (usually linear) consumption func-tions.

Once the importance of structural fac-tors is recognised, a vast new field of useful, scientific economic research is opened up. The effects of variations in the birth-rate, of emigration and of changes in the rate of change of productivity are all of great practical importance and open to relatively easy investigation.

The *Normal Income Hypothesis* we found to be well-substantiated for farmers and business-men in the United States, but we kept an open mind as to how far it ex-tends to other countries or occupations where incomes are more stable. However, even if the hypothesis were valid *only* for these groups (and there is no evidence for this) its importance is established. Friend and Kravis (1957b) estimate (p. 296) that these groups are responsible for 55–65 percent of personal saving in the United States, and (p. 278) that their marginal propensity to save is more than twice that of the rest of the community. As it is well known that their incomes are more variable, it is clear that their be-haviour determines a very large proportion of the variation in personal savings.

This serves to put trade-cycle theory on what one might call "a fully expectational footing." The recent orthodoxy has been an expectational theory of investment *plus* a mechanistic consumption function—now consumers can have their expectations too! We must, however, enter a caution. Employment and trade-cycle theory depend, not on the marginal propensity to consume but on the marginal propensity to *spend*, which may be very much higher. A consumer may well use a temporary increase in his income to purchase some item of durable equipment, thus spending a large part while consuming only a small fraction of the increase. Another way of putting this might be to say that consumers' durables introduce a sort of accelerator effect on the consumer side.

The hypothesis also has implications for the use of budget studies to throw light on consumption behaviour. We have seen that where the Friedman Effect is present and the *Normal Income Hypothesis* holds, a simple regression analysis will give a biased estimate of the income elasticity of consumption. If a partial regression analysis of, say, consumption on current income and a third variable x is made in the same circumstances, even more misleading results can be produced. For a linear function of x and current income may well be significantly more closely correlated with normal income than is current income alone. In this case, x will appear to have a significant effect on consumption, even though there is no causal relation at all. Friedman (1957a, pp. 86–90) gives an excellent discussion of such possibilities.

It is clear that these phenomena make the interpretation of cross-section studies where only current income is recorded extremely hazardous. So far as existing data are concerned, it behoves the research worker to tread warily, with an eye constantly turned towards the possible effects of Normal Income. For future surveys, one hopes that, at the very least, income for several previous years and expected future income will be recorded; it is perhaps too much to hope that cross-section surveys will be replaced by the much more informative continuous budget studies.

REFERENCES

Boulding, K. E. (1950). *A Reconstruction of Economics.*

Brady, D. S., and R. D. Friedman (1947). "Savings and the Income Distribution," *National Bureau of Economic Research Studies in Income and Wealth*, X.

Cramer, J. S. (1958). "Ownership Elasticities of Durable Consumer Goods," *Review of Economic Studies*, XXV.

Fisher, M. R. (1956). "Explorations in Savings Behaviour," *Bulletin of the Oxford Institute of Statistics*, 1956.

Friedman, M. (1957a). *A Theory of the Consumption Function* (Princeton U.P., 1957).

Friend, I., and I. B. Kravis (1957b). "Entrepreneurial Income, Saving and Investment," *American Economic Review*, June 1957.

Friend, I., and I. B. Kravis (1957a). "Consumption Patterns and Permanent Income," *American Economic Review*, Papers and Proceedings, May 1957.

Goldsmith, R. W. (1951). "Trends and Structural Changes in Saving in the Twentieth Century," *Conference on Savings, Inflation and Economic Progress*, University of Minnesota, 1951.

Goldsmith, R. W. (1955). *A Study of Saving in the United States*, Three volumes (Princeton U.P., 1955 and 1956).

Graaff, J. de V. (1950). "Mr. Harrod on Hump Saving," *Economica*, 1950.

Harrod, R. F. (1948). *Towards a Dynamic Economics* (London: Macmillan & Co., 1948). "Lecture Two: The Supply of Saving."

Hicks, J. R. (1939). *Value and Capital.*

Katona, G., and J. A. Fisher. "Post-war Changes in the Income of Identical Consumer Units," *N.B.E.R. Studies in Income and Wealth*, XIII.

Klein, L. R. (Ed.) (1954). *Contributions of Survey Methods to Economics* (New York: Columbia U.P., 1954).

Kuznets, S. (1952). "Proportion of Capital Formation to National Product," *American Economic Review*, Papers and Proceedings, May 1952.

Modigliani, F. (1949). "Fluctuations in the Saving-Income Ratio: A Problem in Economic Forecasting," *N.B.E.R. Studies in Income and Wealth*, XI.

Modigliani, F., and R. E. Brumberg (1953). *Utility Analysis and Aggregate Consumption Functions: An Attempt at Integration*.

Modigliani, F., and R. E. Brumberg (1954). "Utility Analysis and the Consumption Function: An Interpretation of Cross-section Data," *Post-Keynesian Economics*, K. K. Kurihara (ed.) (Rutgers U.P., 1954).

Morgan, J. N. (1951). "The Structure of Aggregate Personal Saving," *Journal of Political Economy*, 1951.

Vickrey, W. (1947), "Resource Distribution Patterns and the Classification of Families," *N.B.E.R. Studies in Income and Wealth*, X.

Watts, H. W. (1958). *Long-run Income Expectations and Consumer Saving* (Cowles Foundation Paper No. 123).

Part III

INVESTMENT

8

Interest Inelasticity of Investment Demand— The Case from Business Attitude Surveys Re-examined*

WILLIAM H. WHITE

From the late 1930's economists have been growing increasingly skeptical of the value of monetary policy for moderating the swings of the business cycle or for controlling inflation. The main source of this

* *

This is a revised version of an article which was originally published, under the same title, in *The American Economic Review*, vol. 46 (September 1956), pp. 565–587. Reprinted by permission of the publisher and author.

In revising the paper, the author has deleted his discussion of the two French surveys (Sections III and IV in the original article) and added a brief review of the NBER survey (Section III) and of some of the more recent surveys (Section VI).

William H. White is affiliated with the International Monetary Fund.

* Opinions expressed are the author's and do not necessarily reflect the official views of either the Fund or the Brookings Institution, which sponsored a revision of this study. Acknowledgments are due to David Finch, Richard Goode, George Gussman, and E. D. W. Spingarn for reading drafts of this paper and for comments.

skepticism lies, with regard to conditions other than deep depression, in the evidence provided by a number of empirical investigations showing that the interest elasticity of demand for investment is extremely small.

These remarks about the [low] interest elasticity of investment have been well substantiated by different types of empirical investigation. Two studies made on the basis of questionnaires submitted to a large sample of business men [by the Oxford Economists' Research Group and by a Harvard Business School investigator (see below)] show conclusively that the interest rate is largely neglected when investment decisions are being made.[1]

[1] L. R. Klein, *The Keynesian Revolution* (New York, 1947), pp. 65–66. Klein has partly revised his own econometric findings, deriving, on the basis of new data, high interest elasticities of investment demand for electric utilities and railroads. See L. R. Klein, "Studies in Investment Behavior," in *Conference on Business Cycles*, Nat. Bur. of Econ. Research (New York, 1951), pp. 233–304.

It seems to me to have been made clear by the empirical studies referred to [the Oxford investigations] that the traditional theory exaggerated the *direct* effect of the rate of interest on investment plans . . .[2]

The hypothesis of low interest elasticity of investment demand may in fact be correct,[3] but a large part of the empirical foundation upon which it has been constructed seems unsound. This paper discusses, first, two leading prewar surveys, the surveys of British businessmen by the Oxford Economists' Research Group; second, a postwar supplement to the Oxford investigations; third, an American survey by a Harvard Business School investigator; fourth, a survey of large firms made for the N.B.E.R. at the end of the 1930's; subsequently, two widely cited postwar surveys of American business are discussed, the surveys by the University of Minnesota Business School and by the McGraw-Hill Department of Economic Surveys. Finally, some evidence from more recent surveys is presented.

[2] J. R. Hicks, "Comment" on "The New Monetary Policy and the Problem of Credit Control" and "Monetary Policy and the Crisis," *Bull. Oxford Univ. Inst. Stat.*, Apr.–May 1952, XIV, 158. (Hicks argues that a sufficient indirect effect on investment could be achieved from moderate increases in interest rates if it were made clear to business that these would be followed if necessary by increases up to the level of 20 percent.)

Among others accepting the various survey findings of low elasticity are R. V. Rosa, "Interest Rates and the Central Bank" in *Money, Trade and Economic Growth* (New York, 1951), pp. 270–72, 275, and G. L. S. Shackle, "Interest-Rates and the Pace of Investment," *Econ. Jour.*, Mar. 1946, LVI, 1, 6, 7; "Bank Rate and the Modernisation of Industry," *Bankers' Magazine*, June 1954, No. 1323, p. 554. D. H. Robertson considers that the neo-Keynesian thinking on the question has been determined by the surveys in conjunction with econometric investigations. See his *Utility and All That* (London, 1952), p. 87. In one instance, publication of the statistically suspect results of an econometric investigation was justified on the ground that these results were similar to those of the surveys (J. R. Meyer and E. Kuh, *The Investment Decision*, Cambridge 1957, esp. 189).

[3] Although the a priori reasoning offered to support it is also open to question.

The survey technique and the evidence it provides remains of great interest today, despite the large amount of econometric evidence becoming available, because of three serious shortcomings of the econometric approach. (1) "Good" econometric results are those which make it unlikely that the reported results are in error by as much as 100 percent (the null hypothesis), but economic policy-making requires that the probability of error in the reported parameters be small even for errors not larger than 50 percent or less. (2) In contrast with the survey approach, econometrics has had extreme difficulty in making the important distinction between the effects of changes in the "cost" and in the "availability" of money (and has also been troubled by changes in structural relationships within its necessarily long periods of observation). (3) The confidence limits customarily published have greatly exaggerated the reliability of econometric findings: If a given goodness of relationship could result by pure chance only 1 time out of 20, then (to overstate for simplification) the 20 alternative formulations of his relationship which the econometrician generally runs through the computer "guarantee" the discovery of the "good" results that are published.

Thus, study of the accumulated survey evidence remains worthwhile not only for the information on behavior it provides but also for the insight it gives into the many pitfalls in the formulation and interpretation of surveys.

I. OXFORD ECONOMISTS' RESEARCH GROUP SURVEYS OF BRITISH BUSINESS

In 1938 there appeared in the *Oxford Economic Papers* the results of a discussion with 37 businessmen on the importance of the cost of capital in investment decisions.[4]

[4] H. D. Henderson, "The Significance of the Rate of Interest" and J. E. Meade and P. W. S. Andrews, "Summary of Replies to Questions on Effects of Interest Rates," *Oxford Econ. Papers,*

Only about one-fourth of them considered that the cost of capital had an effect on investment, and even these considered it— as would of course be expected—less important than other factors. Most of those who denied the effect did so on the ground that they relied on self-financing or that interest is too small an element in comparison with depreciation and obsolescence, or because of the uncertainty of the market for end-products. This study was unsatisfactory because "the nature of the replies which were received might have been affected by the smallness of the sample and by the bias resulting from the prosperity and relative importance of the businesses represented." A broad survey of British industry was then taken by mail questionnaire.[5] By strictly random sample, 1,000 firms (mostly manufacturing firms) were chosen. In addition, 308 questionnaires were sent to public companies (companies whose shares are freely transferrable) selected at random in a few industries not included in the first population, and to all public companies in a few lines containing very small numbers of firms. The questionnaire, which could be answered merely by noting down a few letters in three blanks, asked whether investment in plant expansion, in maintenance of plant, or in stock holdings was ever affected by (changes in) bank rate, bill discount rate, bank overdraft rate, ease of obtaining overdrafts, government security yields, and ease of obtaining new capital

from the public. About 23 percent of the questionnaires were returned.

Almost 25 percent of the replies indicated that the cost of capital was a factor in the decision to invest in plant and equipment or in stocks.[6] The authors take this result as evidence that capital-cost changes have a negligible direct effect on investment demand.

The authors consider even the 25 percent figure an overstatement of the actual attitude of British businessmen—on the ground that practically all of the 77 percent of the recipients who failed to answer the questionnaire probably did so because they had been affected neither by capital cost changes nor by capital or credit rationing and therefore considered the questionnaire silly. An accurate survey, therefore, should show that only somewhere between 6 percent and 25 percent of British businesses consider capital cost a factor in investment. Even such a reduced figure would overstate the significance of capital cost because, as the comments of respondents "almost invariably" show, capital cost is only one among ". . . a number of other determinant factors, some far more influential than lenders' terms . . . this must mean that, of the firms . . . having been at any time marginal in respect of lenders' terms, few are likely to have been marginal borrowers (and investors) in any given short period of time."[7]

The listing of defects in the Oxford survey should be prefaced by a warning that there are uncertainties about the actual composition of this survey's sample (and other surveys' samples) as well as about some of the characteristics of the business universe against which sample populations must be judged; as a result, some of the criticisms presented here have only presumptive, prima-facie validity. These

---

Oct. 1938, I, 1–31, reprinted in *Oxford Studies in the Price Mechanism*, T. Wilson and P. W. S. Andrews, eds. (Oxford, 1951), pp. 16–30. A more detailed evaluation of this survey is found on pages 26–27 of the article cited in footnote 26 below.

[5] P. W. S. Andrews, "A Further Inquiry into the Effects of Rates of Interest," and R. S. Sayers, "Business Men and the Terms of Borrowing," *Oxford Econ. Papers*, Feb. 1940, III, 32–73 and 23–31, reprinted in *Oxford Studies, op. cit.*, pp. 51–67 and 67–74. Subsequent references to articles in footnotes 4 and 5 are to *Oxford Studies* unless otherwise indicated.

[6] Including 3 percent reporting that they were affected by the "facility with which . . . [they] could raise new capital from the public."

[7] Sayers, *op. cit.*, pp. 68–70.

criticisms are not advanced as proof of error in the surveys; they are intended merely to cause a withholding of credence from the survey's challenged findings pending introduction of more convincing evidence.

1. Overweighting of Small Business

The chief defect lies in the Oxford survey's use of an unweighted random sample of the business population (including replies from small private partnerships and sole proprietorships).[8] Randomness is undesirable when the responses are not weighted, because it must cause the sample to be dominated by small firms; these are naturally much more numerous than large ones, whether for industry as a whole or within separate industries. Now the investment carried out by the average small firm must be both minor in comparison with the investment of the average large firm and also, as will be shown, less open to the influence of changing capital costs. But since the objective of the survey was to obtain information on the responsiveness of *aggregate* investment to changes in capital costs, the replies ought to have been weighted in proportion to the respondents' normal (or potential) investments.[9] The appropriate weights might have been very hard to fix; nevertheless, equal weighting creates a serious bias in favor of the small investor. Moreover, the investment of small firms in the aggregate may even be so small a part of total investment that the behavior of small firms as a *group* should receive only a minor part of the total weight instead of the large (and perhaps predominant) part which they actually did receive.

The smallness of the amount of investment per small firm, the predominance of small firms in the business population and the predominance of large firms in total investment are demonstrated by the available data on distribution of manufacturers' capital spending or employment by size of (consolidated) enterprise. In 1935 the just 88 manufacturing enterprises that had 5,000 or more employees accounted for a quarter of all employment in manufacturing. Their share in capital spending is unknown, but data for 1958 indicate that a very small minority made up of big companies must have accounted for half of total capital spending: In 1958 the 0.3 percent of manufacturers that had 5,000 or more employees (180 companies) accounted for 34 percent of employment in manufacturing and still more—51 percent—of capital spending. The 2 percent of companies with 1,000 or more employees had 55 percent of employment and 72 percent of spending. On the other hand, the 80 percent or so of the manufacturers that had under 100 employees accounted for only 16 percent of the employees and a mere 9 percent of the spending.[10] It is clear, therefore, that companies with under 100 employees should now be given only one tenth of the weight (one seventh when those with up to 200 employees are included) in any survey, while the giants with 5,000 or more employees should be given half the weight.

There is another bias introduced by nonweighting; just as random sampling overweights the small firm, so it overweights those firms of any size who are small investors for any reason. In this category are firms in lines of production requiring relatively small amounts of capital and firms in depressed activities, such as the textile industry, which for a number of years preceding the Oxford questionnaire had little or no occasion to enlarge their capital.

Failure to weight replies by size of firm would not be objectionable if there were no

---

[8] Andrews, *op. cit.* p., 53.

[9] A more elaborate weighting system would be preferable because, since only 23 percent of the (randomly distributed) questionnaires were returned, the actual sample may be unrandom.

[10] Derived from *Board of Trade Jour.*, March 8, 1963, pp. 555, 557.

reason for expecting differing responsiveness to changes in the cost of capital according to size of firm. But in actuality there is strong reason for expecting the smaller firms to be less sensitive to changes in the cost of capital. Firms in overexpanded industries, regardless of size, can also be expected not to be sensitive to capital costs. These groups should tend to ignore changes in the cost of capital because they usually rely on self-financing to pay for their investment—and especially for their fixed capital investment.

That relatively small firms are predominantly self-financers is indicated by the well-known difficulty which small firms have in raising capital from the public by bond and share issues. Public unfamiliarity with the firm makes sale of its securities difficult so that, even if underwriters should be willing to sponsor an issue, the cost of the funds will be extremely high. This is especially the case for stock issues. And the inherent dangers for a small firm in the (high) fixed interest charges of a bond issue discourage use of this source of outside capital.[11] Similar reasoning holds for large firms in depressed lines; the relatively small amount of investment they undertake also tends to be self-financed.

The importance of this consideration is revealed by the comments in the replies to the Oxford questionnaire. Explanations were appended by about 70 percent of the respondents who reported being unaffected by the cost or availability of capital. And about half of these explanations gave as reason for ignoring capital costs and the facility of obtaining capital either the fact that plant and inventory investments had been financed by the firm's own resources or that the firms were small.[12]

There is no proof that this half of the negative respondents consisted entirely of small businesses (or firms in the depressed trades). But at least one-third of the group is known to be comprised of small firms (see footnote 12) and it seems plausible that most of the remainder were. One of the businessmen interviewed in the course of the first Oxford survey stated, in response to a question on the importance of self-financing in the determination of

[11] The validity of this reasoning for Britain is shown by F. W. Paish, *Business Finance* (London, 1953), p. 102. The minimum practical size for a single security issue was £100,000 before the war and £150,000 in 1953; smaller issues were "inordinately expensive" (*ibid.*, p. 100). The extent of the merely institutional limitation of access to organized capital markets in the universe from which the sample comes is revealed by the fact that in 1938 only 8½ percent of British corporations ("companies") had the legal right to issue shares publicly (*ibid.*, p. 45). (Some of these firms must have been subsidiaries of security-issuing firms, but allowance for such members of the group would probably be outweighed by the necessary allowance for unincorporated businesses which has not been made.)

For the validity of the above reasoning in the United States, see C. H. Schmidt, "Analyzing the Effects of Business Size on Sources and Uses of Funds," *Conference on Research in Business Finance*, Nat. Bur. of Econ. Research (New York, 1952), p. 38.

[12] Of the 156 negative respondents appending comments, 65 gave as explanation the fact that they relied on their own resources or did not believe in borrowing, etc. Included among these were 18 respondents who also indicated that they were small firms ("small scale," "family business," "private company," etc.). In addition to these 65 firms, 6 others gave their smallness as the sole reason for insensitivity to capital costs. There were 9 more firms which, although providing additional reasons for their capital-cost insensitivity such as the inconsequentiality of interest costs among total costs or in comparison with required profit margins, also reported that they were small or were self-financers. Another 9 stated (as did 5 of the above) that they did compare the rate of return with the cost of capital, but either the latter had not varied, or it had not varied widely enough to have an effect, or else the firm had been unaffected only because it was relying solely on its own resources. (Those making the comparison were negative replies numbers 23, 85, 100 and 137; the others were negative replies numbers 9, 45, 51, 69, 93, 105, 109, 117, 122, 132.) The comments were reproduced in the original presentation of Andrews' report (*Oxford Econ. Papers*, Feb. 1940, III, 48–70), but not in the reprint cited above. Andrews also points out the importance of self-financers among the negative respondents (*op. cit.*, pp. 64–65), but he apparently interprets the situation only as evidence of the great extent to which investment is isolated from the capital markets.

investment, that self-financing fixed the limit to investment much more for small companies than for large companies.[13] Every consideration leads to the conclusion that the "large" or active firms which must dominate total investment during any year would have been borrowers from the public, the banks or the mortgage market at one time or another during the 'twenties or 'thirties. As noted above the large firms are the ones with easy access to outside capital. And outside capital did play a major role in total investment in the period: Whereas

> in the nineteenth century much of the long-term capital for industrial expansion was provided out of the profits of private industrial firms, and by private borrowing from fairly rich individuals with local ... knowledge.... By 1937, though that process was not negligible, it was overshadowed by the expansion of public joint stock companies of which the shares were quoted on the London Stock Exchange.[14]

Thus, unless they were in a depressed industry and for that reason did not invest much, relatively few "large" firms would be likely to be included in that half of the capital-cost-ignoring respondents known to consist either of small or of self-financing firms.

For the other half of the negative respondents, whose comments give few indications of size,[15] the findings must be more uncertain. The likelihood of a bias in favor of small firms does exist, nevertheless, because of the marked tendency for reliance on scientific management to diminish as the size of firm diminishes. Use of scientific management comes close to being a necessary condition (even if perhaps not a sufficient condition) for sensitivity to capital costs. Even if other

factors leading to sensitivity were equal as between large and small firms, the absence of this practically necessary condition in the case of a much larger fraction of the small firms would itself assure relatively less capital-cost sensitivity for small than for large firms. It follows that small firms should (presumptively) claim a disproportionately large share of this remaining group of negative responses. On this ground also, therefore, the Oxford survey's 25 percent finding may be assumed to understate the effectiveness of interest rate changes.[16]

2. Motivation of Nonrespondents

The opinion of one investigator that even the 25 percent figure was too high on the ground that "most" of the recipients who ignored the questionnaire did so because their investment decisions had never been affected by the cost or availability of capital is unconvincing. As the investigator himself noted, other explanations are available for failure to respond, *viz:* impatience because of entanglement in

[16] The limited explicit information on the distribution of large firms between the negative and affirmative respondents tends to corroborate the self-financing and scientific management arguments. Neglecting the 8 public utilities, 7 of which are insensitive to capital cost changes, only 3 negative respondents could be identified as large, while 9 very sensitive members of the much smaller affirmative group were found—by the readiness, reflected in their comments, to issue securities to the public—to be large. (Only 3 very sensitive firms were identifiably small.) The large negative respondents are numbers 26 (which is self-financing), 70 (a small subsidiary of a large firm) and 106. (Numbers 60 and 127 may also be large firms, but, on the other hand, some of these 5 may be public utilities—which are being excluded from consideration.) The large and small affirmative respondents are, respectively, numbers 3, 15, 19, 28, 34, 36, 44, 50, and 55 and numbers 4, 6, and 23. (See Andrews, originally published comments, *loc. cit.*)

A concrete instance of a large British firm that, though drawing on the capital market before the second world war, was insensitive to capital cost changes is provided by P. W. S. Andrews and Elizabeth Brunner, *Capital Development in Steel, A Study of the United Steel Companies, Ltd.* (Oxford, 1951).

[13] Meade and Andrews, *op. cit.*, p. 30.

[14] R. F. Henderson, "The Significance of the New Issue Market for the Finance of Industry," *Econ. Jour.*, Mar. 1948, LVIII, 66.

[15] Some of this group report financing fixed investment with bank overdrafts.

government form-filling, fear of use of the information against the interests of the firm, unconcern with economic theoreticians' projects.[17] And by his own hypothesis, those not affected by capital costs or rationing who did bother to return the questionnaire ought to have done so more perfunctorily than did the respondents who were affected; but the proportion of responses containing additional comments (requested but not required) was practically the same for the former (69 percent) as for the latter group (73 percent).

3. Omission of Any Question on Cost of Funds on the Stock Market

The only question in the Oxford survey touching on the cost of long-term capital asks about the effect of government bond yields on private investment. This obviously would have been less effective in eliciting answers acknowledging the role of long-term capital costs than a direct question on industrial bond yields.[18] More important, no question was asked about the role in investment decisions of the cost of capital on the share market (*e.g.*, the ratio of the company's average earnings per share to the selling price of the shares).

The responsiveness of investment demand to share-capital costs is significant because many firms will at times consider only equity financing for (part of) their investment and because the cost of share capital is, like the bond yield, subject to the influence of monetary policy.[19]

The question on "the facility with which

you can raise new capital from the public" may have been interpreted to cover the cost of share capital, the more so since infacility can be at least partially overcome by payment of a higher return, especially in the case of shares. Nevertheless, as it stands the questionnaire appears to discourage consideration of the role of the cost of share capital in investment decisions; this is particularly the case because two separate questions are asked on the role of bank credit, one on the facility with which bank overdrafts can be obtained and the other on their cost.

4. Influence of Factors Other than Capital Costs

It is argued that a variety of factors operate on investment profitabilities, so that at a given point of time "most" of those entrepreneurs who do consider the cost of capital might find that potential projects are far enough from marginal profitability to be immune to capital cost changes. This is considered, by the Oxford investigators, to have the effect of reducing interest elasticity of demand below whatever value is connoted by the one-quarter sensitivity figure.[20]

It appears, however, that the explanations for a major portion of the instances of nonmarginality are such that the connoted elasticity could be only partially affected: A large portion of the intermittently nonmarginal firms will consist of those that are very submarginal simply

---

[17] Sayers, *op. cit.*, p. 68.

[18] Even among affirmative respondents, only 2 out of the 77 mentioned the yield on government securities as a factor in plant-extension decisions. Andrews, *op. cit.*, p. 61.

[19] Special factors make equity capital costs appear to move independently of debt costs, but movements of the latter must in fact cause some shift of savers between the debt and equity markets in one direction and investors in the other, thereby affecting stock market prices.

[20] Sayers, *op. cit*, pp. 69–70. As indicated above (p. 97), the inference of frequent nonmarginality seems to have been made from the investigator's conclusion that affirmative respondents "almost invariably insist on the presence of a number of other determinant factors, some of them far more influential than lenders' terms." Robertson interprets the reports of the presence of other and stronger factors not as additional evidence of low elasticities but as ground for considering the survey's low-elasticity findings invalid. He argues that respondents thought the questionnaire concerned the extent of correlation between changes in interest rates and observed—rather than *ceteris paribus*—changes in investment. See Robertson, *op. cit.*, p. 87.

because they cannot find (even during prosperous times) enough investment projects which would yield the minimum plausible capital charges. But—provided only that the average capital-cost-sensitive firm does not spend a larger part of its time in the very submarginal, low investing group than does the average insensitive firm—this kind of nonmarginality leaves demand elasticity comparatively little affected. (What is reduced by that submarginality is in great part simply the *volume* of aggregate investment actually going on at any time rather than its elasticity.)

Another large portion of the instances of intermittent insensitivity should consist of cases in which the least profitable (*i.e.*, marginal) project that the firm will consider has a rate of return above the expected levels of capital costs. This is the condition of discontinuity in firms' investment demand curves.[21] Now, although discontinuity entails insensitivity of the volume of investment to changes in capital costs within a certain range, it also means that changes beyond the given range will cause relatively *large* changes in investment. Since the position of this range of indifference will vary among firms, it seems safe to assume that, with large numbers of firms making investment decisions, the average effect will be almost as large as if all firms had continuous demand curves.

There are, of course, many instances of

[21] Expectation theory provides one of the reasons for discontinuity. The entrepreneur has no basis for considering rates of return within a certain range as having other than equal probabilities of being realized; hence changes in the cost of capital within this range will not affect investment demand. See R. F. Harrod, "Comment" (on Harold Pilvin, "Full Capacity versus Full Employment Growth"), *Quart. Jour. Econ.*, Nov. 1953, LXVII, 557–58. The importance of this source of discontinuity may be overrated, for the entrepreneur knows that his expectations concerning the *limits* of the range may themselves prove incorrect; and, as a change in capital costs moves the required rate of return relative to the upper limit of this range, the risk of loss in case that limit was overestimated will change; hence, the willingness to invest will also be changed.

temporary nonmarginality in which the interest elasticity of investment demand is reduced, *e.g.*, where net investment is going on but is restricted to projects that are not directly profit-making (such as investments for generating employee or public good will) or are of absolute necessity for the survival of the enterprise or, although promising returns much below the cost of capital, are carried out because (more than) sufficient internal funds are available. Nevertheless these cases need not appear so often as might be assumed (*cf.* the very large role played by long-term outside capital in the financing of net business investment since the second world war and the likelihood that, assuming conditions at the worst only "moderately" depressed, interest-sensitive firms will tend to make marginal, economic investments simultaneously with their nonmarginal, "noneconomic" investments).

5. Special Conditions of British Industry in the 1930's

A member of the Oxford economists' research group, in a résumé of the interest rate controversy in the reprint of the group's studies, emphasized that the depressed and chaotic conditions of the 'thirties resulted in a "quite extraordinary lack of confidence [which] lasted for years" and made necessary very high rates of risk discount for investment projects. In view of this, "it would have been surprising if businessmen had shown less skepticism in their answers to the Oxford economists."[22] The inference to be made from this analysis is that the study proves interest-inelasticity only for situations in which there exists an enormous collapse of confidence such as was produced by the capping of Britain's struggles in " 'getting back' to pre-war normality" with a deep, prolonged depression. Such an observation

[22] Even though "when in the twenties interest rates were high, businessmen were loud in emphasizing . . . the depressive effects of dear money." R. S. Sayers, "The Rate of Interest as a Weapon of Economic Policy," *Oxford Studies*, p. 14.

by one of the participants in the Oxford survey must be a warning against generalization of the low-elasticity findings.[23]

Again, the value of generalization from the Oxford study may be questionable because, in so far as it *is* representative of its period, the study represents only the behavior of British business before the second world war. The "Working Party" reports on a number of British industries have made it clear that before the war British business was extremely conservative in investment policy. Far from paying attention to such refined considerations as interest rate changes, business tended to ignore opportunities for large profits from technological developments. As *The Economist* put it:

> British industrialists, with a few notable exceptions, have never been 're-equipment minded.' The general attitude towards plant replacement before the war was to scrap a machine only when it could no longer do the job for which it was originally designed. Only rarely was the question asked whether a new machine could do the job better and more economically than an existing one; or whether a new plant layout involving, say, two new machines instead of three installed, would do the job more economically still.[24]

This rather casual attitude toward investment planning was not monopolized by prewar Great Britain. But for a number of other countries that have probably been less affected by it, a finding with respect to British industry may well understate the

sensitivity of investment to changes in capital costs within their own industries.

Wartime experience began ". . . the conversion of the British industrialist to the view that frequent re-equipment and modernisation of plant really does pay."[25] It is to be expected that the great increase in the productive efficiency of British industry since the war promises continuing attention to the possibilities of increasing productive capacity and efficiency. And if investment projects are examined more scientifically today than in the past, it seems likely that the role of the cost of capital will now receive at least more recognition than it has in the past. In fact, evidence provided to the Radcliffe Committee during the late 1950's by the British Chambers of Commerce, the Federation of British Industries, and the chief officers of eight giant firms indicates a potentially significant role for the interest rate; and the Bank of England, which had testified to belief in a weak role, has since reversed its own opinion.[26]

Our discussion suggests the following conclusion: The large firms, which dominate total investment and are presumably most sensitive to capital cost changes, seem to have been seriously underweighted. Moreover, acknowledgment of responsiveness to changes in bond-and-share capital costs was discouraged by exclusion of these from the list of capital costs investigated. In addition, the survey was an unrepresentative one because it was made when business had been suffering "from a quite extraordinary lack of confidence [which] lasted for years" and in a time and country in which scientific management may have been relatively underdeveloped. Finally, the lowness of the implied investment demand elasticities said to follow from the fact that the sensitivity reported was

[23] Sayers, however, continues to support the findings on a priori grounds: Whatever the uniqueness of the conditions in which the findings were made, the latter were symptomatic of the waning of the interest-rate myth—a myth which was a reality in the 19th century and had persisted in the 20th in large part simply because businessmen had continued to believe in it. *Ibid.*, pp. 14–15.

[24] *The Economist*, October 6, 1945, p. 494. See also Great Britain, Board of Trade, *Working Party Reports, Cotton* (London, 1946), pp. 66, 68–69, and *Working Party Reports, Wool* (London, 1947), pp. 85–86. The underdeveloped state of management accounting techniques is reported in Graham Hutton, *We Too Can Prosper*, British Productivity Council (London, 1953), pp. 47, 48.

[25] *The Economist, loc. cit.*

[26] See W. H. White, "Inventory Investment and the Rate of Interest," Brookings Institution Reprint No. 57 (from *Banca Nazionale del Lavoro, Quarterly Review*, June 1961), 6, 32–34, 36.

(assertedly) only intermittent and from the fact that insensitive firms might have tended not to return their questionnaires seems greatly exaggerated; other explanations—such as submarginality and discontinuity—which need not detract from the implied elasticity seem appropriate. These points seem sufficient to justify disregard of the Oxford survey's finding that investment demand is extremely inelastic.

II. HARVARD BUSINESS SCHOOL SURVEY

In 1938 Ebersole published the findings of a survey of the Harvard Business School's collection of actual decisions taken with respect to a great variety of business problems.[27] These "cases" were collected by skilled investigators, with the close cooperation of the firms concerned, for use in the training of business administration students. From 13,100 cases, 93 were found which "involved entrepreneurial problems of business of the type in which interest rates might have been a factor," and of these 63 contained no reference to interest rates or the cost of capital. Of the 30 cases in which the cost of capital was mentioned ". . . there were 20 in which it was not a factor contributing to the decision whether or not to expand or contract [plant or operations] and only 10 instances in which the interest rate or cost of capital funds was recognized as a factor in making the decision." And even for these 10 it was not the sole or decisive factor.[28] From this evidence the investigator tentatively concluded that the cost of capital might be a negligible factor in American business investment decisions.[29]

As in the Oxford survey, the conclusion is made dubious by the failure to weight

entrepreneurs' attitudes by some allowance for the size of their companies. Many of the 13,100 cases must have involved large corporations; but small firms surely must also have been represented because, *e.g.*, a large part of the student body was training for "small" business positions.

Moreover, it is important to recognize that these 83 negative or tacitly negative cases do not denote firms which always disregarded capital costs. Rather they are separate instances of disregard of capital costs. And as has already been pointed out (pp. 101–102), findings based on a sample of individual investment decisions should underestimate actual capital-cost sensitivity. Thus many of the 83 instances of insensitivity could be due to the fact that (a) for those firms that decided to "contract plant or operations," only submarginal projects were available, and (b) for firms that decided to "expand . . . plant or operations," the planned investment volume was at a discontinuous point in the firms' respective (arc-elastic) investment demand curves. As already described, such instances of capital-cost insensitivity detract little from the effectiveness of a high interest rate policy and should be excluded from the survey.[30]

This conclusion must be qualified to allow for cases occurring during depressed periods. The preceding argument remains valid for depression in the sense that the

[27] J. F. Ebersole, "The Influence of Interest Rates upon Entrepreneurial Decisions in Business —A Case Study," *Harvard Bus. Rev.*, Autumn 1938, XVII, 35–40.

[28] *Ibid.*, pp. 38–39.

[29] *Ibid.*, p. 39. See also Sayers, "The Rate of Interest as a Weapon of Economic Policy," *op. cit.*, pp. 1, 5–6.

[30] If capital costs were disregarded in any investment decision only because—not having changed for a time prior to the decision—they were taken for granted as a fixed, "structural" factor, then that instance should also be excluded from the survey sample, for the survey is concerned with the effectiveness of *changes* in capital costs.

The Oxford survey, each respondent to which presumably reported on several investment decisions, is superior in this respect to the Harvard Business School survey, although Shackle ("Interest-Rates and the Pace of Investment," *op. cit.*, pp. 15–16) uses the stability of the consol (perpetual government bond) yield as a partial explanation for the predominance of negative responses in the Oxford survey.

finding of capital-cost insensitivity among low investors still carries no implication of insensitivity on the part of firms that *are* (on the margin of) investing enough to make external financing necessary. However, during depression an abnormally large fraction of firms become submarginal investors. The marginal investors are therefore an abnormally small group; even though capital-cost changes operate on their investment with undiminished effect, the absolute effect—change in volume of investment—must be diminished.

Despite this qualification, complete retention of the low-investing submarginal cases in the sample remains suspect. Those drawn from prosperity years clearly should be given only partial weights. Of course many of the low investment cases will reflect depression conditions and cannot be so eliminated from the survey sample. However, a survey of prosperity years alone would be particularly interesting because it is in prosperity conditions that monetary policy is thought to have the best chance of success. And with the weights of the negative cases caused by submarginality or by discontinuity cut down, there is a presumption that the Harvard findings would be much more favorable to interest rate policy.

Still another consideration justifies the suspicion that the survey is biased against a finding of capital-cost sensitivity. The test of sensitivity is whether the decision to expand or contract "operations or plant" was affected by capital costs. Now in so far as "operations" changes mean something different from plant changes, they must refer to changes in the rate of production not affecting the existing capacity. A significant part of the cases must have consisted of this kind of decision, for the period covered included a majority of subnormal years during which production was falling below or rising towards pre-existing productive capacity. But the only change in existing investment involved here would be a change of inventories. And inventories are generally (on the average) a small fraction of annual production; *e.g.*, 16 percent (since the start of the second world war) of total sales by U.S. manufacturing,[31] and a smaller percentage of total sales in manufacturing plus trade. Thus, with the exception of those firms whose operation consists of the holding of inventory, it is clear that a decision to change the volume of "operations" is practically unaffected by changes in the cost of holding inventory. If a rise in demand made profitable a rise in the volume of production, the deterrent effect of increases in the interest cost of carrying (additional) inventory would perforce be below the threshold of perception.[32]

As regards unrepresentativeness of timing, the investigation surpasses the failure of the Oxford study to reflect the postwar spread of investment planning, for it takes some of its observations from as far back as 1920—a time when the techniques of cost accounting, market survey and business budgeting were extremely primitive.

Finally—as the investigator concedes—in some of the 63 cases not mentioning capital costs the silence may have been caused not by the absence of the factor but by the fact that the case-collector was interested in other aspects of the investment decision (*e.g.*, the role of market research, of technological progress in investment planning, or the role of advertising

[31] *Economic Report of the President*, Jan. 1955, p. 172.

[32] An increase in interest rates of 2 percentage points on debt equal to 16 percent of sales would require the selling price to be raised by only 0.32 percent even if net profit per unit of sales had to be maintained on the marginal sales. And even if the intended expansion in operations were only 5 percent, the effect of this capital cost increase would be almost invisible—unless the product's price elasticity of demand was unusually high. (Where value added by manufacturing rather than total sales by manufacturers is considered the proper basis for the comparison, the selling price increase becomes 0.64 to 0.96 percent.)

in the decision to change the volume of production within the limits of existing capacity).

To summarize, the survey presumably included small firms; in dealing with single investment decisions, it must have included many cases of discontinuity and submarginality, both of which are often irrelevant; it must have contained many cases involving inventory investment—which is likewise irrelevant; it is badly out of date; and, finally, very many of the cases must have been selected to illustrate other aspects of the investment decision than the role of capital costs. These defects seem sufficient to establish that the survey's findings on American business' sensitivity to capital cost changes should be disregarded.

III. NBER SURVEY

The influential interview survey of over 50 large and medium-sized U.S. companies made for the N.B.E.R. by Ruth P. Mack during the great depression found that required minimum rates of return on investment were commonly ignored. When they were used they were fixed at between 20 percent and 50 percent for modernization investments and appeared to be much higher for those modernization investments which included a large element of expansion.

Because the surveyor found such very high required rates of return on the latter, partly-expansion investments, because she found too few instances of such partly expansion projects even among the giant companies interviewed to permit generalization about the levels of returns that were required, and because she explained the extremely low rate of capital spending by depression psychosis rather than by the commonly-assumed "strike of capital" against the New Deal,[33] her careful findings of no role for the interest rate in

the determination of industrial investment should have long since been discarded as totally irrelevant to more normal conditions. In fact, the surveyor herself reported indications that the interest rate might be influential in more normal conditions. And even under depression conditions she found that the larger textile firms who could borrow money at the low interest rates charged by banks were thereby enabled to maintain more modern equipment than other textile firms who would have had to pay the "high" interest rates on equipment loans of 5 percent or 6 percent.[34]

A reminder of just how abnormal the conditions were for surveys made during the great depression is provided by this surveyor's comment that: "Even in this wealthiest and most progressive of countries, the common man and woman lead a poor life in which want and fear play an atrociously major role."[35]

IV. MINNESOTA BUSINESS SCHOOL SURVEY

The University of Minnesota investigation, published in 1950,[36] was based on interviews of officials of 13 firms in the Minneapolis area. The firms covered ranged in size from a few hundred to several thousand employees. The main factor in their investment was found to be the availability of internal financing. Small, weak firms had no access to outside long-term funds while prosperous firms, which could get outside funds easily at reasonable rates, avoided them. Four conditions explain this unwillingness to rely on outside financing: (1) delays and inconvenience in security flotation, (2) unwillingness to release information on the

---

[33] Ruth P. Mack, *The Flow of Business Funds and Consumer Purchasing Power*, New York, 1941, esp. pp. 258, 267–269, 297–298.

[34] *Ibid.*, pp. 255, 262, and pp. 267–268.
[35] *Ibid.*, p. 387.
[36] A. Upgren, *et al.*, *The Minneapolis Project; a Pilot Study of Local Capital Formation* (School of Bus. Admin., Univ. of Minnesota, 1950); and W. W. Heller, "The Anatomy of Investment Decisions," *Harvard Bus. Rev.*, Mar. 1951, XXIX, 99–104.

SHARE OF TOTAL U.S. MANUFACTURING
PLANT AND EQUIPMENT INVESTMENT, BY SIZE CLASS OF INVESTOR, 1952

(1) Gross assets of corporations ($000,000)	(2) Percent of aggregate investment[a]	(3) Percent of all manu-facturing corporations in size class[b]	(4) Average investment per firm, index[c]
0–0.1 ⎱ 0.1–1.0 ⎰	8	50.4 ⎱ 38.9 ⎰	2
1–5	9	7.9	27
5–10	6	1.3	100
10–50	13	1.2	250
50–100	10	0.2	1580
100–	53	0.2	6910

SOURCE: U.S. Department of Commerce, Securities and Exchange Commission, and Bureau of Internal Revenue. Column (3) is from Bur. Internal Revenue, *Statistics of Income for 1951, Part 2* (Washington, 1955), p. 130.

[a] Corporations' investment gross of depreciation and depletion.
[b] Data are for end of 1951 and therefore are not entirely comparable with column (2).
[c] Index of (2) ÷ (3); average investment of $5–$10 million corporations = 100.

firm's activities to banks or the Securities and Exchange Commission, (3) "the dilution of control and per-share earnings" (in the case of stock issues), and (4) the risk involved in fixed-interest obligations plus the prospect of bank intervention in future policy-making (in the case of bond issues).[37]

Computations of the rate of profit on projected investment often were either not made or made without being related (by the self-financers, especially) to the rate of interest.[38]

The Minnesota survey revealed an important, unexpected limitation on the role of capital-cost changes: in over half the firms studied the very high rate of investment during the four years following the war was almost more than management and engineering staffs could handle; in a situation in which otherwise profitable projects had to be passed up, changes in the cost of capital must have had greatly diminished influence on the volume of investment.[39]

It appears, however, that—disregarding 4 companies each of which had 2 security issues 1950–55 and whose inclusion in a sample of firms opposed to external financing therefore requires explanation[40] —the Minnesota sample was dominated by low-investing and atypical firms. First there were the small, weak self-financers who were unable to get outside funds at reasonable rates. There appear to have been 4 in the sample's population.[41] Then

[37] Upgren, *op. cit.*, pp. 21, 29.
[38] *Ibid.*, p. 20.
[39] *Ibid.*, pp. 21–22.

[40] Including 2 firms each having an issue in 1950, the year the Minnesota survey was published, there were 3 firms, each of which has had 2 successive large new-money debt issues or placements and a fourth which has had 3 new money issues (including one issue of common stock). (A fifth firm, having a net worth of $6.3 million in 1949, had raised $1.4 million by private placement in 1948.) See Appendix A to *The Minneapolis Project* (available on request from the publishers) and *Moody's Industrials*, 1950 and 1955.
[41] Two firms exclusively in grain milling, stated to be stagnant, a hosiery and lingerie manufacturer with very low income in 1949, and, presumably, a paint manufacturer with 300 employees. See *Minneapolis Project*, Appendix A.
One firm, presumably a member of this group, stated, "We don't have enough funds to do more than replace the machines that are obviously ready for the scrap heap." See Heller, *op. cit.*, p. 101.

there were the prosperous firms who could get outside funds at reasonable rates but would not do so because of considerations such as unwillingness to reveal their financial position to banks or the Securities and Exchange Commission, and fear of dilution of control of the business if (voting) common shares were issued. These firms comprised, at the most, the 5 of the sample's 13 not already accounted for. It is possible that these firms would not prove to be typical of large investing businesses, for their two motivating considerations hold chiefly for firms that have not had public issues of securities. Practically every "large" corporation will have had public security issues and its financial position will be common knowledge. And the past security issues of most of these firms will have been so large and so widely distributed that fear of dilution of control as a result of new share issues will be the exception. (Moreover, such firms should be able to issue fractional-voting or non-voting shares.)[42]

The statistical evidence on the important role of long-term external finance by medium and large manufacturing firms from 1948 through 1953 reinforces the conclusion that these 5 or fewer self-financers are probably not representative of aggregate investment by medium and large manufacturers.[43]

The Minnesota findings do suggest that small firms are self-financers and that they ignore capital costs. However, it is easily demonstrated that such firms' part in American manufacturing investment is unimportant. The table (p. 107) shows that the concentration of fixed capital formation in manufacturing is as great in the United States as in Great Britain; the largest 2.8 percent of American manufacturing corporations did 82 percent of the investment.[44]

Despite the apparent predominance of small and atypical firms in the Minnesota survey (or perhaps because of the extent to which the dominance is not complete), one of the reasons given for not relying on share issues to finance investment was "dilution of . . . per-share earnings." Dilution of per-share earnings occurs when the "price" paid for share capital—the amount of anticipated earnings required by a buyer of the share per dollar of capital which he provides—is higher than the anticipated rate of return on the extra investment which is financed by the stock sale. The stating of this ground for refusing to raise new funds from the public

---

[42] One of the 5 or fewer self-financers, the largest of the firms in the sample, is known to have been closely held (although having 15,000 stockholders by 1954) and to reflect the attitudes described by the survey. However, this firm's circumstances may be somewhat unusual among large businesses. It was still "essentially a first-generation company" with the directors controlling nearly half the stock. Some millions of dollars worth of stock had to be sold because of estate taxes in 1945 and "Estate taxes might eventually break up these [remaining] holdings. . . ." See "Minnesota Mining in Motion," *Fortune*, Mar. 1949, XXXIX, 93, 172.

It is interesting to note that this firm did make a $20 million issue of debt and preferred stock in 1947. See *Moody's Industrials*, 1950.

[43] The source and use of funds data published annually for all manufacturing corporations by

the *Survey of Current Business* and for 200 medium and large manufacturing corporations by the *Federal Reserve Bulletin* suggest that external financing has amounted (excluding the transactions of negative financers in any year) to perhaps 50 percent of medium and large firms' net fixed investment. This financing must have been spread among firms doing much more than half the investment because the rolls of financers must have been made up of a varying list of firms over the years and because many firms must have used sizable amounts of internal funds along with their external funds.

[44] The largest 2/10 of a percent—200 manufacturing corporations—did 53 percent of the investment.

Employment data must be substituted for investment data if unincorporated firms are to be included in the measure. On this basis the largest 6/10 percent (firms with a minimum of 1,000 and an average of over 4,600 workers) employed well over half of the manufacturing labor force (*Surv. Curr. Bus.*, May 1954, XXXIV, 16, 18, 23).

is an acknowledgment of the importance of capital costs in investment decisions.[45]

The Minnesota finding that shortages in management and engineering staff set the limit to the rate of investment and caused an accumulation of profitable investment projects in over half the firms studied is itself a strong reason for discounting the survey's conclusions.   Only after the temporary shortage and "rationing" phase had ended could there be a valid survey of the importance of a market-mechanism factor such as the price of capital.

V. MCGRAW-HILL SURVEY

A survey made at the end of 1949 by the McGraw-Hill Department of Economic Surveys asked whether American manufacturing firms would expand capital investment in 1950 if common stock prices were 50 percent above the level of November 1949 (*i.e.*, at a price higher than had been reached since 1929).[46] Ninety-three percent of the firms replied that they would not.[47]

The investigation had two peculiarities which make this finding especially significant. Firstly, the sample was biased toward large firms, smaller firms being included only where the large firms surveyed did not dominate total investment sufficiently and it was necessary instead to employ a "representative cross section" of the industry. Secondly, the finding was made for the case of a very large change in the cost of capital (the ratio of expected

per-share earnings to price of shares) in the share market, *viz*: 33 percent.

Nevertheless, most of the negative responses to the McGraw-Hill survey are open to explanations which would leave the survey's findings consistent with the existence of a high interest elasticity of investment demand. In the first place, the study itself reports both the big companies' possession of surplus liquidity and difficulty in arranging security flotations in the limited time allowed as factors in the high ratio of negative responses. Secondly, many of the negative respondents must have experienced the prior limitation on investment created by the postwar shortage of administrative personnel, for the survey was made at the same time as the Minnesota investigation. Again, the respondents did include some small firms, many of which must have been unable to float share issues. More important, the cost of share capital— the per-share earnings share-price ratio— would have been quite high even after the one-third reduction: 9.3 percent net of corporate income taxes (a level higher than in any of the years 1920–21, 1927 through 1940, and 1942 through 1946)[48] or 15 percent before corporate income taxes. Unwillingness or inability to finance additional investment when the cost of financing falls only to 15 percent is quite consistent with a high interest elasticity of investment demand. Many firms were already relying on debt financing at interest costs plus risk charges (to cover the fixed interest burden) of well below 15 percent;[49] such firms obviously could reject a proposal to finance additional investment with another

---

[45] The cost of capital on the stock market was abnormally high at the time the survey was made (see next section); therefore this explanation of unwillingness to borrow is in conformity with expectations.

[46] "Industry's 1950 Capital Spending Plans," *Bus. Week*, Jan. 21, 1950, pp. 73–80 and McGraw-Hill Dept. of Econ. Surveys, *Business Plans for New Plants and Equipment 1950* (New York, 1950).

[47] "Industry's 1950 Capital Spending Plans," *op. cit.*, p. 78.

[48] Federal Reserve System, *Federal Reserve Charts on Bank Credit, Money Rates, and Business, Historical Supplement*, Sept. 1954, p. 54.

[49] The high cost of share capital in comparison with bond capital was in fact a major cause of the very low level of share issues after the second world war. See W. B. Hickman, *The Volume of Corporate Bond Financing since 1900*, Nat. Bur. Econ. Research (New York, 1953), pp. 178–79.

kind of capital the cost of which had fallen only as low as 15 percent. Finally, some firms were presumably the temporary constituents of the normal complement of low investing, submarginal firms whose responses should be given relatively low weights.

VI. THE EVIDENCE FROM MORE RECENT SURVEYS

Some of the more recent studies are briefly discussed below.

1. An interview survey of financiers and executives of large corporations made by Dan T. Smith during the recession-dominated months, Spring 1949—Autumn 1950, confirmed the depression-time findings of the N.B.E.R. survey: there was such great reluctance to issue long-term debt among big industrial companies that it would be done only to finance projects of exceptional urgency or of exceptionally high profitability; hence, even a 3 percentage point change in interest rates would affect very few big companies.[50] But, as the surveyor himself pointed out, the availability of long-term funds at under 3 percent was occasionally an effective inducement, and if the supposedly inevitable postwar depression continued to be postponed, big businesses in the less cyclical lines might again become willing to borrow for other than extraordinary projects—an accurate forecast.[51] Moreover, the Smith interviews appear to indicate that there would be a substantial role for the cost of equity capital (the per-share earnings/share-price ratio) among the big industrial companies once the excessively depressed level of stock prices had improved.[52]

2. That the non-appearance of the postwar depression did reassure business is in-

dicated by the mail survey of Brockie and Grey dealing with the investment selection criteria of companies quoted on the New York Stock Exchange.

The survey found that much more sophisticated investment-selection techniques were in use—and lower rates of return on investment were required—than economists generally supposed. That situation was, of course, favorable to a greater sensitivity to the cost of capital than economists were assuming.[53] While no question appears to have been asked on the influence of the interest rate on the externally-financed parts of the respondents' investment, it was found that 41 percent of the 57 industrial companies who replied took account of the *market* rate of interest in computing the rate of return on proposed *self*-financed investments. If allowances for possible biases and uncertainties about the actual form of the question asked were to permit even 20 of the 41 percent to survive, the Brockie-Grey findings would provide strong support for the view that the cost of debt and equity capital were significant factors in the determination of the volume of *ex*ternally-financed investment.[54]

3. Contrary evidence on the behavior of industrial firms in 1955 is often inferred from the results of a Commerce Department survey of principal reasons for di-

---

[50] Dan T. Smith, *Effects of Taxation: Corporate Financial Policy*, Boston 1952, pp. 7, 36–37.

[51] *Ibid.*, pp. 40, 41, 72.

[52] *Ibid.*, pp. 52, 53, 56, 74.

[53] For evidence on the rapid progress toward use of scientific investment selection techniques by big industrial companies during the second half of the 1950's, and evidence that required rates of return on investment were becoming sufficiently low so that plausible variations in the long-term interest rate could no longer be assumed inconsequential, see W. H. White, "The Changing Criteria in Investment Planning," Brookings Institution Reprint No. 58 (from *Variability of Private Investment in Plant and Equipment, Materials Submitted to the Joint Economic Committee*, 87th Cong., 2nd Session, Pt. II (1962), pp. 1–24).

[54] See W. H. White, "The Rate of Interest, the Marginal Efficiency of Capital and Investment Programming," *Econ. Jour.*, Mar. 1958, LXVIII, 51–59; and W. H. White, "The Rate of Interest, Marginal Efficiency of Capital and Investment Programming—Reply," *Econ. Jour.*, Mar. 1960, LXX, 154–57.

vergences between the amount of 1955 capital spending planned early in the year and the amount actually realized.[55]

Because the rise in the various alternative rates of interest during 1955 was only one half percentage point or less and was concentrated in the second half of the year, it is unreasonable to expect the rise in interest costs to have been the principal cause of the observed reductions in spending. (The minimum spending changes to be investigated had been set at 15 percent for big companies—assets $50 million or more—and 25 percent for others.) The substantial rise in stock prices may have reduced the earnings/price ratio on common stocks by 20 percent by the end of 1955, but while that change may have had a substantial effect on the rate of investment spending by the last quarter of the year, it obviously could not have been powerful enough to account for most of the 15 percent or more increases experienced in the *whole* year's investment by the responding 50 big companies—especially so since over half of the group appears to have increased its investment by 40 percent or more. Actually, the fact that 3 of the 20 or fewer big companies that reported increases of 15–40 percent did offer change in the "cost of outside financing" as principal explanation would seem to be, if anything, strong proof of an important role for the cost of (equity) capital.[56] Because of the smallness of the relevant sample, that inference must be only tentative, however.

4. The monthly questionnaire sent to 200 members of the National Association

of Purchasing Agents who are apparently officers of large U.S. corporations is the source of two of the N.B.E.R.'s "leading indicators", published monthly in the Census Bureau's *Business Cycle Developments*. In addition to the monthly questions on current developments in employment, production, new orders, actual and desired inventory changes, etc., the questionnaire frequently contains special questions; and on four occasions when interest rates were rising there were questions on the effects of interest rates on investment. As these questions were asked over the second half of the 1950's—a period of increasing use of scientific management techniques, which included years of increased resort to external financing, and which saw the termination of almost a quarter century of cheap money—the results should be particularly significant for the evaluation of interest rate policy.[57]

(i) The October 1956 survey received 33 percent of "yes" answers among 96 respondents to the question: "Is the increased cost of borrowing the available scarce money affecting plans for expansion and modernization expenditure?" Since interest rates on new bond issues were still 1 percentage point below their 1957 highs and barriers to paying off the issues within the first 5 or 10 years had not yet become a regular feature of new issues, this result appears to give strong support for the view that interest elasticity is usefully high.

(ii) Early in the recovery from the 1958 recession, 22 percent of the respondents answered affirmatively to the special October question: "What effect is the high cost of borrowing having on the expansion plans of your company?" Although this total included only 6 percentage points of

[55] M. F. Foss and V. Natrella, "Investment Plans and Realization," *Survey of Current Business*, June 1957, pp. 12–18.

[56] This conclusion is, in fact, consistent with the surveyors' own evaluation: that the rapidity of rise in sales during the first three quarters of 1955 and the high corporate liquidity at the start of the year made it quite reasonable for unexpected sales increases to dominate among the explanations received (*ibid.*, p. 13).

[57] Sources for the N.A.P.A. surveys include: *Bulletin of the National Association of Purchasing Agents*, Oct. 31, 1956, p. 1 and Aug. 12, 1959, p. 2; *Journal of Commerce*, Nov. 3, 1958, p. 1; and information provided to the author by the N.A.P.A. Survey Committee.

"considerable" effect and 16 points of just "some" effect, the results can be considered as giving strong support for interest-rate policy because the recession and the high volume of excess capacity in industry were restricting intended capital spending—and especially the specified "expansion" capital spending—to low, self-financeable levels; as noted above, such conditions imply reduced opportunity for the state of the capital market to affect business investment.

In one sense the results may exaggerate the direct influence of the cost of money capital, for (to judge from the industrial composition of the survey committee in 1956) one-eighth of the respondents may have represented public utility firms (the only non-manufacturing group included) and producers of building materials; some of these respondents might have reported the *indirect* effects of the reduced demand for their own products caused by the effect of high interest rates on the availability of funds for house mortgages. Complete exclusion of these industries from the sample does not seem justified, however, because the permitted interest rates on house mortgages had by October 1958 been allowed to rise to more-or-less competitive levels; in any case, such an exclusion would leave the proportion of respondents among the remaining industries whose expansion investment plans were affected at the high figure, for a recession period, of 20 percent.

(iii) The further rise in interest rates to July 1959, perhaps one half percentage point over the levels of October 1958 for both long- and short-term money, caused the N.A.P.A. to pose a similar interest rate question. All that is known of the actual question and the replies is that "80 percent say the increased cost of borrowing money has not affected their ['proposed capital expenditure'] plans at all; 16 percent are deferring some plans, and 4 percent have temporarily stopped

all expansion." In the absence of more detail, it is possible to say only that the 20 percent frequency of effect on capital spending from a rise in borrowing costs of at most ½ percentage point, achieved at a time of relatively low capital spending rates, seems fully consistent with an important role for plausible increases in interest rates at those times when investment was high enough to need restraining.

(iv) Apparently contradictory results were found by the next survey inquiry on interest rates made in February 1960 when interest rates had regained or surpassed their 1957 peaks. With utilities excluded (but building products firms retained because they all reported being *unaffected*), only 8 percent of 135 respondents answered affirmatively to the question: "Have the present high interest rates caused your company to stay out of the money market for needed projects?" But the 8 percent figure is probably biased downward, since the question specified "needed" rather than the more sensitive "marginal" projects, and because the question requires a *negative* answer from those who were affected to the extent of reducing but not eliminating their dependence on the money market.

With self-financers' investment not affectable, the best test of the pervasiveness of interest sensitivity should show the proportion of (would-be) *external* financers that was affected. (The external financing group also merits special consideration because the firm that is doing external financing tends to be doing more than the average amount of capital spending for firms of similar size.) Such data are available for the 1960 N.A.P.A. survey: A far from negligible 22 percent of the affectable respondents did abandon "needed" projects because of high interest rates. The percentage would presumably be made very much higher by allowance for firms which reduced but did not abandon externally-financed "needed" projects and for firms which reduced or abandoned "marginal" externally-financed projects. (Further increases might be required to allow for those respondents who interpreted "money market" as covering the short-term money market only, but reductions would be required for cases of firms which answered in the affirmative because high interest rates caused them to switch from the "money market" to the "equity capital" market.)

In summary, the successive N.A.P.A. surveys appear to provide strong corroborative—but not conclusive—evidence for the view that plausibly high interest rates can be a significant deterrent to the capital spending of the larger businesses which dominate total capital formation in manufacturing. Evidence from other recent surveys which tends to reinforce this conclusion, as well as survey evidence which suggests that the rapidly-affected inventory segment of business investment

is also affectable, has been published elsewhere.[58]

CONCLUSION

In view of all their defects, no definite conclusion can be drawn from the surveys of business attitudes toward capital costs. The surveys do indicate that investment is to *some* degree less interest-elastic than thought by the proponents of interest-rate policy. But they do not establish that the interest elasticity falls *seriously* below what its proponents claimed. Further investigation, taking account of the considerations outlined above, must be carried out before any reliable conclusions can be reached. Computations of the *weighted* shares of affirmative replies in the various enquiries already taken might be a useful first step in such an investigation.

[58] White, "Inventory Investment and the Rate of Interest," *op. cit.*

9

The Acceleration Principle and the Theory of Investment: A Survey[1]

A. D. KNOX

Reprinted from *Economica*, New Series, vol. 19 (August 1952), pp. 269–297, by permission of the publisher and author.

A. D. Knox is affiliated with the International Bank for Reconstruction and Development; he was formerly at the London School of Economics.

I.

Over the past two decades the acceleration principle has played an extremely important part in the theory of investment. Its history, however, takes us back to the early years of this century[2]; and a con-

** **

siderable literature exists on the uses to which it may be put and on the reliability of its explanation of the motives for investment in capital equipment.[3]

The main body of literature centres on the acceleration principle and the trade cycle. Here the popularity of the principle dates from the development of the multiplier and the realisation that neat models could be based on the interaction of these two theories. J. M. Clark drew attention to the possibilities of such models,[4] but

---

[1] I should like to express my thanks for helpful suggestions to Mr. A. W. Phillips, Professor Lionel Robbins, Dr. W. J. L. Ryan, and Mr. Ralph Turvey.

[2] The main early works on the acceleration principle are: A. Aftalion, "La réalité des surproductions générales," *Revue d'Economie Politique*, 1909, pp. 219–220, and *Les Crises Périodiques de Surproduction* (Paris, 1913), tôme II, pp. 356–370; C. F. Bickerdike, "A non-monetary cause of fluctuations in employment," *Economic Journal*, 1914; and J. M. Clark, "Business acceleration and the law of demand: a technical

factor in economic cycles," *Journal of Political Economy*, 1917, and reprinted in American Economic Association, *Readings in Business Cycle Theory* (Philadelphia, 1944), pp. 235–260.

[3] Useful bibliographies are in: G. von Haberler, *Prosperity and Depression* (Geneva, 1941), p. 87; and *Readings, op. cit.*, pp. 460–462.

[4] J. M. Clark, "Additional note on 'Business acceleration and the law of demand'," in *Preface to Social Economics* (New York, 1936) and reprinted in *Readings, op. cit.*, pp. 259–260; and *Strategic Factors in Business Cycles* (New York, 1934), pp. 167–183. See also R. Frisch, "Propagation problems and impulse problems in dynamic economics," in *Essays in Honour of Gustav Cassel* (London, 1933).

they were first fully developed by Lundberg[5] and Harrod.[6] Harrod's work, in particular, aroused considerable interest in the acceleration principle—or the relation, as he called it—for in it the principle was brought to the very forefront of the analysis of the cycle.

It is a relation [wrote Mr. Harrod] which has, indeed, been noted by learned writers often enough. Nonetheless I have the impression that not nearly sufficient importance has, on the whole, been attached to it. Its simplicity, ineluctability, and independence of all special theories as to the workings of the cyclical process demand for it pride of place.[7]

Since 1936 the acceleration principle has been significant in a number of models of the cycle: the rigorous statement of the interaction of the multiplier and the acceleration principle presented by Samuelson,[8] and the later refinements of Bennion,[9] Baumol,[10] Hicks,[11] and Goodwin.[12]

The acceleration principle, as applied to the theory of investment in capital equipment, has been used in two other connexions. In part the theory of pump-

priming rests upon it.[13] More recently the major use of the principle has been with regard to the problem of the long-run growth of an economy. As in the theory of the trade cycle, it has lent itself to the formulation of neat models.[14]

Finally the acceleration principle has also been used to explain investment in stocks[15] and in durable consumers' goods.[16] These applications are not discussed in this survey.

When applied to the explanation of investment in fixed capital, the acceleration principle is said to tell us what will be the behaviour of that part of this investment which is net and induced. These two terms have never been clearly defined in the literature on the acceleration principle; and indeed they do not lend themselves to precise definition. In rough terms, therefore, by net investment is meant an expansion of productive capacity.[17] In-

[5] E. Lundberg, *Studies in the Theory of Economic Expansion* (London, 1937), ch. 9.
[6] R. F. Harrod, *The Trade Cycle: an Essay* (Oxford, 1936), especially ch. 2.
[7] *Op. cit.*, pp. 53–54.
[8] P. A. Samuelson, "A synthesis of the principle of acceleration and the multiplier," *Journal of Political Economy*, 1939; and "Interactions between the multiplier analysis and the principle of acceleration," *Review of Economic Statistics*, 1939. The latter article has been reprinted in *Readings, op. cit.*, pp. 261–269 [also reprinted in this volume, Selection 18].
[9] E. G. Bennion, "The multiplier, the acceleration principle, and fluctuating autonomous investment," *Review of Economic Statistics*, 1945.
[10] W. J. Baumol, "Notes on some dynamic models," *Economic Journal*, 1948.
[11] J. R. Hicks, "Mr. Harrod's dynamic theory", *Economica*, 1949; and *A Contribution to the Theory of the Trade Cycle* (Oxford, 1950).
[12] R. M. Goodwin, "Secular and cyclical aspects of the multiplier and the accelerator," in *Income, Employment and Public Policy: Essays in Honor of Alvin H. Hansen* (New York, 1948); and "The non-linear accelerator and the persistence of business cycles," *Econometrica*, 1951.

[13] E.g., J. M. Clark, *Economics of Planning Public Works* (Washington, 1935); International Labour Office, *Public Investment and Full Employment* (Montreal, 1946); and H. M. Somers, *Public Finance and National Income* (Philadelphia, 1949), ch. 5.
[14] Lundberg, *op. cit.*, p. 180; R. F. Harrod, "An essay in dynamic theory," *Economic Journal*, 1939, and *Towards a Dynamic Economics* (London, 1948), especially ch. 3; E. D. Domar, "Capital expansion, rate of growth and employment," *Econometrica*, 1946, and other articles; Baumol, *op. cit.*; Hicks, *op. cit.*; and S. S. Alexander, "The accelerator as a generator of steady growth," *Quarterly Journal of Economics*, 1949, and "Mr. Harrod's dynamic model," *Economic Journal*, 1950.
[15] M. Abramovitz, *Inventories and Business Cycles* (New York, 1950), pp. 19–26, and the literature mentioned there; and J. Tinbergen, "An acceleration principle for commodity stock-holding and a short cycle resulting from it," in O. Lange *et al.* (eds.), *Studies in Mathematical Economics and Econometrics* (Chicago, 1942).
[16] There is a fairly extensive literature, but the main elements of the theory are outlined in Haberler, *op. cit.*, pp. 92–99.
[17] There is a discussion in part II of this paper on the possibility of distinguishing between net and replacement investment. But since the acceleration principle rests on the assumption that this distinction may be made, the validity of doing so is not questioned for the moment.

duced investment is the portion of net that depends on current movements in output; and thus the acceleration principle relates to investment in existing firms that produce existing types of goods for existing markets.[18] The acceleration principle as applied to net induced investment in a *single firm* may be stated rigorously and *without qualification* by means of a simple equation:

$$C_t \equiv K_t - K_{t-1} = a(O_t - O_{t-1})$$

| Out-put of capital goods | Increase in stock of capital goods | Increase in final output times the accelerator. |

The symbols have the following meanings:

C Current output of capital equipment employed by the firm to make a net increase in its capital stock. In what follows this is referred to simply as output.

K The firm's stock of capital equipment.

O The firm's output of finished products— referred to as final output.

a The accelerator or the coefficient of acceleration. This is the ratio between the current increase in the stock of capital equipment and the current increase in the flow of final output produced with that equipment. The accelerator is assumed to be constant.

$t, t - 1$, etc.   Time periods.

It is useful to express the acceleration principle in this form, for its two parts may readily be seen. The first part—$C_t \equiv K_t - K_{t-1}$—is an identity which tells us the very obvious fact that the current output of capital equipment for net investment is equal to the current increase in the stock of equipment. The second part is a theory of investment. Because the

accelerator is assumed to be constant, there is always a fixed connexion between the current growth of capital stock and the current rise in final output. The validity of the theory of investment depends upon whether we can really assume the accelerator to be constant.

Despite its tautological nature, the first part yields certain useful and important conclusions about the timing and the proportional amplitude of fluctuations in the stock of capital equipment and in the output of the capital goods industries. The identity $C_t \equiv K_t - K_{t-1}$ expresses the fact that because capital equipment is durable[19] the stock of it exceeds the current output.[20] This excess of stock over output has the effect that turning points appear in output before they appear in stock, despite the fact that attempts to change the latter cause movements of the former. The condition that must be satisfied if C_t is to fall just below C_{t-1} is that $(K_t - K_{t-1})$ is less than $(K_{t-1} - K_{t-2})$, but that K_t exceeds K_{t-1}. In other words, the stock of equipment is rising, but not at a sufficiently fast rate to prevent a decline in the output of the capital goods industries.

The excess of stock over output has a further effect in that a given percentage fluctuation in stock means a more than proportionate fluctuation in output; and the more durable the stock the greater is the relative violence of the movements in output. This relationship may be shown by means of a simple arithmetical example. Assume that in period 1 one hundred

[18] The distinction is between induced investment on the one hand and spontaneous or autonomous investment on the other hand. Once expectations are introduced it becomes increasingly difficult to maintain the distinction. But as will be pointed out at the beginning of part II, we cling to the distinction in order to restrict the scope of this paper.

[19] Durability can be adequately defined only with reference to some time period. If we take a sufficiently short period the stock of most goods is greater than the current output. Unfortunately the relevant period for the acceleration period is not clear and is likely to be variable. We must, therefore, fall back on common usage which defines durable goods as those which are not destroyed or transformed in the act of consumption or production.

[20] Were capital equipment not durable, then C_t would be equal to K_t: i.e., $K_{t-1} = 0$.

machines of a particular type exist[21] and that the rate of replacement of these machines is a function solely of age. If they have a lifetime of 10 years then 10 machines are produced each year, so long as the stock of machines remains constant. Now assume a rise in that stock to 110 in period 2, at which level it remains in period 3. Output rises from 10 to 20, and then falls again to 10. A 10 percent increase in stock has led to a 100 percent rise in output, which then returns to its former level.[22] If, on the other hand, the lifetime of these machines is only 2 years, the same 10 percent increase in stock causes in period 2 only a 20 percent rise in output, which in period 3 returns to its former level of 50.

The effects of this purely technical relationship in matters of timing and amplitude are very useful in the analysis of business cycles; and its validity is unquestionable. This paper, therefore, is concerned with the second part of the acceleration principle: the theory of investment. So long as the accelerator is constant, the conclusions about the relationship between K and C apply also, once due allowances have been made for lags, to the timing and amplitude of fluctuations in K and in O. The crucial problem of the acceleration principle is whether the accelerator is constant.

The equation

$$K_t - K_{t-1} = a(O_t - O_{t-1})$$

states the acceleration principle in its most uncompromising form: net induced investment is solely a function of the rate of growth of final output. Stating it in this way enables us to see the mechanism at work. But few writers use this unqualified acceleration principle; and some have rejected the principle outright. More-over, there have been various attempts to test it statistically, and the results of most of these tests have been unfavourable.[23] The next section attempts three things: (*a*) to set out the contending arguments on the modifications that should be made in the simple acceleration principle; (*b*) to assess the relative merits of these arguments, or at least to circumscribe the area of dispute; and (*c*) to seek from this review of the arguments the reasons for the unfavourable results yielded by the statistical tests.[24]

Before passing on to the next section it is necessary to make clear certain assumptions that will be maintained in this paper. The exposition of the acceleration principle related the investment of the single firm to the rate of growth of its output. One assumption is maintained for most of this paper, until it is explicitly abandoned. It is that inventories are ignored, together with such things as the lengthening or shortening of order books. Investment therefore depends equally well on the rate of growth of sales or of output. The second assumption, which is kept throughout, provides for the application of the acceleration principle to the whole economy.

---

[21] Ten machines have been added to the stock in each of the past ten years.

[22] The increase in stock causes a rise in replacement investment only after a lag.

[23] T. Hultgren, *American Transportation in Prosperity and Depression* (New York, 1948), pp. 157ff.; S. Kuznets, "Relation between capital goods and finished products in the business cycle," in *Economic Essays in Honour of Wesley Clair Mitchell* (New York, 1935), pp. 248–267; J. Tinbergen, "Statistical evidence on the acceleration principle," *Economica*, 1938, and *Statistical Testing of Business Cycle Theories* (League of Nations, Geneva, 1938), vol. I, chs. 3 and 5, and vol. II, ch. 2; T. Wilson, *Fluctuations in Income and Employment* (London, 1948), pp. 114ff.

On the other hand, Clark's statistical test yielded quite favourable results for the acceleration principle: *op. cit., Readings*, pp. 245–249. A. S. Manne has argued that a slightly modified version of the principle can be substantiated empirically: "Some notes on the acceleration principle," *Review of Economic Statistics*, 1945.

[24] Even with the advances in econometrics the tools available for empirical testing are still somewhat crude. There is something to be said for occasional "theoretical verifications" of the results of the statistical tests!

Strictly, we should trace the effects of the rate of growth of, say, the output of shirts on the investment of the shirt-makers; the effects of the rate of growth of demand for shirt-making machinery on investment in the firms producing that machinery; and so on. It is doubtful whether we can successfully do so. Therefore, whenever the subsequent analysis deals with the economy as a whole, the assumption to be made is that aggregate net induced investment is related to the rate of growth of national income.[25]

II.

Many writers have criticised the acceleration principle, but no general agreement has emerged from these discussions. The history of discussions on the acceleration principle accounts at least in part for this continuing diversity of opinion. While much has been written on its various potential weaknesses, there have been few controversies in which the contending arguments might be marshalled and set forth as a whole. Issues have been raised for the most part without reference to previous discussions. Further, most writers have restricted their attention to a narrow range of criticisms; and sometimes to only one.

In order to simplify the problem of presenting this scattered and varied material, it is preferable to arrange it analytically rather than chronologically. Further, we may exclude from our terms of reference part of the literature on the acceleration principle. Criticisms of the acceleration principle may roughly be divided into two

categories: those that dispute whether the principle gives a true representation of the forces determining induced investment; and those that, by questioning the importance of induced investment, cast doubt upon some of the more ambitious claims made on behalf of the principle. To settle the issues raised by both types of criticism would require a discussion of the entire theory of investment. Prudence, therefore, suggests that we concentrate on the first group. The problems to be discussed relate to[26]:—

1. surplus capacity;
2. replacement investment; and
3. expectations about demand, and the related questions of prices and profits.

1.

It is not easy to find the rationale for the acceleration principle. It is often called the acceleration principle of derived demand. The theory of derived demand as applied to investment tells us that a rise in the stock of capital equipment will continue only if there is at some stage an increase in consumption.[27] But this is not the same as saying, with the acceleration principle, that a given percentage rise in consumption must be met by an equal percentage rise in the stock of capital equipment. There appeared very soon the qualification that where surplus capacity exists the acceleration principle is not valid. In other words, the necessary assumption for the acceleration principle is that firms should be working at full capacity. J. M. Clark in his first article on the acceleration principle made this assumption quite clear when he wrote:

... the first increase in demand for finished products can be taken care of by utilising

[25] For discussions on this point, see J. M. Clark, *op. cit., Readings*, pp. 252–253; Baumol, *op. cit.*, p. 514 fn.; Hicks, *Trade Cycle, op. cit.*, p. 38; R. M. Bissell, "The rate of interest," *American Economic Review*, supplement, 1938, p. 32. The fullest discussion of this problem is to be found in B. A. Chait, *Les Fluctuations Economiques et l'Interdépendance des Marchés* (Brussels, 1938).

[26] For a complementary approach to the acceleration principle, see S. C. Tsiang, "Accelerator, theory of the firm, and the business cycle," *Quarterly Journal of Economics*, 1951.

[27] Cf. the lengthy discussion in M. Bouniatian, *Les Crises Economiques* (Paris, 1922), esp. pp. 234ff.

the excess producing capacity which an industry using much machinery habitually carries over a period of depression. Thus they do not need to buy more equipment the instant the demand begins to increase.[28]

Many subsequent writers have noted that full capacity is a prerequisite for the acceleration principle but not one that is likely to be satisfied in the early stages of a cyclical upswing. That the accelerator is asymmetrical as between upswing and downswing has been argued by Tinbergen:

> Very strong decreases in consumers' goods production must not occur. If the principle were right, they would lead to a corresponding disinvestment and this can only take place to the extent of replacement. If annual replacement amounts to 10 percent of the stock of capital goods, then a larger decrease in this stock than 10 percent per annum is impossible. A decrease in consumers' goods production of 15 percent could not lead to a 15 percent decrease in physical capital as the acceleration principle would require. It is interesting that this limit is sharper the greater the duration of life of the capital goods considered.[29]

This criticism is generally accepted; and it is agreed that the acceleration principle can make but little contribution to the explanation of the lower turning point. Many writers, however, argue that surplus capacity is exhausted during the upswing.[30] On this view the principle is use-ful for the analysis of the downturn and of long-run growth.

The matter is allowed to rest there by most writers; but not by all. Tinbergen stresses that it is only when production has reached full capacity that "the necessity of the principle's action recurs;"[31] and he argues that statistical evidence shows that this condition is rarely, if ever, satisfied.[32] The arguments and assumptions that have been surveyed so far make this a challenging criticism. Two things, however, must be borne in mind:

(a) The terms "capacity" and "surplus capacity" (and its variants "excess" and "unused" capacity) are much bandied about in discussions of the acceleration principle, but they are not defined.

(b) It is true to say that full capacity is commonly taken as a prerequisite for the acceleration principle, and that this full capacity is apparently looked upon as some *ne plus ultra* beyond which output cannot be expanded without the addition of capital equipment. There are, however, some writers who have queried whether this assumption is consistent with some of the conclusions derived from the acceleration principle; and others who query whether it is a necessary assumption.

---

[28] *Op. cit., Readings*, p. 244.

[29] Tinbergen, *op. cit., Economica*, 1938, p. 165.

[30] E.g., F. A. Burchardt, "The causes of unemployment," in Oxford Institute of Statistics, *The Economics of Full Employment* (Oxford, 1947), p. 29.

Haberler, *op. cit.*, p. 96.

A. H. Hansen, *Fiscal Policy and Business Cycles* (New York, 1941), p. 282.

Hicks, *Trade Cycle, op. cit.*, ch. IV.

W. Röpke, *Crises and Cycles* (London, 1936), p. 104.

Somers, *op. cit.*, p. 102.

Wilson, *op. cit.*, pp. 45–46.

Perhaps a word should be devoted to Manne's treatment of this capacity problem. He seeks to get round the difficulties experienced by the accelerator by relating changes in output to variations in the amount of equipment actually employed. The results of his correlations are much better than those obtained by correlating changes in output with changes in the stock of equipment. This is an interesting way of looking at the principle, but one that smacks a little of tautology. This is particularly so if we take this approach to its logical conclusion and include in the dependent variable not merely variations in the amount of equipment used, but also in the intensity with which it is used. Cf. Manne, *op. cit.*, pp. 94–96.

[31] *Op. cit., Economica*, 1938, p. 166.

[32] *Ibid.*, p. 167, and "Critical remarks on some business cycle theories," *Econometrica*, 1942, p. 139. See also R. G. Hawtrey, review of Bouniatian, *Les Crises Economiques* (ed. 2), *Economic Journal*, 1932, p. 437: "The productive power of the community is *never* fully employed even at times of intense activity. It would seem to follow that the appearance of an increased demand for consumption goods does not in itself require additional capital equipment, but merely the fuller employment of that which already exists." (Hawtrey's italics.)

In its simplest form the acceleration principle postulates that an increase in the rate of growth of output is accompanied simultaneously by a rise in net investment. In its more complex forms there are many variants of the lags involved, but they all agree that the rise in investment does not come first.[33] This is not possible when the economy is working at full capacity. Output cannot rise until additional capital equipment has been produced and installed; and in an economy where the process of production has become very roundabout this gestation period is long. Moreover, the problem is not restricted to one of lags. A long gestation period may cause variations in the accelerator; but this problem is left until II (3).[34]

The second doubt raised in (b) is whether full capacity is a necessary assumption for the acceleration principle. Tinbergen thinks so; Clark does not. He suggests that there is always some surplus capacity in the economy and that it is fully compatible with the acceleration principle.[35] Are we to interpret this as a real conflict of view or merely as a difference of definition? It is not possible to say, because no definitions are given. It will be useful therefore to outline the possible definitions of capacity and to inquire into their implications for the acceleration principle.

At least four principal definitions of capacity appear in various economic writings:

(a) In terms of the single firm, the point at which its average total cost curve becomes vertical. This definition is hardly realistic, for it implies that "all of the strategic factor (plant and machinery) is operated at maximum speed and none is strictly idle for any of the 168 hours in a week."[36]

(b) "Practicable" capacity: i.e., the output that a firm can maintain for a reasonable period with a given plant, making due allowance for such factors as seasonal fluctuations, repairs, obsolescence, and custom and regulations governing hours of work.[37] Capacity here is less than under (a). The definition is more realistic, but precision is lost.

(c) The output at a firm's minimum average total cost. "At that point the differential cost of added output will be equal to the average cost, including all overhead costs on account of the machine itself. Beyond that point it will pay to get more machines. This point might furnish a theoretical measure of capacity, but one that would be hard to apply."[38]

(d) Where marginal cost equals marginal revenue. This is a useful supplement to the other definitions when imperfect competition is under discussion; but for present purposes it has serious drawbacks. So far as firms seek to maximise profits they will usually be operating at capacity in this sense; and an increased demand may lead to a rise in the stock of capital or—equally well if we are discussing the economy—in price. The definition can have little meaning for the acceleration principle and may be ignored.

[33] For a summary, cf. Somers, *op. cit.*, pp. 77–80.
[34] Cf. pp. 130–131.
[35] "Additional note . . . ", *Readings*, *op. cit.*, pp. 256–257. This is a later work than that quoted on pp. 118–119.

[36] R. Noyes, "Certain problems in the empirical study of costs," *American Economic Review*, 1941, p. 482.
[37] The attempt was made to "limit our estimates to what would be practically attainable under conditions of 'sustained simultaneous operations'." E. G. Nourse *et al.*, *America's Capacity to Produce* (Washington, 1934), p. 23.
[38] J. M. Clark, *Studies in the Economics of Overhead Costs* (Chicago, 1923), p. 91. This definition may give the same result as (a) if the average total cost curve has the particular shape attributed to it by some writers: i.e., falling to the point of least cost and then rising vertically. The validity of this hypothesis is questionable and it need not detain us here. Cf. W. J. Eiteman, "Factors determining the location of the least cost point," *American Economic Review*, 1947, and "The least cost point, capacity, and marginal analysis," *ibid.*, 1948; and W. H. Haines, "Capacity production and the least cost point," *ibid.*, 1948.

So much for the definitions—what are their implications for the acceleration principle? When the firms of an economy are working at full capacity in the sense of definition (a) the common view is apparently that the acceleration principle is inexorably valid. As pointed out on page 120 this neglects some problems, which are being left until II (3). At the moment the point at issue is the doubt whether this capacity is often attained. Breakdowns may occur; single shift working may be customary; or the organisations of firms may not be as efficient as possible; and so on. For these same reasons, however, the presence of surplus capacity in the sense (a) does not necessarily invalidate the acceleration principle. There is in fact some *prima facie* reason for using definition (b); but this may be rejected in favour of (c).

The acceleration principle may be given a simple rational basis. It may be interpreted to mean that entrepreneurs will meet a rise in demand by expanding their plant, where the cost of producing the extra output with the existing plant exceeds the operating cost with the enlarged plant plus the costs of purchasing and installing it. If we assume with the acceleration principle that changes in output are the only forces making for investment, we may conclude that there is no incentive for investment before the least cost point is reached,[39] and an increasing incentive the further beyond that point output goes.[40] Definition (c) is the most useful.

This interpretation enables us to reach some tentative conclusions about capacity and the acceleration principle. It is possible to admit the existence of surplus capacity as defined by (a) or (b) and to argue that the acceleration principle is a useful theory. Some such difference on the rationale of the principle may lie at the basis of the divergent views held by Clark and Tinbergen. Even if this is the explanation of the conflict of conclusion, Tinbergen's stress on the volitional nature of investment is justified. There is nothing inevitable about investment, as the simpler version of the acceleration principle would have us believe. Tinbergen, however, presses rather too far the conclusion he derives from the capacity argument.[41] The aspect of the acceleration principle that is challenged by the vagueness of full capacity is its usefulness in explaining the timing of investment. From the moment at which least cost output is passed there is a possibility of investment; but there is no knowing just when the decision to invest will be taken. On the other hand this conclusion does not question the aspect of the acceleration principle that apparently gives it its major appeal. It is only reasonable to expect that when an entrepreneur invests, the amount of his investment is governed in some measure by a comparison of the output he can most efficiently produce with his existing plant and the output at which demand conditions now justify him in aiming. The timing and the volume of investment are not fully independent. But they are sufficiently so to justify this conclusion: provided that output does not fall below the least-cost points of the firms in an economy, we may query the validity of the acceleration principle in explaining the timing of investment but not the volume.

The inadequacy of the acceleration principle in matters of timing is emphasised by other considerations. If net investment is to be strictly a function of the rate of growth of output, then the units into

---

[39] Cf. C. D. Long, *Building Cycles and the Theory of Investment* (Princeton, 1940), pp. 59–60.

[40] It should be remembered that the acceleration principle deals with the investment of existing firms. Cf. p. 116.

[41] *Op. cit.*, *Economica*, 1938, esp. p. 167.

which the stock of capital equipment is divisible must be the same as those into which output is divisible. This point has been developed by Kuznets. On the assumption of perfect foresight, and of a certain period within which plant cannot be varied, he shows that where demand alters during this period the entrepreneur maximises his profits by having a plant of such size that part of it stands idle for some of the time.[42] His analysis suffers, however, in that he does not clearly show what determines this period within which plant is not varied. There are three principal reasons:

(a) The technical factor. Capital equipment may be bulky, and the employment of additional plant is justified only when output has risen considerably.[43] This factor is all the more important because usually what is added is a complex of machines and not a machine.

(b) The extension of plant may interfere with current output directly and will almost certainly do so indirectly through a diversion of managerial energies.[44] There are thus likely to be lulls in investment.

(c) The addition of plant may enhance the entrepreneur's uncertainty. He is now faced with the development of new markets to absorb his expanded output.[45] This factor, however, is possibly unimportant when discussing purely induced investment.

There can be little doubt that investment in the single firm is essentially a discontinuous process. Whether similar lulls will occur in the investment activity of the entire economy is not readily apparent. The process of aggregation may smooth them over; but it is difficult to believe that the timing of investment will be that suggested by the acceleration principle.

The literature on capacity and the acceleration principle is rambling, and in setting out and weighing the various arguments we have rambled with it. Our conclusions may nevertheless be stated briefly. It is not possible to devise a definition of capacity that is both realistic and precise. The acceleration principle, therefore, is not precise; but it draws attention to a possible reason for investment so long as firms are operating along the rising segment of their average total-cost curves. The effects of this lack of precision may be summed up by saying that the acceleration principle is unsatisfactory as an explanation of the timing of investment. It suffers from a further weakness: it is not of much use for explaining the lower turning point. But a rider must be added to this earlier criticism: it is valid only where output in all firms has fallen below their least-cost points.

2.

In his first outline of the acceleration principle[46] Clark assumes that net investment is a function of the rate of growth of output, but that replacement depends on its level. The implications of this thesis about replacement have interested many writers; but largely the assumption itself has been accepted. Pigou notes that as net investment falls replacement may rise and offset the depressing effects of this fall.[47]   Frisch attaches even more im-

---

[42] *Op. cit.*, pp. 231–236.

[43] Long, *op. cit.*, pp. 61–2:" For example, papermaking machines for the manufacture of newsprint paper come only in million dollar units capable of producing one-fourth the requirements of a good-sized plant and characterised by great durability."

[44] Hultgren, *op. cit.*, p. 167, who writes that as a result of such factors "no one railroad typically buys cars in continuous driblets; or at any rate small repetitive purchases can hardly account for any large part of total orders." Cf. also W. W. Heller, "The anatomy of investment decisions," *Harvard Business Review*, March 1951, p. 102: "One of the unforeseen—and most interesting—investment barriers was the bottleneck in top engineering and management talent."

[45] Cf. G. L. S. Shackle, *Expectations, Investment, and Income* (London, 1938), pp. 99–100.

[46] "Business acceleration . . . ," *op. cit.*, *Readings*, p. 238.

[47] A. C. Pigou, *Industrial Fluctuations* (London, 1929, ed. 2), p. 110.

portance to this qualification. He shows that the extent to which replacement may offset net investment depends on (i) the speed with which the rate of growth of output is falling, and (ii) the sizes of the two categories of investment. It is in fact quite conceivable that total capital production may approach some constant level.[48] Since Frisch's statement of the problem, the argument has waxed and waned. Hansen censors Harrod for his neglect of the movements of replacement.[49] Clark[50] and Somers[51] recognise the strict validity of Frisch's criticism, but doubt whether circumstances often arise to make it really important. Samuelson defends the neglect of replacement with an argument[52] that is ingenious but also somewhat spurious in that it equates replacement with depreciation.

No single conclusion emerges from this discussion. This uncertainty about the effects of replacement on the acceleration principle is heightened by the fact that it is not universally accepted that replacement is a function solely of the level of output. Haberler, for example, assumes that it depends on the age of equipment, and that therefore replacement cycles will reflect earlier fluctuations in investment.[53] Kuznets works out the various possible models in some detail.[54] Whether replacement cycles coincide with those in net investment depends on (i) the life of capital equipment, all of which is assumed to last for a constant period, and (ii) the behaviour of gross investment in the relevant past period that is indicated by (i). The importance of the resulting replacement cycles in determining the turning points of gross investment depends on the relative volume of replacement and of net investment: that is, on the past behaviour of gross investment and on the present rate of growth of output.

The age hypothesis has in its turn been qualified in a number of ways in the literature on the acceleration principle:

(a) Somers points out that replacement depends partly on the "extent to which capital goods are used to produce 'finished' products (in so far as depreciation is a function of use, i.e. through wear and tear or direct use in the process of production)."[55]

(b) Kuznets qualifies his assumption about the importance of the age of machines, and shows that, given a constant rate of obsolescence, it will pay to replace earlier at a higher level of output than at a lower.[56] He errs, however, in concluding that this substantiates Frisch's conclusions.[57] Durability and hence age have to be given some place in the theory, as Kuznets recognises when he writes that the level of output will in-

---

[48] R. Frisch, "The interrelation between capital production and consumer-taking," *Journal of Political Economy*, 1931, pp. 649–652, and subsequent articles in *ibid.*, April and October 1932. This criticism of replacement is the issue usually associated with these articles; but, emphasised though it was by Frisch, it was not his principal worry. He was mainly concerned to make quite clear that the acceleration principle did not provide a closed model of the cycle. Cf. also his "Propagation problems . . . ," *op. cit.*

[49] A. H. Hansen, *Full Recovery or Stagnation?* (London, 1938), p. 49.

[50] J. M. Clark, "Capital production and consumer-taking—a reply," *Journal of Political Economy*, 1931, and a later article in *ibid.*, October 1932.

[51] Somers, *op. cit.*, pp. 75–76.

[52] ". . . It would involve double-counting to include in the computation of the national income both consumption and the replacement expenditures imputable as costs of that consumption. Only net investment is "multiplied" to give the national income; as a first approximation Harrod was justified in neglecting replacement in the formal relation." *Op. cit.*, *Journal of Political Economy*, 1939, p. 796. Long, *op. cit.*, pp. 78–82, presents the same argument at greater length.

[53] Haberler, *op. cit.*, p. 91.

[54] Kuznets, *op. cit.*, pp. 221–225. Kuznets reserves the Frisch-Clark assumption for such types of investments as traders' stocks. Cf. *ibid.*, pp. 217–218 and his comment on Frisch's analysis of replacement, p. 219 fn.

[55] Somers, *op. cit.*, p. 74. It should be noted that, contrary to what Somers implies, this yields the same result as the Frisch-Clark hypothesis only by ignoring the age of equipment.

[56] Kuznets, *op. cit.*, pp. 238–243.

[57] *Ibid.*, p. 243.

fluence the replacement of only those items of equipment as are "sufficiently near the end of their average period of life to be affected by the change in the prospective savings from the installation of new units . . ."[58]

(c) Finally, Hicks has adduced two factors on which many elaborate echo effects have been based[59]: (i) capital goods do not have the same life-span, and (ii) they do not even have precise life-spans. From these two qualifications of the age hypothesis he concludes that replacement cycles will after a time become so damped that they may be ignored.[60]

In sum, a survey of the literature on replacement and the acceleration principle yields a bewildering number of conclusions. As with other aspects of the theory of investment, this variety of results reflects the complexity of the subject and our lack of empirical knowledge. The most that we can hope for, therefore, is to narrow somewhat the area of doubt. In particular we may be able to resolve the question whether replacement does or does not falsify conclusions drawn from the acceleration principle, although we may not be able to state the precise extent of this falsification.

We must consider whether it is possible to distinguish clearly between net and replacement investment. What is relevant in determining whether a particular act of investment has added to or merely maintained the stock of capital is "whether a person maintains a stock of non-permanent resources which will secure him an increasing, constant, or decreasing income stream, not whether the stock itself increases, remains constant, or decreases in any of its directly measurable dimen-

sions."[61] This being so we can assess the effects of investment only where it is possible to foresee with certainty the future income stream to be yielded by the new equipment. In the uncertain world of reality this cannot be done. Replacement and net investment cannot be clearly distinguished from one another. This conclusion may be supported by a second argument. By and large, firms when replacing machines install something larger or better.[62] The new equipment is both net investment and replacement. Even if it were possible to determine *ex post* what part of investment is net and what part replacement, the distinction would be artificial. At the same time, we must recognise that the distinction has not been adhered to by so many writers without good reason. It is useful in analysing the motives for investment. There are some motives that are peculiarly concerned with replacing equipment, and others with adding to it.[63] In discussing the rationale of gross investment it is necessary to consider both sets of forces and then the results of their interplay.

The acceleration principle errs in discussing net investment where it should discuss gross. For all that it can be condemned for concentrating on net only when it is shown that the result is a distorted theory of net investment. The problem of distinguishing between net and replacement is *prima facie* evidence that such a distortion exists. To test the adequacy of this conclusion we must now

---

[58] *Ibid.*, p. 241.
[59] The outstanding discussion of these echo effects is probably R. Frisch, "Sammenhengen mellem primaerinvestering og reinvestering" *Statsøkonomisk Tidsskrift*, 1927, pp. 117–152. Cf. also J. Tinbergen, "Annual survey: suggestions on quantitative business cycle theory," *Econometrica*, 1935, pp. 288–291.
[60] Hicks, *Trade Cycle, op. cit.*, pp. 41–42.

[61] F. A. Hayek, *The Pure Theory of Capital* (London, 1941), pp. 300–1.
[62] Cf. R. P. Mack, *The Flow of Business Funds and Consumer Purchasing Power* (New York, 1941), pp. 251–52; and Heller, *op. cit.*, p. 100: "Replacement is seldom made without improvement. A worn-out piece of equipment is rarely replaced with an identical item".
[63] Cf. J. Tinbergen and J. J. Polak, *The Dynamics of Business Cycles* (London, 1950), p. 176; and M. Gort, "The planning of investment: a study of capital budgeting in the electric-power industry, I," *Journal of Business of the University of Chicago*, 1951, p. 85.

examine the nature of the factors that make for replacement. Is there such flexibility in the timing of replacement investment that entrepreneurs undertake it only when it is convenient to add to their plant? Or do they add to their plant when the time is suitable for replacement?

Assuming that firms seek to maximise profits, there is an incentive to replace when the present value of the anticipated stream of profits from the new machines minus that from the old is greater than the price of the new machine minus the "scrap" value of the old.[64] This may be written:

$$\pi_{1t} - \pi_{2t} > P_{1t} - S_{2t} \qquad (1)$$

The subscript 1 refers to the new machines, while 2 refers to the old. The subscript t refers to the time period. π stands for aggregate profit. P is a composite of the purchase price of the new machines and of the total costs of installation. Lastly,

---

[64] This discussion of the motives for replacing equipment is based on:

J. Einarsen, *Reinvestment Cycles and their Manifestation in the Norwegian Shipping Industry* (Oslo, 1938), which contains a useful survey of the earlier literature; and his "Reinvestment cycles," *Review of Economic Statistics*, 1938.

Mack, *op. cit.*, ch. 8.

J. Meuldijk, "Der Englische Schiffbau während der Period 1870–1912 und das Problem des Ersatzbaues," *Weltwirtschaftliches Archiv*, 1940.

National Bureau of Economic Research, *Cost Behavior and Price Policy* (New York, 1943), ch. VII, sections 3 and 4; and appendix C.

R. C. Blanchard, "A replacement policy that shares responsibility," *American Machinist*, 1931, pp. 729–740.

A series of articles by P. T. Norton, G. S. Tracey, R. F. Runge, H. K. Spencer, H. P. Bailey, J. H. Jackson, and D. S. Linton, *ibid.*, 1935.

P. de Wolff, "The demand for passenger cars in the United States," *Econometrica*, 1938.

G. Terborgh, *Dynamic Equipment Policy* (New York, 1949).

S. L. Horner, *et al.*, *Dynamics of Automobile Demand* (General Motors Corporation, 1939).

Cf. also, J. S. Bain, "The relation of the economic life of equipment to reinvestment cycles," *Review of Economic Statistics*, 1939; and B. Caplan, "Premature abandonment of machinery," *Review of Economic Studies*, 1940.

S represents "scrap" value, where that is interpreted to mean (i) the price equipment can fetch on the second-hand market or as junk, and (ii) the alternative uses to which the firm may put it, either by holding it in reserve or by using it for some task requiring less precision.

Equation (1) may be rewritten in terms of operating costs:

$$\sum_{t}^{t+n} \frac{Y}{(1+i)^n} (c_2 - c_1) > P_{1t} - S_{2t} \quad (2)^{[65]}$$

Y is the anticipated stream of output over future periods up to period $t + n$. c_1 is the average cost of production with the new machines, and c_2 with the old. n should represent the economic life of the new equipment. The problem is how to determine *ex ante* this economic life. To do so properly we must be able to foresee the future course of technical development of the equipment over all time.[66] This degree of foresight is impossible, and it appears that in consequence firms fall back on rule-of-thumb methods. n, there-

---

[65] The derivation of equation (2) from (1) is:

$$\pi_{1t} = \sum_{t}^{t+n} \frac{rY}{(1+i)^n} - \sum_{t}^{t+n} \frac{c_1 Y}{(1+i)^n}$$

$$\pi_{2t} = \sum_{t}^{t+n} \frac{rY}{(1+i)^n} - \sum_{t}^{t+n} \frac{c_2 Y}{(1+i)^n}$$

where r is the price at which output sells. Substituting for π_{1t} and π_{2t} in (1),

$$\sum_{t}^{t+n} \frac{rY}{(1+i)^n} - \sum_{t}^{t+n} \frac{c_1 Y}{(1+i)^n} - \sum_{t}^{t+n} \frac{rY}{(1+i)^n}$$
$$+ \sum_{t}^{t+n} \frac{c_2 Y}{(1+i)^n} > P_{1t} - S_{2t}$$

$$\therefore \sum_{t}^{t+n} \frac{Y}{(1+i)^n} (c_2 - c_1) > P_{1t} - S_{2t} \quad (2)$$

[66] We can decide how long to keep the new machine only when we know how soon a superior model will appear. But simply to know the time of appearance of the first superior model is not sufficient. It may pay to ignore it and wait for the second model, if, when the first appears, further developments are regarded as imminent. And so on for the third and subsequent models.

fore, is arbitrary and also short. The bulk of equipment is expected to pay for itself in at most 5 years.[67] Lastly, i is the rate of interest used in discounting.

It is possible to draw some conclusions about the various hypotheses summarised on pp. 122–124 by examining how each of the items in equation (2) is likely to behave during the trade cycle. When we are thinking of the economy as a whole, Y must stand for gross national income. The influence of Y is then clear. It stimulates replacement in the upswing, and stimulates it the more the stronger is the upswing. Similarly Y makes for the postponement of replacement in the downswing. Its influence is possibly stronger than appears from equation (2). It is often difficult to know just when the saving on any machine or group of machines is sufficient to justify replacement.[68] The timing of replacement may be a matter of chance: when somebody in the plant or a visiting salesman happens to notice the possibility of lowering costs by replacing some equipment. More likely, attention is given to replacement when times are good and funds are available. Funds come primarily from gross profits. In so far as these vary with Y, the influence of Y on replacement is strengthened. The pull exerted on replacement by Y is at the basis of Kuznets's qualification of the age hypothesis[69]; and thus possibly, as he argues, underlies the assumption made by other writers that replacement depends solely on the level of output. Undoubtedly, Y has a powerful effect on replacement, but equation (2) also points to the other forces that are at work. We must, therefore, reject this assumption. At the same time, the fluc-

tuations of Y persuade entrepreneurs to take advantage of the flexibility in the life of their plant[70] to put off replacement in the downswing and to concentrate it in the upswing. This suggests that we should reject Hicks's conclusion that replacement cycles are so damped that they may be ignored.[71]

$(c_2 - c_1)$ is subject to a number of influences. The arguments outlined early in section (1),[72] that equipment falls out of use in the downswing and that in consequence Y can rise in the upswing faster than the stock of capital equipment, supports Somers's contention about variations in user cost.[73] User cost is likely to be greater at high levels of output than at low. There is, however, one factor that is likely to counteract the effects of the level of output on wear and tear. In general, maintenance and repairs are curtailed in the downswing, while efforts are bent towards making good the effects of neglect when output is rising.[74] One cannot say unequivocally that user cost will strengthen the tendency for replacement to rise and fall with Y. Moreover, there are forces that make $(c_2 - c_1)$ act in the opposite direction to Y. If replacement is postponed during the depression, c_1 falls relatively to c_2 for two reasons: (i) plant is getting older and therefore c_2 rises; and (ii) technical development is usually not hindered by depression and as a result the potential c_1 is always falling. It is impossible to say just how strong will be the effect of this increase in $(c_2 - c_1)$, for that depends on the rate at which Y is falling relative to the rate at which $(c_2 - c_1)$ is rising. There is no reason why the relation between these rates should be constant from cycle to cycle. It might happen that the increase in

[67] The published evidence relates to American manufacturing industry and is summarised in Terborgh, *op. cit.*, Ch. XII.

[68] This point may be seen very clearly in the articles from the *American Machinist* referred to in fn. 64, p. 125. Cf. N.B.E.R., *op. cit.*, p. 326.

[69] Above, pp. 123–124.

[70] Above, pp. 123–124.

[71] Above, p. 124.

[72] Above, pp. 118ff.

[73] Above, p. 123.

[74] Cf. Hultgren, *op. cit.*, pp. 169–175.

$(c_2 - c_1)$ is sufficient to cause a rise in replacement which would help to explain the lower turning point. It will certainly happen that this increase will hasten the revival of replacement when the upswing begins. On the basis of the factors considered so far, the movement of $(c_2 - c_1)$ will stimulate a considerable bunching of replacement in the early period of the upswing. If such a bunching occurs, $(c_2 - c_1)$ will offset Y in the later part of the upswing, just as it does in the later part of the downswing. This tendency to offset occurs because the early upsurge of replacement leaves industry with comparatively up-to-date equipment. That is to say, c_2 falls sharply and some time must elapse before the gradual fall in c_1 and the gradual rise in c_2 are sufficient to encourage replacement. A temporary lull in replacement is quite plausible, particularly as the other forces that lead to discontinuity of investment are effective here. But as with the upturn, one cannot say whether the fall in $(c_2 - c_1)$ will be soon enough or large enough to explain the downturn. It will help Y in inducing a postponement of replacement where once the downswing has begun. This stronger force making for postponement early in the downswing increases the possibility that $(c_2 - c_1)$ may rise sufficiently to explain the upturn, which in turn makes more plausible the argument that a fall in $(c_2 - c_1)$ accounts for the downturn. But that is all on the assumption that other things are equal; and it is more likely that other things change to at least some extent from cycle to cycle. It assumes, moreover, that the entrepreneur always knows just when replacement is worth while; and, as we have seen, this is by no means always a valid assumption. Finally, it assumes that we are discussing firms that are not growing rapidly. In rapidly expanding firms the age distribution of equipment is likely to be so skewed that no bunching of replacement occurs early

in the upswing.[75] For our present purposes this qualification may be neglected, because it is doubtful whether the acceleration principle has much significance for such firms anyhow.[76] All in all, we must view with caution the thesis that replacement explains the turning points; but it is interesting to note that the movements of $(c_2 - c_1)$ may yield the same effects as the echo theories[77] and without their special assumptions about the lifetime of machines. Indeed, a consideration of the various forces affecting $(c_2 - c_1)$ helps us to see that, while the age structure of equipment is important, replacement cannot be regarded as a simple function of age. Furthermore, $(c_2 - c_1)$ makes it quite clear why it is impossible to accept the thesis that replacement depends solely on Y. One implication of this conclusion is that we cannot accept Frisch's contention that gross investment may approach asymptotically some level and stay there.

The behaviour of P and S need not detain us for long. P consists of the prices of capital equipment and of the costs of installing it. Kalecki's index of the prices of capital goods shows that they do not change much, and that such changes as do occur show no consistent pattern *vis-à-vis* the cycle.[78] The costs of installation include both direct costs and also indirect costs in the form of interference with current production and the diversion of managerial energies. Their effects have already been discussed and the conclusion has been reached that generalisation is hazardous. So far as they may be significant they have already been allowed for in the discussion about $(c_2 - c_1)$. S probably supports the effects of Y. Both the second-hand market and alternative

[75] Cf. Horner, *op. cit.*, chart 12, p. 49.
[76] Cf. p. 116.
[77] See Einarsen *op. cit.*; and Tinbergen, *op. cit.*, *Econometrica*, 1935.
[78] M. Kalecki, *Essays in the Theory of Economic Fluctuations* (London, 1938), p. 39, table 3. This index should, perhaps, be viewed with caution.

opportunities improve as Y rises and deteriorate as it falls. It is difficult, however, to assess the significance of S.

The general conclusion to be derived from this discussion is that we may point to certain factors that have a significant influence on replacement. Furthermore, the analysis shows that we must reject the various hypotheses outlined at the beginning of this section. We cannot regard replacement as a function solely of Y or of age; nor can we safely assume that replacement cycles gently die away. To go beyond this, however, is most difficult. This is so for two reasons: (*a*) we cannot say at what stage of the cycle replacement becomes profitable or unprofitable; and (*b*) even if we knew the answer to this question, we should still be unable to say much on the timing of replacement. The major reason for the first difficulty is the problem of predicting the behaviour of $(c_2 - c_1)$ relative to that of the other forces in the cycle. To do this we should require a closed model, and one based on a more complete theory of investment than the fragment under discussion here. The second difficulty arises from the fact that equation (2) tells us when replacement becomes profitable, but not when the decision to replace is taken. We are thwarted in our attempt to state the behaviour of gross investment influenced by motives for expansion as well as those for replacement. We can say no more, therefore, than that it is difficult, if not impossible, to separate replacement from net investment; and that there are strong forces acting on the motive for replacement. It is in consequence unlikely that gross investment will slavishly follow the pattern suggested by the acceleration principle. It is a weak conclusion, and clearly we must pursue our inquiries further.

3.

In general the acceleration principle is expressed as a theory relating current out-put to current investment. Sometimes lags are introduced and investment is regarded as a function of the changes in output during a past period. A number of critics have made the pertinent comment that no satisfactory theory of investment can be constructed without some provision for expectations. Indeed even the simplest formulation of the acceleration principle contains an implicit assumption about the future behaviour of output: it is expected to remain at the level which it has just reached. There is no dispute whether the assumptions made about anticipations affect the acceleration principle. The difference of opinion turns on the nature of that effect. There are three main schools of thought.

Professor Tinbergen stresses the distorting effects of errors of judgment. The ideal at which the entrepreneur aims in the adjustment of his capital equipment may be "the adaptation as set out by the acceleration principle. But since the adaptation must always be directed towards an unknown future demand for consumers' goods, it is only natural that errors may be committed."[79] The consequence, Tinbergen argues, is that the acceleration principle cannot accurately depict the formation of investment decisions. Other writers take the view that the explicit introduction of expectations helps to explain why statistical studies have in general yielded such unfavourable results for the acceleration principle. Such studies have sought the degree of correlation between all changes in output and all changes in the stock of capital equipment. A. S. Manne has suggested that since the entrepreneur is gifted with a certain measure of foresight he will be able to distinguish, at least in part, between those changes in the demand for his

---

[79] Tinbergen, *Econometrica*, 1942, p. 139; cf. also J. M. Clark, *Strategic Factors, op. cit.*, p. 40; and Pigou, *op. cit.*, p. 108, esp. footnote. Clark and Pigou do not find these errors in forecasting very harmful to the acceleration principle.

product that are purely transitory and those changes that justify some extension or contraction of his plant.[80] If this is so, empirical research must make some distinction between these categories of movements in demand. It will be noted, however, that this attempt to shield the acceleration principle from one criticism reinforces the argument that investment is discontinuous.[81] *Prima facie* another attempt to show that the acceleration principle can be made more useful by the introduction of anticipations is that by Professor Wright. Wright, however, uses the phrase "acceleration principle" to refer to the purely technical relationship outlined on pages 116–117. His introduction of expectations results in a complete rejection of the principle that is being discussed here. "We can take the matter further," he writes, "and divorce [investment] altogether from consumption,"[82] making it depend on autonomous changes in entrepreneurial expectations or on innovations. His attitude, therefore, is more akin to Tinbergen's than to Manne's.

Many writers who refer to the effects of expectations on the acceleration principle are eclectic and recognise that there are valid elements in the arguments for and against the principle.

The supposition which underlies the rigid application of the acceleration principle is that the present level of demand is assumed to rule in the future also. Now it is very doubtful whether it is possible to generalise as to the exact behaviour of producers in this respect. Fortunately for the broad result, however, it is sufficient to indicate a certain range of expectations as probable and to eliminate others as highly unlikely.[83]

There can be no doubt that the eclectic approach is the safest one in view of our very restricted knowledge of how expectations are formed. The position has been summed up very aptly by Bissell: only when we have a workable theory of expectations shall we know just how far the acceleration principle must be qualified.[84] One or two comments, however, are possible in an attempt to limit somewhat the range of uncertainty about anticipations and the acceleration principle.

To some extent memories of the past affect reactions to the events of the present. Firms that have known violent fluctuations in the demand for their output are likely to be hesitant about expanding their plant in the face of a current growth in demand.[85] The result is that during the course of a trade cycle different firms will respond to market changes with differing speeds and to differing degrees; and their various reactions will depend on their past experiences.[86]

[83] Haberler, *op. cit.*, p. 343; and also pp. 102 and 306. Cf. Somers, *op. cit.*, pp. 83–86 and Long, *op. cit.*, pp. 44–55.

[84] Bissell, *op. cit.*, p. 34.

[85] E.g., the policy of the United States Steel Corporation as recorded in S. D. Merlin, *The Theory of Fluctuations in Contemporary Economic Thought*, p. 117, fn. 54. Also, Heller, *op. cit.*, p. 100: "There has been some tendency to regard the 1946–1950 markets as 'too good to be true'. Productive capacity has been held below levels needed to meet peak demands because the long-run plateau was expected to be lower."

[86] In so far as the firms with the most unpleasant memories are in the capital goods industries, some such hesitation to invest even when faced by sharply rising demand must lie at the basis of the explanation of the downturn given by Goodwin, especially in *op. cit.*, *Econometrica*, 1951, and by Clark in *Overhead Costs, op. cit.*, pp. 393–394. Clark and Goodwin suggest that the rate of growth of income is slowed down by this reluctance of the capital goods industries to add to their equipment.

It will be noted that in this section we abandon the simplifying assumption that output and demand may be treated as one.

[80] Manne, *op. cit.*, pp. 96–97. See also, J. W. Angell, *Investment and Business Cycles* (New York, 1941); "Regardless of the state of present demand, entrepreneurs will not increase present capacity unless their anticipations for the future warrant the step." (p. 89, fn.).

Kuznets argues, *op. cit.*, p. 229, that the more durable the capital equipment the more wary will the entrepreneur be before he installs additional equipment in response to a rise in demand. This is true, however, only on certain assumptions about the age structure of existing equipment.

[81] Cf. above, p. 122.

[82] D. McC. Wright, "A neglected approach to the acceleration principle," *Review of Economic Statistics*, 1941, p. 101.

A second factor that delimits somewhat the applicability of the acceleration principle is that firms in their investment policy may be concerned with distant possibilities that are divorced from the current movements of markets.[87] Strictly, however, this takes us into the territory of those criticisms that query the importance of induced investment. This territory is out of bounds.

In the light of these two arguments we may say that the acceleration principle is fully applicable only to induced investment in firms that have not suffered too greatly from ups and downs of demand. With regard to the firms that have not so suffered, we seek here to discuss only one qualification to the acceleration principle. In a world of imperfect foresight what effect has the current level of profits on the confidence with which entrepreneurs view the future? This involves us in the arguments as to the relative merits of the profits principle and the acceleration principle. It is more convenient to consider the effects of profits on anticipations together with these other arguments.

The case for the profits principle, which has been put most forcefully by Tinbergen,[88] rests on two arguments: (a) in the uncertain world of reality the entrepreneur falls back on rule-of-thumb methods in trying to evaluate the future, and the present level of profits provides that rule-of-thumb; and (b) firms prefer internal sources of finance and thus profits must have a dominating influence on investment. He supports his theoretical arguments

with correlation analyses of a number of time series. The profits principle has more than one form. It is sometimes argued that the level of profits determines the level of investment; and sometimes that what is important is the rate of profit, where this "is determined *grosso modo* by the level of national income and the stock of capital equipment."[89] There are arguments in favour of both these theses, but they favour the second more than the first.

Let us examine first profits and their effect on expectations. It is not plausible to argue that expectations will be based solely on the rule-of-thumb provided by the current level of profits. If entrepreneurs are as uncertain as this implies about the future market they are unlikely to invest at all.[90] This argument is strengthened by the fact that some at least of the decisions on an investment project initiated in the present can be put off until the situation is clearer.[91] The most, therefore, that can be said of the effects of profits is that they may distort expectations. It is worth dwelling a little longer on this distortion. It is likely to be the more severe the longer is the gestation period. When the gestation period is long a rise in demand will be met by a rise in price rather than by an increase in output. The individual producer has to decide by how much demand has risen in real terms. It is reasonable to suggest that his vision is likely to be distorted.[92] We are now in a

---

[87] D. H. Robertson, *Essays in Monetary Theory* (London, 1939), p. 179; and Lundberg, *op. cit.*, p. 254. For some empirical evidence that raises doubts about the importance of these long-range anticipations, cf. Gort, *op. cit.*, pp. 81–84. It will be noted, moreover, that the introduction of expectations makes it exceptionally difficult to maintain the distinction between autonomous and induced investment. It is not discussed here in order to limit the scope of this paper.

[88] See in particular, his *Statistical Testing, op. cit., passim*; and Tinbergen and Polak, *op. cit.*, ch. 13.

[89] Kalecki, *op. cit.*, p. 133. Models based on both forms of profits principle are in Tinbergen and Polak, *op. cit.*, pp. 195–206.

[90] On the importance of market forecasts, see W. E. Wright, *Forecasting for Profit* (New York, 1947), pp. 2 and 10; and Heller, *op. cit.*, p. 99.

[91] Gort, *op. cit.*, p. 82; and A. G. Hart, "Anticipations, business planning, and the cycle," *Quarterly Journal of Economics*, 1937, p. 286.

[92] The effects of a long gestation period on expectations is developed at length in Aftalion, *op. cit.*; cf. also J. Tinbergen, "Ein Schiffbauzyklus?" *Weltwirtschaftliches Archiv*, 1931; T. C. Koopmans, *Tanker Freight Rates and Tankship Building* (Haarlem, 1939), pp. 165ff.; and J. A. Schumpeter, *Business Cycles* (New York, 1939), vol. II, pp. 533–535.

better position to see the two horns of the dilemma on which the acceleration principle finds itself.[93] On the one hand, firms may reach capacity in terms of definition (c).[94] Where this happens a case can be made for the acceleration principle, but one which leaves it weak in matters of timing. On the other hand, capacity in terms of definition (a) may be reached. Were the adjustment of plant to changes in output instantaneous, the acceleration principle would explain both the timing and the amount of investment once this capacity was reached. But instantaneous adjustment is not possible. Moreover, the gestation period must grow if, during an upswing, more and more firms reach capacity (a). In short, where there is surplus capacity according to definition (a) the acceleration principle encounters one serious obstacle; and where such surplus capacity does not exist it encounters another.[95]

The above argument, so far as it supports the profits principle, favours the level of profits as a determinant of investment. The case for this variant of the profits principle can be strengthened. The acceleration principle assumes (a) that where a firm needs outside capital for an investment programme it has no hesitation whatever in seeking it, and (b) that the supply of credit is perfectly elastic. We are here concerned with (a).[96] It is an unwarranted assumption. There is some evidence that firms prefer internal sources of finance to borrowing either short or long.[97] Profits are a major source of internal finance. The level of profits is,

therefore, a major factor in determining how much a firm can invest and when it invests. Profits exercise, therefore, over both the amount and the timing of investment, an influence that is permissive,[98] except in so far as the availability of funds stimulates some inquiry into the openings for investment[99] or distorts expectations about such openings.

We must not, however, press too far the argument in favour of the level of profits. Undoubtedly there are strong reasons for looking upon the level of profits as the determinant of investment, but only where the openings for investment exceed the funds available.[100] A particularly important weakness of this variant of the profits principle is that it assumes that so long as profits remain at a given level, investment will continue to be constant regardless of the effects of past investment on the stock of equipment. This is not a valid assumption. "Indeed, if in a given period there is a high level of profitability which induces investment this will not continue for the subsequent period because all investment plans will have already been undertaken under the influence of high profitability in the initial period".[101] This defect can be avoided by taking the rate of profit as the determinant of investment, for then we allow for the stock of capital equipment.

---

[93] Cf. above, p. 120.

[94] Cf. II (1), esp. p. 120.

[95] It was recognition of this obstacle that led J. M. Clark to suggest that there is always some "surplus capacity". Cf. above, p. 120, and *Readings, op. cit.*, pp. 256–257.

[96] For a discussion of (a) and (b) cf. Tsiang, *op. cit.*, pp. 331–335.

[97] See, e.g., the case studies in J. K. Butters and J. Lintner, *Effect of Federal Taxes on Growing Enterprises* (Boston, 1945); and Heller, *op. cit.*, pp. 101–102.

[98] "But as repeated references to reliance on internal funds have indicated, finance is more a barrier to capital investment than a 'thrust' towards new projects." Heller, *op. cit.*, p. 101. See also the answers to the question on the "effect of the abundance or scarcity of liquid resources on investment in fixed plant", in J. E. Meade and P. W. S. Andrews, "Summary of replies to questions on the effects of interest rates," *Oxford Economic Papers*, 1938, pp. 25–8.

[99] Cf. the discussion about replacement on p. 126 above.

[100] It will be noted that once again we encounter the difficulty of distinguishing between induced and autonomous investment. Presumably they are both financed from the same source and thus their movements cannot be fully independent.

[101] M. Kalecki, "A new approach to the problem of business cycles," *Review of Economic Studies*, 1949–50, p. 61.

Within the restricted limits of this survey the determinants of investment may be summed up. We may write:

$$I = \beta(K_D - K_A), \quad \text{where}$$

(a) β is the inverse of the gestation period. Hitherto we have been able to treat the decision to invest and the actual execution of investment as one. The introduction of the gestation period makes it necessary to have a distinction; and I here refers to the process of investment.

(b) K_D is, for want of a better term, the desired level of capital stock.

(c) K_A is that part of the existing equipment that is considered efficient enough to be kept in operation.

This equation differs in certain respects from the acceleration principle. In the first place, it allows for some form of gestation period. In the second place, it differs as regards the timing of the decision to invest and as regards the proposed volume of investment. Thus K_D depends, for timing and amount, not solely on the level of national income but also on profits, which affect it in the ways outlined above.[102] To some extent, the essential characteristic of the acceleration principle is preserved in the difference between K_D and K_A. But, whereas the principle neglects replacement and thus the movements of K_A, those movements are allowed for in $(K_D - K_A)$. Thus I refers to gross investment, the timing and amount of which are strongly influenced by profits. That this is so is plausible in view of the difficulties experienced in II (1) and II (2), where we were discussing the timing of net and replacement investment.

III.

The acceleration principle may be criticised on three counts. It purports to give

[102] The case for the profits principle would be strengthened if costs vary cyclically as has been suggested, e.g., by W. C. Mitchell, *Business Cycles and their Causes* (Berkeley, 1951). The case for this theory is not considered here, as it does not fall within our terms of reference.

a precise explanation of the timing of investment where in fact it is vague. This is the conclusion of II (1); and it is supported in some measure by II (2). This latter section also suggests the inadequacy of any theory of investment that is restricted to net investment. Finally, we argued on p. 121 that there is a strong element of truth in the acceleration principle: namely, that the amount of an entrepreneur's investment is governed in some measure by a comparison of the output he can most efficiently produce with his existing plant and the output at which demand conditions now justify him in aiming. II (3), however, presents the arguments in favour of profits as a determinant of investment, both in matters of timing and of amount. Thus the essential appeal of the acceleration principle is somewhat muted, but mainly in that the level of profits may curb the enthusiasm to invest engendered by the rate of growth of output.

In sum, there is an element of truth in the acceleration principle; but it is an element that is so heavily overlaid by other factors that the acceleration principle by itself is inadequate as a theory of investment. Unfortunately, it is not at all clear what theory we should put in its place. $I = \beta(K_D - K_A)$ meets the criticisms of the acceleration principle; but it is no more than a summary behind which lie some very complex relationships. It is certainly not neat and easy to handle. Much of the appeal of the acceleration principle has lain in these very characteristics, but it may be wondered whether they should always be regarded as commending a theory of investment. There is sufficient similarity in the factors that determine investment from one cycle to the next to enable us to pick out certain salient factors and decide that those are the ones we must watch. There is not sufficient uniformity to justify our attaching fixed coefficients to these factors.

The precise theory is easier to handle, but its precision should make it suspect. The many qualifications with which our conclusions have been hedged are in part an admission of ignorance; in part also they spring from a desire to avoid placing undue emphasis on the constancy of economic life.

Part IV

MONEY, INTEREST,
AND INCOME

10

Mr. Keynes and the "Classics"; A Suggested Interpretation[1]

J. R. HICKS

I.

It will be admitted by the least charitable reader that the entertainment value of Mr. Keynes' *General Theory of Employment* is considerably enhanced by its satiric aspect. But it is also clear that many readers have been left very bewildered by this Dunciad. Even if they are convinced by Mr. Keynes' arguments and humbly acknowledge themselves to have been "classical economists" in the past, they find it hard to remember that they believed in their unregenerate days the things Mr. Keynes says they believed. And there are

* *

Reprinted from *Econometrica*, vol. 5 (April 1937), pp. 147–159, by permission of the publisher and author.

J. R. Hicks is Professor Emeritus at Oxford University; he was formerly at Gonville and Caius College, Cambridge.

[1] Based on a paper which was read at the Oxford meeting of the Econometric Society (September, 1936) and which called forth an interesting discussion. It has been modified subsequently, partly in the light of that discussion, and partly as a result of further discussion in Cambridge.

no doubt others who find their historic doubts a stumbling block, which prevents them from getting as much illumination from the positive theory as they might otherwise have got.

One of the main reasons for this situation is undoubtedly to be found in the fact that Mr. Keynes takes as typical of "Classical economics" the later writings of Professor Pigou, particularly *The Theory of Unemployment*. Now *The Theory of Unemployment* is a fairly new book, and an exceedingly difficult book; so that it is safe to say that it has not yet made much impression on the ordinary teaching of economics. To most people its doctrines seem quite as strange and novel as the doctrines of Mr. Keynes himself; so that to be told that he has believed these things himself leaves the ordinary economist quite bewildered.

For example, Professor Pigou's theory runs, to a quite amazing extent, in real terms. Not only is his theory a theory of real wages and unemployment; but numbers of problems which anyone else would have preferred to investigate in money terms are investigated by Professor Pigou in terms of "wage-goods." The ordinary classical economist has no part in this *tour de force*.

But if, on behalf of the ordinary classical economist, we declare that he would have preferred to investigate many of those problems in money terms, Mr. Keynes will reply that there is no classical theory of money wages and employment. It is quite true that such a theory cannot easily be found in the textbooks. But this is only because most of the textbooks were written at a time when general changes in money wages in a closed system did not present an important problem. There can be little doubt that most economists have thought that they had a pretty fair idea of what the relation between money wages and employment actually was.

In these circumstances, it seems worth while to try to construct a typical "classical" theory, built on an earlier and cruder model than Professor Pigou's. If we can construct such a theory, and show that it does give results which have in fact been commonly taken for granted, but which do not agree with Mr. Keynes' conclusions, then we shall at last have a satisfactory basis of comparison. We may hope to be able to isolate Mr. Keynes' innovations, and so to discover what are the real issues in dispute.

Since our purpose is comparison, I shall try to set out my typical classical theory in a form similar to that in which Mr. Keynes sets out his own theory; and I shall leave out of account all secondary complications which do not bear closely upon this special question in hand. Thus I assume that I am dealing with a short period in which the quantity of physical equipment of all kinds available can be taken as fixed. I assume homogeneous labour. I assume further that depreciation can be neglected, so that the output of investment goods corresponds to new investment. This is a dangerous simplifi-cation, but the important issues raised by Mr. Keynes in his chapter on user cost are irrelevant for our purposes.

Let us begin by assuming that w, the rate of money wages per head, can be taken as given.

Let x, y, be the outputs of investment goods and consumption goods respectively, and N_x, N_y, be the numbers of men employed in producing them. Since the amount of physical equipment specialised to each industry is given, $x = f_x(N_x)$ and $y = f_y(N_y)$, where f_x, f_y, are *given* functions.

Let M be the *given* quantity of money. It is desired to determine N_x and N_y.

First, the price-level of investment goods = their marginal cost = $w(dN_x/dx)$. And the price-level of consumption goods = their marginal cost = $w(dN_y/dy)$.

Income earned in investment trades (value of investment, or simply Investment) = $wx(dN_x/dx)$. Call this I_x.

Income earned in consumption trades = $wy(dN_y/dy)$.

Total income
$$= wx(dN_x/dx) + wy(dN_y/dy).$$
Call this I.

I_x is therefore a given function of N_x, I of N_x and N_y. Once I and I_x are determined, N_x and N_y can be determined.

Now let us assume the "Cambridge Quantity equation"—that there is some definite relation between Income and the demand for money. Then, approximately, and apart from the fact that the demand for money may depend not only upon total Income, but also upon its distribution between people with relatively large and relatively small demands for balances, we can write
$$M = kI.$$

As soon as k is given, total Income is therefore determined.

In order to determine I_x, we need two equations. One tells us that the amount of investment (looked at as demand for capital) depends upon the rate of interest:

$$I_x = C(i).$$

This is what becomes the marginal-efficiency-of-capital schedule in Mr. Keynes' work.

Further, Investment = Saving. And saving depends upon the rate of interest and, if you like, Income. $\therefore I_x = S(i, I)$. (Since, however, Income is already determined, we do not need to bother about inserting Income here unless we choose.)

Taking them as a system, however, we have three fundamental equations,

$$M = kI, \; I_x = C(i), \; I_x = S(i, I),$$

to determine three unknowns, I, I_x, i. As we have found earlier, N_x and N_y can be determined from I and I_x. Total employment, $N_x + N_y$, is therefore determined.

Let us consider some properties of this system. It follows directly from the first equation that as soon as k and M are given, I is completely determined; that is to say, total income depends directly upon the quantity of money. Total employment, however, is not necessarily determined at once from income, since it will usually depend to some extent upon the proportion of income saved, and thus upon the way production is divided between investment and consumption-goods trades. (If it so happened that the elasticities of supply were the same in each of these trades, then a shifting of demand between them would produce compensating movements in N_x and N_y, and consequently no change in total employment.)

An increase in the inducement to invest (i.e., a rightward movement of the schedule of the marginal efficiency of capital, which we have written as $C(i)$ will tend to raise the rate of interest, and so to affect saving. If the amount of saving rises, the amount of investment will rise too; labour will be employed more in the investment trades,

less in the consumption trades; this will increase total employment if the elasticity of supply in the investment trades is greater than that in the consumption-goods trades—diminish it if *vice versa*.

An increase in the supply of money will necessarily raise total income, for people will increase their spending and lending until incomes have risen sufficiently to restore k to its former level. The rise in income will tend to increase employment, both in making consumption goods and in making investment goods. The total effect on employment depends upon the ratio between the expansions of these industries; and that depends upon the proportion of their increased incomes which people desire to save, which also governs the rate of interest.

So far we have assumed the rate of money wages to be given; but so long as we assume that k is independent of the level of wages, there is no difficulty about this problem either. A rise in the rate of money wages will necessarily diminish employment and raise real wages. For an unchanged money income cannot continue to buy an unchanged quantity of goods at a higher price-level; and, unless the price-level rises, the prices of goods will not cover their marginal costs. There must therefore be a fall in employment; as employment falls, marginal costs in terms of labour will diminish and therefore real wages rise. (Since a change in money wages is always accompanied by a change in real wages in the same direction, if not in the same proportion, no harm will be done, and some advantage will perhaps be secured, if one prefers to work in terms of real wages. Naturally most "classical economists" have taken this line.)

I think it will be agreed that we have here a quite reasonably consistent theory, and a theory which is also consistent with the pronouncements of a recognizable group of economists. Admittedly it follows from this theory that you may be able to increase employment by direct inflation; but whether or not you decide to favour that policy still depends upon your judgment about the probable reaction on wages, and also—in a national area—upon your views about the international standard.

Historically, this theory descends from Ricardo, though it is not actually Ricardian; it is probably more or less the theory that was held by Marshall. But with Marshall it was already beginning to be qualified in important ways; his successors have qualified it still further. What Mr. Keynes has done is to lay enormous emphasis on the qualifications, so that they almost blot out the original theory. Let us follow out this process of development.

II.

When a theory like the "classical" theory we have just described is applied to the analysis of industrial fluctuations, it gets into difficulties in several ways. It is evident that total money income experiences great variations in the course of a trade cycle, and the classical theory can only explain these by variations in M or in k, or, as a third and last alternative, by changes in distribution.

(1) Variation in M is simplest and most obvious, and has been relied on to a large extent. But the variations in M that are traceable during a trade cycle are variations that take place through the banks—they are variations in bank loans; if we are to rely on them it is urgently necessary for us to explain the connection between the supply of bank money and the rate of interest. This can be done roughly by thinking of banks as persons who are strongly inclined to pass on money by lending rather than spending it. Their action therefore tends at first to lower interest rates, and only afterwards, when the money passes into the hands of spenders, to raise prices and incomes. "The new currency, or the increase of currency, goes, not to private persons, but to the banking centers; and therefore, it increases the willingness of lenders to lend in the first instance, and lowers the rate of discount. But it afterwards raises prices; and therefore it tends to increase discount."[2] This is superficially satisfactory; but if we endeavoured to give a more precise account of this process we should soon get into difficulties. What determines the amount of money needed to produce a given fall in the rate of interest? What determines the length of time for which the low rate will last? These are not easy questions to answer.

(2) In so far as we rely upon changes in k, we can also do well enough up to a point. Changes in k can be related to changes in confidence, and it is realistic to hold that the rising prices of a boom occur because optimism encourages a reduction in balances; the falling prices of a slump because pessimism and uncertainty dictate an increase. But as soon as we take this step it becomes natural to ask whether k has not abdicated its status as an independent variable, and has not become liable to be influenced by others among the variables in our fundamental equations.

(3) This last consideration is powerfully supported by another, of more purely theoretical character. On grounds of pure value theory, it is evident that the direct sacrifice made by a person who holds a stock of money is a sacrifice of interest; and it is hard to believe that the marginal principle does not operate at all in this field. As Lavington put it:

> The quantity of resources which (an individual) holds in the form of money will be such that the unit of money which is just and only just worth while holding in this form yields him a return of convenience and security equal to the yield of satisfaction derived from the marginal unit spent on consumables, and equal also to the net rate of interest.[3]

[2] Marshall, *Money, Credit, and Commerce*, p. 257.
[3] Lavington, *English Capital Market*, 1921, p. 30. See also Pigou, "The Exchange-value of Legal-tender Money," in *Essays in Applied Economics*, 1922, pp. 179–181.

The demand for money depends upon the rate of interest! The stage is set for Mr. Keynes.

As against the three equations of the classical theory,

$$M = kI, \; I_x = C(i), \; I_x = S(i, I),$$

Mr. Keynes begins with three equations,

$$M = L(i), \; I_x = C(i), \; I_x = S(I).$$

These differ from the classical equations in two ways. On the one hand, the demand for money is conceived as depending upon the rate of interest (Liquidity Preference). On the other hand, any possible influence of the rate of interest on the amount saved out of a given income is neglected. Although it means that the third equation becomes the multiplier equation, which performs such queer tricks, nevertheless this second amendment is a mere simplification, and ultimately insignificant.[4] It is the liquidity preference doctrine which is vital.

For it is now the rate of interest, not income, which is determined by the quantity of money. The rate of interest set against the schedule of the marginal efficiency of capital determines the value of investment; that determines income by the multiplier. Then the volume of employment (at given wage-rates) is determined by the value of investment and of income which is not saved but spent upon consumption goods.

[4] This can be readily seen if we consider the equations

$$M = kI, \; I_x = C(i), \; I_x = S(I),$$

which embody Mr. Keynes' second amendment without his first. The third equation is already the multiplier equation, but the multiplier is shorn of his wings. For since I still depends only on M, I_x now depends only on M, and it is impossible to increase investment without increasing the willingness to save or the quantity of money. The system thus generated is therefore identical with that which, a few years ago, used to be called the "Treasury View." But Liquidity Preference transports us from the "Treasury View" to the "General Theory of Employment."

It is this system of equations which yields the startling conclusion, that an increase in the inducement to invest, or in the propensity to consume, will not tend to raise the rate of interest, but only to increase employment. In spite of this, however, and in spite of the fact that quite a large part of the argument runs in terms of this system, and this system alone, *it is not the General Theory.* We may call it, if we like, Mr. Keynes' *special theory.* The General Theory is something appreciably more orthodox.

Like Lavington and Professor Pigou, Mr. Keynes does not in the end believe that the demand for money can be determined by one variable alone—not even the rate of interest. He lays more stress on it than they did, but neither for him nor for them can it be the only variable to be considered. The dependence of the demand for money on interest does not, in the end, do more than qualify the old dependence on income. However much stress we lay upon the "speculative motive," the "transactions" motive must always come in as well.

Consequently we have for the General Theory

$$M = L(I, i), \; I_x = C(i), \; I_x = S(I).$$

With this revision, Mr. Keynes takes a big step back to Marshallian orthodoxy, and his theory becomes hard to distinguish from the revised and qualified Marshallian theories, which, as we have seen, are not new. Is there really any difference between them, or is the whole thing a sham fight? Let us have recourse to a diagram (Figure 1).

Against a given quantity of money, the first equation, $M = L(I, i)$, gives us a relation between Income (I) and the rate of interest (i). This can be drawn out as a curve (LL) which will slope upwards, since an increase in income tends to raise the demand for money, and an increase in the rate of interest tends to lower it. Further,

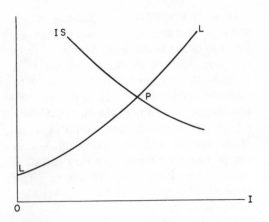

FIGURE 1.

the second two equations taken together give us another relation between Income and interest. (The marginal-efficiency-of-capital schedule determines the value of investment at any given rate of interest, and the multiplier tells us what level of income will be necessary to make savings equal to that value of investment.) The curve *IS* can therefore be drawn showing the relation between Income and interest which must be maintained in order to make saving equal to investment.

Income and the rate of interest are now determined together at *P*, the point of intersection of the curves *LL* and *IS*. They are determined together; just as price and output are determined together in the modern theory of demand and supply. Indeed, Mr. Keynes' innovation is closely parallel, in this respect, to the innovation of the marginalists. The quantity theory tries to determine income without interest, just as the labour theory of value tried to determine price without output; each has to give place to a theory recognising a higher degree of interdependence.

III.

But if this is the real "General Theory," how does Mr. Keynes come to make his remarks about an increase in the inducement to invest not raising the rate of

interest? It would appear from our diagram that a rise in the marginal-efficiency-of-capital schedule must raise the curve *IS*; and, therefore, although it will raise Income and employment, it will also raise the rate of interest.

This brings us to what, from many points of view, is the most important thing in Mr. Keynes' book. It is not only possible to show that a given supply of money determines a certain relation between Income and interest (which we have expressed by the curve *LL*); it is also possible to say something about the shape of the curve. It will probably tend to be nearly horizontal on the left, and nearly vertical on the right. This is because there is (1) some minimum below which the rate of interest is unlikely to go, and (though Mr. Keynes does not stress this) there is (2) a maximum to the level of income which can possibly be financed with a given amount of money. If we like we can think of the curve as approaching these limits asymptotically (Figure 2).

Therefore, if the curve *IS* lies well to the right (either because of a strong inducement to invest or a strong propensity to consume), *P* will lie upon that part of the curve which is decidedly upward sloping, and the classical theory will be a good approximation, needing no more than the qualification which it has in fact re-

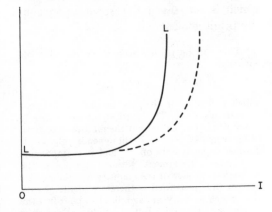

FIGURE 2.

ceived at the hands of the later Marshallians. An increase in the inducement to invest will raise the rate of interest, as in the classical theory, but it will also have some subsidiary effect in raising income, and therefore employment as well. (Mr. Keynes in 1936 is not the first Cambridge economist to have a temperate faith in Public Works.) But if the point *P* lies to the left of the *LL* curve, then the *special* form of Mr. Keynes' theory becomes valid. A rise in the schedule of the marginal efficiency of capital only increases employment, and does not raise the rate of interest at all. We are completely out of touch with the classical world.

The demonstration of this minimum is thus of central importance. It is so important that I shall venture to paraphrase the proof, setting it out in a rather different way from that adopted by Mr. Keynes.[5]

If the costs of holding money can be neglected, it will always be profitable to hold money rather than lend it out, if the rate of interest is not greater than zero. Consequently the rate of interest must always be positive. In an extreme case, the shortest short-term rate may perhaps be nearly zero. But if so, the long-term rate must lie above it, for the long rate has to allow for the risk that the short rate may rise during the currency of the loan, and it should be observed that the short rate can only rise, it cannot fall.[6] This does not only mean that the long rate must be a sort of average of the probable short rates over its duration, and that this average must lie above the current short rate. There is also the more

important risk to be considered, that the lender on long term may desire to have cash before the agreed date of repayment, and then, if the short rate has risen meanwhile, he may be involved in a substantial capital loss. It is this last risk which provides Mr. Keynes' "speculative motive" and which ensures that the rate for loans of indefinite duration (which he always has in mind as *the* rate of interest) cannot fall very near zero.[7]

It should be observed that this minimum to the rate of interest applies not only to one curve *LL* (drawn to correspond to a particular quantity of money) but to any such curve. If the supply of money is increased, the curve *LL* moves to the right (as the dotted curve in Figure 2), but the horizontal parts of the curve are almost the same. Therefore, again, it is this doldrum to the left of the diagram which upsets the classical theory. If *IS* lies to the right, then we can indeed increase employment by increasing the quantity of money; but if *IS* lies to the left, we cannot do so; merely monetary means will not force down the rate of interest any further.

So the General Theory of Employment is the Economics of Depression.

IV.

In order to elucidate the relation between Mr. Keynes and the "Classics," we have invented a little apparatus. It does not

---

[5] Keynes, *General Theory*, pp. 201–202.
[6] It is just conceivable that people might become so used to the idea of very low short rates that they would not be much impressed by this risk; but it is very unlikely. For the short rate may rise, either because trade improves, and income expands; or because trade gets worse, and the desire for liquidity increases. I doubt whether a monetary system so elastic as to rule out both of these possibilities is really thinkable.

[7] Nevertheless something more than the "speculative motive" is needed to account for the system of interest rates. The shortest of all short rates must equal the relative valuation, at the margin, of money and such a bill; and the bill stands at a discount mainly because of the "convenience and security" of holding money—the inconvenience which may possibly be caused by not having cash immediately available. It is the chance that you may want to discount the bill which matters, not the chance that you will then have to discount it on unfavourable terms. The "precautionary motive," not the "speculative motive," is here dominant. But the prospective terms of rediscounting are vital, when it comes to the *difference* between short and long rates.

appear that we have exhausted the uses of that apparatus, so let us conclude by giving it a little run on its own.

With that apparatus at our disposal, we are no longer obliged to make certain simplifications which Mr. Keynes makes in his exposition. We can reinsert the missing i in the third equation, and allow for any possible effect of the rate of interest upon saving; and, what is much more important, we can call in question the sole dependence of investment upon the rate of interest, which looks rather suspicious in the second equation. Mathematical elegance would suggest that we ought to have I and i in all three equations, if the theory is to be really General. Why not have them there like this:

$$M = L(I, i), \ I_x = C(I, i), \ I_x = S(I, i)?$$

Once we raise the question of Income in the second equation, it is clear that it has a very good claim to be inserted. Mr. Keynes is in fact only enabled to leave it out at all plausibly by his device of measuring everything in "wage-units," which means that he allows for changes in the marginal-efficiency-of-capital schedule when there is a change in the level of money wages, but that other changes in Income are deemed not to affect the curve, or at least not in the same immediate manner. But why draw this distinction? Surely there is every reason to suppose that an increase in the demand for consumers' goods, arising from an increase in employment, will often directly stimulate an increase in investment, at least as soon as an expectation develops that the increased demand will continue. If this is so, we ought to include I in the second equation, though it must be confessed that the effect of I on the marginal efficiency of capital will be fitful and irregular.

The Generalized General Theory can then be set out in this way. Assume first of all a given total money Income. Draw a

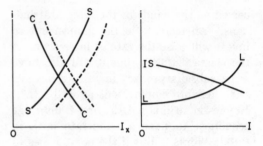

Figure 3.

curve CC showing the marginal efficiency of capital (in money terms) at that given Income; a curve SS showing the supply curve of saving at that *given* Income (Figure 3). Their intersection will determine the rate of interest which makes savings equal to investment at that level of income. This we may call the "investment rate."

If Income rises, the curve SS will move to the right; probably CC will move to the right too. If SS moves more than CC, the investment rate of interest will fall; if CC more than SS, it will rise. (How much it rises and falls, however, depends upon the elasticities of the CC and SS curves.)

The IS curve (drawn on a separate diagram) now shows the relation between Income and the corresponding investment rate of interest. It has to be confronted (as in our earlier constructions) with an LL curve showing the relation between Income and the "money" rate of interest; only we can now generalize our LL curve a little. Instead of assuming, as before, that the supply of money is given, we can assume that there is a given monetary system—that up to a point, but only up to a point, monetary authorities will prefer to create new money rather than allow interest rates to rise. Such a generalized LL curve will then slope upwards only gradually—the elasticity of the curve depending on the elasticity of the monetary system (in the ordinary monetary sense).

As before, Income and interest are determined where the IS and LL curves intersect—where the investment rate of interest equals the money rate. Any change in the inducement to invest or the propensity to consume will shift the *IS* curve; any change in liquidity preference or monetary policy will shift the *LL* curve. If, as the result of such a change, the investment rate is raised above the money rate, Income will tend to rise; in the opposite case, Income will tend to fall; the extent to which Income rises or falls depends on the elasticities of the curves.[8]

When generalized in this way, Mr. Keynes' theory begins to look very like Wicksell's; this is of course hardly surprising.[9] There is indeed one special case where it fits Wicksell's construction absolutely. If there is "full employment" in the sense that any rise in Income immediately calls forth a rise in money wage rates; then it is *possible* that the *CC* and *SS* curves may be moved to the right to exactly the same extent, so that *IS* is horizontal. (I say possible, because it is not unlikely, in fact, that the rise in the wage level may create a presumption that wages will rise again later on; if so, *CC* will probably be shifted more than *SS*, so that *IS* will be upward sloping.) However that may be, if *IS* is horizontal, we do have a perfectly Wicksellian construction;[10] the investment rate becomes Wicksell's *natural rate*, for in this case it may be

thought of as determined by real causes; if there is a perfectly elastic monetary system, and the money rate is fixed below the natural rate, there is cumulative inflation; cumulative deflation if it is fixed above.

This, however, is now seen to be only one special case; we can use our construction to harbour much wider possibilities. If there is a great deal of unemployment, it is very likely that $\partial C/\partial I$ will be quite small; in that case *IS* can be relied upon to slope downwards. This is the sort of Slump Economics with which Mr. Keynes is largely concerned. But one cannot escape the impression that there may be other conditions when expectations are tinder, when a slight inflationary tendency lights them up very easily. Then $\partial C/\partial I$ may be large and an increase in Income tends to *raise* the investment rate of interest. In these circumstances, the situation is unstable at *any* given money rate; it is only an imperfectly elastic monetary system— a rising *LL* curve—that can prevent the situation getting out of hand altogether.

These, then, are a few of the things we can get out of our skeleton apparatus. But even if it may claim to be a slight extension of Mr. Keynes' similar skeleton, it remains a terribly rough and ready sort of affair. In particular, the concept of "Income" is worked monstrously hard; most of our curves are not really determinate unless something is said about the distribution of Income as well as its magnitude. Indeed, what they express is something like a relation between the price-system and the system of interest rates; and you cannot get that into a curve. Further, all sorts of questions about depreciation have been neglected; and all sorts of questions about the timing of the processes under consideration.

The *General Theory of Employment* is a useful book; but it is neither the beginning nor the end of Dynamic Economics.

---

[8] Since $C(I, i) = S(I, i)$,

$$\frac{dI}{di} = - \frac{\partial S/\partial i - \partial C/\partial i}{\partial S/\partial I - \partial C/\partial I}.$$

The savings investment market will not be stable unless $\partial S/\partial i + (-\partial C/\partial i)$ is positive. I think we may assume that this condition is fulfilled.

If $\partial S/\partial i$ is positive, $\partial C/\partial i$ negative, $\partial S/\partial I$ and $\partial C/\partial I$ positive (the most probable state of affairs), we can say that the *IS* curve will be more elastic, the greater the elasticities of the *CC* and *SS* curves, and the larger is $\partial C/\partial I$ relatively to $\partial S/\partial I$. When $\partial C/\partial I > \partial S/\partial I$, the *IS* curve is upward sloping.

[9] Cf. Keynes, *General Theory*, p. 242.

[10] Cf. Myrdal, "Gleichgewichtsbegriff," in *Beiträge zur Geldtheorie*, ed. Hayek.

11

The Quantity Theory
of Money—
A Restatement

MILTON FRIEDMAN

The quantity theory of money is a term evocative of a general approach rather than a label for a well-defined theory. The exact content of the approach varies from a truism defining the term "velocity" to an allegedly rigid and unchanging ratio between the quantity of money—defined in one way or another—and the price level— also defined in one way or another. Whatever its precise meaning, it is clear that the general approach fell into disrepute after the crash of 1929 and the subsequent Great Depression and only recently has been slowly re-emerging into professional respectability.

The present volume is partly a symptom of this re-emergence and partly a continuance of an aberrant tradition. Chicago was one of the few academic centers at

**

Reprinted from *Studies in the Quantity Theory of Money*, edited by Milton Friedman, pp. 3–21, by permission of The University of Chicago Press and author. Copyright 1956 by The University of Chicago.

Milton Friedman teaches at the University of Chicago.

which the quantity theory continued to be a central and vigorous part of the oral tradition throughout the 1930's and 1940's, where students continued to study monetary theory and to write theses on monetary problems. The quantity theory that retained this role differed sharply from the atrophied and rigid caricature that is so frequently described by the proponents of the new income-expenditure approach— and with some justice, to judge by much of the literature on policy that was spawned by quantity theorists. At Chicago, Henry Simons and Lloyd Mints directly, Frank Knight and Jacob Viner at one remove, taught and developed a more subtle and relevant version, one in which the quantity theory was connected and integrated with general price theory and became a flexible and sensitive tool for interpreting movements in aggregate economic activity and for developing relevant policy prescriptions.

To the best of my knowledge, no systematic statement of this theory as developed at Chicago exists, though much can be read between the lines of Simons' and Mints's writings. And this is as it should be, for the Chicago tradition was not a rigid system, an unchangeable orthodoxy, but a way of looking at things. It was a theoretical approach that insisted that money does matter—that any interpretation of short-term movements in economic activity is likely to be seriously at fault if it neglects monetary changes and repercussions and if it leaves unexplained why people are willing to hold the particular nominal quantity of money in existence.

The purpose of this introduction is not to enshrine—or, should I say, inter—a definitive version of the Chicago tradition. To suppose that one could do so would be inconsistent with that tradition itself. The purpose is rather to set down a particular "model" of a quantity theory in an attempt to convey the flavor of the oral tradition which nurtured the remaining essays in this volume [*i.e.*, in *Studies in the Quantity Theory of Money*]. In consonance with this purpose, I shall not attempt to be exhaustive or to give a full justification for every assertion.

1. The quantity theory is in the first instance a theory of the *demand* for money. It is not a theory of output, or of money income, or of the price level. Any statement about these variables requires combining the quantity theory with some specifications about the conditions of supply of money and perhaps about other variables as well.

2. To the ultimate wealth-owning units in the economy, money is one kind of asset, one way of holding wealth. To the productive enterprise, money is a capital good, a source of productive services that are combined with other productive services to yield the products that the enterprise sells. Thus the theory of the demand for money is a special topic in the theory of capital; as such, it has the rather unusual feature of combining a piece from each side of the capital market, the supply of

capital (points 3 through 8 that follow), and the demand for capital (points 9 through 12).

3. The analysis of the demand for money on the part of the ultimate wealth-owning units in the society can be made formally identical with that of the demand for a consumption service. As in the usual theory of consumer choice, the demand for money (or any other particular asset) depends on three major sets of factors: (*a*) the total wealth to be held in various forms—the analogue of the budget restraint; (*b*) the price of and return on this form of wealth and alternative forms; and (*c*) the tastes and preferences of the wealth-owning units. The substantive differences from the analysis of the demand for a consumption service are the necessity of taking account of intertemporal rates of substitution in (*b*) and (*c*) and of casting the budget restraint in terms of wealth.

4. From the broadest and most general point of view, total wealth includes all sources of "income" or consumable services. One such source is the productive capacity of human beings, and accordingly this is one form in which wealth can be held. From this point of view, "the" rate of interest expresses the relation between the stock which is wealth and the flow which is income, so if Y be the total flow of income, and r, "the" interest rate, total wealth is

$$W = \frac{Y}{r} \tag{1}$$

Income in this broadest sense should not be identified with income as it is ordinarily measured. The latter is generally a "gross" stream with respect to human beings, since no deduction is made for the expense of maintaining human productive capacity intact; in addition, it is affected by transitory elements that make it depart more or less widely from the theoretical concept of the stable level of consumption of services that could be maintained indefinitely.

5. Wealth can be held in numerous forms, and the ultimate wealth-owning unit is to be regarded as dividing his wealth among them (point [a] of 3), so as to maximize "utility" (point [c] of 3), subject to whatever restrictions affect the possibility of converting one form of wealth into another (point [b] of 3). As usual, this implies that he will seek an apportionment of his wealth such that the rate at which he *can* substitute one form of wealth for another is equal to the rate at which he is just willing to do so. But this general proposition has some special features in the present instance because of the necessity of considering flows as well as stocks. We can suppose all wealth (except wealth in the form of the productive capacity of human beings) to be expressed in terms of monetary units at the prices of the point of time in question. The rate at which one form can be substituted for another is then simply $1.00 worth for $1.00 worth, regardless of the forms involved. But this is clearly not a complete description, because the holding of one form of wealth instead of another involves a difference in the composition of the income stream, and it is essentially these differences that are fundamental to the "utility" of a particular structure of wealth. In consequence, to describe fully the alternative combinations of forms of wealth that are available to an individual, we must take account not only of their market prices—which except for human wealth can be done simply by expressing them in units worth $1.00—but also of the form and size of the income streams they yield.

It will suffice to bring out the major issues that these considerations raise to consider five different forms in which wealth can be held: (i) money (M), interpreted as claims or commodity units that are generally accepted in payment of debts at a fixed nominal value; (ii) bonds (B),

interpreted as claims to time streams of payments that are fixed in nominal units; (iii) equities (E), interpreted as claims to stated pro-rata shares of the returns of enterprises; (iv) physical non-human goods (G); and (v) human capital (H). Consider now the yield of each.

(i) Money may yield a return in the form of money, for example, interest on demand deposits. It will simplify matters, however, and entail no essential loss of generality, to suppose that money yields its return solely in kind, in the usual form of convenience, security, etc. The magnitude of this return in "real" terms per nominal unit of money clearly depends on the volume of goods that unit corresponds to, or on the general price level, which we may designate by P. Since we have decided to take $1.00 worth as the unit for each form of wealth, this will be equally true for other forms of wealth as well, so P is a variable affecting the "real" yield of each.

(ii) If we take the "standard" bond to be a claim to a perpetual income stream of constant nominal amount, then the return to a holder of the bond can take two forms: one, the annual sum he receives—the "coupon"; the other, any change in the price of the bond over time, a return which may of course be positive or negative. If the price is expected to remain constant, then $1.00 worth of a bond yields r_b per year, where r_b is simply the "coupon" sum divided by the market price of the bond, so $1/r_b$ is the price of a bond promising to pay $1.00 per year. We shall call r_b the market bond interest rate. If the price is expected to change, then the yield cannot be calculated so simply, since it must take account of the return in the form of expected appreciation or depreciation of the bond, and it cannot, like r_b, be calculated directly from market prices (so long, at least, as the "standard" bond is the only one traded in).

The nominal income stream purchased for $1.00 at time zero then consists of

$$r_b(0) + r_b(0) \, d \, \frac{\left(\dfrac{1}{r_b(t)} \right)}{dt}$$

$$= r_b(0) - \frac{r_b(0)}{r_b^2(t)} \cdot \frac{dr_b(t)}{dt} \quad (2)$$

where t stands for time. For simplicity, we can approximate this functional by its value at time zero, which is

$$r_b - \frac{1}{r_b} \frac{dr_b}{dt} \quad (3)$$

This sum, together with P already introduced, defines the real return from holding $1.00 of wealth in the form of bonds.

(iii) Analogously to our treatment of bonds, we may take the "standard" unit of equity to be a claim to a perpetual income stream of constant "real" amount; that is, to be a standard bond with a purchasing-power escalator clause, so that it promises a perpetual income stream equal in nominal units to a constant number times a price index, which we may, for convenience, take to be the same price index P introduced in (i).[1] The nominal return to the holder of the equity can then be regarded as taking three forms: the constant nominal amount he would receive per year in the absence of any change in P; the increment or decrement to this nominal amount to adjust for changes in P; and any change in the nominal price of the equity over time, which may of course arise from changes either in interest rates or in price levels. Let r_e be the market interest rate on equities defined analogously to r_b, namely, as the ratio of the "coupon" sum at any time (the first two items above) to the price of the equity, so $1/r_e$ is the price of

[1] This is an oversimplification, because it neglects "leverage" and therefore supposes that any monetary liabilities of an enterprise are balanced by monetary assets.

an equity promising to pay $1.00 per year if the price level does not change, or to pay

$$\frac{P(t)}{P(0)} \cdot 1$$

if the price level varies according to $P(t)$. If $r_e(t)$ is defined analogously, the price of the bond selling for $1/r_e(0)$ at time 0 will be

$$\frac{P(t)}{P(0)r_e(t)}$$

at time t, where the ratio of prices is required to adjust for any change in the price level. The nominal stream purchased for $1.00 at time zero then consists of

$$r_e(0) \cdot \frac{P(t)}{P(0)} + \frac{r_e(0)}{P(0)} \cdot d \, \frac{\left[\dfrac{P(t)}{r_e(t)} \right]}{dt}$$

$$= r_e(0) \cdot \frac{P(t)}{P(0)} + \frac{r_e(0)}{r_e(t)} \cdot \frac{1}{P(0)} \cdot \frac{dP(t)}{dt}$$

$$- \frac{P(t)}{P(0)} \cdot \frac{r_e(0)}{r_e^2(t)} \cdot \frac{dr_e(t)}{dt} \quad (4)$$

Once again we can approximate this functional by its value at time zero, which is

$$r_e + \frac{1}{P} \frac{dP}{dt} - \frac{1}{r_e} \frac{dr_e}{dt} \quad (5)$$

This sum, together with P already introduced, defines the "real" return from holding $1.00 of wealth in the form of equities.

(iv) Physical goods held by ultimate wealth-owning units are similar to equities except that the annual stream they yield is in kind rather than in money. In terms of nominal units, this return, like that from equities, depends on the behavior of prices. In addition, like equities, physical goods must be regarded as yielding a nominal return in the form of appreciation or depreciation in money value. If we suppose the price level P, introduced earlier, to apply equally to the value of these physical goods, then, at time zero,

$$\frac{1}{P}\frac{dP}{dT} \qquad (6)$$

is the size of this nominal return per $1.00 of physical goods.[2] Together with P, it defines the "real" return from holding $1.00 in the form of physical goods.

(v) Since there is only a limited market in human capital, at least in modern non-slave societies, we cannot very well define in market prices the terms of substitution of human capital for other forms of capital and so cannot define at any time the physical unit of capital corresponding to $1.00 of human capital. There are some possibilities of substituting non-human capital for human capital in an individual's wealth holdings, as, for example, when he enters into a contract to render personal services for a specified period in return for a definitely specified number of periodic payments, the number not depending on his being physically capable of rendering the services. But, in the main, shifts between human capital and other forms must take place through direct investment and disinvestment in the human agent, and we may as well treat this as if it were the only way. With respect to this form of capital, therefore, the restriction or obstacles affecting the alternative compositions of wealth available to the individual cannot be expressed in terms of market prices or rates of return. At any one point in time there is some division between human and non-human wealth in his portfolio of assets; he may be able to

change this over time, but we shall treat it as given at a point in time. Let w be the ratio of non-human to human wealth or, equivalently, of income from non-human wealth to income from human wealth, which means that it is closely allied to what is usually defined as the ratio of wealth to income. This is, then, the variable that needs to be taken into account so far as human wealth is concerned.

6.   The tastes and preferences of wealth-owning units for the service streams arising from different forms of wealth must in general simply be taken for granted as determining the form of the demand function.   In order to give the theory empirical content, it will generally have to be supposed that tastes are constant over significant stretches of space and time. However, explicit allowance can be made for some changes in tastes in so far as such changes are linked with objective circumstances. For example, it seems reasonable that, other things the same, individuals want to hold a larger fraction of their wealth in the form of money when they are moving around geographically or are subject to unusual uncertainty than otherwise.   This is probably one of the major factors explaining a frequent tendency for money holdings to rise relative to income during wartime.   But the extent of geographic movement, and perhaps of other kinds of uncertainty, can be represented by objective indexes, such as indexes of migration, miles of railroad travel, and the like. Let u stand for any such variables that can be expected to affect tastes and preferences (for "utility" determining variables).

7.   Combining 4, 5, and 6 along the lines suggested by 3 yields the following demand function for money:

[2] In principle, it might be better to let P refer solely to the value of the services of physical goods, which is essentially what it refers to in the preceding cases, and to allow for the fact that the prices of the capital goods themselves must vary also with the rate of capitalization, so that the prices of services and their sources vary at the same rate only if the relevant interest rate is constant. I have neglected this refinement for simplicity; the neglect can perhaps be justified by the rapid depreciation of many of the physical goods held by final wealth-owning units.

$$M = f\left(P, r_b - \frac{1}{r_b}\frac{dr_b}{dt}, r_e + \frac{1}{P}\frac{dP}{dt}\right.$$

$$\left. - \frac{1}{r_e}\frac{dr_e}{dt}, \frac{1}{P}\frac{dP}{dt}; w; \frac{Y}{r}; u\right) \qquad (7)$$

A number of observations are in order about this function.

(i) Even if we suppose prices and rates of interest unchanged, the function contains three rates of interest: two for specific types of assets, r_b and r_e, and one intended to apply to all types of assets, r. This general rate, r, is to be interpreted as something of a weighted average of the two special rates plus the rates applicable to human wealth and to physical goods. Since the latter two cannot be observed directly, it is perhaps best to regard them as varying in some systematic way with r_b and r_e. On this assumption, we can drop r as an additional explicit variable, treating its influence as fully taken into account by the inclusion of r_b and r_e.

(ii) If there were no differences of opinion about price movements and interest-rate movements, and bonds and equities were equivalent except that the former are expressed in nominal units, arbitrage would of course make

$$r_b - \frac{1}{r_b}\frac{dr_b}{dt} = r_e + \frac{1}{P}\frac{dP}{dt} - \frac{1}{r_e}\frac{dr_e}{dt} \quad (8)$$

or, if we suppose rates of interest either stable or changing at the same percentage rate,

$$r_b = r_e + \frac{1}{P}\frac{dP}{dt} \quad (9)$$

that is, the "money" interest rate equal to the "real" rate plus the percentage rate of change of prices. In application the rate of change of prices must be interpreted as an "expected" rate of change and differences of opinion cannot be neglected, so we cannot suppose (9) to hold; indeed, one of the most consistent features of inflation seems to be that it does not.[3]

(iii) If the range of assets were to be widened to include promises to pay specified sums for a finite number of time units—"short-term" securities as well as

[3] See Reuben Kessel, "Inflation: Theory of Wealth Distribution and Application in Private Investment Policy" (unpublished doctoral dissertation, University of Chicago).

"consols"—the rates of change of r_b and r_e would be reflected in the difference between long and short rates of interest. Since at some stage it will doubtless be desirable to introduce securities of different time duration (see point 23 below), we may simplify the present exposition by restricting it to the case in which r_b and r_e are taken to be stable over time. Since the rate of change in prices is required separately in any event, this means that we can replace the cumbrous variables introduced to designate the nominal return on bonds and equities simply by r_b and r_e.

(iv) Y can be interpreted as including the return to all forms of wealth, including money and physical capital goods owned and held directly by ultimate wealth-owning units, and so Y/r can be interpreted as an estimate of total wealth, only if Y is regarded as including some imputed income from the stock of money and directly owned physical capital goods. For monetary analysis the simplest procedure is perhaps to regard Y as referring to the return to all forms of wealth other than the money held directly by ultimate wealth-owning units, and so Y/r as referring to total remaining wealth.

8. A more fundamental point is that, as in all demand analyses resting on maximization of a utility function defined in terms of "real" magnitudes, this demand equation must be considered independent in any essential way of the nominal units used to measure money variables. If the unit in which prices and money income are expressed is changed, the amount of money demanded should change proportionately. More technically, equation (7) must be regarded as homogeneous of the first degree in P and Y, so that

$$f\left(\lambda P, r_b, r_e, \frac{1}{P}\frac{dP}{dt} ; w; \lambda Y; u\right)$$
$$= \lambda f\left(P, r_b, r_e, \frac{1}{P}\frac{dP}{dt} ; w; Y; u\right) \quad (10)$$

where the variables within the parentheses have been rewritten in simpler form in accordance with comments 7 (i) and 7 (iii).

This characteristic of the function enables us to rewrite it in two alternative and more familiar ways.

(i) Let $\lambda = 1/P$. Equation (7) can then be written

$$\frac{M}{P} = f\left(r_b, r_e, \frac{1}{P}\frac{dP}{dt}; w; \frac{Y}{P}; u\right) \quad (11)$$

In this form the equation expresses the demand for real balances as a function of "real" variables independent of nominal monetary values.

(ii) Let $\lambda = 1/Y$. Equation (7) can then be written

$$\frac{M}{Y} = f\left(r_b, r_e, \frac{1}{P}\frac{dP}{dt}, w, \frac{P}{Y}, u\right)$$

$$= \frac{1}{v\left(r_b, r_e, \frac{1}{P}\frac{dP}{dt}, w, \frac{Y}{P}, u\right)} \quad (12)$$

or

$$Y = v\left(r_b, r_e, \frac{1}{P}\frac{dP}{dt}, w, \frac{Y}{P}, u\right) \cdot M \quad (13)$$

In this form the equation is in the usual quantity theory form, where v is income velocity.

9. These equations are, to this point, solely for money held directly by ultimate wealth-owning units. As noted, money is also held by business enterprises as a productive resource. The counterpart to this business asset in the balance sheet of an ultimate wealth-owning unit is a claim other than money. For example, an individual may buy bonds from a corporation, and the corporation use the proceeds to finance the money holdings which it needs for its operations. Of course, the usual difficulties of separating the accounts of the business and its owner arise with unincorporated enterprises.

10. The amount of money that it pays business enterprises to hold depends, as for any other source of productive services, on the cost of the productive services, the cost of substitute productive services, and the value product yielded by the productive service. Per dollar of money held, the cost depends on how the corresponding capital is raised—whether by raising additional capital in the form of bonds or equities, by substituting cash for real capital goods, etc. These ways of financing money holdings are much the same as the alternative forms in which the ultimate wealth-owning unit can hold its non-human wealth, so that the variables r_b, r_e, P, and $(1/P)(dP/dt)$ introduced into (7) can be taken to represent the cost to the business enterprise of holding money. For some purposes, however, it may be desirable to distinguish between the rate of return received by the lender and the rate paid by the borrower; in which case it would be necessary to introduce an additional set of variables.

Substitutes for money as a productive service are numerous and varied, including all ways of economizing on money holdings by using other resources to synchronize more closely payments and receipts, reduce payment periods, extend use of book credit, establish clearing arrangements, and so on in infinite variety. There seem no particularly close substitutes whose prices deserve to be singled out for inclusion in the business demand for money.

The value product yielded by the productive services of money per unit of output depends on production conditions: the production function. It is likely to be especially dependent on features of production conditions affecting the smoothness and regularity of operations as well as on those determining the size and scope of enterprises, degree of vertical integration, etc. Again there seem no variables that deserve to be singled out on the present level of abstraction for special attention; these factors can be taken into account by interpreting u as including variables affecting not only the tastes of wealth-owners but also the relevant technological conditions of production. Given the amount of money demanded per unit of output, the total amount demanded is proportional to total output, which can be represented by Y.

11. One variable that has traditionally been singled out in considering the demand for money on the part of business enterprises is the volume of transactions, or of transactions per dollar of final products; and, of course, emphasis on transactions has been carried over to the ultimate wealth-owning unit as well as to the business enterprise. The idea that renders this approach attractive is that there is a mechanical link between a dollar of payments per unit time and the average stock of money required to effect it—a fixed technical coefficient of production, as it were. It is clear that this mechanical approach is very different in spirit from the one we have been following. On our approach, the average amount of money held per dollar of transactions is itself to be regarded as a resultant of an economic equilibrating process, not as a physical datum. If, for whatever reason, it becomes more expensive to hold money, then it is worth devoting resources to effecting money transactions in less expensive ways or to reducing the volume of transactions per dollar of final output. In consequence, our ultimate demand function for money in its most general form does not contain as a variable the volume of transactions or of transactions per dollar of final output; it contains rather those more basic technical and cost conditions that affect the costs of conserving money, be it by changing the average amount of money held per dollar of transactions per unit time or by changing the number of dollars of transactions per dollar of final output. This does not, of course, exclude the pos-

sibility that, for a particular problem, it may be useful to regard the transactions variables as given and not to dig beneath them and so to include the volume of transactions per dollar of final output as an explicit variable in a special variant of the demand function.

Similar remarks are relevant to various features of payment conditions, frequently described as "institutional conditions," affecting the velocity of circulation of money and taken as somehow mechanically determined—such items as whether workers are paid by the day, or week, or month; the use of book credit; and so on. On our approach these, too, are to be regarded as resultants of an economic equilibrating process, not as physical data. Lengthening the pay period, for example, may save bookkeeping and other costs to the employer, who is therefore willing to pay somewhat more than in proportion for a longer than a shorter pay period; on the other hand, it imposes on employees the cost of holding larger cash balances or providing substitutes for cash, and they therefore want to be paid more than in proportion for a longer pay period. Where these will balance depends on how costs vary with length of pay period. The cost to the employee depends in considerable part on the factors entering into his demand curve for money for a fixed pay period. If he would in any event be holding relatively large average balances, the additional costs imposed by a lengthened pay period tend to be less than if he would be holding relatively small average balances, and so it will take less of an inducement to get him to accept a longer pay period. For given cost savings to the employer, therefore, the pay period can be expected to be longer in the first case than in the second. Surely, the increase in the average cash balance over the past century in this country that has occurred for other reasons has been a factor producing a lengthening of pay periods and not the other way around. Or, again, experience in hyperinflations shows how rapidly payment practices change under the impact of drastic changes in the cost of holding money.

12. The upshot of these considerations is that the demand for money on the part of business enterprises can be regarded as expressed by a function of the same kind as equation (7), with the same variables on the right-hand side. And, like (7), since the analysis is based on informed maximization of returns by enterprises, only "real" quantities matter, so it must be homogeneous of the first degree in Y and P. In consequence, we can interpret (7) and its variants (11) and (13) as describing the demand for money on the part of a business enterprise as well as on the part of an ultimate wealth-owning unit, provided only that we broaden our interpretation of u.

13. Strictly speaking, the equations (7), (11), and (13) are for an individual wealth-owning unit or business enterprise. If we aggregate (7) for all wealth-owning units and business enterprises in the society, the result, in principle, depends on the distribution of the units by the several variables. This raises no serious problem about P, r_b, and r_e, for these can be taken as the same for all, or about u, for this is an unspecified portmanteau variable to be filled in as the occasion demands. We have been interpreting $(1/P)(dP/dt)$ as the expected rate of price rise, so there is no reason why this variable should be the same for all, and w and Y clearly differ substantially among units. An approximation is to neglect these difficulties and take (7) and the associated (11) and (13) as applying to the aggregate demand for money, with $(1/P)(dP/dt)$ interpreted as some kind of an average expected rate of change of prices, w as the ratio of total income from non-human wealth to income from human wealth, and Y as aggregate income. This is the procedure that has generally been followed, and it seems the

right one until serious departures between this linear approximation and experience make it necessary to introduce measures of dispersion with respect to one or more of the variables.

14. It is perhaps worth noting explicitly that the model does not use the distinction between "active balances" and "idle balances" or the closely allied distinction between "transaction balances" and "speculative balances" that is so widely used in the literature. The distinction between money holdings of ultimate wealth-owners and of business enterprises is related to this distinction but only distantly so. Each of these categories of money-holders can be said to demand money partly from "transaction" motives, partly from "speculative" or "asset" motives, but dollars of money are not distinguished according as they are said to be held for one or the other purpose. Rather, each dollar is, as it were, regarded as rendering a variety of services, and the holder of money as altering his money holdings until the value to him of the addition to the total flow of services produced by adding a dollar to his money stock is equal to the reduction in the flow of services produced by subtracting a dollar from each of the other forms in which he holds assets.

15. Nothing has been said above about "banks" or producers of money. This is because their main role is in connection with the supply of money rather than the demand for it. Their introduction does, however, blur some of the points in the above analysis: the existence of banks enables productive enterprises to acquire money balances without raising capital from ultimate wealth-owners. Instead of selling claims (bonds or equities) to them, it can sell its claims to banks, getting "money" in exchange: in the phrase that was once so common in textbooks on money, the bank coins specific liabilities into generally acceptable liabilities. But

this possibility does not alter the preceding analysis in any essential way.

16. Suppose the supply of money in nominal units is regarded as fixed or more generally autonomously determined. Equation (13) then defines the conditions under which this nominal stock of money will be the amount demanded. Even under these conditions, equation (13) alone is not sufficient to determine money income. In order to have a complete model for the determination of money income, it would be necessary to specify the determinants of the structure of interest rates, of real income, and of the path of adjustment in the price level. Even if we suppose interest rates determined independently—by productivity, thrift, and the like—and real income as also given by other forces, equation (13) only determines a unique equilibrium level of money income if we mean by this the level at which prices are stable. More generally, it determines a time path of money income for given initial values of money income.

In order to convert equation (13) into a "complete" model of income determination, therefore, it is necessary to suppose either that the demand for money is highly inelastic with respect to the variables in v or that all these variables are to be taken as rigid and fixed.

17. Even under the most favorable conditions, for example, that the demand for money is quite inelastic with respect to the variables in v, equation (13) gives at most a theory of money income: it then says that changes in money income mirror changes in the nominal quantity of money. But it tells nothing about how much of any change in Y is reflected in real output and how much in prices. To infer this requires bringing in outside information, as, for example, that real output is at its feasible maximum, in which case any increase in money would produce the same or a larger percentage increase in prices; and so on.

18. In light of the preceding exposition, the question arises what it means to say that someone is or is not a "quantity theorist." Almost every economist will accept the general lines of the preceding analysis on a purely formal and abstract level, although each would doubtless choose to express it differently in detail. Yet there clearly are deep and fundamental differences about the importance of this analysis for the understanding of short- and long-term movements in general economic activity. This difference of opinion arises with respect to three different issues: (i) the stability and importance of the demand function for money; (ii) the independence of the factors affecting demand and supply; and (iii) the form of the demand function or related functions.

(i) The quantity theorist accepts the empirical hypothesis that the demand for money is highly stable—more stable than functions such as the consumption function that are offered as alternative key relations. This hypothesis needs to be hedged on both sides. On the one side, the quantity theorist need not, and generally does not, mean that the real quantity of money demanded per unit of output, or the velocity of circulation of money, is to be regarded as numerically constant over time; he does not, for example, regard it as a contradiction to the stability of the demand for money that the velocity of circulation of money rises drastically during hyperinflations. For the stability he expects is in the functional relation between the quantity of money demanded and the variables that determine it, and the sharp rise in the velocity of circulation of money during hyperinflations is entirely consistent with a stable functional relation, as Cagan so clearly demonstrates in his essay. On the other side, the quantity theorist must sharply limit, and be prepared to specify explicitly, the variables that it is empirically important to include in the function. For to expand the number of variables regarded as significant is to empty the hypothesis of its empirical content; there is indeed little if any difference between asserting that the demand for money is highly unstable and asserting that it is a perfectly stable function of an indefinitely large number of variables.

The quantity theorist not only regards the demand function for money as stable; he also regards it as playing a vital role in determining variables that he regards as of great importance for the analysis of the economy as a whole, such as the level of money income or of prices. It is this that leads him to put greater emphasis on the demand for money than on, let us say, the demand for pins, even though the latter might be as stable as the former. It is not easy to state this point precisely, and I cannot pretend to have done so. (See item [iii] below for an example of an argument against the quantity theorist along these lines.)

The reaction against the quantity theory in the 1930's came largely, I believe, under this head. The demand for money, it was asserted, is a will-o'-the-wisp, shifting erratically and unpredictably with every rumor and expectation; one cannot, it was asserted, reliably specify a limited number of variables on which it depends. However, although the reaction came under this head, it was largely rationalized under the two succeeding heads.

(ii) The quantity theorist also holds that there are important factors affecting the supply of money that do not affect the demand for money. Under some circumstances these are technical conditions affecting the supply of specie; under others, political or psychological conditions determining the policies of monetary authorities and the banking system. A stable demand function is useful precisely in order to trace out the effects of changes in supply, which means that it is useful only if supply is affected by at least some factors other than those regarded as affecting demand.

The classical version of the objection under this head to the quantity theory is the so-called real-bills doctrine: that changes in the demand for money call forth corresponding changes in supply and that supply cannot change otherwise, or at least cannot do so under specified institutional arrangements. The forms which this argument takes are legion and are still widespread. Another version is the argument that the "quantity theory" cannot "explain" large price rises, because the price rise produced both the increase in demand for nominal money holdings and the increase in supply of money to meet it; that is, implicitly that the same forces affect both the demand for and the supply of money, and in the same way.

(iii) The attack on the quantity theory associated with the Keynesian underemployment analysis is based primarily on an assertion about the form of (7) or (11). The demand for money, it is said, is infinitely elastic at a "small" positive interest rate. At this interest rate, which can be expected to prevail under underemployment conditions, changes in the real supply of money, whether produced by changes in prices or in the nominal stock of money, have no effect on anything. This is the famous "liquidity trap." A rather more complex version involves the shape of other functions as well: the magnitudes in (7) other than "the" interest rate, it is argued, enter into other relations in the economic system and can be regarded as determined there; the interest rate does not enter into these other functions; it can therefore be regarded as determined by this equation. So the only role of the stock of money and the demand for money is to determine the interest rate.

19. The proof of this pudding is in the eating; and the essays in this book [*i.e.*, in *Studies in the Quantity Theory of Money*] contain much relevant food, of which I may perhaps mention three particularly juicy items.

One cannot read Lerner's description of the effects of monetary reform in the Confederacy in 1864 without recognizing that at least on occasion the supply of money can be a largely autonomous factor and the demand for money highly stable even under extraordinarily unstable circumstances.   After three years of war, after widespread destruction and military reverses, in the face of impending defeat, a monetary reform that succeeded in reducing the stock of money halted and reversed for some months a rise in prices that had been going on at the rate of 10 percent a month most of the war! It would be hard to construct a better controlled experiment to demonstrate the critical importance of the supply of money.

On the other hand, Klein's examination of German experience in World War II is much less favorable to the stability and importance of the demand for money. Though he shows that defects in the figures account for a sizable part of the crude discrepancy between changes in the recorded stock of money and in recorded prices, correction of these defects still leaves a puzzlingly large discrepancy that it does not seem possible to account for in terms of the variables introduced into the above exposition of the theory. Klein examined German experience precisely because it seemed the most deviant on a casual examination.   Both it and other wartime experience will clearly repay further examination.

Cagan's examination of hyperinflations is another important piece of evidence on the stability of the demand for money under highly unstable conditions. It is also an interesting example of the difference between a numerically stable velocity and a stable functional relation: the numerical value of the velocity varied enormously during the hyperinflations, but this was a predictable response to the changes in the expected rate of changes of prices.

20.   Though the essays in this book [*i.e.*, in *Studies in The Quantity Theory of Money*] contain evidence relevant to the issues discussed in point 18, this is a by-product rather than their main purpose, which is rather to add to our tested knowledge about the characteristics of the demand function for money. In the process of doing so, they also raise some questions about the theoretical formulation and suggest some modifications it might be desirable to introduce. I shall comment on a few of those without attempting to summarize at all fully the essays themselves.

21.   Selden's material covers the longest period of time and the most "normal" conditions. This is at once a virtue and a vice—a virtue, because it means that his results may be applicable most directly to ordinary peacetime experience; a vice, because "normality" is likely to spell little variation in the fundamental variables and hence a small base from which to judge their effect. The one variable that covers a rather broad range is real income, thanks to the length of the period. The secular rise in real income has been accompanied by a rise in real cash balances per unit of output—a decline in velocity—from which Selden concludes that the income elasticity of the demand for real balances is greater than unity—cash balances are a "luxury" in the terminology generally adopted. This entirely plausible result seems to be confirmed by evidence for other countries as well.

22.   Selden finds that for cyclical periods velocity rises during expansions and falls during contractions, a result that at first glance seems to contradict the secular result just cited.   However, there is an alternative explanation entirely consistent with the secular result. It will be recalled that Y was introduced into equation (7) as an index of wealth. This has important implications for the measure or concept of income that is relevant. What is required

by the theoretical analysis is not usual measured income—which in the main corresponds to current receipts corrected for double counting—but a longer term concept, "expected income," or what I have elsewhere called "permanent income."[4] Now suppose that the variables in the v function of (13) are unchanged for a period. The ratio of Y to M would then be unchanged, provided Y is *permanent* income. Velocity as Selden computes it is the ratio of *measured* income to the stock of money and would not be unchanged. When measured income was above permanent income, measured velocity would be relatively high, and conversely. Now measured income is presumably above permanent income at cyclical peaks and below permanent income at cyclical troughs. The observed positive conformity of measured velocity to cyclical changes of income may therefore reflect simply the difference between measured income and the concept relevant to equation (13).

23. Another point that is raised by Selden's work is the appropriate division of wealth into forms of assets. The division suggested above is, of course, only suggestive. Selden finds more useful the distinction between "short-term" and "long-term" bonds; he treats the former as "substitutes for money" and calls the return on the latter "the cost of holding money." He finds both to be significantly related to the quantity of money demanded. It was suggested above that this is also a way to take into account expectations about changes in interest rates.

Similarly, there is no hard-and-fast line between "money" and other assets, and for some purposes it may be desirable to distinguish between different forms of "money" (e.g., between currency and deposits). Some of these forms of money may pay interest or may involve service charges, in which case the positive or negative return will be a relevant variable in determining the division of money holdings among various forms.

24. By concentrating on hyperinflations, Cagan was able to bring into sharp relief a variable whose effect is generally hard to evaluate, namely, the rate of change of prices. The other side of this coin is the necessity of neglecting practically all the remaining variables. His device for estimating expected rates of change of prices from actual rates of change, which works so well for his data, can be carried over to other variables as well and so is likely to be important in fields other than money. I have already used it to estimate "expected income" as a determinant of consumption,[5] and Gary Becker has experimented with using this "expected income" series in a demand function for money along the lines suggested above (in point 22).

Cagan's results make it clear that changes in the rate of change of prices, or in the return to an alternative form of holding wealth, have the expected effect on the quantity of money demanded: the higher the rate of change of prices, and thus the more attractive the alternative, the less the quantity of money demanded. This result is important not only directly but also because it is indirectly relevant to the effect of changes in the returns to other alternatives, such as rates of interest on various kinds of bonds. Our evidence on these is in some way less satisfactory because they have varied over so much smaller a range; tentative findings that the effect of changes in them is in the expected direction are greatly strengthened by Cagan's results.

[4] See Milton Friedman, *A Theory of the Consumption Function*, forthcoming publication of the Princeton University Press for the National Bureau of Economic Research.

[5] See *ibid.*

One point which is suggested by the inapplicability of Cagan's relations to the final stages of the hyperinflations he studies is that it may at times be undesirable to replace the whole expected pattern of price movements by the rate of change expected at the moment, as Cagan does and as is done in point 5 above. For example, a given rate of price rise, expected to continue, say, for only a day, and to be followed by price stability, will clearly mean a higher (real) demand for money than the same rate of price rise expected to continue indefinitely; it will be worth incurring greater costs to avoid paying the latter than the former price. This is the same complication as occurs in demand analysis for a consumer good when it is necessary to include not only the present price but also past prices or future expected prices. This point may help explain not only Cagan's findings for the terminal stages but also Selden's findings that the inclusion of the rate of change of prices as part of the cost of holding money worsened rather than improved his estimated relations, though it may be that this result arises from a different source, namely, that it takes substantial actual rates of price change to produce firm enough and uniform enough expectations about price behavior for this variable to play a crucial role.

Similar comments are clearly relevant for expected changes in interest rates.

25. One of the chief reproaches directed at economics as an allegedly empirical science is that it can offer so few numerical "constants," that it has isolated so few fundamental regularities. The field of money is the chief example one can offer in rebuttal: there is perhaps no other empirical relation in economics that has been observed to recur so uniformly under so wide a variety of circumstances as the relation between substantial changes over short periods in the stock of money and in prices; the one is invariably linked with the other and is in the same direction; this uniformity is, I suspect, of the same order as many of the uniformities that form the basis of the physical sciences. And the uniformity is in more than direction. There is an extraordinary empirical stability and regularity to such magnitudes as income velocity that cannot but impress anyone who works extensively with monetary data. This very stability and regularity contributed to the downfall of the quantity theory, for it was overstated and expressed in unduly simple form; the numerical value of the velocity itself, whether income or transactions, was treated as a natural "constant." Now this it is not; and its failure to be so, first during and after World War I and then, to a lesser extent, after the crash of 1929, helped greatly to foster the reaction against the quantity theory. The studies in this volume [*i.e.*, in *Studies in the Quantity Theory of Money*] are premised on a stability and regularity in monetary relations of a more sophisticated form than a numerically constant velocity. And they make, I believe, an important contribution toward extracting this stability and regularity, toward isolating the numerical "constants" of monetary behavior. It is by this criterion at any rate that I, and I believe also their authors, would wish them to be judged.

I began this Introduction by referring to the tradition in the field of money at Chicago and to the role of faculty members in promoting it. I think it is fitting to end the Introduction by emphasizing the part which students have played in keeping that tradition alive and vigorous. The essays that follow are one manifestation. Unpublished doctoral dissertations on money are another. In addition, I wish especially to express my own personal appreciation to the students who have participated with me in the Workshop in

Money and Banking, of which this volume is the first published fruit. I owe a special debt to David I. Fand, Phillip Cagan, Gary Becker, David Meiselman, and Raymond Zelder, who have at various times helped me to conduct it.

We all of us are indebted also to the Rockefeller Foundation for financial assistance to the Workshop in Money and Banking. This assistance helped to finance some of the research reported in this book and has made possible its publication.*

* [With the second edition of this volume, Professor Friedman has added the following bibliographical note:

For further and more recent developments in this field, reference may be made to some of my papers in *The Optimum Quantity of Money and Other Essays* (Aldine Publishing Company, 1969) and *Dollars and Deficits* (Prentice-Hall, Inc., 1968).—*Ed.*]

12

The Role of Money
in Keynesian Theory

LAWRENCE S. RITTER

In recent years it has frequently been asserted, primarily by Quantity theorists, that the main characteristic of Keynesian theory is that "money does not matter."[1] The view that "money matters" is held to be the exclusive province of the Quantity theory, and extensive statistical tests are thereupon conducted to demonstrate that the supply of money has had an important influence on the level of economic activity. On this basis, Keynesian theory is, *ipso facto*, declared fallacious.

The purpose of this essay is to examine carefully the role of money in Keynesian theory, in order to evaluate the thesis that

❋ ❋

Reprinted from Deane Carson (ed.), *Banking and Monetary Studies*, sponsored by the U.S. Comptroller of the Currency (Homewood, Illinois: Richard D. Irwin, Inc., 1963), pp. 134–150, by permission of the publisher and author.

Lawrence S. Ritter teaches at New York University.

[1] See, for example, Milton Friedman's statements in *Studies in the Quantity Theory of Money* (Chicago: University of Chicago Press, 1956), p. 3 [reprinted in this volume, pp. 146–147]; *Employment, Growth, and Price Levels*, Hearings before the Joint Economic Committee, U.S. Congress, 1959, pp. 606–7; and *A Program for Monetary Stability* (New York: Fordham University Press, 1960), p. 1.

in the Keynesian system "money does not matter." It turns out that the validity of this point of view depends in large part on which version of Keynesian theory one has in mind, just as the validity of many Keynesian criticisms of the Quantity theory depends on which version of the latter one has in mind.

I. KEYNES WITHOUT MONEY

The most familiar version of Keynesian economics, which we will call Model A, is the elementary simplification of Keynes in which the only determinants of the level of national income are the consumption function and a given volume of investment (including government) spending. Consumption spending is seen as depending mainly upon income, and investment spending is assumed to be given, determined autonomously. Occasionally, in order to include an accelerator effect, investment spending may also be made to depend partly upon income. Within this context, the equilibrium level of national income is found where realized income, resulting from consumption plus investment expenditures, equals anticipated income, on the basis of which spending decisions are made. Alternatively, equilibrium income is that level of income at which planned investment equals planned saving.

It is this simplified model which has been popularized by the widely known "Keynesian cross" diagram, in which either consumption and investment or saving and investment are plotted on the vertical axis, and anticipated income is plotted on the horizontal axis. Equilibrium income is determined where aggregate demand equals anticipated income or, alternatively, where planned investment equals planned saving.[2] This particular analytical system has also been the basis for the bulk of orthodox Keynesian multiplier theory: a sustained increase in autonomous spending is assumed to raise equilibrium income by a multiple of the initial increment in spending. The specific value of the multiplier is determined solely by the size of the marginal propensity to consume. Such an uncomplicated formula for the value of the multiplier can only be derived from an equally uncomplicated frame of reference, such as that outlined above.[3] For if the value of the multiplier depends solely on the size of the marginal propensity to consume, it must be assumed, implicitly or explicitly, that spending is insensitive to such increases in interest rates and tightening of credit availability as would normally accompany an expansion in income.

On the basis of this model, countless public policy recommendations, dealing almost exclusively with the implications of alternative fiscal policies, have been ad-

[2] This has been a standard textbook diagram for well over a decade. See Paul A. Samuelson, *Economics* (5th ed.; New York: McGraw-Hill Book Co., Inc., 1961), chap. xiii, or Abba P. Lerner, *Economics of Employment* (New York: McGraw-Hill Book Co., Inc., 1951), chap. v.

[3] See Paul A. Samuelson, "The Simple Mathematics of Income Determination," in *Income, Employment, and Public Policy* (New York: W. W. Norton & Co., Inc., 1948), pp. 133–55 [reprinted in this volume, Selection 3]; and L. S. Ritter, "Some Monetary Aspects of Multiplier Theory and Fiscal Policy," *Review of Economic Studies*, Vol. XXIII, No. 2 (1956), pp. 126–31.

vanced over the years in the name of Keynesian economics. In this scheme of things, the Quantity theory's characterization of the Keynesian system as one in which "money does not matter" is quite accurate: national income is determined without any reference whatsoever to either the supply of or the demand for money, and public policy prescriptions are confined to the area of fiscal policy. Monetary policy is completely extraneous. That this model evidently commands considerable allegiance, even today, is attested to by the great amount of attention paid in 1962 and 1963 to alternative forms of tax reduction, and to the size of the resulting budget deficit, as compared with the relative lack of interest in how such a deficit should be financed, i.e., whether by monetary creation or otherwise.

II. KEYNES WITH MONEY

Although Model A is probably the most popular version of Keynesian economics, it is not the same economics to be found in Keynes' *The General Theory of Employment, Interest, and Money*. As far as Keynes himself was concerned, and as the title of his major work indicates, money plays a significant role in the determination of income and employment. Let us call the orthodox Keynesian system, as advanced in *The General Theory* and much subsequent literature, Model B.

Most important, Keynes did not assume that investment spending is exogenous, a given datum, but rather that it depends on relationships *within* the system, namely on comparisons between the expected rate of profit and the rate of interest. The rate of interest, in turn, depends on the supply of and demand for money. The demand for money, or liquidity preference, is viewed as consisting of two parts, the demand for idle money balances (with the amount demanded increasing as the rate of interest falls) and the demand for active or transaction balances (with the amount demanded increasing as the level of income rises).

In contrast to the partial Keynesian system, represented by Model A, the complete Keynesian system, Model B, requires that *two* conditions be fulfilled before income can be said to be in equilibrium. Not only must planned investment equal planned saving, as before, but in addition at any moment in time the amount of money people want to hold must equal the supply of money, the amount that is available for them to hold.   If the second condition is not satisfied, the rate of interest will rise or fall, thereby altering the volume of investment and consequently changing the equilibrium level of income.[4]

If, at a given interest rate and income, planned investment equals planned saving but the amount of money desired exceeds (falls short of) the supply, the interest rate will rise (fall), thereby reducing (increasing) investment spending and lowering (raising) the level of income. As the interest rate rises, the desired amount of idle balances contracts, and as income falls the desired amount of active balances contracts, until the amount of money demanded is reduced to the point where it is equal to the given supply.   Thus, the equilibrium level of income eventually is reached, with both planned investment equal to planned saving and the demand for money equal to the supply, but the interest rate is now higher and income now lower than initially postulated.

Here there is room for monetary policy to operate: if the monetary authorities want to prevent upward pressure on the interest rate, and the consequent drop in income, they can increase the supply of money enough to satisfy the demand at the initial interest rate and income level. On the other hand, if they want to permit money income to fall, they can sit back and let nature take its course. Both of these are rather passive policies. More aggressive actions would call for increasing the money supply even more than enough to satisfy the initial demand, in order to stimulate an increase in income rather than merely prevent a decrease; or actually reducing the money supply, even though it is already less than the demand, to provide added impetus to the decline in income.

It is obvious that a policy of doing nothing is but one alternative among a spectrum of possibilities. The Federal Reserve at times seems to suggest that those changes in interest rates which occur when the central bank is passive are none of its doing. It is implied that changes in interest rates which take place when the central bank is holding the money supply constant are solely the result of "free market forces," and are in some sense preferable to changes which result from more active monetary policies. But as long as interest rates could be different if the central bank did something rather than nothing, it follows that interest rates are what they are in part because the central bank prefers them that way.

All this does not mean that the monetary authorities are omnipotent. In the orthodox Keynesian system, monetary policy is important but not always in the same degree.   As a general principle, monetary policy is likely to be *less* effective the more interest-elastic the demand for idle balances (for then a change in the money supply will not succeed in altering the interest

---

[4] The diagrammatics of the complete Keynesian system thus are not contained in the "Keynesian cross," but rather in Hicks' *IS* and *LM* curves. See J. R. Hicks, "Mr. Keynes and the Classics; A Suggested Interpretation," *Econometrica*, Vol. V (1937), pp. 147–59, reprinted in *Readings in the Theory of Income Distribution* (Philadelphia: The Blakiston Co., 1946), pp. 461–76 [also reprinted in this volume, Selection 10]. Also see Alvin H. Hansen, *Monetary Theory and Fiscal Policy* (New York: McGraw-Hill Book Co., Inc., 1949), chap v, and his *A Guide to Keynes* (New York: McGraw-Hill Book Co., Inc., 1953), chap vii. For a concise exposition see Joseph P. McKenna, *Aggregate Economic Analysis* (New York: Holt, Rinehart & Winston, Inc., 1955), chap viii.

rate) and the less interest-elastic the investment and consumption schedules (for then a change in the interest rate will not induce a change in spending). This has typically been construed by most Keynesians to mean that monetary policy is likely to be less effective in combating depression than in stopping inflation. In a severe depression, the public may prefer to hold additional amounts of money at low interest rates rather than lend it out or buy securities, so that the rate of interest may reach a floor below which it will not fall; investment prospects may appear so bleak that reductions in interest rates become of negligible importance; and job prospects may appear so dismal that consumer spending on durable goods is severely inhibited, despite such additions to the public's wealth as are brought about by expanding the stock of money.

In formal Keynesian terms, during severe depressions the interest-elasticity of liquidity preference may become so great as to prevent increases in the supply of money from reducing the interest rate, as they normally would. And investment and consumer spending may become so unresponsive to changes in interest rates and in wealth as to preclude what would be expected to be their normal reactions. In terms of the equation of exchange, $MV = PT$, increases in the money supply would be offset by proportionate reductions in the velocity of money. Under such circumstances, money again "does not matter" in the Keynesian system, in the sense that increases in the money supply beyond a certain point will not affect the volume of spending, and for all practical purposes we are back in the world of Model A above.

It is important to realize, however, that severe depression is only a special case in the general Keynesian system. And even then, *decreases* in the money supply would not be looked upon as trivial. In other instances, the supply of money may be of crucial importance. From the beginning,

for example, it has been a basic tenet of Keynesian doctrine that inflation cannot proceed very far without an increase in the supply of money. Rising incomes are seen as leading to larger demands for transactions balances, which in the absence of increases in the money supply must be drawn from formerly idle balances, inducing a rise in interest rates. This process can continue until idle balances are depleted, or perhaps somewhat further if there is some interest-elasticity in the demand for active balances at high interest rates. But, unless the money supply is increased, the expansion in spending is viewed as having to grind to a halt before too long, because rising interest rates and tightening monetary conditions in general will sooner or later choke off investment spending.[5] Indeed, so strongly has this position been held by some orthodox Keynesians that they have at times objected to the use of monetary policy to stop inflation because of the fear that it is likely to be *too* effective.[6] In brief, in the orthodox Keynesian system sometimes the supply of money is not very important, sometimes it is critically important, and most of the time it is somewhere in between, depending in each instance on the circumstances at hand.

It is rather ironic that Keynes should be the target of a blanket charge by Quantity theorists that he is responsible for propagating the view that "money does not

---

[5] "A rise in prices and incomes leads to an increase in requirements for money balances in active circulation. This tends to reduce the amount available for inactive balances and so causes the rate of interest to rise, which checks investment. The rope which holds the value of money is a limitation on its supply. If the monetary authorities are compelled to increase the supply of money, the rope frays and snaps in their hands." Joan Robinson, *Essays in the Theory of Employment* (Macmillan, 1937), pp. 17–21 (spliced quotation). Also see J. R. Hicks, *op. cit.*, p. 470 [pp. 142–143 in this volume].

[6] See Alvin H. Hansen, *Monetary Theory and Fiscal Policy*, pp. 161–63. For a closely related view see Keynes, *op. cit.*, pp. 322–23.

matter." For in Keynes' own mind he was enlarging the scope of monetary theory, not narrowing it.[7] Before Keynes, prevailing monetary theory in the form of the Quantity theory of money, had been concerned almost exclusively with the determination of the general level of prices, to the neglect of the influence of money on real output and employment. As expressed by Jean Bodin in 1569, through John Locke, David Hume, David Ricardo, John Stuart Mill, and Irving Fisher, the Quantity theory had always stressed that the supply of money determined primarily the absolute price level. The velocity of money was held to be an institutional datum and aggregate real output was assumed at the full employment level by virtue of Say's Law. In terms of the equation of exchange, $MV = PT$, V and T were assumed to be given so that changes in the money supply would result in proportionate changes in prices.[8]

The policy implications of the pre-Keynesian Quantity theory were simple and paralyzing. Increases in the supply of money, even in periods of substantial unemployment, could never achieve any permanent benefit. They could only be harmful, by raising prices proportionately —a view that is deeply imbedded in popular folklore to this day. It is this framework, rather than the Keynesian, which in a fundamental sense views money as

unimportant. Here money is seen as "neutral," a veil behind which "real" forces work themselves out just about as they would in the absence of money. In the Keynesian approach, on the other hand, money also plays a role in the determination of real output. For the first time money becomes more than merely a veil, and a monetary economy is seen as behaving very differently from a barter economy.

III. NEW DEPARTURES

Model C is a lineal descendant of Model B, but comes to rather different conclusions. Although Model C uses most of the orthodox Keynesian apparatus, it is so unorthodox in its handling of selected parts of that apparatus as to make it debatable whether it should be classified as a version of Keynesian theory. Perhaps it should be given a category of its own and called Radcliffism, since it has been most closely associated with the work of the Radcliffe Committee and Professors Gurley and Shaw.[9] In any case, in this model changes in the money supply are seen as no more likely to be effective against inflation than they were against depression in Model B!

The analysis of Model C differs from both previous models in that it does not ignore the liquidity preference function, as A does, nor does it stress the significance of its interest-elasticity, as B does. Rather than being ignored, the liquidity preference function is an integral part of Model C, *but the demand for liquidity is no longer viewed as identical with the demand for*

---

[7] See *The General Theory*, Preface, chap. xvii, and pp. 292–94. On this point see also Dudley Dillard, "The Theory of a Monetary Economy," in Kenneth Kurihara (ed.), *Post-Keynesian Economics* (New Brunswick, N.J.: Rutgers University Press, 1954), pp. 3–30.

[8] As expressed by Irving Fisher, in the most widely accepted pre-Keynesian statement of the Quantity theory: "Since a doubling in the quantity of money will not appreciably affect either the velocity of circulation or the volume of trade, it follows necessarily and mathematically that the level of prices must double. There is no possible escape from the conclusion that a change in the quantity of money must normally cause a proportional change in the price level." Irving Fisher, *The Purchasing Power of Money* (Macmillan, 1911), pp. 156–57 (spliced quotation).

[9] *Report* of the Committee on the Working of the Monetary System (London, 1959), and J. G. Gurley and E. S. Shaw, *Money in a Theory of Finance* (Washington, D.C.: The Brookings Institution, 1960). See also J. G. Gurley, *Liquidity and Financial Institutions in the Postwar Economy*, Study Paper 14, Joint Economic Committee, U.S. Congress (1960); R. S. Sayers, "Monetary Thought and Monetary Policy in England," *Economic Journal*, Vol. LXX, No. 280 (December, 1960), pp. 710–24; and A. B. Cramp, "Two Views on Money," *Lloyds Bank Review*, No. 65 (July, 1962), pp. 1–15.

money. And rather than stressing the importance of the interest-elasticity of the demand schedule for money, attention is directed instead to the likelihood of *shifts* in that schedule. While the orthodox Keynesian literature has a great deal to say about shifts in the investment demand function, through the influence of changes in expectations, it tends to ignore the possibility of shifts in the demand for money, and instead concentrates almost exclusively on its interest-elasticity.

In the orthodox Keynesian system, Model B, the demand for liquidity is synonymous with the demand for money. The ready availability of interest-yielding money substitutes, however, destroys that equation. Such near monies as time deposits, savings and loan shares, and Treasury bills are virtually as liquid as cash and in addition yield an interest return Thus, the demand for money (demand deposits plus currency) may contract even though the demand for liquidity broadly conceived remains stable. Liquidity preference, in other words, may be satisfied partially by holdings of money substitutes in place of money itself.

There are two reasons for the demand for money in the orthodox Keynesian system. In the first place, active money balances are needed for transactions purposes. The demand for active balances is assumed to bear a more or less constant ratio to income, so that an expansion in income will lead to a proportionate increase in the amount of active balances desired. In the second place, idle cash is demanded because of uncertainties regarding the future course of interest rates. Idle cash is held primarily because of the fear that interest rates might rise (bond prices fall), imposing capital losses on bondholders. This is the main reason why Keynes believed that the amount of idle cash desired would increase as the rate of interest falls.[10] The lower

[10] See *General Theory*, pp. 201–2. Also see Day and Beza, *Money and Income* (New York: Oxford University Press, Inc., 1960), pp. 17–20.

the rate of interest, the more it is likely to drop below what are considered "safe" or "normal" levels, leading to the expectation that its future course is likely to be upward, with consequent losses in capital values. Under such circumstances, it is prudent to get out of bonds and into a more liquid asset. In *The General Theory* the only liquid asset available is cash.

The existence of short-term money substitutes, however, provides an alternative to holding money for both of these purposes. With respect to *active* balances, there is no reason to assume that these need be held solely in the form of money. For immediate transactions purposes, there is little alternative to possessing the medium of exchange itself. But for payments scheduled for several months in the future, there are many assets available which can serve as a substitute for holding cash without diminishing liquidity, and which at the same time provide an interest income. Firms with scheduled payments to make at particular dates in the future can hold Treasury bills, sales finance company paper, or repurchase agreements with government securities dealers, for example—all of which can easily be arranged to come due when the cash is needed. The very purpose of tax anticipation bills is to fill just such a need. Similarly, households can hold time deposits, paying interest from date of deposit to date of withdrawal, pending anticipated payments. For possible emergencies, lines of credit can be arranged on a standby basis in place of holding idle cash.

Many other methods exist through which both households and business firms can economize on their average holdings of transactions cash without impairing their liquidity positions. Indeed, there is ample evidence that high short-term interest rates in the postwar period have stimulated the expenditure of considerable ingenuity in the economical management of cash balances, with consequent reductions in the required ratio of active money balances to income. To the extent that this is accomplished, an expansion in income will not lead to a proportionate increase in the amount of transactions cash desired.

With respect to *idle* balances, the existence of short-term money substitutes also provides an alternative to holding cash when it is feared that long-term interest rates might rise (bond prices fall). If it is thought that long-term rates are too low (bond prices too high) for safety, investors need not increase their holdings of idle cash to get liquidity, but instead can purchase Treasury bills or other interest-bearing liquid assets. With highly liquid money substitutes, the concept of a "safe" yield level is almost meaningless and the chance of suffering a capital loss close to nil; indeed, the very definition of a liquid asset is one which can be turned into cash on short notice with little or no loss in dollar value.

The concept of a "safe" yield level is crucial in decisions as to whether or not to buy *long-term* securities, because the existence of uncertainty regarding future long rates gives rise to the fear of taking substantial capital losses (or the hope of making capital gains). But the rationale behind buying *short-term* liquid assets is that if yields rise no loss need be suffered. The securities will mature shortly anyway, and thereby turn into cash at their face value. And, in any event, even if one has no choice but to dispose of them before maturity, the resulting capital losses (or gains) are likely to be small. Unlike long-terms, a rather large change in yields on short-term instruments involves but a small change in their price.[11]

In brief, the amount of money desired may not increase when the rate of interest falls, even though the amount of liquidity desired does increase. At least part of the accumulation of liquidity is likely to take the form of interest-bearing near monies instead of nonearning cash. In comparison with Model B, the demand for idle cash balances will have contracted throughout the range of interest rates, even though the liquidity preference function may have remained stable. Under these circumstances, with both segments of the demand for money susceptible to leftward shifts, monetary policies confined to regulating the supply of money are not likely to be as successful in stemming inflation as orthodox Keynesian theory believes. Since the significant variable is not the supply of money, per se, but rather the supply relative to the demand, the flexibility of demand makes control of the supply, alone, an unreliable instrument through which to affect the level of economic activity. These results do not depend, as in orthodox Keynesian theory, on the short-run interest-elasticity of the demand for money, but rather on shifts in that demand.

In Model B, for example, if the economy is initially in equilibrium, with planned investment equal to planned saving and the demand for money equal to the supply, an exogenous increase in spending will raise money income and increase the amount of transactions cash desired proportionately. Limitation of the money supply—holding it constant—will then automatically result in an excess demand for money, which will

---

[11] A rise in yields from 4 percent to 5 percent on a $1000 face value 30-year bond bearing a 4 percent coupon involves a fall in price from $1000 to $845. A similar rise in yield on a 3-month security of similar coupon involves a fall in price from $1000 to only $997.

The point can be made even more dramatically. Assume, not too unrealistically, that at the extreme long-term yields on government securities might be expected to vary between 2 percent and 6 percent in the forseeable future, and short-term yields between 1 percent and 7 percent. The holder of a $1000 30-year bond bearing a 4 percent

coupon might then anticipate, at the extreme, that its price might possibly vary between the limits of $723 and $1450. For a 3-month security of similar coupon, however, the possible range of price variation would be only from $992 to $1008. In one case possible range of price variation is $727 on a $1000 security, and in the other case it is only $16. Safety of principal is tenuous in the former, and practically assured in the latter.

These figures can be calculated from any bond basis book. See also Burton G. Malkiel, "Expectations, Bond Prices, and the Term Structure of Interest Rates," *Quarterly Journal of Economics*, Vol. LXXVI, No. 2 (May, 1962), pp. 197–218.

raise interest rates, check investment, and thereby bring the expansion in income to a halt. There will probably be some slippage, as the rise in interest rates attracts some funds out of idle cash holdings into transactions balances, with the degree of slippage depending on the interest-elasticity of the demand for idle balances and the specific ratio between active cash and income. But that same rise in interest rates, and the related tightening of monetary conditions in general, will tend to discourage some expenditures. In any event, sooner or later idle balances will be depleted. If the monetary authorities want to accelerate the process, they can provide added impetus by actually reducing the money supply rather than merely holding it stable.

In the world envisaged by Model C, on the other hand, these results are not as likely to be realized. If the required ratio of transactions cash to income contracts as income rises, the expansion in income will not lead to a proportionate increase in the amount of active cash desired. It may not even lead to an absolute increase. Limitation of the money supply then may not produce very much of an excess demand for money, so that upward pressure on interest rates will be negligible, investment will not be checked, and the rise in spending will proceed unhindered. If, at the same time, the demand for idle balances has also shifted to the left, then— regardless of its interest-elasticity—formerly idle balances will become available for transactions use, again with minimal increases in interest rates. Instead of an excess demand for money, there might conceivably be an excess supply, with consequent *downward* pressure on interest rates. Even if the monetary authorities were to actually reduce the supply of money, they might be hard put to keep pace with the contraction in demand. And although idle balances must sooner or later be depleted, this will pose no obstacle to

the continued rise in spending if the desired active cash to income ratio continues to contract.

Of course, the process need not be this straightforward. Models B and C need not be mutually exclusive, but may be combined over several cycles. Interest rates may indeed rise during periods of cyclical expansion, especially if the expansion is vigorous, as spending increases more rapidly than can be accommodated by contractions in the demand schedules for money. However, rising interest rates are likely to stimulate new financial techniques for economizing on cash balances.[12] These techniques of cash management, introduced during periods of tight money, are not likely to be abandoned when rates recede in the subsequent recession. As a result, the contraction in the demand for money may not be clearly evident until the *next* upturn in business conditions. When that upturn comes, the supply of money may be more than ample to finance it, even though, by past standards, it would appear to be less than adequate. In effect, liquidity is accumulated during the recession, in the form of money substitutes instead of money, and is then released when needed to finance expenditures when economic activity revives.

Presumably, the central bank could always reduce the money supply drastically enough to counteract the decline in the demand for money, and thereby produce the results it wants. But with business prospects cloudy, as they generally are, and with past guidelines unreliable indicators of the current adequacy of the money supply, the monetary authorities are usually not sure enough of where they stand to

[12] See Hyman P. Minsky, "Central Banking and Money Market Changes," *Quarterly Journal of Economics*, Vol. LXXI, No. 2 (May, 1957), pp. 171–87; and L. S. Ritter, "The Structure of Financial Markets, Income Velocity, and the Effectiveness of Monetary Policy," *Schweizerische Zeitschrift für Volkswirtschaft und Statistik*, Vol. XCVIII, No. 3 (September, 1962), pp. 276–89.

take decisive action in *any* direction. This inaction is then rationalized by the invocation of moral principles, as ethical values are attributed to the determination of interest rates by "free market forces" and to "minimum intervention" in general.

It is for these reasons that Model C shifts attention away from the money supply narrowly defined to the significance of liquidity broadly conceived. Traditional monetary policy, which is confined to the control of the money supply, is seen as having to give way to a more broadly based liquidity policy if it is to successfully influence economic activity within the context of the present-day financial environment.[13] It is thus Radcliffe monetary theory, rather than orthodox Keynesian theory, which poses the most fundamental challenge to the modern Quantity theory of money.

IV. SUMMARY AND CONCLUSIONS

The differences between orthodox Keynesian theory (Model B), Radcliffe theory (Model C), and the modern Quantity theory of money can be summarized most conveniently in terms of their implications for the behavior of velocity. This simultaneously affords a comparison of their respective evaluations of the effectiveness of monetary policy. For if monetary policy is to be effective—i.e., if changes in the money supply are to produce changes in aggregate spending, and thus in income—then velocity must either remain more or less stable or else move in the same direction as the money supply.

If the phrase "money matters" is to have any operational meaning, it must imply the existence of such conditions. In terms of the equation of exchange, if changes in

M are to produce changes in MV and thus in PT, then V must necessarily remain rather stable or else reinforce the change in M. On the other hand, to the extent that velocity falls when the money supply is increased, or rises when the money supply is decreased, or changes in the absence of changes in the money supply, the effectiveness of monetary policy is correspondingly reduced. If these offsetting changes in velocity are so great that the influence of monetary policy is negligible, then "money does not matter." In between these two extremes lies a continuum of possibilities.

It should be noted that the modern Quantity theory is not precisely the same as the pre-Keynesian Quantity theory. As presented by Milton Friedman, the present-day version of the Quantity theory is no longer strictly an explanation of what determines the price level. Friedman uses the Quantity theory to explain major depressions as well as inflations, so that it is now, like the Keynesian approach, essentially a theory of income determination.[14]

In addition, Friedman accepts variations in velocity as consistent with the Quantity theory. Unlike Irving Fisher, Friedman does not view velocity as an institutional datum, nor as a numerical constant, but rather as a functional relationship in which the demand for money is a function of a number of variables within the system, such as interest rates, income, wealth, and

---

[13] In the words of the Radcliffe Report (paragraph 981, p. 337): "The factor which monetary policy should seek to influence or control is something that reaches far beyond what is known as 'the supply of money.' It is nothing less than the state of liquidity of the whole economy."

[14] In terms of the equation of exchange, T is no longer assumed as given by virtue of Say's Law, so that changes in the supply of money can affect output and employment as well as the price level. See Milton Friedman, "The Quantity Theory of Money—A Restatement," in *Studies in the Quantity Theory of Money* [reprinted in this volume, Selection 11], and Chapter 1 in *A Program for Monetary Stability*. Friedman prefers to view the Quantity theory as a theory of the demand for money rather than a theory of income determination, with the addition of the supply of money necessary before income can be determined. However, this is a purely semantic matter. In the same sense, neither is orthodox Keynesian theory a theory of income determination until the supply of money is given.

expected changes in the price level. Depending on movements in these variables, velocity may vary both cyclically and secularly. This also represents a major shift in emphasis by the Quantity theory in the direction of the Keynesian approach, wherein velocity has *always* been functionally related to such variables.

Nevertheless, the two are still rather far apart. In Friedman's view, under normal circumstances the demand-for-money function is so stable and inelastic that such changes in velocity as do occur will not be very bothersome. Velocity may fall somewhat when the money supply is increased, or rise somewhat when the money supply is decreased, or even change to some extent in the absence of changes in the money supply so as to produce minor fluctuations in income despite stability in the stock of money. But these changes in velocity are assumed to be small. Velocity is no longer seen as constant, but it *is* seen as fluctuating only very moderately.[15] Thus, changes

[15] In Friedman's words: "It is, of course, true that velocity varies over short periods of time. The fact of the matter, however, is that these variations are in general relatively small." *Monetary Policy and Management of the Public Debt*, Hearings before the Joint Economic Committee, U.S. Congress, 1952, p. 720. From the same source, p. 743: "Income velocity is a reasonably stable magnitude. It has been declining over the last century . . . however, the decline appears to have been rather gradual, and income velocity is relatively stable over short periods." From *Studies in the Quantity Theory of Money* (p. 21) [p. 159 in this volume]:

There is an extraordinary empirical stability and regularity to such magnitudes as income velocity that cannot but impress anyone who works extensively with monetary data. This very stability and regularity contributed to the downfall of the Quantity theory, for it was overstated and expressed in unduly simple form. The numerical value of velocity itself, whether income or transactions, was treated as a natural 'constant.' Now this it is not; and its failure to be so, first during and after World War I and then, to a lesser extent, after the crash of 1929, helped greatly to foster the reaction against the Quantity theory. The studies in this volume are premised on a stability and regularity in monetary relations of a more sophisticated form than a numerically constant velocity.

in velocity are not likely to appreciably offset changes in the money supply, and major fluctuations in income are not likely to take place in the absence of major fluctuations in the stock of money. As a result, the modern Quantity theory views monetary policy as highly effective. Aside from minor short-run fluctuations in income, monetary policy is seen as both necessary *and sufficient* for the attainment of economic stability.

Radcliffe monetary theory, on the other hand, looks upon monetary policy in a rather different light:

Though we do not regard the supply of money as an unimportant quantity, we view it as only part of the wider structure of liquidity in the economy. It is the whole liquidity position that is relevant to spending decisions, and our interest in the supply of money is due to its significance in the whole liquidity picture. The fact that spending is not limited by the amount of money in existence is sometimes argued by reference to the velocity of money. It is possible, for example, to demonstrate statistically that during the last few years the volume of spending has greatly increased while the supply of money has hardly changed: the velocity of money has increased. We have not made more use of this concept because we cannot find any reason for supposing, or any experience in monetary history indicating, that there is any limit to velocity.[16]

While the Quantity theory views traditional monetary policy as both necessary and sufficient, and Radcliffe views it as too narrowly conceived to be of much use, Keynesian theory lies in between these two extremes. Sometimes changes in velocity are seen as nullifying changes in the money supply, sometimes they are seen as reinforcing,[17] and most of the time they

[16] Radcliffe, *Report*, pp. 132–33.

[17] "In conditions like those of the last decade, it seems unwise to expect that induced changes in V will largely undo the effects of central bank operations; at times they could be reinforcing. The Radcliffe Report seems to me to give misleading impressions in this regard, whatever its other merits." Paul A. Samuelson, "Reflections on Monetary Policy," *Review of Economics and Statistics*, Vol. XLII, No. 3 (August, 1960), p. 268.

are seen as somewhere in between. The crucial determinants of the behavior of velocity in the orthodox Keynesian system are the interest and wealth-elasticities of the spending and liquidity preference functions, and these are likely to vary depending on the particular historical, institutional, and expectational circumstances at hand. Since velocity is not something the monetary authorities can depend upon, in the sense of being able to reliably anticipate its behavior, monetary policy emerges from the Keynesian system as usually necessary but rarely sufficient for the attainment of national economic objectives.

Although it is not the purpose of this paper to evaluate the implications of the empirical evidence, a brief look, in closing, at the postwar movements in velocity

would not be inappropriate. As Figure 1 indicates, velocity has fluctuated between an annual rate of 1.93 in the first quarter of 1946 and 3.87 in the fourth quarter of 1962.[18] Over the period as a whole, velocity has shown a marked upward trend, with fluctuations about that trend coinciding with cyclical fluctuations in general business conditions. Each cyclical peak in velocity has typically been accompanied by rising interest rates and other signs of monetary stringency, leading observers to believe that velocity could not rise much

[18] In the first quarter of 1963, the latest data available at the time of writing, velocity reached a post-1929 high of 3.88. It should be noted that with our present money supply of about $150 billion, even so small an absolute change in velocity as 0.1 would correspond to a change in gross national product of $15 billion.

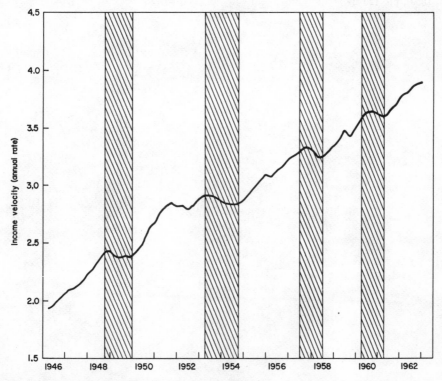

FIGURE 1. INCOME VELOCITY, QUARTERLY, 1946–1962.

Income velocity is the quotient of gross national product divided by the average money supply over the period, both seasonally adjusted. The money supply is defined as demand deposits, adjusted, plus currency outside banks. Shaded areas indicate periods of recession in general business conditions.

further, that it was close to its upper limit.[19] But then, after a slight decline during recession periods, velocity has promptly resumed its upward climb as soon as business conditions have turned up again. Not only has velocity risen to successively higher peaks from cycle to cycle, but in each period of business recovery it has equaled or exceeded its prior-cycle peak *within only two quarters* after recovery has begun.

How much higher can velocity rise? Recent levels of velocity, approaching a turnover rate of 4 times per annum, are comparable to previous peaks of 4 reached in 1919 and again in 1929. This has once again revived speculation that velocity is approaching its upper limit. However, as

[19] See, for example, L. S. Ritter, "Income Velocity and Anti-Inflationary Monetary Policy," *American Economic Review*, Vol. XLIX, No. 1 (March, 1959), pp. 120–29.

of late 1962 and early 1963, liquidity has appeared to be ample throughout the economy, no upward pressure has been evident on interest rates, and the money and capital markets have been characterized more by ease than by tightness. There is thus less evidence today that velocity is approaching a ceiling than there was six years ago, when velocity was around 3.3. Recent increases in velocity would appear to stem from a decrease in the demand for money, rather than a scarcity of supply, indicating that there is probably considerable room for further advance still remaining.

The "extraordinary empirical stability" that Quantity theorists find in the behavior of velocity is revealed only to the disciples. But whether the Radcliffe Report is correct, that for all practical purposes velocity has no upper limit whatsoever, remains to be seen.

13

Liquidity Preference as Behavior Towards Risk[1]

J. TOBIN

One of the basic functional relationships in the Keynesian model of the economy is the liquidity preference schedule, an inverse relationship between the demand for cash balances and the rate of interest. This aggregative function must be derived from some assumptions regarding the behavior of the decision-making units of the economy, and those assumptions are the concern of this paper. Nearly two decades of drawing downward-sloping liquidity preference curves in textbooks and on classroom blackboards should not blind us to the basic implausibility of the behavior they describe. Why should anyone hold the non-interest bearing obligations of the government instead of its interest bearing obligations? The apparent irrationality of holding cash is the same, moreover, whether the interest rate is 6 percent, 3 percent or $\frac{1}{2}$ of 1 percent. What needs to be explained is not only the existence of a demand for cash when its yield is less than the yield

❋ ❋

Reprinted from *The Review of Economic Studies*, vol. 25 (February 1958), pp. 65–86, by permission of the publisher and author.

J. Tobin teaches at Yale University.

[1] I am grateful to Challis Hall, Arthur Okun, Walter Salant, and Leroy Wehrle for helpful comments on earlier drafts of this paper.

on alternative assets but an inverse relationship between the aggregate demand for cash and the size of this differential in yields.[2]

1. TRANSACTIONS BALANCES AND INVESTMENT BALANCES

Two kinds of reasons for holding cash are usually distinguished: transactions reasons and investment reasons.

1.1 Transactions Balances: Size and Composition

No economic unit—firm or household or government—enjoys perfect synchronization between the seasonal patterns of its flow of receipts and its flow of expenditures.

[2] "... in a world involving no transaction friction and no uncertainty, there would be no reason for a spread between the yield on any two assets, and hence there would be no difference in the yield on money and on securities ... in such a world securities themselves would circulate as money and be acceptable in transactions; demand bank deposits would bear interest, just as they often did in this country in the period of the twenties." Paul A. Samuelson, *Foundations of Economic Analysis* (Cambridge: Harvard University Press, 1947), p. 123. The section, pp. 122–124, from which the passage is quoted makes it clear that liquidity preference must be regarded as an explanation of the existence and level not of the interest rate but of the differential between the yield on money and the yields on other assets.

The discrepancies give rise to balances which accumulate temporarily, and are used up later in the year when expenditures catch up. Or, to put the same phenomenon the other way, the discrepancies give rise to the need for balances to meet seasonal excesses of expenditures over receipts. These balances are *transactions balances*. The aggregate requirement of the economy for such balances depends on the institutional arrangements that determine the degree of synchronization between individual receipts and expenditures. Given these institutions, the need for transactions balances is roughly proportionate to the aggregate volume of transactions.

The obvious importance of these institutional determinants of the demand for transactions balances has led to the general opinion that other possible determinants, including interest rates, are negligible.[3] This may be true of the size of transactions balances, but the composition of transactions balances is another matter. Cash is by no means the only asset in which transactions balances may be held. Many transactors have large enough balances so that holding part of them in earning assets, rather than in cash, is a relevant possibility. Even though these holdings are always for short periods, the interest earnings may be worth the cost and inconvenience of the financial transactions involved. Elsewhere[4] I have shown that, for such transactors, the proportion of cash in trans-

actions balances varies inversely with the rate of interest; consequently this source of interest-elasticity in the demand for cash will not be further discussed here.

1.2 Investment Balances and Portfolio Decisions

In contrast to transactions balances, the investment balances of an economic unit are those that will survive all the expected seasonal excesses of cumulative expenditures over cumulative receipts during the year ahead. They are balances which will not have to be turned into cash within the year. Consequently the cost of financial transactions—converting other assets into cash and vice versa—does not operate to encourage the holding of investment balances in cash.[5] If cash is to have any part in the composition of investment balances, it must be because of expectations or fears of loss on other assets. It is here, in what Keynes called the speculative motives of investors, that the explanation of liquidity preference and of the interest-elasticity of the demand for cash has been sought.

The alternatives to cash considered, both in this paper and in prior discussions of the subject, in examining the speculative motive for holding cash are assets that differ from cash only in having a variable market yield. They are obligations to pay stated cash amounts at future dates, with no risk of default. They are, like cash, subject to changes in real value due to fluctuations in the price level. In a broader perspective, all these assets, including cash, are merely minor variants of the same species, a species we may call monetary assets—marketable, fixed in money value, free of default risk. The differences of members

---

[3] The traditional theory of the velocity of money has, however, probably exaggerated the invariance of the institutions determining the extent of lack of synchronization between individual receipts and expenditures. It is no doubt true that such institutions as the degree of vertical integration of production and the periodicity of wage, salary, dividend, and tax payments are slow to change. But other relevant arrangements can be adjusted in response to money rates. For example, there is a good deal of flexibility in the promptness and regularity with which bills are rendered and settled.

[4] "The Interest Elasticity of the Transactions Demand for Cash," *Review of Economics and Statistics*, vol. 38 (August 1956), pp. 241–247.

[5] Costs of financial transactions have the effect of deterring changes from the existing portfolio, whatever its composition; they may thus operate against the holding of cash as easily as for it. Because of these costs, the *status quo* may be optimal even when a different composition of assets would be preferred if the investor were starting over again.

of this species from each other are negligible compared to their differences from the vast variety of other assets in which wealth may be invested: corporate stocks, real estate, unincorporated business and professional practice, etc. The theory of liquidity preference does not concern the choices investors make between the whole species of monetary assets, on the one hand, and other broad classes of assets, on the other.[6] Those choices are the concern of other branches of economic theory, in particular theories of investment and of consumption. Liquidity preference theory takes as given the choices determining how much wealth is to be invested in monetary assets and concerns itself with the allocation of these amounts among cash and alternative monetary assets.

Why should any investment balances be held in cash, in preference to other monetary assets? We shall distinguish two possible sources of liquidity preference, while recognizing that they are not mutually exclusive. The first is inelasticity of expectations of future interest rates. The second is uncertainty about the future of interest rates. These two sources of liquidity preference will be examined in turn.

2. INELASTICITY OF INTEREST RATE EXPECTATIONS

2.1 Some Simplifying Assumptions

To simplify the problem, assume that there is only one monetary asset other than cash, namely consols. The current yield of consols is r per "year". $1 invested in consols today will purchase an income of $r per "year" in perpetuity. The yield of cash is assumed to be zero; however, this is not essential, as it is the current and expected differentials of consols over cash that matter. An investor with a given total

[6] For an attempt by the author to apply to this wider choice some of the same theoretical tools that are here used to analyze choices among the narrow class of monetary assets, see "A Dynamic Aggregative Model", *Journal of Political Economy*, vol. 63 (April 1955), pp. 103–115.

balance must decide what proportion of this balance to hold in cash, A_1, and what proportion in consols, A_2. This decision is assumed to fix the portfolio for a full "year".[7]

2.2 Fixed Expectations of Future Rate

At the end of the year, the investor expects the rate on consols to be r_e. This expectation is assumed, for the present, to be held with certainty and to be independent of the current rate r. The investor may therefore expect with certainty that every dollar invested in consols today will earn over the year ahead not only the interest $r, but also a capital gain or loss g:

$$g = \frac{r}{r_e} - 1 \qquad (2.1)$$

For this investor, the division of his balance into proportions A_1 of cash and A_2 of consols is a simple all-or-nothing choice. If the current rate is such that $r + g$ is greater than zero, then he will put everything in consols. But if $r + g$ is less than zero, he will put everything in cash. These conditions can be expressed in terms of a critical level of the current rate r_c, where:

$$r_c = \frac{r_e}{1 + r_e} \qquad (2.2)$$

[7] As noted above, it is the costs of financial transactions that impart inertia to portfolio composition. Every reconsideration of the portfolio involves the investor in expenditure of time and effort as well as of money. The frequency with which it is worth while to review the portfolio will obviously vary with the investor and will depend on the size of his portfolio and on his situation with respect to costs of obtaining information and engaging in financial transactions. Thus the relevant "year" ahead for which portfolio decisions are made is not the same for all investors. Moreover, even if a decision is made with a view to fixing a portfolio for a given period of time, a portfolio is never so irrevocably frozen that there are no conceivable events during the period which would induce the investor to reconsider. The fact that this possibility is always open must influence the investor's decision. The fiction of a fixed investment period used in this paper is, therefore, not a wholly satisfactory way of taking account of the inertia in portfolio composition due to the costs of transactions and of decision making.

At current rates above r_c, everything goes into consols; but for r less than r_c, everything goes into cash.

2.3 Sticky and Certain
Interest Rate Expectations

So far the investor's expected interest-rate r_e has been assumed to be completely independent of the current rate r. This assumption can be modified so long as some independence of the expected rate from the current rate is maintained. In Figure 1, for example, r_e is shown as a function of r, namely $\varphi(r)$. Correspondingly $r_e/1 + r_e$ is a function of r. As shown in the figure, this function $\varphi/1 + \varphi$ has only one intersection with the 45° line, and at this intersection its slope $\varphi'/(1 + \varphi)^2$ is less than one. If these conditions are met, the intersection determines a critical rate r_c such that if r exceeds r_c the investor holds no cash, while if r is less than r_c he holds no consols.

2.4 Differences of Opinion
and the Aggregate Demand for Cash

According to this model, the relationship of the individual's investment demand for cash to the current rate of interest would be the discontinuous step function shown by the heavy vertical lines $LMNW$ in Figure 2. How then do we get the familiar Keynesian liquidity preference function, a smooth, continuous inverse relationship between the demand for cash and the rate of interest? For the economy as a whole,

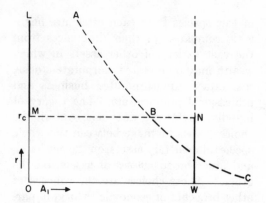

FIGURE 2. INDIVIDUAL DEMAND FOR CASH ASSUMING CERTAIN BUT INELASTIC INTEREST RATE EXPECTATIONS.

such a relationship can be derived from individual behavior of the sort depicted in Figure 2 by assuming that individual investors differ in their critical rates r_c. Such an aggregate relationship is shown in Figure 3.

At actual rates above the maximum of individual critical rates the aggregate demand for cash is zero, while at rates below the minimum critical rate it is equal to the total investment balances for the whole economy. Between these two extremes the demand for cash varies inversely with the rate of interest r. Such a relationship is shown as $LMN\Sigma W$ in Figure 3. The demand for cash at r is the total of investment balances controlled by investors whose critical rates r_c exceed r. Strictly speaking, the curve is a step function; but, if the number of investors is large, it

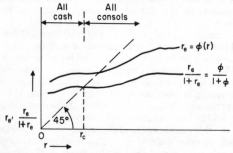

FIGURE 1. STICKINESS IN THE RELATION BETWEEN EXPECTED AND CURRENT INTEREST RATE.

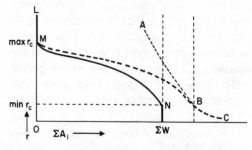

FIGURE 3. AGGREGATE DEMAND FOR CASH ASSUMING DIFFERENCES AMONG INDIVIDUALS IN INTEREST RATE EXPECTATIONS.

can be approximated by a smooth curve. Its shape depends on the distribution of dollars of investment balances by the critical rate of the investor controlling them; the shape of the curve in Figure 3 follows from a unimodal distribution.

2.5 Capital Gains or Losses and Open Market Operations

In the foregoing analysis the size of investment balances has been taken as independent of the current rate on consols r. This is not the case if there are already consols outstanding. Their value will depend inversely on the current rate of interest. Depending on the relation of the current rate to the previously fixed coupon on consols, owners of consols will receive capital gains or losses. Thus the investment balances of an individual owner of consols would not be constant at W but would depend on r in a manner illustrated by the curve ABC in Figure 2.[8] Similarly, the investment balances for the whole economy would follow a curve like ABC in Figure 3, instead of being constant at ΣW. The demand for cash would then be described by $LMBC$ in both figures. Correspondingly the demand for consols at any interest rate would be described by the horizontal distance between $LMBC$ and ABC. The value of consols goes to infinity as the rate of interest approaches zero; for this reason, the curve BC may never reach the horizontal axis. The size of investment balances would be bounded if the monetary assets other than cash consisted of bonds with definite maturities rather than consols.

According to this theory, a curve like $LMBC$ depicts the terms on which a central bank can engage in open-market opera-

tions, given the claims for future payments outstanding in the form of bonds or consols. The curve tells what the quantity of cash must be in order for the central bank to establish a particular interest rate. However, the curve will be shifted by open market operations themselves, since they will change the volume of outstanding bonds or consols. For example, to establish the rate at or below $min\ r_c$, the central bank would have to buy all outstanding bonds or consols. The size of the community's investment balances would then be independent of the rate of interest; it would be represented by a vertical line through, or to the right of, B, rather than the curve ABC. Thus the new relation between cash and interest would be a curve lying above LMB, of the same general contour as $LMN\Sigma W$.

2.6 Keynesian Theory and its Critics

I believe the theory of liquidity preference I have just presented is essentially the original Keynesian explanation. The *General Theory* suggests a number of possible theoretical explanations, supported and enriched by the experience and insight of the author. But the explanation to which Keynes gave the greatest emphasis is the notion of a "normal" long-term rate, to which investors expect the rate of interest to return. When he refers to uncertainty in the market, he appears to mean disagreement among investors concerning the future of the rate rather than subjective doubt in the mind of an individual investor.[9] Thus Kaldor's correction of

---

[8] The size of their investment balances, held in cash and consols may not vary by the full amount of these changes in wealth; some part of the changes may be reflected in holdings of assets other than monetary assets. But presumably the size of investment balances will reflect at least in part these capital gains and losses.

[9] J. M. Keynes, *The General Theory of Employment, Interest, and Money* (New York: Harcourt Brace, 1936), Chapters 13 and 15, especially pp. 168–172 and 201–203. One quotation from p. 172 will illustrate the point: "It is interesting that the stability of the system and its sensitiveness to changes in the quantity of money should be so dependent on the existence of a *variety* of opinion about what is uncertain. Best of all that we should know the future. But if not, then, if we are to control the activity of the economic system by changing the quantity of money, it is important that opinions should differ."

Keynes is more verbal than substantive when he says, "It is ... not so much the *uncertainty* concerning future interest rates as the *inelasticity* of interest expectations which is responsible for Mr. Keynes' 'liquidity preference function,' ..."[10]

Keynes' use of this explanation of liquidity preference as a part of his theory of underemployment equilibrium was the target of important criticism by Leontief and Fellner. Leontief argued that liquidity preference must necessarily be zero *in equilibrium*, regardless of the rate of interest. Divergence between the current and expected interest rate is bound to vanish as investors learn from experience; no matter how low an interest rate may be, it can be accepted as "normal" if it persists long enough. This criticism was a part of Leontief's general methodological criticism of Keynes, that unemployment was not a feature of equilibrium, subject to analysis by tools of static theory, but a phenomenon of disequilibrium requiring analysis by dynamic theory.[11] Fellner makes a similar criticism of the logical appropriateness of Keynes' explanation of liquidity preference for the purposes of his theory of underemployment equilibrium. Why, he asks, are interest rates the only variables to which inelastic expectations attach? Why don't wealth owners and others regard predepression price levels as "normal" levels to which prices will return? If they did, consumption and investment demand would respond to reductions in money wages and prices, no matter how strong and how elastic the liquidity preference of investors.[12]

[10] N. Kaldor, "Speculation and Economic Stability," *Review of Economic Studies*, vol. 7 (1939), p. 15.
[11] W. Leontief, "Postulates: Keynes' General Theory and the Classicists", Chapter XIX in S. Harris, editor, *The New Economics* (New York: Knopf, 1947), pp. 232–242. Section 6, pp. 238–239, contains the specific criticism of Keynes' liquidity preference theory.
[12] W. Fellner, *Monetary Policies and Full Employment* (Berkeley: University of California Press, 1946), p. 149.

These criticisms raise the question whether it is possible to dispense with the assumption of stickiness in interest rate expectations without losing the implication that Keynesian theory drew from it. Can the inverse relationship of demand for cash to the rate of interest be based on a different set of assumptions about the behavior of individual investors? This question is the subject of the next part of the paper.

3. UNCERTAINTY, RISK AVERSION, AND LIQUIDITY PREFERENCE

3.1 The Locus of Opportunity for Risk and Expected Return

Suppose that an investor is not certain of the future rate of interest on consols; investment in consols then involves a risk of capital gain or loss. The higher the proportion of his investment balance that he holds in consols, the more risk the investor assumes. At the same time, increasing the proportion in consols also increases his expected return. In the upper half of Figure 4, the vertical axis represents expected return and the horizontal axis risk. A line such as OC_1 pictures the fact that the investor can expect more return if he assumes more risk. In the lower half of Figure 4, the left-hand vertical axis measures the proportion invested in consols. A line like OB shows risk as proportional to the share of the total balance held in consols.

The concepts of expected return and risk must be given more precision.

The individual investor of the previous section was assumed to have, for any current rate of interest, a definite expectation of the capital gain or loss g (defined in expression (2.1) above) he would obtain by investing one dollar in consols. Now he will be assumed instead to be uncertain about g but to base his actions on his estimate of its probability distribution. This probability distribution, it will be assumed, has an expected value of zero and is independent of the level of r, the current rate on consols. Thus the investor considers a

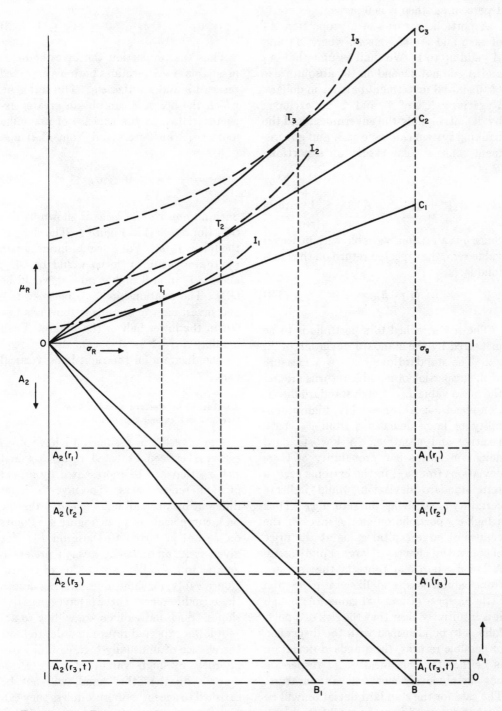

FIGURE 4.   PORTFOLIO SELECTION AT VARIOUS INTEREST RATES AND BEFORE AND
AFTER TAXATION.

doubling of the rate just as likely when rate is 5 percent as when it is 2 percent, and a halving of the rate just as likely when it is 1 percent as when it is 6 percent.

A portfolio consists of a proportion A_1 of cash and A_2 of consols, where A_1 and A_2 add up to 1. We shall assume that A_1 and A_2 do not depend on the absolute size of the initial investment balance in dollars. Negative values of A_1 and A_2 are excluded by definition; only the government and the banking system can issue cash and government consols. The return on a portfolio R is:

$$R = A_2(r + g) \qquad 0 \le A_2 \le 1 \quad (3.1)$$

Since g is a random variable with expected value zero, the expected return on the portfolio is:

$$E(R) = \mu_R = A_2 r \qquad (3.2)$$

The risk attached to a portfolio is to be measured by the standard deviation of R, σ_R. The standard deviation is a measure of the dispersion of possible returns around the mean value μ_R. A high standard deviation means, speaking roughly, high probability of large deviations from μ_R, both positive and negative. A low standard deviation means low probability of large deviations from μ_R; in the extreme case, a zero standard deviation would indicate certainty of receiving the return μ_R. Thus a high-σ_R portfolio offers the investor the chance of large capital gains at the price of equivalent chances of large capital losses. A low-σ_R portfolio protects the investor from capital loss, and likewise gives him little prospect of unusual gains. Although it is intuitively clear that the risk of a portfolio is to be identified with the dispersion of possible returns, the standard deviation is neither the sole measure of dispersion nor the obviously most relevant measure. The case for the standard deviation will be further discussed in section 3.3 below.

The standard deviation of R depends on the standard deviation of g, σ_g, and on the amount invested in consols:

$$\sigma_R = A_2 \sigma_g \qquad 0 \le A_2 \le 1 \quad (3.3)$$

Thus the proportion the investor holds in consols A_2 determines both his expected return μ_R and his risk σ_R. The terms on which the investor can obtain greater expected return at the expense of assuming more risk can be derived from (3.2) and (3.3):

$$\mu_R = \frac{r}{\sigma_g} \sigma_R \qquad 0 \le \sigma_R \le \sigma_g \quad (3.4)$$

Such an *opportunity locus* is shown as line OC_1 (for $r = r_1$) in Figure 4. The slope of the line is r_1/σ_g. For a higher interest rate r_2, the opportunity locus would be OC_2; and for r_3, a still higher rate, it would be OC_3. The relationship (3.3) between risk and investment in consols is shown as line OB in the lower half of the Figure. Cash holding $A_1(=1 - A_2)$ can also be read off the diagram on the right-hand vertical axis.

3.2 Loci of Indifference between Combinations of Risk and Expected Return

The investor is assumed to have preferences between expected return μ_R and risk σ_R that can be represented by a field of indifference curves. The investor is indifferent between all pairs (μ_R, σ_R) that lie on a curve such as I_1 in Figure 4. Points on I_2 are preferred to those on I_1; for given risk, an investor always prefers a greater to a smaller expectation of return. Conceivably, for some investors, *risk-lovers*, these indifference curves have negative slopes. Such individuals are willing to accept lower expected return in order to have the chance of unusually high capital gains afforded by high values of σ_R. *Risk-averters*, on the other hand, will not be satisfied to accept more risk unless they can also expect greater expected return. Their indifference curves will be positively sloped. Two kinds of risk-averters need to be distinguished. The first type, who may be called *diversifiers* for reasons that will become clear below, have indifference curves that are concave upward, like those in Figure 4. The second type, who may be called *plungers*, have indifference curves that are upward sloping, but either linear or convex upward.

3.3 Indifference Curves as Loci of Constant Expected Utility of Wealth

The reader who is willing to accept the indifference fields that have just been introduced into the analysis may skip to section 3.4 without losing the main thread of the argument. But these indifference curves need some explanation and defence. Indifference curves between μ_R and σ_R do not necessarily exist. It is a simplification to assume that the investor chooses among the alternative probability distributions of R available to him on the basis of only two parameters of those distributions. Even if this simplification is accepted, the mean and standard deviation may not be the pair of parameters that concern the investor.

3.3.1 One justification for the use of indifference curves between μ_R and σ_R would be that the investor evaluates the future of consols only in terms of some two-parameter family of probability distributions of g. For example, the investor might think in terms of a range of equally likely gains or losses, centered on zero. Or he might think in terms that can be approximated by a normal distribution. Whatever two-parameter family is assumed—uniform, normal, or some other—the whole probability distribution is determined as soon as the mean and standard deviation are specified. Hence the investor's choice among probability distributions can be analyzed by μ_R-σ_R indifference curves; any other pair of independent parameters could serve equally well.

If the investor's probability distributions are assumed to belong to some two-parameter family, the shape of his indifference curves can be inferred from the general characteristics of his utility-of-return function. This function will be assumed to relate utility to R, the percentage growth in the investment balance by the end of the period. This way of formulating the utility function makes the investor's indifference map, and therefore his choices of proportions of cash and consols, independent of the absolute amount of his initial balance.

On certain postulates, it can be shown that an individual's choice among probability distributions can be described as the maximization of the expected value of a utility function.[13] The ranking of probability distributions with respect to the expected value of utility will not be changed if the scale on which utility is measured is altered either by the addition of a constant or by multiplication by a positive constant. Consequently we are free to choose arbitrarily the zero and unit of measurement of the utility function $U(R)$ as follows: $U(0) = 0$; $U(-1) = -1$.

Suppose that the probability distribution of R can be described by a two-parameter density function $f(R; \mu_R, \sigma_R)$. Then the

---

[13] See Von Neumann, J. and Morgenstern, O., *Theory of Games and Economic Behavior*, 3rd Edition (Princeton: Princeton University Press, 1953), pp. 15–30, pp. 617–632; Herstein, I. N. and Milnor, J., "An Axiomatic Approach to Measurable Utility", *Econometrica*, vol. 23 (April 1953), pp. 291–297; Marschak, J., "Rational Behavior, Uncertain Prospects, and Measurable Utility", *Econometrica*, vol. 18 (April 1950), pp. 111–141; Friedman, M. and Savage, L. J., "The Utility Analysis of Choices Involving Risk", *Journal of Political Economy*, vol. 56 (August 1948), pp. 279–304, and "The Expected Utility Hypothesis and the Measurability of Utility", *Journal of Political Economy*, vol. 60 (December 1952), pp. 463–474. For a treatment which also provides an axiomatic basis for the subjective probability estimates here assumed, see Savage, L. J., *The Foundations of Statistics* (New York: Wiley, 1954).

expected value of utility is:

$$E[U(R)] = \int_{-\infty}^{\infty} U(R)f(R; \mu_R, \sigma_R) \, dR \quad (3.5)$$

Let $\qquad z = \dfrac{R - \mu_R}{\sigma_R}$

$$E[U(R)] = E(\mu_R, \sigma_R)$$
$$= \int_{-\infty}^{\infty} U(\mu_R + \sigma_R z)f(z; 0, 1) \, dz \quad (3.6)$$

An indifference curve is a locus of points (μ_R, σ_R) along which expected utility is constant. We may find the slope of such a locus by differentiating (3.6) with respect to σ_R:

$$0 = \int_{-\infty}^{\infty} U'(\mu_R + \sigma_R z)\left[\frac{d\mu_R}{d\sigma_R} + z\right]$$
$$\times f(z; 0, 1) \, dz$$

$$\frac{du_R}{d\sigma_R} = -\frac{\int_{-\infty}^{\infty} zU'(R)f(z; 0, 1) \, dz}{\int_{-\infty}^{\infty} U'(R)f(z; 0, 1) \, dz} \quad (3.7)$$

$U'(R)$, the marginal utility of return, is assumed to be everywhere non-negative. If it is also a decreasing function of R, then the slope of the indifference locus must be positive; an investor with such a utility function is a risk-averter. If it is an increasing function of R, the slope will be negative; this kind of utility function characterizes a risk-lover.

Similarly, the curvature of the indifference loci is related to the shape of the utility function. Suppose that (μ_R, σ_R) and (μ_R', σ_R') are on the same indifference locus, so that $E(\mu_R, \sigma_R) = E(\mu_R, \sigma_R)$. Is $[(\mu_R + \mu_R')/2, (\sigma_R + \sigma_R')/2]$ on the same locus, or on a higher or a lower one? In the case of declining marginal utility we know that for every z:

$$\tfrac{1}{2}U(\mu_R + \sigma_R z) + \tfrac{1}{2}U(\mu_R' + \sigma_R' z)$$

$$< U\left(\frac{\mu_R + \mu_R'}{2} + \frac{\sigma_R + \sigma_R'}{2}z\right)$$

Consequently $E[(\mu_R + \mu_R')/2, (\sigma_R + \sigma_R')/2]$

is greater than $E(\mu_R, \sigma_R)$ or $E(\mu_R', \sigma_R')$, and $[(\mu_R + \mu_R')/2, (\sigma_R + \sigma_R')/2]$, which lies on a line between (μ_R, σ_R) and (μ_R', σ_R'), is on a higher locus than those points. Thus it is shown that a risk-averter's indifference curve is necessarily concave upwards, provided it is derived in this manner from a two-parameter family of probability distributions and declining marginal utility of return. All risk-averters are diversifiers; plungers do not exist. The same kind of argument shows that a risk-lover's indifference curve is concave downwards.

3.3.2 In the absence of restrictions on the subjective probability distributions of the investor, the parameters of the distribution relevant to his choice can be sought in parametric restrictions on his utility-of-return function. Two parameters of the utility function are determined by the choice of the utility scale. If specification of the utility function requires no additional parameters, one parameter of the probability distribution summarizes all the information relevant for the investor's choice. For example, if the utility function is linear $[U(R) = R]$, then the expected value of utility is simply the expected value of R, and maximizing expected utility leads to the same behavior as maximizing return in a world of certainty. If, however, one additional parameter is needed to specify the utility function, then two parameters of the probability distribution will be relevant to the choice; and so on. Which parameters of the distribution are relevant depends on the form of the utility function.

Focus on the mean and standard deviation of return can be justified on the assumption that the utility function is quadratic. Following our conventions as to utility scale, the quadratic function would be:

$$U(R) = (1 + b)R + bR^2 \quad (3.8)$$

Here $0 < b < 1$ for a risk-lover, and

$-1 < b < 0$ for a risk-averter. However (3.8) cannot describe the utility function for the whole range of R, because marginal utility cannot be negative. The function given in (3.8) can apply only for:

$$(1 + b) + 2bR \geqq 0$$

that is, for:

$$R \geqq - \left(\frac{1 + b}{2b}\right) (b > 0) \quad \text{(Risk-lover)}$$
$$(3.9)$$
$$R \leqq - \left(\frac{1 + b}{2b}\right) (b < 0) \quad \text{(Risk-averter)}$$

In order to use (3.8), therefore, we must exclude from the range of possibility values of R outside the limits (3.9). At the maximum investment in consols ($A_2 = 1$), $R = r + g$. A risk-averter must be assumed therefore, to restrict the range of capital gains g to which he attaches nonzero probability so that, for the highest rate of interest r to be considered:

$$r + g \leqq - \left(\frac{1 + b}{2b}\right) \quad (3.10)$$

The corresponding limitation for a risk-lover is that, for the lowest interest rate r to be considered:

$$r + g \geqq - \left(\frac{1 + b}{2b}\right) \quad (3.11)$$

Given the utility function (3.8), we can investigate the slope and curvature of the indifference curves it implies. The probability density function for R, $f(R)$, is restricted by the limit (3.10) or (3.11); but otherwise no restriction on its shape is assumed.

$$E[U(R)] = \int_{-\infty}^{\infty} U(R)f(R)\,dR$$
$$= (1 + b)\mu_R + b(\sigma_R^2 + \mu_R^2)$$
$$(3.12)$$

Holding $E[U(R)]$ constant and differentiating with respect to σ_R to obtain the slope

of an indifference curve, we have:

$$\frac{d\mu_R}{d\sigma_R} = \frac{\sigma_R}{-\dfrac{1 + b}{2b} - \mu_R} \quad (3.13)$$

For a risk-averter, $-[(1 + b)/2b]$ is positive and is the upper limit for R, according to (3.9); $-[(1 + b)/2b]$ is necessarily larger than μ_R. Therefore the slope of an indifference locus is positive. For a risk-lover, on the other hand, the corresponding argument shows that the slope is negative.

Differentiating (3.13) leads to the same conclusions regarding curvature as the alternative approach of section 3.3.1, namely that a risk-averter is necessarily a diversifier.

$$\frac{d^2\mu_R}{d\sigma_{R^2}} = \frac{1 + \left(\dfrac{d\mu_R}{d\sigma_R}\right)^2}{-\dfrac{1 + b}{2b} - \mu_R} \quad (3.14)$$

For a risk-averter, the second derivative is positive and the indifference locus is concave upwards; for a risk-lover, it is concave downwards.

3.4 Effects of Changes in the Rate of Interest

In section 3.3 two alternative rationalizations of the indifference curves introduced in section 3.2 have been presented. Both rationalizations assume that the investor (1) estimates subjective probability distributions of capital gain or loss in holding consols, (2) evaluates his prospective increase in wealth in terms of a cardinal utility function, (3) ranks alternative prospects according to the expected value of utility. The rationalization of section 3.3.1 derives the indifference curves by restricting the subjective probability distributions to a two-parameter family. The rationalization of section 3.3.2 derives the indifference curves by assuming the utility function to be quadratic within the relevant range. On either rationalization, a risk-averter's indifference curves must be concave upwards, characteristic of the diversifiers of section 3.2, and those of a risk-lover concave downwards. If the category defined as *plungers* in 3.2 exists at all, their indifference curves must be determined by some process other than those described in 3.3.

The opportunity locus for the investor is described in 3.1 and summarized in equation (3.4). The investor decides the amount to invest in consols so as to reach the highest indifference curve permitted by his opportunity-locus. This maximization may be one of three kinds:

I. Tangency between an indifference curve and the opportunity locus, as illustrated by points T_1, T_2, and T_3 in Figure 4. A regular maximum of this kind can occur only for a risk-averter, and will lead to diversification. Both A_1, cash holding, and A_2, consol holding, will be positive. They too are shown in Figure 4, in the bottom half of the diagram, where, for example, $A_1(r_1)$ and $A_2(r_1)$ depict the cash and consol holdings corresponding to point T_1.

II. A corner maximum at the point $\mu_R = r, \sigma_R = \sigma_g$, as illustrated in Figure 5. In Figure 5 the opportunity locus is the ray OC, and point C represents the highest expected return and risk obtainable by the investor i.e. the expected return and risk from holding his entire balance in consols. A utility maximum at C can occur either

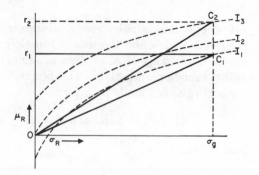

FIGURE 6. "PLUNGERS": OPTIMUM PORT-FOLIO AT MINIMUM OR MAXIMUM RISK AND EXPECTED RETURN.

for a risk-averter or for a risk-lover. I_1 and I_2 represent indifference curves of a diversifier; I_2 passes through C and has a lower slope, both at C and everywhere to the left of C, than the opportunity locus. I'_1 and I'_2 represent the indifference curves of a risk-lover, for whom it is clear that C is always the optimum position. Similarly, a plunger may, if his indifference curves stand with respect to his opportunity locus as in Figure 6 (OC_2) plunge his entire balance in consols.

III. A corner maximum at the origin, where the entire balance is held in cash. For a plunger, this case is illustrated in Figure 6 (OC_1). Conceivably it could also occur for a diversifier, if the slope of his indifference curve at the origin exceeded the slope of the opportunity locus. However, case III is entirely excluded for investors whose indifference curves represent the constant-expected-utility loci of section 3.3. Such investors, we have already noted, cannot be plungers. Furthermore, the slope of all constant-expected-utility loci at $\sigma_R = 0$ must be zero, as can be seen from (3.7) and (3.13).

We can now examine the consequences of a change in the interest rate r, holding constant the investor's estimate of the risk of capital gain or loss. An increase in the interest rate will rotate the opportunity locus OC to the left. How will this affect the investor's holdings of cash and consols?

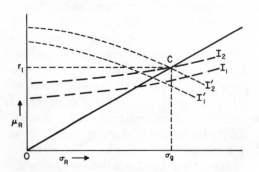

FIGURE 5. "RISK-LOVERS" AND "DIVERSI-FIERS": OPTIMUM PORTFOLIO AT MAXIMUM RISK AND EXPECTED RETURN.

We must consider separately the three cases.

I. In Figure 4, OC_1, OC_2, and OC_3 represent opportunity loci for successively higher rates of interest. The indifference curves I_1, I_2, and I_3 are drawn so that the points of tangency T_1, T_2, and T_3, correspond to successively higher holdings of consols A_2. In this diagram, the investor's demand for cash depends inversely on the interest rate.

This relationship is, of course, in the direction liquidity preference theory has taught us to expect, but it is not the only possible direction of relationship. It is quite possible to draw indifference curves so that the point of tangency moves left as the opportunity locus is rotated counterclockwise. The ambiguity is a familiar one in the theory of choice, and reflects the ubiquitous conflict between income and substitution effects. An increase in the rate of interest is an incentive to take more risk; so far as the substitution effect is concerned, it means a shift from security to yield. But an increase in the rate of interest also has an income effect, for it gives the opportunity to enjoy more security along with more yield. The ambiguity is analogous to the doubt concerning the effect of a change in the interest rate on saving; the substitution effect argues for a positive relationship, the income effect for an inverse relationship.

However, if the indifference curves are regarded as loci of constant expected utility, as derived in section 3.3, part of this ambiguity can be resolved. We have already observed that these loci all have zero slopes at $\sigma_R = 0$. As the interest rate r rises from zero, so also will consul holding A_2. At higher interest rates, however, the inverse relationship may occur.

This reversal of direction can, however, [be] virtually excluded in the case of the quadratic utility function (section 3.3.2). The condition for a maximum is that the slope of an indifference locus as given by

(3.13) equal the slope of the opportunity locus (3.4).

$$\frac{r}{\sigma_g} = \frac{A_2 \sigma_g}{-\dfrac{1+b}{2b} - A_2 r};$$

$$A_2 = \frac{r}{r^2 + \sigma_g^2}\left(-\frac{1+b}{2b}\right) \tag{3.15}$$

Equation (3.15) expresses A_2 as a function of r, and differentiating gives:

$$\frac{dA_2}{dr} = \frac{\sigma_g^2 - r^2}{(\sigma_g^2 + r^2)^2}\left(-\frac{1+b}{2b}\right); \tag{3.16}$$

$$\frac{r}{A_2}\frac{dA_2}{dr} = \frac{\sigma_g^2 - r^2}{\sigma_g^2 + r^2}$$

Thus the share of consols in the portfolio increases with the interest rate for r less than σ_g. Moreover, if r exceeds σ_g, a tangency maximum cannot occur unless r also exceeds g_{max}, the largest capital gain the investor conceives possible (see 3.10).[14] The demand for consols is less elastic at high interest rates than at low, but the elasticity is not likely to become negative. II and III. A change in the interest rate cannot cause a risk-lover to alter his position, which is already the point of maximum risk and expected yield. Conceivably a "diversifier" might move from a corner maximum to a regular interior maximum in response either to a rise in the interest rate or to a fall. A "plunger" might find

[14] For this statement and its proof, I am greatly indebted to my colleague Arthur Okun. The proof is as follows:
If $r^2 \geq \sigma_g^2$, then by (3.15) and (3.10):

$$1 \geq A_2 \geq \frac{r}{2r^2}\left(-\frac{1+b}{2b}\right) \geq \frac{1}{2r}(r + g_{max})$$

From the two extremes of this series of inequalities it follows that $2r \geq r + g_{max}$ or $r \geq g_{max}$. Professor Okun also points out that this condition is incompatible with a tangency maximum if the distribution of g is symmetrical. For then $r \geq g_{max}$ would imply $r + g_{min} \geq 0$. There would be no possibility of net loss of consols and thus no reason to hold any cash.

his position altered by an increase in the interest rate, as from r_1 to r_2 in Figure 6; this would lead him to shift his entire balance from cash to consols.

3.5 Effects of Changes in Risk

Investor's estimates σ_g of the risk of holding monetary assets other than cash, "consols," are subjective. But they are undoubtedly affected by market experience, and they are also subject to influence by measures of monetary and fiscal policy. By actions and words, the central bank can influence investors' estimates of the variability of interest rates; its influence on these estimates of risk may be as important in accomplishing or preventing changes in the rate as open-market operations and other direct interventions in the market. Tax rates, and differences in tax treatment of capital gains, losses, and interest earnings, affect in calculable ways the investor's risks and expected returns.   For these reasons it is worth while to examine the effects of a change in an investor's estimate of risk on his allocation between cash and consols.

In Figure 7, T_1 and $A_2(r_1, \sigma_g)$ represent the initial position of an investor, at interest rate r_1 and risk σ_g. OC_1 is the opportunity locus (3.4), and OB_1 is the risk-consols relationship (3.3). If the investor now cuts his estimate of risk in half, to $\sigma_g/2$, the opportunity locus will double in slope, from OC_1 to OC_2, and the investor will shift to point T_2.   The risk-consols relationship will have also doubled in slope, from OB_1 to OB_2.   Consequently point T_2 corresponds to an investment in consols of $A_2(r_1, \sigma_g/2)$.   This same point T_2 would have been reached if the interest rate had doubled while the investor's risk estimate σ_g remained unchanged.   But in that case, since the risk-consols relationship would remain at OB_1, the corresponding investment in consols would have been only half as large, i.e., $A_2(2r_1, \sigma_g)$.   In general, the following relationship exists between the elasticity of the demand for consols with respect to risk and its elasticity with respect to the interest rate:

$$\frac{\sigma_g}{A_2}\frac{dA_2}{d\sigma_g} = -\frac{r}{A_2}\frac{dA_2}{dr} - 1 \qquad (3.17)$$

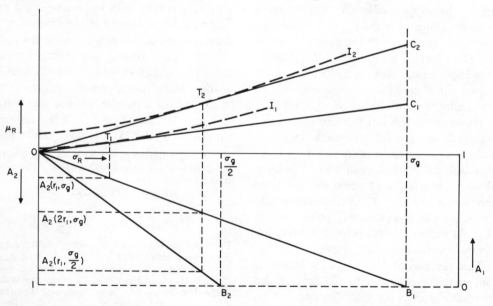

FIGURE 7. COMPARISON OF EFFECTS OF CHANGES IN INTEREST RATE (R) AND IN "RISK" (σ_g) ON HOLDING OF CONSOLS.

The implications of this relationship for analysis of effects of taxation may be noted in passing, with the help of Figure 7. Suppose that the initial position of the investor is T_2 and $A_2(2r_1, \sigma_g)$. A tax of 50 percent is now levied on interest income and capital gains alike, with complete loss offset provisions. The result of the tax is to reduce the expected net return per dollar of consols from $2r_1$ to r_1 and to reduce the risk to the investor per dollar of consols from σ_g to $\sigma_g/2$. The opportunity locus will remain at OC_2, and the investor will still wish to obtain the combination of risk and expected return depicted by T_2. To obtain this combination, however, he must now double his holding of consols, to $A_2(r_1, \sigma_g/2)$; the tax shifts the risk-consols line from OB_1 to OB_2. A tax of this kind, therefore, would reduce the demand for cash at any market rate of interest, shifting the investor's liquidity preference schedule in the manner shown in Figure 8. A tax on interest income only, with no tax on capital gains and no offset privileges for capital losses, would have quite different effects. If the Treasury began to split the interest income of the investor in Figure 7 but not to share the risk, the investor would move from his initial position, T_2 and $A_2(2r_1, \sigma_g)$; to T_1 and $A_2(r_1, \sigma_g)$. His demand for cash at a given market rate of interest would be increased and his liquidity preference curve shifted to the right.

3.6 Multiple Alternatives to Cash

So far it has been assumed that there is only one alternative to cash, and A_2 has represented the share of the investor's balance held in that asset, "consols". The argument is not essentially changed, however, if A_2 is taken to be the aggregate share invested in a variety of non-cash assets, e.g. bonds and other debt instruments differing in maturity, debtor, and other features. The return R and the risk σ_g on "consols" will then represent the

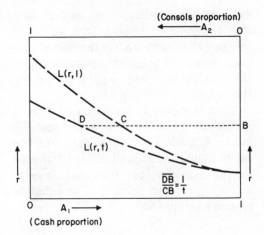

(Consols proportion)

FIGURE 8. EFFECT OF TAX (AT RATE $1 - t$) ON LIQUIDITY PREFERENCE FUNCTION.

average return and risk on a composite of these assets.

Suppose that there are m assets other than cash, and let $x_i(i = 1, 2, \ldots m)$ be the amount invested in the ith of these assets. All x_i are non-negative, and $\sum_{i=l}^{m} x_i = A_2 \leqq 1$. Let r_i be the expected yield, and let g_i be the capital gain or loss, per dollar invested in the ith asset. We assume $E(g_i) = 0$ for all i. Let v_{ij} be the variance or covariance of g_i and g_j as estimated by the investor.

$$v_{ij} = E(g_i g_j)(i, j, = 1, 2, \ldots m) \quad (3.18)$$

The over-all expected return is:

$$\mu_R = A_2 r = \sum_{i=1}^{m} x_i r_i \quad (3.19)$$

The over-all variance of return is:

$$\sigma_R^2 = A_2^2 \sigma_g^2 = \sum_{i=1}^{m} \sum_{j=1}^{m} x_i x_j v_{ij} \quad (3.20)$$

A set of points x_i for which $\sum_{i=1}^{m} x_i r_i$ is constant may be defined as a *constant-return locus*. A constant-return locus is linear in the x_i. For two assets x_1 and x_2, two loci are illustrated in Figure 9. One locus of combinations of x_1 and x_2 that give the same expected return μ_R is the line from μ_R/r_2 to μ_R/r_1, through C; another locus, for a higher constant, μ_R', is the parallel line from $\mu_{R'}/r_2$ to $\mu_{R'}/r_1$, through C'.

A set of points x_i for which σ_R^2 is constant may be defined as a *constant-risk locus*. These loci are ellipsoidal. For two assets x_1 and x_2, such a locus is illustrated by the quarter-ellipse from $\sigma_R/\sqrt{v_{22}}$ to $\sigma_R/\sqrt{v_{11}}$, through point C. The equation of such an ellipse is:

$$x_1^2 v_{11} + 2x_1 x_2 v_{12} + x_2^2 v_{22} = \sigma_R^2 = \text{constant}$$

Another such locus, for a higher risk level, σ_R', is the quarter-ellipse from $\sigma_{R'}/\sqrt{v_{22}}$ to $\sigma_R'/\sqrt{v_{11}}$ through point C'.

From Figure 9, it is clear that C and C' exemplify *dominant* combinations of x_1 and x_2. If the investor is incurring a risk of $\sigma\mathbf{a}$, somewhere on the ellipse through C, he will [at C] have the highest possible expectation of return available to him at that level of risk. The highest available expected return is represented by the constant-expected-return line tangent to the ellipse at C. Similarly C' is a dominant point: it would not be possible to obtain a higher expected return than at C' without incurring additional risk, or to diminish risk without sacrificing expected return.

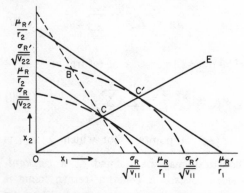

FIGURE 9. DOMINANT COMBINATIONS OF TWO ASSETS.

In general, a dominant combination of assets is defined as a set x_i which minimizes σ_R^2 for μ_R constant:

$$\sum_i \left(\sum_j v_{ij} x_j \right) x_i - \lambda \left(\sum_i r_i x_i - \mu_R \right) = \min$$
$$(3.21)$$

where λ is a Lagrange multiplier. The conditions for the minimum are that the x_i satisfy the constraint (3.19) and the following set of m simultaneous linear equations, written in matrix notation:

$$[v_{ij}]\,[x_i] = [\lambda r_i] \qquad (3.22)$$

All dominant sets lie on a ray from the origin. That is, if $[x_i^{(0)}]$ and $[x_i^{(1)}]$ are dominant sets, then there is some non-negative scalar κ such that $[x_i^{(1)}] = [\kappa x_i^{(0)}]$. By definition of a dominant set, there is some $\lambda^{(0)}$ such that:

$$[v_{ij}]\,[x_i^{(0)}] = [\lambda^{(0)} r_i]$$

and some $\lambda^{(1)}$ such that:

$$[v_{ij}]\,[x_i^{(1)}] = [\lambda^{(1)} r_i]$$

Take $\kappa = \lambda^{(1)}/\lambda^{(0)}$. Then:

$$[v_{ij}]\,[\kappa x_i^{(0)}] = [\kappa\lambda^{(0)} r_i] = [\lambda^{(1)} r_i] = [v_{ij}]\,[x_i^{(1)}]$$

At the same time,

$$\sum_i r_i x_i^{(0)} = \mu_R^{(0)} \text{ and } \sum_i r_i x_i^{(1)} = \mu_R^{(1)}$$

Hence, $\mu_R^{(1)} = \kappa\mu_R^{(0)}$. Conversely, every set on this ray is a dominant set. If $[x_i^{(0)}]$ is a dominant set, then so is $[\kappa x_i^{(0)}]$ for any non-negative constant κ. This is easily proved. If $[x_i^{(0)}]$ satisfies (3.19) and (3.22) for $\mu_R^{(0)}$ and $\lambda^{(0)}$, then $[\kappa x_i^{(0)}]$ satisfies (3.19) and (3.22) for $\lambda^{(\kappa)} = \kappa\lambda^{(0)}$ and $\mu_R^{(\kappa)} = \kappa\mu_R^{(0)}$. In the two dimensional case pictured in Figure 9, the dominant pairs lie along the ray $OCC'E$.

There will be some point on the ray (say E in Figure 9) at which the investor's holdings of non-cash assets will exhaust his investment balance $\left(\sum_i x_i = 1\right)$ and leave nothing for cash holding. Short of that point the balance will be divided among cash and non-cash assets in proportion to the distances along the ray; in Figure 9 at point C for example, OC/OE of the balance would be non-cash, and CE/OE cash. But the convenient fact that has just been proved is that the proportionate composition of the non-cash assets is independent of their aggregate share of the investment balance. This fact makes it possible to describe the investor's decisions as if there were a single non-cash asset, a composite formed by combining the multitude of actual non-cash assets in fixed proportions.

Corresponding to every point on the ray of dominant sets is an expected return μ_R and risk σ_R; these pairs (μ_R, σ_R) are the opportunity locus of sections 3.1 and 3.4. By means of (3.22), the opportunity locus can be expressed in terms of the expected return and variances and covariances of the non-cash assets: Let:

$$[V_{ij}] = [V_{ij}]^{-1}$$

Then:

$$\mu_R = \lambda \sum_i \sum_j r_i r_j V_{ij} \qquad (3.23)$$

$$\sigma_R^2 = \lambda^2 \sum_i \sum_j r_i r_j V_{ij} \qquad (3.24)$$

Thus the opportunity locus is the line:

$$\mu_R = \sigma_R \sqrt{\sum_i \sum_j r_i r_j V_{ij}} = \sigma_R \frac{r}{\sigma_g}$$
$$(3.25)$$

This analysis is applicable only so long as cash is assumed to be a riskless asset. In the absence of a residual riskless asset, the investor has no reason to confine his choices to the ray of dominant sets. This may be easily verified in the two-asset case. Using Figure 9 for a different purpose now, suppose that the entire investment balance must be divided between x_1 and x_2. The

point (x_1, x_2) must fall on the line $x_1 + x_2 = 1$, represented by the line through BC in the diagram. The investor will not necessarily choose point C. At point B, for example, he would obtain a higher expected yield as well as a higher risk; he may prefer B to C. His opportunity locus represents the pairs (μ_R, σ_R) along the line through $BC(x_1 + x_2 = 1)$ rather than along the ray OC, and is a hyperbola rather than a line. It is still possible to analyze portfolio choices by the apparatus of (μ_R, σ_R) indifference and opportunity loci, but such analysis is beyond the scope of the present paper.[15]

It is for this reason that the present analysis has been deliberately limited, as stated in section 1.2, to choices among monetary assets. Among these assets cash is relatively riskless, even though in the wider context of portfolio selection, the risk of changes in purchasing power, which all monetary assets share, may be relevant to many investors. Breaking down the portfolio selection problem into stages at different levels of aggregation—allocation first among, and then within, asset categories—seems to be a permissible and perhaps even indispensable simplification both for the theorist and for the investor himself.

4. IMPLICATIONS OF THE ANALYSIS FOR LIQUIDITY PREFERENCE THEORY

The theory of risk-avoiding behavior has been shown to provide a basis for

[15] A forthcoming book by Harry Markowitz, *Techniques of Portfolio Selection*, will treat the general problem of finding dominant sets and computing the corresponding opportunity locus, for sets of securities all of which involve risk. Markowitz's main interest is prescription of rules of rational behavior for investors; the main concern of this paper is the implications for economic theory, mainly comparative statics, that can be derived from assuming that investors do in fact follow such rules. For the general nature of Markowitz's approach, see his article, "Portfolio Selection", *Journal of Finance*, Vol. VII, No. 1 (March 1952), pp. 77–91.

liquidity preference and for an inverse relationship between the demand for cash and the rate of interest. This theory does not depend on inelasticity of expectations of future interest rates, but can proceed from the assumption that the expected value of capital gain or loss from holding interest-bearing assets is always zero. In this respect, it is a logically more satisfactory foundation for liquidity preference than the Keynesian theory described in section 2. Moreover, it has the empirical advantage of explaining diversification—the same individual holds both cash and "consols"—while the Keynesian theory implies that each investor will hold only one asset.

The risk aversion theory of liquidity preference mitigates the major logical objection to which, according to the argument of section 2.6, the Keynesian theory is vulnerable. But it cannot completely meet Leontief's position that in a strict stationary equilibrium liquidity preference must be zero unless cash and consols bear equal rates. By their very nature consols and, to a lesser degree, all time obligations contain a potential for capital gain or loss that cash and other demand obligations lack. Presumably, however, there is some length of experience of constancy in the interest rate that would teach the most stubbornly timid investor to ignore that potential. In a pure stationary state, it could be argued, the interest rate on consols would have been the same for so long that investors would unanimously estimate σ_g to be zero. So stationary a state is of very little interest. Fortunately the usefulness of comparative statics does not appear to be confined to comparisons of states each of which would take a generation or more to achieve. As compared to the Keynesian theory of liquidity preference, the risk aversion theory widens the applicability of comparative statics in aggregative analysis; this is all that need be claimed for it.

The theory, however, is somewhat ambiguous concerning the direction of relationship between the rate of interest and the demand for cash. For low interest rates, the theory implies a negative elasticity of demand for cash with respect to the interest rate, an elasticity that becomes larger and larger in absolute value as the rate approaches zero. This implication, of course, is in accord with the usual assumptions about liquidity preference. But for high interest rates, and especially for individuals whose estimates σ_g of the risk of capital gain or loss on "consols" are low, the demand for cash may be an increasing, rather than a decreasing, function of the interest rate. However, the force of this reversal of direction is diluted by recognition, as in section 2.5, that the size of investment balances is not independent of the current rate of interest r. In section 3.4 we have considered the proportionate allocation between cash and "consols" on the assumption that it is independent of the size of the balance. An increase in the rate of interest may lead an investor to desire to shift towards cash. But to the extent that the increase in interest also reduces the value of the investor's consol holdings, it automatically gratifies this desire, at least in part.

The assumption that investors expect on balance no change in the rate of interest has been adopted for the theoretical reasons explained in section 2.6 rather than for reasons of realism. Clearly investors do form expectations of changes in interest rates and differ from each other in their expectations. For the purposes of dynamic theory and of analysis of specific market situations, the theories of sections 2 and 3 are complementary rather than competitive. The formal apparatus of section 3 will serve just as well for a non-zero expected capital gain or loss as for a zero expected value of g. Stickiness of interest rate expectations would mean that the expected value of g is a function of the rate of interest r, going down when r goes down and rising when r goes up. In addition to the rotation of the opportunity locus due to a change in r itself, there would be a further rotation in the same direction due to the accompanying change in the expected capital gain or loss. At low interest rates expectation of capital loss may push the opportunity locus into the negative quad-rant, so that the optimal position is clearly no consols, all cash. At the other extreme, expectation of capital gain at high interest rates would increase sharply the slope of the opportunity locus and the frequency of no cash, all consols positions, like that of Figure 6. The stickier the investor's expectations, the more sensitive his demand for cash will be to changes in the rate of interest.

14

Liquidity Functions in the American Economy[1]

MARTIN BRONFENBRENNER and THOMAS MAYER

This study analyzes liquidity functions (demand for money) in the American Economy. Total money holdings and idle balances are treated as alternative variables. In Part I an aggregative liquidity function is analyzed twice, once using interest rates and wealth as independent variables and once using last year's idle

✳ ✳

Reprinted from *Econometrica*, vol. 28 (October 1960), pp. 810–834, by permission of the publisher and authors.

Martin Brofenbrenner teaches at the Carnegie-Mellon University; he was formerly at the University of Minnesota.
Thomas Mayer teaches at the University of California, Davis; he was formerly at Michigan State University.

[1] Earlier versions of this paper were presented to the Michigan Academy of Science, Arts and Letters, Ann Arbor, March, 1958, and the August, 1958, meeting of the Econometric Society. The research was supported by the Bureau of Business and Economic Research and the All-University Research Fund, Michigan State University. The aggregate analysis is the primary responsibility of Mr. Bronfenbrenner, the disaggregate analysis of Mr. Mayer. The authors are indebted for helpful comments to Roy Radner, John H. Kareken, James W. Angell and Paul Strassmann and to their research assistants Lloyd D. Orr and Reijo Aho.

balances as a third independent variable. Very good fits were obtained in both cases.

In Part II the liquidity function is disaggregated by major holders. Only one independent variable, the rate of interest, is used. Most emphasis is on year-to-year changes. Estimates obtained in this way are compared to those of a naive model. Finally the elasticity of the liquidity functions at various levels of interest rates is analyzed. Neither the data nor theoretical considerations give any reason for expecting a liquidity trap.

I. INTRODUCTION

The Keynesian system of aggregative economics rests, in its empirical aspects, on three major statistical foundations. One is the consumption function or propensity to consume, relating consumption to disposable income. The second is the investment function or marginal efficiency of capital, relating investment to interest rates. The third is the liquidity function, or liquidity preference, relating money holdings to interest rates.[2]

In the generation since the first appearance of the *General Theory*, none of these three functions has been left in the simplified form in which Keynes presented it. The consumption function has received until recently the lion's share of attention; three developments have dominated post-Keynesian research. One has been the addition of supplementary variables (including lags and ratchet effects). Another has been segmentation of the Keynesian aggregates. A third has been the drawing of distinctions between short- and long-run functions. The goal has been greater empirical realism, as measured by the goodness of statistical fit. Paradoxically, however, in the consumption-function case, one result has been the development of a rival theory as aggregative as Keynes's own, and with as few independent variables.[3]

Turning to liquidity functions, we hope in this study to improve their statistical fits to American data, operating along the lines just mentioned for the consumption function. In the first section, additional variables are added to the Keynesian pair (money stock and interest rates) for the entire American economy. In the second section, only the two Keynesian variables are used, but attention is concentrated on shorter time periods and on sub-groups within the American economy. Both

sections are concerned with five fundamental questions of liquidity theory:

1. Is there a definite observable liquidity function, i.e., a relation between money holdings and interest rates?
2. Assuming this function to exist, what is its interest-elasticity?
3. Assuming this function to exist, what is its stability over time?
4. If shifts over time are observed, what are their causes, i.e., what other variables are important?
5. Does the liquidity function appear to impose an observable floor to interest rates?

II. NOTES ON THE LITERATURE

Before we present our own results, a brief resume of some earlier work appears worthwhile. Many of the earliest attempts to quantify the Keynesian liquidity function took the indirect form of establishing a positive correlation between interest rates and the velocity of circulation of money.[4] For the United Kingdom, however, A. J. Brown computed from British data as early as 1939, and by surprisingly "modern" methods, what appears to be the first true statistical liquidity function in the economic literature.[5] More influential, at least in America, has been a later and simpler study by James Tobin.[6] Tobin defined idle

---

[2] Compare Lawrence R. Klein, "The Empirical Foundations of Keynesian Economics," in K. K. Kurihara (ed.), *Post-Keynesian Economics* (New Brunswick: Rutgers University Press, 1954), p. 277: "Three accepted pillars of the Keynesian system are (1) the propensity to consume, (2) the marginal efficiency of capital, and (3) liquidity-preference."

[3] Milton Friedman, *A Theory of the Consumption Function* (Princeton: Princeton University Press, 1957), esp. ch. 3. Friedman has also applied similar methods to the liquidity function in a paper which appeared only after the present article was completed ("The Demand for Money: Some Theoretical and Empirical Results," *Journal of Political Economy*, August, 1959, pp. 327–352).

[4] For the United Kingdom, Kalecki, "The Short-Term Rate of Interest and the Velocity of Cash Circulation," *Review of Economic Statistics* (May, 1941), pp. 97–99; Kalecki, *Theory of Economic Dynamics* (New York: Rinehart, 1954), pp. 76 f.; for the United States, J. N. Behrman, "The Short Term Interest Rate and the Velocity of Circulation," *Econometrica*, (April, 1948), pp. 185–190 and 370.

[5] A. J. Brown, "Interest, Prices, and the Demand Schedule for Idle Money," (originally published in 1939), in Thomas Wilson and P. W. S. Andrews (eds.), *Oxford Studies in the Price Mechanism* (Oxford: Oxford University Press, 1951), pp. 32–41.

[6] James Tobin, "Liquidity Preference and Monetary Policy," (originally published in 1947) in Arthur Smithies and J. Keith Butters (eds.), *Readings in Fiscal Policy* (Homewood, Illinois: Richard D. Irwin, 1955), pp. 245–47. A Tobin-type liquidity function has even found its way into an elementary text, Paul T. Homan, Albert

balances somewhat arbitrarily as the difference between total deposits and the quotient of total debits and the maximum (1929) velocity of circulation.[7] (The Tobin method makes idle balances zero by definition in 1929.) He then plotted idle balances against interest rates, with no other variables entering the relations, and obtained, for the period ending in 1945, excellent graphical representations of Keynesian liquidity functions—not linear, as in the Brown study, but roughly hyperbolic, as had been assumed in many presentations of the Keynesian system.[8] For subsequent years, unfortunately, the fit was much less good, even when Tobin's method was refined by deflating deposit figures for price changes.

Much subsequent work avoids arbitrary classifications of balances as active or idle.[9] It relates *total* money or deposit holdings to interest rates, income, and other variables, without distinguishing

active from idle elements. This assumes a single liquidity function of the type:

$$M = L(Y, r, a)$$

rather than such standard neo-Keynesian formulations as

$$M = L_1(Y) + L_2(r)$$

or

$$M = L_1(Y, r, b) + L_2(r, c)$$

where the L_1 are separate functions of disparate mathematical forms, and where a, b, and c are collections of other exogenous variables which may overlap or even coincide.

L. R. Klein's successive macroeconomic models of the American economy illustrate the development of ideas regarding liquidity functions. In his Cowles Commission study of 1950, Klein made an idiosyncratic distinction between active and idle balances; he identified the former with demand and the latter with time deposits.[10] To explain the behavior of time deposits measured in current prices over the period 1921–41, his independent variables were corporate bond yields current and lagged one year, a negative time trend, and the prior year's volume of time deposits, a ratchet term. The equation is linear.[11] In his 1955 study with A. S. Goldberger, Klein utilizes the insights of Tobin and others in separating idle from active balances more meaningfully.[12] He

---

G. Hart, and Arnold W. Sametz, *The Economic Order* (New York: Harcourt Brace and Company, 1958), pp. 488–490. For Great Britain, A. M. Khusro has fitted a Tobin-type function in his "Investigation of Liquidity Preference," *Yorkshire Bulletin of Economic and Social Research* (January, 1952), pp. 3 f., before passing to further complexities.

[7] A similar definition had been used earlier by James W. Angell, *Investment and Business Cycles* (New York: McGraw-Hill, 1941), pp. 339–340.

[8] For example, Oscar Lange, "The Rate of Interest and the Optimum Propensity to Consume," (originally published 1938), in Gottfried Haberler (ed.), *Readings in Business Cycle Theory* (Philadelphia: Blakiston, 1944), p. 173; Franco Modigliani, "Liquidity Preference and the Theory of Interest and Money," (originally published 1944) in Friedrich A. Lutz and L. W. Mints (eds.), *Readings in Monetary Theory* (Philadelphia: Blakiston, 1951), pp. 199, 201, and 203.

[9] A good bibliography through 1955 is found in Hans Brems, "A Solution of the Keynes-Hicks-Hansen Non-Linear Employment Model," *Quarterly Journal of Economics* (May, 1956), pp. 306–308. (This also includes references to Scandinavian literature.) See also H. F. Lydall, "Income, Assets, and the Demand for Money," *Review of Economics and Statistics* (February, 1958), pp. 1–14, as an example of a cross-section rather than a time-series study.

[10] Lawrence R. Klein, *Economic Fluctuations in the United States, 1921–1941* (Cowles Commission Monograph No. 11; New York: John Wiley and Sons, 1950), pp. 132 f.

[11] *Ibid.*, pp. 105, 110.

[12] L. R. Klein and A. S. Goldberger, *An Econometric Model of the United States, 1929–1952* (Amsterdam: North-Holland Publishing Company, 1955), pp. 23–28. A preliminary presentation is also found in Klein, "Empirical Foundations of Keynesian Economics," *op. cit.*, pp. 315, 318.

also introduces a distinction between household and business balances. His explanatory variable for households is the difference between the current value of the long-term interest rate and a "minimum possible" rate which he takes as two percent. His money figures are now deflated; his equation is now a logarithmic straight line; ratchet and trend terms have both disappeared.[13] For business balances Klein applies a similar method, using the aggregate wage bill rather than a national income aggregate as his basis for separating idle from active balances. Here his explanatory variables are the amount of price change in the current year, the short-term interest rate, and business idle balances lagged one year; his equation is linear.[14]

III. THE AGGREGATE FUNCTION

Our aggregative study covers the period 1919–56 inclusive. In the major portion of the study the dependent variable (X_1) is the logarithm of an estimate of deflated[15] idle balances computed *a la* Tobin with minor modifications. To derive it, private GNP (i.e., total GNP minus government purchases of goods and services)[16] was

divided by private money holdings.[17] The resulting velocity estimate has its maximum value of 4.022 in 1926 (not 1929). GNP for each year was then divided by this maximum velocity figure to obtain an estimate of active balances, and by subtracting these active balances from total balances we obtained an estimate of idle balances.[18]

As independent variables we chose three which had been suggested by economic theory, by earlier studies, or by promising two-way scatter diagrams reproduced as Figures 1–3.[19] The first of these is the interest rate. Just as it is possible to measure the price of strawberries either in fresh or frozen form, it is legitimate to

[13] Klein and Goldberger, *op. cit,.* pp. 53, 64, 92, 107–8.

[14] *Ibid.,* pp. 53, 65, 92, 108.

[15] The deflator used is the Department of Commerce GNP deflator. See *Survey of Current Business* (July, 1959), Table 41, p. 25.

[16] A series for private GNP from 1919 to 1928 inclusive in 1939 prices may be found in J. W. Kendrick, "National Productivity and Its Long Term Projection," in Conference on Research in Income and Wealth, *Studies in Income and Wealth*, Vol. XVI (Princeton: Princeton University Press, 1954), Table 4, pp. 82 f. For 1929 and subsequent years we used the (not entirely comparable) Department of Commerce series, *Survey of Current Business* (July, 1957), Table 40, pp. 25 f. Undeflated deposit series are from Federal Reserve Board, *Banking and Monetary Statistics* (Washington, 1943), Table 9, pp. 34 f., supplemented by *Economic Report of the President* (1957), p. 165, and *Federal Reserve Bulletin* (December, 1957), p. 1376.

[17] These are defined as currency outside banks plus demand deposits other than Government or interbank deposits. Time deposits were excluded because they bear substantial interest. Liquidity functions are designed to measure, among other things, the influence of interest rates on interest-free money holdings. Inclusion of interest-bearing components in money holdings would muddy the waters. (Insofar as some American banks paid nominal interest on demand deposits until the early thirties, inclusion of these deposits muddies them slightly.)

[18] Since idle balances are zero by definition in 1926, X_1 for 1926 should be $-\infty$. For convenience in calculation, we used the value of 0.1 (billion dollars) for 1926 idle balances, yielding an X_1 of -1.0000 for 1926. It should be noted that this method of isolating idle balances assumes that transactions balances are a linear function of income. While this is an oversimplification (Cf. William J. Baumol, "The Transactions Demand for Cash: An Inventory Theoretic Approach," *Quarterly Journal of Economics*, November, 1952, pp. 545–556) it is hoped that it does not create too serious an error.

[19] In addition to the variables used, the following three variables were tried and rejected because of poor fit: lagged interest rates, lagged national wealth, and the rate of change of the price level. The last named series has, however, been used by A. J. Brown, *op. cit.*, and later by Philip Cagan in modified form as the major explanation of the behavior of the money supply in several European hyperinflations, "The Monetary Dynamics of Hyperinflation," in Milton Friedman (ed.), *Studies in the Quantity Theory of Money* (Chicago: University of Chicago Press, 1956), pp. 35, 37. (Cagan's explanatory variable is not the *observed* but the *expected* rate of price changes.)

measure the cost liquidity either for a long or short term by using a long or a short term interest rate.[20] We chose to use the short rate here, and used the 4–6 months commercial paper rate. Besides being available readily, this rate is nearly free of risk and appreciation factors, and it is also more sensitive to economic changes than are longer term rates.

The second independent variable used is the logarithm of national wealth, more specifically Dr. Goldsmith's series on total national wealth in 1929 prices.[21] Government-owned wealth was not excluded, but rather used as a proxy for the government securities omitted from the wealth of the private sector.[22] The fourth variable used, a ratchet, is the logarithm of prior year idle balances.

[20] This means that the liquidity function here analyzed differs somewhat from that of Keynes, who apparently used the long-term rate exclusively.

[21] To save space the description of statistical sources and details of the methods used have been omitted here, but mimeographed copies of this material are available upon application to Mr. Mayer.

[22] An alternative procedure would have been to subtract Government wealth from Goldsmith's estimate and to add back Treasury estimates of non-bank holdings of Government securities.

An alternative presentation departs from the Angell-Tobin model by using the logarithm of *total* private deposits as X_1 and the logarithm of its lagged value as X_4. In this model an additional variable, X_5, the logarithm of private GNP, has been added.

Figures 1–3 show the arithmetic relationship of the dependent variable with each of the independent variables separately.

In Figure 1, using only the interest rate, a roughly hyperbolic function fits the data quite well over the period 1919–46,[23] but an entirely different function fits the subsequent observations. The scatter diagram of idle balances and national wealth (Figure 2) suggests three separate functions: a horizontal line, 1919–30, a vertical line, 1930–45, and a *slightly* downward sloping line, 1945–56. Figure 3, the scatter diagram of given year and prior year idle balances, shows a close fit through the thirty-seven year period, which suggests a high degree of inertia in money habits.

[23] Compare Tobin, *op. cit.*, Charts 2–5, pp. 244–246, covering periods 1922–1941, 1922–1944, and 1942–1945 for various areas of the United States. The roughly hyperbolic fits to the arithmetical data naturally suggest double-logarithmic straight lines.

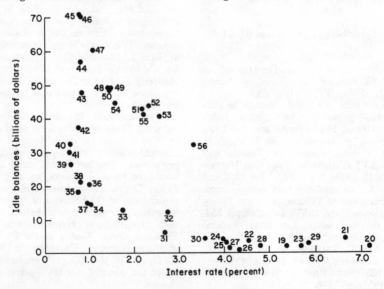

FIGURE 1. IDLE BALANCES AND INTEREST RATES 1919–1956.

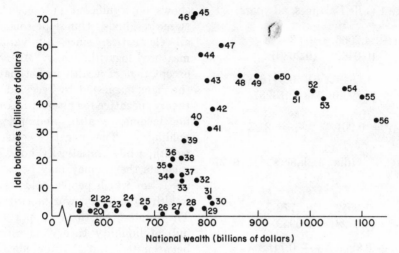

FIGURE 2. IDLE BALANCES AND NATIONAL WEALTH 1919–1956.

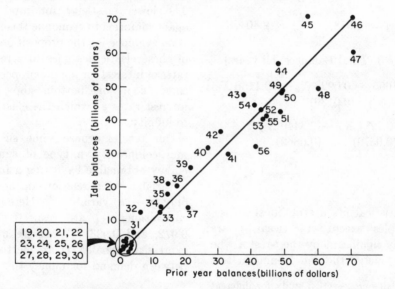

FIGURE 3. IDLE BALANCES RATCHET EFFECT 1919–1956.

We made three separate statistical estimates of liquidity functions. The first two are estimates of the demand for idle balances and employ the modified Tobin technique: income is not one of the independent variables. The third is an estimate of the demand for all private cash balances, and income is one of the independent variables. The first two estimates differ in that the first includes the years 1926 and 1927, while the second excludes them. (In 1926, the Tobin technique fixes the volume of idle balances as zero, whose logarithm we have treated as though the volume were fixed at $0.1 billion. In 1927, the same value enters as a lagged variable.)

The results are as follows, the figures in parentheses being standard errors:[24]

[24] The variables are, to repeat: X_1, log of deflated cash balances; X_2, log of the commercial paper rate; X_3, log of deflated national wealth; X_4, X_1 of the prior year; and (in the third estimate) X_5, log of deflated private GNP.

Estimate 1 (Idle Balances, all years):

$$X_1 = -4.2066 - 0.5304\,X_2$$
$$(0.0482)\quad(0.2030)$$

$$+ 1.6849\,X_3 + 0.5416\,X_4$$
$$(0.8906)\qquad(0.1323)$$

$$r_{1.234} = 0.901,\qquad \frac{\delta^2}{s^2} = 2.23$$

Estimate 2 (Idle Balances, 1926–27 omitted):

$$X_1 = -1.9552 - 0.2772\,X_2$$
$$(0.0198)\quad(0.0952)$$

$$+ 0.8269\,X_3 + 0.7158\,X_4$$
$$(0.4313)\qquad(0.0793)$$

$$r_{1.234} = 0.978,\qquad \frac{\delta^2}{s^2} = 2.40$$

Estimate 3 (Total Balances, all years):

$$X_1 = 0.1065 - 0.0928\,X_2 - 0.1158\,X_3$$
$$(0.0032)\quad(0.0139)\qquad(0.0883)$$

$$+ 0.7217\,X_4 + 0.3440\,X_5$$
$$(0.0576)\qquad(0.0862)$$

$$r_{1.2345} = 0.997,\qquad \frac{\delta^2}{s^2} = 1.91$$

The statistical fits are obviously close. All variables except X_3 (wealth) are statistically significant by the t-test at the 1 percent level;[25] the von Neumann test shows no significant auto-correlation between residuals. Our slope coefficients are all elasticities, since all variables are measured logarithmically. All coefficients except that of wealth in Estimate 3 have the signs suggested by received economic theory; negative for interest rates, positive for income, wealth, and prior money holdings. The negative elasticity for wealth, while statistically not significant, suggests that money may be an "inferior asset," of which people hold less as their wealth (and credit-worthiness) increases. The interest elasticity in particular, the nub of liquidity theory, is estimated at between 0.3 and 0.5 for idle balances, slightly less than 0.1 for total balances.[26] The lower elasticity for total balances again conforms to economic theory. There is no evidence for the proposition that any of these elasticities goes to zero for high rates of interest, or for the proposition that some "floor" or "bottom stop" exists for interest rates at which the elasticity goes to infinity.

Our results arouse some suspicion of multicollinearity, a type of spurious accuracy obtainable by fitting a function in n variables to a relationship or model in only $(n - k)$ variables.[27] Here the simple correlations r_{14} are respectively 0.875, 0.972, and 0.993. What we may have, expressed verbally, is an inertia relation between demand for money this year and

[25] In Lydall's cross-section study for different income and asset classes in a single year in Great Britain, the wealth variable was clearly significant (*op. cit.*, p. 6). The interest rate, furthermore, could not enter directly, being a constant for all observations. It is possible, as implied in Lydall's appendix (*ibid.*, p. 14) that in time series fluctuations in wealth would reflect inversely fluctuations in interest rates, since wealth is largely evaluated by capitalizing expected income at expected interest rates. Our own correlations between observed wealth and observed interest rates, while negative, are so low (-0.303, -0.289, -0.303, respectively) as to cast doubt on the efficacy of Lydall's indirect method of taking into account interest rate changes via the wealth variable.

[26] Lydall's indirectly-computed estimate of the interest elasticity of demand for bank deposits in Great Britain is 2.72 (*ibid.*, p. 11), which we do not attempt to reconcile with our own results. See also A. J. Brown, *The Great Inflation, 1939–1951* (London: Oxford University Press, 1955), pp. 204–07, for higher estimates.

[27] For two elementary introductions to the collinearity problem, see Mordecai Ezekiel, *Methods of Correlation Analysis* (Second Edition: New York: Wiley, 1941), p. 448, and E. F. Beach, *Economic Models: An Exposition* (New York: Wiley, 1957), pp. 171–175, 182–184. The standard treatment remains Ragnar Frisch, *Statistical Confluence Analysis* (Oslo: Universitetets Konomiske Institutt, 1934), *passim*.

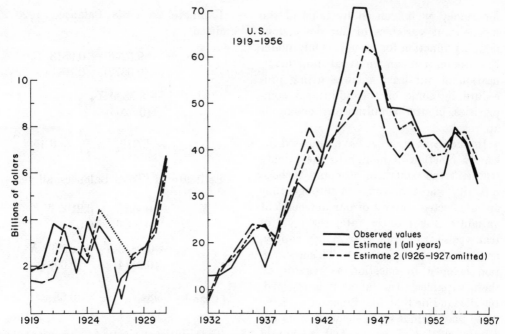

FIGURE 4. IDLE BALANCES: OBSERVED AND ESTIMATED VALUES.

last, with the other independent variables largely superfluous window-dressing. This suspicion is to some extent dispelled by the considerable uniformity among the three sets of numerical results.

Figure 4 compares actual and computed values of X_1 (idle balances) for the first two estimates. The fits to the arithmetic data are generally close (especially in the case of the second estimate), although naturally not so close as would be similar fits to the logarithmic data. There is a clear tendency for the fluctuations of computed values to display smaller amplitudes than the fluctuations of the actual data, and also to lag for a year at peaks and troughs. These are normal attributes of estimates relying heavily on ratchet terms; the first deficiency is also usual for moving averages. The fits are not good during the years of World War II (reflecting accumulation of cash for patriotic reasons and postwar purchases), but they are not so poor as to justify omission of these years

from our study. The period 1941–45 is accordingly included on the same basis as other years.

IV. IDENTIFICATION PROBLEM

Before accepting this function in any of its variants as representing a liquidity function (a structural equation of the demand for money in a more general economic model) we face an *identification problem*.[28] Supposing the function to be useful for prediction purposes, how do we know that it is not rather a supply curve, or perhaps a hybrid between the two? Our procedure cannot be said to meet this challenge. Rather it avoids the challenge by assumption. It is tantamount to specifying the form of the supply function

[28] The most readily available treatment of the identification problem is probably by Lawrence R. Klein, *A Textbook of Econometrics* (Evanston, Ill., and White Plains, N.Y.: Row Peterson, 1953), ch. 3, sec. 3, pp. 92–100.

for money as influenced by none of the independent variables of our demand or liquidity function for money. Only under this assumption can we avoid some modification of our least squares fitting procedure by some of the additional complexities of the simultaneous equations approach.

Implicitly at least, we have supposed the supply function of money to the private sector of the American economy to be a quantity whose movements through time are unaffected by any of our independent variables (the interest rate, the level of real wealth, the prior year money supply, or the level of real income). This assumption is open to question as regards all these variables. Insofar as it is rejected, the demand or liquidity function we have fitted may include some elements from the supply side, and be in fact a hybrid monstrosity. Our best hope is that our hybrids are approximately 99-44/100 percent pure demand or liquidity function. Their coefficients seem to point in this direction.

We may, however, interpret the lagged variables X_4 as reflecting supply relationships rather than demand inertia. The "supply relationship" is in this view the unwillingness of the monetary authority to permit sharp year-to-year changes in the money supply. If we interpret the ratchet variable in this way, X_4 must be omitted from our liquidity functions or demand curves for money. When this is done we have, corresponding to the three estimates above (page 198):

Estimate 1a (Idle Balances, all years):

$$X_1 = -\ 9.9740 - 1.1172\ X_2$$
$$(0.0580)\quad (0.1731)$$

$$+\ 3.9330\ X_3$$
$$(0.8442)$$

$$r_{1.23} = 0.848, \qquad \frac{\delta^2}{s^2} = 0.93$$

Estimate 2a (Idle Balances, 1926–27 omitted):

$$X_1 = -\ 9.5246 - 0.9518\ X_2$$
$$(0.0372)\quad (0.1093)$$

$$+\ 3.7830\ X_3$$
$$(0.5205)$$

$$r_{1.23} = 0.919, \qquad \frac{\delta^2}{s^2} = 0.45$$

Estimate 3a (Total Balances, all years):

$$X_1 = -\ 0.4958 - 0.2160\ X_2$$
$$(0.0076)\quad (0.0234)$$

$$-\ 0.1859\ X_3 + 1.2992\ X_5$$
$$(0.2114)\qquad (0.0963)$$

$$r_{1.235} = 0.984, \qquad \frac{\delta^2}{s^2} = 0.68$$

These interest elasticities are more than double their counterparts in Estimates 1–3, and remain higher for idle than for total balances. The "inferior asset" position of total balances is repeated in Estimate 3a but its statistical significance is not improved. The multiple correlation coefficients are all lower, but that for total balances holds up surprisingly well. A statistical warning is given by the von Neumann coefficients, which are all less than unity. This implies significant autocorrelation of the residuals—a not unexpected result, in view of the strong ratchet effects observed earlier.

V. DISAGGREGATED FUNCTIONS

The liquidity function was disaggregated in two ways. The first was by disaggregation over time and examination of year to year changes. This was done because for policy purposes the short-run liquidity function may at times be more important than the long-run one. Moreover, by analyzing year to year changes, one can observe some interesting shifts in the liquidity function and its elasticity.

Second, separate liquidity functions were computed for several major economic sectors.[29] They were first computed for corporations and then for individuals plus unincorporated businesses combined[30] to see if only corporations have liquidity functions. Then individuals and unincorporated businesses were analyzed separately. Finally, since time deposits are sometimes included in the money supply, an analysis for all holders based on this alternative definition of money was included to see if our results would also apply to this broader definition of money. We therefore computed separate liquidity functions for the following:

1. All private holders combined.[31]
2. Corporations.
3. Individuals plus unincorporated businesses.
4. Individuals.
5. Unincorporated businesses.
6. All holders—alternative definition of money.

No data on money holdings as usually defined are available for individuals and unincorporated business separately; for these two sectors time deposits are included in money. Moreover, the separate data for these individuals and unincorporated businesses are subject to a large margin of error.

The independent variables used are again idle balances, computed as described above, and total money holdings relative to income, as expressed by the Cambridge k.[32] Only one independent variable is used explicitly in this section. This is the short-term interest rate, measured by the 4–6 months commercial paper rate before World War II, and by the Treasury bill rate after the War. Since there is a significant return on time deposits a rate adjusted for this return, as well as the unadjusted rate, was used for the analysis of the alternative definition of money.[33] One of the other independent variables of the aggregated analysis, last year's idle balances, was introduced implicitly by using year-to-year changes. In the computations based on the Cambridge k income was also introduced implicitly. The only variable completely omitted in this section is the stock of wealth.

To take account of possible lags different models were computed using zero, six months and one year lags for income, and using the current month's interest rate and the average interest rate for the last twelve months. Distributed lags were not used. To reduce the computational burden these lag models were not computed for all sectors; for individuals and unincorporated businesses separately, the data are too poor to justify a multiplicity of lag

---

[29] All money figures are deflated by the consumers' price index, which unlike the GNP deflator, is available in monthly form.

[30] Throughout this analysis, the money holdings of non-profit institutions are included with those of individuals, because separate data for individuals are not available.

[31] Private holders are defined as all holders except the Federal Government.

[32] In both cases income figures are needed for the computations. Unfortunately, no accurate income concept is available for any of the sectors other than "all holders" and "individuals." For individuals and unincorporated business combined total *money* income was used. This is not a good measure, since a shift from unincorporated business to the corporate form affects the numerator but not the denominator of the fraction M/Y. For corporations, gross income was used, because a corporation's need for transactions balances is more closely related to its gross than to its net income. (For example, a corporation's demand for transaction balances does not become zero if it has no net income, and does not become negative if the corporation has a net loss.) The k used for corporations is therefore the reciprocal of the corporation's transactions velocity, not of its income velocity. No income figures for unincorporated businesses were available and hence a wealth variable, total assets, was used instead.

[33] The adjustment consists of taking total interest paid on all deposits and dividing this by the money supply. This average rate of return on money is then subtracted from the short-term interest rate. For more detailed discussion see the mimeographed appendix described in footnote 21.

models, and only a one year lag was used. Similarly, preliminary analysis for corporations suggested that the current month's interest rate gives a better fit than the yearly rate, and only this rate was used.

The period covered by the analysis of all holders is 1913–1957 with the period of World War II excluded as abnormal.[34] For the other sectors only the interwar period was analyzed.

Before turning to the results, the reader must be warned again about the identification problem. To what extent do the observed points of intersection between supply and demand curves for money represent a single demand curve traced out by shifting supply curves? This problem is important for the derivation of a forecasting equation, but it is even more serious for the interpretation of the function, and the measurement of its elasticity. Fortunately, there is some evidence suggesting, though not proving conclusively, that the scatter of the points results *primarily* from shifts in the supply curve, and hence gives a fairly reasonable picture of the demand curve for funds with a possible bias in its estimate of elasticity.

First, assume that the shifts in the supply curve and demand curve are not correlated.[35] Then, if we have a stable upward sloping supply curve and a fluctuating downward sloping demand curve, the

points would lie on the supply curve. On the other hand, if the demand curve is stable and the supply curve shifting, the demand curve would emerge and, finally, if shifts in both curves are equally important, the points would tend to have a random distribution. As will be shown subsequently, negative slopes predominate, hence shifts in supply appear to predominate over shifts in demand.

Second, the relation found could not be merely the result of time trends in both money holdings and the interest rates, since our relation holds in a number of cases where the shifts could not be a simple function of time.[36] For example, in Figure 5, the observation for 1917 lies *between* those for 1915 and 1916; this type of relationship occurs quite frequently. This could not have happened if the increase in k and the decrease in interest rates had merely resulted from a monotonic time trend in both variables.

Third, there appears to be some consistency in the shift of the curves; the liquidity curve seems to shift in the same direction several times. Thus, in Figure 5 during the interwar period there were six separate liquidity curves, and each one of these curves is to the left of the previous one. Finally, there is *some* similarity among the slopes of the curves; it would take a very special shift of supply and demand curves to produce this if both had shifted substantially. In view of these factors the scatter diagrams of interest rates and money holding will be treated as reasonable approximations to demand curves for money.

Now for the results. Figures 5 and 6 are scatter diagrams relating the interest rate to the Cambridge k and to idle money holdings. To isolate short-run functions, all points for three or more *consecutive*

[34] The World War I period was not excluded because conditions were substantially different from those of World War II. In the first war there was an open inflation, but in the second war suppressed inflation. Hence money holdings were abnormally high in World War II, but not in World War I.

[35] It is not possible to determine the validity of the assumption of uncorrelated supply and demand curve shifts. James W. Angell has suggested (*op. cit.*, ch. 2) that both supply and demand curves are substantially affected by expectations, favorable anticipations shifting both the supply curve and the demand curve to the right. In this case, the result depends upon the relative size of these shifts.

[36] For a discussion of this point, see A. J. Brown, "The Liquidity-Preference Schedules of the London Clearing Banks," *Oxford Economic Papers*, Number 1 (1938), pp. 54–55.

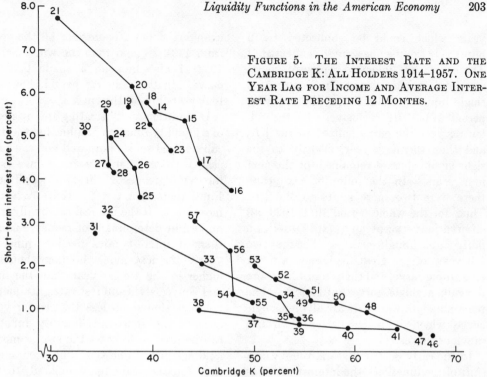

FIGURE 5. THE INTEREST RATE AND THE CAMBRIDGE K: ALL HOLDERS 1914–1957. ONE YEAR LAG FOR INCOME AND AVERAGE INTEREST RATE PRECEDING 12 MONTHS.

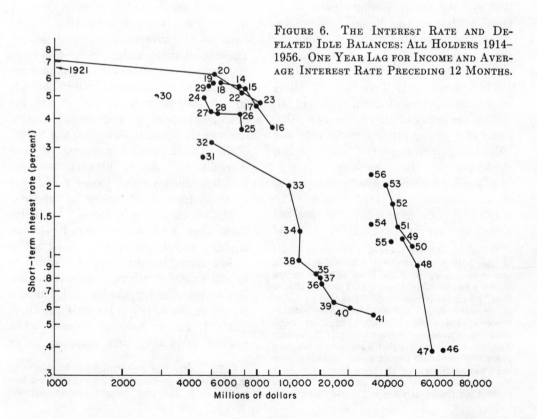

FIGURE 6. THE INTEREST RATE AND DEFLATED IDLE BALANCES: ALL HOLDERS 1914–1956. ONE YEAR LAG FOR INCOME AND AVERAGE INTEREST RATE PRECEDING 12 MONTHS.

years which could be connected by a negatively sloping line were so connected.[37] These lines are taken to represent short-run liquidity functions. In Figure 5, a single liquidity function fits the five year period 1914–1918 inclusive. In the following year the curve shifted to the left, and then the next year, slightly to the right again where it remained for the next four years. In the following six years, there were two more shifts to the left. Thus, for the whole period 1914–1929, all observations except one (1919) fell on fairly stable liquidity curves. The first two full years of the great depression are not on a stable curve, and then from 1932 there is again a single curve until 1936. The remaining interwar years are all on a single curve which is much flatter than the previous curves.

In the early post-war years, there was a shift of the function—the interest rate was the same in 1946 and 1947, but k differed slightly. All the remaining eleven years, however, fall on two liquidity functions. Nonetheless, the good fits for the post-war years may represent the spurious correlation of independent time trends. After 1947 there were only three years of falling interest rates. One of them, 1954, did not fall on the previous curve; the two other years of declining interest rates, 1949 and 1955, fell on their respective functions, but the slopes show discontinuity.

A similar pattern for idle balances is shown logarithmically in Figure 6. The only major differences in the pre-war period are that a single liquidity curve (of changing slope) accounts for all the years from 1924–28, and that the whole period 1932–41 also falls on a single liquidity curve. In the post-war period, however, four years are off the curves.

In addition to illustrating the existence of a liquidity function graphically, the data can be used to see how well one can forecast with the liquidity function. Such forecasts are tested in two ways here. First, there is a test for the *direction* of movement. If the interest rate really is an important determinant of money holdings then, if interest rates decline from one year to the next, money holdings should be higher in the second year than the first, and conversely if interest rates rise money holdings should be less the second year. Second, the short-run liquidity function can be used to forecast the size of money holdings in any one year, and accuracy of this forecast can be compared to the accuracy of a naive model forecast.[38]

Table 1 shows that Keynesian liquidity theory gives a good prediction of the direction of movement in money holdings. These predictions can be compared to those of a naive model. Our naive model assumes a random relation between money holdings and the interest rate, so that in half the cases money holdings and the interest rate move in the opposite direction, and in half of the cases in the same direction. If there is really no relation between the two variables, such a naive model would give a correct forecast 50 percent of the time.

The results shown in Table 1 are better than this, and hence the Keynesian liquidity hypothesis appears to be useful in forecasting the direction of movements in real money holdings. More than this, Table 1 provides support for the Keynesian attack on Say's law. If, as is shown in Table 1, money holdings increase when interest rates fall, then increases in *ex*

[37] The use of three years as a minimum period of time is of course arbitrary but preferable to a two year period. If there is *no* real correlation between two variables there is a 50 percent chance that two observations can be connected by a line of negative slope. With three observations, however, the probability of a negative slope resulting from chance elements is only 25 percent. This chance of error is still high but to use four years as a minimum period would probably have been too restrictive for *short-run* functions. As it happens, however, there are only two functions each of less than four years in Figures 5 and 6.

[38] To reduce the computational burden only the lag models performing best on the first test were used in this and the subsequent analyses.

TABLE 1

ACCURACY OF FORECAST OF DIRECTION

Lag model	Time deposits not included in money					All holders—time deposits included in money	
	All holders	Corporations	Individuals and miscellaneous	Individuals	Unincorporated businesses	Unadjusted interest rate	Adjusted interest rate[a]
RIGHT FORECAST AS PERCENT OF ALL FORECASTS Money holdings as percent of income							
Average interest rate for previous 12 months:							
1 year lag for income	86%[b]		78%[b]	74%[b]	63%	78%[b]	66%
½ year lag for income	81[b]		89				
No lag for income	61		69				
Interest rate of current month:							
1 year lag for income	65	65	67				
½ year lag for income	76[b]	67	80[b]				
No lag for income	82[b]	57	72[b]				
Idle Balances							
Average interest rate for previous 12 months:							
1 year lag for income	86[b]		74[b]	81[b]	58	89[b]	71[b]
½ year lag for income	81[b]		89[b]				
No lag for income	62		78[b]				
Interest rate of current month:							
1 year lag for income	64	65	62				
½ year lag for income	76[b]	67	80[b]				
No lag for income	79[b]	62	79[b]				

Note: Cases in which one variable changed and the other remained constant are not included. Blank spaces denote coefficient not computed.

[a] Interest rate adjusted for interest paid on deposits.
[b] Significant at the 5 percent level. Includes several cases in which the probability is exactly 5 percent.

ante savings do not lead automatically to an equivalent increase in investment, and hence it follows that "demand for commodities *is* demand for labor."[39]

[39] This does not completely settle the issue, however, for if prices would be sufficiently flexible, a decrease in the propensity to spend would lead to an increase in the real quantity of money sufficient to satisfy the increased demand for hoards. As will be shown below, the liquidity preference function is not very elastic, hence for relatively small declines in the propensity to spend, relatively small price declines might suffice.

Table 1 also shows that the responsiveness of money holdings to interest rate changes is not merely an attribute of financial corporations, but is widespread in the economy. Every one of the sectors shows a negative, though by no means always a significant, relation of interest rates and money holdings. However, the disaggregation by sectors does little or nothing to improve the accuracy of the forecasts. The forecasts for individuals and unincorporated businesses are no better than those for all holders, and the forecasts for the other sectors are worse.[40]

The second test of the short-run liquidity function is to forecast the size of money holdings. The short-run function can be used to forecast this by measuring the elasticity or slope between any two years and then multiplying this elasticity or slope of the function by the change in interest rates between the second and the third year. If the elasticity or slope is constant, the resulting forecast would be without error; and the actual error thus reflects the short-run instability of the function. This error can again be compared to that of a naive model.[41] According to the naive model, money holdings are constant—hence year-to-year changes in money holdings measure the error of the naive model.

Table 2 compares the two forecasts for the all holder functions.[42] The first two columns compare the two models by showing the proportion of the years in which

each function gives a better forecast. These results are mixed. The liquidity functions for all holders are better than the naive model but the differences are not significant at the 5 percent level. Many of the sector forecasts are worse than the naive model.

Turning to the mean size of the errors, the situation is worse. In all but one case the liquidity functions have higher mean errors than the naive model. But the mean error is not a good measure. In many cases it is high because of a few extreme observations. To avoid the effects of such few extreme cases the median errors were also computed.

Here the situation looks better. For the slopes, the liquidity functions do better than the naive model in all four "all holders" cases. This difference is significant at the 10 percent level for the Cambridge k and at the 20 percent level for idle balances. For the alternative definition of money the differences are significant at the 10 percent level in both cases.[43] The disaggregated functions again perform badly.

In addition to testing the forecasts obtainable from the liquidity function, the data also make it possible to analyze the elasticity and slope of the function. As is

[40] For the corporate sector it might reflect an instability of the function. Since corporations on the whole have *relatively* easy access to money market information it would not be surprising if their liquidity function would shift frequently. The poor results for individuals and unincorporated businesses could easily result from the weakness of the data—as stated above, the allocation of the money holdings of individuals plus incorporated businesses among its two components is based on worse data than the rest of the study.

[41] Elasticities were again computed by logarithms; those years in which the natural number was zero were omitted from the analysis. Since the slopes and elasticities are taken as constant in the forecasting model, this model is in a way close to a naive model. Basically, there are four possible models. First, there is the naive model described above; second, there is a model based on the assumption that some *average* relation between money holdings and interest rates will continue to hold in the future—this is the model of the aggregate function. Third, there is the model used here which projects, not the average relationship, but the relation in the last year. The fourth model, which is not used here, would take into account such factors as expectations and the structure of assets and claims.

[42] A similar analysis was tried for the other sectors but the results were quite disappointing.

[43] The significance test used is the median test described in Sidney Siegel, *Nonparametric Statistics for the Behavioral Sciences* (New York: McGraw-Hill Book Company, Inc., 1956) pp. 111–115. Comparing the various methods, the forecasting error is much greater for idle balances than for the Cambridge k, but this is merely a reflection of the fact the fluctuation of idle balances is greater, at least when computed by the above method. The naive model error for idle balances is more than twice as great as the naive model error for the Cambridge k; the forecast model errors, however, are not quite twice those of the Cambridge k, and hence show a greater improvement over the naive model. The inclusion of time deposits reduces the median error of the forecast relative to the naive model error. Finally, there is not much to choose between the elasticity and the slope models, though it should be noted that of the six cases where the forecast is better than the naive model, the slope model gives the best forecast in four.

TABLE 2

FORECAST ERRORS

	Percent of years with better forecasts for liquidity models than naive model[a]		Mean error as percent of actual value			Median error as percent of actual value		
			Liquidity function			Liquidity function		
	Elasticity	Slope	Naive model	Elasticity	Slope	Naive model	Elasticity	Slope
Cambridge k								
All holders	60%	53%	7.3%	12.2%	9.7%	5.8%	6.6%	5.2%
All holders—time deposits included in money	50	50	6.7	17.4	12.7	5.6	5.6	4.3
Idle Balances								
All holders	56	59	15.4	43.8	19.6	12.1	11.7	9.4
All holders—time deposits included in money	59	62	14.1	78.7	25.4	12.3	8.8	9.1

[a] Cases where both models gave equally accurate forecasts are excluded from both the numerator and denominator.

shown in Table 3, these short run slopes and elasticities are surprisingly low. For the Cambridge *k* of all holders the greatest single elasticity is 3.6 and even the third quartile elasticity is less than unity.[44] As in the aggregate function idle balances show a substantially greater elasticity than the Cambridge *k*, but even here the

median and third quartile for all holders exceed unity by only a small amount.

VI. A LIQUIDITY TRAP?

An important characteristic frequently attributed to the liquidity function is that at low rates of interest the demand for money becomes infinitely elastic.[45] The

[44] It is most unlikely that the smallness of these elasticities can be explained by the identification error. Even if half the figures are not genuine elasticities and if all of the erroneously included figures are clustered in the lower half of the distribution, the median of the true elasticities would be the figure now shown as the third quartile, and for all holders this figure is less than unity for the Cambridge *k* and not much more than unity for idle balances. Moreover, as can be seen from the range, not a single one of the figures for the Cambridge *k* is very large. The only way these data could be made consistent with the view that the elasticities are quite large, is to argue that due to shifts of the function not a single one of the large true elasticities was included in the table. But if shifts of the function are so frequent, the two-variable liquidity function is of only limited use.

[45] Although the liquidity trap and absolute preference were emphasized by Keynes, their history (though without relation to interest rates) really goes back *somewhat* further. "No one, when he has got sufficient furniture for his house, dreams of making further purchases on this head, but of silver no one ever yet possessed so much that he was forced to cry 'enough'. On the contrary, if ever anybody does become possessed of an immoderate amount he finds as much pleasure in digging a hole in the ground and hoarding it as in the actual employment of it." Thus wrote Xenophon (or pseudo-Xenophon—the attribution is uncertain). Quoted in G. W. Botsford and E. G. Sihler, *Hellenic Civilization* (New York: Columbia University Press, 1915), p. 437. Perhaps Xenophon should be called the first Keynesian.

TABLE 3   ELASTICITIES AND SLOPES OF THE LIQUIDITY FUNCTIONS

(all elasticities and slopes are negative)

	Elasticity					Slope[a]					Number of cases
	Mean	1st quartile	Median	3rd quartile	Range	Mean	1st quartile	Median	3rd quartile	Range	
	Cambridge k[b]										
All holders	.64	.19	.34	.67	0- 3.58	17.78%	2.91%	8.21%	22.60%	.44-115.00	30
Corporations	.59	—[c]	.20	—[c]	.03- 4.93	1.67	—[c]	.39	—[c]	.06- 5.83	14
Individuals plus unincorporated business	.74	.18	.49	1.29	.06- 2.15	9.39	.94	2.76	9.64	.24- 73.00	24
Individuals	.42	.08	.34	.52	.03- 1.33	5.43	2.18	3.34	6.61	.74- 20.95	20
Unincorporated business	1.13	—[c]	.51	—[c]	.08- 5.68	20.17	—[c]	3.41	—[c]	.27-144.00	16
All holders—time deposits included in money	.71	.28	.41	.69	.07- 3.15	28.93	6.82	17.41	36.27	1.15-143.00	26
	Idle Balances (millions of dollars)										
All holders	2.11	.63	1.07	1.23	.14-16.87	28,555	2,191	5,716	24,297	247-266,647	27-29[d]
Corporations	4.50	—[c]	.81	—[c]	.13-41.21	4,067	—[c]	790	—[c]	120- 16,314	12-14[d]
Individuals plus unincorporated business	3.63	.65	1.58	5.58	.25-14.83	14,472	730	3,158	8,112	82-186,500	22-24[d]
Individuals	3.21	.58	1.93	5.65	.15-12.39	899	1,528	2,785	6,875	184- 90,100	20-21[d]
Unincorporated business	3.32	—[c]	1.25	—[c]	.14-22.59	8,255	—[c]	907	—[c]	18- 67,300	15
All holders—time deposits included in money	1.64	.42	.79	1.87	.09- 9.64	25,334	4,031	8,279	31,466	607-170,533	27-29[d]

[a] Slopes unlike elasticities are expressed in the units of measurement, i.e., absolute values for the interest rate and the percent change in money holdings as a percent change of income for the Cambridge k or in millions of dollars for the idle balances.

[b] For unincorporated business, assets rather than income are used: details of the income concept are available from the authors.

[c] Omitted due to small number of observations.

[d] First number refers to elasticities, the second to slopes.

TABLE 4

Coefficients of Rank Correlation
between the Interest Rate and the
Elasticities and Slopes of the
Liquidity Function

	Elasticity	Slope
Cambridge *k*	+.16	—.52[a]
Idle balances	+.37	—.73[a]

[a] Significant at the 1 percent level. The other coefficients are not significant even at the 5 percent level.

data of Table 3 make it possible to test whether there was such a *tendency* during the period studied. Specifically, the hypothesis to be tested is that the elasticity of the all holders function was greater at low interest rates than at high ones. Table 4 shows that this was not the case. The correlation coefficient between the elasticities and the rates is neither significant nor of the "correct" (negative) sign.[46] This does not mean, of course, that the liquidity schedule could never become completely elastic even at a zero interest rate. However, the absence of a negative correlation in a period when interest rates were at times quite low casts doubt on, if not the truth, then at least the relevance of the liquidity trap proposition, and hence makes it worth while to re-examine its theoretical underpinnings.

There are essentially three reasons why the interest elasticity might be greater at low interest rates than at high ones. First, if people hold some idea of a "normal" interest rate, then the lower the interest rate is at any given time, the greater is the chance that it will rise again, and the

[46] This conclusion differs from that reached by Henry A. Latané who found *k* to be less inelastic at low interest rates though he does not indicate whether the difference in the elasticities is significant. ("Cash Balances and the Interest Rate," *Review of Economics and Statistics,* November 1954, p. 460.) We know of no reason for this difference; Latané's data and methods differ in several respects from ours.

greater is the amount by which it can be expected to rise. Second, if the interest rate is already low it cannot fall much further, and hence the potential capital gain from holding securities is less at a low interest rate than at high ones. This results in less willingness to hold securities as interest rates fall. Finally, there is the argument that as interest rates approach the cost of dealing in securities the demand for money must become infinite. All of these arguments are open to criticism.

The argument from expectations is open to the objection that a decline in interest rates may lead to expectations of subsequent further declines. What is relevant here is not the long term rate (about which there may well be stabilizing expectations) but rather the short term rate; for if someone expects long term rates to rise he need not hold cash, but can hold bills instead. And for the short term rate an expected "normal" level is less likely to be significant than for the long rate. If there is such an expected normal level for the long rate it is determined by long run considerations of normal business conditions. For the short rate, however, it is current conditions rather than normal conditions which are relevant. And at a time when interest rates are abnormally low, conditions too are likely to be abnormal. The lower the rate of interest falls, the more abnormal conditions are likely to be, and hence the less reason there is to expect interest rates to rise again during the life of a Treasury bill.

The argument about the potential capital gain at different interest rates is also not convincing. It seems to relate to the level of demand for money, rather than to the elasticity of this demand. The absence of any possibility of a significant capital gain at low interest rates may make people less willing to hold securities, but this does not tell us anything about the *elasticity* of the schedule. Moreover, if we take capital losses into account too, the argument does not necessarily hold even for the *level* of demand. It is true that potential capital gain is less if the interest rate is low than if it is high. But the same applies to capital losses. This can be illustrated better in terms of opportunity costs than of capital values. For example, assume that the interest rate is initially 10 percent. Then if the interest rate rises by half of itself, i.e., to 15 percent, the opportunity loss on a one year $1000 certificate is $50, but if the interest rate falls by half the opportunity gain is also $50. Similarly, if the interest rate had been 1 percent originally, the $5 loss resulting from 50 percent interest rate increase would be just equal to the gain resulting from a 50 percent decrease in interest rates. The critical assumption here is that the interest rate changes by a given percent of itself rather than by an absolute amount. Given this condition high and low interest rates are on a par as far as capital gains and losses are concerned, whereas if interest rates decline by a *given amount* then the lower the interest rate, the less the possible amount of decline can be. On an *a priori* basis, it is of course not possible to say which of these two assumptions is better.

Finally, there is the argument that at some low rate of interest the demand for money may become infinitely elastic. While this argument sounds plausible on the surface, it does involve an aggregation problem. For any one person there is a certain cost (both psychic and financial) of buying securities, and at an interest rate just equal to that cost his demand for securities is zero (i.e., his demand for money is infinitely elastic). For a group of people together, however, there is no single cost of investment (per dollar of investment), and hence different persons will drop out of the security market at different interest rates. There is no reason to assume that the demand for money will necessarily become elastic at any point

until the last man has dropped out of the security market.[47] Thus, while for each person separately the demand for money may become infinitely elastic at a certain interest rate, this conclusion does not necessarily follow for a group of people except in special cases.

It follows that on theoretical grounds there is little reason to expect the liquidity preference schedule to become elastic at low interest rates. And the above data suggest that during the period covered (and over the rates of interest covered) the schedule did in fact not become more elastic as interest rates fell. The *slope* of the schedule did increase, and while this might give the *appearance* of an increasing elasticity it is, of course, quite consistent with a constant, or even a decreasing, elasticity. Fortunately, for Keynesian theory, some of the propositions based on an increasing elasticity can be reformulated in terms of an increasing slope. The low mean level of the elasticity, and its failure to grow at low interest rates, suggests, however, that Patinkin's real balance effect (here the Keynes effect) may be quite significant in the bond market.

VII. CONCLUSION

As long ago as 1917 Pigou stated that demand for money was a function of, among other things, the interest rate. What Keynes did in 1936 was to attempt a grand simplification by focusing attention on only two determinants of the demand for money, income and interest rates. While this has turned out to be a very fruitful insight it was too great a simpli-

[47] This statement is not strictly correct; actually at certain points the curve would become elastic before the market is down to one man. Consider, for example, a market with two potential security buyers. As the interest rate falls by an amount just enough to induce one of the two people to leave the market, the curve is likely to be elastic. But clearly, as soon as there is a significant number of people in the market this possibility disappears.

fication, and much subsequent work on the liquidity function consisted of putting additional variables back into the function. This study shows that most of the fluctuation in idle balance holdings can be accounted for by changes in the stock of wealth and last year's idle balances, with all variables measured logarithmically.

When the function is disaggregated, a liquidity function can be found for some of the major sectors of the economy. While this relation is stable enough to allow one to forecast the direction of changes in money holdings from a knowledge of changes in the interest rate, it is not stable enough to allow one to forecast the change in the *size* of money holdings or idle balances.

For the period covered, the liquidity function was generally interest inelastic. Moreover, the elasticity does not appear to grow as interest rates fall—nor do there seem to be any strong *a priori* reasons for it to do so.

Part V

WAGE RATES,
THE PRICE LEVEL,
AND
EMPLOYMENT

15

Money Wage Rates and Employment

JAMES TOBIN

What is the effect of a general change in money wage rates on aggregate employment and output?[1] To this question, crucial both for theory and for policy, the answers of economists are as unsatisfactory as they are divergent. A decade of Keynesian economics has not solved the problem, but it has made clearer the assumptions concerning economic behavior on which the answer depends. In this field, perhaps even more than in other aspects of the *General Theory*, Keynes' contribution lies in clarifying the theoretical issues at stake rather than in providing an ultimate solution.

James Tobin teaches at Yale University; he was formerly at Harvard University.

[1] This question concerns the effects of a general change in money wage rates which is expected to be permanent. A fall in money wage rates which is expected to be followed by further reductions will discourage output and employment, and a rise which is expected to continue will stimulate output and employment. On these propositions there is no disagreement.

PRE-KEYNESIAN SOLUTIONS TO THE MONEY WAGE PROBLEM

How considerable this contribution is can be appreciated from a brief review of pre-Keynesian attempts to solve the problem.[2] These solutions rested on one of the following assumptions: (a) that the price level is unchanged,[3] (b) that aggregate money demand (MV) is unchanged,[4] or (c) that some component of aggregate money demand, e.g., non-wage-earners' expenditure, is unchanged.[5] Naturally, if

[2] It should be noted that R. F. Harrod ("Review of Professor Pigou's *Theory of Unemployment*," EJ, XLIV, March, 1934, p. 19) anticipated the Keynesian solution.

[3] J. R. Hicks, *The Theory of Wages* (London, Macmillan, 1936), pp. 211–2.

[4] Cf. Hicks, "Mr. Keynes and the Classics; A Suggested Interpretation," EC, V, April, 1937, p. 147 [reprinted in this volume, pp. 137 ff.].

[5] A Smithies, "Wage Policy in the Depression," *Economic Record*, December, 1935, p. 249.

A. C. Pigou, *Theory of Unemployment* (London, Macmillan, 1933), pp. 100–106.

In "Real and Money Wage Rates in Relation to Unemployment" (EJ, XLVII, September, 1937, p. 405), Pigou relaxed this assumption to provide in effect that non-wage-earners' money expenditure, although not constant, is uniquely determined

money demand is assumed to be maintained in any of these ways, the conclusion follows easily that a money wage cut will increase, and a money wage rise diminish, total employment and output. These assumptions, or any variant of them, beg the central question raised by the fact that money wage-rate changes are double-edged. They change money costs, but they change at the same time money incomes and hence money expenditures. Even the money expenditures of non-wage-earners cannot be assumed unchanged, for their incomes depend in part on the expenditures of wage-earners.

THE RÔLE OF THE CONSUMPTION FUNCTION IN KEYNES' SOLUTION

Keynes replaced these assumptions with a proposition which, whatever its short-comings, is certainly a more plausible description of actual economic behavior. This proposition is his consumption function: that *real* consumption expenditure is a unique function of *real* income, with the marginal propensity to consume positive but less than unity. So far as consumption expenditure alone is concerned, therefore, Keynes concluded that a change in money wage rates could not affect the volume of employment and output. Because the marginal propensity to consume is less than unity, any increase in output and real income would fail to generate enough of an increase in real consumption expenditure to purchase the additional output. Any decrease in output and real income would cause, for the same reason, an excess of

aggregate real demand over supply. The result of a change in money wage rates would be, still considering only reactions via consumption expenditure, a proportionate change in prices and money incomes and no change in employment, output, real incomes, or real wage rates.

These are the implications of Keynes' systematic theory. In the course of remarks which are, from the standpoint of his systematic theory, *obiter dicta*, Keynes considered two possible effects of a money wage cut on the propensity to consume: "redistribution of real income (a) from wage-earners to other factors entering into marginal prime cost whose remuneration has not been reduced, and (b) from entrepreneurs to rentiers to whom a certain income fixed in terms of money has been guaranteed."[6] The effects on consumption of the second type of transfer, (b), Keynes thought doubtful and apparently unimportant. The first type of transfer, (a), from wage-earners to other prime factors, would, if it occurred, be likely to diminish the propensity to consume; it would, therefore, be unfavorable to employment. However, Keynes overestimated the likelihood of such a redistribution of income. Maintenance of the prices of other variable factors in the face of a wage cut would encourage substitution of labor for these factors; such substitution would not only be directly favorable to employment of labor but would also diminish or reverse the transfer of income from labor to non-wage-earners. On the other hand, if the owners of other variable factors sought to avoid such substitution, they would, as Lerner has shown, reduce their prices in the same proportion as the wage rate and consequently would not gain income at the expense of labor.[7]

---

by the volume of employment. This variant has the same significance as the three assumptions discussed in the text. Later, under the prodding of Nicholas Kaldor ("Professor Pigou on Money Wages in Relation to Unemployment," EJ, XLVII, December, 1937, p. 745), Pigou in "Money Wages and Unemployment" (EJ, XLVIII, March, 1938, p. 134), accepted in essence the Keynesian position.

[6] *General Theory*, p. 262.
[7] Problems raised by the existence of variable factors other than labor are discussed below, pp. 219, 221–2.

EFFECTS OF MONEY WAGE RATE CHANGES
ON INVESTMENT

The possibility remains that a change in money wage rates may induce a change in the other component of Keynes' effective demand, real investment. So far as real investment is itself dependent on the level of real income or the volume of real consumption expenditure, there is clearly no reason for such a change. Likewise, the marginal efficiency of capital, so far as it is objectively determined by the amount of additional output which can result from an increment of capital, is not altered by a change in money wage rates. Three types of reactions on the rate of real investment are left:

(a) Conceivably, a change in money wage rates may affect that delicate phenomenon, the state of business confidence. However, the direction of this influence cannot be predicted in a general theory.[8] Individual business men making investment decisions may be impressed chiefly by the fact that a money wage cut reduces their costs. On the other hand, a fall in wages and prices embarasses entrepreneurs by increasing the real burden of their debt. Without underrating the importance of these types of reactions, therefore, Keynes had to exclude them from his theoretical structure.[9]

(b) In an open economy, a change in the general wage rate and price level will affect the balance of trade. A reduction of money wage rates and prices will stimulate demand for exports and shift domestic demand to home goods in preference to imports. Such a change in the balance of trade is equivalent to an increase in real investment and has a multiplied effect on home real income and employment. This effect may be strengthened by a worsening of the terms of trade, which increases the employment necessary to obtain the equilibrium level of real income and real saving. A rise in money wage rates would have the opposite effects. On this score there is little dispute. These effects may be nullified, however, by similar wage adjustments in other countries or by changes in exchange rates.

(c) A change in the level of money wage rates, prices, and money incomes alters in the same direction the demand for cash balances for transactions purposes. With an unchanged quantity of money, a reduction of money wage rates leaves a larger supply of money to satisfy the demand for cash balances from precautionary and speculative motives. The result is a reduction in the rate of interest, which should lead to an increase in the rate of real investment. Similarly a rise in money wage rates increases the interest rate and restricts real investment. It was only by this circuitous route that Keynes found any generally valid theoretical reason for expecting in a closed economy a relationship between money wage rates and employment.

THE CENTRAL THESIS
OF THE *GENERAL THEORY*

Such is the Keynesian solution to the money wage problem. It is important to view it in the broad setting of the *General Theory*. Keynes set himself the goal of establishing, first, that there may be involuntary unemployment of labor and, second, that there may be no method open to labor to remove such unemployment by making new money wage bargains. There may be involuntary unemployment because additional labor would be offered at the going money wage rate at the same or lower real wage rates.[10] Labor, beset by a "money illusion," will permit its real wage to be reduced by price rises without leaving the

[8] Except in the case discussed in footnote 1 above, or in the opposite case when wage expectations are inelastic.

[9] He considered the various possibilities in detail. *General Theory*, chap. 19, especially pp. 262–4.

[10] *General Theory*, chap. 2. See footnote 18 below.

market, even when it will not accede to the same reduction in its real wage by a money wage cut. At the same time, labor is powerless to take advantage of the potential demand for its services at lower real wage rates, because a reduction in the money wage may not lead to a reduction in the real wage.

The linkage between money wage rates and employment via the rate of interest appears to destroy the second half of this central thesis. For, if money wage rates were flexible, they could presumably fall enough to lower the rate of interest to a level which would induce the volume of investment necessary to maintain full employment. This linkage is, however, extremely tenuous. It can be broken at either of the following points: (a) The interest elasticity of the demand for cash balances may be infinite; (b) the interest elasticity of the demand for investment may be zero.[11] Condition (a) is likely to be approximated at low interest rates, and condition (b) is supported by the evidence that interest calculations play an insignificant part in business investment decisions. The Keynesian thesis that labor cannot erase unemployment by revising its money wage bargains is, therefore, not seriously damaged by admitting the effect of money wage rates on the demand for cash balances.

ASSUMPTIONS OF KEYNESIAN MONEY WAGE THEORY

It is damaged, however, by removal of certain of the restrictive assumptions of the Keynesian model; and their removal is

[11] F. Modigliani ("Liquidity Preference and the Theory of Interest and Money" EC, XII, January, 1944, pp. 45–89) emphasizes that except when condition (a), which he calls the "Keynesian case," is satisfied, unemployment is attributable to an improper relationship between the quantity of money and the money wage rate, i.e., to rigid wages. He does not mention that condition (b) would constitute another and very important exception to the wage rigidity explanation of unemployment.

logically necessary because they clash with other basic assumptions. To demonstrate this, the main assumptions of Keynesian money wage theory will be examined. They are: (1) that real wages are a decreasing function of the volume of employment, (2) that labor is the only variable factor of production, (3) that pure competition exists throughout the economy or that the degree of monopoly is constant, (4) that "money illusion" affects the supply function for labor, and (5) that "money illusion" does not occur in other supply and demand functions.

1. Diminishing Marginal Productivity

Adopting the traditional postulate of diminishing marginal productivity, Keynes assumed that real wage rates and employment are inversely related. Consequently, an increase in employment at the same money wage can occur only if there is a rise in prices sufficient to compensate business firms for the increase in marginal costs associated with an expansion of output. For this reason, the question whether labor will accept increased employment at a reduced real wage brought about by such a price rise becomes Keynes' criterion for the existence of involuntary unemployment. Keynes ventured the guess that real wages and money wages would usually be found to move in opposite directions, since money wages usually rise in periods of increasing employment and fall when employment is decreasing.[12] This conjecture provoked several statistical investigations designed to check the traditional postulate.[13] Statistically these investiga-

[12] *General Theory*, pp. 9–10.

[13] J. T. Dunlop ("The Movement of Real and Money Wages," EJ, XLVIII, September, 1938, p. 413) and L. Tarshis ("Changes in Real and Money Wages," EJ, XLIX, March, 1939, p. 150) concluded, from English and U.S. experience respectively, that Keynes was wrong in his conjecture and that real and money wage rates generally moved in the same direction. J. H. Richardson ("Real Wage Movements," EJ, XLIX,

tions were inconclusive;[14] in any case the issue, though of great interest in itself, is not crucial for Keynes' central thesis. Equilibrium with decreasing marginal costs throughout most of the economy is conceivable in a world of monopolies. In such an economy, the involuntary nature of unemployment at a given money wage would be even clearer than on Keynes' definition. Increased employment would not be purchased at the expense of a higher cost of living but would yield higher real wages. The question raised by the second proposition of Keynes' central thesis—can unemployment be removed by a money wage cut?—remains the same whether increasing or decreasing marginal productivity prevails.

2. No Variable Factors Other than Labor

The assumption that labor is the only variable factor is more serious. By this simplification, Keynes rules out the possibility of substitution as a result of money wage rate changes. If the possibility of substitution between labor and other factors is admitted, the Keynesian solution of the money wage problem can be saved only by introducing another assumption. Paradoxically, this postulate is that all factors other than labor are fully employed and that their prices are completely flexible. Then their prices will always change in the same direction and proportion as the money wage rate.[15] If the money wage

rate increases, business firms will attempt to economize on labor by substituting other factors. But since these other factors are already fully employed, attempted substitution can only result in bidding their prices up until the incentive to substitute vanishes. Likewise, if there is a cut in the money wage rate, business firms will attempt to substitute labor and reduce the employment of other factors. But since the prices of these factors are perfectly flexible, this substitution will be prevented by a lowering of the prices of these factors to keep them fully employed. If the price of any other factor were rigid, a change in the money wage rate would cause substitution between labor and that factor. A money wage cut would increase the employment of labor and a money wage rise reduce it.

3. Pure Competition or Constant Degree of Monopoly

Under conditions of pure competition, prices would be free to move up or down in the same ratio as the money wage rate, as Keynesian theory requires. Under monopolistic conditions, these proportionate price movements can occur only if the degree of monopoly—the ratio of the difference between price and marginal cost to price—remains the same. Monopolistic conditions lead to price rigidity and stickiness. Consequently a cut in the money wage rate will increase the degree of monopoly. Disregarding other results of the money wage cut, the increase in the degree of monopoly will increase the relative share of the national income going to non-wage-earners. Since non-wage-earners may be assumed to have a lower marginal propensity to consume than wage-earners, this redistribution of income reduces the real demand for consumption goods. In this respect, a money wage cut is detrimental to employment and output. A money wage rise has the opposite effect. This is presumably the *rationale* of the arguments of

---

September, 1939, p. 425) supported the traditional, here also the Keynesian, position. M. Kalecki (*Essays in the Theory of Economic Fluctuations,* London, Allen & Unwin, 1939) held that approximately constant marginal costs prevail.

[14] Cf. R. Ruggles, "Relative Movements of Real and Money Wage Rates," QJE, LIV, November, 1940, pp. 130–149.

[15] Cf. A. P. Lerner, "Mr. Keynes' *General Theory of Employment, Interest, and Money,*" ILR, XXXIV, October, 1936, p. 435; "The Relation of Wage Policies and Price Policies," AER, *Supplement,* March, 1939, p. 158; *The Economics of Control,* New York, Macmillan, 1946, chap. 23, especially pp. 287–8.

proponents of raising wages as an anti-depression policy.[16]

Rigidities in the prices of other factors of production, including unfinished goods and services, also lead to the substitution effects discussed in the previous section. The substitution effects of a money wage cut not only tend to increase employment directly, but also limit or prevent entirely the adverse effects on consumption expenditure from redistribution of income. Even though the degree of monopoly is increased, the increase in employment due to substitution tends to maintain labor's relative share. Monopolists in the finished and near-finished goods markets gain, possibly at the expense of labor but certainly at the expense of the sellers of factors with rigid prices, including the monopolists of unfinished products. Between the marginal propensities to consume of these two groups of non-wage-earners—monopolists in the final stages of production and monopolists in the early stages plus landlords and other property-owners—there is little to choose. Taking substitution effects into account weakens the argument that because of price rigidities a money wage cut redistributes income adversely to consumption expenditure. Indeed, if the elasticity of substitution is high enough, the redistribution of income may be favorable to consumption.

4. "Money Illusion" in the Supply of Labor

Economic theory is usually predicated on the premise that, given their schedules of preferences for goods and services and leisure, individuals behave consistently and "rationally." A consumer is not supposed to alter his expenditure pattern when his income doubles, if the prices of the things he buys all double at the same time. Nor is a business firm expected to change its output, if the price of its product and the prices of all factors it employs change in the same proportion. Generalized, this premise

[16] Kalecki, *op. cit.*, chap. 3, especially pp. 80–86.

is what Leontief calls the "homogeneity postulate," namely, that all supply and demand functions, with prices taken as independent variables, are homogeneous functions of the zero degree.[17] Applied to the supply of labor, this postulate means that a proportionate change in the money wage and in all current prices will leave the supply of labor unchanged. Considering the real wage rate as the ratio between the money wage rate and the current price level of goods consumed by wage-earners, the postulate means that a given real wage rate will bring forth the same amount of labor whatever the level of the money wage rate—that labor will react in the same way towards a 10 percent cut in its real wage whether this cut is accomplished by a reduction of its money wage rate or by a rise in current prices. Any other behavior seems inconsistent and "non-rational," based on a "money illusion" attributing importance to dollars *per se* rather than on an understanding of their real value.

Clearly one of Keynes' basic assumptions —Leontief calls it *the* fundamental assumption—is that "money illusion" occurs in the labor supply function.[18] Labor does attach importance to the money wage rate *per se*, and more labor will be supplied at the same real wage the higher the money wage. This assertion concerning the be-

[17] W. Leontief, "The Fundamental Assumption of Mr. Keynes' Monetary Theory of Unemployment," QJE, LI, November, 1936, p. 192.

[18] Leontief (*op. cit.*), pointed out also that the wording of Keynes' definition of involuntary unemployment does not necessarily repudiate the "homogeneity postulate." ("Men are involuntarily unemployed if, in the event of a small rise in the price of wage-goods relatively to the money wage, both the aggregate supply of labor willing to work for the current money wage and the aggregate demand for it at that wage would be greater than the existing volume of employment." *General Theory*, p. 15.) It could be interpreted to mean merely that the supply schedule for labor with respect to its real wage is negatively inclined. To Keynes' definition should be added the condition that the amount of labor demanded at the lower real wage must be greater than or equal to the amount supplied.

havior of wage-earners is indispensable to Keynes in establishing the existence of involuntary unemployment.

What are the reasons for such "non-rational" behavior on the part of labor? First, high money wage rates are a concrete and immediate accomplishment of the leadership of individual unions. The object of individual labor groups in wage bargaining is to protect and if possible to advance their wages relative to other groups. Each union will resist a cut in money wages in order to avoid a relative reduction in real wages. The cost of living is a remote phenomenon, apparently beyond the control of organized labor, certainly beyond the control of any single bargaining unit. Money wage bargains must be made for periods during which the cost of living may frequently change. Second, wage-earners have obligations fixed in terms of money: debts, taxes, contractual payments such as insurance premiums. These obligations are a greater burden when money wage rates are cut, even though all current prices may fall proportionately. Third, labor may have inelastic price expectations; a certain "normal" price level, or range of price levels, may be expected to prevail in the future, regardless of the level of current prices.[19] With such price expectations, it is clearly to the advantage of wage-earners to have, with the same current real income, the highest possible current money income. For the higher their money incomes the greater will be their money savings and, therefore, their expected command over future goods. Wage-earners with inelastic price expectations will resist money wage cuts even when prices are falling, not only because they fear that wages will not rise again when prices rise but also because the expected price rise would reduce the real value of their current saving. Fourth, labor may be genuinely ignorant of the

course of prices or naïvely deceived by the "money illusion." Judged by labor's consciousness of the cost of living in the United States in 1946, this explanation, if it ever was important, is not now significant. Altogether, the support for Keynes' assumption in regard to the supply of labor is convincing; his denial of the "homogeneity postulate" for the labor supply function constitutes a belated theoretical recognition of the facts of economic life.

5. Absence of "Money Illusion" Elsewhere in the Economy

Wage-earners are the only inhabitants of the Keynesian economy who are so foolish or so smart, as the case may be, as to act under the spell of the "money illusion." They are under its spell only in their capacity as suppliers of labor. The "homogeneity postulate" is denied for the labor supply function; for all other demand and supply functions it is retained. Without the retention of the "homogeneity postulate" for all supply and demand functions except the labor supply function, the Keynesian money wage doctrine cannot be maintained. The dependence of the doctrine on this procedure and the justification for the procedure will be considered for (a) the supply functions of other factors, and (b) the consumption function.

(a) *Supply of Other Factors.* When the existence of variable factors other than labor is admitted, Keynesian theory requires that these factors be fully employed and that their prices be perfectly flexible.[20] This is where the "homogeneity postulate" —the assumption of "rational" behavior— enters with respect to the supply functions of these factors. If the sellers of these factors were, like the sellers of labor, influenced by the "money illusion," their prices would be rigid like wages and there could be unemployment of these factors. A change in the money wage rate could

---

[19] Hicks, *Value and Capital* (Oxford, 1939), pp. 269–272.

[20] P. 219 above.

then alter the employment of labor by causing substitution between labor and other factors.

Keynes, since he assumes away the existence of other factors, presents no reasons for this distinction between labor and other factors. Lerner, however, asserts that it is "plausible and in conformity with the assumption of rationality of entrepreneurs and capital-owners, who would rather get something for the use of their property than let it be idle, while labor has non-rational money-wage demands."[21] It is important to note what is included in "other factors": not only the services of land, other natural agents, and existing items of capital equipment, but also services and unfinished goods which are the products of some firms but serve as inputs for other firms. The sellers of these factors have much the same reasons as wage-earners for having "non-rational" money-price demands. Perhaps to a greater extent than labor, they have obligations fixed in terms of money. If their price expectations are inelastic, they have the same interest in high money rates of remuneration, whatever their current real returns, to protect their current savings against future price rises. They too must make money bargains for the sale of their services, contracts which will last over a period of many possible price level changes. Business firms which control the supply of intermediate goods and services often attempt to stabilize money-prices, letting their output and sales fluctuate widely. Such price rigidities are money-price demands on the part of entrepreneurs analogous in effect to the "non-rational" money-wage demands of labor.

The "money illusion" will frequently influence the suppliers of other factors. Consequently there can be price rigidities in all markets and fluctuations in the use of all factors of production. In such an economy the money wage rate is an independent determinant of the volume of employment.

(*b*) *Consumption Decisions.* The Keynesian consumption function, which is crucial to the Keynesian solution to the money wage problem,[22] is framed in real terms: real consumption expenditure is uniquely determined by real income.[23] It is not affected, for example, by a doubling of money income and of all prices. This is the application of the "homogeneity postulate" to the consumption function. If "money illusion" occurred in consumption and saving decisions, real consumption expenditure would depend on the level of money income as well as on the level of real income, just as the supply of labor depends on the money wage rate as well as on the real wage. A change in the money wage rate, changing the level of money incomes and prices, would alter the real demand for consumption goods and therefore affect the volume of both output and employment. Here again, therefore, retention of the "homogeneity postulate" is an essential assumption for Keynesian money wage doctrine.

But if wage-earners are victims of a "money illusion" when they act as sellers of labor, why should they be expected to become "rational" when they come in to the market as consumers? Most of the reasons which compel them to behave "non-rationally" in making money wage bargains would logically compel them to act "non-rationally" as consumers. And if, as argued above, labor has no corner on such non-rationality, the whole body of consumers would be influenced by the "money illusion."

In which direction would the "money illusion" be expected to operate on the consumption function? With real income given, will an increase in money income cause an increase or a decrease in real consumption expenditure? The logic of the

---

[21] "Relation of Wage Policies and Price Policies," AER, *Supplement*, March, 1939, p. 163.

[22] P. 216 above.

[23] This is the significance of Keynes' use of wage-units.

other assumptions of Keynesian theory leads to an inverse relationship between money income and real consumption expenditure, with real income constant. For wage-earners are assumed to feel worse off when their money wages are cut; and when consumers feel worse off, they are supposed to devote a greater part of their real incomes to consumption and less to saving.

Consistency with other Keynesian assumptions is not, however, the most weighty argument in favor of such a relationship. One reason for non-homogeneous behavior in the supply of labor, we have seen, is the holding of inelastic price expectations. Such price expectations will also influence current consumption expenditure. If current prices are below the "normal" level expected to prevail in the future, consumers will substitute present purchases for future purchases, save less now and plan to save more in the future. If current prices are above expected future prices, consumers will reduce present consumption expenditure in favor of future expenditure, increase current saving at the expense of future saving. From the same real income, real consumption expenditure will be less the higher the current level of money incomes and prices. Inelasticity of price expectations is, therefore, one source of an inverse relationship between money income and real consumption expenditure out of a given real income.

If price expectations are not inelastic, a different but equally effective reason for the same relationship comes into operation. It is now widely recognized that the volume of accumulated savings held by consumers affects their propensity to consume.[24] The greater the volume of such holdings, the more consumers have already satisfied their desire to save, the greater the part of a given current income which will be

spent for consumption. These assets are, except for equities, fixed or very nearly fixed in money value. Now if current price changes are expected to persist, a general decline in money prices and incomes will increase the real value of accumulated savings, and a general rise in money prices and incomes will reduce their real value. An increase in the real value of these assets should increase the propensity to consume, and a decrease in their value reduce it.[25] Such behavior on the part of consumers is quite consistent and rational; it appears to be the consequence of a "money illusion" only when current prices and incomes are taken as the sole variables relevant to consumption decisions.

Assuming that real consumption expenditure is, for these reasons, an inverse function of the level of money income, as well as a direct function of real income *à la* Keynes, a decrease in money wage rates must lead to an expansion of output and employment, and an increase in money wage rates to a curtailment of output and employment. A money wage cut, for example, will cause a general decline in prices and money incomes. This decline will stimulate an increase in the real demand for consumption goods and thereby cause a general expansion of output, real

[24] Cf., for example, A. P. Lerner, "Functional Finance and the Federal Debt," *Social Research*, X, February, 1943, p. 49 [reprinted in this volume, p. 359].

[25] Since the assets held by consumers are the debts of other economic units, price changes affecting the real value of consumers' assets will also affect the real burden of debt. Changes in the real burden of debt may influence business investment decisions. The resulting changes in investment will act in the opposite direction from the changes in consumption described in the text. (Keynes [*General Theory*, p. 264] and Hicks [*Value and Capital*, p. 264] both considered the possible depressing influence of price and wage reductions in increasing the burden of debt without mentioning the favorable effects of the increased real wealth of creditors.) But only part of consumers' assets are, directly or indirectly, business debts; the assets of private economic units exceed private debt by the total of public debt, the monetary gold reserve, and the supply of government-issued currency. Hence, a given price change will cause a greater change in the real value of consumers' assets than in the burden of business debt.

income, and employment. In the new equilibrium, prices will be lower: they will fall less than the money wage if increasing marginal costs prevail, and more than the money wage if decreasing marginal costs predominate. In the latter case, the expansion of output and employment will be greater either because more substitution of present for future consumption is induced or because the increase in real value of accumulated savings is larger. A rise in the money wage rate, of course, has the opposite effects.

These effects of changes in the money wage rate are superimposed on the substitution effects already discussed and act on the employment of labor in the same direction.

CONCLUSION

The central thesis of the *General Theory* contains two complementary propositions: first, that because labor has "non-rational" money wage demands, involuntary unemployment of labor is possible; second, that labor is in any case powerless to remedy this unemployment by altering its money wage bargains. (The second proposition Keynes qualifies by admitting the possibilities of reactions on employment via the rate of interest, but this qualification, for reasons given above, is of limited practical importance.) The second proposition of the central thesis rests on assumptions logically inconsistent with the assumption contained in the first; and the premises of the second proposition are as unrealistic as the assumption underlying Keynes' labor supply function is realistic. If Keynes' denial of the "homogeneity postulate" is extended to supply and demand functions other than the labor supply function—if, in other words, "money illusion" operates elsewhere than on the sellers' side of the labor market—then employment is inversely affected by money wage rate changes. Labor is not powerless to reduce

unemployment by reducing its money wage demands. Changes in employment follow from changes in the money wage because of substitution between labor and other factors and because of the effects of "money illusion" on real consumption expenditure. The substitution effect can be avoided only by assuming, as in the *General Theory*, that labor is the only variable factor or, if other factors are considered, by assuming that the suppliers of these factors, unlike labor, have no "non-rational" money-price demands. The consumption effect can be avoided only by assuming that wage-earners—and the suppliers of other factors if they are admitted to behave like wage-earners—act "rationally" as buyers even though they are "non-rational" as sellers, and by neglecting the effect of inelastic price expectations or accumulated savings on the propensity to consume. These two effects, or either one of them alone, make the money wage rate a determinant of the volume of employment. The consumption effect makes it also a determinant of the level of output and real income.

To summarize, a change in the money wage rate may alter the level of employment in the following ways:

1. By its effect on business confidence, which is not theoretically predictable, a change in the money wage rate may alter the volume of real investment.
2. In an open economy, a wage cut will have an effect equivalent to an expansion of investment by increasing the balance of trade. A wage rise will have the opposite results and affect employment adversely.
3. By reducing the demand for cash balances, a wage cut *may* reduce the rate of interest; reduction of the interest rate *may* stimulate investment and employment. A wage rise may have the opposite effects.
4. A wage cut may induce substitution of labor for other factors, and a wage rise may diminish employment by causing substitution of other factors for labor.
5. A wage cut may cause an increase in the real demand for consumption goods and therefore in both output and employment. Increased consumption demand would

result either from substitution of present consumption for future consumption, when price expectations are inelastic, or from the increased real value of accumulated savings. A wage rise would have the contrary effect.

6. An effect contrary in direction to the four preceding possibilities is that a money wage cut will, because of price rigidities, redistribute income adversely to labor and thereby reduce the propensity to consume. For similar reasons, a money wage rise would be favorable to employment. This effect will be the stronger the weaker is the substitution effect; if substitution is considerable, it may be entirely absent.

Solution of the money wage problem was greatly advanced by replacing arbitrary assumptions concerning the price level or the level of money expenditure with Keynes' analysis of effective demand. Further progress towards a solution, and ultimately towards a quantitative solution, depends on refinement and extension, both theoretical and statistical, of the basic Keynesian system. What are the variables other than real rates of remuneration affecting the supply of labor and of other factors of production, and what effects do these variables have? What variables other than real income determine real consumption expenditure, and how? What variables lie behind the marginal efficiency of capital, and how do they enter business investment calculations? Only when economists have more satisfactory answers to these broader questions will they be able to give an acceptable solution to the money wage problem.

16

Price Flexibility and Full Employment*

DON PATINKIN

At the core of the Keynesian polemics of the past ten years and more is the relationship between price flexibility and full employment. The fundamental argument of Keynes is directed against the belief that price flexibility can be depended upon to generate full employment automatically. The defenders of the classical tradition, on the other hand, still insist upon this automaticity as a basic tenet.

During the years of continuous debate on this question, the issues at stake have been made more precise. At the same time, further material on the question of flexibility has become available. This paper is essentially an attempt to incorporate this new material, and, taking advantage of the perspective offered by time, to analyze the present state of the debate.

From *Readings in Monetary Theory*, selected by a Committee of the American Economic Association (New York: The Blakiston Company, 1951), pp. 252–283. This is a revised version of an article which was originally published, under the same title, in *The American Economic Review*, vol. 38 (September 1948), pp. 543–564. Reprinted by permission of the publishers and author.
All the changes, references to reprinting, and brackets were inserted in the 1951 revision of the article.

Don Patinkin teaches at the Hebrew University.

In Part I, the problem of price flexibility and full employment is presented from a completely static viewpoint. Part II then goes on to discuss the far more important dynamic aspects of the problem. Finally, in Part III, the implications of the discussion for the Keynesian-classical polemic are analyzed. It is shown that over the years these two camps have really come closer and closer together. It is argued that the basic issue separating them is the rapidity with which the economic system responds to price variations.

I. STATIC ANALYSIS

1. The traditional interpretation of Keynesian economics is that it demon-

* In the process of writing this paper the author acknowledges having benefited from stimulating discussions with Milton Friedman, University of Chicago, and Alexander M. Henderson, University of Manchester. (Advantage has been taken of this reprinting to correct and modify several parts of the article. The major changes are the following: the addition of the latter part of the last paragraph of § 5, as a result of discussions with Milton Friedman; the addition of paragraphs three and four of § 6, as a result of comments by Donald Gordon, Franco Modigliani, and Norman Ture; the correction of the last paragraph of § 6 and Table 1 of § 11 in accordance with Herbert Stein's comment on the original article in the *American Economic Review*, XXXIX (1949), 725–26; and the addition of the last three paragraphs of § 14, in the attempt to clarify some points left ambiguous in the original article. All significant additions are enclosed in brackets.)

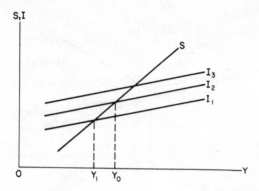

FIGURE 1.

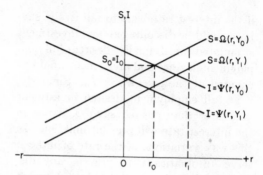

FIGURE 2.

strates the absence of an automatic mechanism assuring the equality of desired savings and investment at full employment. The graphical meaning of this interpretation is presented in a simplified form in Figure 1. Here desired real savings (S) and investment (I) are each assumed to depend only on the level of real income (Y). I_1, I_2, and I_3 represent three possible positions of the investment schedule. Y_0 is the full employment level of real income. If the investment desires of individuals are represented by the curve I_1, desired savings at full employment are greater than desired investment at full employment. This means that unemployment will result: the level of income will drop to Y_1, at which income desired savings and investment are equal. Conversely, if I_3 is the investment curve, a situation of overemployment or inflation will occur: people desire to invest more at full employment than the amount of savings will permit. Only if the investment schedule happened to be I_2 would full employment, desired investment and savings be equal. But since investment decisions are independent of savings decisions, there is no reason to expect the investment schedule to coincide with I_2. Hence there is no automatic assurance that full employment will result.

2. The classical answer to this attack is that desired savings and investment depend on the rate of interest, as well as the level of real income; and that, granted flexibility, variations in the interest rate serve as

an automatic mechanism insuring full employment.

The argument can be interpreted as follows: the savings and investment functions (representing what people desire to do) are written as

$$S = \Omega(r, Y)$$
$$I = \Psi(r, Y)$$

where r represents the rate of interest.

Consider now Figure 2. On this graph there can be drawn a whole family of curves relating savings and investment to the rate of interest—one pair for each level of real income. In Figure 2, these pairs of curves are drawn for the full employment income, Y_0, and for the less than full employment income, Y_1. On the assumption that for a given rate of interest people will save and invest more at a higher level of income, the investment curve corresponding to $Y = Y_0$ is drawn above that corresponding to $Y = Y_1$; similarly for the two savings curves. The curves also reflect the assumption that, for a given level of real income, people desire to save more and invest less at higher rates of interest.

Consider now the pair of curves corresponding to the full employment income Y_0. If in Figure 2 the interest rate were r_1, then it would be true that individuals would desire to save more at full employment than they would desire to invest. But, assuming no rigidities in the interest rate, this would present no difficulties. For if the interest rate were to fall freely, savings would be discouraged, and investment stimulated until finally desired full employment savings and investment would be equated at the level $S_0 = I_0$. Similarly, if at full employment desired investment is greater than desired savings, a rise in the interest rate will prevent inflation. In this way variations in the rate of interest serve automatically to prevent any discrepancy between desired full employment investment and savings, and thus to assure full employment.

This argument can also be presented in terms of Figure 1: assume for simplicity that desired investment depends on the rate of interest as well as the level of real income, while desired savings depends only on the latter. Then downward variations in the interest rate can be counted on to raise the investment curve from, say, I_1 to I_2. That is, at any level of income people can be encouraged to invest more by a reduction in the rate of interest. Similarly, upward movements of the interest rate will shift the investment curve from, say, I_3 to I_2. Thus desired full employment savings and investment will always be equated.

3. The Keynesian answer to this classical argument is that it greatly exaggerates the importance of the interest rate. Empirical evidence has accumulated in support of the hypothesis that variations in the rate of interest have little effect on the amount of desired investment. (That savings are insensitive to the interest rate is accepted even by the classical school.) This insensitivity has been interpreted as a reflection of the presence of widespread uncertainty.[1] The possible effect of this insensitivity on the ability of the system automatically to

[1] *Cf.* Oscar Lange, *Price Flexibility and Employment* (Bloomington, Indiana, Principia Press, 1945), p. 85 and the literature cited there. For an excellent theoretical discussion of this insensitivity, *cf.* G. L. S. Shackle, "Interest Rates and the Pace of Investment," *Economic Journal*, Vol. LVI (1946), pp. 1–17.

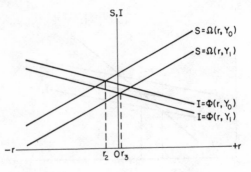

FIGURE 3.

generate full employment is analyzed in Figure 3. For simplicity the savings functions corresponding to different levels of income are reproduced from Figure 2. But the investment functions are now represented as being much less interest-sensitive than those in Figure 2. If the situation in the real world were such as represented in Figure 3, it is clear that interest rate variations could never bring about full employment. For in an economy in which there are negligible costs of storing money, the interest rate can never be negative.[2] But from Figure 3 we see that the only way the interest rate can equate desired full employment savings and investment is by assuming the negative value r_2. Hence it is impossible for the full employment national income Y_0 to exist: for no matter what (positive) rate of interest may prevail, the amount people want to save at full employment exceeds what they want to invest. Instead there will exist some less than full employment income (say) Y_1 for which desired savings and investment can be brought into equality at a positive rate of interest, (say) r_3 (*cf.* Figure 3).

Thus once again the automaticity of the system is thrown into question. Whether the system will generate full employment depends on whether the full employment

[2] Note that in a dynamic world of rising prices, the effective rate of interest may become negative. But even here the *anticipated* effective rate cannot be negative. For in that event there would again be an infinite demand for money.

savings and investment functions intersect at a positive rate of interest. But there is no automatic mechanism to assure that the savings and investment functions will have the proper slopes and positions to bring about such an intersection.[3]

4. Sometimes attempts are made to defend the classical position by arguing that the investment function is really higher (or the savings function lower) than represented by the Keynesians—so that desired full employment savings and investment can be equated at a positive rate of interest (*cf.* Figure 3). But this is beside the point. [The fundamental disagreement between Keynesian and classical economics lies in the former's denial of the automaticity of full employment posited by the latter.] Hence a successful restatement of the classical position must demonstrate the existence of some automatic mechanism which will always bring about full employment. Thus to argue that *if* the investment or saving function is at a certain level, full employment will be brought about is irrelevant; what must be shown is that there exist forces which will *automatically* bring the investment or saving functions to the required level. In other words, the issue at stake is not the *possible*, but the *automatic*, generation of full employment.

5. [To the Keynesian negative interest rate argument replies have been made by both Haberler and Pigou.[4] Just as the crude Keynesian argument of § 1 was answered by introducing a new variable—the rate of interest—into the savings function, so the more refined argument of § 3 is countered by the introduction of yet another variable—the real value of cash balances held by the individuals in the economy. Thus, denoting the amount of money in the economy M_1 (assumed to remain constant) and the absolute price level by p, Pigou's saving schedule is written as

$$S = \Gamma\left(r, Y, \frac{M_1}{p}\right).]$$

His argument is as follows: if people would refuse to save anything at negative and zero rates of interest, then the desired savings schedule would intersect the desired investment schedule at a positive rate of interest regardless of the level of income (*cf.* Figure 3). The willingness to save even without receiving interest, or even at a cost, must imply that savings are not made solely for the sake of future income (*i.e.*, interest) but also for "the desire for possession as such, conformity to tradition or custom and so on."[5] But the extent to which an individual wishes to save out of current income for reasons other than the desire of future income is inversely related to the real value of his cash balances.[6] If this is sufficiently large, all his secondary desires for saving will be fully satisfied. At this point the only reason he will continue to save out of current income is the primary one of anticipated future interest payments. In other words, if the real value of cash balances is sufficiently large, the savings function becomes zero at a positive rate of interest, regardless of the income level.

---

[3] [I have discussed this whole question of the contrast between the classical and Keynesian positions in greater detail elsewhere. *Cf.* "Involuntary Unemployment and the Keynesian Supply Function," *Economic Journal* LIX (1949), 376–78.]

[4] [G. Haberler, *Prosperity and Depression* (League of Nations, Geneva, 1941), 3rd ed., pp. 242, 389, 403, 491–503.]

A. C. Pigou, "The Classical Stationary State," *Economic Journal*, LIII (1943), 343–51; "Economic Progress in a Stable Environment," *Economica*, n. s. XIV (1947), 180–90. Although these articles deal only with a stationary state, their basic argument can readily be extended to the case in which net investment is taking place.

[In the subsequent text, I shall follow the exposition of Pigou; but the argument holds also with respect to Haberler.]

[5] *Ibid.*, p. 346.

[6] And all his other assets too. But the introduction of these other assets does not change Pigou's argument; while concentration on money assets brings out its (the argument's) basic aspect. *Cf.* below, § 6.

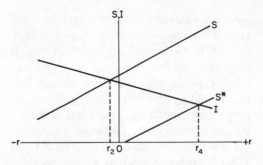

FIGURE 4.

A graphical interpretation of this argument is presented in Figure 4. Here S and I are the full-employment savings and investment curves of Figure 3 (*i.e.*, those corresponding to $Y = Y_0$), and r_2 is again the negative rate of interest at which they are equal. Pigou then argues that by increasing the real value of cash balances, the full employment savings curve shifts to the right until it is in such a position that no savings are desired except at positive rates of interest. This is represented by the savings curve S^*, which becomes zero for a positive rate of interest. (In fact, S^* shows dissaving taking place for sufficiently low rates of interest.) The full employment savings curve S^* clearly intersects the full employment investment curve I at the positive rate of interest r_4. Thus by changing the real value of cash balances, desired full employment savings and investment can always be equated at a positive rate of interest.

How can we be sure that real cash balances will automatically change in the required direction and magnitude? Here Pigou brings in his assumptions of flexible wage and price levels, and a constant stock of money in circulation. If full employment saving exceeds investment, national income begins to fall, and unemployment results. If workers react to this by decreasing their money wages, then the price level will also begin to fall. As the latter continues to fall, the real value of the constant stock of money increases correspond-

ingly. Thus, as the price level falls, the full employment saving function continuously shifts to the right until it intersects the full employment investment function at a positive rate of interest.[7]

This is the automatic mechanism on which Haberler and Pigou rely to assure full employment. It is essential to note that it will operate regardless of the interest-elasticities of the savings and investment functions—provided they are not both identically zero. [It should also be emphasized, as Haberler does, that although this argument has been presented above as an answer to Keynes, it is of much older origin. In particular, it is implicit in classical theorizing on the quantity theory of money. The crucial step in this analysis, it will be recalled, comes at the point where it is argued that as a result of increasing the amount of money in the economy, individuals' cash balances are larger than desired at the existing price level, so that they will attempt to reduce these real bal-

---

[7] The exact price level is determined when to our preceding four equations is added the liquidity preference equation, $M_0 = (r, Y, p)$, where M_0 represents the given amount of money in the system. (As will be shown in the next section, the "stock of money" relevant for the liquidity equation is completely different from the "stock of money" relevant for the Pigou analysis of the savings function; hence the use of two different symbols—M_0 and M_1.) We then have the complete system of five equations in five variables:

$$I = \Phi(r, Y)$$
$$S = \Gamma\left(r, Y, \frac{M_1}{p}\right)$$
$$I = S$$
$$Y = Y_0$$
$$M_0 = \Lambda(r, Y, p).$$

Under the Pigovian assumptions this system is consistent; its equations are satisfied for a positive rate of interest.

[The workings of a more general system of equations under the Pigovian assumption are described in detail in Parts IV and V of the reference cited in footnote 3 above. In this more detailed treatment, the full employment level, Y_0, is not arbitrarily defined—as is done in the present paper—but emerges instead from the economic behavior functions themselves.]

ances by increasing their money expenditures. The main contribution of Haberler and Pigou is to show how this set of forces must, and can, be introduced into the Keynesian analytical apparatus.]

6. The inner mechanism and distinctive characteristic of the Pigou analysis can be laid bare by considering it from a larger perspective. It is obvious that a price reduction has a stimulating effect on creditors. But, restricting ourselves to the private sector of a closed economy, to every stimulated creditor there corresponds a discouraged debtor. Hence from this viewpoint the net effect of a price reduction is likely to be in the neighborhood of zero. The neatness of the Pigou approach lies in its utilizing the fact that although the private sector considered in isolation is, on balance, neither debtor nor creditor, when considered in its relationship to the government, it *must be* a net "creditor." This is due to the fact that the private sector always holds money, which is a (non-interest bearing) "debt" of government. If we assume that government activity is not affected by the movements of the absolute price level,[8] then the net effect of a price decline must always be stimulatory.[9] The community gains at the "expense" of a gracious government, ready, willing, and able to bear the "loss" of the increased value of its "debt" to the public.

More precisely, not every price decline need have this stimulating effect. For we must consider the effect of the price decline on the other assets held by the individual. If the decline reduces the real value of these other assets (*e.g.*, houses and other forms of consumer capital; stock shares; etc.) to an extent more than offsetting the increased value of real cash balances,[10] then the net effect will be discouraging. But the important point is that no matter what our initial position, *there exists* a price level sufficiently low so that the total real value of assets corresponding to it is greater than the original real value. Consider the extreme case in which the value of the other assets becomes arbitrarily small.[11] Clearly even here the real value of the fixed stock of money can be made as large as desired by reducing the price level sufficiently. Thus, to be rigorous, the statement in the preceding paragraph should read: "There always exists a price decline such that its effect is stimulatory." From this and the analysis of the preceding section, we can derive another statement which succinctly summarizes the results of the Pigou analysis: "In the static classical model, regardless of the position of the investment schedule, there always exists a sufficiently low price level such that full employment is generated." In any event, it is clearly sufficient to concentrate (as Pigou has done) on cash balances alone.[12]

[This analysis is subject to at least two reservations, neither one of which has been considered by Haberler or Pigou. First of all, we have tacitly been assuming that the depressing effect of a price decline on a debtor is roughly offset by its stimulating effect on a creditor; hence the private sector, being on balance a creditor with respect to the government, can ultimately

---

[8] Pigou makes this assumption when he writes the investment function (which presumably also includes government expenditure) as independent of the absolute price level. *Cf.* footnote 7 above.

[9] It must be emphasized that I am abstracting here from all dynamic considerations of the effect on anticipations, etc. These will be discussed in Part II of the paper.

[10] A necessary (but not sufficient) condition for this to occur is that the price level of assets falls in a greater proportion than the general price level.

[11] I am indebted to M. Friedman for this example.

[12] *Cf.* above, footnote 6. Another possible reason for Pigou's emphasis on cash balances to the exclusion of other assets is that the relative illiquidity of the latter makes them less likely to be used as a means of satisfying the "irrational" motives of saving. Hence the inverse relationship between other assets and savings out of current income might not be so straightforward as that between real cash balances and savings.

be stimulated by a price decline. But allowance must be made for the possibility of a differential reaction of debtors and creditors. That is, if debtors are discouraged by a price decline much more than creditors are encouraged, it may be possible that there exists no price decline which would have an encouraging effect on expenditures. In brief, the Keynesian aggregative analysis followed by Pigou overlooks the possibility of microeconomic "distribution effects."

Secondly, we have so far considered only the effects of a change in real balances on household behavior; that is, on the consumption (or, its counterpart, the savings) function. It seems only natural to extend the analysis to include the influence of real cash balances on firms, and, hence, on the investment function as well. However, this extension cannot be made automatically, inasmuch as the respective motivations of firms and households are not necessarily the same. Nevertheless, it does seem reasonable to assume that investment decisions of firms are favorably influenced by a higher level of real balances. Once we take account of firms, the differential reactions mentioned in the preceding paragraph become increasingly significant. If firms are, on balance, debtors with respect to households and government, then a persistent price decline will cause a wave of bankruptcies. This will have a seriously depressing effect upon the economy which may not be offset by the improved status of creditors. Furthermore, in most cases of bankruptcy the creditors also lose. For these reasons it is not at all certain that a price decline will result in a positive net effect on the total expenditures (consumption plus investment) function. On this point much further investigation—of a theoretical as well as an empirical nature—is required.]

From the preceding analysis we can also see just exactly what constitutes the "cash balance" whose increase in real value pro-

vides the stimulatory effect of the Pigou analysis. This balance clearly consists of the net obligation of the government to the private sector of the economy. That is, it consists primarily of the total interest- and non-interest-bearing government debt held outside the treasury and central bank, [plus the net amount owed by the central bank to member banks]. Thus, by excluding demand deposits and including government interest-bearing debt and member bank reserves, it differs completely from what is usually regarded as the stock of money.

These same conclusions can be reached through a somewhat different approach. Begin with the ordinary concept of the stock of money as consisting of hand-to-hand currency and demand deposits. Consider now what changes must be made in order to arrive at the figure relevant for the Pigou analysis. Clearly, government interest-bearing debt must be added, since a price decline increases its value. Now consider money in the form of demand deposits. To the extent that it is backed by bank loans and discounts, the gains of deposit holders are offset by the losses of bank debtors.[13] Thus the net effect of a price decline on demand deposits is reduced to its effect on the excess of deposits over loans, or (approximately) on the reserves of the banks held in the form of hand-to-hand currency [and deposits in the central bank]. Finally, hand-to-hand currency held by individuals outside the banking system is added in, and we arrive at exactly the same figure as in the preceding paragraph.

For convenience denote the stock of money relevant for the Pigou analysis by M_1. Note that this is completely different from M_0 of footnote 7: for M_0 is defined in the usual manner as hand-to-hand currency plus demand deposits. This distinc-

[13] *Cf.* M. Kalecki, "Professor Pigou on 'The Classical Stationary State'—A Comment," *Economic Journal*, LIV (1944), 131–32.

tion is of fundamental importance. [One of its immediate implications is that central bank open-market operations which do not change the market price of government bonds affect the economic system only through the liquidity preference equation.] Since such operations merely substitute one type of government debt (currency) for another (bonds), they have no effect on M_1 and hence no direct effect on the amount of savings. [Even when open market purchases do cause an increase in the price of government bonds, the changes in M_0 and M_1 will not, in general, be equal. The increase in M_0 equals the total amount of money expended for the purchase of the bonds; the increase in M_1 equals the increase in the value of bonds (both of those bought and those not bought by the central bank) caused by the open-market operations.[14] Corresponding statements can be made for open-market sales.]

7. How does the Pigou formulation compare with the original classical theory?[15] Although both Pigou and the "classics" stress the importance of "price flexibility," they mean by this term completely different things. The "classics" are talking about flexibility of relative prices; Pigou is talking about flexibility of absolute prices. The classical school holds that the existence of long-run unemployment is *prima facie* evidence of rigid wages. The only way to eliminate unemployment is, then, by reducing *real* wages. (Since workers can presumably accomplish this end by reducing their *money* wage, this position has implicit in it the assumption of a constant price level—[or at least one falling relatively less than wages].) Pigou now recognizes that changing the relative price of labor is not enough, and that the absolute price level itself must vary. In fact, a strict interpretation of Pigou's position would indicate that unemployment can be eliminated even if real wages remain the same or even rise (namely, if the proportionate fall in prices is greater than or equal to that of wages); for in any case the effect of increased real value of cash balances is still present.[16]

The Pigou analysis also differs from those interpretations of the classical position which, following Keynes, present the effect of a wage decrease as acting through the liquidity preference equation to increase the real value of M_0 and thereby reduce the rate of interest; this in turn stimulates both consumption and investment expenditures—thus generating a higher level of national income. To this effect, Pigou now adds the direct stimulus to consumption expenditures provided by the price decline and the accompanying increase in real balances. Consequently, even if the savings and investment functions are completely insensitive to changes in the rate of interest (so that the effect through the liquidity equation is completely inoperative), a wage decrease will still be stimulatory through its effect on real balances and hence on savings.

---

[14] [It might be argued that through its effect on the interest rate, open-market purchases affect the value of assets other than government securities; hence, this change in value should also be included in the change in M_1. This is a point which deserves further investigation. The main question is whether there exists an offset to this improvement in the position of bondholders of private corporations.]

[15] Pigou, of course, introduces the absolute price level into the analysis of the real sector of the economy, whereas classical economics insists that this sector must be considered on the basis of relative prices alone. [As I have shown elsewhere, on this point classical economics is definitely wrong. For, in a money economy, the demand for any good must, in general, depend on the absolute price level, as well as on relative prices. This is a direct result of utility maximization. *Cf.* "Money in General Equilibrium Theory: Critique and Reformulation," *Econometrica*, XVIII (1950), and references cited there.]

[16] The role of real wages in Pigou's system is very ambiguous. At one point (p. 348, bottom) he assumes that reduced money wages will also decrease real wages. At another (p. 349, lines 20–38) no such assumption seems to be involved. "As money wage-rates fall . . . prices fall and go on falling." *Ibid.*

8. Before concluding this part of the paper, one more point must be clarified. The explicit assumption of the Pigou analysis is that savings are directly related to the price level, and therefore inversely related to the size of real cash balances. This assumption by itself is, on *a priori* grounds, quite reasonable; [indeed, in a money economy it is a direct implication of utility maximization (above, note 15)]. But it must be emphasized that even if we disregard the reservations mentioned in the preceding sections, this assumption is insufficient to bring about the conclusion desired by Pigou. For this purpose he *implicitly* makes an additional, and possibly less reasonable, assumption. Specifically, in addition to postulating explicitly the direction of the relationship between savings and the price level, he also implies something about its *intensity*.

The force of this distinction is illustrated by Figure 5. Here S and I are the full employment savings and investment curves of Figure 3 (*i.e.*, those corresponding to $Y = Y_0$) for a fixed price level, p_0. The other savings curves, S_1, S_2, S_3, S_4, represent the full employment savings schedules corresponding to the different price levels p_1, p_2, p_3, p_4, respectively. In accordance with the Pigou assumption, as the price level falls, the savings function shifts over to the right. (That is p_1, p_2, p_3, p_4, are listed in descending order.) But it may well be that as the real value of

their cash balances continues to increase, people are less and less affected by this increase. That is, for each successive increase in real balances (for each successive price level decline) the savings function moves less and less to the right, until eventually it might respond only infinitesimally, no matter how much prices fall. In graphical terms, as the price decline continues, the savings function might reach S_3 as a limiting position. That is, no matter how much the price level might fall, the savings function would never move to the right of S_3.[17] In such an event the declining price level would fail to bring about full employment. The validity of the Pigou argument thus depends on the additional assumption that the intensity of the inverse relationship between savings and real cash balances is such that it will be possible to shift over the savings function to a position where it will intercept the investment function at a positive rate of interest: say, S_4 (*cf.* Figure 5).

What is at issue here is the reaction of individuals with already large real balances to further increases in these balances. Consider an individual with a cash balance of a fixed number of dollars. As the price

[17] Mathematically this may be stated as follows. Write the savings function as

$$S = \Gamma(r, p, Y).$$

(*Cf.* footnote 7, above.) Pigou's explicit assumption is

$$\Gamma_p(r, p, Y) > 0$$

where Γ_p is the partial derivative of S with respect to p. Let $Y = Y_0$ represent the full employment income. Then the argument here is that the savings function, Γ, may still be of a form such that

$$\lim_{p \to 0} \Gamma(r, p, Y_0) = \Gamma^*(r, Y_0)$$

for any fixed r—where Γ^* is any curve which intersects the investment curve at a negative rate of interest. (In the argument of the text, Γ^* is taken to be S_3 in Figure 5.) Pigou tacitly assumes that the savings function approaches no such limit; or that if it does, the limiting function intersects the investment function at a positive rate of interest.

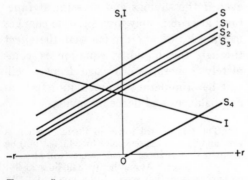

FIGURE 5.

falls, the increased real value of these dollars must be allocated between the alternatives of an addition to either consumption and/or real balances.[18] How the individual will actually allocate the increase clearly depends on the relative marginal utilities of these two alternatives. If we are willing to assume that the marginal utility of cash balances approaches zero with sufficient rapidity relative to that of consumption, then we can ignore the possibility of the savings curve reaching a limiting position such as in Figure 5. That is, we would be maintaining the position that by increasing the individual's balances sufficiently, he will have no further incentive to add to these balances; hence he will spend any additional real funds on consumption, so that we can make him consume any amount desired. If, on the other hand, we admit the possibility that, for sufficiently large consumption, the decrease in the marginal utility of cash balances is accompanied by a much faster decrease in the marginal utility of consumption, then the individual will continuously use most of the additional real funds (made available by the price decline) to add to his balances. In this event, the situation of Figure 5 may well occur.

9. I do not believe we have sufficient evidence—either of an *a priori* or empirical[19] nature—to help us answer the question raised in the preceding paragraph. The empirical evidence available is consistent with the hypothesis that the effect of real balances on savings is very weak. But even granted the truth of this hypothesis, it casts no light on the question raised here. What we want to know is what

happens to the effect of real balances on savings as these real balances increase in size. Even if the effect were arbitrarily small, but remained constant regardless of the size of real balances, there could be no convergence of savings functions like that pictured in Figure 5. In the face of this lack of evidence, we have to be satisfied with the conclusion that, subject to the [reservations of §§ 6 and 8, Haberler and Pigou have] demonstrated the automaticity of full employment within the framework of the classical static model[20]—the main mechanism by which this is brought about being the effect of a price decline on cash balances.

The statement of this conclusion immediately raises the interesting question of how this set of forces, [emphasized by Haberler and Pigou,] could have been overlooked by Keynesian economists, in general, and Keynes himself, in particular. Questions of this type can rarely be answered satisfactorily—and perhaps should not even be asked. Nevertheless, I think it is both possible and instructive to trace through the exact chain of errors in Keynes's reasoning which caused him to overlook these factors.

I submit the hypothesis that Keynes recognized the influence of assets on saving (consumption), but unfortunately thought of this influence only in terms of physical capital assets. This was his fundamental error.[21] From it immediately followed that in his main discussion of the (short-run) consumption function, where he assumed a *constant* stock of capital, the possible influence of assets was not (and

---

[18] I am abstracting here from the possible third alternative, investment.

[19] Empirical studies on the effect of real balances on savings have been made by L. R. Klein, "The Use of Econometric Models as a Guide to Economic Policy," *Econometrica*, Vol. XV (1947), pp. 122–25. Klein's procedure was incorrect in that he used a series for M_0, instead of M_1 in fitting his equations (*cf.* last paragraph of § 6 above).

[20] It must be re-emphasized that this conclusion holds only for static analysis. The modifications that must be introduced once dynamic factors enter are discussed in Part II.

[21] Note that there are really two distinct errors involved here. The first is the obvious one of the exclusion of monetary assets. The second is that what is relevant for the influence on saving is not the *physical* asset, but its *real* value in terms of some general price level.

could not) even be considered.[22] But as soon as Keynes discussed a period sufficiently long for noticeable capital growth, the influence of assets on savings was immediately recognized.[23] Even here, Keynes could not come to the same conclusion as Pigou. For Keynes restricted himself to physical assets, and thus rightfully pointed out that it would be "an unlikely coincidence" that just the correct amount of assets should exist—*i.e.*, that amount which would push over the savings function to such a position where full employment could be generated. Compare this with the determinate process by which just exactly the "correct amount" of real cash balances is brought into existence in the Pigou analysis. (See above, § 5, paragraph 4.)

This exclusion of physical assets from the short-run consumption function was subconsciously extended to all kinds of assets. Here was the last link in the chain of errors. For later when Keynes began to examine the effects of increased real cash balances (brought about either by price declines or increases in the amount of money), he did not even consider their possible influence on consumption. Instead, he concentrated exclusively on their tendency, through the liquidity function, to lower interest rates.[24] (*Cf.* above, § 7, last paragraph.)

[22] J. M. Keynes, *The General Theory of Employment, Interest, and Money* (New York, Harcourt, Brace, and Co., 1936), Chap. 8. See especially pp. 91-5, where Keynes considers the possible influence of other factors besides income on consumption, and does not even mention assets.

[23] *Ibid.*, p. 218, second paragraph.

[24] *Ibid.*, pp. 231-34, 266. The following passage is especially interesting:

It is, therefore, on the effect of a falling wage- and price-level on the *demand for money* that those who believe in the self-adjusting quality of the economic system must rest the weight of their argument; though I am not aware that they have done so. If the quantity of money is itself a function of the wage- and price-level, there is, indeed, nothing to hope for in this direction. But if the quantity of money is virtually fixed, it is evident that its quantity in

Looking back on the nature of these errors, we cannot but be struck by the irony that they should have emanated from the man who did most to demonstrate the fundamental inseparability of the real and monetary sectors of our economy.

II. DYNAMIC ANALYSIS:
THE QUESTION OF POLICY

10. [The Haberler-Pigou analysis discussed in Part I makes two contributions. First, in its emphasis on the effects of a price on savings *via* its effects on real balances, it introduces into the Keynesian analytical apparatus a set of forces hitherto overlooked by the latter. (For convenience this will be referred to as the Pigou effect— though, as mentioned at the end of § 5 above, it is of much older origin.) Secondly, it proceeds to draw the implications of this set] of forces for static analysis, and summarizes its results in the following theorem (*cf.* §§ 5 and 6): *There always exists a sufficiently low price level such that, if expected to continue indefinitely,*[25] *it will generate full employment.*[26] (For convenience this will be referred to as the Pigou Theorem.) The purpose of this part of the paper is to accomplish a third objective: *viz.*, to draw the implications of the Pigou effect for dynamic analysis and policy formulation. It must be emphasized that the Pigou Theorem tells us nothing about the dynamic and policy aspects which interest us in this third objective. (This point is discussed in greater detail in § 12.)

Specifically, consider a full employment situation which is suddenly terminated by a downswing in economic activity. The question I now wish to examine is the use-

terms of wage-units can be indefinitely increased by a sufficient reduction in money wages . . . (*Ibid.*, p. 266. Italics not in original.)

[25] This qualifying phrase incorporates in it the restriction of the Pigou argument to static analysis.

[26] I am overlooking here the reservations discussed in §§6 and 8 above.

fulness of a policy which consists of maintaining the stock of money constant, allowing the wage and price levels to fall, and waiting for the resulting increase in real balances to restore full employment.

At the outset it must be made clear that the above policy recommendation is *not* to be attributed to Pigou. His interest is purely an intellectual one, in a purely static analysis. As he himself writes: ". . . The puzzles we have been considering . . . are academic exercises, of some slight use perhaps for clarifying thought, but with very little chance of ever being posed on the chequer board of actual life."[27]

In reality, Pigou's disavowal of a deflationary policy (contained in the paragraph from which the above quotation is taken) is not nearly as thoroughgoing as might appear on the first reading. The rejection of a price decline as a practical means of combatting unemployment may be due to: (a) the conviction that dynamic considerations invalidate its use as an immediate policy, regardless of its merits in static analysis; (b) the conviction that industrial and labor groups, sometimes with the assistance of government, prevent the price flexibility necessary for the success of a deflationary policy. A careful reading of Pigou's disclaimer indicates that he had only the second of these alternatives in mind; *i.e.*, that he felt that the policy would not work because it would not be permitted to work. What I hope to establish in this part of the essay is the first alternative: namely, that even granted full flexibility of prices, it is still highly possible that a deflationary policy will not work, due to the dynamic factors involved.

Nevertheless, nothing in this part of the paper is intended (or even relevant) as a criticism of Pigou, since the latter has clearly abstained from the problem of policy formulation. If sometimes the terms

[27] "Economic Progress in a Stable Environment," *Economica*, n. s. XIV (1947), 188.

"Pigou effect" and "Pigou Theorem" are used in the following discussion, they should be understood solely as shorthand notations for the concepts previously explained.

11. The analysis of this section is based on the following two assumptions: (a) One of the prerequisites of a successful anti-depression policy is that it should be able to achieve its objective rapidly (say, within a year). (b) Prices cannot fall instantaneously; hence, the larger the price level fall necessary to bring about full employment *via* the Pigou effect, the longer the time necessary for the carrying out of the policy. (If no price fall can bring about full employment, then we can say that an infinite amount of time is necessary for the carrying out of the policy.)

There are at least two factors which act toward lengthening the period necessary to carry out a policy based on the Pigou effect. The first is the possibility that the effect of an increase in cash balances on consumption is so small, that very large increases (very great price declines) will be necessary. [Certainly there is a burden of proof on the supporters of a policy of absolute price flexibility to show that this is not so;] that the economic system is sufficiently responsive to make the policy practical. So far no one has presented the required evidence.

The second factor is a result of the price decline itself. In dynamic analysis we must give full attention to the role played by price expectations and anticipations in general. It is quite possible that the original price decline will lead to the expectation of further declines. Then purchasing decisions will be postponed, aggregate demand will fall off, and the amount of unemployment increased still more. In terms of Figures 1 and 3, the savings function will rise (consumption will be decreased) and the investment function fall, further aggravating the problem of achieving full employment. This was the point

[TABLE 1]

Year	Money in circulation Outside Treasury and Federal Reserve System	Market value of government interest-bearing debt held outside government agencies and the Federal Reserve System	Member bank deposits in the Federal Reserve System	Non-member bank deposits in the Federal Reserve System	Other Federal Reserve accounts	Reserve Bank credit outstanding excluding that based on Treasury U.S. government securities	Treasury deposits in member and non-member banks	Postal savings	Net balances (M_1) $(1)+(2)$ $+(3)+(4)$ $+(5)-(6)$ $-(7)+(8)$	Cost of living index (p)	Net real balances $\frac{M_1}{p}$ $(9)-(10)$	Real national income
	(1)	(2)	(3)	(4)	(5)	(6)	(7)	(8)	(9)	(10)	(11)	(12)
1929	4.5	14.5	2.4	0.0	0.4	1.3	0.4	0.2	20.2	1.22	16.6	89.9
1930	4.2	13.9	2.4	0.0	0.4	0.5	0.3	0.2	20.4	1.19	17.1	76.3
1931	4.7	15.1	2.3	0.1	0.4	0.6	0.4	0.6	22.1	1.09	20.3	66.3
1932	5.3	16.0	2.1	0.1	0.4	0.6	0.4	0.9	23.7	.98	24.2	54.2

All money figures are in billions of dollars.
Data for series (1), (3), (4), (5), (6) were obtained from *Banking and Monetary Statistics*, p. 368. On pp. 360–67 of this book their interrelationships are discussed. For (7) see *ibid.*, pp. 34–5. For (8) see *Statistical Abstract of the United States*, 1947, p. 419.
Being unable to find an official series for (2), I used the following procedure: Total outstanding government debt at face value was classified according to maturities (0–5 years, 5–10, and over 10) on the basis of *Banking and Monetary Statistics*, p. 511. These classifications were multiplied by price indexes for government bonds with maturities of more than 3 and less than 4 years, more than 6 and less than 9, and more than 10, respectively (Standard and Poor, *Statistics: Security Price Index Record*, 1948 edition, pp. 139–44). The sum of these products was used as an estimate of the market value of the total government debt. The ratio of this to the face value of the total debt was computed, and this ratio applied to the face value of government debt held outside the Treasury and Federal Reserve System (*Banking and Monetary Statistics*, p. 512) to yield an estimate of the required series.
Series (10): Bureau of Labor Statistics, cost of living index, *Survey of Current Business*, Supplement, 1942, p. 16.
Series (12): National income in billions of 1944 dollars. J. Dewhurst and Associates, *America's Needs and Resources* (New York, The Twentieth Century Fund, 1947), p. 697.]

on which Keynes was so insistent.[28] Furthermore, the uncertainty about the future generated by the price decline will increase the liquidity preference of individuals. Thus if we consider an individual possessing a fixed number of dollars, and confronted with a price decline which increases the real value of these dollars, his uncertainty will make him more inclined to employ these additional real funds to increase his real balances, than to increase his expenditures.[29] In other words, the uncertainty created by the price decline might cause people to accumulate indefinitely large real cash balances, and to increase their expenditures very little if at all. [Finally, the bankruptcies caused by the inability of creditors to carry the increased real burden of their debt (above, § 6) will strengthen the pessimistic outlook for the future. The simultaneous interaction of these three forces] will further exacerbate these difficulties. For as the period of price decline drags itself out, anticipations for the future will progressively worsen, and uncertainties further increase. The end result of letting the Pigou effect work itself out may be a disastrous deflationary spiral, continuing for several years without ever reaching any equilibrium position. Certainly our past experiences should have sensitized us to this danger.

Because of these considerations I feel that it is impractical to depend upon the Pigou effect as a means of policy: the required price decline might be either too large (factor one), or it might be the initial step of an indefinite deflationary spiral (factor two).

On this issue, it may be interesting to investigate the experience of the United States in the 1930's. In Table 1, net balances are computed for the period 1929–32

according to the definition in § 6. As can be seen, although there was a 19 per cent *increase* in real balances from 1930 to 1931, real national income during this period *decreased* by 13 per cent. Even in the following year, when a further increase of 19 per cent in real balances took place, real income proceeded to fall by an additional 18 per cent. For the 1929–1932 period as a whole there was an increase in real balances of 46 per cent, and a decrease in real income of 40 per cent.

It will, of course, be objected that these data reflect the presence of "special factors," and do not indicate the real value of the Pigou effect. But the pertinent question which immediately arises is: To what extent were these "special factors" necessary, concomitant results of the price decline itself! If the general feeling of uncertainty and adverse anticipations that marked the period is cited as one of these "special factors," the direct relationship between this and the decline in price level itself certainly cannot be overlooked. Other proposed "special factors" must be subjected to the same type of examination. The data of the preceding table are not offered as conclusive evidence. But they are certainly consistent with the previously stated hypothesis of the impracticability of using the Pigou effect as a means of policy; and they certainly throw the burden of proof on those who argue for its practicality.

12. The argument of the preceding section requires further explanation on at least one point. In the discussion of the "second factor" there was mentioned the possibility of an indefinitely continuing spiral of deflation and unemployment. But what is the relation between this possibility and the Pigou Theorem (*cf.* § 10) established in Part I? The answer to this question may be expressed as follows:

On the downswing of the business cycle it might be interesting to know that there exists a sufficiently low price level which,

---

[28] See his discussion of changes in money wages, *op. cit.*, pp. 260–69, especially p. 263. *Cf.* also J. R. Hicks, *Value and Capital* (Oxford, Oxford University Press, 1939), and O. Lange, *op. cit.*

[29] *Cf.* above, § 8, last paragraph.

if it were expected to continue existing indefinitely, would bring about full employment. Interesting, but, for policy purposes, irrelevant. For due to perverse price expectations and the dynamics of deflationary spirals, it is impossible to reach (or, once having reached, to remain at) such a position.

The implication of these remarks can be clarified by consideration of the cobweb theorem for the divergent case. Assume that a certain market can be explained in terms of the cobweb theorem. It is desired to know whether (assuming unchanged demand and supply curves) the designated market will ever reach a stationary position; that is, whether it will settle down to a unique price that will continue indefinitely to clear the market. This question is clearly divided into two parts: (a) does there exist such a price, and (b) if it does exist, will the market be able to attain it. In the case of the cobweb presented in Figure 6 it is clear that such a price does exist. For if the price p_0 had always existed and were expected to exist indefinitely, it would continuously clear the market. But Figure 6 represents the case of a divergent cobweb; hence the market will never be able to reach the price p_0. In brief, even though p_0 exists, it is irrelevant to the workings of the market. The analogy to the argument of the preceding paragraph is obvious.[30]

---

[30] The distinction of this section can be expressed in rigorous mathematical form using the dynamic system which has become familiar through the work of Samuelson and Lange (P. A. Samuelson, "The Stability of Equilibrium: Comparative Statics and Dynamics," *Econometrica*, Vol. IX [1941], pp. 97–120; Lange, *op. cit.*, pp. 91 ff.). Consider a single market and let D, S, and p represent the demand, supply and price of the particular good, respectively. Let t represent time. Then we can write this system as

(a) $D = f(p)$ demand function
(b) $S = g(p)$ supply function
(c) $\dfrac{dp}{dt} = h(D\text{-}S)$ market adjusting function

III.   CONCLUSIONS

13.   The conclusions of this paper can be summarized as follows: in a static world with a constant stock of money,[31] price flexibility assures full employment. (I abstract here again from the difficulties raised

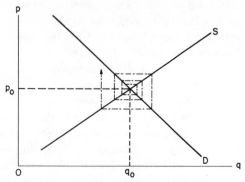

FIGURE 6.

The last equation has the property that

(d) $\operatorname{sign} \dfrac{dp}{dt} = \operatorname{sign} (D\text{-}S)$

i.e., price rises with excess demand and falls with excess supply. Consider now the static system identical with (a) − (c), except that it replaces (c) by (e) $D = S$. As long as (e) is not satisfied, we see from (d) that the system will not be in stationary equilibrium, but will continue to fluctuate. Thus the existence of a solution to the static system (a), (b), (e) (*i.e.*, the consistency of (a), (b), (e)) is a *necessary* condition for the existence of a stationary solution for the dynamic system (a), (b), (c). But this is not a sufficient condition. For the static system (a), (b), (e) may have a consistent solution which, if the dynamic system is not convergent, will never be reached.

Thus Pigou has completed only half the task. Setting aside the difficulties of § 8, we can accept his proof of the *consistency* of the *static* classical system. But that still leaves completely unanswered the question of whether the classical *dynamic* system will converge to this consistent solution. In this and the preceding section I have tried to show why such convergence may not occur in the real world. (I have discussed these issues in greater detail elsewhere. *Cf.* footnote 3, above.)

[31] Throughout Part III, unless otherwise indicated, "stock of money" is to be understood in the M_1 sense of the last paragraph of § 6.

in §§ 6 and 8.) But in the real dynamic world in which we live, price flexibility with a constant stock of money might generate full employment only after a long period; or might even lead to a deflationary spiral of continuous unemployment. On either of these grounds, a full employment policy based on a constant stock of money and price flexibility does not seem to be very promising.

All that this means is that our full employment policy cannot be the fairly simple one of maintaining a constant stock of money and waiting for the economic system to generate full employment automatically through price declines. Other policies will be required. One possible alternative policy can be inferred from the Haberler-Pigou analysis itself: there are two ways to increase real balances. One is to keep the money stock constant and permit prices to fall. An equally effective way is to maintain the price level constant, and increase the stock of money by creating a government deficit.[32] This method of increasing real balances has the added advantage of avoiding one of the difficulties encountered previously (§ 11), for a policy of stabilizing the price level by increasing money stocks avoids some of the dangers of uncertainty and adverse anticipation accompanying general price declines. Nevertheless, there still remains the other difficulty—that individuals may not be very sensitive to increases in real balances. If this turned out to be true, we would have to seek still other policies.

14. [On the basis of the analysis presented in this paper it is possible to re-

[32] Considered from this perspective, the Pigou analysis presents in a rigorous fashion part of the theoretical framework implicit in the fiscal-monetary policy of the Simons-Mints position. *Cf.* the recently published collection of essays of Henry C. Simons, *Economic Policy for a Free Society* (Chicago, University of Chicago Press, 1948); and Lloyd W. Mints, "Monetary Policy," *Review of Economic Statistics*, Vol. XXVIII (1946), pp. 60–9.

examine the question which has been a favorite one of economists these past years: namely,] What is the distinctive characteristic of Keynesian analysis? It certainly cannot be the claim to have demonstrated the possibility of the coexistence of underemployment equilibrium and flexible prices. This, in its day, served well as a rallying cry. But now it should be definitely recognized that this is an indefensible position. For flexibility means that the money wage falls with excess supply, and rises with excess demand; and equilibrium means that the system can continue on through time without change. Hence, *by definition*, a system with price flexibility cannot be in equilibrium if there is any unemployment;[33] [but, like any other proposition that must be true by definition, this one, too, is uninteresting, unimportant, and uninformative about the real problems of economic policy].

Nor should Keynesian economics be interpreted as asserting that just as an underemployment equilibrium is impossible, so, too, in a static system may a full-employment equilibrium be impossible. That is, the static system may be at neither

[33] This can be expressed mathematically in the following way: let N^S and N^D be the amounts of labor supplied and demanded, respectively; w, the money wage rate; and t, time. Then a flexible dynamic system will, by definition, contain an equation of the general type

$$\frac{dw}{dt} = f(N^D - N^S)$$

where

$$\text{sign} \frac{dw}{dt} = \text{sign} (N^D - N^S).$$

If by equilibrium is meant a situation such that

$$\frac{dw}{dt} = 0$$

then clearly this system cannot be in equilibrium unless

$$N^D - N^S = 0$$

i.e., unless there is full employment.

an underemployment equilibrium, nor a full-employment equilibrium. In other words, the static system may be inconsistent. (This is the negative interest rate argument of § 3.) For Pigou's and Haberler's discussion of the effect of a declining price level on real balances shows how this inconsistency is removed. It is, of course, still possible to maintain this interpretation of Keynes on the basis of the reservations of §§ 6 and 8. But I think this is neither necessary nor advisable. For the real significance of the Keynesian contribution can be realized only within the framework of *dynamic* economics. Whether or not an underemployment equilibrium exists; whether or not full employment equilibrium always will be generated in a static system—all this is irrelevant. The fundamental issue raised by Keynesian economics is the *stability of the dynamic system:* its ability to return automatically to a full-employment equilibrium within a reasonable time (say, a year) if it is subjected to the customary shocks and disturbances of a peacetime economy. In other words, what Keynesian economics claims is that the economic system may be in a position of underemployment *dis*equilibrium (in the sense that wages, prices, and the amount of unemployment are continuously changing over time) for long, or even indefinite, periods of time.

But this is not sufficient to characterize the Keynesians. Everyone agrees that there exist dynamic systems which will not automatically generate full employment. What distinguishes one economic school from the other is the system (or systems) to which this lack of automaticity is attributed. If the Keynesian message is applied to an economic system with no monetary policy (if such a thing is possible to define), then it is purely trivial. For few would claim automaticity of full employment for such a system. Keynesian theory acquires meaning only when applied to systems with more intelligent monetary

policies. Here an element of arbitrariness is introduced; for what is termed "Keynesian" depends entirely on the choice of the monetary policy to be used as a criterion.

On the basis of Keynes' writings, I believe it is clear that he was primarily interested in attacking the policy of assuring full employment by manipulation of the interest rate through open market operations.[34] But to Keynes, this policy was equivalent to one of wage flexibility;[35] for (he erroneously thought) the only effect of a wage decline was to increase the real value of the stock of money (in the M_0, not M_1, sense; *cf.* above, last paragraph of § 6) and thereby decrease the rate of interest—just as in open market operations. As we have pointed out above (end of §§ 6 and 7), these policies are really not equivalent. For open market operations may change only M_0, whereas a wage and price decline change the real value of M_1 as well. Hence, open market operations may act only through the liquidity preference equation, whereas a policy of price flexibility acts also through the savings function (*cf.* above, footnote 7 and end of §§ 6 and 7).

Let us now assume that even if Keynes had recognized the distinction between open market and wage flexibility policies (*i.e.*, if he had recognized the Pigou effect) he still would have continued to reject the latter as a means of assuring full employment. This is not an unreasonable assumption; for most of the objections cited above (§ 11) against the use of a policy based on the Pigou effect, are the very same ones that Keynes uses in arguing against open market operations.[36]

[34] *Cf.* Keynes, *op. cit.*, pp. 231–34; 266–67.

[35] "There is, therefore, no ground for the belief that a flexible wage policy is capable of maintaining a state of continuous full employment;— any more than for the belief that an open market monetary policy is capable, unaided, of achieving this result. The economic system cannot be made self-adjusting along these lines." (*Ibid.*, p. 267.)

[36] *Cf.* the passages cited in footnote 34, above.

Granted this assumption, I believe it is useful to identify the Keynesian position against one which maintains that full employment can be automatically achieved *via* the Pigou effect by maintaining a constant stock of money, and providing for wage and price flexibility. It is now possible to delineate three distinct theoretical formulations of the Keynesian position—differing in varying degrees from the classical one: (a) Most opposed to the classical position is the Keynesian one which states that even if there were no problem of uncertainty and adverse anticipations (that is, even if there were a static system), and even if we were to allow an infinite amount of time for adjustment, a policy of price flexibility would still not assure the generation of full employment. (This is the negative interest rate argument of §§ 3 and 8; [or the argument based on differential creditor-debtor responses of § 6].)

(b) Then there is the position which states that, in a static world, price flexibility would always assure full employment. But in a dynamic world of uncertainty and adverse anticipations, even if we were to allow an infinite adjustment period, there is no certainty that full employment will be generated. That is, we may remain indefinitely in a position of underemployment disequilibrium. (c) Finally, there is the Keynesian position, closest to the "classics," which states that even with uncertainty full employment would eventually be generated by a policy of price flexibility; but the length of time that might be necessary for the adjustment makes the policy impractical.

Although these positions are quite distinct theoretically, their policy implications are very similar. (In what way would the policies of a man advocating position (a) differ from those of a man advocating (c) and stating that the adjustment would take ten years?) The policies would in general be directed at influencing the consumption and investment functions themselves, in addition to manipulating the amount of money. Thus the policies may advocate tax reductions to stimulate consumption and investment (the Simons-Mints school); or may insist on direct government investment to supplement private investment (Hansen, *et al.*). In this way we could cross-classify Keynesian positions according to their advocated policies, as well as their theoretical foundations.

[Finally, it should be noted that none of the preceding three formulations of the Keynesian position is dependent upon the assumption of wage rigidities. This assumption is frequently, and erroneously, attributed to Keynesian economics as a result of two related misconceptions as to its nature. First of all, as we have seen, the attempt to interpret Keynes' analysis of unemployment within a static equilibrium framework makes it mandatory, by definition, to assume the existence of wage rigidities. The dynamic approach followed in this paper obviates this necessity.

A second implication of restricting ourselves to static equilibrium analysis is that *involuntary* unemployment can, *by definition*, exist only if there are wage rigidities. For if there were no wage rigidities, the wage level could assume any value; and for each such value there would be a corresponding, and presumably different, amount of labor supplied. Thus at the intersection point of the demand and supply curves—the only point of interest in static equilibrium analysis—workers are providing all the labor they wish to at the equilibrium wage. There can be no question of involuntary unemployment. Only if there are wage rigidities—a minimum wage w_0, below which the workers refuse to go—can the situation be different. For then the supply curve of labor is parallel to the quantity axis at the height w_0 until a certain point (say) N_1, is reached; only afterwards does the curve begin to rise. If the demand curve is now assumed to intersect the supply curve in its horizontal portion at, say, the quantity N_0, then we can say that *involuntary* unemployment to the extent $N_1 - N_0$ exists; for at the equilibrium wage rate, w_0, workers desire to provide a maximum of N_1 units of labor, and are instead providing only N_0.

However, once we throw off the restrictions of static equilibrium analysis, we also free ourselves of the necessity of assuming wage rigidity as a necessary precondition of involuntary unemployment. For, during any given period of time, the dynamic workings of the system may well keep the workers at a point *off their supply curve*. In this departure from the supply curve lies the *involuntariness* of the unemployment. The important point here is that this situation can exist regardless of the shape of the supply curve; that is, even if wages are not rigid. One's view on the length of time such a situation can continue clearly depends on one's choice of the three alternative Keynesian positions delineated above. All this has been dealt with at length elsewhere,[37] and there is no need for any further repetition here.[38]]

[37] *Cf.* reference cited in footnote 3 above.

[38] It might be added that in the light of Chapter 19 of the *General Theory*—the chapter which provides the climax to Keynes' argument, and which explicitly examines the effects of wage flexibility—it is difficult to understand how wage rigidities can be considered a basic assumption of the Keynesian theory of unemployment. From this chapter it is quite clear that wage rigidities are *not* an *assumption* of Keynes' analysis, but rather a policy conclusion that follows from his investigation of the probable effects of *wage flexibility*.

Further explicit evidence that Keynes, in his theory of unemployment, was concerned with a regime of flexible prices is provided by the following passage from the *General Theory* (p. 191): "in the extreme case where money wages are assumed to fall without limit in face of involuntary unemployment ... there will, it is true, be only two possible long period positions—full employment and the level of employment corresponding to the rate of interest at which liquidity preference becomes absolute (in the event of this being less than full employment)."

17

The Relation between Unemployment and the Rate of Change of Money Wage Rates in the United Kingdom, 1861–1957*

A. W. PHILLIPS

I. HYPOTHESIS

When the demand for a commodity or service is high relatively to the supply of it we expect the price to rise, the rate of rise being greater the greater the excess demand. Conversely when the demand is low relatively to the supply we expect the price to fall, the rate of fall being greater

Reprinted from *Economica*, New Series, vol. 25 (November 1958), pp. 283–299, by permission of the publisher and author.

A. W. Phillips teaches at the Australian National University; he was formerly at the London School of Economics.

* This study is part of a wider research project financed by a grant from the Ford Foundation. The writer was assisted by Mrs. Marjory Klonarides. Thanks are due to Professor E. H. Phelps Brown, Professor J. E. Meade and Dr. R. G. Lipsey for comments on an earlier draft.

the greater the deficiency of demand. It seems plausible that this principle should operate as one of the factors determining the rate of change of money wage rates, which are the price of labour services. When the demand for labour is high and there are very few unemployed we should expect employers to bid wage rates up quite rapidly, each firm and each industry being continually tempted to offer a little above the prevailing rates to attract the most suitable labour from other firms and industries. On the other hand it appears that workers are reluctant to offer their services at less than the prevailing rates when the demand for labour is low and unemployment is high so that wage rates fall only very slowly. The relation between unemployment and the rate of change of wage rates is therefore likely to be highly non-linear.

It seems possible that a second factor influencing the rate of change of money wage rates might be the rate of change of the demand for labour, and so of unemployment. Thus in a year of rising business activity, with the demand for labour increasing and the percentage unemployment decreasing, employers will be bidding more vigorously for the services of labour than they would be in a year during which the average percentage unemployment was the same but the demand for labour was not increasing. Conversely in a year of falling business activity, with the demand for labour decreasing and the percentage unemployment increasing, employers will be less inclined to grant wage increases, and workers will be in a weaker position to press for them, than they would be in a year during which the average percentage unemployment was the same but the demand for labour was not decreasing.

A third factor which may affect the rate of change of money wage rates is the rate of change of retail prices, operating through cost of living adjustments in wage rates. It will be argued here, however, that cost of living adjustments will have little or no effect on the rate of change of money wage rates except at times when retail prices are forced up by a very rapid rise in import prices (or, on rare occasions in the United Kingdom, in the prices of home-produced agricultural products). For suppose that productivity is increasing steadily at the rate of, say, 2 percent per annum and that aggregate demand is increasing similarly so that unemployment is remaining constant at, say, 2 percent. Assume that with this level of unemployment and without any cost of living adjustments wage rates rise by, say, 3 percent per annum as the result of employers' competitive bidding for labour and that import prices and the prices of other factor services are also rising by 3 percent per annum. Then retail prices will be rising on average at the rate of about 1 percent per annum (the rate of

change of factor costs minus the rate of change of productivity). Under these conditions the introduction of cost of living adjustments in wage rates will have no effect, for employers will merely be giving under the name of cost of living adjustments part of the wage increases which they would in any case have given as a result of their competitive bidding for labour.

Assuming that the value of imports is one fifth of national income, it is only at times when the annual rate of change of import prices exceeds the rate at which wage rates would rise as a result of competitive bidding by employers by more than five times the rate of increase of productivity that cost of living adjustments become an operative factor in increasing the rate of change of money wage rates. Thus in the example given above a rate of increase of import prices of more than 13 percent per annum would more than offset the effects of rising productivity so that retail prices would rise by more than 3 percent per annum. Cost of living adjustments would then lead to a greater increase in wage rates than would have occurred as a result of employers' demand for labour and this would cause a further increase in retail prices, the rapid rise in import prices thus initiating a wage-price spiral which would continue until the rate of increase of import prices dropped significantly below the critical value of about 13 percent per annum.

The purpose of the present study is to see whether statistical evidence supports the hypothesis that the rate of change of money wage rates in the United Kingdom can be explained by the level of unemployment and the rate of change of unemployment, except in or immediately after those years in which there was a very rapid rise in import prices, and if so to form some quantitative estimate of the relation between unemployment and the rate of change of money wage rates. The periods 1861–1913, 1913–1948 and 1948–1957 will be considered separately.

II. 1861–1913

Schlote's index of the average price of imports[1] shows an increase of 12.5 percent in import prices in 1862 as compared with the previous year, an increase of 7.6 percent in 1900 and in 1910, and an increase of 7.0 percent in 1872. In no other year between 1861 and 1913 was there an increase in import prices of as much as 5 percent. If the hypothesis stated above is correct the rise in import prices in 1862 may just have been sufficient to start up a mild wage-price spiral, but in the remainder of the period changes in import prices will have had little or no effect on the rate of change of wage rates.

A scatter diagram of the rate of change of wage rates and the percentage unemployment for the years 1861–1913 is shown in Figure 1. During this time there were 6½ fairly regular trade cycles with an average period of about 8 years. Scatter diagrams for the years of each trade cycle are shown in Figures 2 to 8. Each dot in the diagrams represents a year, the average rate of change of money wage rates during the year being given by the scale on the vertical axis and the average

unemployment during the year by the scale on the horizontal axis. The rate of change of money wage rates was calculated from the index of hourly wage rates constructed by Phelps Brown and Sheila Hopkins,[2] by expressing the first central difference of the index for each year as a percentage of the index for the same year. Thus the rate of change for 1861 is taken to be half the difference between the index for 1862 and the index for 1860 expressed as a percentage of the index for 1861, and similarly for other years.[3] The percentage unemployment figures are those calculated by the Board of Trade and the Ministry of Labour[4] from trade union returns. The corresponding percentage employment figures are quoted in Beveridge, *Full Employment in a Free Society*, Table 22.

It will be seen from Figures 2 to 8 that there is a clear tendency for the rate of change of money wage rates to be high when unemployment is low and to be low or negative when unemployment is high. There is also a clear tendency for the rate of change of money wage rates at any given level of unemployment to be above the average for that level of unemployment when unemployment is decreasing during the upswing of a trade cycle and to be below the average for that level of unemployment when unemployment is increasing during the downswing of a trade cycle.

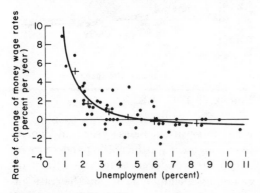

FIGURE 1. 1861–1913.

[1] W. Schlote, *British Overseas Trade from 1700 to the 1930's*, Table 26.

[2] E. H. Phelps Brown and Sheila Hopkins, "The Course of Wage Rates in Five Countries, 1860–1939," *Oxford Economic Papers*, June, 1950.

[3] The index is apparently intended to measure the average of wage rates during each year. The first central difference is therefore the best simple approximation to the average absolute rate of change of wage rates during a year and the central difference expressed as a percentage of the index number is an appropriate measure of the average percentage rate of change of wage rates during the year.

[4] *Memoranda upon British and Foreign Trade and Industrial Conditions* (Second Series) (Cd. 2337), B.P.P. 1905, Vol. 84; *21st Abstract of Labour Statistics, 1919–1933* (Cd. 4625), B.P.P. 1933–34, Vol. 26.

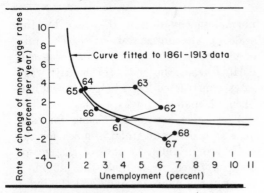

FIGURE 2. 1861–1868.

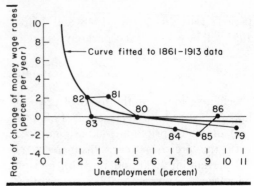

FIGURE 4a. 1879–1886, USING BOWLEY'S
WAGE INDEX FOR THE YEARS 1861–1886.

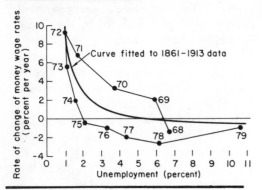

FIGURE 3. 1868–1879.

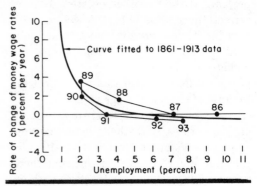

FIGURE 5. 1886–1893.

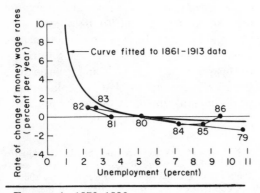

FIGURE 4. 1879–1886.

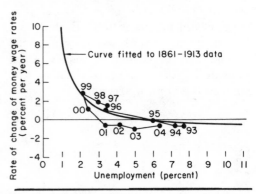

FIGURE 6. 1893–1904.

The crosses shown in Figure 1 give the average values of the rate of change of money wage rates and of the percentage unemployment in those years in which unemployment lay between 0 and 2, 2 and 3, 3 and 4, 4 and 5, 5 and 7, and 7 and 11 percent respectively (the upper bound being included in each interval). Since each interval includes years in which unemployment was increasing and years in which it was decreasing the effect of changing unemployment on the rate of change of wage rates tends to be cancelled out by this averaging, so that each cross gives an approximation to the rate of change of wages which would be associated

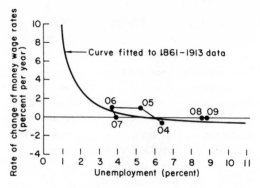

FIGURE 7.   1904–1909.

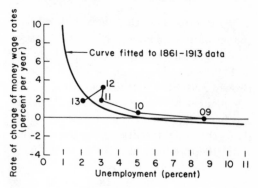

FIGURE 8.   1909–1913.

with the indicated level of unemployment if unemployment were held constant at that level.

The curve shown in Figure 1 (and repeated for comparison in later diagrams) was fitted to the crosses. The form of equation chosen was

$$y + a = bx^c$$

or

$$\log (y + a) = \log b + c \log x$$

where y is the rate of change of wage rates and x is the percentage unemployment. The constants b and c were estimated by least squares using the values of y and x corresponding to the crosses in the four intervals between 0 and 5 percent unemployment, the constant a being chosen by trial and error to make the curve pass as close as possible to the remaining two crosses in the intervals between 5 and 11 percent unemployment.[5] The equation of

---

[5] At first sight it might appear preferable to carry out a multiple regression of y on the variables x and dx/dt. However, owing to the particular form of the relation between y and x in the present case it is not easy to find a suitable linear multiple regression equation. An equation of the form $y + a = bx^c + k[(1/x^m)(dx/dt)]$ would probably be suitable. If so the procedure which has been adopted for estimating the relation that would hold between y and x if dx/dt were zero is satisfactory, since it can easily be shown that $(1/x^m) \cdot (dx/dt)$ is uncorrelated with x or with any power of x provided that x is, as in this case, a trend-free variable.

the fitted curve is

$$y + 0.900 = 9.638x^{-1.394}$$

or

$$\log (y + 0.900) = 0.984 - 1.394 \log x$$

Considering the wage changes in individual years in relation to the fitted curve, the wage increase in 1862 (see Figure 2) is definitely larger than can be accounted for by the level of unemployment and the rate of change of unemployment, and the wage increase in 1863 is also larger than would be expected. It seems that the 12.5 percent increase in import prices between 1861 and 1862 referred to above (and no doubt connected with the outbreak of the American civil war) was in fact sufficient to have a real effect on wage rates by causing cost of living increases in wages which were greater than the increases which would have resulted from employers' demand for labour and that the consequent wage-price spiral continued into 1863. On the other hand the increases in import prices of 7.6 percent between 1899 and 1900 and again between 1909 and 1910 and the increase of 7.0 percent between 1871 and 1872 do not seem to have had any noticeable effect on wage rates. This is consistent with the hypothesis stated above about the effect of rising import prices on wage rates.

Figure 3 and Figures 5 to 8 show a very clear relation between the rate of change of wage rates and the level and rate of change of unemployment,[6] but the relation hardly appears at all in the cycle shown in Figure 4. The wage index of Phelps Brown and Sheila Hopkins from which the changes in wage rates were calculated was based on Wood's earlier index,[7] which shows the same stability during these years. From 1880 we have also Bowley's index of wage rates.[8] If the rate of change of money wage rates for 1881 to 1886 is calculated from Bowley's index by the same method as was used before, the results shown in Figure 4a are obtained, giving the typical relation between the rate of change of wage rates and the level and rate of change of unemployment. It seems possible that some peculiarity may have occurred in the construction of Wood's index for these years. Bowley's index for the remainder of the period up to 1913 gives results which are broadly similar to those shown in Figures 5 to 8, but the pattern is rather less regular than that obtained with the index of Phelps Brown and Sheila Hopkins.

From Figure 6 it can be seen that wage rates rose more slowly than usual in the upswing of business activity from 1893 to 1896 and then returned to their normal pattern of change; but with a temporary increase in unemployment during 1897. This suggests that there may have been exceptional resistance by employers to wage increases from 1894 to 1896, culminating in industrial strife in 1897. A

glance at industrial history[9] confirms this suspicion. During the 1890's there was a rapid growth of employers' federations and from 1895 to 1897 there was resistance by the employers' federations to trade union demands for the introduction of an eight-hour working day, which would have involved a rise in hourly wage rates. This resulted in a strike by the Amalgamated Society of Engineers, countered by the Employers' Federation with a lock-out which lasted until January 1898.

From Figure 8 it can be seen that the relation between wage changes and unemployment was again disturbed in 1912. From the monthly figures of percentage unemployment in trade unions[10] we find that unemployment rose from 2.8 percent in February 1912 to 11.3 percent in March, falling back to 3.6 percent in April and 2.7 percent in May, as the result of a general stoppage of work in coal mining. If an adjustment is made to eliminate the effect of the strike on unemployment the figure for the average percentage unemployment during 1912 would be reduced by about 0.8 percent, restoring the typical pattern of the relation between the rate of change of wage rates and the level and rate of change of unemployment.

From a comparison of Figures 2 to 8 it appears that the width of loops obtained in each trade cycle has tended to narrow, suggesting a reduction in the dependence of the rate of change of wage rates on the rate of change of unemployment. There seem to be two possible explanations of this. First, in the coal and steel industries before the first world war sliding scale adjustments were common, by which wage rates were linked to the prices of the products.[11] Given the tendency of product prices to rise with an increase in business

[6] Since the unemployment figures used are the averages of monthly percentages, the first central difference is again the best simple approximation to the average rate of change of unemployment during a year. It is obvious from an inspection of Fig. 3 and Figs. 5 to 8 that in each cycle there is a close relation between the deviations of the points from the fitted curve and the first central differences of the employment figures, though the magnitude of the relation does not seem to have remained constant over the whole period.

[7] See Phelps Brown and Sheila Hopkins, *loc. cit.*, pp. 264–5.

[8] A. L. Bowley, *Wages and Income in the United Kingdom since 1800*, Table VII, p. 30.

[9] See B. C. Roberts, *The Trades Union Congress, 1868–1921*, Chapter IV, especially pp. 158–162.

[10] *21st Abstract of Labour Statistics, 1919–1933*, *loc. cit.*

[11] I am indebted to Professor Phelps Brown for pointing this out to me.

activity and fall with a decrease in business activity, these agreements may have strengthened the relation between changes in wage rates and changes in unemployment in these industries. During the earlier years of the period these industries would have fairly large weights in the wage index, but with the greater coverage of the statistical material available in later years the weights of these industries in the index would be reduced. Second, it is possible that the decrease in the width of the loops resulted not so much from a reduction in the dependence of wage changes on changes in unemployment as from the introduction of a time lag in the response of wage changes to changes in the level of unemployment, caused by the extension of collective bargaining and particularly by the growth of arbitration and conciliation procedures. If such a time lag existed in the later years of the period the wage change in any year should be related, not to average unemployment during that year, but to the average unemployment lagged by, perhaps, several months. This would have the effect of moving each point in the diagrams horizontally part of the way towards the point of the preceding year and it can easily be seen that this would widen the loops in the diagrams. This fact makes it difficult to discriminate at all closely between the effect of time lags and the effect of dependence of wage changes on the rate of change of unemployment.

III.   1913–1948

A scatter diagram of the rate of change of wage rates and percentage unemployment for the years 1913–1948 is shown in Figure 9. From 1913 to 1920 the series used are a continuation of those used for the period 1861–1913. From 1921 to 1948 the Ministry of Labour's index of hourly wage rates at the end of December of each year[12] has been used, the percentage

change in the index each year being taken as a measure of the average rate of change of wage rates during that year. The Ministry of Labour's figures for the percentage unemployment in the United Kingdom[13] have been used for the years 1921–1945. For the years 1946–1948 the unemployment figures were taken from the *Statistical Yearbooks* of the International Labour Organisation.

It will be seen from Figure 9 that there was an increase in unemployment in 1914 (mainly due to a sharp rise in the three months following the commencement of the war). From 1915 to 1918 unemployment was low and wage rates rose rapidly. The cost of living was also rising rapidly and formal agreements for automatic cost of living adjustments in wage rates became widespread, but it is not clear whether the cost of living adjustments were a real factor in increasing wage rates or whether they merely replaced increases which would in any case have occurred as a result of the high demand for labour. Demobilisation brought increased unemployment in 1919 but wage rates continued to rise rapidly until 1920, probably as a result of the rapidly rising import prices, which reached their peak in 1920, and consequent cost of living adjustments in wage rates. There was then a sharp increase in unemployment from 2.6 percent in 1920 to 17.0 percent in 1921, accompanied by a fall of 22.2 percent in wage rates in 1921. Part of the fall can be explained by the extremely rapid increase in unemployment, but a fall of 12.8 percent in the cost of living, largely a result of falling import prices, was no doubt also a major factor. In 1922 unemployment was 14.3 percent and wage rates fell by 19.1 percent. Although unemployment was high in this year it was decreasing, and the major part of the large fall in wage rates must be explained by the fall of 17.5 per-

---

[12] *Ministry of Labour Gazette*, April, 1958, p. 133.

[13] *Ibid.*, January, 1940 and subsequent issues.

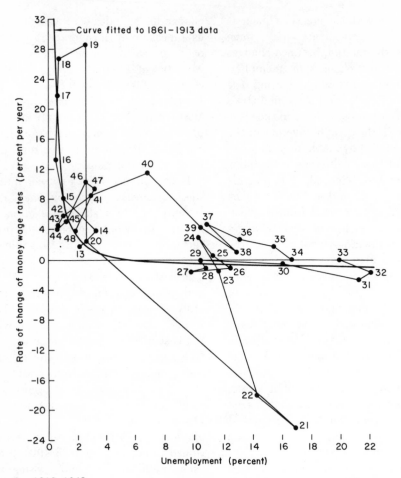

FIGURE 9.   1913–1948.

cent in the cost of living index between 1921 and 1922. After this experience trade unions became less enthusiastic about agreements for automatic cost of living adjustments and the number of these agreements declined.

From 1923 to 1929 there were only small changes in import prices and in the cost of living. In 1923 and 1924 unemployment was high but decreasing. Wage rates fell slightly in 1923 and rose by 3.1 percent in 1924. It seems likely that if business activity had continued to improve after 1924 the changes in wage rates would have shown the usual pattern of the recovery phase of earlier trade cycles. However, the decision to check demand in an at-

tempt to force the price level down in order to restore the gold standard at the pre-war parity of sterling prevented the recovery of business activity and unemployment remained fairly steady between 9.7 percent and 12.5 percent from 1925 to 1929. The average level of unemployment during these five years was 10.94 percent and the average rate of change of wage rates was −0.60 percent per year. The rate of change of wage rates calculated from the curve fitted to the 1861–1913 data for a level of unemployment of 10.94 percent is −0.56 percent per year, in close agreement with the average observed value. Thus the evidence does not support the view, which is sometimes expressed, that the policy of forcing the price level down failed because of increased resistance to downward movements of wage rates. The actual results obtained, given the levels of unemployment which were held, could have been predicted fairly accurately from a study of the pre-war data, if anyone had felt inclined to carry out the necessary analysis.

The relation between wage changes and unemployment during the 1929–1937 trade cycle follows the usual pattern of the cycles in the 1861–1913 period except for the higher level of unemployment throughout the cycle. The increases in wage rates in 1935, 1936 and 1937 are perhaps rather larger than would be expected to result from the rate of change of employment alone and part of the increases must probably be attributed to cost of living adjustments. The cost of living index rose 3.1 percent in 1935, 3.0 percent in 1936 and 5.2 percent in 1937, the major part of the increase in each of these years being due to the rise in the food component of the index. Only in 1937 can the rise in food prices be fully accounted for by rising import prices; in 1935 and 1936 it seems likely that the policies introduced to raise prices of home-produced agricultural produce played a significant part in increasing food prices and so the cost of living index and wage rates. The extremely uneven geographical distribution of unemployment may also have been a factor tending to increase the rapidity of wage changes during the upswing of business activity between 1934 and 1937.

Increases in import prices probably contributed to the wage increases in 1940 and 1941. The points in Figure 9 for the remaining war years show the effectiveness of the economic controls introduced. After an increase in unemployment in 1946 due to demobilisation and in 1947 due to the coal crisis, we return in 1948 almost exactly to the fitted relation between unemployment and wage changes.

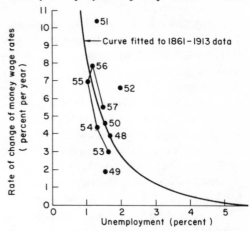

FIGURE 10. 1948–1957.

IV. 1948–1957

A scatter diagram for the years 1948–1957 is shown in Figure 10. The unemployment percentages shown are averages of the monthly unemployment percentages in Great Britain during the calendar years indicated, taken from the *Ministry of Labour Gazette*. The Ministry of Labour does not regularly publish figures of the percentage unemployment in the United Kingdom; but from data published in the *Statistical Yearbooks* of the International Labour Organisation it appears that unemployment in the United Kingdom was fairly consistently about 0.1 percent higher than that in Great Britain throughout this period. The wage index used was the index of weekly wage rates, published monthly in the *Ministry of Labour Gazette*, the percentage change during each calendar year being taken as a measure of the average rate of change of money wage rates during the year. The Ministry does not regularly publish an index of hourly wage rates;[14] but an index of normal weekly hours published in the *Ministry of Labour Gazette* of September 1957 shows a reduction of 0.2 percent in 1948 and in 1949 and an average annual reduction of

[14] An index of hourly wage rates covering the years considered in this section is, however, given in the *Ministry of Labour Gazette* of April, 1958.

approximately 0.04 percent from 1950 to 1957. The percentage changes in hourly rates would therefore be greater than the percentage changes in weekly rates by these amounts.

It will be argued later that a rapid rise in import prices during 1947 led to a sharp increase in retail prices in 1948 which tended to stimulate wage increases during 1948, but that this tendency was offset by the policy of wage restraint introduced by Sir Stafford Cripps in the spring of 1948; that wage increases during 1949 were exceptionally low as a result of the policy of wage restraint; that a rapid rise in import prices during 1950 and 1951 led to a rapid rise in retail prices during 1951 and 1952 which caused cost of living increases in wage rates in excess of the increases that would have occurred as a result of the demand for labour, but that there were no special factors of wage restraint or rapidly rising import prices to affect the wage increases in 1950 or in the five years from 1953 to 1957. It can be seen from Figure 10 that the point for 1950 lies very close to the curve fitted to the 1861–1913 data and that the points for 1953 to 1957 lie on a narrow loop around this curve, the direction of the loop being the reverse of the direction of the loops shown in Figures 2 to 8. A loop in this direction could result from a time lag in the adjustment of wage rates. If the rate of change of wage rates during each calendar year is related to unemployment lagged seven months, i.e. to the average of the monthly percentages of unemployment from June of the preceding year to May of that year, the scatter diagram shown in Figure 11 is obtained. The loop has now disappeared and the points for the years 1950 and 1953 to 1957 lie closely along a smooth curve which coincides almost exactly with the curve fitted to the 1861–1913 data.

In Table 1 below the percentage changes in money wage rates during the years

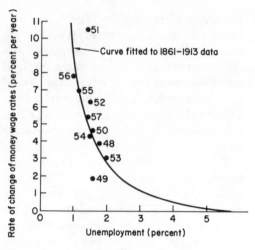

FIGURE 11. 1948–1957, WITH UNEMPLOYMENT LAGGED 7 MONTHS.

1948–1957 are shown in column (1). The figures in column (2) are the percentage changes in wage rates calculated from the curve fitted to the 1861–1913 data corresponding to the unemployment percentages shown in Figure 11, i.e. the average percentages of unemployment lagged seven months. On the hypothesis that has been used in this paper, these figures represent the percentages by which wage rates would be expected to rise, given the level of employment for each year, as a result of employers' competitive bidding for labour, i.e. they represent the "demand pull" element in wage adjustments. The relevant figure on the cost side in wage negotiations is the percentage increase shown by the retail price index in the month in which the negotiations are proceeding over the index of the corresponding month of the previous year. The average of these monthly percentages for each calendar year is an appropriate measure of the "cost push" element in wage adjustments, and these averages[15] are given in column (3). The percentage

---

[15] Calculated from the retail price index published in the *Monthly Digest of Statistics*. The figure for 1948 is the average of the last seven months of the year.

TABLE 1

	(1) Change in wage rates	(2) Demand pull	(3) Cost push	(4) Change in import prices
1947	..	..	..	20.1
1948	3.9	3.5	7.1	10.6
1949	1.9	4.1	2.9	4.1
1950	4.6	4.4	3.0	26.5
1951	10.5	5.2	9.0	23.3
1952	6.4	4.5	9.3	−11.7
1953	3.0	3.0	3.0	− 4.8
1954	4.4	4.5	1.9	5.0
1955	6.9	6.8	4.6	1.9
1956	7.9	8.0	4.9	3.8
1957	5.4	5.2	3.8	− 7.3

change in the index of import prices[16] during each year is given in column (4).

From Table 1 we see that in 1948 the cost push element was considerably greater than the demand pull element, as a result of the lagged effect on retail prices of the rapid rise in import prices during the previous year, and the change in wage rates was a little greater than could be accounted for by the demand pull element. It would probably have been considerably greater but for the co-operation of the trade unions in Sir Stafford Cripps' policy of wage restraint. In 1949 the cost element was less than the demand element and the actual change in wage rates was also much less, no doubt as a result of the policy of wage restraint which is generally acknowledged to have been effective in 1949. In 1950 the cost element was lower than the demand element and the actual wage change was approximately equal to the demand element.

Import prices rose very rapidly during 1950 and 1951 as a result of the devaluation of sterling in September 1949 and the outbreak of the Korean War in 1950. In consequence the retail price index rose rapidly during 1951 and 1952 so that the cost element in wage negotiations considerably exceeded the demand element.

[16] *Board of Trade Journal.*

The actual wage increase in each year also considerably exceeded the demand element so that these two years provide a clear case of cost inflation.

In 1953 the cost element was equal to the demand element and in the years 1954 to 1957 it was well below the demand element. In each of these years the actual wage increase was almost exactly equal to the demand element. Thus in these five years, and also in 1950, there seems to have been pure demand inflation.   ·

V. CONCLUSIONS

The statistical evidence in Sections II to IV above seems in general to support the hypothesis stated in Section I, that the rate of change of money wage rates can be explained by the level of unemployment and the rate of change of unemployment, except in or immediately after those years in which there is a sufficiently rapid rise in import prices to offset the tendency for increasing productivity to reduce the cost of living.

Ignoring years in which import prices rise rapidly enough to initiate a wage-price spiral, which seem to occur very rarely except as a result of war, and assuming an increase in productivity of 2 percent per year, it seems from the relation fitted to the data that if aggregate demand were kept at a value which would maintain a stable level of product prices the associated level of unemployment would be a little under $2\frac{1}{2}$ percent. If, as is sometimes recommended, demand were kept at a value which would maintain stable wage rates the associated level of unemployment would be about $5\frac{1}{2}$ percent.

Because of the strong curvature of the fitted relation in the region of low percentage unemployment, there will be a lower average rate of increase of wage rates if unemployment is held constant at a given level than there will be if unemployment is allowed to fluctuate about that level.

These conclusions are of course tentative. There is need for much more detailed research into the relations between unemployment, wage rates, prices and productivity.

Part VI

FLUCTUATIONS
AND GROWTH

18

Interactions between the Multiplier Analysis and the Principle of Acceleration

PAUL A. SAMUELSON

Few economists would deny that the "multiplier" analysis of the effects of governmental deficit spending has thrown some light upon this important problem. Nevertheless, there would seem to be some ground for the fear that this extremely simplified mechanism is in danger of hardening into a dogma, hindering progress and obscuring important subsidiary relations and processes. It is highly desirable, therefore, that model sequences, which operate under more general assumptions, be investigated, possibly including the conventional analysis as a special case.[1]

* *

Reprinted by permission of the publishers and author from *The Review of Economic Statistics*, vol. 21 (May 1939), pp. 75–78. Cambridge, Mass.: Harvard University Press, Copyright, 1939, by the President and Fellows of Harvard College.

Paul A. Samuelson teaches at the Massachusetts Institute of Technology; he was formerly at Harvard University.

[1] The writer, who has made this study in connection with his research as a member of the Society of Fellows at Harvard University, wishes to express his indebtedness to Professor Alvin H. Hansen of Harvard University at whose suggestion the investigation was undertaken.

In particular, the "multiplier," using this term in its usual sense, does *not* pretend to give the relation between total national income induced by governmental spending and the original amount of money spent. This is clearly seen by a simple example. In any economy (not necessarily our own) where any dollar of governmental deficit spending would result in a hundred dollars less of private investment than would otherwise have been undertaken, the ratio of total induced national income to the initial expenditure is overwhelmingly negative, yet the "multiplier" in the strict sense must be positive. The answer to the puzzle is simple. What the multiplier does give is the ratio of the total increase in the national income to the total amount of investment, governmental and private. In other words, it does *not* tell us how much is to be multiplied. The effects upon private investment are often regarded as tertiary influences and receive little systematic attention.

In order to remedy the situation in some measure, Professor Hansen has developed a new model sequence which ingeniously combines the multiplier analysis with that of the *acceleration* principle or *relation*. This is done by making additions to the national income consist of three components: (1) governmental deficit spending, (2) private consumption expenditure induced by previous public expenditure, and (3) induced private investment, assumed according to the familiar acceleration principle to be proportional to the time increase of consumption. The introduction of the last component accounts for the novelty of the conclusions reached and also the increased complexity of the analysis.

A numerical example may be cited to illuminate the assumptions made. We assume governmental deficit spending of one dollar per unit period, beginning at some initial time and continuing thereafter. The marginal propensity to consume, a, is taken to be one-half. This is taken to mean that the consumption of any period is equal to one-half the national income of the previous period. Our last assumption is that induced private investment is proportional to the increase in consumption between the previous and the current period. This factor of proportionality or *relation*, β, is provisionally taken to be equal to unity; i.e., a time increase in consumption of one dollar will result in one dollar's worth of induced private investment.

In the initial period when the government spends a dollar for the first time, there will be no consumption induced from previous periods, and hence the addition to the national income will equal the one dollar spent. This will yield fifty cents of consumption expenditure in the second period, an increase of fifty cents over the consumption of the first period, and so according to the *relation* we will have fifty cents worth of induced private investment. Finally, we must add the new dollar of expenditure by the govern-

ment. The national income of the second period must therefore total two dollars. Similarly, in the third period the national income would be the sum of one dollar of consumption, fifty cents induced private investment, and one dollar current governmental expenditure. It is clear that given the values of the marginal propensity to consume, a, and the *relation*, β, all succeeding national income levels can be easily computed in succession. This is done in detail in Table 1 and illustrated in Chart 1. It will be noted that the introduction of the acceleration principle causes our series to reach a peak at the 3rd year, a trough at the 7th, a peak at the 11th, etc. Such oscillatory behavior could not occur in the conventional model sequences, as will soon become evident.

For other chosen values of a and β similar model sequences can be developed. In Table 2 national income totals are given for various selected values of these coefficients. In the first column, for example, the marginal propensity to consume is assumed to be one-half, and the *relation* to be equal to zero. This is of special interest because it shows the conventional multiplier sequences to be special cases of the more general Hansen analysis. For this case no oscillations are possible. In

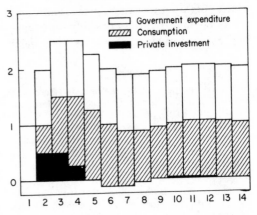

CHART 1. GRAPHIC REPRESENTATION OF DATA IN TABLE 1. (UNIT: ONE DOLLAR).

TABLE 1

THE DEVELOPMENT OF NATIONAL INCOME AS A RESULT OF A CONTINUOUS LEVEL OF
GOVERNMENTAL EXPENDITURE WHEN THE MARGINAL PROPENSITY TO CONSUME EQUALS
ONE HALF AND THE RELATION EQUALS UNITY

(unit: one dollar)

Period	Current governmental expenditure	Current consumption induced by previous expenditure	Current private investment proportional to time increase in consumption	Total national income
1	1.00	0.00	0.00	1.00
2	1.00	0.50	0.50	2.00
3	1.00	1.00	0.50	2.50
4	1.00	1.25	0.25	2.50
5	1.00	1.25	0.00	2.25
6	1.00	1.125	−0.125*	2.00
7	1.00	1.00	−0.125	1.875
8	1.00	0.9375	−0.0625	1.875
9	1.00	0.9375	0.00	1.9375
10	1.00	0.96875	0.03125	2.00
11	1.00	1.00	0.03125	2.03125
12	1.00	1.015625	0.015625	2.03125
13	1.00	1.015625	0.00	2.015625
14	1.00	1.0078125	−0.0078125	2.00

* Negative induced private investment is interpreted to mean that for the system as a whole there
is *less* investment in this period than there otherwise would have been. Since this is a marginal
analysis, superimposed implicitly upon a going state of affairs, this concept causes no difficulty.

the second column the oscillations in the
national income are undamped and regular.
In column three things are still worse; the
oscillations are explosive, becoming larger
and larger but always fluctuating around
an "average value." In the fourth column
the behavior is no longer oscillatory but
is explosive upward approaching a compound interest rate of growth.

By this time the investigator is inclined
to feel somewhat disorganized. A variety
of qualitatively different results emerge in
a seemingly capricious manner from minor
changes in hypotheses. Worse than this,
how can we be sure that for still different
selected values of our coefficients new and
stronger types of behavior will not emerge?
Is it not even possible that if Table 2 were
extended to cover more periods, new types

of behavior might result for these selected
coefficients?

Fortunately, these questions can be
given a definite negative answer. Arithmetical methods cannot do so since we
cannot try all possible values of the coefficients nor compute the endless terms of
each sequence. Nevertheless, comparatively simple algebraic analysis can be
applied which will yield all possible qualitative types of behavior and enable us
to unify our results.

The national income at time t, Y_t, can
be written as the sum of three components:
(1) governmental expenditure, g_t, (2) consumption expenditure, C_t, and (3) induced
private investment, I_t.

$$Y_t = g_t + C_t + I_t$$

TABLE 2

MODEL SEQUENCES OF NATIONAL INCOME FOR SELECTED VALUES OF MARGINAL
PROPENSITY TO CONSUME AND RELATION

(*unit: one dollar*)

Period	$a = .5$ $\beta = 0$	$a = .5$ $\beta = 2$	$a = .6$ $\beta = 2$	$a = .8$ $\beta = 4$
1	1.00	1.00	1.00	1.00
2	1.50	2.50	2.80	5.00
3	1.75	3.75	4.84	17.80
4	1.875	4.125	6.352	56.20
5	1.9375	3.4375	6.6256	169.84
6	1.9688*	2.0313	5.3037	500.52
7	1.9844	.9141	2.5959	1,459.592
8	1.9922	− .1172	− .6918	4,227.704
9	1.9961	.2148	−3.3603	12,241.1216

* Table is correct to four decimal places.

But according to the Hansen assumptions

$$C_t = aY_{t-1}$$
$$I_t = \beta[C_t - C_{t-1}] = a\beta Y_{t-1} - a\beta Y_{t-2}$$

and

$$g_t = 1$$

Therefore, our national income can be rewritten

$$Y_t = 1 + a[1 + \beta]Y_{t-1} - a\beta Y_{t-2}$$

In words, if we know the national income for two periods, the national income for the following period can be simply derived by taking a weighted sum. The weights depend, of course, upon the values chosen for the marginal propensity to consume and for the *relation*.

This is one of the simplest types of difference equations, having constant coefficients and being of the second order. The mathematical details of its solution need not be entered upon here. Suffice it to say that its solution depends upon the roots—which in turn depend upon the

coefficients a and β—of a certain equation.[2] It can be easily shown that the whole field of possible values of a and β can be divided into four regions, each of which gives qualitatively different types of behavior. In Chart 2 these regions are plotted. Each point in this diagram represents a selection of values for the marginal propensity to consume and the *relation*. Corresponding to each point there will be a model sequence of national income through time. The qualitative properties of this sequence depend upon whether the point is in Region A, B, C, or D.[3] The properties of each region can be briefly summarized.

[2] Actually, the solution can be written in the form
$$Y_t = \frac{1}{1 - a} + a_1[x_1]^t + a_2[x_2]^t$$

where x_1 and x_2 are roots of the quadratic equation
$$x^2 - a[1 + \beta]x + a\beta = 0,$$

and a_1 and a_2 are constants dependent upon the a's and β's chosen.

[3] Mathematically, the regions are demarcated by the conditions that the roots of the equation referred to in the previous footnote be real or complex, greater or less than unity in absolute value.

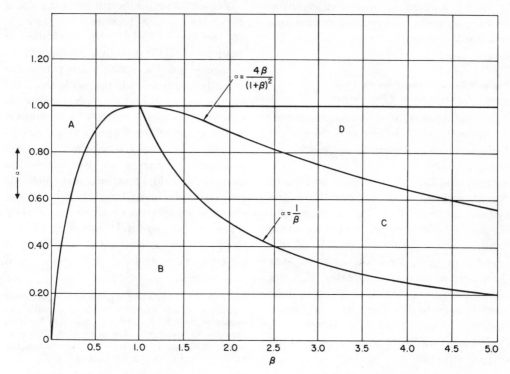

CHART 2. DIAGRAM SHOWING BOUNDARIES OF REGIONS YIELDING DIFFERENT QUALITATIVE BEHAVIOR OF NATIONAL INCOME.

Region A (relatively small values of the relation)

If there is a constant level of governmental expenditure through time, the national income will approach asymptotically a value $(1/1 - a)$ times the constant level of governmental expenditure. A single impulse of expenditure, or any amount of expenditure followed by a complete cessation, will result in a gradual approach to the original zero level of national income. (It will be noted that the asymptote approached is identically that given by the Keynes-Kahn-Clark formula. Their analysis applies to points along the a axis and is subsumed under the more general Hansen analysis.) Perfectly periodic net governmental expenditure will result eventually in perfectly periodic fluctuations in national income.

Region B

A constant continuing level of governmental expenditure will result in damped oscillatory movements of national income, gradually approaching the asymptote $(1/1 - a)$ times the constant level of government expenditure. (Cf. Table 1.) Governmental expenditure in a single or finite number of periods will result eventually in damped oscillations around the level of income zero. Perfectly regular periodic fluctuations in government expenditure will result eventually in fluctuations of income of the same period.

Region C

A constant level of governmental expenditure will result in *explosive*, ever increasing oscillations around an asymptote computed as above. (Cf. column 3 of

Table 2.) A single impulse of expenditure or a finite number of expenditure impulses will result eventually in explosive oscillations around the level zero.

Region D (large values of the marginal propensity to consume and the relation)

A constant level of governmental expenditure will result in an ever increasing national income, eventually approaching a compound interest rate of growth. (Cf. column 4 of Table 2.) A single impulse of net investment will likewise send the system up to infinity at a compound interest rate of growth. On the other hand, a single infinitesimal unit of disinvestment will send the system ever downward at an increasing rate. This is a highly unstable situation, but corresponds most closely to the pure case of pump-priming, where the total increase in national income bears no finite ratio to the original stimulus.

The limitations inherent in so simplified a picture as that presented here should not be overlooked.[4] In particular, it assumes that the marginal propensity to consume and the *relation* are constants; actually these will change with the level of income, so that this representation is strictly a *marginal* analysis to be applied to the study of small oscillations. Nevertheless, it is more general than the usual analysis. Contrary to the impression commonly held, mathematical methods properly employed, far from making economic theory more abstract, actually serve as a powerful liberating device enabling the entertainment and analysis of ever more realistic and complicated hypotheses.

[4] It may be mentioned in passing that the formal structure of our problem is identical with the model sequences of Lundberg, and the dynamic theories of Tinbergen. The present problem is so simple that it provides a useful introduction to the mathematical theory of the latter's work.

19

Economic Progress and Declining Population Growth

ALVIN H. HANSEN

The main papers and the round tables in this year's program, like those of a year ago, concern a single, though broadly inclusive, subject. A year ago we considered the various factors which influence *fluctuations* in the rate of investment, income and employment. In selecting the topic for this year we have turned away in large measure from the ever-present and all-absorbing problem of cyclical fluctuations and have set ourselves the task of probing the problems of structural change in our economy, involving among other things also how these structural changes in various countries have affected the cycle itself. In the main sessions and in the round-table discussions various aspects of "The Changing American Economy" are considered—changes in the structure and functioning of our economic institu-

Reprinted from *The American Economic Review,* vol. 29 (March 1939), pp. 1–15, by permission of the publisher and author. Presidential address delivered at the Fifty-first Annual Meeting of the American Economic Association, Detroit, Michigan, December 28, 1938.

Alvin H. Hansen is Professor Emeritus at Harvard University.

tions. The topic is, however, so vast that even in a meeting as large as ours it is quite impossible to include all aspects pertinent to the subject; and doubtless many members will feel that important segments of the problem have been overlooked by our program committee.

One may ask: "Is there any special reason why in the year 1938 we should devote our attention as economists to the general subject "The Changing Character of the American Economy"? Throughout the modern era, ceaseless change has been the law of economic life. Every period is in some sense a period of transition. The swift stream of events in the last quarter century offers, however, overwhelming testimony in support of the thesis that the economic order of the western world is undergoing in this generation a structural change no less basic and profound in character than that transformation of economic life and institutions which we are wont to designate loosely by the phrase "the Industrial Revolution." We are passing, so to speak, over a divide which separates the great era of growth and expansion of the nineteenth century from an era which no man, unwilling to embark on pure conjecture, can as yet characterize with clarity or precision. We are moving swiftly out of the order in which those of our generation were brought up, into no one knows what.

Overwhelmingly significant, but as yet all too little considered by economists, is the profound change which we are currently undergoing in the rate of population growth. In the decade of the nineteen-twenties the population of the United States increased by 16,000,000—an absolute growth equal to that of the pre-war decade and in excess of any other decade in our history. In the current decade we are adding only half this number to our population, and the best forecasts indicate a decline to a third in the decade which we are about to enter.

Inadequate as the data are, it appears that the prodigious growth of population in the nineteenth century was something unique in history. Gathering momentum with the progress of modern science and transportation, the absolute growth in western Europe mounted decade by decade until the great World War; and in the United States it reached the highest level, as I have just noted, in the post-war decade. The upward surge began with relatively small accretions which rapidly swelled into a flood. But the advancing tide has come to a sudden halt and the accretions are dwindling toward zero.

Thus, with the prospect of actual contraction confronting us, already we are in the midst of a drastic decline in the rate of population growth. Whatever the future decades may bring, this present fact is already upon us; and it behooves us as economists to take cognizance of the significance of this revolutionary change in our economic life.

Schooled in the traditions of the Malthusian theory, economists, thinking in terms of static economics, have typically placed an optimistic interpretation upon the cessation of population growth. This indeed is also the interpretation suggested by the National Resources Committee which recently has issued an exhaustive statistical inquiry into current and prospective changes in population growth. In a fundamental sense this conclusion is, I think, thoroughly sound; for it can scarcely be questioned that a continued growth of population at the rate experienced in the nineteenth century would rapidly present insoluble problems. But it would be an unwarranted optimism to deny that there are implicit in the current drastic shift from rapid expansion to cessation of population growth, serious structural maladjustments which can be avoided or mitigated only if economic policies, appropriate to the changed situation, are applied. Indeed in this shift must be sought a basic cause of not a few of the developments in our changing economy.

Adam Smith regarded growth of population as at once a consequence and a cause of economic progress. Increasing division of labor would, he argued, bring about greater productivity, and this would furnish an enlarged revenue and stock, from which would flow an enlarged wages fund, an increased demand for labor, higher wages, and so economic conditions favorable for population growth. Now a growing population, by widening the market and by fostering inventiveness, in turn facilitated, he thought, division of labor and so the production of wealth. Thus he arrived at an optimistic conclusion. Population growth, he held, stimulated progress and this in turn stimulated further growth and expansion. In contrast, the pessimistic analyses of Malthus and Ricardo stressed the limitation of natural resources and the danger of an increasing population's pressing down the margin of cultivation to a point at which real income would be reduced to a bare subsistence level. In this static analysis the more dynamic approach of Adam Smith was quite forgotten. If we wish to get a clear insight into the economic consequences of the current decline in population growth, it is necessary to return to the suggestion of Adam Smith and to explore more fully the causal interconnection between economic progress, capital formation and population growth.

Economic analysis from the earliest development of our science has been concerned with the rôle played by economic progress. Various writers have included under this caption different things; but for our purpose we may say that the constituent elements of economic progress are (a) inventions, (b) the discovery and development of new territory and new resources, and (c) the growth of population. Each of these in turn, severally and in combination, has opened investment outlets and caused a rapid growth of capital formation.

The earlier economists were concerned chiefly with the effect of economic progress upon the volume of output, or in other words, upon the level of real income. For them economic progress affected the economic life mainly, if not exclusively, in terms of rising productivity and higher real income per capita.

Not until the very end of the nineteenth century did an extensive literature arise which stressed the rôle of economic progress as a leading, if not the main, factor causing fluctuations in employment, output, and income. Ricardo had indeed seen that there was some relation between economic progress and economic instability; but it was left for Wicksell, Spiethoff, Schumpeter, Cassel, and Robertson to elaborate the thesis that economic fluctuations are essentially a function of economic progress.

More recently the rôle of economic progress in the maintenance of full employment of the productive resources has come under consideration. The earlier economists assumed that the economic

system tended automatically to produce full employment of resources. Some unemployment there was periodically, owing to the fluctuations incident to the business cycle; but in the upswing phase of the cyclical movement the economy was believed to function in a manner tending to bring about full recovery—maximum output and employment. This view was inspired by a century in which the forces of economic progress were powerful and strong, in which investment outlets were numerous and alluring. Spiethoff saw clearly that technological progress, the development of new industries, the discovery of new resources, the opening of new territory were the basic causes of the boom, which in turn was the progenitor of depression. Indeed he believed that once the main resources of the globe had been discovered and exploited, once the whole world had been brought under the sway of the machine technique, the leading disturbing factors which underlie the fluctuations of the cycle would have spent their force and an era of relative economic stability would ensue. But he did not raise the question whether such stability would be achieved at a full-employment and full-income level.

The business cycle was *par excellence* the problem of the nineteenth century. But the main problem of our times, and particularly in the United States, is the problem of full employment. Yet paradoxical as it may seem, the nineteenth century was little concerned with, and understood but dimly, the character of the business cycle. Indeed, so long as the problem of full employment was not pressing, it was not necessary to worry unduly about the temporary unemployment incident to the swings of the cycle. Not until the problem of full employment of our productive resources from the long-run, secular standpoint was upon us, were we compelled to give serious consideration to those factors and forces in our economy which tend to make business recoveries weak and anaemic and which tend to prolong and deepen the course of depressions. This is the essence of secular stagnation—sick recoveries which die in their infancy and depressions which feed on themselves and leave a hard and seemingly immovable core of unemployment.

In every great crisis the struggle of contending groups maneuvering for an advantageous position amidst rapid change whips up the froth and fury of political and social controversy. Always there is present the temptation to explain the course of events in terms of the more superficial phenomena which are frequently manifestations rather than causes of change. It is the peculiar function of the economist however to look deeper into the underlying economic realities and to discover in these, if possible, the causes of the most obstinate problem of our time—the problem of under-employment. Fundamental to an understanding of this problem are the changes in the "external" forces, if I may so describe them, which underlie economic progress—changes in the character of technological innovations, in the availability of new territory, and in the growth of population.

The expanding economy of the last century called forth a prodigious growth of capital formation. So much was this the case, that this era in history has by common consent been called the capitalistic period. No one disputes the thesis that without this vast accumulation of capital we should never have witnessed the great rise in the standard of living achieved since the beginning of the Industrial Revolution. But it is not the effect of capital formation upon real income to which I wish especially to direct attention. What I wish to stress in this paper is rather the rôle played by the process of capital formation in securing at each point in this ascending income scale fairly full employment of the productive re-

sources and therefore the maximum income possible under the then prevailing level of technological development. For it is an indisputable fact that the prevailing economic system has never been able to reach reasonably full employment or the attainment of its currently realizable real income without making large investment expenditures. The basis for this imperious economic necessity has been thoroughly explored in the last half century in the great literature beginning with Tugan-Baranowsky and Wicksell on saving and investment. I shall not attempt any summary statement of this analysis. Nor is this necessary; for I take it that it is accepted by all schools of current economic thought that full employment and the maximum currently attainable income level cannot be reached in the modern free enterprise economy without a volume of investment expenditures adequate to fill the gap between consumption expenditures and that level of income which could be achieved were all the factors employed. In this somewhat truistic statement I hope I have succeeded in escaping a hornets' nest of economic controversy.

Thus we may postulate a consensus on the thesis that in the absence of a positive program designed to stimulate consumption, full employment of the productive resources is essentially a function of the vigor of investment activity. Less agreement can be claimed for the rôle played by the rate of interest on the volume of investment. Yet few there are who believe that in a period of investment stagnation an abundance of loanable funds at low rates of interest is alone adequate to produce a vigorous flow of real investment. I am increasingly impressed with the analysis made by Wicksell who stressed the prospective rate of profit on new investment as the active, dominant, and controlling factor, and who viewed the rate of interest as a passive factor, lagging behind the profit rate. This view is moreover in accord with competent business judgment.[1] It is true that it is necessary to look beyond the mere *cost* of interest charges to the indirect effect of the interest rate structure upon business expectations. Yet all in all, I venture to assert that the rôle of the rate of interest as a determinant of investment has occupied a place larger than it deserves in our thinking. If this be granted, we are forced to regard the factors which underlie economic progress as the dominant determinants of investment and employment.

A growth in real investment may take the form either of a deepening of capital or of a widening of capital, as Hawtrey has aptly put it. The deepening process means that more capital is used per unit of output, while the widening process means that capital formation grows *pari passu* with the increase in the output of final goods. If the ratio of real capital to real income remains constant, there is no deepening of capital; but if this ratio is constant and real income rises, then there is a widening of capital.

According to Douglas[2] the growth of real capital formation in England from 1875 to 1909 proceeded at an average rate of two per cent per annum; and the rate of growth of capital formation in the United States from 1890 to 1922 was four per cent per annum. The former is less than the probable rate of increase of output in England, while the latter is somewhat in excess of the annual rise of production in the United States. Thus, during the last fifty years or more, capital formation for

each economy as a whole has apparently consisted mainly of a widening of capital. Surprising as it may seem, as far as we may judge from such data as are available, there has been little, if any, deepening of capital. The capital stock has increased approximately in proportion to real income. This is also the conclusion of Gustav Cassel;[3] while Keynes[4] thinks that real capital formation in England may have very slightly exceeded the rise in real income in the period from 1860 to the World War. If this be true, it follows that, in terms of the time element in production, which is the very essence of the capital concept, our system of production is little more capitalistic now than fifty or seventy-five years ago. It requires, in other words, a period of employment of our productive resources no longer than formerly to reproduce the total capital stock. The "waiting," so to speak, embodied in our capital accumulations is no greater today than half a century or more ago. Capital has indeed grown relative to labor. Thus the technical coefficient of production, with respect to capital, has increased. While this indicates a more intensive application of capital relative to the other factors, it does not necessarily imply any deepening of capital.

In important areas the capital stock has not increased significantly even in relation to population. This is notably true in the service industries. Moreover, in the field of housing real capital has little more than kept pace with population growth. In manufacturing as a whole it is certainly true that real capital formation has not only far outstripped population but has also risen more rapidly than physical product. The studies of Douglas for the United States and Australia show that real

[1] *Cf.* J. E. Meade and P. W. S. Andrews, "Summary of Replies to Questions on Effects of Interest Rates," *Oxford Econ. Papers*, no. 1; also J. Franklin Ebersole, "The Influence of Interest Rates upon Entrepreneurial Decisions in Business —A Case Study," *Harvard Bus. Rev.*, vol. xvii, pp. 35–39. The indirect effect on valuation is perhaps overlooked.

[2] Paul H. Douglas, *The Theory of Wages*, Macmillan, 1934, pp. 464–5.

[3] Gustav Cassel, *On Quantitative Thinking in Economics*, Oxford, 1935, chapter 6.

[4] J. M. Keynes, "Some Economic Consequences of a Declining Population," *Eugenics Review*, April, 1937.

fixed capital invested in manufacturing increased more rapidly than physical output of manufactured goods.   On the other hand, Carl Snyder's[5] data, which run in terms of value of invested capital and value of product, indicate that for important separate industries, such as textiles, iron and steel, and petroleum, capital has grown little or no faster than output since about 1890.   With respect to the automobile industry, according to his findings, capital investment has risen no more rapidly than value of product, while in the electrical industries, invested capital increased at a slower rate than output after 1907.   Considering the economy as a whole, including fields of economic activity other than manufacturing, there is no good evidence that the advance of technique has resulted in recent decades, certainly not in any significant measure, in any deepening of capital. Apparently, once the machine technique has been developed in any field, further mechanization is likely to result in an increase in output at least proportional to and often in excess of the net additions to real capital.   Though the deepening process is all the while going on in certain areas, elsewhere capital-saving inventions are reducing the ratio of capital to output.

In order to get some insight into the effect of population growth upon capital formation, it is necessary to consider the rôle it plays in conjunction with other factors in the widening and deepening process.   The widening of capital is a function of an increase in final output, which in turn is due partly to an increase in population and partly to an increase in per capita productivity, arising from causes other than a larger use of capital per unit of output.   On the other hand, the deepening of capital results partly from cost-reducing changes in technique, partly (though this is probably a much less significant factor) from a reduction in the rate of interest, and partly from changes in the character of the output as a whole, with special reference to the amount of capital required to produce it.

Now the rate of population growth must necessarily play an important rôle in determining the character of the output; in other words, the composition of the flow of final goods.   Thus a rapidly growing population will demand a much larger per capita volume of new residential building construction than will a stationary population.   A stationary population with its larger proportion of old people may perhaps demand more personal services; and the composition of consumer demand will have an important influence on the quantity of capital required.   The demand for housing calls for large capital outlays, while the demand for personal services can be met without making large investment expenditures.   It is therefore not unlikely that a shift from a rapidly growing population to a stationary or declining one may so alter the composition of the final flow of consumption goods that the ratio of capital to output as a whole will tend to decline.

In the beginning stages of modern capitalism both the deepening and the widening processes of capital formation were developing side by side.   But in its later stages the deepening process, taking the economy as a whole, rapidly diminished.   And now with the rapid cessation of population growth, even the widening process may slow down.   Moreover it is possible that capital-saving inventions may cause capital formation in many industries to lag behind the increase in output.

An interesting problem for statistical research would be to determine the proportion of investment in the nineteenth century which could be attributed (a) to population growth, (b) to the opening up of new territory and the dis-

---

[5] Carl Snyder, "Capital Supply and National Well-Being," *Am. Econ. Rev.*, June, 1936.

covery of new resources, and (c) to technical innovations. Such an analysis it has not been possible for me to make, and I shall venture only a few rough estimates together with some qualitative judgments. With respect to population growth some insight into the problem may perhaps be gained by considering first the rôle of population growth in the rise of aggregate real income. The various estimates agree that the annual rate of growth of physical output up to the World War was roughly three per cent in western Europe and nearly four per cent in the United States. Of this average annual increase something less than half of the three per cent increase in western Europe can be attributed to population growth, while something more than half of the annual increase in the United States can be assigned to the increase in the labor supply. Thus it appears that per capita output has increased both in western Europe and in the United States at approximately one and one-half per cent per annum. This increase can be attributed mainly to changes in technique and to the exploitation of new natural resources.

We have already noted that capital formation has progressed at about the same rate as the rise in aggregate output. Thus, as a first approximation, we may say that the growth of population in the last half of the nineteenth century was responsible for about forty per cent of the total volume of capital formation in western Europe and about sixty per cent of the capital formation in the United States. If this is even approximately correct, it will be seen what an important outlet for investment is being closed by reason of the current rapid decline in population growth.

Obviously the growth of population affects capital formation most directly in the field of construction, especially residential building. From decade to decade the increase in the number of dwellings had maintained a close relation to the increase in population. In the decade of the twenties, however, the increase in houses ran about twenty-five per cent in excess of previous decennial increases in relation to population. According to Kuznets, during the seven prosperous years 1923 to 1929, a quarter of the net capital formation was residential building. But the effect of population growth on capital formation is, of course, felt in other spheres as well. This is notably true of all the various municipal and public utilities, and also of the manufacture of essential consumers' goods.

An interesting excursus would lead us into a consideration of the problem how far an increase in population itself contributed to a more efficient technique and so was in part responsible for the rise in per capita real income. According to the older Malthusian view, the growth of population would act counter to the effect of technological progress upon per capita productivity, and would thus slow down the rise in per capita real income. If this were correct, population growth considered by itself alone would tend to check the rise in per capita consumption, and this in turn, *via* the so-called *Relation*, would affect the volume of capital formation. According to the optimum population theory, however, it may not infrequently be the case, and indeed probably was during the greater part of the nineteenth century, that population growth itself facilitated mass production methods and accelerated the progress of technique. If this be correct, population growth was itself responsible for a part of the rise in per capita real income, and this, *via* the influence of a rising consumption upon investment, stimulated capital formation. Thus it is quite possible that population growth may have acted both directly and indirectly to stimulate the volume of capital formation.

It is not possible, I think, to make even an approximate estimate of the proportion of the new capital created in the nineteenth century which was a direct consequence of the opening up of new territory. The development of new countries was indeed so closely intertwined with the growth of population that it would be difficult to avoid double counting. What proportion of new capital formation in the United States went each year into the western frontier we do not know, but it must have been very considerable. Apparently about one-fourth of the total capital accumulations of England were invested abroad by 1914, and one-seventh of those of France.

These figures, while only suggestive, point unmistakably to the conclusion that the opening of new territory and the growth of population were together responsible for a very large fraction—possibly somewhere near one-half—of the total volume of new capital formation in the nineteenth century. These outlets for new investment are rapidly being closed. The report on *Limits of Land Settlement* by President Isaiah Bowman and others may be regarded as conclusive in its findings that there are no important areas left for exploitation and settlement. So far as population is concerned, that of western Europe has already virtually reached a standstill; but that in eastern Europe, notably in Russia, is still growing, and so also is that in the Orient. And much of this area will probably experience a considerable industrialization. But it is not yet clear how far the mature industrial countries will participate in this development through capital export. Russia still has a long way to go before she becomes completely industrialized; but foreign capital is not likely to play any significant rôle in this process. India will offer some opportunity for British investment, but the total is likely to be small relative to the volume of British foreign investments in the nineteenth century. China and the Orient generally offer, in view of the present and prospective turmoil

in that area, relatively meager investment opportunities. At all events, no one is likely to challenge the statement that foreign investment will in the next fifty years play an incomparably smaller rôle than was the case in the nineteenth century.

Thus the outlets for new investment are rapidly narrowing down to those created by the progress of technology. To be sure, the progress of technology itself played in the nineteenth century a decisive rôle in the opening of new territory and as a stimulus to population growth. But while technology can facilitate the opening of new territory, it cannot create a new world or make the old one bigger than it is. And while the advance of science, by reducing the death rate, was a major cause of the vast nineteenth-century increase in population, no important further gains in this direction can possibly offset the prevailing low birth rate. Thus the further progress of science can operate to open investment outlets only through its direct influence on the technique of production.

We are thus rapidly entering a world in which we must fall back upon a more rapid advance of technology than in the past if we are to find private investment opportunities adequate to maintain full employment. Should we accept the advice of those who would declare a moratorium on invention and technical progress, this one remaining avenue for private investment would also be closed. There can be no greater error in the analysis of the economic trends of our times than that which finds in the advance of technology, broadly conceived, a major cause of unemployment. It is true that we cannot discount the problem of technological unemployment, a problem which may be intensified by the apparently growing importance of capital-saving inventions. But, on the other side, we cannot afford to neglect that type of innovation which creates new industries and which thereby opens new outlets for real investment. The problem of our generation is, above all, the problem of inadequate private investment outlets. What we need is not a slowing down in the progress of science and technology, but rather an acceleration of that rate.

Of first-rate importance is the development of new industries. There is certainly no basis for the assumption that these are a thing of the past. But there is equally no basis for the assumption that we can take for granted the rapid emergence of new industries as rich in investment opportunities as the railroad, or more recently the automobile, together with all the related developments, including the construction of public roads, to which it gave rise. Nor is there any basis, either in history or in theory, for the assumption that the rise of new industries proceeds inevitably at a uniform pace. The growth of modern industry has not come in terms of millions of small increments of change giving rise to a smooth and even development. Characteristically it has come by gigantic leaps and bounds. Very often the change can best be described as discontinuous, lumpy, and jerky, as indeed D. H. Robertson has so vividly done. And when a revolutionary new industry like the railroad or the automobile, after having initiated in its youth a powerful upward surge of investment activity, reaches maturity and ceases to grow, as all industries finally must, the whole economy must experience a profound stagnation, unless indeed new developments take its place. It is not enough that a mature industry continues its activity at a high level on a horizontal plane. The fact that new railroad mileage continued to be built at about the same rate through the seventies, eighties and nineties was not sufficient. It is the *cessation of growth* which is disastrous. It is in connection with the growth, maturity and decline of

great industries that the principle of acceleration operates with peculiar force. And when giant new industries have spent their force, it *may* take a long time before something else of equal magnitude emerges. In fact nothing has emerged in the decade in which we are now living. This basic fact, together with the virtual cessation of public investment by state and local government bodies, as indicated by a decline of $2,000,000,000 in their net public debt since 1932, explains in large measure the necessary rise in federal expenditures.[6]

Spiethoff was quite right when he argued that a vigorous recovery is not just spontaneously born from the womb of the preceding depression. Some small recovery must indeed arise sooner or later merely because of the growing need for capital replacement. But a full-fledged recovery calls for something more than the mere expenditure of depreciation allowances. It requires a large outlay on new investment, and this awaits the development of great new industries and new techniques. But such new developments are not currently available in adequate volume. It is my growing conviction that the combined effect of the decline in population growth, together with the failure of any really important innovations of a magnitude sufficient to absorb large capital outlays, weighs very heavily as an explanation for the failure of the recent recovery to reach full employment. Other factors are certainly significant and important, particularly our failure to control the cost structure and to grapple effectively with specific situations, such as those presented by the railroads and by building construction.

We have noted that the approaching cessation of population growth and the disappearance of new territory for settlement and exploitation may cut off a half or more of the investment outlets which

[6] *Debts and Recovery 1929 to 1937*, The Twentieth Century Fund, 1938, p. 230.

we were wont to make in the past. We are thus compelled to fall back upon that measure of capital formation which is associated with the advance of technique and the rise in per capita output. But current institutional developments are restricting even this outlet. The growing power of trade unions and trade associations, the development of monopolistic competition, of rivalry for the market through expensive persuasion and advertising, instead of through price competition, are factors which have rightly of late commanded much attention among economists. There is, moreover, the tendency to block the advance of technical progress by the shelving of patents.

Under vigorous price competition, new cost-reducing techniques were compulsorily introduced even though the scrapping of obsolete but undepreciated machinery entailed a capital loss. But under the monopoly principle of obsolescence new machines will not be introduced until the undepreciated value of the old machine will at least be covered by the economies of the new technique. Thus progress is slowed down, and outlets for new capital formation, available under a more ruthless competitive society, are cut off. Capital losses which could not be avoided under rigorous price competition can be and are avoided under an economic system more closely integrated by intercorporate association and imperfect competition. If we are to save the one remaining outlet for private capital formation, deliberate action of a far bolder character than hitherto envisaged must be undertaken in order to make the price system and free enterprise sufficiently responsive to permit at least that measure of capital formation to which the rate of technological progress had accustomed us in the past.

Yet even though this much was achieved, it is necessary to recognize that such a rate of progress would not provide sufficient investment outlets to give us full employment of our resources. With a stationary population we could maintain as rapid a rise in per capita real income as that experienced in the past, by making annually only half the volume of new investment to which we have been accustomed. A volume of investment adequate to provide full employment could give us an annual percentage increase in per capita output greatly in excess of any hitherto attained.

Various measures have been offered to maintain full employment in the absence of an adequate rate of technological progress and of the development of new industries. Consumption may be strengthened by the relief from taxes which drain off a stream of income which otherwise would flow into consumption channels. Public investment may usefully be made in human and natural resources and in consumers' capital goods of a collective character designed to serve the physical, recreational and cultural needs of the community as a whole. But we cannot afford to be blind to the unmistakable fact that a solution along these lines raises serious problems of economic workability and political administration.

How far such a program, whether financed by taxation or by borrowing, can be carried out without adversely affecting the system of free enterprise is a problem with which economists, I predict, will have to wrestle in the future far more intensely than in the past. Can a rising public debt owned internally be serviced by a scheme of taxation which will not adversely affect the marginal return on new investment or the marginal cost of borrowing? Can any tax system, designed to increase the propensity to consume by means of a drastic change in income distribution, be devised which will not progressively encroach on private investment?[7]

[7] Joseph J. Spengler, "Population Movements, Employment, and Income," *Southern Econ. Jour.*, Oct., 1938.

As so often in economic life, we are confronted by a dilemma. Continued unemployment on a vast scale, resulting from inadequate private investment outlets, could be expected sooner or later to lead straight into an all-round regimented economy. But so also, by an indirect route and a slower process, might a greatly extended program of public expenditures. And from the standpoint of economic workability the question needs to be raised how far such a program can be carried out in a democratic society without raising the cost structure to a level which prevents full employment. Thus a challenge is presented to all those countries which have not as yet submitted to the yoke of political dictatorship. In one of our round tables we are discussing divergencies in the success of governmental spending in democratic countries and in totalitarian states. Totalitarian states have the great advantage that they can rigorously check the advance of costs, including wage rates, while engaging in an expansionist program of public investment. Democratic countries cannot in modern times escape from the influence exerted by organized groups upon the operation of the price system. From the standpoint of the workability of the system of free enterprise, there emerges the problem of sovereignty in democratic countries confronted in their internal economies with powerful groups—entrepreneurial and wage-earning—which have robbed the price system of that impersonal and non-political character idealized in the doctrine of laissez-faire. It remains still to be seen whether political democracy can in the end survive the disappearance of the automatic price system.

Thus we are confronted with various alternatives. On the one side, there is the proposal to risk a negative governmental policy in the expectation that the recuperative forces to which we have long been accustomed will, in the absence of political interference, re-assert themselves. On the other side, there is the proposal to go forward under full steam with unrestrained governmental expansion until full employment has been reached. Those who have no doubts whatever about the correctness of their economic analyses will not hesitate to make a bold choice of policy. But others, impressed with the stubborn economic realities of a rapidly changing world, on the one side, and the frailties of human nature in its power to make the appropriate adaptation to change, on the other, will not be so sure, and may prefer to take a course that risks neither a negative policy nor a breakdown of collective management.

With respect to the permissible rôle of public expenditures, I should like to suggest that the problem might usefully be posed in terms of the national income. In 1929 our national income was about $80,000,000,000. Taking account of the prevailing lower level of prices, on the one side, and the additions to the labor force, on the other, we may perhaps set the income which should currently give us approximately full employment at about $80,000,000,000. At the bottom of the Great Depression the national income had fallen from $80,000,000,000 to $40,000,000,000. So drastic a decline in the national income we could not again afford to risk. The consequences for the vitality and workability of the economic system are too serious to contemplate. I suggest—the figures are only a rough approximation—that we cannot afford to let our income fall materially below $65,000,000,000, or say $60,000,000,000 as a minimum. A scale of net income-creating governmental expenditures adequate to prevent a fall in income below this level can, it seems to me, scarcely be questioned, and would currently, I believe, command the support of most economists. As the national income, however, approaches $70,000,000,000, I suggest that the net income-creating governmental expenditures ought to be tapered off. As we approach this income level, the economic situation becomes increasingly explosive. Bottle-necks begin to appear. Costs rise. Labor aggressively demands wage increases. Rising costs lead to inventory speculation. We encounter the familiar vicious spiral of rising costs and rising prices with growing inefficiency. At this level the spending program becomes relatively ineffective as a means to raise the real income of the community. This danger point is clearly reached sooner in a democratic country than in a totalitarian state. At what precise point it is reached depends upon the degree of discipline and self-restraint which the various economic groups have achieved or can achieve under democratic institutions. What I am suggesting is that in the United States the upper limit of tolerance in terms of social and economic stresses and strains may be set at around $70,000,000,000. At the $60,000,000,000 income level we can afford to spend heavily to forestall any further decline.

The objection will almost certainly be raised that the argument which I have directed against continued governmental spending to the point of full employment, could equally well be directed against private investment, once the upper danger zone has been reached. I should doubt the validity of this criticism. If the government continues to pour out funds at a lavish rate, wage-earners and employers alike are prone to take the easy course which leads to higher costs and higher prices. But if reliance could not be placed upon a stream of purchasing power external to business itself, we could expect, I think, a more vigorous resistance to un-

economic cost-raising demands. Public spending is the easiest of all recovery methods, and therein lies its danger. If it is carried too far, we neglect to attack those specific maladjustments without the removal of which we cannot attain a workable cost-price structure, and therefore we fail to achieve the otherwise available flow of private investment.

There are no easy answers to the problems that confront us. And because this is true, economists will not perform their function if they fail to illuminate the rapidly shifting course of economic development, and through such neglect unwittingly contribute to a dangerous lag in adjustments to change. Equally they will not perform their function if they fail to disclose the possible dangers which lurk in the wake of vastly enlarged governmental activities. Choices indeed must be made, and scientific analysis and painstaking research can aid by exploring the probable consequences of alternative choices. The problems which I have raised offer a challenge to our profession. The great transition, incident to a rapid decline in population growth and its impact upon capital formation and the workability of a system of free enterprise, calls for high scientific adventure along all the fronts represented by the social science disciplines.*

* [With the second edition of this volume, Professor Hansen has added the following postscript: In essence, my stagnation thesis contends that the U.S. propensity to save outruns the inducement to invest. Vast governmental outlays, induced partly by three wars, have indeed in large part filled the gap. Still, despite the greatly enlarged role of government, we averaged 4.7 per cent unemployment in 1947–1968 inclusive. No one can claim that the "self-sustaining economy" has proven its capacity to produce full employment.—*Ed.*]

20

Expansion and Employment[1]

EVSEY D. DOMAR

"A slow sort of a country," said the Queen. "Now, *here*, you see, it takes all the running *you* can do, to keep in the same place. If you want to get somewhere else, you must run at least twice as fast as that."
Lewis Carroll: *Through the Looking Glass*

In these days of labor shortages and inflation, a paper dealing with conditions needed for full employment and with the threat of deflation may well appear out of place. Its publication at this time is due partly to a two-year lag between the first draft and the final copy; also to the widely held belief that the present inflation is a temporary phenomenon, and that once it

* *

Reprinted from *The American Economic Review*, vol. 37 (March 1947), pp. 34–55, by permission of the publisher and author.

Evsey D. Domar teaches at the Massachusetts Institute of Technology; he was formerly at the Carnegie Institute of Technology.

[1] This paper forms a sequence to my earlier article on "The 'Burden' of the Debt and the National Income," published in this *Review*, Vol. XXXIV, No. 5 (Dec., 1944), pp. 798–827. Though their titles seem different, the two papers are based on the same logical foundation and treat a common subject: the economic rôle of growth.

is over, the old problem of deflation and unemployment may possibly appear before us again.

Our comfortable belief in the efficacy of Say's Law has been badly shaken in the last fifteen years. Both events and discussions have shown that supply does not automatically create its own demand. A part of income generated by the productive process may not be returned to it; this part may be saved and hoarded. As Keynes put it, "Unemployment develops ... because people want the moon; men cannot be employed when the object of desire (*i.e.*, money) is something which cannot be produced...."[2] The core of the problem then is the public's desire to hoard. If no hoarding takes place, employment can presumably be maintained.

This sounds perfectly straight and simple; and yet it leaves something unexplained. Granted that absence of hoarding is a *necessary* condition for the maintenance of full employment, is it also a *sufficient* condition? Is the absence of hoarding *all*

[2] John M. Keynes, *The General Theory of Employment Interest and Money* (New York, 1936), p. 235.

that is necessary for the avoidance of unemployment? This is the impression *The
General Theory* gives. And yet, on a different plane, we have some notions about an
increasing productive capacity which must
somehow be utilized if unemployment is
to be avoided. Will a mere absence of
hoarding assure such a utilization? Will
not a continuous increase in expenditures
(and possibly in the money supply) be
necessary in order to achieve this goal?

The present paper deals with this problem. It attempts to find the conditions
needed for the maintenance of full employment over a period of time, or more exactly,
the rate of growth of national income which
the maintenance of full employment requires. This rate of growth is analyzed in
Section I. Section II is essentially a digression on some conceptual questions and
alternative approaches. It may be omitted
by the busy reader. Section III is concerned with the *dual* character of the investment process; that is, with the fact
that investment not only generates income
but also increases productive capacity.
Therefore the effects of investment on employment are less certain and more complex
than is usually supposed. In Section IV
a few examples from existing literature on
the subject are given, and Section V contains some concluding remarks. The most
essential parts of the paper are presented
in Sections I and III.

As in many papers of this kind, a number
of simplifying assumptions are made. Most
of them will become apparent during the
discussion. Two may be noted at the outset. First, events take place simultaneously, without any lags. Second, income,
investment and saving are defined in the
net sense, *i.e.*, over and above depreciation.
The latter is understood to refer to the cost
of replacement of the depreciated asset by
another one of *equal* productive capacity.
These assumptions are not entirely essential to the argument. The discussion could
be carried out with lags, and, if desired, in

gross terms or with a different concept of
depreciation. Some suggestions along these
lines are made in Section II. But it is
better to begin with as simple a statement
of the problem as possible, bearing in mind
of course the nature of assumptions made.

I. THE RATE OF GROWTH

It is perfectly clear that the requirement
that income paid out should be returned
to the productive process, or that savings
be equal to investment, or other expressions of the same idea, are simply formulas
for the retention of the income *status quo*.
If underemployment was present yesterday, it would still remain here today. If
yesterday's income was at a full employment level, that *income level* would be
retained today. It may no longer, however,
correspond to full employment.

Let yesterday's full employment income
equal an annual rate of 150 billion dollars,
and let the average propensity to save
equal, say, 10 percent. If now 15 billions
are annually invested, one might expect
full employment to be maintained. But
during this process, capital equipment of
the economy will have increased by an
annual rate of 15 billions—for after all,
investment *is* the formation of capital.[3]
Therefore, the productive capacity of the
economy has also increased.

The effects of this increase on employment will depend on whether or not *real
income* has also increased. Since money

[3] The identification of investment with capital
formation is reasonably safe in a private economy
where only a small part of resources is disposed of
by the government. When this part becomes
substantial, complications arise. This question
will be taken up again in Section II. Meanwhile,
we shall disregard it and divide total national
income, irrespective of source, into investment
(*i.e.*, capital formation) and consumption.

The term "national income" is understood here
in a broad sense, as total output minus depreciation, and does not touch on current controversies
regarding the inclusion or exclusion of certain
items. Perhaps "net national product" would be
more appropriate for our purposes.

income has remained, as assumed, at the 150 billion annual level, an increase in real income can be brought about only by a corresponding fall in the general price level. This indeed has been the traditional approach to problems of this kind, an approach which we shall have to reject here for the following reasons:

1. The presence of considerable monopolistic elements (in industry and labor) in our economy makes unrealistic the assumption that a falling *general* price level could be achieved without interfering with full employment. This of course does not exclude *relative* changes among prices. As a matter of fact, if industries subject to a faster-than-average technological progress do not reduce their prices to some extent, a constant general price level cannot be maintained.
2. For an economy saddled with a large public debt and potentially faced (in peacetime) with serious employment problems, a falling price level is in itself undesirable.
3. A falling price level can bring about a larger real income only in the special case when prices of consumers' goods fall more rapidly than those of investment goods. For otherwise (with a constant propensity to save) money income will be falling as fast or faster than the price level, and real income will be falling as well. To prevent money income from falling so rapidly, the volume of real investment would have to keep rising—a conclusion which will be presently reached in the more general case.
4. Finally, the assumption of a falling general price level would obscure—and I believe quite unnecessarily—the main subject we are concerned with here.

For these reasons, a *constant general price level* is assumed throughout this paper. But, from a theoretical point of view, this is a convenience rather than a necessity. The discussion could be carried on with a falling or a rising price level as well.

To come back to the increase in capacity. If both money and real national income thus remain fixed at the 150 billion annual level, the creation of the new capital equipment will have one or more of the following effects: (1) The new capital remains unused; (2) The new capital is used at the expense of previously constructed capital, whose labor and/or markets the new capital has taken away; (3) The new capital is substituted for labor (and possibly for other factors).

The first case represents a waste of resources. That capital need not have been constructed in the first place. The second case—the substitution of new capital for existing capital (before the latter is worn out, since investment is defined here in the net sense)—takes place all the time and, in reasonable magnitudes, is both unavoidable and desirable in a free dynamic society. It is when this substitution proceeds on a rather large scale that it can become socially wasteful; also, losses sustained or expected by capital owners will make them oppose new investment—a serious danger for an economy with considerable monopolistic elements.

Finally, capital may be substituted for labor. If this substitution results in a *voluntary* reduction in the labor force or in the length of the work week, no objections can be raised. Such a process has of course been going on for many years. But in our economy it is very likely that at least a part of this substitution—if carried on at an extensive scale—will be involuntary, so that the result will be unemployment.

The tools used in this paper do not allow us to distinguish between these three effects of capital formation, though, as will appear later, our concepts are so defined that a voluntary reduction in the number of man-hours worked is excluded. In general, it is not unreasonable to assume that in most cases all three effects will be present (though not in constant proportions), and that capital formation not accompanied by an increase in income will result in unemployed capital and labor.

The above problems do not arise in the standard Keynesian system because of its explicit assumption that employment is a function of national income, an assumption which admittedly can be justified only over short periods of time. Clearly, a full employment income of 1941 would cause considerable unemployment today. While Keynes' approach—the treatment of employment as a function of income—is a reasonable first approximation, we shall go a step further and assume instead that *the percentage of labor force employed is a function of the ratio between national income and productive capacity*. This should be an improvement, but we must admit the difficulties of determining productive capacity, both conceptually and statistically. These are obvious and need not be elaborated. We shall mean by productive capacity the total output of the economy at what is usually called full employment (with due allowance for frictional and seasonal unemployment), such factors as consumers' preferences, price and wage structures, intensity of competition, and so on being given.

The answer to the problem of unemployment lies of course in a growing income. If after capital equipment has increased by (an annual rate of) 15 billions an income of 150 billions leaves some capacity unused, then a higher magnitude of income can be found—say 155 or 160 billions—which will do the job. There is nothing novel or startling about this conclusion. The idea that a capitalist economy needs growth goes back, in one form or another, at least to Marx. The trouble really is that the idea of growth is so widely accepted that people rarely bother about it. It is always treated as an afterthought, to be added to one's speech or article if requested, but very seldom incorporated in its body. Even then it is regarded as a function of some abstract technological progress which somehow results in increasing productivity per man-hour, and which takes place quite independently of capital formation. And yet, our help in the industrialization of undeveloped countries will take the form not only of supplying technical advice and textbooks, but also of actual machinery and goods. Certainly the 80 odd billion dollars of net capital formation created in the United States in the period 1919–29 had a considerable effect on our productive capacity.[4]

A change in productive capacity of a country is a function of changes in its natural resources (discovery of new ones or depletion of others), in its labor force (more correctly, man-hours available), capital and the state of technique.[5] Since changes in natural resources and technique are very difficult concepts, we can express changes in total capacity via changes in the quantity and productivity of labor or of capital. The traditional approach builds around labor. The several studies of the magnitude of total output corresponding to full employment, made in the last few years, consisted in multiplying the expected labor force (subdivided into several classes) by its expected average productivity.[6] This procedure did not imply that the other three factors (natural resources, technology and capital) remained constant; rather that their variations were all reflected in the changes in productivity of labor.

It is also possible to put capital in the center of the stage and to estimate variations in total capacity by measuring the changes in the quantity of capital and in its productivity, the latter reflecting changes currently taking place in natural resources, technology and the labor force. From a practical point of view, the labor approach has obvious advantages, at least in some problems, because labor is a more

[4] This figure, in 1929 prices, is taken from Simon Kuznets, *National Income and Its Composition*, Vol. I (New York, 1941), p. 268. The actual figure was 79.1 billion dollars.

[5] Taking other conditions listed [earlier on this page] as given.

[6] See for instance E. E. Hagen and N. B. Kirkpatrick, "The National Output at Full Employment in 1950," *Amer. Econ. Rev.*, Vol. XXXIV, No. 4 (Sept., 1944), pp. 472–500.

homogeneous and easily measurable factor. But from a theoretical point of view, the capital approach is more promising and for this reason: the appearance of an extra workman or his decision to work longer hours *only* increases productive capacity without, however, generating any income to make use of this increase. But the construction of a new factory has a *dual* effect: *it increases productive capacity and it generates income.*

The emphasis on this dual character of the investment process is the essence of this paper's approach to the problem of employment. If investment increases productive capacity and also creates income, what should be the magnitude of investment, or at what rate should it grow, in order to make the increase in income equal to that of productive capacity?[7] Couldn't an equation be set up one side of which would represent the increase (or the rate of increase) of productive capacity, and the other—that of income, and the solution of which would yield the required *rate of growth?*

We shall attempt to set up such an equation. It will be first expressed in symbolic form, and later (on p. 283) illustrated by a numerical example.

Let investment proceed at an annual rate of I, and let annual productive capacity (net value added) per dollar of newly created capital be equal on the average to s. Thus if it requires, say, 3 dollars of capital to produce (in terms of annual net value added) one dollar of output, s will equal one-third or 33.3 percent per year. It is not meant that s is the same in all firms or industries. It depends of course on the nature of capital constructed and on many other factors. Its treatment here as a given magnitude is a simplification which can be readily dispensed with.

The productive capacity of I dollars invested will thus be Is dollars per year. But it is possible that the operation of new capital will take place, at least to some

extent, at the expense of previously constructed plants, with which the new capital will compete both for markets and for factors of production (mainly labor). If as a result, the output of existing plants must be curtailed, it would be useless to assert that the productive capacity of the *whole economy* has increased by Is dollars per year.[8] It has actually increased by a smaller amount which will be indicated by $I\sigma$.[9] σ may be called the *potential social average productivity of investment.* Such a long name calls for an explanation.

1. As stated above, σ is concerned with the increase in productive capacity of the whole society and not with the productive capacity per dollar invested in the new plants taken by themselves, that is with s. A difference between s and σ indicates a certain misdirection of investment, or—more important—that investment proceeds at too rapid a rate as compared with the growth of labor and technological progress. This question will be taken up again in Section II.

2. σ should not be confused with other related concepts, such as the traditional marginal productivity of capital. These concepts are usually based on a *ceteris paribus* assumption regarding the quantity of other factors and the state of technique. It should be emphasized that the use of σ does not imply in the least that labor, natural resources and technology remain fixed. It would be more correct therefore to say that σ indicates the increase in productive capacity which *accompanies* rather than which is caused by each dollar invested.

[7] This statement of the problem presupposes that full employment has already been reached and must only be maintained. With a small extra effort we could begin with a situation where some unemployment originally existed.

[8] These comparisons must of course be made at a full employment level of national income. See also pp. 284–286.

[9] We are disregarding here external economies obtained by existing plants from the newly constructed ones.

3. For our purposes, the most important property of σ is its *potential character*. It deals not with an increase in national income but with that of the *productive potential* of the economy. A high σ indicates that the economy *is capable* of increasing its output relatively fast. But whether this increased capacity will actually result in greater output or greater unemployment, depends on the behavior of money income.

The expression $I\sigma$ is the supply side of our system; it is the increase in output which the economy *can* produce. On the demand side we have the multiplier theory, too familiar to need any elaboration, except for the emphasis on the obvious but often forgotten fact that, with any given marginal propensity to save, to be indicated by α, an increase in national income is not a function of investment, but of the *increment* in investment. If investment today, however large, is equal to that of yesterday, national income of today will be just equal and not any larger than that of yesterday. All this is obvious, and is stressed here to underline the lack of symmetry between the effects of investment on productive capacity and on national income.

Let investment increase at an absolute annual rate of ΔI (*e.g.*, by two billion per year), and let the corresponding absolute annual increase in income be indicated by ΔY. We have then

$$\Delta Y = \Delta I \frac{1}{\alpha} \qquad (1)$$

where $1/\alpha$ is of course the multiplier.

Let us now assume that the economy is in a position of a full employment equilibrium, so that its national income equals its productive capacity.[10] To retain this position, income and capacity should increase at the same rate. The annual increase in potential capacity equals $I\sigma$. The annual increase in actual income is expressed by $\Delta I(1/\alpha)$. Our objective is to

[10] See note 7.

make them equal. This gives us the fundamental equation

$$\Delta I \frac{1}{\alpha} = I\sigma \qquad (2)$$

To solve this equation, we multiply both sides by α and divide by I, obtaining

$$\frac{\Delta I}{I} = \alpha\sigma \qquad (3)$$

The left side of expression (3) is the absolute annual increase (or the absolute rate of growth) in investment—ΔI—divided by the volume of investment itself; or in other words, it is the relative increase in investment, or the annual percentage rate of growth of investment. Thus the maintenance of full employment requires that investment grow at the annual percentage rate $\alpha\sigma$.

So much for investment. Since the marginal propensity to save—α—is assumed to be constant, an increase in income is a constant multiple of an increase in investment (see expression [1]). But in order to remain such a constant multiple of investment, income must also grow at the same annual percentage rate, that is at $\alpha\sigma$.*

To summarize, the maintenance of a continuous state of full employment requires that *investment and income grow at a constant annual percentage (or compound interest) rate* equal to the product of the marginal propensity to save and the average (to put it briefly) productivity of investment.[11]

* [In the 1957 reprinting of this article, Professor Domar pointed out that "for income and investment to grow at the same relative rate, the average propensity to save must be constant and hence equal to the marginal." The word "marginal" before the propensity to save should therefore be deleted. See his *Essays in the Theory of Economic Growth* (New York: Oxford University Press, 1957), p. 91.—*Ed.*]

[11] The careful reader may be disturbed by the lack of clear distinction between increments and rates of growth here and elsewhere in the text. If some confusion exists, it is due to my attempt

This result can be made clearer by a numerical example. Let $\sigma = 25$ percent per year, $\alpha = 12$ percent, and $Y = 150$ billions per year. If full employment is to be maintained, an amount equal to $150 \times (12/100)$ should be invested. This will raise productive capacity by the amount invested times σ, *i.e.*, by $150 \times (12/100) \times (25/100)$, and national income will have to rise by the same annual amount. But the relative rise in income will equal the absolute increase divided by the income itself, *i.e.*,

$$\frac{150 \times \dfrac{12}{100} \times \dfrac{25}{100}}{150} = \frac{12}{100} \times \frac{25}{100}$$

$$= \alpha\sigma = 3 \text{ percent} \quad (4)$$

These results were obtained on the assumption that α, the marginal propensity to save, and σ, the average productivity of investment, remain constant. The reader can see that this assumption is not necessary for the argument, and that the whole problem can be easily reworked with variable α and σ. Some remarks about a changing α are made on p. 288.

The expression (3) indicates (in a very simplified manner) conditions needed for the maintenance of full employment over a period of time. It shows that it is not sufficient, in Keynesian terms, that savings of yesterday be invested today, or, as it is often expressed, that investment offset saving. Investment of today must always exceed savings of yesterday. A mere absence of hoarding will not do. An injection of new money (or dishoarding) must take place every day. Moreover, this injection

must proceed, in absolute terms, at an accelerated rate. The economy must continuously expand.[11a]

II. THE ARGUMENT RE-EXAMINED

The busy reader is urged to skip this section and proceed directly to Section III. The present section is really a long footnote which re-examines the concepts and suggests some alternative approaches. Its purpose is, on the one hand, to indicate the essential limitations of the preceding discussion, and on the other, to offer a few suggestions which may be of interest to others working in this field.

It was established in Section I that the maintenance of full employment requires income and investment to grow at an annual compound interest rate equal to $\alpha\sigma$. The meaning of this result will naturally depend on those of α and σ. Unfortunately neither of them is devoid of ambiguity.

The marginal propensity to save—α—is a relatively simple concept in a private economy where only a small part of resources is handled by the government. National income can be divided, without too much trouble, into investment and consumption, even though it is true that the basis for this distinction is often purely formal.[12] But on the whole it sounds quite reasonable to say that if marginal propensity to save is α, then an α fraction of an increase in income is saved by the public and invested in income-producing assets.

When a substantial part of the economy's resources is disposed of by the government, two interpretations of the marginal pro-

---

to express these concepts in non-mathematical form. Actually they all should be stated in terms of rates of growth (derivatives in respect to time). For a more serious treatment of this point, as well as for a more complete statement of the logic of the paper, see my article "Capital Expansion, Rate of Growth, and Employment," *Econometrica*, Vol. XIV (Apr., 1946), pp. 137–47.

[11a] After this paper was sent to the printer, I happened to stumble on an article by R. F. Harrod, published in 1939, which contained a number of ideas similar to those presented here. See "An Essay in Dynamic Theory," *Econ. Jour.*, Vol. XLIX (Apr., 1939), pp. 14–33.

[12] Thanks are due to George Jaszi for his persistent efforts to enlighten me on this subject. The division of national income into investment and consumption is really a more difficult task than my text might imply.

pensity to save, or of savings and investment in general, appear possible. The first is to continue dividing the total output, whether produced by government or by private business, into consumption and investment. This method was implicitly followed in this paper. But a question arises regarding the meaning and stability of α. It makes sense to say that a person or the public saves, in accordance with the size of their incomes, their habits, expectations, etc., a certain, though not necessarily constant, fraction of an increment in their *disposable* (*i.e.*, after income and social security taxes) income, but can a similar statement be made regarding total national income, a good part of which is not placed at the disposal of the public? Also it is not easy to divide government expenditures into consumption and investment.

The other method would limit α to disposable income only, and then provide for government expenditures separately. It would be necessary then to find out the effects of these expenditures on productive capacity.

Depreciation raises another problem. Since all terms are defined here in the net sense, the meaning and magnitude of α will also depend on those of depreciation, irrespective of the choice between the above two methods. Depreciation has been defined here (see page 278) as the cost of replacement of a worn out asset by another one with an equal productive capacity. While this approach is about as bad or as good as any other, the difficulty still remains that businesses ordinarily do not use this definition, and therefore arrive at a different estimate of their net incomes, which in turn determine their propensity to save.

I do not have ready answers to these questions, though I do not consider them insurmountable. I am mentioning them here partly in order to indicate the limitations of the present argument, and also as obstacles which will have to be overcome if a more exact analysis is undertaken.

σ is even more apt to give rise to ambiguities. s, from which it springs, has been used, in one form or another, in economic literature before, particularly in connection with the acceleration principle.[13] Here it indicates the annual amount of income (net value added) which can be produced by a dollar of newly created capital. It varies of course among firms and industries, and also in space and time, though a study recently made seems to indicate that it has been quite stable, at least in the United States and Great Britain, over the last 70 years or so.[14] Whether s has or has not been relatively stable is not essential for our discussion. The real question is whether such a concept has meaning, whether it makes sense to say that a given economy or a plant has a certain capacity. Traditional economic thinking would, I fear, be against such an approach. Unfortunately, it is impossible to discuss this question here. I believe that our actual experience during the last depression and this war, as well as a number of empirical studies, show that productive capacity, both of a plant and of the whole economy is a meaningful concept, though this capacity, as well as the magnitude of s, should be treated as a *range* rather than as a single number.

In some problems s may be interpreted as the minimum annual output per dollar invested which will make the investment worth undertaking. If this output falls below s, the investor suffers a loss or at least a disappointment, and may be unwilling to replace the asset after it has depreciated.

[13] See for instance Paul A. Samuelson, "Interactions between the Multiplier Analysis and the Principle of Acceleration," *Rev. Econ. Stat.*, Vol. XXI (May, 1939), pp. 75–79 [reprinted in this volume, Selection 18]; also R. F. Harrod, *The Trade Cycle* (Oxford, 1936). These authors, however, used not the ratio of income to capital, but of consumption to capital, or rather the reciprocal of this ratio.

[14] See Ernest H. Stern, "Capital Requirements in Progressive Economies," *Economica*, n.s., Vol. XII (Aug., 1945), pp. 163–71.

All these doubts apply to σ even more than to s. As explained on page 281, σ differs from s by indicating the annual increment in capacity of the *whole economy* per dollar invested, rather than that of the newly created capital taken by itself. The possible difference between s and σ is due to the following reasons:

1. The new plants are not operated to capacity because they are unable to find a market for their products.

2. Old plants reduce their output because their markets are captured by new plants.

As productive capacity has no meaning except in relation to consumers' preferences, in both of the above cases productive capacity of the country is increased by a smaller amount than could be produced by the new plants; in the limiting case it is not increased at all, and $\sigma = 0$, however high s may be. But it must be made clear that the test of whether or not σ is below s can be made only under conditions (actual or assumed) of full employment. If markets are not large enough because of insufficiency of effective demand due to unemployment, it cannot yet be concluded that σ is below s.

3. The first two cases can take place irrespective of the volume of current investment. A more important case arises when investment proceeds at such a rapid rate that a shortage of other factors relative to capital develops. New plants may be unable to get enough labor, or more likely, labor (and other factors) is transferred to new plants from previously constructed ones, whose capacity therefore declines. In its actual manifestation, case 3 can hardly be separated from cases 1 and 2, because to the individual firm affected the difference between s and σ always takes the form of a cost-price disparity. The reason why we are trying to separate the first two cases from the third lies in the bearing of this distinction on practical policy. The first two cases arise from an error of judgment on the part of investors

(past or present) which is, at least to some extent, unavoidable and not undesirable. The struggle for markets and the replacement of weaker (or older) firms and industries by stronger (or newer) ones is the essence of progress in a capitalist society. The third case, on the other hand, may result from poor fiscal policy. It constitutes an attempt to invest too much, to build more capital than the economy can utilize even at full employment. Such a situation can develop if an economy with a high propensity to save tries to maintain full employment by investing all its savings into capital goods. But it should be made clear that the expressions "too much capital" or "high propensity to save" are used in a relative sense—in comparison with the growth of other factors, that is natural resources, labor and technology.

The use of σ certainly does not imply that these factors remain fixed. As a matter of fact, it would be very interesting to explore the use of a more complex function as the right side of expression (2) instead of $I\sigma$, a function in which the growth of labor, natural resources, and technology would be presented explicitly, rather than through their effects on σ.[15] I did not attempt it because I wished to express the idea of growth in the simplest possible manner. One must also remember that in the application of mathematics to economic problems, diminishing returns appear rapidly, and that the construction of complex models requires so many specific assumptions as to narrow down their applicability.

And yet it may be interesting to depart in another direction, namely to introduce lags. In this paper both the multiplier effect and the increase in capacity are supposed to take place simultaneously and without any lag. Actually, the multiplier

[15] Some work along these lines has been done by J. Tinbergen. See his "Zur Theorie der langfristigen Wirtschaftsentwicklung" in the *Weltwirtschaftliches Archiv*, Vol. LV (May, 1942), pp. 511–49.

may take some time to work itself out, and certainly the construction of a capital asset takes time. In a secular problem these lags are not likely to be of great importance, but they may play an essential rôle over the cycle. We shall return to this question on pages 289–290.

Finally, it is possible to approach the problem of growth from a different point of view. It was established here that the rate of growth required for a full employment equilibrium to be indicated by r is equal to

$$r = \alpha\sigma \tag{5}$$

so that if α and σ are given, the rate of growth is determined. But the equation (5) can also be solved for α in terms of r and σ, and for σ in terms of r and α. Thus if it is believed that r should be treated as given (for instance by technological progress), and if it is also decided to keep σ at a certain level, perhaps not too far from s, then it is possible to determine $\alpha = r/\sigma$, as being that marginal propensity to save which can be maintained without causing either inflation or unemployment. This approach was actually used by Ernest Stern in his statistical study of capital requirements of the United Kingdom, the United States and the Union of South Africa.[16] I also understand from Tibor de Scitovsky that he used the same approach in a study not yet published.

It is also possible to treat r and α as given and then determine what $\sigma = r/\alpha$ would have to be. Each approach has its own advantages and the choice depends of course on the nature of the problem in hand. The essential point to be noticed is the relationship between these three variables r, α, and σ, and the fact that if any two of them are given, the value of the third needed for the maintenance of full employment is determined; and if its actual value differs from the required one, inflation

[16] Stern, *op. cit.*

in some cases and unused capacity and unemployment in others will develop.

III. THE DUAL NATURE OF THE INVESTMENT PROCESS

We shall continue the discussion of growth by returning to expression (2) on page 282,

$$\Delta I \frac{1}{\alpha} = I\sigma$$

which is fundamental to our whole analysis. As a matter of fact, the statement of the problem in this form (2) appears to me at least as important as its actual solution expressed in (3). To repeat, the left part of the equation shows the annual increment in national income and is the demand side; while the right part represents the annual increase in productive capacity and is the supply side. Alternatively, the left part may be called the "multiplier side," and the right part the "σ side."

What is most important for our purposes is the fact that investment appears on both sides of the equation; that is, it has a *dual effect:* on the left side it generates income via the multiplier effect; and on the right side it increases productive capacity—the σ effect. The explicit recognition of this dual character of investment could undoubtedly save much argument and confusion. Unless some special assumptions are made, the discussion of the effects of investment on profits, income, employment, etc., cannot be legitimately confined to one side only. For the generation of income and the enlargement of productive capacity often have diametrically opposed effects, and the outcome in each particular case depends on the special circumstances involved.[17]

[17] The effects of labor saving machinery on employment of labor is a good case in point. Some economists, particularly those connected with the labor movement, insist that such machines displace labor and create unemployment. Their opponents are equally sure that the

Analyzing expression (2) further, we notice that even though investment is present on both its sides, it does not take the same form: for on the σ side we have the *amount* of investment as such; but on the multiplier side we have not the amount of investment but its annual increment, or its absolute *rate of increase*.

The amount of investment (always in the net sense) may remain constant, or it may go up or down, but so long as it remains positive (and except for the rare case when $\sigma \leqq 0$) productive capacity increases. But if income is to rise as well, it is not enough that just any amount be invested: *an increase in income is not a function of the amount invested; it is the function of the increment of investment.* Thus the whole body of investment, so to speak, increases productive capacity, but only its very top—the increment—increases national income.

In this probably lies the explanation why inflations have been so rare in our economy in peacetime, and why even in relatively prosperous periods a certain degree of underemployment has usually been present. Indeed, it is difficult enough to keep investment at some reasonably high level year after year, but the requirement that it always be rising is not likely to be met for any considerable length of time.

Now, if investment and therefore income do not grow at the required rate, unused capacity develops. Capital and labor become idle. It may not be apparent why investment by increasing productive capacity creates unemployment of labor. Indeed, as was argued on page 279, this need not always be the case. Suppose national income remains constant or rises very slowly

while new houses are being built. It is possible that new houses will be rented out at the expense of older buildings and that no larger rents will be paid than before; or that the new houses will stand wholly or partly vacant with the same result regarding the rents.[18] But it is also possible, and indeed very probable, that the complete or partial utilization of the new buildings which are usually better than the old ones, will require the payment of larger rents, with the result that less income will be left for the purchase of, say clothing; thus causing unemployment in the clothing trades. So the substitution of capital for labor need not take the obvious form of labor-saving machinery; it may be equally effective in a more circuitous way.

The unemployment of men is considered harmful for obvious reasons. But idle buildings and machinery, though not arousing our humanitarian instincts, can be harmful because their presence inhibits new investment. Why build a new factory when existing ones are working at half capacity? It is certainly not necessary to be dogmatic and assert that no plant or house should ever be allowed to stand idle, and that as soon as unused capacity develops the economy plunges into a depression. There is no need, nor is it possible or desirable, to guarantee that every piece of capital ever constructed will be fully utilized until it is worn out. When population moves from Oklahoma to California, some buildings in Oklahoma will stand idle; or when plastics replace leather in women's handbags, the leather industry may suffer. Such changes form the very life of a free dynamic society, and should not be interfered with. The point is that there be no vacant houses while prospective tenants are present but cannot afford to live in

---

introduction of labor saving devices reduces costs and generates income, thus increasing employment. Both sides cite ample empirical evidence to prove their contentions, and neither side is wrong. But both of them present an incomplete picture from which no definite conclusion can be derived.

[18] It is worth noticing that in both cases the construction of the new houses represents a misdirection of resources, at least to some extent. But a complete avoidance of such misdirection is perfectly impossible and even undesirable.

them because they are unemployed. And they are unemployed because income and investment do not grow sufficiently fast.

The extent to which unused capacity, present or expected, inhibits new investment greatly depends on the structure of industry and the character of the economy in general. The more atomistic it is, the stronger is competition, the more susceptible it is to territorial, technological and other changes, the smaller is the effect of unused capacity on new investment. One firm may have an idle plant, while another in the same industry builds a new one; steel may be depressed while plastics are expanding. It is when an industry is more or less monopolized, or when several industries are financially connected, that unused capacity presents a particularly serious threat to new investment.

Strictly speaking, our discussion so far, including equation (2), was based on the assumption that α remained constant. If α varies within the time period concerned, the relation between investment and income becomes more involved. What the left side of the equation (2) requires is that *income* increase; and investment must grow only in so far as its growth is necessary for the growth of income. So if α declines sufficiently fast, a growing income can be achieved with a constant or even falling investment. But years of declining α have evidently been offset by others of rising α, because whatever information is available would indicate that over the last seventy years or so prior to this war the percentage of income saved was reasonably constant, possibly with a slight downward trend.[19] Therefore, in the absence of direct government interference, it would seem better not to count too much on a falling α, at least for the time being.

In general, a high α presents a serious danger to the maintenance of full employment, because investment may fail to grow at the required high rate, or will be physically unable to do so without creating a substantial difference between s and σ. This difference indicates that large numbers of capital assets become unprofitable and their owners suffer losses or at least disappointments (see page 285). Space does not permit me to develop this idea at greater length here.[20] But it must be emphasized that what matters is not the magnitude of α taken by itself, but its relation to the growth of labor, natural resources, and technology. Thus a country with new resources, a rapidly growing population, and developing technology is able to digest, so to speak, a relatively large α, while absence or at least a very slow growth of these factors makes a high α a most serious obstacle to full employment.[21] But the problem can be attacked not only by lowering α, but also by speeding up the rate of technological progress, the latter solution being much more to my taste. It must be remembered, however, that technological progress makes it *possible* for the economy to grow, without guaranteeing that this growth will be realized.

In a private capitalist society where α cannot be readily changed, a higher level of income and employment at any given time can be achieved only through increased investment. But investment, as an employment creating instrument, is a mixed blessing because of its σ effect. The economy finds itself in a serious dilemma: if sufficient investment is not forthcoming today, unemployment will be here today. But if enough is invested today, still more will be needed tomorrow.

It is a remarkable characteristic of a capitalist economy that while, on the whole,

[19] See Simon Kuznets, *National Product since 1869*, National Bureau of Economic Research (mimeo., 1945), p. II-89. I do not mean that we must always assume a constant α; rather that we lack sufficient proof to rely on a falling one.

[20] See my paper, *Econometrica*, Vol. XIV, particularly pp. 142–45.
[21] *Cf*. Alvin H. Hansen, *Fiscal Policy and the Business Cycle* (New York, 1941), particularly Part IV.

unemployment is a function of the difference between its actual income and its productive capacity, most of the measures (*i.e.*, investment) directed towards raising national income also enlarge productive capacity. It is very likely that the increase in national income will be greater than that of capacity, but the whole problem is that the increase in income is temporary and presently peters out (the usual multiplier effect), while capacity has been increased for good. So that as far as unemployment is concerned, investment is at the same time a cure for the disease and the cause of even greater ills in the future.[22]

IV. AN ECONOMIC EXCURSION

It may be worth while to browse through the works of several economists of different schools of thought to see their treatment of the σ and of the multiplier effects of investment. It is not suggested to make an exhaustive study, but just to present a few examples.

Thus in Marshall's *Principles* capital and investment are looked upon as productive instruments (the σ effect), with little being said about monetary (that is, income or price) effects of investment.[23] The same attitude prevails in Fisher's *Nature of Capital and Income*,[24] and I presume in the great majority of writings not devoted to the business cycle. It is not that these writers were unaware of monetary effects of investment (even though they did not have the multiplier concept as such), but such questions belonged to a different field, and the problem of aggregate demand was supposed to be taken care of by some variation of Say's Law.

In the business cycle literature we often find exactly an opposite situation. The whole Wicksellian tradition treated economic fluctuations as a result of monetary effects of excessive investment. It is curious that all this investment did not lead to increased output which would counteract its inflationary tendencies. Indeed, as one reads Hayek's *Prices and Production*, one gets an impression that these investment projects never bear fruit and are, moreover, abandoned after the crisis. The σ effect is entirely absent, or at least appears with such a long lag as to make it inoperative. Prosperity comes to an end because the banking system refuses to support inflation any longer.[25]

σ fares better in the hands of Aftalion.[26] His theory of the cycle is based upon, what I would call, a time lag between the multiplier and the σ effects. Prosperity is started by income generated by investment in capital goods (the multiplier effect), while no increase in productive capacity has taken place as yet. As investment projects are completed, the resulting increase in productive capacity (the σ effect) pours goods on the market and brings prosperity to an end.

---

[22] That income generating effects of investment are temporary and that new and larger amounts must be spent to maintain full employment, has been mentioned in economic and popular literature a number of times. Particular use has been made of this fact by opponents of the so-called deficit financing, who treat government expenditures as a "shot in the arm" which must be administered at an ever increasing dose. What they fail to realize is that exactly the same holds true for private investment.

[23] Marshall was very careful, however, to distinguish between the substitution of a particular piece of machinery for particular labor, and the replacement of labor by capital in general. The latter he regarded impossible, because the construction of capital creates demand for labor, essentially a sort of a multiplier effect. See *Principles of Economics*, 8th ed. (London, 1936), p. 523.

[24] Irving Fisher, *The Nature of Capital and Income* (New York, 1919).

[25] Friedrich A. Hayek, *Prices and Production* (London, 1931). I don't mean to say that Professor Hayek is not aware that capital is productive; rather that he did not make use of this fact in his theory of the business cycle. See, however, his "The 'Paradox' of Saving," *Economica*, Vol. XI (May, 1931), pp. 125–69.

[26] Albert Aftalion, "The Theory of Economic Cycles Based on the Capitalistic Technique of Production," *Rev. Econ. Stat.*, Vol. IX (Oct., 1927), pp. 165–70. This short article contains a summary of his theory.

A similar approach is used by Michal Kalecki. The essence of his model of the business cycle consists in making profit expectations, and therefore investment, a function (with appropriate lags) of the relation between national income and the stock of capital. During the recovery, investment and income rise, while the accumulation of capital lags behind. Presently, however, due to the structure of the model, the rise of income stops while capital continues to accumulate. This precipitates the downswing.[27]

Space does not allow us to analyze the works of a number of other writers on the subject, among whom Foster and Catchings should be given due recognition for what is so clumsy and yet so keen an insight.[28] I am also omitting the whole Marxist literature, in which capital accumulation plays such an important rôle, because that would require a separate study. The few remaining pages of this section will be devoted to Hobson and Keynes.

Hobson's writings contain so many interesting ideas that it is a great pity he is not read more often.[29] Anti-Keynesians probably like him not much more than they do Keynes, while Keynesians are apt to regard the *General Theory* as the quintessence of all that was worth while in economics before 1936, and may not bother to read earlier writings. I may say that Keynes's own treatment of Hobson, in spite of his generous recognition of the latter's works, may have substantiated this impression.[30]

Even though both Keynes and Hobson were students of unemployment, they actually addressed themselves to two different problems. Keynes analyzed what happens when savings (of the preceding period) are not invested. The answer was—unemployment, but the statement of the problem in this form might easily give the erroneous impression that if savings were invested, full employment would be assured. Hobson, on the other hand, went a step further and stated the problem in this form: suppose savings are invested. Will the new plants be able to dispose of their products? Such a statement of the problem was not at all, as Keynes thought, a mistake.[31] It was a statement of a different, and possibly also a deeper, problem.

Hobson was fully armed with the σ effect of investment, and he saw that it could be answered only by growth. His weakness lay in a poor perception of the multiplier effect and his analysis lacked rigor in general. He gave a demonstration rather than a proof. But the problem to which he addressed himself is just as alive today as it was fifty and twenty years ago.[32]

This discussion, as I suspect almost any other, would be obviously incomplete without some mention of Keynes's treatment of the σ and of the multiplier effects. Keynes's approach is very curious: as a matter of fact, he has two: the familiar

---

[27] Michal Kalecki, *Essays in the Theory of Economic Fluctuations* (New York, 1939). See particularly the last essay "A Theory of the Business Cycle," pp. 116–49. What Mr. Kalecki's model shows in a general sense is that accumulation of capital cannot proceed for any length of time in a trendless economy (*i.e.*, an economy with a secularly constant income). His other results depend upon the specific assumptions he makes.

[28] William T. Foster and Waddill Catchings, *Profits* (Boston and New York, 1925). This book is the most important of their several published works. It is interesting to note that they did come to the conclusion that ". . . as long as capital facilities are created at a sufficient rate, there need be no deficiency of consumer income. To serve that purpose, however, facilities must be increased at a constantly accelerating rate" (p. 413). This they regarded quite impossible.

[29] I am particularly referring to his *Economics of Unemployment* (London, 1922) and *Rationalization and Unemployment* (New York, 1930).

[30] See *The General Theory*, pp. 364–71.

[31] *Ibid.*, pp. 367–68.

[32] Contrary to popular impression, Hobson does not advocate a maximum reduction in the propensity to save. What he wants is to reduce it to a magnitude commensurable with requirements for capital arising from technological progress—an interesting and reasonable idea.

short-run analysis, and another one which may be called a long-run one.[33]

Keynes's short-run system (later expressed so admiringly by Oscar Lange[34]) is based on "... given the existing skill and quantity of available labor, the existing quality and quantity of available equipment, the existing technique, the degree of competition, the tastes and habits of the consumer ..."[35] Productive capacity thus being given, employment becomes a function of national income, expressed, to be sure, not in money terms but in "wage units." A wage unit, the remuneration for "an hour's employment of ordinary labor" (page 41), is of course a perfect fiction, but some such device must be used to translate real values into monetary and *vice versa*, and one is about as good or as bad as another. The important point for our purposes is the assumption that the amount of equipment (*i.e.*, capital) in existence is given.

Now, the heart of Keynesian economics is the argument that employment depends on income, which in turn is determined by the current volume of investment (and the propensity to save). But investment (in the net sense) is nothing else but the rate of change of capital. Is it legitimate then first to assume the quantity of capital as given, and then base the argument on its rate of change? If the quantity of capital changes, so does (in a typical case) productive capacity, and if the latter changes it can be hardly said that employment is solely determined by the size of national income, expressed in wage units or otherwise. Or putting it in the language of this paper, is it safe and proper to analyze the relation between investment and employment without taking into account the σ effect?

The answer depends on the nature of the problem in hand. In this particular case, Keynes could present two reasons for his disregard of the σ effect. He could assume that the latter operates with at least a one period lag, the period being understood here as the whole time span covered by the discussion.[36] Or he could argue that over a typical year the net addition (*i.e.*, net investment) to the stock of capital of a society, such as England or the United States, will hardly exceed some 3 or 5 percent; since this increment is small when compared with changes in income, it can be disregarded.[37]

Both explanations are entirely reasonable provided of course that the period under consideration is not too long. A five-year lag for the σ effect would be difficult to defend, and an increase in the capital stock of some 15 or 20 percent can hardly be disregarded. I am not aware that Keynes did present either of these explanations; but there is just so much one can do in four hundred pages at any one time.

It would be perfectly absurd to say that Keynes was not aware of the productive qualities of capital. In the *long run* he laid great stress on it, possibly too great. All through the *General Theory* we find grave concern for the diminishing marginal efficiency of capital due, in the long run, to its increasing quantity.[38] There is so much of this kind of argument as to leave the reader puzzled in the end. We are told that marginal efficiency of capital depends

[33] This whole discussion is based on *The General Theory* and not on Keynes's earlier writings.

[34] Oscar Lange, "The Rate of Interest and the Optimum Propensity to Consume," *Economica*, n.s., Vol. V (Feb., 1938), pp. 12–32. This otherwise excellent paper has a basic defect in the assumption that investment is a function of consumption rather than of the rate of change of consumption.

[35] *The General Theory*, p. 245. See also pp. 24 and 28.

[36] This again is not quite safe unless some provision for investment projects started in preceding periods and finished during the present period is made.

[37] The second assumption is specifically made by Professor Pigou in his *Employment and Equilibrium* (London, 1941), pp. 33–34.

[38] See for instance pp. 31, 105–106, 217, 219, 220–21, 324, and 375.

on its scarcity. Well and good. But scarcity relative to what? It could become less scarce relative to other factors, such as labor, so that the marginal productivity of capital in the real sense (*i.e.*, essentially our σ) declined. But then on page 213 we read: "If capital becomes less scarce, the excess yield will diminish, without its having become less productive—at least in the physical sense."

Why then does the marginal efficiency of capital fall? Evidently because capital becomes less scarce relative to income.[39] But why cannot income grow more rapidly if labor is not the limiting factor? Could it be only a matter of poor fiscal policy which failed to achieve a faster growing income? After all we have in investment an income generating instrument; if investment grows more rapidly, so does income. This is *the* multiplier effect of investment on which so much of the *General Theory* is built.

I don't have the answer. Is it possible that, while Keynes disregarded the σ effect in the short-run analysis, he somehow omitted the multiplier effect from the long-run?

V. CONCLUDING REMARKS

A traveller who sat in the economic councils of the United States and of the Soviet Union would be much impressed with the emphasis placed on investment and technological progress in both countries. He would happily conclude that the differences between the economic problems of a relatively undeveloped socialist economy and a highly developed capitalist economy are really not as great as they are often made to appear. Both countries want investment and technological progress. But if he continued to listen to the debates, he would presently begin to wonder. For in the Soviet Union investment

and technology are wanted in order to enlarge the country's productive capacity. They are wanted essentially as labor-saving devices which would allow a given task to be performed with less labor, thus releasing men for other tasks. In short, they are wanted for their σ effects.

In the United States, on the other hand, little is said about enlarging productive capacity. Technological progress is wanted as the creator of investment opportunities, and investment is wanted because it generates income and creates employment. It is wanted for its multiplier effect.

Both views are correct and both are incomplete. The multiplier is not just another capitalist invention. It can live in a socialist state just as well and it has been responsible for the inflationary pressure which has plagued the Soviet economy all these years, since the first five-year plan. And similarly, σ is just as much at home in one country as in another, and its effect —the enlarged productive capacity brought about by accumulation of capital—has undoubtedly had much to do with our peacetime unemployment.

But what is the solution? Shall we reduce σ to zero and also abolish technological progress thus escaping from unemployment into the "nirvana" of a stationary state? This would indeed be a defeatist solution. It is largely due to technology and savings that humanity has made the remarkable advance of the last two hundred years, and now when our technological future seems so bright, there is less reason to abandon it than ever before.

It is possible that α has been or will be too high as compared with the growth of our labor force, the utilization of new resources, and the development of technology. Unfortunately, we have hardly any empirical data to prove or disprove this supposition. The fact that private investment did not absorb available savings in the past does not prove that they could not be utilized in other ways (*e.g.*,

[39] There is a third possibility, namely that income is redistributed against the capitalists, but Keynes makes no use of it.

by government), or even that had private business invested them these investments would have been unprofitable; the investing process itself might have created sufficient income to justify the investments. What is needed is a study of the magnitudes of s, of the difference between s and σ which can develop without much harm and then of the value of α which the economy can digest at its full employment rate of growth.

Even if the resulting magnitude of α is found to be considerably below the existing one, a reduction of α is only one of the two solutions, the speeding up of technological progress being the other. But it must be remembered that neither technology, nor of course saving, guarantee a rise in income. What they do is to place in our hands the *power* and the ability of achieving a growing income. And just as, depending upon the use made of it, any power can become a blessing or a curse, so can saving and technological progress, depending on our economic policies, result in frustration and unemployment or in an ever expanding economy.

21

Domar
and Dynamic Economics
R. F. HARROD

1. I have had reasons for believing that perplexities of the kind set forth by Mr. Oshima in the foregoing article [in *The Economic Journal*, September 1959] have been shared by other workers in the field, and his expression of them may be taken as a suitable opportunity for me to attempt a further elucidation of these and kindred matters.

2. I should like to take advantage of it to extend my fraternal greetings to Professor Domar. I have for long felt a lively appreciation of his work, and for my unseemly delay in expressing that on paper I can only plead that there was no occasion that struck me as suitable. He paid a generous tribute to my work more than seven years ago.[1] From the beginning he realised that the correct analysis of a growing economy required far-reaching changes in some of our traditional habits of thinking;

* *

ing; and, independently of me,[2] he provided an equation, formally identical (see below) with one that I had previously furnished, which, I believe, must remain central to growth theory. Since the date A.D. of a formulation is of no importance, our names have rightly been jointly associated with this equation. I would claim that my first contribution to growth theory, as we both understand it, and as it is now, albeit slowly, coming to be understood by others, appeared in *Economica* in August 1934.[3] In the years before that it seemed to be becoming clear that the traditional concepts of static economies would not serve to demonstrate decisively which of the rival monetary theories of Keynes and von Hayek was correct; yet from the practical point of view of the maxims of central banking it was vitally important to do so. The view was voiced that the matter might really be indeterminate—depending on "who got to the telephone first." The position, so it seemed to me, was entirely transformed, if one assessed the rival the-

Reprinted from *The Economic Journal*, vol. 69 (September 1959), pp. 451–464, by permission of the publisher and author.

R. F. Harrod is Reader Emeritus at Oxford University.

[1] *American Economic Review, Papers and Proceedings*, Vol. 42, No. 2 (May 1952), p. 481.

[2] Cf. his statement, *Essays in the Theory of Economic Growth*, p. 92, n. 11a [p. 283 in this volume].

[3] "Expansion of Credit in an Advancing Community." Reprinted as Essay 11 in *Economic Essays* (Macmillan, 1952).

ories by their application to a growing economy, and this I sought to explain in the afore-mentioned article. Two years later I published my *Trade Cycle*, which showed that the effects of the accelerator and the multiplier are intimately inter-locked.[4] The attempt to reduce the doc-trines of that book to better order and to extricate what was most essential resulted in the formulation of a theory of which the afore-mentioned equation was a central feature.[5]

3. This equation must be considered primarily as the expression of certain neces-sary relations between elements in a steadily growing economy. The validity of the equation is consistent with rival causal theories of growth, although not with all theories that have been suggested. It is to be stressed that, subject to two relatively minor reservations to be mentioned, Do-mar's equation is identical with mine. Confusion has been caused by the fact that he introduced it by considering the increase of production rendered possible by new investment; he designates the potential increase of output per unit of new invest-ment by the symbol σ. I, on the other hand, make no explicit reference to this increased productivity, but, looking at the same fact from the opposite point of view, considered how many units of new invest-ment are required, on the assumption that the new investment is properly utilised, to produce an extra unit of output; this I designated C_r.[6] My approach was quite reasonably regarded as giving expression to the acceleration principle, about which Domar appeared to say nothing. If we

carefully note the fact that Domar's σ is valued on the basis that the new invest-ment is properly utilised—it is in Domar's words the measure of a "potential"—and the fact that my C_r is valued on the basis that the new investment is no more nor less than that required to produce a growth of output, *i.e.*, that it is properly utilised, it is evident that

$$\sigma = \frac{1}{C_r}$$

As, subject to the two reservations to be mentioned, there are no other terms in the Domar equation that are not in mine, nor terms in my equation that are not in Domar's, it is clear that the equations are identical.

4. One of the reservations referred to in the last paragraph is as follows. Domar states his equation in its most familiar form as

$$\frac{\Delta I}{I} = \alpha\sigma$$

where σ is as stated above, α is the fraction of income saved and I investment. My equation makes no reference to ΔI or I, but runs

$$G_w = \left(\frac{\Delta Y}{Y}\right)_w = \frac{s}{C_r}$$

where Y stands for income, the suffix w indicates that the equation defines condi-tions for a steady rate of growth, or a mov-ing equilibrium, and s is the same as Domar's α.

5. The formal identity of the two equa-tions is preserved, owing to Domar's as-sumption that

$$\frac{\Delta I}{I} = \frac{\Delta Y}{Y}$$

I make no such assumption, and my equa-tion is accordingly more general than his.

---

[4] For an early attempt to define dynamic theory, see also the last two pages of a paper which I read at a meeting of the Econometric Society in Oxford in 1936 (*Econometrica*, January 1937; republished in *Economic Essays* as Essay 12).

[5] "An Essay in Dynamic Theory," *Economic Journal*, March 1939. Essay 13 in *Economic Essays*.

[6] In *Towards a Dynamic Economics;* in the *Essay* it was designated simply C.

In my equilibrium equation there is no reference, explicit or implicit, to ΔI or I. In my equation expressing certain necessary relations in an actual rate of growth, viz., $G = s/C$, there is an implicit reference to I, since C is defined as $I/\Delta Y$; but there is still no reference, explicit or implicit, to ΔI. I may add here, in relation to Mr. Rose's interesting article,[7] of which I shall have something to say presently, where, in an endeavour to restate my doctrines, he refers to the amount of outstanding capital (and to its rates of increase), that I have never made any reference, explicit or implicit, to the amount of outstanding capital. These omissions were not accidental, but deliberate and the result of careful thought before I composed my *Essay*. These various values, of which I took no cognisance, will, of course, have to be brought in and play their part in a complete dynamic theory; the omissions were due to the desire to achieve great *generality* as befits a very fundamental proposition. Failure to notice that I do not refer at all to these values must betoken some lack of understanding of my thought. To extend the list of omissions yet further, be it noted that, although I sometimes referred loosely to capital goods in the *Essay*, the theory expounded in it draws no distinction between capital goods and consumer goods. (The first time that I brought the distinction in is on the last page of my *Supplement on Dynamic Theory*.[8]) This is very carefully stressed in the *Essay*. "Circulating and fixed capital are lumped together" (p. 18).[9] "It may be well to emphasise at this point that no distinction is drawn in this theory between capital goods and consumption goods" (p. 18).[10] In *Towards a Dynamic Economics* I also said explicitly: "C is the addition to capital, but need not consist exclusively, or even

mostly, of capital goods. It is merely the accretion during the period of all goods . . ." (p. 80). Consequently the distinction that Mr. Rose draws between two variant interpretations of my theory is not tenable.[11] He writes, "the primary source of instability [viz., according to one interpretation] is in the effect of excess demand or supply on production decisions, not [as according to the other interpretation] in the effect of growing capital shortage or redundancy on investment decisions." As in my theory capital goods and consumer goods are lumped together, an "excess demand" is one and the same thing as "capital shortage," since "capital" includes stocks of consumer goods, and no distinction can be drawn between "production decisions" and "investment decisions." I revert to this matter below.

6. To return to Domar, I believe that he worked in terms of the increment of investment, because he was anxious to show that investment must itself grow if the economy is to grow. In order to bring this out clearly in his formulation, he made the restrictive, but not otherwise objectionable, assumption that the rate of growth of investment is the same as the rate of growth of income.

7. Mr. Oshima affirms that Professor Domar's equation explicitly includes the multiplier and implies that mine does not, or, if not that, at least that the multiplier does not play so large a role in it as in Domar's equation. I cannot agree to this, nor perceive any difference in this regard between myself and Domar. s in my equation, as stated above, is the reciprocal of the multiplier, and the magnitude of ΔY varies, *ceteris paribus*, directly with that of s. I do not see how one could make the multiplier play a greater role!

8. Mr. Oshima states that we both assume that the marginal propensity to save is equal to the average propensity to save. There can be no such assumption in my

---

[7] "The Possibility of Warranted Growth," *Economic Journal*, June 1959.

[8] *Economic Essays*, Essay 14.

[9] *Economic Essays*, p. 258.

[10] *Op. cit.*, p. 259.

[11] *Economic Journal*, June 1959, p. 317.

equation, as there is no reference, explicit or implicit, to the marginal propensity to save in it. (Another deliberate omission.) Domar tells us that he assumes equality of the marginal and average propensities, and this is presumably tied up with his assumption that $\Delta I/I = \Delta Y/Y$.

9. It may occasion surprise that the marginal propensity to save plays no part in my equation. I would say that such a surprise would be an *ignoratio elenchi*. I lay great stress on the importance of this, because from the beginning it has seemed to me that one of the great services that the formal definition of a dynamic branch of economics could render would be to prevent mistakes about dimensions.

Theorists of static economics, including Keynes, proceeded for long without perceiving (or anyhow without thinking it practically important) that a theory of static equilibrium is self-contradictory unless it assumes that savings = investment = zero. If we wish to postulate that saving is, and continues to be, positive, that entails that the economy is growing; we can no longer work in terms of a static equilibrium, but instead must use the concept of a steady rate of growth. If the fraction of income saved is constant, then, *ceteris paribus*, the steady rate of growth remains constant. My equation purported to specify what the steady rate of growth at a given point of time would be, given the values of the dynamic determinants.[12] I did not dare venture beyond that. It seemed prudent to tackle one thing at a time.

The fraction of income saved (average propensity to save) may rise temporarily in consequence of the trade cycle or owing to other disturbances; such changes are not relevant to the determination of the value of a steady growth rate. But it may be desirable to postulate a steady continuing

[12] Cf. "The analysis relates to a single point of time"—in "An Essay in Dynamic Theory," p. 24 (*Essays*, p. 267).

rise in the fraction of income saved: Some time ago it would have been held confidently that such a rise would be normal in a growing economy, but doubt has been cast on that. If a rising average propensity to save has to be postulated, this, *ceteris paribus*, entails an *accelerating* growth of income. In order to maintain growth, it would not merely be necessary, as Domar so strongly urges, for ΔI to be positive, but it would be necessary that $\Delta I_{t_2} > \Delta I_{t_1}$. I did not venture, nor, I believe, did Domar —at least in his central articles—on the economics of accelerating (or decelerating) growth.

10. So much for the identity of our equation, still subject to one further reservation shortly to be discussed. But its formulation is by no means the full tale of my thinking, which utilised it, nor indeed of that of Domar. When we go further in comparing our theories we find further similarities, as well as differences; I by no means wish to follow a precedent that may occur to the minds of some readers and to stress the difference between us. I will first point out a further similarity, to which I do not think that attention has been drawn. Those who have studied my theory know that the distinction between the "warranted" rate of growth, as expressed in my equation, and the "natural" rate of growth is central to it. I see a kinship between my distinction between these two rates and Domar's distinction between his concepts, σ and s.

Of my two growth rates it is the natural rate that is to be regarded as the welfare optimum. The warranted rate is the path on which the supply and demand for goods and services will remain in equilibrium, given the propensity to save; thus the economy could move along the warranted rate with great and growing "involuntary" unemployment in Keynes' sense. It is the natural rate that implies full employment. The actual rate of growth may be below both.

The natural rate is also the maximum sustainable rate, although the actual rate may go above it in phases of the trade cycle, when unemployed are being brought back into work, or when high marginal earnings, only worth paying in periods of high inflationary pressure, attract people to paid occupations who are not normally available for them. According to me, the difference between the gradients of the natural and warranted rates has to be considered in close relation to the instability principle, *i.e.*, the presence of centrifugal prices on either side of the warranted rate. (Mr. Rose's remarks on this are discussed below.) If the warranted rate is above the natural rate, the actual rate must be below the warranted rate for most of the time, and the centrifugal forces pull it further down, causing frequent periods of unemployment. (This is the dynamised version of the stagnation thesis.) If the natural rate is above the warranted rate, full employment may be achieved more frequently owing to the upward pull of the centrifugal forces, but only at the cost of inflation. The target of policy should be to bring the warranted rate as near as possible to the natural rate.[13]

In certain passages, however, Domar makes it plain that his rate of growth

$$r = \alpha\sigma$$

is for him a target rate and would sustain full employment. This caused me to look very closely at the concept σ. I believe that the rate specified by Domar's equation is really my "natural" rate; what is peculiar is that he should have defined it by what are (apparently) the same terms that I used to define my "warranted" rate, the very essence of which is that it may give trouble by being different from the natural rate. My warranted rate is simply the dynamised version of Keynes' excess

or deficiency of aggregate effective demand in relation to what is required for full employment. The key to this puzzle is, I believe, to be found in Domar's concept of σ. Domar uses the symbol s for the ratio of the net value added by new projects of production to the capital invested in the projects. "But the productive capacity of the whole economy may increase by a smaller amount, because the operations of these new projects may involve a transfer of labor (and other factors) from other plants, whose productive capacity is therefore reduced."[14] σ makes allowance for this fact and is the net potential *social* average productivity of the new capital. σ is taken to be usually less than s. We need not bother with Domar's point that this may be so owing to a mis-direction of investment. Apart from that, the shortfall of σ compared with s is due to the fact that there is a "lack of balance between the propensity to save on the one hand, and the growth of labor, discovery of natural resources, and technological progress on the other."[15]   If only there was enough labour, etc., the economy could grow at $r = \alpha s$, which is really my "warranted" rate; but the lack of labour, etc., compresses potential growth to $r = \alpha\sigma$, my "natural" rate.

The result of this shortage of labour, etc., according to Domar, is that, fixed capital having been made to match existing savings, some pre-existing equipment has to be "junked"; too many stands having been created, some can just not be used; this junking process has a crucial and sinister role in Domar's scheme of things. It may be useful to relate the junking process to my equation.

Let us first suppose that the extinction of the amount of pre-existing equipment, as required by Domar, is due, not to competitive pressures, as postulated by him,

---

[13] It is to be noted that Mr. Kaldor holds that in the long run these will be brought together by a shift of income distribution.

[14] *Essays in the Theory of Economic Growth*, p. 73.
[15] *Op. cit.*, p. 79.

but to periodic enemy action; this continuing enemy action would raise the amount of new capital required to sustain a given increase of output in the economy; it would raise the value of my C_r. Thus, if, in the absence of enemy action, the warranted rate $G_w = s/C_r$ were above the natural rate, enemy action of the correct intensity would, by raising C_r, reduce G_w to the natural rate. Then the warranted rate would be equal to the natural rate and all could go forward smoothly.

But in fact there is no enemy action. Domar supposes that: (i) for a time enough investment is undertaken to absorb all saving at a full employment level, and that (ii) in consequence of more stands being created than there is labour to fill them, some of the pre-existing stands are junked. But the matter does not rest there; the junking process may well have a discouraging effect on the propensity to invest. If previously growth had proceeded in accordance with $\Delta I/I = \Delta Y/Y = \sigma\alpha$, the reduction in investment will cause growth to fall below this level.

In my terminology what has happened in this case is that the fact of the warranted rate (that required to absorb saving) being above the natural rate (that required, having regard to technological progress, to maintain full employment) has caused the actual rate to fall below either. In Domar's terminology it is the excess of s over σ that, by leading to junking, causes the actual rate to fall below $s\alpha$ and $\sigma\alpha$. It is clear that the theories are very near together. The excess of s over σ is really another way of expressing what I have expressed by the excess of the warranted over the natural rate.

By parenthesis I should like to say that, in my judgment, Domar deals in rather too cavalier a way with junking. He recognises that it may be resisted by monopolists; he recognises that an excessive rate of junking may be socially undesirable (presumably by requiring too much mobility of labour); and he recognises the important point that it may reduce the future propensity to invest and thus cause a lapse from the path of steady growth. But otherwise he seems to look favourably, in a rather loose way, on junking; he seems to imply that, apart from the aforementioned drawbacks, the more junking the better. He does not seem to appreciate that a high rate of junking might be bad from a purely productivity point of view.

In fact, from the productivity point of view, there is an optimum rate of junking. Let us suppose, to simplify the argument, that the labour force is stationary and that no new natural resources are discovered. Progress would then consist: (i) in providing new-type stands, by investment, on which more old-type goods could be produced per unit of labour than before, and (ii) in the event of the demand for the old-type goods not being sufficiently elastic to absorb all the labour previously employed on them, in providing stands, by investment, for the released labour to produce new-type goods. New-type stands under (i) should, from a welfare point of view, and, if capitalist expectations and calculations are correct, will, be produced only if the cost of making old-type goods on the new-type stands, including interest and amortisation on them, is less than the cost of making those goods on the old stands free of interest and amortisation. The amount of investment required to produce all the new-type stands under (i), as justified by this computation, depends on technical progress. The amount of investment required to produce stands for the production of new-type goods depends on technical progress and on the amount of labour released under (i). There is no *a priori* reason why the amount of investment required under (i) and (ii) together should be sufficient to absorb saving at full employment. I characterise such a state of affairs as one in which the warranted rate is above the natural rate. According to me this state of affairs causes the actual rate to fall below both natural and warranted rates; so it does according to Domar, but by a slightly different mechanism. If the labour force were increasing sufficiently, such a situation would not arise, since the surplus saving would be mopped up in providing extra stands for the new hands. The actual and warranted rates can stand above the natural rate for a period in the trade cycle when unemployed labour is being re-absorbed. But this must in due course come to an end.

Domar, on the other hand, appears to envisage that for a period new stands will be created (presumably in a spirit of gay optimism) to the full number permitted by the saving available, regardless of the question of their profitability; then, if there are too many stands altogether, some old ones will be junked. But suppose that, in order to mop up all savings by creating new stands, one makes some that are not more profitable than the old, on the basis of the computation mentioned above; then the old will not necessarily be junked; all stands may be under-employed. This will have an even more depressing effect than a high rate of junking on the future propensity to invest.

Domar writes:

> I am not prepared to say whether we already are or shall be soon faced with a serious difference between s and σ, though I doubt that was an important problem in the past, except perhaps for the short boom years. My own guess is that we shall be more concerned with the disparity between $\alpha\sigma$ and r [the actual rate of growth], that is, with the failure of income to grow at the required rate.[16]

(We are dealing here, of course, with an excessive propensity to save, not with the dilemma of the under-developed countries.) In my opinion there are not two separate phenomena here, but one phenomenon.

[16] *Essays in the Theory of Economic Growth*, p. 81.

In my view it is the excess of s over σ that *causes* r to fall below $\alpha\sigma$.

11. The tendency of an excess of the warranted rate over the natural rate to cause chronic depression depends on the instability principle; otherwise a community tending to excess saving might continue to bump along the ceiling of full employment. (I judge that Domar broadly endorses the instability principle.)   Accordingly, this may be a suitable point at which to comment on Mr. Rose's criticism of that principle.[17] He takes me to task for denying that my theory implies lags—and Domar makes a similar denial—holding that it does imply a lag in the adjustment of the amount of capital to the need for it. I do not deny that. Language is apt to be influenced by time and circumstance. What I was seeking to stress was that my trade-cycle theory—if it can be dignified with that name—was not of the same genus as those theories which econometricians were developing with great vigour at that time, and which, I doubt not, must be a part of the full and final theory of growth; these essentially depended on systematic lags between variables in a model which generated an oscillation, explosive or damped. There was danger that my instability principle might become confused with such theories, to which it really has no direct relation.

But I do deny that investment on any given day can be identical with the amount of investment that people want to have on that day, *unless* they are on the line of warranted growth. Only if people are on that line will *ex-post* investment in a given period be equal to the investment that is needed to bring the total amount of capital, fixed and circulating, up to no more nor less than the level that people deem they require to have in that period. If people find that on a given day, or, to be more realistic, in a given month, they have less capital, whether fixed or circulating, than

[17] *Economic Journal*, June 1959, pp. 319–21.

they require in order most conveniently to execute turnover at its current level, there is nothing they can do to rectify that within the month. What they can do is to place extra orders, or, to step up their own production. The essence of the instability principle is that this will make capital still more short in the following period. The idea that they can have whatever capital, fixed and circulating, they require in a given short period, by taking some action in that period, is unacceptable. I conclude that Rose's criticism of the instability principle can be safely rejected.

12. Rose's thought appears to rest on a distinction between fixed and circulating capital, and it may be expedient to consider that. Let us suppose that, after a period of progress on the line of warranted growth, there is a divergence from it in an upward direction. This may be due to a chance aberration. Such an eventuality must be allowed as possible, since the economy consists of a great concourse of entrepreneurs, all working in conditions of uncertainty, and in particular industries, each of which may be growing at a different rate. It is essential to the idea of a static equilibrium, that, subject to the possibility of cobweb action, etc., it is stable, in the sense that chance divergences from it will be corrected in due course and a return to the previous positions secured. In the case of the dynamic equilibrium it is important to remember that a divergence may be due, not to a change in the behaviour of any entrepreneur, or of a group of entrepreneurs, but to a change in the values of the dynamic determinants themselves. These are, of course, always changing. This is analogous to the point, which Wicksell made so often, that the divergence of the market rate of interest from the natural rate, as defined by him, was less often due to a change of attitude on the part of the bankers in extending credit and more often to a change in the forces that determine the natural rate.

Let us suppose that, on the occasion of such a chance divergence, fixed capital is found to be short, taking the overall average of all entrepreneurs, but stocks of consumer goods not so. Let us suppose that extra orders for fixed capital are placed in consequence, but no extra orders for consumer goods. Rose is not wrong in thinking that this may redress the balance between capital goods and consumer goods on hand; it is possible that the orders for extra capital goods might be so extensive as to redress the shortage of capital goods; but, if this happens, it can only be by creating a shortage of circulating capital (consumer goods), which will be greater in value than the previous shortage of fixed capital. It is this fact that justified my lumping capital goods and consumer goods together for the purpose of formulating the dynamic theorem in its most general possible form.

13. While I hold that the instability theorem is safe, in the sense that the warranted rate of growth is surrounded by centrifugal forces and that a chance divergence from the warranted rate will be accentuated, I do not claim to have made any thorough-going analysis of the regions lying farther afield from the warranted rate.

There is no doubt that an explosive expansion will eventually be checked by the ceiling of full employment, at which growth has to be slowed down to the natural rate. Professor Hicks has brought that fact into play in his study. (Incidentally it is to be noted that the British boom of 1954/55 broke through the full-employment ceiling by temporarily bringing into employment people not normally seeking it.) It has been observed that booms sometimes terminate before the full-employment ceiling is reached. Domar has drawn attention to terminations of expansion in the United States in 1907, 1929 and 1937 considerably below the ceiling.[18] He draws a moral from them which I do not find acceptable.

[18] *Op. cit.*, p. 117.

He raises the question whether it is possible for the American economy to sustain an advance on the line of growth indicated by his equation. I would put that question in the form—is the warranted rate there above the natural rate? If it is, then, according to Domar's thinking, one would expect an actual advance to be checked by labour shortage, and, if it was not so checked on the three occasions cited, that suggests to his mind that the warranted rate was not unachievable on account of labour shortage and that the lapse from it was due to *other* reasons than its being impossibly high in relation to labour availability. In what follows I seek to examine that argument closely.

14. The possibility of a boom terminating before the full-employment ceiling is reached has naturally been present to my mind from the beginning, and I have given two reasons why that might happen. I propose to add a third reason, which may be even more important.

15. The first reason I gave was that a boom might in due course temporarily raise the propensity to save considerably above its normal level. It will be evident that a rise in the rate of growth above its warranted level (G_w) cannot in a moderate period of time be accompanied by an equiproportional rise in the fraction of income saved (s), even if, for all values of Y above normal, the whole of ΔY was saved. Accordingly, capital would remain in short supply. But after a time a strong rise in s (due to profit inflation) could overtake the rise in G; this could bring the boom to an end before the ceiling of full employment was reached. I have suggested that this is the reason why a boom accompanied by an unrestrained price inflation might peter out more quickly than one in which excess demand was reflected mainly in delayed delivery. In the former kind the profit inflation and the temporary rise in s are greater. I incline to think, however, that variation in s may be more relevant in

explaining why a slump may come to an end—s may have a great decline in a severe slump—than why a boom may do so.

16. My second, and probably more important, reason was that the actual rate of growth begins to decline well before the ceiling of full employment is reached, owing to decreasing mobility of labour, as unemployment declines, and the appearance of bottlenecks that are due to shortages of specific types of capital. Growth, having moved freely forward in the early stages of boom at a rate well above the warranted rate, may begin to decline and thus fall below the warranted rate, even when there is still a sizeable reserve of unemployed labour; thus the boom is brought to an end and a recession rendered inevitable.

17. In order to explain the third possible reason for this phenomenon it is needful to take a wider view. In my original *Essay* I distinguished between those orders governed by the acceleration principle, those that are dependent rather on the current level of income (designated by me as k, where k is a fraction of income) and those unrelated to either (designated K). Professor Hicks has developed the distinction between the first and last mentioned, calling the former "induced" and the latter "autonomous" investment. For the instability principle to be valid, all that is required is that *some* current orders should be dependent on the acceleration principle. In the more refined account of the instability principle given in my *Supplement*, I have stated the assumption required as follows: "The more general assumption is simply that the entrepreneur will order more, the lower the ratio of his stocks and equipment to current put-through, and this I take to be safe."[19] This does not imply that there are no other forces governing his current level of orders.

I have suggested that we must not suppose a hard-and-fast line between induced and autonomous investment. Orders that,

[19] *Economic Essays*, p. 283.

in relation to a short and mild slump, should be regarded as belonging to the autonomous (K) category, may come up for review, if the slump is severe and prolonged. This is an aspect of the vicious-circle process of a depression; the more the types of investment are that are reconsidered for downward revision in consequence of a recession, the stronger the forces of recession will be; and the stronger the recession, the more the types of investment are that will be considered for downward revision. The opposite process may occur in the boom phase; a prolonged period of expansion may make people take a buoyant view and set more long-range projects going.

But in the boom there is another aspect. People may become more buoyant, but they may also become more sceptical. In the early phase of a boom one may, and indeed must, suppose that their long-range views are unaffected by it, so that the felt shortage of capital, fixed and/or circulating, which is caused by the boom, induces them to increase orders. This increase of orders cannot mitigate, but must, by itself, increase the felt shortage of capital, fixed and/or circulating. But as the boom proceeds, their view of the longer future may come in as a counteracting influence. They may begin to ask themselves whether demand can continue to increase at the rate at which it has recently been doing. Even if the experienced shortage of capital continues unabated, they may begin to hesitate about placing increased orders, anyhow for fixed capital, on the ground that calls upon its utilisation are not likely to continue to increase at their existing and recent rate. In the case of fixed capital at least, they must have regard to its utilisation over its expected length of life. These hesitations caused by attention to the longer future may bring the boom to an end before full employment is reached.

18. I will first deal with the relevance of this point to Domar's doubts. Consider the hypothesis that lack of full employment in the United States before the War was due to the warranted rate being above the natural rate, or in other words, that the rate of growth required by Domar's formula just *could* not be achieved permanently because labour (along with technical progress) was not growing fast enough to render that possible. Domar rules out this explanation on the ground that three booms broke before any labour shortage was apparent. But one must also look at the prospective demand side. I take the following figures merely to illustrate the argument. Let us suppose that in the United States as was for a longish period 4 percent and that this rate of growth, or a higher one, was achieved in boom periods. Let us further suppose (*my* hypothesis, on which the premature termination of booms, in Domar's view, throws doubts) that the maximum sustainable rate of progress in the United States over this longish period, having regard to technical progress and population increase, was, say, 3 percent. During the boom period we suppose that fixed capital was increased at 4 percent or more with confidence, since the revival, accompanied by re-employment of labour, was bringing demand up at that rate. This rate of 4 percent or more is, of course, an average; entrepreneurs in expanding industries may have based themselves on a much higher rate of prospective increase. Let us call the boom-period rate of increase x, where x has a different value in each industry. After a period of expansion canny entrepreneurs may have said to themselves that they could not believe that the x rate of expansion could continue indefinitely; and these would accordingly slow down their rate of increase of fixed capital, although there was still a shortage of it, and thus bring the boom to an end. And why should the entrepreneurs think that the x rate of expansion could not continue? Because the 4 percent (or higher) rate of expansion in the economy as a whole could

not continue. Population increase and technical progress were just not sufficient to allow aggregate output to expand at that rate indefinitely, and therefore aggregate effective demand could not expand at that rate indefinitely. Thus the canny entrepreneurs would have been proved right in their scepticism. But if the increase of output allowed by technical progress and population increase had been 4 percent p.a., then the entrepreneurs would have been wrong in their scepticism. Thus the fundamental reason why the entrepreneurs were right to be sceptical was that the maximum increase in demand that could possibly be sustained indefinitely was 3 percent in the aggregate, viz., below the x percent recently current in each industry, and below the aggregate 4 percent (recently achieved or exceeded), as represented by Domar's αs. This perfectly correct attitude of scepticism could serve to bring the boom to an end before full employment was reached. But if the natural rate had been as high as 4 percent, viz., not less than the warranted rate, the entrepreneurs' scepticism would have been groundless and the expansion could have continued. The natural rate being below the warranted rate (taken to be 4 percent) would thus have served to push the actual rate below either, *before* any labour shortage had begun to be felt; the low level of the natural rate operated through the fact that the insufficient rate of increase of demand sustainable indefinitely cast its shadow backwards, and reasonably and rightly deterred entrepreneurs from ordering as much as would have been needed to keep the increase going forward at its sustainable rate. Accordingly, I hold that the termination of booms before labour shortage began to be felt is not a reason for denying that it was the warranted rate being above the natural rate that prevented either being achieved for more than ephemeral boom periods. The insufficient expansion of the labour force (or of technical progress)

checked expansion because it meant that a correct prognosis of the maximum possible increase of demand was not sufficient to justify sufficient ordering in the present. Be it noted that this check would have operated, even if the entrepreneurs had been thoroughly optimistic, not assuming that any recession was coming, but assuming only that demand would not continue indefinitely to grow at more than the maximum possible sustainable rate.

It is fair to observe that Domar anticipates this point. "It is possible to argue that ... such a situation ... was foreseen by the entrepreneurs who reduced their commitments in advance." He adds, "but without sufficient evidence, almost anything could just as well be said." It is always desirable to have factual evidence; but it does not seem reasonable to dismiss in so cavalier a way the hypothesis that the entrepreneurs did what they ought to have done on a correct prognosis.

19. This may be the appropriate point to refer to a criticism by Professor Baumol.[20] He suggests that the instability principle would not operate, if only entrepreneurs kept a firm grasp of what was likely to happen in the long period and based their policy on that. "It is even possible that entrepreneurs will generally believe in the 'normalcy' of the economy and so will regard any case of overproduction as a temporary phenomenon soon likely to disappear." It is evident that my preceding paragraph makes some concession to Professor Baumol's point of view (which presumably applies to underproduction also). I have suggested that, despite a continuing experienced shortage of capital, fixed and/or circulating, entrepreneurs may abate their rate of ordering, because they regard the current tempo of advance of demand for their products as abnormal and not capable of being sustained indefinitely. But I suggest that it would be pushing this argument much too far to

[20] *Economic Dynamics*, pp. 53–4.

regard it as obviating the instability principle. For it to do that, one would have to suppose entrepreneurs having fixed and rigid views about the future, on which they based their current action, and not being influenced at all by current experience. This is rendered the more unlikely when we consider that each industry, and each sector of an industry, has its own problems and uncertainties, its own current rate of expansion and its own projected future rate of expansion, which may be different. In view of this, it is, I would even say, absurd to suppose that each firm will go forward on the basis of its own view about the future and disregard current experience. We know that an upward deviation in the rate of growth will cause a shortage of fixed and/or circulating capital in relation to current requirements on the overall average. The incidence of the shortage will probably be uneven as between industries and firms. I submit that we must suppose that, on the overall average, firms, faced by a novel shortage, will place more orders than they otherwise would. And this will cause a further deviation from the path of warranted growth. In fine, the instability principle will operate.

It would be most inappropriate to make any comments on the far-reaching views set out by Mrs. Robinson[21] and Mr. Kaldor[22] at the end of what is primarily a tidying-up article; the omission to do so must therefore not be taken to imply lack of regard for them. If my views come to constitute a limb of those "Principles of Dynamic Economics," which we still await, then it is important that their scope and limitations should be understood with precision.

[21] *The Accumulation of Capital* (Macmillan, 1956).

[22] "A Model of Economic Growth," *Economic Journal*, December 1957.

22

A New Model
of Economic Growth

NICHOLAS KALDOR
and JAMES A. MIRRLEES

I.

The purpose of this paper is to present a "Keynesian" model of economic growth which is an amended version of previous attempts put forward by one of the authors in three former publications.[1] This new theory differs from earlier theories mainly in the following respects:

1. it gives more explicit recognition to the fact that technical progress is infused into the economic system through the creation

Reprinted from *The Review of Economic Studies*, vol. 29 (June 1962), pp. 174–192, by permission of the publisher and authors.

Nicholas Kaldor teaches at King's College, Cambridge.

James A. Mirrlees teaches at Nuffield College, Oxford; he was formerly at Trinity College, Cambridge.

[1] Cf. N. Kaldor, "Alternative Theories of Distribution," *Review of Economic Studies*, 1955–56 (reprinted in *Essays on Value and Distribution*, pp. 228–236). "A Model of Economic Growth," *Economic Journal*, December 1957 (reprinted in *Essays in Economic Stability and Growth*, pp. 256–300) and "Capital Accumulation and Economic Growth" (presented in Corfu, September 1958 and published in *The Theory of Capital*, Macmillan, 1961, pp. 177–220). N. Kaldor's ideas in connection with the present model were worked out during his tenure as Ford Research Professor in Economics in Berkeley, California.

of new equipment, which depends on current (gross) investment expenditure. Hence the "technical progress function" has been re-defined so as to exhibit a relationship between the rate of change of gross (fixed) investment per operative and the rate of increase in labour productivity on *newly installed* equipment;

2. it takes explicit account of obsolescence, caused by the fact that the profitability of plant and equipment of any particular "vintage" must continually diminish in time owing to the competition of equipment of superior efficiency installed at subsequent dates; and it assumes that this *continuing obsolescence is broadly foreseen by entrepreneurs* who take it into account in framing their investment decision. The model also assumes that, irrespective of whether plant and equipment has a finite physical life-time or not, its *operative* life-time is determined by a complex of economic factors which govern the rate of obsolescence, and not by physical wear and tear;

3. in accordance with this, the behavioural assumptions concerning the investors' attitudes to uncertainty in connection with investment decisions and which are set out below, differ in important respects from those made in the earlier models;

4. account is also taken, in the present model, of the fact that some proportion of the existing stock of equipment disappears each year through physical

causes—accidents, fire, explosions, etc.—and this gives rise to some "radioactive" physical depreciation in addition to obsolescence;

5. since, under continuous technical progress and obsolescence, there is no way of measuring the "stock of capital" (measurement in terms of the historical cost of the surviving capital equipment is irrelevant; in terms of historical cost *less* accrued "obsolescence" is question-begging, since the allowance for obsolescence, unlike the charge for physical wear and tear, etc., depends on the share of profits, the rate of growth, etc., and cannot therefore be determined independently of all other relations), the model avoids the notion of a quantity of capital, and its corollary, the rate of capital accumulation, as variables of the system; it operates solely with the value of current gross investment (gross (fixed) capital expenditure per unit of time) and its rate of change in time. The macro-economic notions of income, income per head, etc., on the other hand are retained.

II.

The present model is analogous to the earlier models in the following main features:

1. like all "Keynesian" economic models, it assumes that "savings" are passive—the level of investment is based on the volume of investment decisions made by entrepreneurs, and is independent of the propensities to save; it postulates an economy in which the mechanism of profit and income generation will create sufficient savings (at any rate within certain limits or "boundaries") to balance the investment which entrepreneurs decide to undertake;

2. the model relates to an isolated economy with continuous technical progress, and with a steady rate of increase in the working population, determined by exogeneous factors;

3. the model assumes that investment is primarily *induced* by the growth in production itself, and that the underlying conditions are such that growth-equilibrium necessarily carries with it a state of continuous full employment. This will be the case when the purely 'endogeneous'

growth rate (as determined by the combined operation of the accelerator and the multiplier) which is operative under conditions of an unlimited supply of labour, is appreciably higher than the "natural rate of growth," which is the growth of the "labour potential" (i.e., the *sum* of the rate of growth of the labour force and of (average) labour productivity). In that case, starting from any given state of surplus labour and underemployment, continued growth, as determined by these endogeneous factors, will necessarily lead to full employment sooner or later; and once full employment rules, continued growth involves that the "accelerator-multiplier" mechanism becomes "tethered" (through variations in the share of profits and through the imposition of a quasi-exogeneous growth rate in demand) to the natural rate of growth.

III.

In a situation of continuing full employment the volume of investment decisions for the economy as a whole will be governed by the number of workers who become available, per unit period, to "man" new equipment, and by the amount of investment per operative. It may be assumed that each entrepreneur, operating in imperfectly competitive markets, aims at the maximum attainable growth of his own business (subject as we shall explain below, to the maintenance of a satisfactory rate of return on the capital employed) and for that reason prefers to maintain an appreciable amount of excess capacity so as to be able to exploit any chance increase in his selling power either by increasing his share of the market or by invading other markets. However, when gross investment per period is in excess of the number of workers becoming available to "man" new equipment, the degree of excess capacity must steadily rise; hence whatever the desired relationship between capacity and output, sooner or later a point will be reached when the number of workers available for operating new equipment exerts a dominating influence (via the mechanism of the accelerator) on the volume of investment decisions in the economy.[2]

We shall assume that the equipment of any given vintage is in "limitational" relationship to labour—i.e. that it is not possible to increase the productivity of labour by reducing the number of workers employed in connection with already existing equipment (though it is possible that productivity would, on the contrary, be *reduced* by such a reduction, on account of its being associated with a higher ratio of overhead to prime labour). This does not mean that the equipment of any vintage requires a fixed amount of labour to keep it in operation. The latter would assume the case not only of "fixed co-efficients" but of complete indivisibility of the plant and equipment as well.

Writing n_t for the number of workers available to operate new equipment per unit period and i_t for the amount of investment per operative on machines of vintage t, and I_t for gross investment in fixed capital

$$i_t \equiv \frac{I_t}{n_t} \qquad (1)$$

We shall use the symbols Y_t for the gross national product at t, N_t for the working population, and y_t for output per head, so that

$$y_t \equiv \frac{Y_t}{N_t}$$

IV.

We shall assume that "machines" of each vintage are of constant physical ef-

ficiency during their lifetime, so that the growth of productivity in the economy is entirely due to the infusion of new "machines" into the system through (gross) investment.[3] Hence our basic assumption is a technical progress function which makes the annual rate of growth of productivity per worker *operating on new equipment* a function of the rate of growth of investment per worker, i.e., that

$$\dot{p}_t/p_t = f(\dot{i}_t/i_t) \text{ with } f(0) > 0,$$
$$f' > 0, f'' < 0 \qquad (2)$$

This function is illustrated in Figure 1. It is assumed that a constant rate of investment per worker over time will itself increase productivity per worker; but that the rate of growth of productivity will also be an increasing function of the rate of growth of investment per worker, though at a diminishing rate.[4]

Both output per operative and investment per operative are measured in terms

---

[2] We may assume that for the average, or representative, firm, sales grow at the same rate as production in the economy as a whole. But there will always be of course the exceptional firms who grow at a higher rate, and sub-average firms who grow at a lower rate. Investment in all cases serves the purpose of keeping productive capacity in some desired relationship with expected sales.

[3] It is probable that in addition to "embodied" technical progress there is some "disembodied" technical progress as well, resulting from increasing know-how in the use of existing machinery. On the other hand it is also probable that the physical efficiency of machinery declines with age (on account of higher repair and maintenance expenditures, etc.); our assumption of constant physical efficiency thus implies that these two factors just balance each other.

[4] It should be noted that the "technical progress function" in this model relates to the rate of growth of output per man-hour of the workers operating newly installed equipment (the equipment resulting from the investment of period t), *not* to the rate of growth of productivity in the economy in general (though in full steady growth equilibrium, as we shall see, the two will correspond to each other); and to the rate of growth of gross investment per worker from year to year, not the rate of accumulation of capital (which may not be a meaningful or measurable quantity). It is plausible that, with technical progress, the same investment per operative should yield a higher output per operative in successive years; and that this rate of growth will be enhanced, within limits, when the value of investment per operative is increasing over time.

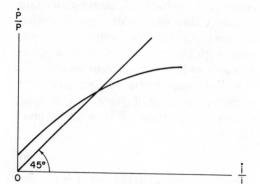

$\frac{\dot{P}}{P}$

45°

O

$\frac{i}{i}$

FIGURE 1.

V.

of money values deflated by an index of the prices of "wage goods" (i.e., consumption goods which enter into the wage-earners' budget). This means that changes in the prices of equipment goods in terms of wage-goods (and also of such consumption goods which only enter into consumption out of profits) will in general cause shifts in the *f*-function. Provided, however, that there is a reasonably stable trend in the prices of these latter goods in terms of wage goods, we can still conceive of the function as stable in time for any particular value of I_t/Y_t in money terms, and the system may still possess a steady growth equilibrium with a constant (equilibrium) value of I_t/Y_t. A full demonstration of this would require, however, a fully fledged 2-sector model in which the technical progress functions of the consumption goods sector and the capital goods sector, the distribution of employment and of savings between the two sectors, etc., are all treated separately. Since this would go far beyond the scope of this paper, it is better to assume, for the present purposes, that the rate of technical progress, as measured by productivity growth, is the same in all sectors, and hence that relative prices remain constant; bearing in mind, however, that the model could probably be extended to cover a wider range of possibilities.

With regard to the manner in which entrepreneurs meet risk and uncertainty, we shall make two important assumptions. In the first place we shall assume that entrepreneurs will only invest in their own business in so far as this is consistent with maintaining the earning power of their fixed assets above a certain minimum, a minimum which, in their view, represents the earning power of fixed assets in the economy in general. This is because, if the earnings of a particular firm are low in relation to the capital employed, or if they increase at a lower rate than the book value of the fixed assets, fixed assets will take up an increasing proportion of the total resources of the firm (including its potential borrowing power) at any given rate of growth, with the result that the financial position of the firm will become steadily weaker, with enhanced risks of bankruptcy or take-over bids. Hence we may assume that the sum of the expected profits anticipated from operating the equipment during its anticipated period of operation (or lifetime), T, will earn after full amortisation, a rate of profit that is at least equal to the assumed rate of profit on new investment in the economy generally. Hence for any particular investor

$$i_t \leq \int_t^{t+T} e^{-(\rho+\delta)(\tau-t)}(p_t - w_\tau^*)\, d\tau \quad (3)$$

where ρ stands for what the entrepreneur assumes the general rate of profit to be, w_τ^* for the expected rate of wages which is a rising function of future time[5] and δ

[5] In a golden age equilibrium, the inequality (3) should be replaced by an equality, and since all the variables will be determined independently by the other equations, (3) can then be taken as determining the rate of profit on investment. Cf. p. 312 below.

is the rate of "radioactive" decay of machines (we take it that the investor assumes his machine is an average machine).[6]

In the second place, under conditions of continuing technical progress, the expectations concerning the more distant future (whether in regard to money wages or in regard to the prices—or demands—of the particular products produced by a firm, both of which are projected in w_τ^*) are regarded as far more hazardous or uncertain than the expectations for the near future, where the incidence of unforseeable major new inventions or discoveries is less significant. Hence investment projects which qualify for adoption must pass a further test—apart from the test of earning a satisfactory rate of profit—and that is that the cost of the fixed assets must be "recovered" within a certain period—i.e., that the gross profit earned in the first h years of its operation must be sufficient to repay the cost of investment. Hence

$$i_t \leq \int_t^{t+h} (p_t - w_\tau^*) \, d\tau \qquad (4)$$

VI.

We shall assume, for the purposes of this model, that (3) is satisfied whenever (4) is satisfied—hence in (4) the $=$ sign will apply, i.e., the undiscounted sum of profits over h periods must be equal to i_t. There is plenty of empirical evidence that the assumption underlying (4) is a generally

---

[6] Our equation (3) thus postulates conditions under which the amount of "finance" available to the firm is considerably greater than its fixed capital expenditure, so that the firm is free to vary its total investment expenditure per unit of time; and that it will adopt projects which pass the tests of adequacy as indicated by (3) even though it could earn a higher *rate* of profit on projects involving a smaller volume of investment and yielding a smaller *total* profit. (In other words we assume that the firm is guided by the motive of maximising the rate of profit on the shareholders' equity, which involves different decisions from the assumption of maximising the rate of profit on its fixed investment.)

recognised method of meeting the uncertainty due to obsolescence in modern business, though the value of h may vary with the rate of technical progress, and also as between different sectors. (In the U.S. manufacturing industry h is normally taken as 3 years; but in other sectors—e.g., public utilities—it is much higher.)[7]

VII.

It is assumed, as in the earlier Keynesian growth models, that the savings which finance business investment come out of profits, and that a constant proportion, s, of *gross* profits are saved.[8] Hence (dividing income into two categories, profits and wages, which comprise all forms of non-business income) the share of (gross)

---

[7] The assumptions represented by these two equations should be contrasted with the assumptions made in "Capital Accumulation and Economic Growth," according to which

$$\frac{P}{K} = r + \rho$$

$$\rho = \xi(v)(\xi' > 0)$$

where P/K the rate of profit, r the money rate of interest, ρ the risk premium, v the capital/output ratio. ρ was assumed to be a rising function of v, because v reflects the ratio of fixed to circulating capital, and investment in the former is considered far more risky or "illiquid" than investment in the latter. The present assumptions are not inconsistent with the former hypothesis concerning the higher returns demanded on fixed investments; but they also take into account that the "riskiness" of the investment in fixed capital will be all the greater the longer the period over which the cost of the investment is 'recovered' out of the profits—a matter which depends not only on the capital/output ratio (or rather, the investment/output ratio) but also on the share of gross profits in output. "Gross profits" should for this purpose be calculated net of other charges, including a notional interest charge on the 'liquid' business assets (i.e., the investment in circulating capital associated with the investment in fixed capital).

[8] Savings out of wages are ignored—i.e, they are assumed to be balanced by non-business (personal) investment (i.e., residential construction). The assumption that business savings are a constant proportion of *gross* profits (after tax) is well supported by data relating to gross corporate savings.

profits, π_t, in the gross national product will be given by the equation

$$\pi_t = \frac{1}{s}\frac{I_t}{Y_t} \qquad (5)$$

which, in virtue of equation (1), reduces to

$$\pi_t = \frac{r}{s}\frac{i_t}{y_t} \qquad (5a)$$

where r is defined by

$$r_t = n_t/N_t$$

where N_t is the total labour force at time t and n_t, as earlier defined, is the number of workers available to operate new equipment per unit period.

We shall assume that once equipment is installed the number of workers operating it will only fall in time by the physical wastage of equipment, caused by accidents, fires, etc.—until the whole of the residual equipment is scrapped on account of obsolescence. Writing δ for the rate of (radioactive) depreciation per unit period, and $T(t)$ for the age of the equipment which is retired at t (i.e., the lifetime of equipment as governed by obsolescence), we have the following relationship for the distribution of the labour force:

$$N_t = \int_{t-T}^{t} n_\tau e^{-\delta(t-\tau)}\,d\tau \qquad (6)$$

and for total output

$$Y_t = \int_{t-T}^{t} p_\tau n_\tau e^{-\delta(t-\tau)}\,d\tau \qquad (7)$$

Since output Y_t is divided into two categories of income only, wages and profits, the residue left after profits is equal to the total wages bill. Writing w_t for the rate of wages at t, we further have

$$Y_t(1 - \pi_t) = N_t w_t \qquad (8)$$

Finally, since equipment will only be employed so long as its operation more than covers prime costs, the profit on the oldest yet surviving machinery must be zero. Hence

$$p_{t-T} = w_t \qquad (9)$$

We shall assume that population grows at the constant rate λ, hence

$$N_t = \lambda N_t \qquad (10)$$

We shall also assume that businessmen anticipate that wages in terms of output units will rise in the foreseeable future at the same rate as they have been rising during the past l periods.

Hence the expected wage rate at a future time T will be

$$w_T^* = w_t\left(\frac{w_t}{w_{t-l}}\right)^{(T-t)/l} \qquad (11)$$

Finally, the model is subject to two constraints (or "boundary conditions") which are known from earlier models:

$$w_t \geq w_{min}$$
$$\pi \geq m$$

In other words, the wage rate resulting from the model must be above a certain minimum (determined by conventional subsistence needs) and at the same time the share of profits resulting from the model must be higher than a certain minimum (the so-called "degree of monopoly" or "degree of imperfect competition").

VIII.

The above system gives 10 independent equations (regarding (3) only as a boundary condition) which are sufficient to determine the 10 unknowns; I_t, i_t, n_t, p_t, w_t, $w^*{}_t$, π_t, T, y_t, N_t, given the parameters, s, h, δ and λ, and the function f.

We shall investigate whether this system yields a solution in terms of a steady growth (or golden age) equilibrium where the rate of growth of output per head is equal to the rate of growth of productivity on new equipment and both are equal to the rate of growth of (fixed) investment per worker, and to the rate of growth of wages; i.e., where

$$\dot{p}/p = \dot{y}/y = \dot{i}/i = \dot{w}/w$$

and where the share of investment in output I/Y, the share of profits in income π, and the period of obsolescence of equipment, T, remain constant. Finally we shall show that there is a unique rate of profit on investment in a steady growth equilibrium.

The assumptions about the technical progress function imply that there is *some* value $\dot{p}/p$ (let us call it γ) at which

$$\dot{p}/p = \dot{i}/i = \gamma$$

Equilibrium is only possible when this holds.

If we integrate equation (4) using (11), we see that

$$i_t = hp_t - w_t \frac{e^{vh} - 1}{v} \qquad (12)$$

where v is the expected rate of growth of w. Hence p could only grow faster than i in the long run if w was growing faster than p: that would imply a continuous reduction in T, which would lead to unemployment and stagnation before T fell to h (at which point the rate of profit would be negative). On the other hand, p cannot grow more slowly than i in the long run, since w cannot fall below w_{min} (and there would in fact be an inflation crisis before that point was reached).

It is clear too that, so long as $\dot{w}/w$ does not diverge too far from $\dot{p}/p$, $\dot{i}/i$ would increase if it were less than $\dot{p}/p$, and decrease if it were greater than $\dot{p}/p$. For if

$\dot{p}/p$ were less than γ, it would breed, by equation (4), a rate of growth of investment, $\dot{i}/i$ that would require higher $\dot{p}/p$, and so on, until the equilibrium position is reached. A similar mechanism would be at work if $\dot{p}/p$ were greater than γ. Thus the equilibrium would in general be stable; but instability cannot be excluded, and a movement away from equilibrium would be possible in either of the two ways described above. For example a downward drift of the technical progress function might allow the rate of growth of p to fall off, and remain below the rate of growth of w (which reflects the rate of growth of y over the recent past) sufficiently long until with falling investment, unemployment and stagnation set in.[9] Conversely an upward shift in the technical progress function might lead to an inflationary situation at which investment, by one means or another, would be compressed below that indicated by (4) and (3).

Hence, excluding the case where $\dot{p}/p$ is significantly different from $\dot{w}/w$, when

$$\frac{\dot{p}}{p} \gtrless \frac{\dot{i}}{i}$$

there will be a convergent movement until (12) is obtained.

IX.

It will be convenient to deduce two further relations from the above equations. The first one relates to n_t, the amount of labour available for new equipment: it is obtained by differentiating (6) with respect to t.

$$n_t = \dot{N}_t + \delta N_t + n_{t-T}\left(1 - \frac{dT}{dt}\right)e^{-\delta T} \qquad (13)$$

[9] For example, a slowing down of technical progress in the late 1920's may have been responsible for that "sudden collapse of the marginal efficiency of capital" which led to the crisis and stagnation of the 1930's.

This equation says that n_t will be composed of three elements: (i) the growth in working population, $\dot{N}_t$; (ii) the labour released by physical wastage of equipment all vintages, which is δN_t; (iii) and finally the labour released by the retirement of obsolete equipment.

Differentiating equation (7) in the same way we obtain

$$\dot{Y}_t = p_t n_t - p_{t-T} n_{t-T} \left(1 - \frac{dT}{dt}\right) \times e^{-\delta T} - \delta Y_t$$

Substituting w_t for p_{t-T} in accordance with (9) and using (13) this becomes

$$\dot{Y}_t = p_t n_t - w_t (n_t - \dot{N}_t - \delta N_t) - \delta Y_t$$

Dividing both sides by $Y_t = N_t y_t$ we obtain

$$\frac{\dot{Y}_t}{Y_t} = r \frac{p_t}{y_t} - \frac{w_t}{y_t}(r - \lambda - \delta) - \delta$$

Using

$$\frac{\dot{Y}_t}{Y_t} = \frac{\dot{y}_t}{y_t} + \lambda$$

and re-arranging we finally obtain

$$\frac{\dot{y}_t}{y_t} + \lambda + \delta = r \frac{p_t}{y_t} - (r - \lambda - \delta)\frac{w_t}{y_t} \tag{14}$$

X.

In order that entrepreneurial expectations should be fulfilled, it is necessary that wages should grow at constant rate in time, β.

$$\frac{\dot{w}_t}{w_t} = \beta \text{ (constant)} \tag{15}$$

We shall now proceed to demonstrate that when β is constant, T will also be constant, provided that

$$\gamma < (s/h) - \lambda - \delta$$

It follows from (9) that

$$\frac{\dot{w}_t}{w_t} = \frac{\dot{p}_{t-T}}{p_{t-T}}\left(1 - \frac{dT}{dt}\right)$$

Hence

$$1 - \frac{dT}{dt} = \frac{\beta}{\gamma}, \text{ a constant}$$

Integrating with respect to t we obtain

$$T = T_0 + \left(1 - \frac{\beta}{\gamma}\right)t \tag{16}$$

where T_0 is the lifetime of equipment at some initial date, $t = 0$.

Substituting (16) into (13) and remembering that $r_t = n_t/N_t$, we obtain

$$r_t = \lambda + \delta + r_{t-T} e^{-(\lambda+\delta)T}\frac{\beta}{\gamma} \tag{17}$$

In order to show that, in a state of steady growth equilibrium $T = T_0$ and $\beta = \gamma$, we shall first consider the cases where $\beta \neq \gamma$.

(i) When $\gamma < \beta$, clearly steady growth cannot continue since entrepreneurs' profits would become negative sooner or later.

(ii) When $\gamma > \beta$, it follows from equation (16) that T becomes indefinitely large with time (and perhaps this is enough to dispose of this case, since for most goods there may be a maximum physical lifetime, quite apart from obsolescence). In any case this implies, in accordance with (17), that r ultimately tends to $\lambda + \delta$; and since w/y must tend to zero, so that the share of profits, π, tends towards unity.

$$i/y \text{ tends to } \frac{s}{\lambda + \delta} \tag{18}$$

Also from (4):

$$i/p \text{ tends to } h$$

Hence from (14):

$$\dot{y}/y \text{ tends to } \frac{s}{h} - \lambda - \delta$$

(18) shows that y ultimately grows at the same rate as i, which grows at the rate γ.

Therefore

$$\gamma = \frac{s}{h} - \lambda - \delta \qquad (19)$$

which implies, in Harrod's terms, that the "natural rate" (here, $\gamma + \lambda + \delta$) is equal to what the "warranted rate" would be if wages were zero and profits absorbed the whole output (since then s would equal the proportion of Y saved, and $h = i/p$).

XI.

It is easy to see that in fact the rate of growth of output per head cannot in the long run be greater than this quantity $(s/h) - \lambda - \delta$. By (5), i/y can rise no higher, ultimately, than s/r; hence by (4), even if (as might happen ultimately) the wage rate were negligible in relation to output per head, p/y could not be greater than $s/(rh)$. Turning to equation (14), we see that it implies the inequality

$$\dot{y}_t/y_t + \lambda + \delta \leq r \cdot \frac{s}{rh} = \frac{s}{h}$$

Hence there can be no steady growth equilibrium unless

$$\gamma \leq \frac{s}{h} - \lambda - \delta$$

Normally we would not expect to have to worry about this constraint, for the quantity s/h will be large—especially when we remember that h will be small when there is a high rate of growth. If it is asked what would happen if the equilibrium growth rate given by the technical progress function really did fail to satisfy this inequality, the answer must be that the wage rate would be driven down to its minimum level and entrepreneurs would then find themselves unable to invest as much as the prospects would warrant: the equality (4) would become an inequality again. The rest of the discussion

will be carried on under the assumption that the equilibrium rate of growth γ does satisfy this inequality.

We can see that, quite apart from the unrealistic value of γ implied by equation (19), equilibrium with $\gamma > \beta$ is a freak case; the slightest shift in γ would either render equilibrium impossible, or make it possible only with $\beta = \gamma$.

XII.

(iii) It is clear from the above that steady growth equilibrium will involve

$$\beta = \gamma$$

in which case it also involves a constant T. (17) has now become

$$r_t = \lambda + \delta + r_{t-T} \, e^{-(\lambda + \delta)T}$$

where T is constant, so that r_t will tend to the equilibrium value

$$r = \frac{\lambda + \delta}{1 - e^{-(\lambda + \delta)T}} \qquad (20)$$

From equation (5)

$$y_t = w_t + \frac{r}{s} i_t$$

so that, since r is constant in equilibrium, y_t also grows at the equilibrium growth rate γ. It is convenient to write this last equation as

$$\frac{r}{s} \frac{i}{y} + \frac{w}{y} = 1 \qquad (21)$$

In equilibrium, expectations are fulfilled, so that $w_t^* = w_t$. Since $w_t = w_0 e^{\beta t} = w_0 e^{\gamma t}$ (where w_0 is the wage rate at some initial time), the integral in equation (4) can be evaluated, so that

$$i_t = h p_t - \frac{e^{\gamma h} - 1}{\gamma} w_t$$

which we can write

$$\frac{1}{h}\frac{i}{y} + \frac{e^{\gamma h} - 1}{\gamma h}\frac{w}{y} - \frac{p}{y} = 0 \qquad (22)$$

(14) can now be rewritten

$$(r - \lambda - \delta)\frac{w}{y} - r\frac{p}{y} = -(\gamma + \lambda + \delta) \qquad (23)$$

Equations (21), (22), (23) can be treated as three simultaneous equations for i/y, w/y, and p/y (which are all constants in a state of steady growth).

Now equation (9) provides an equation for T:

$$e^{\gamma T} = \frac{p}{w} = \frac{p/y}{w/y} \qquad (24)$$

Using the values of r, p/y, w/y found by solving (21), (22) and (23), we obtain:

$$e^{\gamma T} = \frac{1 - \frac{h(\gamma + \lambda + \delta)}{s}\frac{e^{\gamma h} - 1}{\gamma h} + \frac{\gamma}{r}}{1 - \frac{h(\gamma + \lambda + \delta)}{s}} \qquad (25)$$

And from (20), since

$$e^{\gamma T} = [e^{-(\lambda + \delta)T}]^{-\gamma/(\lambda + \delta)}$$

$$e^{\gamma T} = \left[1 - \frac{\lambda + \delta}{r}\right]^{-\gamma/(\lambda + \delta)} \qquad (26)$$

(25) and (26) determine T and r simultaneously in terms of the parameters λ, δ, h, s, and the steady growth rate γ (which was determined by the technical progress function). Equation (20) is not valid when $\lambda + \delta = 0$. In that case we go back to equation (6); integration gives

$$rT = 1 \qquad (27)$$

which replaces (26) in this particular case.

XIII

Although (25) and (26) are rather cumbersome equations, numerical solution for particular values of the parameters presents no particular difficulty. Once T and r are calculated, simultaneous solution of (23) and (24) yields the values of p/y and w/y (the share of wages). Then i/y is found from (22). A demonstration of the existence of a unique meaningful solution to the equations is given in the Appendix.

If capital stock were valued at historic cost, without any allowance for reduction in value through obsolescence, we should have

$$K = \int_{t-T}^{t} i_\tau n_\tau e^{-\delta(t-\tau)}\, d\tau$$

and

$$Y = \int_{t-T}^{t} p_\tau n_\tau e^{-\delta(t-\tau)}\, d\tau \qquad (28)$$

so that the aggregate capital-output ratio,

$$\frac{K}{Y} = \frac{i}{p},$$

since this latter is constant.

However, when obsolescence is *foreseen* the knowledge of the share of profits, π, and of the historical cost of invested capital as shown by (28), does not enable us to calculate either net profits or the rate of profit on capital. The value of capital at any one time will be lower than K_t by the accrued provision made for obsolescence, and the appropriate obsolescence provision—which must take into account the annual reduction in the profits earned on equipment of a given vintage, as well as the retirement of equipment when it becomes T years old—cannot be calculated without knowing the capital on which the profit is earned, which in turn cannot be known without knowing the rate of profit.

XIV.

In a state of fully-fledged golden age equilibrium, where (1) expectations are (in general) fulfilled and the expected profit on new investments is therefore the same as the realised profit, and (2) the rate of profit earned on all investment will be the same, the inequality (3) above can be replaced by an equality and regarded as an additional equation determining ρ (since i_t, p_t, w_t and T are all determined by the other equations of the system).

$$i_t = \int_0^T e^{-(\rho+\delta)\tau}(p_t - W_{t+\tau}).\,d\tau \qquad (3a)$$

ρ is constant, so the familiar relation

$$\gamma + \lambda = \rho\sigma \qquad (29)$$

where σ is the proportion of *net* profits saved, holds; for it is easy to check that the value of capital—in terms of output to come—grows at the equilibrium growth rate $\gamma + \lambda$, and that ρ defined by (3a) is equal to the ratio of net profit to the stock of capital. In general, of course, σ depends on ρ, and is best calculated from the relation (29). But when $s = 1$, i.e., when all (gross) profits are invested, σ must also be equal to unity, so that the rate of profit is equal to the rate of growth of output: $\rho = \gamma + \lambda$. On the face of it, it is not clear that this value of ρ satisfies (3a): yet it must do. To show that it does, we use the fact that total output,

$$Y_t = \int_0^T p_{t-\tau} n_{t-\tau} e^{-\delta\tau}\, d\tau$$

$$= p_t n_t \int_0^T e^{-(\gamma+\lambda+\delta)\tau}\, d\tau$$

Thus, when we put $\rho = \gamma + \lambda$ in the right hand side of (3a), we get:

$$\frac{y_t}{r_t} - w_t \int_0^T e^{-(\lambda+\delta)\tau}\, d\tau$$

This last integral $=$

$$(1 - e^{-(\lambda+\delta)T})/(\lambda + \delta) = 1/r$$

by equation (20). Hence the right hand side of equation (3a) is equal to $(y_t - w_t)/r$, which is equal to i_t when $s = 1$ (by equation (21)).

If $s \neq 1$, we must find ρ from equation (3a). If we perform the integration (which we can do, since p and w are growing exponentially), we get the following relation, which can be solved numerically for $\rho + \delta$:

$$\frac{i}{y} = \frac{1 - e^{-(\rho+\delta)T}}{\rho + \delta}\frac{p}{y} - \frac{1 - e^{-(\rho+\delta-\gamma)T}}{\rho + \delta - \gamma}\frac{w}{y} \qquad (30)$$

Outside a golden age equilibrium a rate of profit on investment does not exist except in the sense of an *assumed* rate of profit, based on a mixture of convention and belief, which enables entrepreneurs to decide whether any particular project passes the test of adequate profitability.

XV. SOME NUMERICAL RESULTS

The following are the solutions of the equations for various arbitrarily selected values of the parameters.[10]

For the U.S. in the 1950's, reasonable values of the parameters are $\gamma = 2$ to $2\frac{1}{2}$ percent, $\lambda + \delta = 2 - 4$ percent, $s = .66$, $h = 4$ to 5 years. The average lifetime of equipment in manufacturing industry has been estimated at 17 years. π as indicated by the ratio of gross corporate profit after tax to the gross income originating in corporations after corporation tax has been 21 percent, and the ratio of business fixed capital to business gross product around 1.5. These, as the table shows, are close

[10] We are indebted to Mr. D. G. Champernowne for programming these calculations, and to the Director of the Mathematical Laboratory of Cambridge University for making the computer available.

For $s = 0.66$:

h years	$\lambda + \delta\%$	$\gamma\%$	T years	r	$\pi\%$	$I/Y\%$	i/p	$\rho + \delta\%$
	2	2	8.03	.135	8.0	5.3	.367	21.7
		2.5	8.15	.133	10.1	6.7	.459	22.1
3		3	8.27	.131	12.2	8.1	.551	22.4
	4	2	8.68	.136	8.9	5.9	.401	23.0
		2.5	8.82	.135	11.2	7.5	.501	23.4
		3	8.97	.133	13.5	9.0	.601	23.7
	2	2	11.20	.100	11.2	7.5	.672	17.0
		2.5	11.44	.098	14.1	9.6	.839	17.3
4		3	11.68	.096	17.1	11.4	1.006	17.6
	4	2	12.54	.101	12.9	8.6	.759	18.2
		2.5	12.84	.100	16.3	10.9	.948	18.6
		3	13.15	.098	19.8	13.2	1.136	18.9
	2	2	14.69	.078	14.6	9.7	1.080	14.1
		2.5	15.10	.077	18.5	12.3	1.348	14.4
5		3	15.53	.075	22.4	14.9	1.615	14.7
	4	2	17.13	.081	17.8	11.9	1.267	15.4
		2.5	17.71	.079	22.5	15.0	1.579	15.7
		3	18.34	.077	27.4	16.4	1.888	16.0

Some representative values for different s:

s	h	$\lambda + \delta\%$	$\gamma\%$	T	r	$\pi\%$	$I/Y\%$	i/p	$\rho + \delta\%$
.33	3	2	2	20.66	.059	20.4	6.8	.955	30.6
			2.5	21.26	.058	25.6	8.5	1.169	30.8
.50	4	4	2	19.98	.073	20.7	10.3	1.207	21.7
			2.5	20.66	.071	26.2	13.1	1.490	22.0
			3	21.42	.070	31.8	15.9	1.765	22.3
	5	2	2	22.61	.055	22.2	11.1	1.655	17.0
			2.5	23.47	.053	28.1	14.0	2.038	17.3
			3	24.41	.052	34.1	17.0	2.407	17.6
1.00	4	4	2.5	6.08	.185	7.7	7.7	.387	6.5
			3	6.22	.182	9.4	9.4	.474	7.0
		2	2.5	7.28	.148	9.0	9.0	.561	4.5
			3	7.49	.144	11.1	11.1	.691	5.0
	5	4	2.5	8.20	.143	10.4	10.4	.662	6.5
			3	8.44	.140	12.7	12.7	.812	7.0

to the results of the model when $s = .66$, $h = 5$, $\lambda + \delta = 4$ percent, and when γ is $2 - 2.5$ percent.[11]

The rate of profit on investment, on the other hand, appears rather high. However it must be remembered that our equation (3) derives the rate of (net) profit from the stream of gross profit *after* tax, and not (as is usually done) from the gross profit before tax. This involves a smaller provision for obsolescence, and consequently a higher net profit, than in the usual method of calculation. It also implies that in "grossing up" for tax, the relevant rate is the effective tax charge on profits before depreciation, and not the rate of tax on profits net of depreciation. Hence, if the tax on corporation profits is one third of gross profits before tax, a rate of net profit (net of tax) of 12.5 percent (assuming $\lambda = 1$ percent, $\delta = 3$ percent) corresponds to a rate of net profit *before* tax of 18.5 percent.[12]

It can be seen from the figures, too, that π and i/p are quite sensitive to changes in the technical progress function (i.e. in γ), and highly sensitive to changes in s and h, but stable for changes in λ and δ. T is only sensitive to changes in s and h, but *not* to γ. These results may sound surprising at first. One would expect T to be inversely related to γ, and one would also expect $r (= n_t/N_t)$ to be positively correlated with $(\lambda + \delta)$. However, a rise in γ leads to a rise in i/p, and hence of π, which more than compensates for the rise in γ in determining the associated change

in T; a rise in $(\lambda + \delta)$ reduces (as between one steady growth equilibrium and another) the amount of labour released through obsolescence in relation to the current labour force (since the labour force T years ago was that much smaller, when λ is larger; and of the equipment built T years ago so much less survives to be scrapped when δ is larger) so that it compensates for the increase in $(\lambda + \delta)$, leaving the value of r pretty much the same.

XVI. GENERAL CONCLUSIONS

The model shows technical progress—in the specific form of the rate of improvement of the design, etc., of newly produced capital equipment—as the main engine of economic growth, determining not only the rate of growth of productivity but—together with other parameters—also the rate of obsolescence, the average lifetime of equipment, the share of investment in income, the share of profits, and the relationship between investment and potential output (i.e., the "capital/output ratio" on new capital).

The model is Keynesian in its mode of operation (entrepreneurial expenditure decisions are primary; incomes, etc., are secondary) and severely *non*-neo-classical in that technological factors (marginal productivities or marginal substitution ratios) play no role in the determination of wages and profits. A "production function" in the sense of a single-valued relationship between *some* measure of capital, K_t, the labour force N_t and of output Y_t (all at time t) clearly does not exist. Everything depends on past history, on how the collection of equipment goods which comprises K_t has been built up. Thus Y_t will be greater for a given K_t (as measured by historical cost) if a greater part of the existing capital stock is of more recent creation; this would be the case, for example, if the rate of

[11] It should be borne in mind, of course, that no allowance was made in the model for net investment in working capital (inventory accumulation) which would affect the values of T, π, I/Y and i/p, but the effect of which can be subsumed in h. Equally, the model assumes that government savings and investment are equal—i.e., that there is no financial surplus or deficit arising out of government operations, and that personal savings and personal investments (mainly in housing) are equal.

[12] U.S. estimates put the average rate of profit on (business) investment 16 percent before tax and 8 percent after tax.

growth of population has been accelerating.

Whilst "machines" earn quasi-rents which are all the smaller the older they are (so that, for the oldest surviving machine, the quasi-rents are zero) it would be wrong to say that the position of the marginal "machine" determines the share of quasi-rents (or gross profits) in total income. For the total profit is determined quite independently of the structure of these "quasi-rents" by equation (5), i.e., by the factors determining the share of investment in output and the proportion of profits saved and therefore the position of the "marginal" machine is itself fully determined by the other equations of the system. It is the macro-economic condition specified in (5), and not the age-and-productivity structure of machinery, which will determine what the (aggregate) share of quasi-rents will be.

This technical progress function is quite consistent with a technological "investment function", i.e., a functional relationship (shifting in time) between investment per worker and output per worker.[13] However, owing to anticipated obsolescence and to uncertainty, it would not be correct to say that the "marginal product" of investment, dp_t/di_t, plays a role in determining the amount per man. Since the profitability of operating the equipment is expected to diminish in time, the marginal addition to the stream of profits (which we may call the "marginal value produc-

tivity") will be something quite different from the marginal product in the technological sense, and unlike the latter, it will not be a derivative of a technological function alone but will depend on the whole system of relationships. Further, owing to the prevailing attitude to uncertainty, it would not even be correct to say that "profit-maximising" will involve adding to investment per man until the marginal increment in anticipated profits, discounted at the ruling rate of interest or at some "assumed" rate of profit becomes equal to the marginal addition to investment. Whenever the desire to recover the cost of investment within a certain number of years—owing to the greater uncertainty of the more distant future—becomes the operative restriction (as is assumed in equation (4)), investment per man will be cut short before this marginal condition is satisfied.

The inequality (3) together with equation (4) enables us to specify an investment function in terms of the parameters of the system which determine both n_t and i_t without regard to the relationship between the expected rate of profit on investment and the rate of interest. In previous "Keynesian" models the existence of an independent investment function was closely tied to the postulate of some relationship between the "marginal efficiency" of investment and—an independently determined—rate of interest. This was a source of difficulty, since it either caused such models to be "over-determined"[14] or else it required the postulate that the capital/output ratio (or the amount of investment per worker) itself varied with the excess of the rate of profit over the money rate of interest.[15] The weakness of this latter approach has been

---

[13] On the relationship of a technical progress function and a production function cf. John Black, "The Technical Progress Function and The Production Function," *Economica*, May 1962. Whilst it is possible to make assumptions under which a technical progress function is merely one way of representing an (ex-ante) production function of constant elasticity which shifts at some pre-determined rate in time, the postulate of a technical progress function is also consistent with situations in which the rate of technical progress does not proceed at some pre-determined rate (where the shift of the "curve" is bound up with the movement *along* the "curve") and where therefore one cannot associate a unique production function with a given "state" of knowledge.

[14] Cf. R. C. O. Matthews, "The Rate of Interest in Growth Models," *Oxford Economic Papers*, October 1960, pp. 249–268.

[15] Cf. Kaldor, "Capital Accumulation and Economic Growth," *op. cit.*, pp. 217 ff.

that it assigned too much importance to the rate of interest. So long as one could assume that the rate of interest was a constant, determined by some psychological minimum (the "pure" liquidity preference of Keynesian theory), this did not matter very much. But it was unsatisfactory to rely on the *excess* of the rate of profit over the rate of interest as an important element—determining the chosen capital/output ratio and through that, the other variables—considering that this excess is under the control of the monetary authorities; if the authorities were to follow a policy of keeping the money rate of interest in some constant relationship to the rate of profit—which they may be easily tempted to do—this would have endowed them with an importance in the general scheme of things which is quite contrary to common experience.

The present model, by contrast allows the money rate of interest to move up and down, without the slightest effect on investment decisions, provided such movements do not violate certain constraints.[16] This is in much better accord with the oft-repeated assertions of business men (both in the U.K. and the U.S.) that the rate of interest has *no* influence on their investment decisions at least as far as investment in fixed capital is concerned.

Finally there is the question how far the postulate of a "technical progress function" as specified in (2) implies some restraint on the *nature* of technological change. Every change in the rate of investment per worker implies a change in the extent to which new ideas ("innovations") are actually exploited. Since the "capital saving" innovations—which increase the output/capital ratio as well as the output/labour ratio—are much more profitable to the

[16] For it must still remain true, of course, that the expected rate of profit on (fixed) investment must exceed the rate of interest by more than some minimum compensation for the "illiquidity" or other risks.

entrepreneur than the "labour-saving" ones that yield the same rate of increase in labour productivity, clearly the former are exploited first and the balance of technological change will appear more "capital-using" (all the less "capital-saving") the greater the rate of increase in investment per man. There is therefore always *some* rate of increase in investment per worker which allows output per man to grow at the same rate as investment per man and in that sense takes on the appearance of "neutral" technical progress; to assume that this rate of increase in investment per man remains unchanged over time implies also assuming that the relative importance of "capital saving" and "capital using" innovations in the total flow of innovations remains unchanged. To assume this is really implied in the assumption that the rate of technical progress is *constant;* since a growing incidence of "capital saving" innovations is the same thing as an upward drift in the technical progress function, and *vice versa.* Therefore the only sense in which the technical progress function postulates some "neutral" technical progress is the sense in which "unneutral" technical progress necessarily involves either a continuous acceleration or deceleration in the rate of increase in productivity for any given value of $\dot{i}/i$.

The main "practical" conclusion for economic policy that emerges from this model is that any scheme leading to the accelerated retirement of old equipment (such as a tax on the use of obsolete plant and equipment) is bound to accelerate for a temporary period the rate of increase in output per head $\dot{y}/y$, since it will increase n_t (the number of workers "available" for new machines) and hence I_t; and will thus involve a reduction in p_t/y_t. A more permanent cure, however, requires stimulating the technical dynamism of the economy (*raising* the technical progress function) which is not only (or perhaps mainly) a matter of more scientific education and more expenditure on research, but of higher quality business management which is more alert in searching for technical improvements and less resistant to their introduction.

APPENDIX

We must enquire whether the solution of the equations for a state of steady growth is unique. Equation (25) is a linear equation for $e^{\gamma T}$ in terms of $1/r$; it can be represented on a diagram, with $1/r$ measured along one axis and $e^{\gamma T}$ along the other, by a straight line.

Equation (26), on the other hand, represents a curve of increasing slope (as shown in the diagram). The curve representing equation (26), BB', passes through the point $e^{\gamma T} = 1$, $1/r = 0$; AA', which represents equation (25), has $e^{\gamma T} < 1$ when $1/r = 0$.

We shall prove that (1) AA', in fact cuts BB', and cuts it in two points, to which correspond the values r_1 and r_2 of r, and T_1 and T_2 of T; (2) $T_1 < h$, so that this case is in fact impossible (for entrepreneurs will make losses). It follows that there is a single possible steady growth state.

(1) To prove that AA' does not fail to cut BB', we show that there are points of BB' lying *below* AA'. Let x be the value of $1/r$ corresponding to $T = h$ on the

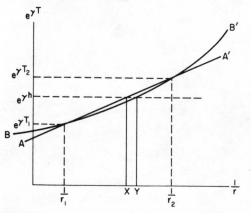

FIGURE 2.

curve AA' (i.e., found by solving equation (25)); and let y be the value of $1/r$ corresponding to $T = h$ on the curve BB' (i.e., found by solving equation (26)).

Then

$$\gamma x = e^{\gamma h}\left[1 - \frac{h(\gamma + \lambda + \delta)}{s}\right]$$
$$+ \frac{h(\gamma + \lambda + \delta)}{s}\frac{e^{\gamma h} - 1}{\gamma h} - 1$$

$$= e^{\gamma h} - 1 - \frac{(\gamma + \lambda + \delta)}{\gamma s}$$
$$\times [\gamma h \cdot e^{\gamma h} - e^{\gamma h} + 1]$$

$$= \gamma h + \tfrac{1}{2}(\gamma h)^2 + \tfrac{1}{6}(\gamma h)^3 + \ldots$$
$$- \frac{\gamma + \lambda + \delta}{\gamma s}[\tfrac{1}{2}(\gamma h)^2$$
$$+ \tfrac{1}{3}(\gamma h)^3 + \tfrac{1}{8}(\gamma h)^4 + \ldots]$$

$$= \gamma h + \tfrac{1}{2}(\gamma h)^2\left[1 - \frac{\gamma + \lambda + \delta}{\gamma s}\right]$$
$$+ \tfrac{1}{6}(\gamma h)^3\left[1 - 2\frac{\gamma + \lambda + \delta}{\gamma s}\right]$$

$$+ \tfrac{1}{24}(\gamma h)^4\left[1 - 3\frac{\gamma + \lambda + \delta}{\gamma s}\right]$$
$$+ \ldots$$

Clearly $\gamma + \lambda + \delta > \gamma s$, so that all the terms in square brackets are negative. Hence:

$$\gamma x < \gamma h - \tfrac{1}{2}(\gamma h)^2\left[\frac{\gamma + \lambda + \delta}{\gamma s} - 1\right]$$

so that

$$\gamma x < \gamma h - \tfrac{1}{2}\gamma h^2.(\lambda + \delta) \qquad (31)$$

since $s \leq 1$.

Also,

$$\gamma y = \frac{\gamma}{\lambda + \delta}(\lambda + \delta)y = \frac{\gamma}{\lambda + \delta}$$
$$\times [1 - e^{-(\lambda + \delta)h}]$$

$$> \frac{\gamma}{\lambda + \delta}[(\lambda + \delta)h - \tfrac{1}{2}(\lambda + \delta)^2 h^2]$$

$$= \gamma h - \tfrac{1}{2}\gamma h^2(\lambda + \delta)$$

which, as we have just shown, $> \gamma x$. Hence $y > x$; which is to say, that when $T = h$, the curve BB' lies to the right of AA'. Hence AA' meets BB'; for AA' cuts the $e^{\gamma T}$-axis below BB', and BB' eventually rises above AA'.

(2) It also follows from the fact that BB' lies to the right of AA' when $T = h$ that one of the points at which AA' and BB' cut has $t < h$; i.e., $T_1 < h$. Thus only T_2 (which is $> h$) is a possible value for T.

What we have shown is that there exists a single possible solution to our equations for the state of steady growth at rate γ. [The case $\lambda + \delta = 0$ follows in the same way; from (31), $\gamma x < \gamma h$; and $h = y$ in this case.]

23

Technical Change and the Aggregate Production Function*

ROBERT M. SOLOW

In this day of rationally designed econometric studies and super-input-output tables, it takes something more than the usual "willing suspension of disbelief" to talk seriously of the aggregate production function. But the aggregate production function is only a little less legitimate a concept than, say, the aggregate consumption function, and for some kinds of long-run macro-models it is almost as indispensable as the latter is for the short-run. As long as we insist on practicing macro-economics we shall need aggregate relationships.

Even so, there would hardly be any justification for returning to this old-fashioned topic if I had no novelty to suggest. The new wrinkle I want to describe is an elementary way of segre-

** **

gating variations in output per head due to technical change from those due to changes in the availability of capital per head. Naturally, every additional bit of information has its price. In this case the price consists of one new required time series, the share of labor or property in total income, and one new assumption, that factors are paid their marginal products. Since the former is probably more respectable than the other data I shall use, and since the latter is an assumption often made, the price may not be unreasonably high.

Before going on, let me be explicit that I would not try to justify what follows by calling on fancy theorems on aggregation and index numbers.[1] Either this

[1] Mrs. Robinson in particular has explored many of the profound difficulties that stand in the way of giving any precise meaning to the quantity of capital ("The Production Function and the Theory of Capital," *Review of Economic Studies*, Vol. 21, No. 2), and I have thrown up still further obstacles (*ibid.*, Vol. 23, No. 2). Were the data available, it would be better to apply the analysis to some precisely defined production function with many precisely defined inputs. One can at least hope that the aggregate analysis gives some notion of the way a detailed analysis would lead.

Reprinted by permission of the publishers and author from *The Review of Economics and Statistics*, vol. 39 (August 1957), pp. 312–320. Cambridge, Mass.: Harvard University Press, Copyright, 1957, by the President and Fellows of Harvard College.

Robert M. Solow teaches at the Massachusetts Institute of Technology.

*I owe a debt of gratitude to Dr. Louis Lefeber for statistical and other assistance, and to Professors Fellner, Leontief, and Schultz for stimulating suggestions.

kind of aggregate economics appeals or it doesn't.   Personally I belong to both schools. If it does, I think one can draw some crude but useful conclusions from the results.

THEORETICAL BASIS

I will first explain what I have in mind mathematically and then give a diagrammatic exposition. In this case the mathematics seems simpler. If Q represents output and K and L represent capital and labor inputs in "physical" units, then the aggregate production function can be written as:

$$Q = F(K, L; t) \qquad (1)$$

The variable t for time appears in F to allow for technical change. It will be seen that I am using the phrase "technical change" as a shorthand expression for *any kind of shift* in the production function. Thus slowdowns, speedups, improvements in the education of the labor force, and all sorts of things will appear as "technical change."

It is convenient to begin with the special case of *neutral* technical change. Shifts in the production function are defined as neutral if they leave marginal rates of substitution untouched but simply increase or decrease the output attainable from given inputs.   In that case the production function takes the special form

$$Q = A(t)f(K, L) \qquad (1a)$$

and the multiplicative factor $A(t)$ measures the cumulated effect of shifts over time. Differentiate (1a) totally with respect to time and divide by Q and one obtains

$$\frac{\dot{Q}}{Q} = \frac{\dot{A}}{A} + A\frac{\partial f}{\partial K}\frac{\dot{K}}{Q} + A\frac{\partial f}{\partial L}\frac{\dot{L}}{Q}$$

where dots indicate time derivatives. Now

define $w_k = (\partial Q/\partial K)(K/Q)$ and $w_l = (\partial Q/\partial L)(L/Q)$ the relative shares of capital and labor, and substitute in the above equation (note that $\partial Q/\partial K = A\,\partial f/\partial K$, etc.) and there results:

$$\frac{\dot{Q}}{Q} = \frac{\dot{A}}{A} + w_k\frac{\dot{K}}{K} + w_l\frac{\dot{L}}{L} \qquad (2)$$

From time series of $\dot{Q}/Q$, w_k, $\dot{K}/K$, w_l and $\dot{L}/L$ or their discrete year-to-year analogues, we could estimate $\dot{A}/A$ and thence $A(t)$ itself.   Actually an amusing thing happens here. Nothing has been said so far about returns to scale. But if all factor inputs are classified either as K or L, then the available figures always show w_k and w_l adding up to one. Since we have assumed that factors are paid their marginal products, this amounts to assuming the hypotheses of Euler's theorem. The calculus being what it is, we might just as well assume the conclusion, namely that F is homogeneous of degree one. This has the advantage of making everything come out neatly in terms of intensive magnitudes. Let $Q/L = q$, $K/L = k$, $w_l = 1 - w_k$; note that $\dot{q}/q = \dot{Q}/Q - \dot{L}/L$ etc., and (2) becomes

$$\frac{\dot{q}}{q} = \frac{\dot{A}}{A} + w_k\frac{\dot{k}}{k} \qquad (2a)$$

Now all we need to disentangle the technical change index $A(t)$ are series for output per man-hour, capital per man-hour, and the share of capital.

So far I have been assuming that technical change is neutral. But if we go back to (1) and carry out the same reasoning we arrive at something very like (2a), namely

$$\frac{\dot{q}}{q} = \frac{1}{F}\frac{\partial F}{\partial t} + w_k\frac{\dot{k}}{k} \qquad (2b)$$

It can be shown, by integrating a partial differential equation, that if $\dot{F}/F$ is independent of K and L (actually under constant returns to scale only K/L matters) then (1) has the special form (1a) and shifts in the production function are neutral. If in addition $\dot{F}/F$ is constant in time, say equal to a, then $A(t) = e^{at}$ or in discrete approximation $A(t) = (1 + a)^t$.

The case of neutral shifts and constant returns to scale is now easily handled graphically. The production function is completely represented by a graph of q against k (analogously to the fact that if we know the unit-output isoquant, we know the whole map). The trouble is that this function is shifting in time, so that if we observe points in the (q, k) plane, their movements are compounded out of movements along the curve and shifts of the curve. In Chart 1, for instance, every ordinate on the curve for $t = 1$ has been multiplied by the same factor to give a neutral upward shift of the production function for period 2. The problem is to estimate this shift from knowledge of points P_1 and P_2. Obviously it would be quite misleading to fit a curve through raw observed points like P_1, P_2 and others. But if the shift factor for each point of time can be estimated, the observed points can be corrected for technical change, and a production function can then be found.[2]

The natural thing to do, for small changes, is to approximate the period 2 curve by its tangent at P_2 (or the period 1 curve by its tangent at P_1). This yields an approximately corrected point P_{12}, and an estimate for $\Delta A/A$, namely $P_{12}P_1/q_1$. But $k_1P_{12} = q_2 - \partial q/\partial k\,\Delta k$ and hence $P_{12}P_1 = q_2 - q_1 - \partial q/\partial k\,\Delta k = \Delta q - \partial q/\partial k\,\Delta k$ and $\Delta A/A = P_{12}P_1/q_1 = \Delta q/q - \partial q/\partial k(k/q)\Delta k/k = \Delta q/q - w_k\,\Delta k/k$

---

[2] Professors Wassily Leontief and William Fellner independently pointed out to me that this "first-order" approximation could in principle be improved. After estimating a production function corrected for technical change (see below), one could go back and use it to provide a second approximation to the shift series, and on into further iterations.

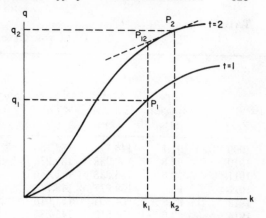

CHART 1.

which is exactly the content of (2a). The not-necessarily-neutral case is a bit more complicated, but basically similar.

AN APPLICATION TO THE U.S.: 1909–1949

In order to isolate shifts of the aggregate production function from movements along it, by use of (2a) or (2b), three time series are needed: output per unit of labor, capital per unit of labor, and the share of capital. Some rough and ready figures, together with the obvious computations, are given in Table 1.

The conceptually cleanest measure of aggregate output would be real net national product. But long NNP series are hard to come by, so I have used GNP instead. The only difference this makes is that the share of capital has to include depreciation. It proved possible to restrict the experiment to private non-farm economic activity. This is an advantage (a) because it skirts the problem of measuring government output and (b) because eliminating agriculture is at least a step in the direction of homogeneity. Thus my q is a time series of real private non-farm GNP per manhour, Kendrick's valuable work.

The capital time series is the one that will really drive a purist mad. For present purposes, "capital" includes land, mineral deposits, etc. Naturally I have used

TABLE 1

DATA FOR CALCULATION OF $A(t)$

Year	% labor force employed (1)	Capital stock ($ mill.) (2)	Col. 1 × Col. 2 (3)	Share of property in income (4)	Priv. nonfarm GNP per man-hour (5)	Employed capital per man-hour (6)	$\Delta A/A$ (7)	$A(t)$ (8)
1909	91.1	146,142	133,135	.335	$.623	$2.06	−.017	1.000
1910	92.8	150,038	139,235	.330	.616	2.10	.039	.983
1911	90.6	156,335	141,640	.335	.647	2.17	.002	1.021
1912	93.0	159,971	148,773	.330	.652	2.21	.040	1.023
1913	91.8	164,504	151,015	.334	.680	2.23	.007	1.064
1914	83.6	171,513	143,385	.325	.682	2.20	−.028	1.071
1915	84.5	175,371	148,188	.344	.669	2.26	.034	1.041
1916	93.7	178,351	167,115	.358	.700	2.34	−.010	1.076
1917	94.0	182,263	171,327	.370	.679	2.21	.072	1.065
1918	94.5	186,679	176,412	.342	.729	2.22	.013	1.142
1919	93.1	189,977	176,869	.354	.767	2.47	−.076	1.157
1920	92.8	194,802	180,776	.319	.721	2.58	.072	1.069
1921	76.9	201,491	154,947	.369	.770	2.55	.032	1.146
1922	81.7	204,324	166,933	.339	.788	2.49	.011	1.183
1923	92.1	209,964	193,377	.337	.809	2.61	.016	1.196
1924	88.0	222,113	195,460	.330	.836	2.74	.032	1.215
1925	91.1	231,772	211,198	.336	.872	2.81	−.010	1.254
1926	92.5	244,611	226,266	.327	.869	2.87	−.005	1.241
1927	90.0	259,142	233,228	.323	.871	2.93	−.007	1.235
1928	90.0	271,089	243,980	.338	.874	3.02	.020	1.226
1929	92.5	279,691	258,714	.332	.895	3.06	−.043	1.251
1930	88.1	289,291	254,865	.347	.880	3.30	.024	1.197
1931	78.2	289,056	226,042	.325	.904	3.33	.023	1.226
1932	67.9	282,731	191,974	.397	.879	3.28	.011	1.198
1933	66.5	270,676	180,000	.362	.869	3.10	.072	1.211
1934	70.9	262,370	186,020	.355	.921	3.00	.039	1.298
1935	73.0	257,810	188,201	.351	.943	2.87	.059	1.349
1936	77.3	254,875	197,018	.357	.982	2.72	−.010	1.429
1937	81.0	257,076	208,232	.340	.971	2.71	.021	1.415
1938	74.7	259,789	194,062	.331	1.000	2.78	.048	1.445
1939	77.2	257,314	198,646	.347	1.034	2.66	.050	1.514
1940	80.6	258,048	207,987	.357	1.082	2.63	.044	1.590
1941	86.8	262,940	228,232	.377	1.122	2.58	.003	1.660
1942	93.6	270,063	252,779	.356	1.136	2.64	.016	1.665
1943	97.4	269,761	262,747	.342	1.180	2.62	.071	1.692
1944	98.4	265,483	261,235	.332	1.265	2.63	.021	1.812
1945	96.5	261,472	252,320	.314	1.296	2.66	−.044	1.850
1946	94.8	258,051	244,632	.312	1.215	2.50	−.017	1.769
1947	95.4	268,845	256,478	.327	1.194	2.50	.016	1.739
1948	95.7	276,476	264,588	.332	1.221	2.55	.024	1.767
1949	93.0	289,360	269,105	.326	1.275	2.70	. . .	1.809

NOTES AND SOURCES:

Column (1): Percentage of labor force employed. 1909–26, from Douglas, *Real Wages in the United States* (Boston and New York, 1930), 460. 1929–49, calculated from *The Economic Almanac*, 1953–54 (New York, 1953), 426–28.

Column (2): Capital stock. From Goldsmith, *A Study of Saving in the United States*, Vol. 3 (Princeton, 1956), 20–21, sum of columns 5, 6, 7, 9, 12, 17, 22, 23, 24.

Column (3): (1) × (2).

Goldsmith's estimates (with government, agriculture, and consumer durables eliminated). Ideally what one would like to measure is the annual flow of capital services. Instead one must be content with a less utopian estimate of the stock of capital goods in existence. All sorts of conceptual problems arise on this account. As a single example, if the capital stock consisted of a million identical machines and if each one as it wore out was replaced by a more durable machine of the same annual capacity, the stock of capital as measured would surely increase. But the maximal flow of capital services would be constant. There is nothing to be done about this, but something must be done about the fact of idle capacity. What belongs in a production function is capital in use, not capital in place. Lacking any reliable year-by-year measure of the utilization of capital I have simply reduced the Goldsmith figures by the fraction of the labor force unemployed in each year, thus assuming that labor and capital always suffer unemployment to the same percentage. This is undoubtedly wrong, but probably gets closer to the truth than making no correction at all.[3]

The share-of-capital series is another hodgepodge, pieced together from various sources and ad hoc assumptions (such as Gale Johnson's guess that about 35 percent of non-farm entrepreneurial income is a return to property). Only after these

[3] Another factor for which I have not corrected is the changing length of the work-week. As the work-week shortens, the intensity of use of existing capital decreases, and the stock figures overestimate the input of capital services.

computations were complete did I learn that Edward Budd of Yale University has completed a careful long-term study of factor shares which will soon be published. It seems unlikely that minor changes in this ingredient would grossly alter the final results, but I have no doubt that refinement of this and the capital time-series would produce neater results.

In any case, in (2a) or (2b) one can replace the time-derivatives by year-to-year changes and calculate $\Delta q/q - w_k \, \Delta k/k$. The result is an estimate of $\Delta F/F$ or $\Delta A/A$, depending on whether these relative shifts appear to be neutral or not. Such a calculation is made in Table 1 and shown in Chart 2. Thence, by arbitrarily setting $A(1909) = 1$ and using the fact that $A(t+1) = A(t) \, (1 + \Delta A(t)/A(t))$ one can successively reconstruct the $A(t)$ time series, which is shown in Chart 3.

I was tempted to end this section with the remark that the $A(t)$ series, which is meant to be a rough profile of technical

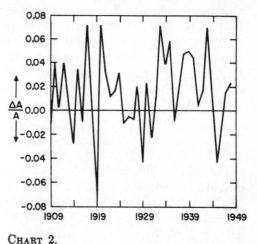

CHART 2.

Column (4): Share of property in income. Compiled from *The Economic Almanac*, 504–505; and Jesse Burkhead, "Changes in the Functional Distribution of Income," *Journal of the American Statistical Association*, Vol. 48 (June 1953), 192–219. Depreciation estimates from Goldsmith, 427.

Column (5): Private nonfarm GNP per man-hour, 1939 dollars. Kendrick's data, reproduced in *The Economic Almanac*, 490.

Column (6): Employed capital per man-hour. Column (3) divided by Kendrick's man-hour series, *ibid.*

Column (7): $\Delta A/A = \Delta(5)/(5) - (4) \times \Delta(6)/(6)$.

Column (8): From (7).

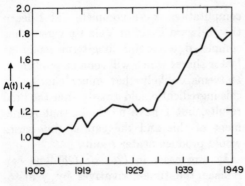

CHART 3.

change, at least looks reasonable. But on second thought I decided that I had very little prior notion of what would be "reasonable" in this context. One notes with satisfaction that the trend is strongly upward; had it turned out otherwise I would not now be writing this paper. There are sharp dips after each of the World Wars; these, like the sharp rises that preceded them, can easily be rationalized. It is more suggestive that the curve shows a distinct levelling-off in the last half of the 1920's. A sustained rise begins again in 1930. There is an unpleasant sawtooth character to the first few years of the $\Delta A/A$ curve, which I imagine to be a statistical artifact.

THE OUTLINES
OF TECHNICAL CHANGE

The reader will note that I have already drifted into the habit of calling the curve of Chart 2 $\Delta A/A$ instead of the more general $\Delta F/F$. In fact, a scatter of $\Delta F/F$ against K/L (not shown) indicates no trace of a relationship. So I may state it as a formal conclusion that over the period 1909–49, shifts in the aggregate function netted out to be approximately neutral. Perhaps I should recall that I have defined neutrality to mean that the shifts were pure scale changes, leaving marginal rates of substitution unchanged at given capital/labor ratios.

Not only is $\Delta A/A$ uncorrelated with K/L, but one might almost conclude from the graph that $\Delta A/A$ is essentially constant in time, exhibiting more or less random fluctuations about a fixed mean. Almost, but not quite, for there does seem to be a break at about 1930. There is some evidence that the average rate of progress in the years 1909–29 was smaller than that from 1930–49. The first 21 relative shifts average about 9/10 of one percent per year, while the last 19 average $2\frac{1}{4}$ percent per year. Even if the year 1929, which showed a strong downward shift, is moved from the first group to the second, there is still a contrast between an average rate of 1.2 percent in the first half and 1.9 percent in the second. Such *post hoc* splitting-up of a period is always dangerous. Perhaps I should leave it that there is some evidence that technical change (broadly interpreted) may have accelerated after 1929.

The over-all result for the whole 40 years is an average upward shift of about 1.5 percent per year. This may be compared with a figure of about .75 percent per year obtained by Stefan Valavanis-Vail by a different and rather less general method, for the period 1869–1948.[4] Another possible comparison is with the output-per-unit-of-input computations of Jacob Schmookler,[5] which show an increase of some 36 percent in output per unit of input between the decades 1904–13 and 1929–38. Our $A(t)$ rises 36.5 percent between 1909 and 1934. But these are not really comparable estimates, since Schmookler's figures include agriculture.

As a last general conclusion, after which I will leave the interested reader to his own impressions, over the 40 year period

[4] S. Valavanis-Vail, "An Econometric Model of Growth, U.S.A. 1869–1953," *American Economic Review, Papers and Proceedings*, XLV (May 1955), 217.
[5] J. Schmookler, "The Changing Efficiency of the American Economy, 1869–1938," this *Review* (August 1952), 226.

output per man-hour approximately doubled. At the same time, according to Chart 2, the cumulative upward shift in the production function was about 80 percent. It is possible to argue that about one-eighth of the total increase is traceable to increased capital per man-hour, and the remaining seven-eighths to technical change. The reasoning is this: real GNP per man-hour increased from $.623 to $1.275. Divide the latter figure by 1.809, which is the 1949 value for $A(t)$, and therefore the full shift factor for the 40 years. The result is a "corrected" GNP per man-hour, net of technical change, of $.705. Thus about 8 cents of the 65 cent increase can be imputed to increased capital intensity, and the remainder to increased productivity.[6]

Of course this is not meant to suggest that the observed rate of technical progress would have persisted even if the rate of investment had been much smaller or had fallen to zero. Obviously much, perhaps nearly all, innovation must be embodied in new plant and equipment to be realized at all. One could imagine this process taking place without net capital formation as old-fashioned capital goods are replaced by the latest models, so that the capital-labor ratio need not change systematically. But this raises problems of definition and measurement even more formidable than the ones already blithely ignored. This whole area of interest has been stressed by Fellner.

For comparison, Solomon Fabricant[7] has estimated that over the period 1871–1951 about 90 percent of the increase in output per capita is attributable to technical progress. Presumably this figure is based on the standard sort of output-per-unit-of-input calculation.

It might seem at first glance that calculations of output per unit of resource input provide a relatively assumption-free way of measuring productivity changes. Actually I think the implicit load of assumptions is quite heavy, and if anything the method proposed above is considerably more general.

Not only does the usual choice of weights for computing an aggregate resource-input involve something analogous to my assumption of competitive factor markets, but in addition the criterion output ÷ a weighted sum of inputs would seem tacitly to *assume* (a) that technical change is neutral and (b) that the aggregate production function is *strictly* linear. This explains why numerical results are so closely parallel for the two methods. We have already verified the neutrality, and as will be seen subsequently, a strictly linear production function gives an excellent fit, though clearly inferior to some alternatives.[8]

THE AGGREGATE PRODUCTION FUNCTION

Returning now to the aggregate production function, we have earned the right to write it in the form (1a). By use of the (practically unavoidable) assumption of

[6] For the first half of the period, 1909–29, a similar computation attributes about one-third of the observed increase in GNP per man-hour to increased capital intensity.

[7] S. Fabricant, "Economic Progress and Economic Change," *34th Annual Report of the National Bureau of Economic Research* (New York, 1954).

[8] For an excellent discussion of some of the problems, see M. Abramovitz "Resources and Output Trends in the U.S. since 1870," *American Economic Review, Papers and Proceedings*, XLVI (May 1956), 5–23. Some of the questions there raised could in principle be answered by the method used here. For example, the contribution of improved quality of the labor force could be handled by introducing various levels of skilled labor as separate inputs. I owe to Prof. T. W. Schultz a heightened awareness that a lot of what appears as shifts in the production function must represent improvement in the quality of the labor input, and therefore a result of real capital formation of an important kind. Nor ought it be forgotten that even straight technical progress has a cost side.

constant returns to scale, this can be further simplified to the form

$$q = A(t)f(k, 1) \qquad (3)$$

which formed the basis of Chart 1. It was there noted that a simple plot of q against k would give a distorted picture because of the shift factor $A(t)$. Each point would lie on a different member of the family of production curves. But we have now provided ourselves with an estimate of the successive values of the shift factor. (Note that this estimate is quite *independent* of any hypothesis about the exact shape of the production function.) It follows from (3) that by plotting $q(t)/A(t)$ against $k(t)$ we reduce all the observed points to a *single* member of the family of curves in Chart 1, and we can then proceed to discuss the shape of $f(k, 1)$ and reconstruct the aggregate production function. A scatter of q/A against k is shown in Chart 4.

Considering the amount of *a priori* doctoring which the raw figures have undergone, the fit is remarkably tight. Except, that is, for the layer of points which are obviously too high. These maverick observations relate to the seven last years of the period, 1943–49. From the way they

lie almost exactly parallel to the main scatter, one is tempted to conclude that in 1943 the aggregate production function simply shifted. But the whole earlier procedure was designed to purify those points from shifts in the function, so that way out would seem to be closed. I suspect the explanation may lie in some systematic incomparability of the capital-in-use series. In particular during the war there was almost certainly a more intensive use of capital services through two- and three-shift operation than the stock figures would show, even with the crude correction that has been applied. It is easily seen that such an underestimate of capital inputs leads to an overestimate of productivity increase. Thus in effect each of the affected points should really lie higher and toward the right. But further analysis shows that, for the orders of magnitude involved, the net result would be to pull the observations closer to the rest of the scatter.

At best this might account for 1943–1945. There remains the postwar period. Although it is possible that multi-shift operation remained fairly widespread even after the war, it is unlikely that this could be nearly enough to explain the whole discrepancy.[9] One might guess that accelerated amortization could have resulted in an underestimate of the capital stock after 1945. Certainly other research workers, notably Kuznets and Terborgh, have produced capital stock estimates which rather exceed Goldsmith's at the end of the period. But for the present, I leave this a mystery.*

[9] It is cheering to note that Professor Fellner's new book voices a suspicion that the postwar has seen a substantial increase over prewar in the prevalence of multi-shift operation. See *Trends and Cycles in Economic Activity* (New York, 1956), 92.

* [This "mystery" turned out to have resulted from a computational error. The corrected figures (as given in Warren P. Hogan, "Technical Progress and Production Functions," *The Review*

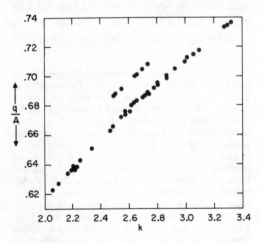

CHART 4.

In a first version of this paper, I resolutely let the recalcitrant observations stand as they were in a regression analysis of Chart 4, mainly because such casual amputation is a practice I deplore in others. But after some experimentation it seemed that to leave them in only led to noticeable distortion of the results. So, with some misgivings, in the regressions that follow I have omitted the observations for 1943–1949. It would be better if they could be otherwise explained away.

Chart 4 gives an inescapable impression of curvature, of persistent but not violent diminishing returns. As for the possibility of approaching capital-saturation, there is no trace on this gross product level, but even setting aside all other difficulties, such a scatter confers no particular license to guess about what happens at higher K/L ratios than those observed.

As for fitting a curve to the scatter, a Cobb-Douglas function comes immediately to mind, but then so do several other parametric forms, with little to choose among them.[10] I can't help feeling that little or nothing hangs on the choice of functional form, but I have experimented with several. In general I limited myself to two-parameter families of curves, linear in the parameters (for computational con-

venience), and at least capable of exhibiting diminishing returns (except for the straight line, which on this account proved inferior to all others).

The particular possibilities tried were the following:

$$q = a + \beta k \qquad (4a)$$
$$q = a + \beta \log k \qquad (4b)$$
$$q = a - \beta/k \qquad (4c)$$
$$\log q = a + \beta \log k \qquad (4d)$$
$$\log q = a - \beta/k. \qquad (4e)$$

Of these, ($4d$) is the Cobb-Douglas case; ($4c$ and e) have upper asymptotes; the semilogarithmic ($4b$) and the hyperbolic ($4c$) must cross the horizontal axis at a positive value of k and continue ever more steeply but irrelevantly downward (which means only that some positive k must be achieved before any output is forthcoming, but this is far outside the range of observation); ($4e$) begins at the origin with a phase of increasing returns and ends with a phase of diminishing returns—the point of inflection occurs at $k = \beta/2$ and needless to say all our observed points come well to the right of this.

The results of fitting these five curves to the scatter of Chart 4 are shown in Table 2.

of Economics and Statistics, vol. 40 (November 1958), p. 407) are as follows:

	$A(t)$	q/A
1943	1.733	.681
1944	1.856	.682
1945	1.895	.684
1946	1.812	.671
1947	1.781	.670
1948	1.810	.675
1949	1.853	.688

—*Ed.*]

[10] A discussion of the same problem in a different context is to be found in Prais and Houthakker, *The Analysis of Family Budgets* (Cambridge, England, 1955), 82–88. See also S. J. Prais, "Non-Linear Estimates of the Engel Curves," *Review of Economic Studies*, No. 52 (1952–53), 87–104.

TABLE 2

Curve	a	β	r
$4a$	.438	.091	.9982
b	.448	.239	.9996
c	.917	.618	.9964
d	−.729	.353	.9996
e	−.038	.913	.9980

The correlation coefficients are uniformly so high that one hestitates to say any more than that all five functions, even the linear one, are about equally good at representing the general shape of the observed points. From the correlations alone, for what they are worth, it appears that the Cobb-Douglas function (4d) and the semilogarithmic (4b) are a bit better than the others.[11]

Since all of the fitted curves are of the form $g(y) = a + \beta h(x)$, one can view them all as linear regressions and an interesting test of goodness of fit proposed by Prais and Houthakker (*ibid.*, page 51) is available. If the residuals from each regression are arranged in order of increasing values of the independent variable, then one would like this sequence to be disposed "randomly" about the regression line. A strong "serial" correlation in the residuals, or a few long runs of positive residuals alternating with long runs of negative residuals, would be evidence of just that kind of smooth departure from linearity that one would like to catch. A test can be constructed using published tables of critical values for runs of two kinds of elements.

[11] It would be foolhardy for an outsider (or maybe even an insider) to hazard a guess about the statistical properties of the basic time series. A few general statements can be made, however. (a) The natural way to introduce an error term into the aggregate production function is multiplicatively: $Q = (1 + u) F(K, L; t)$. In the neutral case it is apparent that the error factor will be absorbed into the estimated $A(t)$. Then approximately the error in $\Delta A/A$ will be $\Delta u/1 + u$. If u has zero mean, the variance of the estimated $\Delta A/A$ will be approximately $2(1 - \rho)$ var u, where ρ is the first autocorrelation of the u series. (b) Suppose that marginal productivity distribution doesn't hold exactly, so that

$$K/Q \, \partial Q/\partial K = w_k + v,$$

where now v is a random deviation and w_k is the share of property income. Then the error in the estimated $\Delta A/A$ will be $v \, \Delta k/k$, with variance $(\Delta k/k)^2$ var v. Since K/L changes slowly, the multiplying factor will be very small. The effect is to bias the estimate of $\Delta A/A$ in such a way as to lead to an overestimate when property receives less than its marginal product (and k is increasing). (c) Errors in estimating $A(t)$ enter in a relatively harmless way so far as the regression analysis is concerned. Errors of observation in k will be more serious and are likely to be large. The effect will of course be to bias the estimates of β downward.

This has been done for the linear, semilogarithmic, and Cobb-Douglas functions. The results strongly confirm the visual impression of diminishing returns in Chart 4, by showing the linear function to be a systematically poor fit. As betwen (4b) and (4d) there is little to choose.[12]

A NOTE ON SATURATION

It has already been mentioned that the aggregate production function shows no signs of levelling off into a stage of capital-saturation. The two curves in Table 2 which have upper asymptotes (c and e) happen to locate that asymptote at about the same place. The limiting values of q are, respectively, .92 and .97. Of course these are both true asymptotes, approached but not reached for any finite value of k. It could not be otherwise: no analytic function can suddenly level off and become constant unless it has always been constant. But on the other hand, there is no reason to expect nature to be infinitely differentiable. Thus any conclusions extending beyond the range actually observed in Chart 4 are necessarily treacherous. But, tongue in cheek, if we take .95 as a guess at the saturation level of q, and use the *linear* function (4a) (which will get there first) as a lower-limit guess at the saturation level for k, it turns out to be about 5.7, more than twice its present value.

But all this is in terms of *gross output*, whereas for analytic purposes we are interested in the *net* productivity of capital. The difference between the two is depreciation, a subject about which I do not feel able to make guesses. If there were more certainty about the meaning of existing estimates of depreciation, especially over long periods of time, it would have been

[12] The test statistic is R, the total number of runs, with small values significant. For (4a), $R = 4$; for (4b), $R = 13$. The 1% critical value in both cases is about 9.

better to conduct the whole analysis in terms of net product.

However, one can say this. Zero net marginal productivity of capital sets in when gross marginal product falls to the "marginal rate of depreciation," i.e., when adding some capital adds only enough product to make good the depreciation on the increment of capital itself. Now in recent years NNP has run a bit over 90 percent of GNP, so capital consumption is a bit under 10 percent of gross output. From Table 1 it can be read that capital per unit of output is, say, between 2 and 3. Thus annual depreciation is between 3 and 5 percent of the capital stock. Capital-saturation would occur whenever the gross marginal product of capital falls to .03–.05. Using (4b), this would happen at K/L ratios of around 5 or higher, still well above anything ever observed.[13]

---

[13] And this is under relatively pessimistic assumptions as to how technical change itself affects the rate of capital consumption. A warning is in order here: I have left Kendrick's GNP data in 1939 prices and Goldsmith's capital stock figures in 1929 prices. Before anyone uses the β's of Table 2 to reckon a yield on capital or any similar number, it is necessary to convert Q and K to a comparable price basis, by an easy calculation.

SUMMARY

This paper has suggested a simple way of segregating shifts of the aggregate production function from movements along it. The method rests on the assumption that factors are paid their marginal products, but it could easily be extended to monopolistic factor markets. Among the conclusions which emerge from a crude application to American data, 1909–49, are the following:

1. Technical change during that period was neutral on average.
2. The upward shift in the production function was, apart from fluctuations, at a rate of about one percent per year for the first half of the period and 2 percent per year for the last half.
3. Gross output per man hour doubled over the interval, with $87\frac{1}{2}$ percent of the increase attributable to technical change and the remaining $12\frac{1}{2}$ percent to increased use of capital.
4. The aggregate production function, corrected for technical change, gives a distinct impression of diminishing returns, but the curvature is not violent.

Part VII

POLICY ISSUES

24

A Monetary and Fiscal Framework for Economic Stability*

MILTON FRIEDMAN

During the late 19th and early 20th centuries, the problems of the day were of a kind that led economists to concentrate on the allocation of resources and, to a lesser extent, economic growth, and to pay little attention to short-run fluctuations of a cyclical character. Since the Great Depression of the 1930's, this emphasis has been reversed. Economists now tend to concentrate on cyclical movements, to act and talk as if any improvement, however slight, in control of the cycle justified any sacrifice, however

✱✱

Reprinted from *The American Economic Review*, vol. 38 (June 1948), pp. 245–264, by permission of the publisher and author.

Milton Friedman teaches at the University of Chicago.

*An earlier version of this paper was presented before the Econometric Society on September 17, 1947, at a meeting held in conjunction with the International Statistical Conferences in Washington, D.C. I am deeply indebted for helpful criticisms and constructive suggestions to Arthur F. Burns, Aaron Director, Albert G. Hart, H. Gregg Lewis, Lloyd W. Mints, Don Patinkin, and George J. Stigler.

large, in the long-run efficiency, or prospects for growth, of the economic system. Proposals for the control of the cycle thus tend to be developed almost as if there were no other objectives and as if it made no difference within what general framework cyclical fluctuations take place. A consequence of this attitude is that inadequate attention is given to the possibility of satisfying both sets of objectives simultaneously.

In constructing the monetary and fiscal framework proposed in this paper, I deliberately gave primary consideration to long-run objectives. That is, I tried to design a framework that would be appropriate for a world in which cyclical movements, other than those introduced by "bad" monetary and fiscal arrangements, were of no consequence. I then examined the resulting proposal to see how it would behave in respect of cyclical fluctuations. It behaves surprisingly well; not only might it be expected not to contribute to cyclical fluctuations, it tends to offset them and therefore seems to offer considerable promise of providing a tolerable degree of short-run economic stability.

This paper is devoted to presenting the part of the analysis dealing with the implications of the proposal for cyclical stability. Nonetheless, in view of the motivation of the proposal it seems well to begin by indicating the long-run objectives adopted as a guide, even though a reasonably full discussion of these long-run objectives would not be appropriate here.

The basic long-run objectives, shared I am sure by most economists, are political freedom, economic efficiency, and substantial equality of economic power. These objectives are not, of course, entirely consistent and some compromise among them may be required. Moreover, objectives stated on this level of generality can hardly guide proximate policy choices. We must take the next step and specify the general institutional arrangements we regard best suited for the attainment of these objectives. I believe—and at this stage agreement will be far less widespread—that all three objectives can best be realized by relying, as far as possible, on a market mechanism within a "competitive order" to organize the utilization of economic resources. Among the specific propositions that follow from this general position, three are particularly relevant: (1) Government must provide a monetary framework for a competitive order since the competitive order cannot provide one for itself. (2) This monetary framework should operate under the "rule of law" rather than the discretionary authority of administrators. (3) While a truly free market in a "competitive order" would yield far less inequality than currently exists, I should hope that the community would desire to reduce inequality even further. Moreover, measures to supplement the market would need to be taken in the interim. For both purposes, general fiscal measures (as contrasted with specific

intervention) are the most desirable non-free-market means of decreasing inequality.

The extremely simple proposal which these long-run objectives lead me to advance contains no new elements. Indeed, in view of the number of proposals that have been made for altering one or another part of the present monetary or fiscal framework, it is hard to believe that anything completely new remains to be added. The combination of elements that emerges is somewhat less hackneyed; yet no claim of originality can be made even for this. As is perhaps not surprising from what has already been said, the proposal is something like the greatest common denominator of many different proposals. This is perhaps the chief justification for presenting it and urging that it receive full professional discussion. Perhaps it, or some variant, can approach a minimum program for which economists of the less extreme shades of opinion can make common cause.

This paper deals only with the broad outlines of the monetary and fiscal framework and neglects, or deals superficially with, many difficult, important, and closely related problems. In particular, it neglects almost entirely the transition from the present framework to that outlined here; the implications of the adoption of the recommended framework for international monetary arrangements; and the special requirements of war finance. These associated problems are numerous and serious and are likely to justify compromise at some points. It seems well, however, to set forth the ultimate ideal as clearly as possible before beginning to compromise.

I. THE PROPOSAL

The particular proposal outlined below involves four main elements: the first relates to the monetary system; the second, to government expenditures on goods and services; the third, to government transfer payments; and the fourth, to the tax structure. Throughout, it pertains entirely to the federal government and all references to "government" should be so interpreted.[1]

1. A reform of the monetary and banking system to eliminate both the private creation or destruction of money and discretionary control of the quantity of money by central bank authority. The private creation of money can perhaps best be eliminated by adopting the 100 per cent reserve proposal, thereby separating the depository from the lending function of the banking system.[2] The adoption of 100 per cent reserves would also reduce the discretionary powers of the reserve system by eliminating rediscounting and existing powers over reserve requirements. To complete the elimination of the major weapons of discretionary authority, the existing powers to engage in open market operations and the existing direct controls over stock market and consumer credit should be abolished.

These modifications would leave as the chief monetary functions of the banking system the provision of depository facilities, the facilitation of check clearance, and the like; and as the chief function of the monetary authorities, the creation of money to meet government deficits or the retirement of money when the government has a surplus.[3]

2. A policy of determining the volume of government expenditures on goods and services—defined to exclude transfer expenditures of all kinds—entirely on the basis of the community's desire, need, and willingness to pay for public services. Changes in the level of expenditure should be made solely in response to alterations in the relative value attached by the community to public services and private consumption. No attempt should be made to vary expenditures, either directly or inversely, in response to cyclical fluctuations in business activity. Since the community's basic objectives would presumably change only slowly—except in time of war or immediate threat of war—this policy would, with the same exception, lead to a relatively stable volume of expenditures on goods and services.[4]

3. A predetermined program of transfer expenditures, consisting of a statement of the conditions and terms under which relief and assistance and other transfer payments will be granted.[5] Such a program

---

[1] The reason for restricting the discussion to the federal government is simply that it alone has ultimate monetary powers, not any desire to minimize the role of smaller governmental units. Indeed, for the achievement of the long-run objectives stated above it is highly desirable that the maximum amount of government activity be in the hands of the smaller governmental units to achieve as much decentralization of political power as possible.

[2] This proposal was advanced by Henry C. Simons. See his *A Positive Program for Laissez-Faire: Some Proposals for a Liberal Economic Policy*, Public Policy Pamphlet No. 15 (Univ. of Chicago Press, 1934); "Rules *vs.* Authorities in Monetary Policy," *Jour. Pol. Econ.*, Vol. XLIV (Feb., 1936), pp. 1–30. Both of these are reprinted in Henry C. Simons, *Economic Policy for a Free Society* (Chicago, Univ. of Chicago Press, 1948).

[3] The adoption of 100 per cent reserves is essential if the proposed framework is to be entirely automatic. It should be note however, that the same results could, in principle, be achieved in a fractional reserve system through discretionary authority. In order to accomplish this, the monetary authorities would have to adopt the rule that the quantity of money should be increased only when the government has a deficit, and then by the amount of the deficit, and should be decreased only when the government has a surplus, and then by the amount of the surplus.

[4] The volume of expenditures might remain stable either in money or real terms. The principle of determining the volume of expenditures by the community's objectives would lead to a stable real volume of expenditures on current goods and services. On the other hand, the usual legislative procedure in budget making is to grant fixed sums of money, which would lead to stability of money expenditures and provides a slight automatic contra-cyclical flexibility. If the volume of real expenditures were stabilized, money expenditures would vary directly with prices.

[5] These transfer payments might perhaps more appropriately be regarded as negative revenue.

is exemplified by the present system of
social security under which rules exist for
the payment of old-age and unemployment insurance. The program should be
changed only in response to alterations in
the kind and level of transfer payments the
community feels it should and can afford
to make. The program should not be
changed in response to cyclical fluctuations
in business activity. Absolute outlays,
however, will vary automatically over the
cycle. They will tend to be high when unemployment is high and low when unemployment is low.[6]

4. A progressive tax system which
places primary reliance on the personal
income tax. Every effort should be made
to collect as much of the tax bill as possible at source and to minimize the delay
between the accrual of the tax liability
and the actual collection of the tax.
Rates, exemptions, etc., should be set in
light of the expected yield at a level of
income corresponding to reasonably full
employment at a predetermined price
level. The budget principle might be either
that the hypothetical yield should balance
government expenditure, including transfer payments (at the same hypothetical
level of income) or that it should lead to a
deficit sufficient to provide some specified
secular increase in the quantity of money.[7]

[6] It may be hoped that the present complex
structure of transfer payments will be integrated
into a single scheme co-ordinated with the income
tax and designed to provide a universal floor to
personal incomes. But this is a separate issue.

[7] These specifications about the hypothetical
level of income to be used and the budget principle
to be followed are more definite and dogmatic
than is justified. In principle, the economic system
could ultimately adjust to any tax structure and
expenditure policy, no matter what level of income
or what budget principle they were initially based
on, provided that the tax structure and expenditure policy remained stable. That is, there corresponds some secular position appropriate to each
possible tax structure and expenditure policy.
The best level of income and the best budget
principle to choose depend therefore on short-run
adjustment considerations: what choice would
require the least difficult adjustment? Moreover,
the level of income and budget principle must be

The tax structure should not be varied in
response to cyclical fluctuations in business
activity, though actual receipts will, of
course, vary automatically.[8] Changes in
the tax structure should reflect changes in
the level of public services or transfer payments the community chooses to have. A
decision to undertake additional public
expenditures should be accompanied by a
revenue measure increasing taxes. Calculations of both the cost of additional public
services or transfer payments and the
yield of additional taxes should be made
at the hypothetical level of income suggested above rather than at the actual
level of income. The government would

chosen jointly: the same final result can obviously
be obtained by combining a high hypothetical income with a surplus budget principle or a low
hypothetical income with a deficit budget principle
or by any number of intermediate combinations.
My own conjecture is that the particular level of
income and budget principles suggested above are
unlikely to lead to results that would require
radical short-run adjustments to attain the corresponding secular position. Unfortunately, our
knowledge about the relevant economic interrelationships is too meager to permit more than
reasonably informed conjecture. See Section IV
below, especially footnote 22.

[8] The principle of setting taxes so as to balance
the budget at a high level of employment was
suggested by Beardsley Ruml and H. Chr. Sonne,
Fiscal and Monetary Policy, National Planning
Pamphlet no. 35 (July, 1944).

Since the present paper was written, the Committee for Economic Development has issued a
policy statement in which it makes essentially the
same tax and expenditure recommendations—that
is, it calls for adoption of a stable tax structure
capable of balancing the budget at a high level of
employment, a stable expenditure policy, and
primary reliance on automatic adjustments of
absolute revenue and expenditures to provide
cyclical stability. They call this policy the
"stabilizing budget policy." The chief difference
between the present proposal and the C.E.D.
proposal is that the C.E.D. is silent on the monetary framework and almost silent on public debt
policy, whereas the present proposal covers both.
Presumably the C.E.D. plans to cover monetary
and debt policy in separate statements still to be
issued. See *Taxes and the Budget: A Program for
Prosperity in a Free Economy*, a statement on
national policy by the Research and Policy Committee of the Committee for Economic Development (Nov., 1947).

thus keep two budgets: the stable budget, in which all figures refer to the hypothetical income, and the actual budget. The principle of balancing outlays and receipts at a hypothetical income level would be substituted for the principle of balancing actual outlays and receipts.

II. OPERATION OF THE PROPOSAL

The essence of this fourfold proposal is that it uses automatic adaptations in the government contribution to the current income stream to offset, at least in part, changes in other segments of aggregate demand and to change appropriately the supply of money. It eliminates discretionary action in response to cyclical movements as well as some extraneous or perverse reactions of our present monetary and fiscal structure.[9] Discretionary action is limited to the determination of the hypothetical level of income underlying the stable budget; that is, essentially to the determination of a reasonably attainable objective. Some decision of this kind is unavoidable in drawing up the government's budget; the proposal involves a particular decision and makes it explicit. The determination of the income goal admittedly cannot be made entirely objective or mechanical. At the same time, this determination would need to be made only at rather long intervals—perhaps every five or ten years—and involves a minimum of forecasting. Further, as will be indicated later, errors in the income goal tend to be automatically neutralized and do not require a redetermination of the goal.

[9] For example, the tendency under the existing system of fractional reserve banking for the total volume of money to change when there is a change in the proportion of its total stock of money the community wishes to hold in the form of deposits; the tendency to reduce tax rates and increase government expenditures in booms and to do the reverse in depressions; and the tendency for the government to borrow from individuals at the same time as the Federal Reserve System is buying government bonds on the open market.

Under the proposal, government expenditures would be financed entirely by either tax revenues or the creation of money, that is, the issue of non-interest-bearing securities. Government would not issue interest-bearing securities to the public; the Federal Reserve System would not operate in the open market. This restriction of the sources of government funds seems reasonable for peacetime. The chief valid ground for paying interest to the public on government debt is to offset the inflationary pressure of abnormally high government expenditures when, for one reason or another, it is not feasible or desirable to levy sufficient taxes to do so. This was the justification for wartime issuance of interest-bearing securities, though, perversely, the rate of interest on these securities was pegged at a low level. It seems inapplicable in peacetime, especially if, as suggested, the volume of government expenditures on goods and services is kept relatively stable. Another reason sometimes given for issuing interest-bearing securities is that in a period of unemployment it is less deflationary to issue securities than to levy taxes. This is true. But it is still less deflationary to issue money.[10]

[10] See Henry C. Simons, "On Debt Policy," *Jour. Pol. Econ.*, Vol. LII (Dec., 1944), pp. 356–61.

This paragraph deliberately avoids the question of the payment of interest to banks on special issues of government bonds, as has been proposed in some versions of the 100 per cent reserve proposal. The fundamental issue involved in judging such proposals is whether government should subsidize the use of deposit money and a system of check clearance and if so, what form the subsidy should take.

The large volume of government bonds now outstanding raises one of the most serious problems in accomplishing the transition from the present framework. This problem would be eased somewhat by the monetization of bonds that would occur in the process of going over to 100 per cent reserves. But there would still remain a substantial volume. Two alternatives suggest themselves: (1) freeze the volume of debt at some figure, preferably by converting it into perpetuities ("consols"); (2) use the monetization of the debt

Deficits or surpluses in the government budget would be reflected dollar for dollar in changes in the quantity of money; and, conversely, the quantity of money would change only as a consequence of deficits or surpluses. A deficit means an increase in the quantity of money; a surplus, a decrease.[11]

Deficits or surpluses themselves become automatic consequences of changes in the level of business activity. When national money income is high, tax receipts will be large and transfer payments small; so a surplus will tend to be created, and the higher the level of income, the larger the surplus. This extraction of funds from the current income stream makes aggregate demand lower than it otherwise would be and reduces the volume of money, thereby tending to offset the factors making for a further increase in income. When national money income is low, tax receipts will be small and transfer payments large, so a deficit will tend to be created, and the lower the level of income, the larger the deficit. This addition of funds to the current income stream makes aggregate demand higher than it otherwise would be and increases the quantity of money, thereby tending to offset the factors making for a further decline in income.

The size of the effects automatically produced by changes in national income

obviously depends on the range of activities government undertakes, since this will in turn determine the general order of magnitude of the government budget. Nonetheless, an essential element of the proposal is that the activities to be undertaken by government be determined entirely on other grounds. In part, this element is an immediate consequence of the motivation of the proposal. The motivation aside, however, it seems a desirable element of any proposal to promote stability. First, there is and can be no simple, reasonably objective, rule to determine the optimum share of activity that should be assigned to government— short of complete socialization—even if stability were the only objective. Changes in circumstances are likely to produce rapid and erratic variations in the share that seems desirable. But changes in the share assigned government are themselves likely to be destabilizing, both directly and through their adverse effects on anticipations. The attempt to adapt the magnitude of government operations to the requirements of stability may therefore easily introduce more instability than it corrects. Second, the share of activity assigned government is likely to have far more important consequences for other objectives—particularly political freedom and economic efficiency—than for stability.[11a] Third, means other than changes in the share of activity assigned government are readily available for changing the size of the reaction to changes in income, if experience under the proposal should prove this desirable. And some of these means need not have anything like

---

as a means of providing a secular increase in the quantity of money. Under the second plan, which, on a first view, seems more attractive, the principle of balancing the stable budget would be adopted and the government would commit itself to retiring, through the issuance of new money, a predetermined amount of the public debt annually. The amount to be retired would be determined so as to achieve whatever secular increase in the quantity of money seemed desirable. This problem, however, requires much additional study.

[11] These statements refer, of course, to the ultimate operation of the proposal. Under the second of the alternatives suggested in the preceding footnote, the change in the quantity of money during the transitional period would equal the excess of government expenditures over receipts plus the predetermined amount of money issued to retire debt.

[11a] An example of the relevance of these two points is provided by the tendency during the 'thirties to recommend an increase in the progressiveness of the tax structure as a means of increasing the propensity to consume and hence, it was argued, employment. Applied to the postwar period, the same argument would call for a shift to regressive taxes, yet I wonder if many economists would wish to recommend regressive taxes on these grounds.

the same consequences for other objectives.

Under the proposal, the aggregate quantity of money is automatically determined by the requirements of domestic stability. It follows that changes in the quantity of money cannot also be used—as they are in a fully operative gold standard—to achieve equilibrium in international trade. The two criteria will by no means always require the same changes in the quantity of money; when they conflict, one or the other must dominate. The decision, implicit in the framework recommended, to select domestic stability means that some other technique must be used to bring about adjustments to changes in the conditions of international trade. The international arrangement that seems the logical counterpart of the proposed framework is flexible exchange rates, freely determined in foreign exchange markets, preferably entirely by private dealings.[11b]

III. EFFECT OF PROPOSAL UNDER PRESENT INSTITUTIONAL CONDITIONS

The fluctuations in the government contribution to the income stream under the proposed monetary and fiscal framework are clearly in the "right" direction. Nonetheless, it is not at all clear that they would, without additional institutional modifications, necessarily lead either to reasonably full employment or to a reasonable degree of stability. Rigidities in prices are likely to make this proposal, and indeed most if not all other proposals for attaining cyclical stability, inconsistent with reasonably full employment; and,

[11b] Though here presented as a byproduct of the proposed domestic framework, flexible exchange rates can be defended directly. Indeed, it would be equally appropriate to present the proposed domestic framework as a means of implementing flexible exchange rates. The heart of the matter is that domestic and international monetary and trade arrangements are part of one whole.

when combined with lags in other types of response, to render extremely uncertain their effectiveness in stabilizing economic activity.

A. Price Rigidities

Under existing circumstances, when many prices are moderately rigid, at least against declines, the monetary and fiscal framework described above cannot be expected to lead to reasonably full employment of resources, even though lags in other kinds of response are minor. The most that can be expected under such circumstances is a reasonably stable or moderately rising level of money income. As an extreme example, suppose that the economy is in a relatively stable position at reasonably full employment and with a roughly balanced actual government budget and that the great bulk of wage rates are rigid against downward pressure. Now, let there be a substantial rise in the wage rates of a particular group of workers as a consequence either of trade union action or of a sharp but temporary increase in the demand for that type of labor or decrease in its supply, and let this higher wage rate be rigid against downward pressure. Employment of resources as full as previously would imply a higher aggregate money income since, under the assumed conditions of rigidity, other resources would receive the same amount as previously whereas the workers whose wage rates rose would receive a larger aggregate amount if fully employed. But if this higher money income, which also of course would imply a higher price structure, were attained, the government would tend to have a surplus since receipts would rise by more than expenditures. There is nothing that has occurred that would, in the absence of other independent changes, offset the deflationary effect of the surplus. The assumed full employment position would not therefore be an equilibrium position. If attained by accident, the resultant budgetary surplus would reduce effective demand and, since prices are assumed rigid, the outcome could only be unemployment. The equilibrium level of income will be somewhat higher than before, primarily because transfer payments to the unemployed will be larger, so that some of the unemployment will be offset. But there is no mechanism for offsetting the rest. The only escape from this situation is to permit inflation.

As is widely recognized, the difficulty just described is present also in most other monetary and fiscal proposals; they, too, can produce full employment under such circumstances only by inflation. This dilemma often tends, however, to be concealed in their formulation, and, in practice, it seems fairly likely that inflation would result. The brute fact is that a rational economic program for a free enterprise system (and perhaps even for a collectivist system) must have flexibility of prices (including wages) as one of its cornerstones. This need is made clear by a proposal like the present. Moreover, the adoption of such a proposal would provide some assurance against cumulative deflation and thereby tend to make flexibility of prices a good deal easier to achieve since government support for monopolistic practices of special occupational and industrial groups derives in large measure from the obvious waste of general deflation and the need for protection against it.

B. Lags in Response

Our economy is characterized not only by price rigidities but also by significant lags in other types of response. These lags make impossible any definitive statement about the actual degree of stability likely to result from the operation of the monetary and fiscal framework described above. One could reasonably expect smaller fluctuations than currently exist; though our ignorance about lags and about the fundamental causes of business fluctuations prevents complete confidence even in this outcome. The lag between the creation of a government deficit and its effects on the behavior of consumers and producers could conceivably be so long and variable that the stimulating effects of the deficit were often operative only after other factors had already brought about a recovery rather than when the initial decline was in progress. Despite intuitive feelings to the contrary, I do not believe we know enough to rule out completely this possibility. If it were realized, the proposed framework could intensify rather than mitigate cyclical fluctuations; that is, long and variable lags could convert the fluctuations in the government contribution to the income stream into the equivalent of an additional random disturbance.[12]

About all one can say about this possibility is that the completely automatic proposal outlined above seems likely to do less harm under the circumstances envisaged than alternative proposals which provide for discretionary action in addition to automatic reactions. There is a strong presumption that these discretionary actions will in general be subject to longer lags than the automatic reactions and hence will be destabilizing even more frequently.

The basis for this presumption can best be seen by subdividing into three parts the total lag involved in any action to offset a disturbance: (1) the lag between the need for action and the recognition of this need; (2) the lag between recognition of the need for action and the taking of action; and (3) the lag between the action and its effects.

The first lag, which is nonexistent for automatic reactions of the kind here proposed, could be negative for dis-

[12] See Milton Friedman, "Lerner on the Economics of Control," *Jour. Pol. Econ.*, Vol. LV, No. 5 (Oct., 1947), p. 414, especially footnote 12.

cretionary proposals if it were possible to forecast accurately the economic changes that would occur in the absence of government action. In view of the record of forecasters, it hardly needs to be argued that it would be better to shun forecasting and rely instead on as prompt an evaluation of the current situation as possible. The lag between the need for action and the recognition of that need then becomes positive. Its exact magnitude depends on the particular discretionary proposal, though the past record of contemporary interpreters of business conditions indicates that it is not likely to be negligible.[13]

The second lag is present even for automatic reactions because all taxes will not or cannot be collected at source simultaneously with the associated payments, and transfer payments will not or cannot be made immediately without some kind of a waiting period or processing period. It is clear, however, that this lag can be reduced to a negligible time by appropriate construction and administration of the system of taxes and transfer payments. For discretionary action, the length of the lag between the recognition of the need for action and the taking of action depends very much on the kind of action taken. Action can be taken very promptly to change the form or amount of the community's holdings of assets by open market purchases or sales of securities or by changes in rediscount rates or reserve requirements. A considerably longer time is required to change the net contribution of the government to the income stream by changing the tax structure. Even though advance prescription for alternative possibilities eliminates any delay in deciding what changes to make in tax rates, exemptions, kinds of taxes levied, or the like, administrative considerations will enforce a substantial delay before the change becomes effective. Taxpayers,

businesses or individuals acting as intermediaries in collecting the taxes, and tax administrators must all be informed of the change and be given an opportunity to make the appropriate adjustments in their procedures; new forms must be printed or at least circulated; and so on.

The longest delay of all is likely to be involved in changing the net contribution of government to the income stream by changing government expenditure policy, particularly for goods and services. No matter how much advance planning may have been done, the rate of expenditure cannot be stepped up or curtailed overnight unless the number of names on the payroll is to be the only basis in terms of which the expenditure is to be controlled or judged. Time is involved in getting projects under way with any degree of efficiency; and considerable waste in ceasing work on projects abruptly.

The third lag, that between the action and its effects, is present and significant both for automatic reactions and discretionary actions, and little if anything can be done about it by either legal or administrative reform of the fiscal and monetary structure.[14] We have no trustworthy empirical evidence on the length of this lag for various kinds of action, and much further study of this problem is clearly called for. Some clues about the direction such study should take are furnished by *a priori* considerations which suggest, as a first approximation, that the order of the various policies with respect to the length of this lag is the reverse of their order with respect to the length of the lag between the recognition of the need for action and the taking of action. Changes in government expenditures on goods and services lead to almost immediate changes in the employment of the resources used to produce those goods and

---

[13] *Ibid.*, p. 414, especially footnote 11.

[14] Reforms of other types, for example, reforms increasing the flexibility of prices, might affect this lag.

services.   They have secondary effects
through the changes thereby induced in
the expenditures of the individuals owning
the resources so employed.

The lag in these induced changes might
be expected to be less than the lag in the
adjustment of expenditures to changed
taxes or to a changed amount or form of
asset holdings. Changes in taxes make the
disposable incomes of individuals larger or
smaller than they would otherwise be.
Individuals might be expected to react to
a change in disposable income as a result
of a tax change only slightly less rapidly
than to a change in disposable income as a
result of a change in aggregate income.

These indications are, however, none too
trustworthy.   There are likely to be important indirect effects that depend on
such things as the kinds of goods and
services directly affected by changed
government expenditures, the incidence of
the changes in disposable income that
result from changed expenditures or taxes,
and the means employed to finance
government deficits.   For example, if
deficits are financed through increases in
the quantity of money and surpluses are
used to reduce the quantity of money,
part of the effect of changes in government
expenditures or taxes will be produced by
changes in interest rates and the kind
and volume of assets held by the community. The entire effect of open-market
operations, changes in rediscount rates and
reserve requirements, and the like will be
produced in this way, and it seems likely
that these effects would take the longest
to make themselves felt.

The automatic reactions embodied in
the proposal here advanced operate in part
like tax changes—in so far as tax receipts
vary—and in part like expenditure changes
—in so far as transfer payments vary; and
like both of these, some part of their
effect is through changes in the quantity
of money.   One might expect, therefore,
that the lag between action and its effects

would be roughly the same for automatic
reactions as for discretionary tax changes,
a good deal shorter for automatic reactions
than for discretionary monetary changes,
and somewhat longer for automatic reactions than for discretionary changes in
government expenditures on goods and
services.

This analysis, much of which is admittedly highly conjectural, suggests that the
total lag is definitely longer for discretionary monetary or tax changes than for
automatic reactions, since each of the three
parts into which the total lag has been
subdivided is longer.   There is doubt
about the relative length of the total lag
only for discretionary expenditure changes.
Even for these, however, it seems doubtful
that the shorter lag between action and its
effects can more than offset the longer lag
between the need for action and the taking
of action.

Given less extreme conditions than those
required to convert the present proposal
into a destabilizing influence, the reduction
achieved in the severity of fluctuations
would depend on the extent and rapidity
of price adjustments, the nature of the
responses of individuals to these price
changes and to the changes in their incomes
and asset holdings resulting from the
induced surpluses or deficits, and the lags
in such responses. If these were such as to
make the system operate reasonably well,
the improvement would tend to be cumulative, since the experience of damped
fluctuations would lead to patterns of
expectations on the part of both business-
men and consumers that would make it
rational for them to take action that would
damp fluctuations still more. This favorable result would occur, however, only if
the proposed system operated reasonably
well without such aid; hence, in my view,
this proposal, and all others as well, should
be judged primarily on their direct effects,
not on their indirect effects in stimulating
a psychological climate favorable to stabil-

ity. It must be granted, however, that the present proposal is less likely to stimulate such a favorable psychological climate than a proposal which has a simpler and more easily understood goal, for example, a proposal which sets a stable price level as its announced goal. *If the business world were sufficiently confident of the ability of the government to achieve the goal*, it would have a strong incentive to behave in such a way as greatly to simplify the government's task.

IV. IMPLICATIONS OF THE PROPOSAL IF PRICES ARE FLEXIBLE AND LAGS IN RESPONSE MINOR

The ideal possibilities of the monetary and fiscal framework proposed in this paper, and the stabilizing economic forces on which these possibilities depend, can be seen best if we put aside the difficulties that have been detaining us and examine the implications of the proposal in an economy in which prices of both products and factors of production are flexible[15] and lags in other types of response are minor. In such an economy, the monetary and fiscal system described above would tend toward an equilibrium characterized by reasonably full employment.

To describe the forces at work, let us suppose that the economy is initially in a position of reasonably full employment with a balanced actual budget and is

[15] The concept of flexible prices, though one we use continually and can hardly avoid using, is extremely difficult to define precisely. Fortunately, a precise definition is not required for the argument that follows. All that is necessary for the argument is that there be a "substantial" range of prices that are not "rigid" because of long-term contracts or organized noncontractual agreements to maintain price and that these prices should react reasonably quickly to changes in long-run conditions of demand or supply. It is not necessary that there be "perfect" flexibility of prices, however that might be defined, or that contracts involving prices be subject to change at will, or that every change in long-run conditions of demand or supply be reflected instantaneously in market price.

subjected to a disturbance producing a decline in aggregate money demand that would be permanent if no other changes occurred.[16] The initial effect of the decline in aggregate demand will be a decline in sales and the piling up of inventories in at least some parts of the economy, followed shortly by unemployment and price declines caused by the attempt to reduce inventories to the desired level. The lengthening of the list of unemployed will increase government transfer payments; the loss of income by the unemployed will reduce government tax receipts. The deficit created in this way is a net contribution by the government to the income stream which directly offsets some of the decline in aggregate demand, thereby preventing unemployment from becoming as large as it otherwise would and serving as a shock absorber while more fundamental correctives come into play.

These more fundamental correctives, aside from changes in relative prices and interest rates, are (1) a decline in the general level of prices which affects (a) the real value of the community's assets and (b) the government contribution to the income stream, and (2) an increase in the stock of money.

The decline in the general level of prices that follows the initial decline in aggregate demand will clearly raise the real value of the community's stock of money and government bonds since the nominal value of these assets will not decrease. The real value of the remainder of the community's assets may be expected to remain roughly the same, so the real value of the total stock of assets will rise.[17] The rise in the real value of assets

[16] The same analysis would apply to disturbances producing only a temporary decline. The reason for assuming a permanent decline is to trace through the entire process of adjustment to a new equilibrium position.

[17] If the real value of other assets of the community should fall, this would simply mean that the price level would have to fall farther in order

will lessen the need for additional saving and hence increase the fraction of any given level of real income that the community will wish to consume. This force, in principle, would alone be sufficient to assure full employment even if the government maintained a rigidly balanced actual budget and kept the quantity of money constant, since there would presumably always be some price level at which the community could be made to feel rich enough to spend on consumption whatever fraction or multiple of its current income is required to yield an aggregate demand sufficient to permit full employment.

This effect of a lower price level in increasing the fraction of current private (disposable) income devoted to consumption is reinforced by its effect on the government's contribution to the income stream. So long as the price level, and with it money income, is below its initial level, the government will continue to run a deficit. This will be true even if employment is restored to its initial level, so that transfer payments and loss in tax receipts on account of unemployment are eliminated. The tax structure is progressive, and exemptions, rates, etc., are expressed

to raise the real value of the community's total stock of assets. Note that under the proposed framework, all money in the community is either a direct government obligation (nondeposit currency) or is backed one hundred per cent by a direct government obligation (deposits in the central bank). If this analysis were to be applied to a fractional reserve system, the assets whose aggregate real value could be guaranteed to rise with no directly offsetting fall in the real value of private assets would be the total amount of government obligations (currency and bonds) held outside the treasury and central bank. On this and what follows, see A. C. Pigou, "The Classical Stationary State," *Econ. Jour.*, Vol. LIII (Dec., 1943), pp. 342–51, and "Economic Progress in a Stable Environment," *Economica*, n.s. XIV (Aug., 1947), pp. 180–90; and Don Patinkin, "Price Flexibility and Full Employment," to be published in the September, 1948 number of this *Review* [reprinted in this volume, Selection 16].

in absolute dollar amounts. Receipts will therefore fall more than in proportion to the fall in the price level; expenditures, at most, proportionately.[18] Because of the emergence of such a deficit, the price decline required to restore employment will be smaller than if the government were to maintain a rigidly balanced actual budget, and this will be true even aside from the influence of the deficit on the stock of money. The reason is that the price level will have to fall only to the point at which the amount the community desires to add to its hoards equals the government deficit, rather than to the point at which the community desires to add nothing to its hoards.[19]

[18] The effect of the lower price level on expenditures depends somewhat on the precise expenditure and transfer policy adopted. If, as is called for by the principle of determining the expenditure program by the community's objectives, the real volume of government expenditures on goods and services is kept cyclically stable and if the program of transfer payments is also stated in real terms, expenditures will decline proportionately. If government expenditures on goods and services are kept cyclically stable in dollar terms, or the program of transfer expenditures is stated in dollar terms, expenditures will decline less than proportionately.

[19] If the real volume of government expenditures on goods and services is kept cyclically stable and the transfer program is also stated in real terms, the aggregate expenditures of government under fixed expenditure and transfer programs would tend to be the same fraction of the full-employment income of society no matter what the price level. This fraction would be the maximum net contribution the government could make to the income stream no matter how low prices, and with them money income and government receipts, fell. Consequently, this force alone would be limited in magnitude and might not, even in principle, be able to offset every disturbance. If either program is in absolute terms, there would be no limit to the fraction that the government contribution could constitute of the total income stream.

An alternative way to describe this effect is in terms of the relation between the expected expenditures and receipts of consumers, business, and government. It is a condition of equilibrium that the sum of the desired expenditures of these groups equal the sum of their receipts. If the government maintains a rigidly balanced budget, equilibrium requires that consumers and business

The decline in the price level may restore the initial level of employment through the combined effects of the increased average propensity to consume and the government deficit. But so long as a deficit exists, the position attained is not an equilibrium position. The deficit is financed by the issue of money. The resultant increase in the aggregate stock of money must further raise the real value of the community's stock of assets and hence the average propensity to consume. This is the same effect as that discussed above except that it is brought about by an increase in the absolute stock of money rather than by a decline in prices. Like the corresponding effect produced by a decline in prices, the magnitude of this effect is, in principle, unlimited. The rise in the stock of money and hence in the average propensity to consume will tend to raise prices and reduce the deficit. If we suppose no change to occur other than the one introduced to start the analysis going, the final adjustment would be attained when prices had risen sufficiently to yield a roughly balanced actual budget.

A disturbance increasing aggregate money demand would bring into play the same forces operating in the reverse direction: the increase in employment would reduce transfer payments and raise tax receipts, thus creating a surplus to offset part of the increase in aggregate demand; the rise in prices would decrease the real value of the community's stock of money and hence the fraction of current income spent on consumption; the rise in prices would also mean that even after "overemployment" was eliminated, the government would run

a surplus that would tend to offset further the initial increase in aggregate demand;[20] and, finally, the surplus would reduce the stock of money.

As this analysis indicates, the proposed fiscal and monetary framework provides defense in depth against changes in aggregate demand. The first line of defense is the adjustment of transfer payments and tax receipts to changes in employment.[20a] This eases the shock while the defense is taken over by changes in prices. These raise or lower the real value of the community's assets and thereby raise or lower the fraction of income consumed. They also produce a government deficit or surplus in addition to the initial deficit or surplus resulting from the effect of changes in employment or transfer payments and tax receipts. The final line of defense is the cumulative effect of the deficits or surpluses on the stock of money. These changes in the stock of money tend to restore prices to their initial level. In some measure, of course, these defenses all operate simultaneously; yet their main effects are likely to occur in the temporal order suggested in the preceding discussion.

[20] The limit to the possible effect of the surplus on the current income stream would be set by the character of the tax structure, since there would probably be some maximum percentage of the aggregate income that could be taken by taxes no matter how high the price level and the aggregate income.

[20a] It should be noted that this is the only effect taken into account by Musgrave and Miller in their calculations of the possible magnitude of the effect of automatic variations in government receipts and expenditures. (R. A. Musgrave and M. H. Miller, "Built-in Flexibility," this *Review*, March, 1948, pp. 122–28.) They conclude that "the analysis here provided lends no justification to the view now growing in popularity that 'built-in flexibility' can do the job alone and that deliberate countercyclical fiscal policy can be dispensed with." While this is a valid conclusion, it does not justify rejecting the view that "built-in flexibility" can do the job alone, since the "analysis here provided" takes no account of what have been termed above the "more fundamental correctives."

together plan to spend what they receive (*i.e.*, not seek to add to their money hoards). If the government runs a deficit, consumers and business together need not plan to spend all they receive; equilibrium requires that their planned expenditures fall short of their receipts by the amount of the deficit (*i.e.*, that they seek to add to their hoards per period the amount of the deficit).

Even given flexible prices, the existence of the equilibrating mechanism described does not of course mean that the economy will in fact achieve relative stability. This depends in addition on the number and magnitude of the disturbances to which the economy is subject, the speed with which the equilibrating forces operate, and the importance of such disequilibrating forces as adverse price expectations. If the lags of response are minor, and initial perverse reactions unimportant, adjustments would be completed rapidly and there would be no opportunity for disequilibria to cumulate, so that relative stability would be attained. Even in this most favorable case, however, the equilibrating mechanism does not prevent disturbances from arising and does not counteract their effects instantaneously—as, indeed, no system can in the absence of ability to predict everything in advance with perfect accuracy. What the equilibrating mechanism does accomplish is, first, to keep governmental monetary and fiscal operations from themselves contributing disturbances and, second, to provide an automatic mechanism for adapting the system to the disturbances that occur.

Given flexible prices, there would be a tendency for automatic neutralization of any errors in the hypothetical income level assumed or in the calculations of the volume of expenditures and revenues at the hypothetical income level. Further, it would ultimately be of no great importance exactly what decision was reached about the relation to establish between expenditures and revenue at the hypothetical income level (*i.e.*, whether exactly to balance, to strive for a deficit sufficient to provide a predetermined secular increase in the quantity of money, etc.). Suppose, for example, that errors in the assumed income level, the calculated volume of expenditures and receipts, and the relation established between expenditures and

receipts combined to produce a deficit larger than was consistent with stable prices. The resulting inflationary pressure would be analogous to that produced by an external disturbance and the same forces would come into play to counteract it. The result would be that prices would rise and the level of income tend to stabilize at a higher level than the hypothetical level initially assumed.

Similarly, the monetary and fiscal framework described above provides for adjustment not only to cyclical changes but also to secular changes. I do not put much credence in the doctrine of secular stagnation or economic maturity that is now so widely held. But let us assume for the sake of argument that this doctrine is correct, that there has been such a sharp secular decline in the demand for capital that, at the minimum rate of interest technically feasible, the volume of investment at a full-employment level of income would be very much less than the volume of savings that would be forthcoming at this level of income and at the current price level.[21] The result would simply be that the equilibrium position would involve a recurrent deficit sufficient to provide the hoards being demanded by savers. Of course, this would not really be a long-run equilibrium position, since

---

[21] Because of the effect discussed above of price changes on the real value of assets, and in this way on the average propensity to consume, it seems to me that such a state of affairs would not lead to secular unemployment even if the quantity of money were kept constant, provided that prices are flexible (which is the reason for including the qualification "at the current price level" in the sentence to which this footnote is attached). But I am for the moment accepting the point of view of those who deny the existence or importance of this equilibrating force. Moreover, if the quantity of money were constant, the adjustment would be made entirely through a secular decline in prices, admittedly a difficult adjustment. Once again changes in the government contribution to the income stream and through this in the quantity of money can reduce the extent of the required price change.

the gradual increase in the quantity of money would increase the aggregate real value of the community's stock of money and thereby of assets, and this would tend to increase the fraction of any given level of real income consumed. As a result, there would tend to be a gradual rise in prices and the level of money income and a gradual reduction in the deficit.[22]

V. CONCLUSION

In conclusion, I should like to emphasize the modest aim of the proposal. It does not claim to provide full employment in the absence of successful measures to make prices of final goods and of factors of production flexible. It does not claim to eliminate entirely cyclical fluctuations in output and employment. Its claim to serious consideration is that it provides a stable framework of fiscal and monetary action, that it largely eliminates the uncertainty and undesirable political implications of discretionary action by governmental authorities, that it provides for adaptation of the governmental sector to changes occurring in other sectors of the economy of a kind designed to offset the

[22] This and the preceding paragraph, in particular, and this entire section, in general, suggest a problem that deserves investigation and to which I have no satisfactory answer, namely, the characteristics of the system of equations implicit in the proposal and of their equilibrium solution. It is obvious that under strictly stationary conditions, including a stationary population, the equilibrium solution would involve constancy of prices, income per head, etc., and a balanced actual budget. The interesting question is whether there is any simple description of the equilibrium solution under specified dynamic situations. For example, are there circumstances, and if so what are they, under which the equilibrium solution will tend to involve constant money income per head with declining prices, or constant prices with rising money income per head, etc.? It is obvious that no such simple description will suffice in general, but there may well be broad classes of circumstances under which one or another will.

effects of these changes, and that the proposed fiscal and monetary framework is consistent with the long-run considerations stated at the outset of this paper. It is not perhaps a proposal that one would consider at all optimum if our knowledge of the fundamental causes of cyclical fluctuations were considerably greater than I, for one, think it to be; it is a proposal that involves minimum reliance on uncertain and untested knowledge.

The proposal has of course its dangers. Explicit control of the quantity of money by government and explicit creation of money to meet actual government deficits may establish a climate favorable to irresponsible government action and to inflation. The principle of a balanced stable budget may not be strong enough to offset these tendencies. This danger may well be greater for this proposal than for some others, yet in some measure it is common to most proposals to mitigate cyclical fluctuations. It can probably be avoided only by moving in a completely different direction, namely, toward an entirely metallic currency, elimination of any governmental control of the quantity of money, and the re-enthronement of the principle of a balanced actual budget.

The proposal may not succeed in reducing cyclical fluctuations to tolerable proportions. The forces making for cyclical fluctuations may be so stubborn and strong that the kind of automatic adaptations contained in the proposal are insufficient to offset them to a tolerable degree. I do not see how it is possible to know now whether this is the case. But even if it should prove to be, the changes suggested are almost certain to be in the right direction and, in addition, to provide a more satisfactory framework on which to build further action.

A proposal like the present one, which is concerned not with short-run policy but with structural reform, should not be urged on the public unless and until it has withstood the test of professional criticism. It is in this spirit that the present paper is published.*

* [With this reprinting of his article, Professor Friedman has added the following note:

A decade after this article was published, I gave a series of lectures at Fordham University presenting detailed proposals for the reform of our monetary institutions and policy. In the final lecture I referred to the proposal presented in this article as follows: "The research I have done since this proposal was published gives me no reason to doubt that it would work well; that it would provide a stable monetary background which would render major fluctuations well-nigh impossible, would not exacerbate minor fluctuations, and might even alleviate them. But I have become increasingly persuaded that the proposal is more sophisticated and complex than is necessary, that a much simpler rule would also produce highly satisfactory results and would have two great advantages: first, its simplicity would facilitate the public understanding and backing that is necessary if the rule is to provide an effective barrier to opportunistic 'tinkering'; second, it would largely separate the monetary problem from the fiscal and hence would require less far-reaching reform over a narrower area.

"The simpler rule is that the stock of money be increased at a fixed rate year-in and year-out without any variation in the rate of increase to meet cyclical needs. This rule could be adopted by the Reserve System itself. Alternatively, Congress could instruct the Reserve System to follow it. If it were adopted without any other changes in our monetary arrangements, the Reserve System would have much discretion in the precise techniques used to increase the stock of money and it could achieve the objective only with an appreciable though not large margin of error—perhaps one-half to one percentage point. If the other changes I have recommended were made, the area of discretion would be narrowed radically and so would the margin of error.

"To make the rule specific, we need (1) to define the stock of money to which it refers, (2) to state what the fixed rate of increase should be or how it should be determined, (3) to state what if any allowance should be made for intra-year or seasonal movements."

I then went on to discuss these three points. See the published version of the lectures, Milton Friedman, *A Program for Monetary Stability* (Fordham University Press, 1960). —*Ed.*]

25

Functional Finance
and the Federal Debt

ABBA P. LERNER

Apart from the necessity of winning the war, there is no task facing society today so important as the elimination of economic insecurity. If we fail in this after the war the present threat to democratic civilization will arise again. It is therefore essential that we grapple with this problem even if it involves a little careful thinking and even if the thought proves somewhat contrary to our preconceptions.

In recent years the principles by which appropriate government action can maintain prosperity have been adequately developed, but the proponents of the new principles have either not seen their full logical implications or shown an over-solicitousness which caused them to try to save the public from the necessary mental exercise. This has worked like a boomerang. Many of our publicly minded men who have come to see that deficit spending actually works still oppose the permanent maintenance of prosperity because in their

Reprinted from *Social Research*, vol. 10 (February 1943), pp. 38–51, by permission of the publisher and author.

Abba P. Lerner teaches at the University of California, Berkeley; he was formerly at the New School for Social Research.

failure to see *how* it all works they are easily frightened by fairy tales of terrible consequences.

I.

As formulated by Alvin Hansen and others who have developed and popularized it, the new fiscal theory (which was first put forward in substantially complete form by J. M. Keynes in England) sounds a little less novel and absurd to our preconditioned ears than it does when presented in its simplest and most logical form, with all the unorthodox implications expressly formulated. In some cases the less shocking formulation may be intentional, as a tactical device to gain serious attention. In other cases it is due not to a desire to sugar the pill but to the fact that the writers themselves have not seen all the unorthodox implications—perhaps subconsciously compromising with their own orthodox education. But now it is these compromises that are under fire. Now more than ever it is necessary to pose the theorems in the purest form. Only thus will it be possible to clear the air of objections which really are concerned with awkwardnesses that appear only when the new theory is forced into the old theoretical framework.

Fundamentally the new theory, like almost every important discovery, is extremely simple. Indeed it is this simplicity which makes the public suspect it as too slick. Even learned professors who find it hard to abandon ingrained habits of thought have complained that it is "merely logical" when they could find no flaw in it. What progress the theory has made so far has been achieved not by simplifying it but by dressing it up to make it more complicated and accompanying the presentation with impressive but irrelevant statistics.

The central idea is that government fiscal policy, its spending and taxing, its borrowing and repayment of loans, its issue of new money and its withdrawal of money, shall all be undertaken with an eye only to the *results* of these actions on the economy and not to any established traditional doctrine about what is sound or unsound. This principle of judging only by *effects* has been applied in many other fields of human activity, where it is known as the method of science as opposed to scholasticism. The principle of judging fiscal measures by the way they work or function in the economy we may call *Functional Finance.*

The first financial responsibility of the government (since nobody else can undertake that responsibility) is to keep the total rate of spending in the country on goods and services neither greater nor less than that rate which at the current prices would buy all the goods that it is possible to produce. If total spending is allowed to go above this there will be inflation, and if it is allowed to go below this there will be unemployment. The government can increase total spending by spending more itself or by reducing taxes so that the taxpayers have more money left to spend. It can reduce total spending by spending less itself or by raising taxes so that taxpayers

have less money left to spend. By these means total spending can be kept at the required level, where it will be enough to buy the goods that can be produced by all who want to work, and yet not enough to bring inflation by demanding (at current prices) *more* than can be produced.

In applying this first law of Functional Finance, the government may find itself collecting more in taxes than it is spending, or spending more than it collects in taxes. In the former case it can keep the difference in its coffers or use it to repay some of the national debt, and in the latter case it would have to provide the difference by borrowing or printing money. In neither case should the government feel that there is anything especially good or bad about this result; it should merely concentrate on keeping the total rate of spending neither too small nor too great, in this way preventing both unemployment and inflation.

An interesting, and to many a shocking, corollary is that taxing is *never* to be undertaken merely because the government needs to make money payments. According to the principles of Functional Finance, taxation must be judged only by its effects. Its main effects are two: the taxpayer has less money left to spend and the government has more money. The second effect can be brought about so much more easily by printing the money that only the first effect is significant. Taxation should therefore be imposed only when it is desirable that the taxpayers shall have less money to spend, for example, when they would otherwise spend enough to bring about inflation.

The second law of Functional Finance is that the government should borrow money only if it is desirable that the public should have less money and more government bonds, for these are the *effects* of government borrowing. This might be desirable if otherwise the rate of interest would be reduced too low (by attempts on the part of the holders of the cash to lend it out) and induce too much investment, thus bringing about inflation. Conversely, the government should lend money (or repay some of its debt) only if it is desirable to increase the money or to reduce the quantity of government bonds in the hands of the public. When taxing, spending, borrowing and lending (or repaying loans) are governed by the principles of Functional Finance, any excess of money outlays over money revenues, if it cannot be met out of money hoards, must be met by printing new money, and any excess of revenues over outlays can be destroyed or used to replenish hoards.

The almost instinctive revulsion that we have to the idea of printing money, and the tendency to identify it with inflation, can be overcome if we calm ourselves and take note that this printing does not affect the amount of money *spent*. That is regulated by the first law of Functional Finance, which refers especially to inflation and unemployment. The printing of money takes place only when it is needed to implement Functional Finance in spending or lending (or repayment of government debt).[1]

In brief, Functional Finance rejects completely the traditional doctrines of "sound finance" and the principle of trying to balance the budget over a solar year or any other arbitrary period. In their place it prescribes: first, the adjustment of total spending (by everybody in the economy, including the government) in order to eliminate both unemployment and inflation, using government spending when total spending is too low and taxation when total spending is too high; second, the adjustment of public holdings of money and of government bonds, by government borrowing or debt repayment, in order to

[1] Borrowing money from the banks, on conditions which permit the banks to issue new credit money based on their additional holdings of government securities, must be considered for our purpose as printing money. In effect the banks are acting as agents for the government in issuing credit or bank money.

achieve the rate of interest which results in the most desirable level of investment; and, third, the printing, hoarding or destruction of money as needed for carrying out the first two parts of the program.

II.

In judging the formulations of economists on this subject it is difficult to distinguish between tact in smoothing over the more staggering statements of Functional Finance and insufficient clarity on the part of those who do not fully realize the extremes that are implied in their relatively orthodox formulations. First there were the pump-primers, whose argument was that the government merely had to get things going and then the economy could go on by itself. There are very few pump-primers left now. A formula similar in some ways to pump-priming was developed by Scandinavian economists in terms of a series of cyclical, capital and other special budgets which had to be balanced not annually but over longer periods. Like the pump-priming formula it fails because there is no reason for supposing that the spending and taxation policy which maintains full employment and prevents inflation must necessarily balance the budget over a decade any more than during a year or at the end of each fortnight.

As soon as this was seen—the lack of any guarantee that the maintenance of prosperity would permit the budget to be balanced even over longer periods—it had to be recognized that the result might be a continually increasing national debt (if the additional spending were provided by the government's borrowing of the money and not by printing the excess of its spending over its tax revenues). At this point two things should have been made clear: first, that this possibility presented no danger to society, no matter what unimagined heights the national debt might reach, so long as Functional Finance maintained the proper level of total demand for current output; and second (though this is much less important), that there is an automatic tendency for the budget to be balanced in the long run as a *result* of the application of Functional Finance, even if there is no place for the *principle* of balancing the budget. No matter how much interest has to be paid on the debt, taxation must not be applied unless it is necessary to keep spending down to prevent inflation. The interest can be paid by borrowing still more.

As long as the public is willing to keep on lending to the government there is no difficulty, no matter how many zeros are added to the national debt. If the public becomes reluctant to keep on lending, it must either hoard the money or spend it. If the public hoards, the government can print the money to meet its interest and other obligations, and the only effect is that the public holds government currency instead of government bonds and the government is saved the trouble of making interest payments. If the public spends, this will increase the rate of total spending so that it will not be necessary for the government to borrow for this purpose; and if the rate of spending becomes too great, *then* is the time to tax to prevent inflation. The proceeds can then be used to pay interest and repay government debt. In every case Functional Finance provides a simple, quasi-automatic response.

But either this was not seen clearly or it was considered too shocking or too logical to be told to the public. Instead it was argued, for example by Alvin Hansen, that as long as there is a reasonable ratio between national income and debt, the interest payment on the national debt can easily come from taxes paid out of the increased national income created by the deficit financing.

This unnecessary "appeasement" opened the way to an extremely effective opposition to Functional Finance. Even men who

have a clear understanding of the mechanism whereby government spending in times of depression can increase the national income by several times the amount laid out by the government, and who understand perfectly well that the national debt, when it is not owed to other nations, is not a burden on the nation in the same way as an individual's debt to other individuals is a burden on the individual, have come out strongly against "deficit spending."[2] It has been argued that "it would be impossible to devise a program better adapted to the systematic undermining of the private-enterprise system and the hastening of the final catastrophe than 'deficit spending.'"[3]

These objections are based on the recognition that although every dollar spent by the government may create several dollars of income in the course of the next year or two, the effects then disappear. From this it follows that if the national income is to be maintained at a high level the government has to keep up its contribution to spending for as long as private spending is insufficient by itself to provide full employment. This might mean an indefinite continuation of government support to spending (though not necessarily at an increasing rate); and if, as the "appeasement" formulation suggests, all this spending comes out of borrowing, the debt will keep on growing until it is no longer in a "reasonable" ratio to income.

This leads to the crux of the argument. If the interest on the debt must be raised out of taxes (again an assumption that is unchallenged by the "appeasement" formulation) it will in time constitute an important fraction of the national income. The very high income tax necessary to collect this amount of money and pay it to the holders of government bonds will dis-

[2] An excellent example of this is the persuasive article by John T. Flynn in *Harper's Magazine* for July 1942.
[3] Flynn, *ibid.*

courage risky private investment, by so reducing the net return on it that the investor is not compensated for the risk of losing his capital. This will make it necessary for the government to undertake still more deficit financing to keep up the level of income and employment. Still heavier taxation will then be necessary to pay the interest on the growing debt—until the burden of taxation is so crushing that private investment becomes unprofitable, and the private enterprise economy collapses. Private firms and corporations will all be bankrupted by the taxes, and the government will have to take over all industry.

This argument is not new. The identical calamities, although they are now receiving much more attention than usual, were promised when the first income tax law of one penny in the pound was proposed. All this only makes it more important to evaluate the significance of the argument.

III.

There are four major errors in the argument against deficit spending, four reasons why its apparent conclusiveness is only illusory.

In the first place, the same high income tax that reduces the return on the investment is deductible for the loss that is incurred if the investment turns out a failure. As a result of this the *net* return on the risk of loss is unaffected by the income tax rate, no matter how high that may be. Consider an investor in the $50,000-a-year income class who has accumulated $10,000 to invest. At 6 percent this would yield $600, but after paying income tax on this addition to his income at 60 cents in the dollar he would have only $240 left. It is argued, therefore, that he would not invest because this is insufficient compensation for the risk of losing $10,000. This argument forgets that if the $10,000 is all lost, the net loss to the investor, after he has deducted his income

tax allowance, will be only $4,000, and the rate of return on the amount he actually risks is still exactly 6 percent; $240 is 6 percent of $4,000. The effect of the income tax is to make the rich man act as a kind of agent working for society on commission. He receives only a part of the return on the investment, but he loses only a part of the money that is invested. Any investment that was worth undertaking in the absence of the income tax is still worth undertaking.

Of course, this correction of the argument is strictly true only where 100 percent of the loss is deductible from taxable income, where relief from taxation occurs at the same rate as the tax on returns. There is a good case against certain limitations on permissible deduction from the income tax base for losses incurred, but that is another story. Something of the argument remains, too, if the loss would put the taxpayer into a lower income tax bracket, where the rebate (and the tax) is at a lower rate. There would then be some reduction in the net return as compared with the potential net loss. But this would apply only to such investments as are large enough to threaten to impoverish the investor if they fail. It was for the express purpose of dealing with this problem that the corporation was devised, making it possible for many individuals to combine and undertake risky enterprises without any one person having to risk all his fortune on one venture. But quite apart from corporate investment, this problem would be met almost entirely if the maximum rate of income tax were reached at a relatively low level, say at $25,000 a year (low, that is, from the point of view of the rich men who are the supposed source of risk capital). Even if all income in excess of $25,000 were taxed at 90 percent there would be no discouragement in the investment of any part of income over this level. True, the net return, after payment of tax, would be only one-tenth of the nominal interest payments, but the amount risked by the investors would also be only ten percent of the actual capital invested, and therefore the net return on the capital actually risked by the investor would be unaffected.

In the second place, this argument against deficit spending in time of depression would be indefensible even if the harm done by debt were as great as has been suggested. It must be remembered that spending by the government increases the *real* national income of goods and services by several times the amount spent by the government, and that the burden is measured not by the amount of the interest payments but only by the inconveniences involved in the process of transferring the money from the taxpayers to the bondholders. Therefore objecting to deficit spending is like arguing that if you are offered a job when out of work on the condition that you promise to pay your wife interest on a part of the money earned (or that your wife pay it to you) it would be wiser to continue to be unemployed, because in time you will be owing your wife a great deal of money (or she will be owing it to you), and this might cause matrimonial difficulties in the future. Even if the interest payments were really lost to society, instead of being merely transferred within the society, they would come to much less than the loss through permitting unemployment to continue. That loss would be several times as great as the *capital* on which these interest payments have to be made.

In the third place, there is no good reason for supposing that the government would have to raise all the interest on the national debt by current taxes. We have seen that Functional Finance permits taxation only when the *direct* effect of the tax is in the social interest, as when it prevents excessive spending or excessive investment which would bring about inflation. If taxes imposed to prevent inflation do not result in sufficient proceeds, the interest on the debt can be met by borrowing or

printing the money. There is no risk of inflation from this, because if there were such a risk a greater amount would have to be collected in taxes.

This means that the absolute size of the national debt does not matter at all, and that however large the interest payments that have to be made, these do not constitute any burden upon society as a whole. A completely fantastic exaggeration may illustrate the point. Suppose the national debt reaches the stupendous total of ten thousand billion dollars (that is, ten trillion, $10,000,000,000,000), so that the interest on it is 300 billion a year. Suppose the real national income of goods and services which can be produced by the economy when fully employed is 150 billion. The interest alone, therefore, comes to twice the real national income. There is no doubt that a debt of this size would be called "unreasonable." But even in this fantastic case the payment of the interest constitutes no burden on society. Although the real income is only 150 billion dollars the money income is 450 billion—150 billion in income from the production of goods and services and 300 billion in income from ownership of the government bonds which constitute the national debt. Of this money income of 450 billion, 300 billion has to be collected in taxes by the government for interest payments (if 10 trillion is the legal debt limit), but after payment of these taxes there remains 150 billion dollars in the hands of the taxpayers, and this is enough to pay for all the goods and services that the economy can produce. Indeed it would do the public no good to have any more money left after tax payments, because if it spent more than 150 billion dollars it would merely be raising the prices of the goods bought. It would not be able to obtain more goods to consume than the country is able to produce.

Of course this illustration must not be taken to imply that a debt of this size is at all likely to come about as a result of the application of Functional Finance. As will be shown below, there is a natural tendency for the national debt to stop growing long before it comes anywhere near the astronomical figures that we have been playing with.

The unfounded assumption that current interest on the debt must be collected in taxes springs from the idea that the debt must be kept in a "reasonable" or "manageable" ratio to income (whatever that may be). If this restriction is accepted, *borrowing* to pay the interest is eliminated as soon as the limit of "reasonableness" is reached, and if we further rule out, as an indecent thought, the possibility of *printing* the money, there remains only the possibility of raising the interest payments by taxes. Fortunately there is no need to assume these limitations so long as Functional Finance is on guard against inflation, for it is the fear of inflation which is the only rational basis for suspicion of the printing of money.

Finally, there is no reason for assuming that, as a result of the continued application of Functional Finance to maintain full employment, the government must always be borrowing more money and increasing the national debt. There are a number of reasons for this.

First, full employment *can* be maintained by printing the money needed for it, and this does not increase the debt at all. It is probably advisable, however, to allow debt and money to increase together in a certain balance, as long as one or the other has to increase.

Second, since one of the greatest deterrents to private investment is the fear that the depression will come before the investment has paid for itself, the guarantee of permanent full employment will make private investment much more attractive, once investors have got over their suspicions of the new procedure. The greater private investment will diminish the need for deficit spending.

Third, as the national debt increases, and with it the sum of private wealth, there will be an increasingly yield from taxes on higher incomes and inheritances, even if the tax rates are unchanged. These higher tax payments do not represent reductions of spending by the taxpayers. Therefore the government does not have to use these proceeds to maintain the requisite rate of spending, and it can devote them to paying the interest on the national debt.

Fourth, as the national debt increases it acts as a self-equilibrating force, gradually diminishing the further need for its growth and finally reaching an equilibrium level where its tendency to grow comes completely to an end. The greater the national debt the greater is the quantity of private wealth. The reason for this is simply that for every dollar of debt owed by the government there is a private creditor who owns the government obligations (possibly through a corporation in which he has shares), and who regards these obligations as part of his private fortune. The greater the private fortunes the less is the incentive to add to them by saving out of current income. As current saving is thus discouraged by the great accumulation of past savings, spending out of current income increases (since spending is the only alternative to saving income). This increase in private spending makes it less necessary for the government to undertake deficit financing to keep total spending at the level which provides full employment. When the government debt has become so great that private spending is enough to provide the total spending needed for full employment, there is no need for any deficit financing by the government, the budget is balanced and the national debt automatically stops growing. The size of this equilibrium level of debt depends on many things. It can only be guessed at, and in the very roughest manner. My guess is that it is between 100 and 300

billion dollars. Since the level is a result
and not a principle of Functional Finance
the latitude of such a guess does not matter; it is not needed for the application of
the laws of Functional Finance.

Fifth, if for any reason the government
does not wish to see private property grow
too much (whether in the form of government bonds or otherwise) it can check this
by taxing the rich instead of borrowing
from them, in its program of financing
government spending to maintain full employment. The rich will not reduce their
spending significantly, and thus the effects
on the economy, apart from the smaller
debt, will be the same as if the money had
been borrowed from them. By this means
the debt can be reduced to any desired
level and kept there.

The answers to the argument against
deficit spending may thus be summarized
as follows:

The national debt does not have to keep on
   increasing;
Even if the national debt does grow, the
   interest on it does not have to be raised out
   of current taxes;
Even if the interest on the debt is raised out
   of current taxes, these taxes constitute
   only the interest on only a fraction of the
   benefit enjoyed from the government
   spending, and are not lost to the nation
   but are merely transferred from taxpayers
   to bondholders;
High income taxes need not discourage investment, because appropriate deductions for
   losses can diminish the capital actually
   risked by the investor in the same proportion as his net income from the investment
   is reduced.

IV.

If the propositions of Functional Finance
were put forward without fear of appearing
too logical, criticisms like those discussed
above would not be as popular as they

now are, and it would not be necessary to
defend Functional Finance from its friends.
An especially embarrassing task arises
from the claim that Functional Finance
(or deficit financing, as it is frequently but
unsatisfactorily called) is primarily a defense of private enterprise. In the attempt
to gain popularity for Functional Finance,
it has been given other names and declared
to be essentially directed toward saving
private enterprise. I myself have sinned
similarly in previous writings in identifying
it with democracy,[4] thus joining the army
of salesmen who wrap up their wares in the
flag and tie anything they have to sell to
victory or morale.

Functional Finance is not especially related to democracy or to private enterprise.
It is applicable to a communist society
just as well as to a fascist society or a
democratic society. It is applicable to any
society in which money is used as an important element in the economic mechanism. It consists of the simple principle
of giving up our preconceptions of what is
proper or sound or traditional, of what "is
done," and instead considering the *functions* performed in the economy by government taxing and spending and borrowing
and lending. It means using these instruments simply as instruments, and not as
magic charms that will cause mysterious
hurt if they are manipulated by the wrong
people or without due reverence for tradition. Like any other mechanism, Functional Finance will work no matter who
pulls the levers. Its relationship to democracy and free enterprise consists simply in
the fact that if the people who believe in
these things will not use Functional
Finance, they will stand no chance in the
long run against others who will.

[4] In "Total Democracy and Full Employment,"
Social Change (May 1941).

26

Inflationary Depression and the Regulation of Administered Prices

ABBA P. LERNER

Inflation, by which I mean a condition of rising prices, may be the result of action either by buyers or by sellers. We are much more familiar with inflation caused by buyers trying to buy more goods than are available, that is, spending more money than can buy (at current prices) the available supply of goods. When this happens, prices are bid up to the level at which the buyers are no longer trying to buy more than is available. The market is then cleared with every buyer able to buy as much as he wants to buy. If, as a result of this development, there arises a still further increase in the amount of money spent by the buyers, perhaps because they have received more money as sellers of something

* *

From *The Relationship of Prices to Economic Stability and Growth. Compendium of Papers Submitted by Panelists Appearing before the Joint Economic Committee*, 85th Congress, 2d Session (Washington: U.S. Government Printing Office, 1958), pp. 257–268. Reprinted by permission of the author.
Abba P. Lerner teaches at the University of California, Berkeley; he was formerly at the Johns Hopkins University and Roosevelt University.

else, we have a continuing inflationary process.

Such a process cannot go very far unless there is an increase in the supply of money. Otherwise, with the rising prices, the public finds that the stock of money is too small for the greater volume of transactions, in monetary terms, that is going on. Many people then reduce their buying or increase their selling (so as to hold on to or to get hold of more money) and this tends to stop the inflationary process. But if the monetary authorities increase the supply of money, or permit the supply of money to be increased, then the inflationary process can continue.

Because we are much more familiar with this particular type of inflation, we have tended to assume that it is the only kind. This has led to the habit of considering an increase in the supply of money not as merely one of the necessary conditions for an inflationary process to be able to continue, but as the cause of the inflation, which it need not be. Our overoccupation with this particular type of inflation has also led many economists, including my-self, to use the word "inflation" not only to stand for the condition of rising prices, but also to stand for "excess demand," the attempt to buy more goods than are avail-able at the current prices, which is the cause of this type of inflation.

This extension of the meaning of the word inflation would be quite harmless if it were true, as it apparently was assumed to be true, that rising prices could come about only as a result of excess demand by buyers. This usage furthermore had the advantage of permitting the condemnatory word inflation to be used for attacking a condition in which prices were prevented from rising, as by price controls, when the economy would be better served if they were permitted to rise. Such price control under conditions of excess demand could then be called a kind of inflation—repressed inflation—which can be even more harmful to the economy, and to society in general, than an open inflation with rising prices. So it seemed like a good idea to identify inflation with a condition of excess demand, whether the resulting tendency for prices to rise was permitted to express itself or not. Repressed inflation could therefore be called a certain kind of inflation and given a blacker name, and this seemed harmless even though it was something like calling an anti-Communist a certain kind of Communist.

But excess demand by buyers is not the only possible cause of a condition of rising prices. Prices may rise not because of the pressure of buyers who are finding it diffi-cult to buy all they want to buy at the current prices. Prices may rise because of pressures by sellers who insist on raising their prices even though they may find it not especially easy to sell. We would then have not a buyer-induced inflation but a seller-induced inflation. To distinguish this from the kind of inflation we have dis-cussed above, and which we may call a

buyers' inflation (or demand inflation), we may call this kind of inflation a sellers' inflation.

If sellers' inflation is possible as well as buyers' inflation, it is not such a good idea to use the word "inflation" to stand for excess demand. That use of language tends to suggest that if there is no "inflation" in the sense of excess demand, there can be no inflation in the sense of rising prices. It leaves us with no way of describing the kind of situation in which we find ourselves when prices are rising because of upward pressure by sellers, and the authorities, in endeavoring to stop the rise in prices, have taken steps which have been very effective in removing excess demand, but which have not removed the upward pressure on prices from the sellers' side. Indeed such measures as budgetary restraint and tight money can be so effective in removing ex-cess demand that they can overdo this and remove some demand that is not in excess. They would bring about a condition of de-ficient demand, or not enough demand to enable us to make full use of our productive potential. Nevertheless, prices may keep on rising. The net result would be both inflation and depression at the same time—prices rising—even though we are not fully utilizing our available labor force and pro-ductive potential.

This appears paradoxical only because of our habit of using 1 word, "inflation," to represent 2 different things, rising prices and excess demand, that do not necessarily have to go together in the actual world.

The distinction between buyers' inflation and sellers' inflation is related to but is not exactly the same as the distinction between demand inflation and cost inflation. While demand inflation seems to be synonymous with buyers' inflation, cost inflation sug-gests that there is a difference between cost, on the one hand, and profits, on the other, in their operation on price. This is especially true when the phrases "cost-push inflation" or "wage-cost inflation" are used as synonymous with "cost inflation." The impression is given that the whole of the blame falls on labor or on trade unions. When trade unions raise wages by more than can be absorbed by increasing productivity, costs rise. The employer then seems to be completely innocent of "profit inflation" in passing on the increase in costs as long as he does not increase his rate of markup, i.e., as long as he does not increase the prices he charges for the product in a greater proportion than his costs have increased.

There is, however, no essential asymmetry between the wage element and the profit element in the price asked for the product. A sellers' inflation could just as well be started by an increase not in the wage asked, but in the percentage of markup of price above cost. Prices would rise and wages would then be raised by workers in attempts to maintain (or restore) their original buying power. Business would then "innocently" raise their prices again only in proportion to the increase in their costs, and we would have the inflation upon us as well as boring discussions about who started it first and the famous chicken and egg.

The "who started it first" debate is a complete waste of time because there is no original situation in which there was a "just" or "normal" distribution of the product between wages and profits. Any increase can be seen either as the disturbance which bears the full responsibility for the inflation, or as nothing but the correction of an inequity perpetrated in previous history—all depending on the point of view. The term "sellers' inflation," by treating wages and profits on exactly the same footing, avoids the fruitless game of mutual recrimination. Sellers' inflation takes place whenever wage earners and profit takers together attempt to get shares that amount to more than 100 percent of the selling price. When the sum of what they try to get comes to more than 100 percent of the selling price it is futile to ask whether this is because the wages demanded are too high or whether it is because the profits insisted on are too great. No matter where justice may lie between the 2 claims, the only significant thing for our problem is that the sum of the claims is more than 100 percent. That is what causes the inflation.

It is, of course, impossible for the two parties to succeed in getting more than 100 percent of the proceeds between them, but it is precisely on an impossibility such as this that any continuing process depends. Buyers' inflation is similarly built on an attempt to reach the impossible. In that case, it is the attempt of buyers to buy more than 100 percent of the goods than can be made available. Their attempt bids up prices, but since that does not (and cannot) succeed in enabling them to obtain more than 100 percent of the goods that there are available to be got, they continue the attempt and we have the continuing process of buyers' inflation. In our case, the impossibility that generates the process is the attempt of wage earners and profit takers between them to get more than 100 percent of the money proceeds from the sale of the product. Each increases the part he tries to take, by increasing wages or by increasing prices. Since they cannot succeed, they keep on raising wages and prices and so we have the continuing process of sellers' inflation.

There is great resistance to recognizing the possibility of sellers' inflation. Sometimes, this takes the form of saying that there must have been some excess buyers' demand or prices could not have risen. This begs the whole question. Since it assumes, without apparently thinking it necessary to provide any support for the assumption, that the only possible cause of rising prices is excess buyers' demand, the argument assumes what it wants to prove.

A more sophisticated version of this argument points out that if output shrinks by less than the increase in prices, and this is usually the case during a sellers' inflation, there must have been an increase in the total amount spent in buying the output. The arithmetically irrefutable increase in expenditure is then triumphantly exhibited as the excess buyers' demand that is responsible for the inflation. Expenditure is the same thing as buyers' demand, but an increase in expenditure is not the same thing as excess buyers' demand. An increase is not the same thing as an excess. An excess of demand by buyers induces the price increases—it is the cause of the price increases. An increase in expenditure could be induced by—it could be the result of the increases in prices brought about by the pressure of sellers. If there is no increase in expenditure the number of units of goods bought must fall in the same proportion as the price per unit is raised by the sellers. A 10 percent increase in prices would thus result in a fall in output of about 10 percent. This involves depression and unemployment that the authorities naturally seek to remedy by monetary and fiscal measures. Such remedies all involve increases in money expenditure, so that even if only a part of the unemployment is corrected (and this is usually the case because of the authorities' reluctance to undertake inflationary measures when prices are rising), we would observe an increase in total expenditure. Buyers' demand, however, instead of being excessive, could still be deficient, i.e., it could still be insufficient to enable the potential output of the economy to be sold (at the prices demanded by the sellers). An observed increase in total expenditure is therefore no proof that the price rise is due to excess buyers' demand. The increase in expenditure could have been induced by attempts by the authorities to keep down unemployment induced by price increases imposed by the sellers. In a sellers' inflation, an increase in expenditure is perfectly compatible with deficient buyers' demand.

A still more sophisticated argument along the same lines goes on to claim that even if prices are being raised by the insistence of sellers rather than by the pressure of buyers, the orthodox measures of reducing total demand would still check the inflation. By reducing total expenditure, or perhaps by merely refusing to permit the increase in total expenditure needed to accommodate the increased prices, the authorities would bring about depression and unemployment. This would stop the sellers from increasing prices. The question then resolves itself into how much unemployment would be necessary to stop the sellers' inflation, and whether it is morally desirable or politically possible for the authorities to induce or permit unemployment of the required volume and duration.

It has been suggested that even if the authorities are not really prepared to bring about the degree of depression necessary to negate the pressure of sellers' inflation, they could still do the trick by solemnly announcing a policy of refusing to provide the increase in expenditure called for by a continuing sellers' inflation. The threatened unemployment would then sober the sellers into calling off their inflationary wage and price increases.

It seems pretty certain first that such declarations would not be believed and that the bluff would quickly be called. But, even if it were believed as regards the economy as a whole, that would not prevent any specific wages or prices from being raised while the local conditions still permitted this. It would perhaps even aggravate the wage and price increases as each tried to get his increase quickly, while the local going was still good.

All this brings us to the perhaps only too obvious conclusion that sellers' inflation cannot be cured or prevented by measures directed against excess demand by buyers. It can be successfully treated only by attacking the pressure on prices by sellers.[1]

Before we can consider just how one can attack the pressure on prices by sellers, it would be desirable to get a perspective on the whole problem by a quick look at the general theory of inflation and deflation. A somewhat schematic formulation of the development of thought on this subject shows four theoretical models of the operation of the economy.

Model A assumes perfectly flexible prices and wages, so that any excess of buyers' demands makes prices and wages rise, and any deficiency of buyers' demand (through the unemployment that results) makes prices and wages fall, until price stability and full employment are restored. Both monetary policy and fiscal policy are unimportant, or even unnecessary. As long as the volume of money is kept fairly stable

[1] In an outstanding article which concentrates on showing the inadequacy and superficiality of proposals to prevent inflation by monetary and fiscal policies and declarations, Prof. Sumner H. Slichter seems to suggest that the distinction between buyers' inflation and sellers' inflation is a futile fantasy. Thus he says (using a somewhat different terminology), "Much time has been wasted in recent years in discussing whether inflation is demand inspired or cost inspired. (Some 70 or 80 years ago, the Austrian theory of value produced a similar debate as to whether demand or cost determines the value; the argument ended suddenly when it dawned on the economists that each blade in a pair of scissors cuts)." ("On the Side of Inflation," *Harvard Business Review*, September/October 1957, p. 32.)

However, the inapplicability of this analogy jumps to the eye in his very next sentence which shows that it can make sense to distinguish between the blades, since he goes on to say, "Thus changes in the price level may originate either with shifts in the demand schedules or with shifts in the supply schedules," and in another article, Professor Slichter definitely alines himself with the sellers' inflation blade in declaring that: "There is no evidence that prices are rising ahead of costs and are pulling costs up. The evidence is all the other way: that prices are being sluggishly adjusted to slowly rising costs." ("Government Spending Can Reduce Taxes," *Harvard Business Review*, July/August 1957, p. 106.)

by some automatic device such as the gold standard, the price level will automatically adjust itself so as to yield full employment with price stability and without inflation.

Model B embodies the recognition that we do not have the degree of price flexibility in the downward direction to make complete laissez faire a satisfactory monetary and fiscal policy. Unemployment (caused by deficient buyers' demand) does not reduce the wage and price level quickly enough to the level needed to restore full employment. The process is rather complex. To achieve the task, unemployment must reduce the wage level, and thereby the price level, to the degree necessary to increase the value of the existing stock of money (as each dollar becomes more valuable) to the extent necessary to increase expenditure in real terms (as each dollar spent constitutes more real purchasing power) to the volume necessary to give a satisfactory level of employment. This process can last for years, during which time prices and wages are falling as different resistances to the reductions are gradually overcome. Meanwhile, there continues an expectation of price and wage reductions still to come. This expectation induces investors as well as consumers to postpone their expenditures as long as prices are still falling, so that buyers' demand is reduced still further and the depression can get very much worse before it gets better.

The recognition of the nature of such a process leads to the abandonment of laissez faire in monetary and fiscal policy. Instead of waiting for the price level to fall until it has adjusted itself to the volume of money expenditure, a policy is developed of adjusting the volume of money expenditure to the existing price level, so as to reach and maintain a satisfactory level of employment at the current prices.

This switch from laissez faire to an active monetary and fiscal policy is also applied in the opposite direction to deal with excess buyers' demand. Although there is not the same resistance to price and wage increases as there is to price and wage decreases, the necessary adjustment to excess buyers' demand by rising prices still takes time. It is no instantaneous adjustment (if only because of the existence of long-term contracts, and because of attempts to stop profiteering by preventing the necessary price increases) and so it causes disturbances that are unjust and reduce the efficiency of the economy. The policy is therefore applied in both directions, providing for increasing the volume of money expenditure whenever necessary to prevent or correct an insufficiency of buyers' demand; and for decreasing the volume of money expenditure whenever that is necessary to prevent or correct an excess of buyers' demand.

The volume of expenditure may be adjusted either by working on the stock of money (by monetary policy) or by working on the velocity of circulation of money (by fiscal policy), or by some combination of the two.

Model B, which is, of course, the Keynesian general theory of employment policy, differs from model A primarily in incorporating a policy of increasing or decreasing demand, if it should become too little or too great. (It has a steering wheel to keep the car on the road.) Because of this difference, a secondary distinction arises. With policy coming into the picture, it becomes important which of two instruments of policy is to be used, monetary policy or fiscal policy. Model B makes use of both instruments. (The car can use either kerosene or gasoline.)

Model C is not really a new model. It rather consists of a series of publicity releases of model B dolled up to emphasize one or another of its qualities as if this were a new invention that made model B obsolete. One very crude pamphlet of this series emphasizes the ability of model C to cut down on demand, if it becomes excessive or threatens to become excessive,

seeming to imply that model B was a depression model, which could work only in the direction of increasing demand, if it became deficient or threatened to become deficient. (Model C has a steering wheel that can be turned to the right.)

A more refined variant of model C, let us call it model C*, is concerned with the relative effectiveness of monetary policy and of fiscal policy in different circumstances. An economy may be so saturated with money so that further increases in the stock of money would not be effective in increasing expenditure, and reductions in the stock would have no significant effect in reducing total expenditure. (This is sometimes expressed, though not explained, by saying that changes in the money supply would be offset by opposing changes in the velocity of circulation.) Monetary policy is then useless and expenditure can be increased or decreased only by fiscal policy—by the Government increasing or decreasing its own expenditure, e.g. on public works, or permitting others to spend more by reducing taxes or forcing them to spend less by increasing taxes.

It is then suggested that model B works only in this case which is called the Keynesian case. It should more properly be called Keynesian special case (of the Keynesian general theory) when it is appropriate to concentrate entirely on fiscal measures to increase or decrease expenditure on consumption and investment. (Only gasoline can be used.)

In this kind of situation, even extreme price flexibility is unable to restore or maintain the desired level of real demand, because it operates, after all, as nothing but a roundabout way of increasing or decreasing the real volume of money in terms of buying power. It is a kind of automatic monetary policy which is useless for the same reasons as other monetary policy is useless, when the economy is so saturated with money that changing the quantity has no appreciable effect.

When the economy is at the other extreme from being saturated with money, and money is very tight, the situation is naturally reversed. Fiscal measures for increasing expenditure on consumption or investment are ineffective, because an increase in expenditure anywhere in the economy, say in Government expenditure on public works, results in an increase in demand for money to hold in connection with the increased volume of transactions. In the very tight money situation, this raises the rate of interest, or in some other way reduces expenditure somewhere else. Similarly, a decrease in expenditure anywhere releases holdings of money which permit an increase of expenditure somewhere else. Fiscal policy then is helpless, and what is called for is monetary policy to increase or decrease the money supply. (Only kerosene can be used.) This case is then called the Classical case, as if it were one in which the Keynesian theory does not apply and where model B should be replaced by model C* (which can burn kerosene). This case should more properly be called the Classical special case (of the Keynesian general theory). The Keynesian theory (model B) covers both situations in which fiscal policy is strategic (when model B uses gasoline), and situations in which monetary policy is strategic (when model B uses kerosene), as well as the more normal situations when both policies are effective (when model B can make use of both fuels, mixing the proportions to suit the terrain).

Model D is a genuinely different model, in which unemployment not only fails to make prices and wages fall quickly enough to serve as a cure for the unemployment, but is even unable to prevent prices and wages from continuing to rise. When we have strong trade unions with the power to raise wages, strong corporations with the power to set prices administratively, and a general atmosphere in which it is considered normal, natural and only fair for wages to

be increased regularly, and by amounts greater than the average increase in productivity or in the share of the product that labor can obtain, prices increase, and the economy is subject to sellers' inflation. It is now no longer a question of whether fiscal policy or monetary policy is more effective in regulating the volume of buyers' demand or expenditure, since the inflation is caused not by excess buyers' demand, but by the existence of powerful institutions and mores that enable sellers to insist on and obtain continually higher prices. The widespread and generous feeling that workers are entitled to the increases in wages that they get is made much easier by a recognition that any raise need not be taken out of profits, since it is possible, as well as proper, to "pass it along" to the ultimate purchaser in higher prices. Indeed, it is usually considered only right that profits, in dollars, should be increased so as to protect real profits from the declining value of the dollar.

We have already mentioned the argument that a really firm refusal on the part of the monetary authorities to prevent the volume of money from increasing, no matter what happened, would bring the sellers to their senses. Realizing, or discovering, that they will not be able to sell so much if they raise their prices, they will refrain from raising prices, and they will not grant, or ask for, wage increases that raise costs by more than can be squeezed out of profits.

There are several reasons why this is not practical. In the first place, the policy of firmly or obstinately holding the money supply constant does not prevent excess buyers' demand from coming about. It does not even prevent an increase in total expenditure. This is because the policy of holding the money supply constant is essentially a kind of monetary policy, and we may be in the Keynesian special case where monetary policy is not effective. That we are at the present time in such a situation is suggested by the fact that, while the supply of money has been held fairly stable in recent years, the volume of expenditure has continually increased. (Another way of expressing this, which is more common perhaps because it sounds like an explanation, is to say that the velocity of circulation has increased and that this has frustrated the restrictive monetary policy.)

There is, of course, a limit to the degree to which expenditure can increase without an accompanying increase in the money stock, and if the inflation were a buyers' inflation it would come to an end when this limit was reached (i.e., when the velocity of circulation could not increase any more). But where the inflation is a sellers' inflation, it does not stop at that point. After the increase in prices has absorbed all the increase in expenditure that is compatible with a constant money stock (i.e., that can be attributed to an increase in the velocity of circulation) it continues to increase. The increase in prices goes on further until it has reduced real expenditure and employment sufficiently to overcome the institutional forces that enable sellers to demand higher and higher prices. The question is how strong are these institutions? or, in other words, how severe a state of depression and unemployment would have to be maintained in order to destroy these institutions or to induce sellers not to use their power to raise prices; and how able and willing the authorities would be to bring about and maintain this degree of depression and unemployment?

The continuing increase in wages and prices in the present depression would be some indication that it would require quite a severe and prolonged depression to change people's notions of what is the proper development of wage rates (and of the corresponding prices, since the right of wages to increase goes together with the right of profits at least not to fall). It would take perhaps an even more severe

level of unemployment to destroy the power of labor to force the wage increases on more reluctant employers who grant wage increases only when they feel they are forced to—i.e., that they would lose more from the strikes and other weapons of the trade unions than they would lose by agreeing to the higher wages (and passing them on).

At the same time, a policy of full employment seems to have won a firm place in the country's economic policy (even though its application may be rather shaky), not only because of the general acceptance of the desirability of prosperity, for human as well as for international political reasons, but because neither political party can afford the blame for even a mild depression. With such a setup, there is no need to worry whether the cure is worse than the disease—whether the depression would be more harmful than the inflation that it would prevent. This cure is not one that any government would carry out or even seriously attempt to carry out.

None of the problems of sellers' inflation or of inflationary depression could arise in a perfectly competitive economy, because in a perfectly competitive economy, we cannot have the institutions and mores that give sellers the power to push prices up. In a perfectly competitive economy, all that is needed for stability of the price level is a monetary and fiscal policy to keep buyers' demand from becoming either excessive or deficient. No one holds back any product from the market—or can establish a price which results in some of the potential product or the available labor not being taken off the market, so that unless there is excess buyers' demand, prices cannot rise, and if there is a deficient buyers' demand, prices must fall. Unless there is full utilization of resources, we cannot have inflation, and if there is a depression (or recession), we will have deflation (i.e., falling prices). In a perfectly competitive economy, we cannot have inflation and depression at the same time.

But where prices are administered by decrees of large firms, and wages are administered by joint decrees of powerful unions, together with powerful employers or employer groups, the situation is different. Sellers' inflation is a byproduct of the process; and, together with sellers' inflation, we can also have depression—indeed we will have depression with our sellers' inflation, just to the degree that the authorities try to cure the inflation by reducing ("excess") demand.

In an economy where there are both administered and competitive sectors, the phenomenon of sellers' inflation can spill over from the administered to the competitive part. It can even happen that the contagion of sellers' inflation in the competitive sector is more pronounced than in the administered sector. There is then a tendency to assume that the sellers' inflation thesis has thereby been disproved. Actually, this does not prove anything either way in the debate that can rage as to whether the inflation is a sellers' inflation or a buyers' inflation.

The contagion can be explained as follows. Prices and wages being raised in the administered sector but not in the competitive sector, there will be a switch in demand from the products of the administered sector to the products of the competitive sector. There is then a deficiency of demand in the administered sector and an excess of demand in the competitive sector. With factors of production immobile, there is unemployment in the administered sector, but there it does not cause either prices or wages to fall so that the unemployment persists. Attempts to reduce total spending, so as to check the rise in the overall price level, would increase still further the unemployment in the administered sector (while removing some,

or all, of the excess demand in the competitive sector). Pressure is then put on the Government to alleviate the depression; and, in doing so, it must create enough demand to maintain the higher price level in both sectors.

As the economy gets used to such a process, in which wages and prices are rising all the time, an increase in strategic or key prices or wage rates in the administered sector come to be recognized all over the economy as presaging a general rise in prices. The competitive sector then does not wait for the excess demand to appear. Its workers demand higher wages, its employers expect to be able to get the higher prices out of which to be able to pay the higher wages, and they grant the increases and raise the prices. They do not have to go into the elaborate calculations of what output and price maximize profit. They have the businessman's rough rule of thumb of a more or less traditional markup on their cost. This brings them straight away to the position that would be reached after the excess demand has materialized and has been validated and adjusted by the monetary policy undertaken by the authorities to cure or prevent the unemployment threatened by the increase in wages and prices in the administered sector.

The economist is tempted to draw diagrams showing the point of maximum profits of a firm, competitive or monopolist, and to demonstrate, in classical vein, that an increase in wages will move that point to the left, reducing the optimum output of the firm and causing the firm to restrict output and to raise the price by less than the increase in cost. This should cause unemployment which, in the competitive sector, would restore the previous price and wage levels. The sellers' inflation has disappeared into thin air.

The answer to this, in classical vein, is that the demand will not remain the same, because the phenomenon is not happening only to an individual firm (in which case it would be proper to assume the conditions of demand to be unchanged), but that the monetary and fiscal authorities, in providing additional overall demand to cure or prevent the unemployment in the administered sector, will raise every demand curve so that the firm will be able to sell as much as before and provide the same employment as before, even though the price is sufficiently higher to enable the higher wage to be paid. Profits, or the gap between cost and price, will also be higher, of course, although in real terms, allowing for the fall in the value of the dollar, everything will be just the same as in the beginning.

The answer in the businessman's language is that he has to increase his price in proportion to the increase in costs, in applying his regular markup; and his experience is that since this is happening to everybody, including his competitors, and employment in the country is more or less being maintained, he will be able to pass it on to the consumer.

Although the infection starts with the administered sector of the economy, there is no reason why the epidemic should not hit the competitive (and nonadministered monopolistic) sectors of the economy sometimes more severely and sometimes less severely than it hits the administered sector. This is why the observation that prices rise more or rise less in the unadministered sector than in the administered sector proves nothing at all either way as to whether the inflation is a buyers' inflation or a sellers' inflation. But only a sellers' inflation is compatible with a depression.

The inflation and the inflationary depression that result from administered wages and prices have important similarities to, and are no less socially harmful than, the monopolistic exploitation that would result from the administration of excessive prices by public utilities. We have gone a long way toward eliminating the latter evil by the regulation of prices that may be set by public utilities for the services they supply. The same kind of device can be used to eliminate the former evil. Just as the public utility prices can be and are being regulated so as to prevent monopolistic exploitation, so administered prices and wages can and should be regulated, so as to prevent sellers' inflation and the depression it may bring with it.

The regulation of administered prices and wages so as to prevent sellers' inflation would have to follow somewhat different lines. It would not be directly concerned as to whether there is more than or less than a fair rate of return on investments. That would be left to the strong competitive forces that still prevail in our economy. Nor would any other regulations whatsoever be involved other than price regulation. The function of the regulation here proposed would be only to prevent restrictive prices or wages from being administered. A restrictive price is one that results in the demand for a product falling below capacity output. A restrictive wage is one that results in less than full employment in the specific labor market to which it applies. With a monetary and fiscal policy concentrating on the maintenance of adequate buyers' demand for full employment at a constant price level, while preventing buyers' inflation, it would be possible for wages per hour to rise on the average at the same rate as productivity per hour, with aggregate profits rising too at the same pace as aggregate wages and aggregate output (except that increases in the degree of competition, which might be induced, could reduce the share going to profits and increase the share going to labor).

The regulatory body would therefore have to follow a set of rules which would do the following things:

1. They would permit an administered price increase only when production and

sales are at capacity. Such price increases should not be withheld on account of profits being high.

2. They would enforce decreases in administered prices whenever production and sales are significantly below capacity. A price decrease should not be waived on account of profits being low, or even negative on this item in the firm's output, as long as the price more than covers current operating costs (more strictly short period marginal costs).

3. They would permit increases in administered wages in general at a rate equal to the average trend of increase in national productivity.

4. They would permit increases in administered wages greater than this wherever the labor market is tight—with say less than half the national average rate of unemployment.

5. They would permit only smaller increases in administered wages, or no increases at all, where the labor market is slack—with say more than twice the national average rate of unemployment. (The expected continuing increase in product per head makes it possible to avoid reductions in money wages although it is unavoidable, for price stability, that some prices must fall if others rise.)

This is, of course, not a fully worked out solution ready for immediate application. There remains much to be developed—such as generally acceptable criteria of capacity of different firms and industries and generally acceptable measures of slackness or tightness in particular labor markets, or measures for dealing with possible at-tempts by monopolistic industries to restrict the installation of capacity, if they are prevented from restricting the utilization of existing capacity. (This would bring out the existence of a specific monopoly situation that calls for treatment quite apart from the problem of inflation.) The intensification of competition which the regulation would enforce would also, in some instances, lead to the elimination of high cost competitors. While the public would benefit from the increased efficiency of the economy—in higher wages and lower prices—such elimination of competition would conflict with certain existing so-called antitrust policies that have become in effect anticompetition policies and need to be reconsidered.

There remain also important problems of organization and administration of the regulatory body, as well as the need for widespread and intensive public discussion to bring about the familiarity with, and the understanding of, the nature of the proposed regulation which is essential for its effective operation in a democracy. And in the course of such examination and debate, important developments, changes and improvements are to be expected. Nevertheless, the general lines indicated seem to be inevitable if sellers' inflation is to be attacked directly and if we are not to depend on irrelevant nostrums or pious exhortation because we do not dare to attack the problem at its roots.

27

Analytical Aspects
of Anti-Inflation Policy

PAUL A. SAMUELSON

and   ROBERT M. SOLOW

I.

Just as generals are said to be always fighting the wrong war, economists have been accused of fighting the wrong inflation. Thus, at the time of the 1946–48 rise in American prices, much attention was focused on the successive rounds of wage increases resulting from collective bargaining. Yet probably most economists are now agreed that this first postwar rise in prices was primarily attributable to the pull of demand that resulted from wartime accumulations of liquid assets and deferred needs.

This emphasis on demand-pull was somewhat reinforced by the Korean war run-up of prices after mid-1950. But just by the time that cost-push was becoming discredited as a theory of inflation, we ran into the rather puzzling phenomenon of the 1955–58 upward creep of prices, which seemed to take place in the last part of

✳ ✳

Reprinted from *The American Economic Review*, vol. 50 (May 1960), pp. 177–194, by permission of the publisher and authors.

Paul A. Samuelson and Robert M. Solow teach at the Massachusetts Institute of Technology.

the period despite growing overcapacity, slack labor markets, slow real growth, and no apparent great buoyancy in over-all demand.

It is no wonder then that economists have been debating the possible causations involved in inflation: demand-pull versus cost-push; wage-push versus more general Lerner "sellers' inflation"; and the new Charles Schultze theory of "demand-shift" inflation. We propose to give a brief survey of the issues. Rather than pronounce on the terribly difficult question as to exactly which is the best model to use in explaining the recent past and predicting the likely future, we shall try to emphasize the types of evidence which can help decide between the conflicting theories. And we shall be concerned with some policy implications that arise from the different analytical hypotheses.

History of the Debate:
The Quantity Theory and Demand-Pull

The preclassical economists grew up in an environment of secularly rising prices. And even prior to Adam Smith there had grown up the belief in at least a simplified quantity theory. But it was in the neoclassical thought of Walras, Marshall, Fisher, and others that this special version of demand determination of the absolute level of money prices and costs reached its most developed form.

We can oversimplify the doctrine as follows. The real outputs, inputs, and relative prices of goods and factors can be thought of as determined by a set of competitive equations which are independent of the absolute level of prices. As in a barter system, the absolute level of all prices is indeterminate and inessential because of the "relative homogeneity" properties of these market relations. To fix the absolute scale factor, we can if we like bring in a neutral money. Such money, unlike coffee or soap, being valued only for what it will buy and not for its intrinsic utility, will be exactly doubled in demand if there is an exact doubling of all prices. Because of this important "scale homogeneity," fixing the total of such money will, when applied to our already determined real system of outputs, factors, and relative prices, fix the absolute level of all prices; and changes in the total of such money must necessarily correspond to new equilibria of absolute prices that have moved in exact proportion, with relative prices and all real magnitudes being quite unaffected.[1]

As Patinkin and others have shown, the above doctrines are rather oversimplified, for they do not fully analyze the intricacies involved in the demand for money; instead they ignore important (and predictable) changes in such proportionality

[1]But as Hume had early recognized, the periods of rising prices seemed to give rise to at least transient stimulus to the economy as active profit seekers gained an advantage at the expense of the more inert fixed-income, creditor, and wage sectors. The other side of this Hume thesis is perhaps exemplified by the fact that the post-Civil War decades of deflation were also periods of strong social unrest and of relatively weak booms and long periods of heavier-than-average depressions—as earlier National Bureau studies have suggested.

coefficients as velocity of circulation. But by World War I, this particular, narrow version of demand-pull inflation had more or less triumphed. The wartime rise in prices was usually analyzed in terms of rises in the over-all money supply. And the postwar German inflation was understood by non-German economists in similar terms.

But not all economists ever agree on anything. Just as Tooke had eclectically explained the Napoleonic rise in prices partially in terms of the war-induced increase in tax, shipping, and other costs, so did Harold G. Moulton and others choose to attribute the World War I price rises to prior rises in cost of production. And it is not without significance that the great neoclassical Wicksell expressed in the last years of his life some misgivings over the usual version of wartime price movements, placing great emphasis on movements in money's velocity induced by wartime shortages of goods.

Of course, the neoclassical writers would not have denied the necessary equality of competitive costs and prices. But they would have regarded it as superficial to take the level of money costs as a predetermined variable. Instead, they would argue, prices and factor costs are simultaneously determinable in interdependent competitive markets; and if the level of over-all money supply were kept sufficiently in check, then the price level could be stabilized, with any increases in real costs or any decreases in output being offset by enough backward pressure on factor prices so as to leave final money costs and prices on the average unchanged.

Many writers have gone erroneously beyond the above argument to untenable conclusions such as the following: A rise in defense expenditure matched by, say, excise taxes cannot raise the price level if the quantity of money is held constant; instead it must result in enough decrease in wage and other factor costs to offset exactly the rise in tax costs. Actually, however, such a fiscal policy change could be interpreted as a reduction in the combined public and private thriftiness; with M constant, it would tend to swell the volume of total spending, putting upward pressure on interest rates and inducing a rise in money velocity, and presumably resulting in a higher equilibrium level of prices. To roll back prices to their previous level would take, even within the framework of a strictly competitive neoclassical model, a determined reduction in previous money supply. (This illustrates the danger of going from the innocent hypothesis, that a balanced change in all prices might in the long run be consistent with no substantive changes in real relations, to an overly simple interpretation of a complicated change that is actually taking place in historical reality.)

While the above example of a tax-induced price rise that takes place within a strict neoclassical model might be termed a case of cost-push rather than demand-pull, it does not really represent quite the same phenomena that we shall meet in our later discussion of cost-push. This can perhaps be most easily seen from the remark that, if one insisted on holding prices steady, conventional demand reduction methods would work very well, within the neoclassical model, to offset such cost-push.

Demand-Pull à la Keynes

Aside from the neoclassical quantity theory, there is a second version of demand-pull associated with the theories of Keynes. Before and during the Great Depression, economists had become impressed with the institutional frictions and rigidities that made for downward inflexibilities in wages and prices and which made any such deflationary movements socially painful. Keynes's *General Theory* can, if we are willing to oversimplify, be thought of as a systematic model which uses downward inflexibility of wages and prices to convert any reduction in money spending into a real reduction in output and employment rather than a balanced reduction in all prices and factor costs. (This is overly simple for at least the following reasons: in the pessimistic, depression version of some Keynesians, a hyperdeflation of wages and prices would not have had substantive effects in restoring employment and output, because of infinite elasticity of liquidity preference and/or zero elasticity of investment demand; in the general form of the *General Theory*, and particularly after Pigou effects of the real value of money had been built in, if you could engineer a massive reduction in wages and costs, there would have been some stimulating effects on consumption, investment, and on real output; finally, a careful neoclassical theory, which took proper account of rigidities and which analyzed induced shifts of velocity in a sophisticated way, might also have emerged with similar valid conclusions.)

While the Keynesian theories can be said to differ from the neoclassical theories with respect to analysis of deflation, Keynes himself was willing to assume that attainment of full employment would make prices and wages flexible upward. In *How to Pay for the War* (1940), he developed a theory of inflation which was quite like the neoclassical theory in its emphasis upon the demand-pull of aggregate spending even though it differed from that theory in its emphasis on total spending flow rather than on the stock of money. His theory of "demanders' inflation" stemmed primarily from the fact that government plus investors plus consumers want, in real terms, among them, more than 100 percent of the wartime or boomtime available producible output. So prices have to rise to cheat the slow-to-spend of their desired shares. But the price rise closes the inflationary gap only temporarily, as the higher price level breeds higher incomes all around and the real gap reopens itself continually. And so the inflation goes on, at a rate determined by the degree of shifts to profit, the rapidity and extent of wage adjustments to the rising cost of living, and ultimately by the extent to which progressive tax receipts rise enough to close the gap. And, we may add, that firmness by the central bank in limiting the money supply might ultimately so increase credit tightness and so lower real balances as to bring consumption and investment spending into equilibrium with available civilian resources at some higher plateau of prices.

Cost-Push and Demand-Shift Theories of Inflation

In its most rigid form, the neoclassical model would require that wages fall whenever there is unemployment of labor and that prices fall whenever excess capacity exists in the sense that marginal cost of the output that firms sell is less than the prices they receive. A more eclectic model of imperfect competition in the factor and commodity markets is needed to explain the fact of price and wage rises before full employment and full capacity have been reached.

Similarly, the Keynes model, which assumes stickiness of wages even in the face of underemployment equilibrium, rests on various assumptions of imperfect competition. And when we recognize that, considerably before full employment of labor and plants has been reached, modern prices and wages seem to show a tendency to drift upward irreversibly, we see that the simple Keynesian system must be modified even further in the direction of an imperfect competition model.

Now the fact that an economic model in some degree involves imperfect competition does not necessarily imply that the concepts of competitive markets give little insight into the behavior of relative prices, resources allocations, and profitabilities.

To some degree of approximation, the competitive model may cast light on these important real magnitudes, and for this purpose we might be content to use the competitive model. But to explain possible cost-push inflation, it would seem more economical from the very beginning to recognize that imperfect competition is the essence of the problem and to drop the perfect competition assumptions.

Once this is done, we recognize the qualitative possibility of cost-push inflation. Just as wages and prices may be sticky in the face of unemployment and overcapacity, so may they be pushing upward beyond what can be explained in terms of levels and shifts in demand. But to what degree these elements are important in explaining price behavior of any period becomes an important quantitative question. It is by no means always to be expected that by observing an economy's behavior over a given period will we be able to make a very good separation of its price rise into demand and cost elements. We simply cannot perform the controlled experiments necessary to make such a separation; and Mother Nature may not have economically given us the scatter and variation needed as a substitute for controlled experiments if we are to make approximate identification of the causal forces at work.

Many economists have argued that cost-push was important in the prosperous 1951–53 period, but that its effects on average prices were masked by the drop in flexible raw material prices. But again in 1955–58, it showed itself despite the fact that in a good deal of this period there seemed little evidence of over-all high employment and excess demand. Some holders of this view attribute the push to wage boosts engineered unilaterally by strong unions. But others give as much or more weight to the co-operative action of all sellers—organized and unorganized labor, semimonopsonistic managements, oligopolistic sellers in imperfect commodity markets—who raise prices and costs in an attempt by each to maintain or raise his share of national income, and who, among themselves, by trying to get more than 100 percent of the available output, create "seller's inflation."

A variant of cost-push is provided by Charles Schultze's "demand-shift" theory of inflation. Strength of demand in certain sectors of the economy—e.g., capital goods industries in 1955–57—raises prices and wages there. But elsewhere, even though demand is not particularly strong, downward inflexibility keeps prices from falling, and market power may even engineer a price-wage movement imitative in a degree of the sectors with strong demand. The result is an upward drift in average prices—with the suggestion that monetary and fiscal policies restrictive enough to prevent an average price rise would have to be so very restrictive as to produce a considerable level of unemployment and a significant drop in production.

II.

Truths and Consequences:
The Problem of Identification

The competing (although imperfectly competing) theories of inflation appear to be genuinely different hypotheses about observable facts. In that case one ought to be able to distinguish empirically between cost and demand inflation. What are the earmarks? If I believe in cost-push, what should I expect to find in the facts that I would not expect to find were I a believer in demand-pull? The last clause is important. It will not do to point to circumstances which will accompany any inflation, however caused. A test must have what statisticians call power against the main alternative hypotheses.

Trite as these remarks may seem, they need to be made. The clichés of popular discussion fall into the trap again and

again. Although they have been trampled often enough by experts, the errors revive. We will take the time to point the finger once more. We do this because we want to go one step further and argue that this problem of identification is exceedingly difficult. What appear at first to be subtle and reliable ways of distinguishing cost-induced from demand-induced inflation turn out to be far from airtight. In fact we are driven to the belief that aggregate data, recording the *ex post* details of completed transactions, may in most circumstances be quite insufficient. It may be necessary first to disaggregate.

Common Fallacies

The simplest mistake—to be found in almost any newspaper discussion of the subject—is the belief that if money wages rise faster than productivity, we have a sure sign of cost-inflation. Of course the truth is that in the purest of excess-demand inflation wages will rise faster than productivity; the only alternative is for the full increase in the value of a fixed output to be siphoned off into profits, without this spilling over into the labor market to drive wages up still further. This error is sometimes mixed with the belief that it is possible over long periods for industries with rapid productivity increase to pay higher and increasingly higher wages than those where output per man-hour grows slowly. Such a persistent and growing differential is likely eventually to alter the skill- or quality-mix of the labor force in the different industries, which casts doubt on the original productivity comparison.

One sometimes sees statements to the effect that increases in expenditure more rapid than increases in real output necessarily spell demand inflation. It is simple arithmetic that expenditure outrunning output by itself spells only price increases and provides no evidence at all about the source or cause of the inflation. Much of the talk about "too much money chasing too few goods" is of this kind.

A more solemn version of the fallacy goes: An increase in expenditure can come about only through an increase in the stock of money or an increase in the velocity of circulation. Therefore the only possible causes of inflation are M and V and we need look no further.

Further Difficulties

It is more disconcerting to realize that even some of the empirical tests suggested in the professional literature may have little or no cutting power in distinguishing cost from demand inflation.

One thinks automatically of looking at the timing relationships. Do wage increases seem to precede price increases? Then the general rise in prices is caused by the wage-push. Do price increases seem to precede wage increases? Then more likely the inflation is of the excess-demand variety, and wages are being pulled up by a brisk demand for labor or they are responding to prior increases in the cost of living. There are at least three difficulties with this argument. The first is suggested by replacing "wage increase" by "chicken" and "price increase" by "egg." The trouble is that we have no normal initial standard from which to measure, no price level which has always existed and to which everyone has adjusted; so that a wage increase, if one occurs, must be autonomous and not a response to some prior change in the demand for labor. As an illustration of the difficulty of inference, consider average hourly earnings in the basic steel industry. They rose, relative to all manufacturing, from 1950 on, including some periods when labor markets were not tight. Did this represent an autonomous wage-push? Or was it rather a delayed adjustment to the decline in steel wages relative to all manufacturing, which took place during the war, presumably as

a consequence of the differential efficiency of wage control? And why should we take 1939 or 1941 as a standard for relative wages? And so on.

A related problem is that in a closely interdependent economy, effects can precede causes. Prices may begin to ease up because wage rates are expected to. And more important, as wage and price increases ripple through the economy, aggregation may easily distort the apparent timing relations.

But even if we could find the appearance of a controlled experiment, if after a period of stability in both we were to notice a wage increase to a new plateau followed by a price increase, what could we safely conclude? It would be immensely tempting to make the obvious diagnosis of wage-push. But consider the following hypothetical chain of events: Prices in imperfect commodity markets respond only to changes in costs. Labor markets are perfectly competitive in effect, and the money wage moves rapidly in response to shifts in the demand for labor. So any burst of excess demand, government expenditure, say, would cause an increased demand for labor; wages would be pulled up; and only then would prices of commodities rise in response to the cost increase. So the obvious diagnosis might be wrong. In between, if we were clever, we might notice a temporary narrowing of margins, and with this information we might piece together the story.

Consider another sophisticated inference. In a single market, price may rise either because the demand curve shifts to the right or because the supply curve shifts to the left in consequence of cost increases. But in the first case, output should increase; in the second case, decline. Could we not reason, then, that if prices rise, sector by sector, with outputs, demand-pull must be at work? Very likely we can, but not with certainty. In the first place, as Schultze has argued, it is possible that certain sectors face excess demand, without there being aggregate pressure; those sectors will indeed show strong price increases and increases in output (or pressure on capacity). But in a real sense, the source of inflation is the failure of other sectors, in which excess capacity develops, to decrease their prices sufficiently. And this may be a consequence of "administered pricing," rigid markups, rigid wages and all the paraphernalia of the "new" inflation.

To go deeper, the reasoning we are scrutinizing may fail because it is illegitimate, even in this industry-by-industry way, to use partial equilibrium reasoning. Suppose wages rise. We are led to expect a decrease in output. But in the modern world, all or most wages are increasing. Nor is this the first time they have done so. And in the past, general wage and price increases have not resulted in any decrease in aggregate real demand—perhaps the contrary. So that even in a single industry supply and demand curves may not be independent. The shift in costs is accompanied by, indeed may bring about, a compensating shift in the subjectively-viewed demand curve facing the industry. And so prices may rise with no decline and possibly an increase in output. If there is anything in this line of thought, it may be that one of the important causes of inflation is—inflation.

The Need for Detail

In these last few paragraphs we have been arguing against the attempt to diagnose the source of inflation from aggregates. We have also suggested that sometimes the tell-tale symptoms can be discovered if we look not at the totals but at the parts. This suggestion gains force when we recognize, as we must, that the same general price increase can easily be the consequence of different causes in different sectors. A monolithic theory may have its simplicity and style riddled by exceptions. Is there any reason, other than a desire for symmetry, for us to believe that the same reasoning must account for the above-average increase in the price of services and the above-average increase in the price of machinery since 1951 or since 1949? Public utility prices undoubtedly were held down during the war, by the regulatory process; and services ride along on income-elastic demand accompanied by a slower-than-average recorded productivity increase. A faster-than-average price increase amounts to the corrective relative-price change one would expect. The main factor in the machinery case, according to a recent Joint Economic Committee study, appears to have been a burst of excess demand occasioned by the investment boom of the mid-fifties. And to give still a third variant, Eckstein and Fromm in another Joint Economic Committee study suggest that the above-average rise in the wages of steelworkers and the prices of steel products took place in the face of a somewhat less tight labor and product market than in machinery. They attribute it to a joint exercise of market power by the union and the industry. Right or wrong, it is mistaken theoretical tactics to deny this possibility on the grounds that it cannot account for the price history in other sectors.

Some Things It Would Be Good to Know

There are at least two classical questions which are relevant to our problem and on which surprisingly little work has been done: One is the behavior of real demand under inflationary conditions and the other is the behavior of money wages with respect to the level of employment. We comment briefly on these two questions because there seems to us to be some doubt that ordinary reversible behavior equations can be found, and this very difficulty points up an important question we have mentioned earlier: that a period of high demand and rising prices molds attitudes, expectations, even institutions in such a way as to bias the future in favor of further inflation. Unlike some other economists, we do not draw the firm conclusion that unless a firm stop is put, the rate of price increase must accelerate. We leave it as an open question: It may be that creeping inflation leads only to creeping inflation.

The standard way for an inflationary gap to burn itself out short of hyperinflation is for the very process of inflation to reduce real demands. The mechanisms, some dubious, some not, are well known: the shift to profit, real-balance effects, tax progression, squeeze on fixed incomes. If price and wage increases have this effect, then a cost-push inflation in the absence of excess demand inflicts unemployment and excess capacity on the system. The willingness to bear the reduced real demand is a measure of the imperfectness of markets permitting the cost-push. But suppose real demands do not behave in this way? Suppose a wage-price rise has no effect on real demand, or a negligible one, or even a slight positive one? Then not only will the infliction not materialize, but the whole distinction between cost-push and demand-pull begins to evaporate. But is this possible? The older quantity theorists would certainly have denied it; but the increase in velocity between 1955 and 1957 would have surprised an older quantity theorist.

We do not know whether real demand behaves this way or not. But we think it important to realize that the more the recent past is dominated by inflation, by high employment, and by the belief that both will continue, the more likely is it that the process of inflation will preserve or even increase real demand, or the more heavily the monetary and fiscal authorities may have to bear down on demand in the interests of price stabilization. Real-income consciousness is a powerful force. The pressure on real balances from high prices will be partly relieved by the ex-

pectation of rising prices, as long as interest rates in an imperfect capital market fail to keep pace. The same expectations will induce schoolteachers, pensioners, and others to try to devise institutions to protect their real incomes from erosion by higher prices. To the extent that they succeed, their real demands will be unimpaired. As the fear of prolonged unemployment disappears and the experience of past full employment builds up accumulated savings, wage earners may also maintain their real expenditures; and the same forces may substantially increase the marginal propensity to spend out of profits, including retained earnings. If there is anything to this line of thought, the empirical problem of verification may be very difficult, because much of the experience of the past is irrelevant to the hypothesis. But it would be good to know.

The Fundamental Phillips Schedule
Relating Unemployment and Wage Changes

Consider also the question of the relation between money wage changes and the degree of unemployment. We have A. W. Phillips' interesting paper [reprinted in this volume, Selection 17] on the U.K. history since the Civil War (our Civil War, that is!). His findings are remarkable, even if one disagrees with his interpretations.

In the first place, the period 1861–1913, during which the trade-union movement was rather weak, shows a fairly close relationship between the percent change in wage rates and the fraction of the labor force unemployed. Due allowance must be made for sharp import-price-induced changes in the cost of living, and for the normal expectation that wages will be rising faster when an unemployment rate of 5 percent is reached on the upswing than when it is reached on the down-swing. In the second place, with minor exceptions, the same relationship that fits for 1861–1913 also seems to fit about as well for 1913–48 and 1948–57.   And finally Phillips concludes that the money wage level would stabilize with 5 percent unemployment; and the rate of increase of money wages would be held down to the 2–3 percent rate of productivity increase with about $2\frac{1}{2}$ percent of the labor force unemployed.

Strangely enough, no comparably careful study has been made for the U.S. Garbarino's 1950 note is hardly a full-scale analysis, and Schultze's treatment in his first-class Joint Committee monograph is much too casual. There is some evidence that the U.S. differs from the U.K. on at least two counts. If there is any such relationship characterizing the American labor market, it may have shifted somewhat in the last fifty to sixty years. Secondly, there is a suggestion that in this country it might take 8 to 10 percent unemployment to stabilize money wages.

But would it take 8 to 10 percent unemployment forever to stabilize the money wage? Is not this kind of relationship also one which depends heavily on remembered experience? We suspect that this is another way in which a past characterized by rising prices, high employment, and mild, short recessions is likely to breed an inflationary bias—by making the money wage more rigid downward, maybe even perversely inclined to rise during recessions on the grounds that things will soon be different.

There may be no such relation for this country. If there is, why does it not seem to have the same degree of long-run invariance as Phillips' curve for the U.K.? What geographical, economic, sociological facts account for the difference between the two countries? Is there a difference in labor mobility in the two countries? Do the different tolerances for unemployment reflect differences in income level, union organization, or what? What policy decisions might conceivably lead to a decrease in the critical unemployment rate at which wages begin to rise or to rise too fast?   Clearly a careful study of this problem might pay handsome dividends.

III.

A Closer Look at the American Data

In spite of all its deficiencies, we think the accompanying scatter diagram in Figure 1 is useful. Where it does not provide answers, it at least asks interesting questions. We have plotted the yearly percentage changes of average hourly earnings in manufacturing, including supplements (Rees's data) against the annual average percentage of the labor force unemployed.

The first defect to note is the different coverages represented in the two axes. Duesenberry has argued that postwar wage increases in manufacturing on the one hand and in trade, services, etc., on the other, may have quite different explanations: union power in manufacturing and simple excess demand in the other sectors. It is probably true that if we had an unemployment rate for manufacturing alone, it would be somewhat higher during the postwar years than the aggregate figure shown. Even if a qualitative statement like this held true over the whole period, the increasing weight of services in the total might still create a bias. Another defect is our use of annual increments and averages, when a full-scale study would have to look carefully into the nuances of timing.

A first look at the scatter is discouraging; there are points all over the place. But perhaps one can notice some systematic effects. In the first place, the years from 1933 to 1941 appear to be *sui generis:* money wages rose or failed to fall in the face of massive unemployment. One may attribute this to the workings of the New Deal (the 20 percent wage increase of

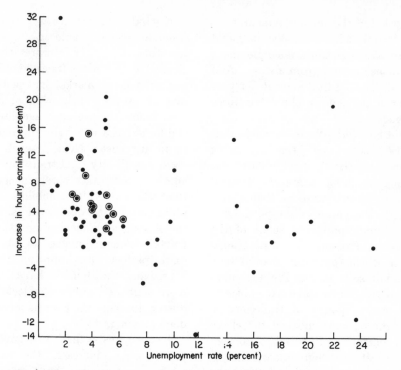

FIGURE 1. PHILLIPS SCATTER DIAGRAM FOR THE UNITED STATES. (THE CIRCLED POINTS ARE FOR RECENT YEARS.)

1934 must represent the NRA codes); or alternatively one could argue that by 1933 much of the unemployment had become structural, insulated from the functioning labor market, so that in effect the vertical axis ought to be moved over to the right. This would leave something more like the normal pattern.

The early years of the first World War also behave atypically although not so much so as 1933–39. This may reflect cost-of-living increases, the rapidity of the increase in demand, a special tightness in manufacturing, or all three.

But the bulk of the observations—the period between the turn of the century and the first war, the decade between the end of that war and the Great Depression, and the most recent ten or twelve years— all show a rather consistent pattern. Wage rates do tend to rise when the labor market is tight, and the tighter the faster. What is most interesting is the

strong suggestion that the relation, such as it is, has shifted upward slightly but noticeably in the forties and fifties. On the one hand, the first decade of the century and the twenties seem to fit the same pattern. Manufacturing wages seem to stabilize absolutely when 4 or 5 percent of the labor force is unemployed; and wage increases equal to the productivity increase of 2 to 3 percent per year is the normal pattern at about 3 percent unemployment. This is not so terribly different from Phillips' results for the U.K., although the relation holds there with a greater consistency. We comment on this below.

On the other hand, from 1946 to the present, the pattern is fairly consistent and consistently different from the earlier period. The annual unemployment rate ranged only narrowly, from 2.5 percent in 1953 to 6.2 percent in 1958. Within that range, as might be expected, wages rose faster the lower the unemployment rate. But one would judge now that it would take more like 8 percent unemployment to keep money wages from rising. And they would rise at 2 to 3 percent per year with 5 or 6 percent of the labor force unemployed.

It would be overhasty to conclude that the relation we have been discussing represents a reversible supply curve for labor along which an aggregate demand curve slides. If that were so, then movements along the curve might be dubbed standard demand-pull, and shifts of the curve might represent the institutional changes on which cost-push theories rest. The apparent shift in our Phillips curve might be attributed by some economists to the new market power of trade-unions. Others might be more inclined to believe that the expectation of continued full employment, or at least high employment, is enough to explain both the shift in the supply curve, if it is that, and the willingness of employers (conscious that what they get from a work force is partly dependent on its morale and its turnover) to pay wage increases in periods of temporarily slack demand.

This latter consideration, however, casts real doubt on the facile identification of the relationship as merely a supply-of-labor phenomenon. There are two parties to a wage bargain.

U.S. and U.K. Compared

A comparison of the American position with Phillips' findings for the U.K. is interesting for itself and also as a possible guide to policy. Anything which will shift the relationship downward decreases the price in unemployment that must be paid when a policy is followed of holding down the rate of wage and price increase by pressure on aggregate demand.

One possibility is that the trade-union leadership is more "responsible" in the U.K.; indeed the postwar policy of wage restraint seems visible in Phillips' data. But there are other interpretations. It is clear that the more fractionated and imperfect a labor market is, the higher the over-all excess supply of labor may have to be before the average wage rate becomes stable and the less tight the relation will be in any case. Even a touch of downward inflexibility (and trade-unionism and administered wages surely mean at least this) will make this immobility effect more pronounced. It would seem plausible that the sheer geographical compactness of the English economy makes its labor market more perfect than ours in this sense. Moreover, the British have pursued a more deliberate policy of relocation of industry to mop up pockets of structural unemployment.

This suggests that any governmental policy which increases the mobility of labor (geographical and industrial) or improves the flow of information in the labor market will have anti-inflationary effects as well as being desirable for other reasons. A quicker but in the long run probably less efficient approach might be for the government to direct the regional distribution of its expenditures more deliberately in terms of the existence of local unemployment and excess capacity.

The English data show a quite clearly nonlinear (hyperbolic) relation between wage changes and unemployment, reflecting the much discussed downward inflexibility. Our American figures do not contradict this, although they do not tell as plain a story as the English. To the extent that this nonlinearity exists, as Duesenberry has remarked, a given average level of unemployment over the cycle will be compatible with a slower rate of wage increase (and presumably price increase) the less wide the cyclical swings from top to bottom.

A less obvious implication of this point of view is that a deliberate low-pressure policy to stabilize the price level may have a certain self-defeating aspect. It is clear from experience that interregional and interindustrial mobility of labor depends heavily on the pull of job opportunities elsewhere, more so than on the push of local unemployment. In effect the imperfection of the labor market is increased, with the consequences we have sketched.

IV.

We have concluded that it is not possible on the basis of a priori reasoning to reject either the demand-pull or cost-push hypothesis, or the variants of the latter such as demand-shift. We have also argued that the empirical identifications needed to distinguish between these hypotheses may be quite impossible from the experience of macrodata that is available to us; and that, while use of microdata might throw additional light on the problem, even here identification is fraught with difficulties and ambiguities.

Nevertheless, there is one area where policy interest and the desire for scientific understanding for its own sake come together. If by deliberate policy one engineered a sizable reduction of demand or refused to permit the increase in demand that would be needed to preserve high employment, one would have an experiment that could hope to distinguish between the validity of the demand-pull and the cost-push theory as we would operationally reformulate those theories. If a small relaxation of demand were followed by great moderations in the march of wages and other costs so that the social cost of a stable price index turned out to be very small in terms of sacrificed high-level employment and output, then the demand-pull hypothesis would have received its most important confirmation. On the other hand, if mild demand repression checked cost and price increases not at all or only mildly, so that

considerable unemployment would have to be engineered before the price level updrift could be prevented, then the cost-push hypothesis would have received its most important confirmation. If the outcome of this experience turned out to be in between these extreme cases—as we ourselves would rather expect—then an element of validity would have to be conceded to both views; and dull as it is to have to embrace eclectic theories, scholars who wished to be realistic would have to steel themselves to doing so.

Of course, we have been talking glibly of a vast experiment. Actually such an operation would be fraught with implications for social welfare. Naturally, since they are confident that it would be a success, the believers in demand-pull ought to welcome such an experiment. But, equally naturally, the believers in cost-push would be dead set against such an engineered low-pressure economy, since they are equally convinced that it will be a dismal failure involving much needless social pain. (A third school, who believes in cost-push but think it can be cured or minimized by orthodox depressing of demand, think that our failure to make this experiment would be fraught with social evil by virtue of the fact that they expect a creep in prices to snowball into a trot and then a gallop.)

Our own view will by now have become evident. When we translate the Phillips' diagram showing the American pattern of wage increase against degree of unemployment into a related diagram showing the different levels of unemployment that would be "needed" for each degree of price level change, we come out with guesses like the following:

1. In order to have wages increase at no more than the $2\frac{1}{2}$ percent per annum characteristic of our productivity growth, the American economy would seem on the basis of twentieth-century and postwar experience to have to undergo something

like 5 to 6 percent of the civilian labor force's being unemployed. That much unemployment would appear to be the cost of price stability in the years immediately ahead.

2. In order to achieve the nonperfectionist's goal of high enough output to give us no more than 3 percent unemployment, the price index might have to rise by as much as 4 to 5 percent per year. That much price rise would seem to be the necessary cost of high employment and production in the years immediately ahead.

All this is shown in our price-level modification of the Phillips curve, Figure 2. The point *A*, corresponding to price stability, is seen to involve about 5½ percent unemployment; whereas the point *B*, corresponding to 3 percent unemployment, is seen to involve a price rise of about 4½ percent per annum. We rather expect that the tug of war of politics will end us up in the next few years somewhere in

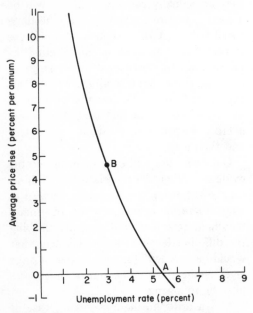

FIGURE 2. MODIFIED PHILLIPS CURVE FOR THE UNITED STATES. THIS SHOWS THE MENU OF CHOICE BETWEEN DIFFERENT DEGREES OF UNEMPLOYMENT AND PRICE STABILITY, AS ROUGHLY ESTIMATED FROM THE LAST TWENTY-FIVE YEARS OF AMERICAN DATA.

between these selected points. We shall probably have some price rise and some excess unemployment.

Aside from the usual warning that these are simply our best guesses we must give another caution. All of our discussion has been phrased in short-run terms, dealing with what might happen in the next few years. It would be wrong, though, to think that our Figure 2 menu that relates obtainable price and unemployment behavior will maintain its same shape in the longer run. What we do in a policy way during the next few years might cause it to shift in a definite way.

Thus, it is conceivable that after they had produced a low-pressure economy, the believers in demand-pull might be disappointed in the short run; i.e., prices might continue to rise even though unemployment was considerable. Nevertheless, it might be that the low-pressure demand would so act upon wage and other expectations as to shift the curve downward in the longer run—so that over a decade, the economy might enjoy higher employment with price stability than our present-day estimate would indicate.

But also the opposite is conceivable. A low-pressure economy might build up within itself over the years larger and larger amounts of structural unemployment (the reverse of what happened from 1941 to 1953 as a result of strong war and postwar demands). The result would be an upward shift of our menu of choice, with more and more unemployment being needed just to keep prices stable.

Since we have no conclusive or suggestive evidence on these conflicting issues, we shall not attempt to give judgment on them. Instead we venture the reminder that, in the years just ahead, the level of attained growth will be highly correlated with the degree of full employment and high-capacity output.

But what about the longer run? If the per annum rate of technical progress were about the same in a low- and high-pressure economy, then the initial loss in output in going to the low-pressure state would never be made up; however, in relative terms, the initial gap would not grow but would remain constant as time goes by. If a low-pressure economy could succeed in improving the efficiency of our productive factors, some of the loss of growth might be gradually made up and could in long enough time even be more than wiped out. On the other hand, if such an economy produced class warfare and social conflict and depressed the level of research and technical progress, the loss in growth would be compounded in the long run.

A final disclaimer is in order. We have not here entered upon the important question of what feasible institutional reforms might be introduced to lessen the degree of disharmony between full employment and price stability. These could of course involve such wide-ranging issues as direct price and wage controls, anti-union and antitrust legislation, and a host of other measures hopefully designed to move the American Phillips curves downward and to the left.

28

The International
Monetary Mechanism*

J. E. MEADE

When one considers the adequacy of the existing international monetary mechanism there are two functions to be studied: (i) the provision of adequate international monetary *Liquidity* and (ii) the working of an efficient mechanism of *Adjustment* of international balances of payments. The problem of Liquidity is to ensure that the central monetary authorities have sufficient direct or indirect calls upon each other's currencies to enable temporary unbalances in foreign payments to be accommodated without undue strain. The problem of Adjustment is to ensure that threatened lasting unbalances in foreign payments are avoided by some appropriate structural change in the economy. Liquidity and Adjustment are, as I shall stress, very closely related. Nevertheless they have

* *

Reprinted from *The Three Banks Review*, no. 63 (September 1964), pp. 3–25, by permission of the publisher and author.

J. E. Meade is affiliated with Christ's College, Cambridge.

*This article is a revised version of a paper presented to the Eleventh Annual Monetary Conference of the American Bankers Association held in Vienna, May 1964. It is a sequel to my article entitled "The Future of International Trade and Payments" published in *The Three Banks Review*, June 1961.

often been considered separately; and in my view in recent discussions Adjustment has received much less attention than Liquidity. This, I think, has been a serious mistake; and I shall therefore start with an examination of Adjustment mechanisms.

Let us suppose then that some country is threatened with a lasting disequilibrium in its balance of international payments. I ought, I suppose, at this point to define precisely what I mean by 'a lasting disequilibrium in its balance of payments'. This I shall not attempt to do largely on the familiar principle that, since everyone knows an elephant when one sees one, it is a waste of time and effort to undertake the extremely difficult task of giving a precise definition of what constitutes elephantitude. But broadly speaking what I have in mind by a 'lasting disequilibrium in a country's balance of payments' is a state of affairs in which there is in process a substantial worsening (or improvement) of the direct or indirect call which that country's central monetary authority can make upon the currencies of other countries and in which there is every prospect that this worsening (or improvement) will continue unless something special is done to stop it. Its net international Liquidity is going up or down and threatens to continue to do so unless some special Adjustment is made. The problem of Adjustment is the problem of devising a policy which will have a lasting effect upon its balance of international payments. In my view there are six possibilities.

(1) The first possibility is to do nothing about it. This is always a real possibility for the surplus country. Its monetary authorities sit back and allow its international liquidity position to improve without limit. It would be possible to devise systems of international payment which also made it possible for the authorities in the deficit country to sit back and do nothing. For example, a Clearing Union of the Keynesian type in which deficit countries could overdraw their accounts without limit and surplus countries could accumulate deposits without limit would be of this type; it would provide an unlimited and automatic lending by the surplus countries to the deficit countries to the exact extent necessary to finance any continuing surpluses or deficits in international payments.

This is not a system which I would advocate. Nevertheless it is worth mentioning for three reasons.

First, an understanding of the real reason why this mechanism alone is bad does much to explain the basic requirements of a good mechanism of Adjustment. It is bad because it automatically adjusts international capital movements to whatever happen to be the other items in the balance of payments. But it is perfectly possible for a rich developed country to be in balance-of-payments deficit; with a fixed exchange rate it has only to indulge in a sufficiently rapid domestic inflation of money prices and costs to achieve this position. It is perfectly possible for a poor primary-producing country whose main export happens to be in good demand to achieve a surplus on its balance of payments. But it is certainly wrong that there should be an automatic continuing flow of

capital funds from the poor to the rich to balance their international accounts. The rich developed country should generate a surplus and the poor underdeveloped country a deficit on its balance of current payments so that real capital resources flow from the developed to the underdeveloped country.

Second, an examination of this system reminds one that in this respect present arrangements are one-sided. The surplus country can always sit back and do nothing about it while the deficit country cannot in present conditions indefinitely lose reserves. A reformed international monetary system should undoubtedly aim at making the surplus countries as responsible for removing their surpluses as the deficit countries are for removing their deficits. This is not to say that in all circumstances both types of country should be equally responsible for the adjustment. But just as in generally inflationary conditions the deficit countries should have the main duty to reduce their excess demands on the world's resources, so in generally deflationary conditions the surplus countries should have the main duty to increase their deficient demands on the world's resources.

Third, while Adjustment should not be avoided through any system of unlimited provision of Liquidity, there is, of course, a very close connection between the two, which we shall have to stress later. Completely unlimited Liquidity is only the extreme form of very ample Liquidity. The more ample is the provision of Liquidity, the less rapidly need the chosen instruments for permanent Adjustment operate. This is of the greatest importance because, as we shall suggest below, the most acceptable means of Adjustment may be slow in operation. To discard objectionable means of Adjustment in favour of acceptable, but slowly operating, means of Adjustment will be possible only if there is very ample Liquidity in the world. This is the fundamental relationship between the twin problems of Liquidity and Adjustment. It is not possible to answer the question whether there is sufficient Liquidity in the world without knowing what means of Adjustment are to be used in the future.

(2) A second approach to the problem of Adjustment is through the direct control of international capital movements and the direct planning of foreign aid to fit in with the other items in a country's balance of payments. A deficit country can limit its outflow of capital or cut down its foreign aid, while a surplus country can raise its foreign aid. This is a bad system for a reason which should by now be clear. There is no reason to believe that the country which happens to have a balance-of-payments surplus is in any real sense richer or basically more capable of providing aid to underdeveloped countries than is the country which happens to have a deficit on its balance of payments. It is wrong that the former should provide more, and the latter less, capital funds and aid merely because the former have surpluses and the latter deficits on their balances of payments. This is not to say that there should be no planning for the movement of funds from developed to underdeveloped countries. On the contrary, on what may very broadly be called 'infant-industry' or, better still, 'infant-economy' grounds, there is, I think, a strong case for the governments of the developed countries to take steps to encourage private capital to flow out from them into the undeveloped, rather than into other developed, economies. And there is a still stronger case for international discussion to determine both an adequate scale for total financial aid to underdeveloped countries and also a fair basis for the share in that total which each individual developed country should undertake. But these things should not be argued on balance-of-payments grounds. Ability to provide funds should be measured by a country's real wealth and development,

not by what surplus it happens to have on its balance of payments. Need to receive funds should be measured by a country's poverty and underdevelopment, not by what happens to the size of its balance-of-payments deficit. Some other mechanism should be found to adjust balances of payments to those movements of funds which are themselves the reflection of real ability to pay or need to receive.

(3) A third main means of adjustment of balances of payments is the use of trade controls. Deficit countries can restrict imports by quantitative licensing or by raising import taxes and can subsidise exports. Surplus countries can remove import taxes and export subsidies with the specific intention of worsening their balance of trade. This method is open to very serious objection. It is obviously likely to be very one-sided; it is the deficit countries which will have to raise trade restrictions, since the surplus countries are much less likely to lower their trade restrictions on balance-of-payments grounds. But the system is open to much more serious objection. A sane world commercial system would be one in which the underdeveloped countries had exceptional freedoms to restrict imports on infant-industry and similar grounds, while the highly developed industrialised countries removed their barriers to their imports both from each other and from the underdeveloped countries. This would constitute a great free trade area in which the developed countries could enjoy economies of scale without monopoly and it would provide the underdeveloped countries with a huge open market for their primary products and for their new manufactures. Some slow progress has already been made towards this sort of system; and this year (1964) with the UN Conference on Trade and Development and the 'Kennedy round' of tariff bargaining under the GATT provides an opportunity for a decisive step forward. It would be most inimical to this idea if developed coun-

tries used import restrictions on balance-of-payments grounds.

(4) The fourth means of adjustment is perhaps the truly orthodox method. The monetary and budgetary authorities in deficit countries could restrain the total level of money demand for goods and services by a dear-money policy and by budgetary surpluses engendered through high taxes and low government expenditures. The authorities in surplus countries could take monetary and budgetary measures to inflate their domestic expenditure. The demand for goods and services and so for imports is thus deflated in the deficit countries and inflated in the surplus countries. There is, however, an extremely powerful objection to this method of adjustment. It means, of course, that the national governments must abandon the use of monetary and budgetary policies for the maintenance of full employment and the promotion of economic growth. Except by the merest fluke you cannot kill two birds with one stone. A country with fairly heavy unemployment and a slow rate of growth but with a deficit on its balance of payments must choose whether it will use its domestic financial policies to inflate demand in the interests of domestic economic expansion or to deflate demand in the interests of its balance of payments. It cannot do both.[1]

The use of monetary and budgetary inflations and deflations of total domestic demand for goods and services for the purpose of preserving balance-of-payments equilibrium rather than for the purpose of maintaining domestic employment and

[1] Within very narrow limits it may be possible to use monetary policy and budgetary policy as two separate stones to kill the two birds of balance-of-payments disequilibrium and of domestic stagnation. Thus a dear-money policy may be employed to attract funds from abroad in order to deal with a balance-of-payments deficit while a reduction in taxation and a budget deficit raises total demand at home. But there are very strict limits to the possibility of such divorce between monetary and budgetary policies.

economic growth might do little harm in a world in which money prices and costs, and in particular money wage rates, were extremely flexible. If a slight restriction of demand leading to a slight rise in unemployment led to a rapid and extensive decline in money wage rates, costs and prices, then a structural readjustment of a country's cost-price structure *vis-à-vis* competing countries could be achieved at little cost by this weapon. But in the real world such money prices and costs do not have this degree of flexibility. A prolonged damping of economic activity may be needed to get a slow and gradual readjustment of the money price-cost structure. In present conditions main reliance on this weapon for balance-of-payments adjustment is too costly in the sacrifice of economic expansion which it may involve.

Moreover, it is of great importance to the underdeveloped countries that the rich developed industrialised countries should not rely primarily on the instrument of domestic monetary and budgetary policies for the attainment of balance-of-payments equilibrium. Once again such policies are likely to be one-sided in that the surplus countries need not inflate their demands, but the deficit countries will be driven to deflate their demands. This can give the system a deflationary bias. The welfare of many underdeveloped countries depends upon their being able to sell their products in buoyant and expanding markets in the developed countries. A developed country which uses its domestic financial policies for the maintenance of its own domestic employment and economic growth is helping its poorer neighbours as well as itself.

It is often argued nowadays of the United States that the dilemma which we have posed between the use of domestic financial policies for internal and for external purposes is a false one. Domestic reflation of demand, so it is argued, will make domestic industry more profitable and this will attract for investment in

United States industry capital funds which would otherwise have been invested in other more prosperous countries; and this change in the flow of capital will more than offset the strain which increased demand in the USA will certainly put upon the US balance of trade. I am not sure whether this argument is true. But if it were true, it would not dispose of the case against the use of domestic inflation and deflation as the main instrument of control over the balance of payments. It would only alter the nature of the dilemma. For consider the case of a country which was suffering from a heavy level of unemployment and slow growth domestically but had a surplus on its balance of payments. Should it now inflate demand in order to achieve a domestic economic expansion? But this—if the present argument be true—by increasing the profitability of its industries would attract funds from abroad, increase the surplus on its balance of payments, and enlarge the deficits of other countries. No, you cannot count on killing two birds with one stone.

(5) We need another stone which will provide our fifth method of adjustment, namely a policy for directly raising or lowering money prices, wages, and costs without relying on the indirect slow process of inflation or deflation of demand for this purpose,—what has come to be called an 'incomes policy'. If we add this to our domestic monetary and budgetary policies, we have what is undoubtedly the ideal means of Adjustment. The authorities could then inflate or deflate domestic demand through their monetary and budgetary policies so as to achieve the desired level of domestic employment and the best attainable rate of economic growth. If there were simultaneously a deficit on the balance of payments, this could be corrected through incomes policy by a reduction in the rate of rise of money wage rates so that, with increasing productivity, the country's prices and costs were reduced relatively to those of other competing countries. Simultaneously it would be desirable that the authorities in the surplus countries should raise the rate of rise of money wage rates, prices and costs through their incomes policy.

This theoretically ideal system is marred only by the fact that it has so far proved totally impracticable. I am a long-haired economist usually to be found up above the clouds star-gazing from an armchair at the top of an ivory tower. But even so I cannot compete in unreality with those many practical men who seem nowadays to be telling us that this is the way to deal with our problems. Consider what it involves. Suppose that in country A output per head is growing at 4 percent per annum and money wage rates are rising at 3 percent per annum, while in country B output per head is rising at 3 percent per annum while money wage rates are rising at 4 percent per annum. The governments of both countries might have achieved these results only by heroic action and might with justification both be congratulating themselves upon their success in combining growth with relative price-cost stability. Nevertheless B's costs would be rising 2 percent per annum relatively to A's costs per unit of output. In a decade B's costs will be 20 percent above A's costs.

By what additional wave of what additional magic wand can the government of B, without deliberately engineering a severe financial deflation and heavy unemployment, reduce the rate of rise of its money wage rates from 4 to 2 percent per annum? And remember always that the magic wand must be of a kind which effectively reduces the average rise of wages to 2 percent without preventing individual wage rates from rising more rapidly where labour is exceptionally scarce and less rapidly where it is exceptionally plentiful. The rate of rise of money wage rates cannot in fact with modern institutions be put up or down like bank rate, the rate of income tax—or, for that matter, the rate of exchange.

(6) Indeed alterations in foreign exchange rates provide the sixth method of Adjustment. Although I favour a much greater use of this method, I do not wish to pretend that it is without its difficulties. Extreme advocates of completely flexible exchange rates do claim that the system solves completely both the problems of Liquidity and of Adjustment. Their argument runs as follows. A country is in deficit; its exchange rate will in consequence depreciate; this will make its exports cheaper in foreign currencies and will make its imports dearer in its own currency; its exports will thus be promoted and its imports discouraged and thus Adjustment will be achieved; true, this Adjustment may take time and in the meanwhile the excess demand for foreign currencies will cause an excessive depreciation of the currency; but in this case private speculators will realise that this temporary depreciation is more than will be required in the long run to achieve Adjustment and they will, therefore, purchase the depreciated currency at its present bargain price; they will thus provide temporary funds to cover the present deficit; private speculative funds will thus meet any need for Liquidity.

I do not hold this extreme view. In the short run, flows of trade may be rather insensitive to moderate changes in relative prices. If in consequence there are large variations in exchange rates, some speculators may behave in a perverse manner and intensify these variations by selling an already heavily depreciated currency from a fear that it will depreciate still further. This fear may engender its own justification. In countries which are highly dependent upon foreign trade for their supplies of essential commodities a severe depreciation of the currency may appreciably raise the cost of living by raising the price of imports; if this rise in the cost of living itself causes a rise in wage rates,

the consequent rise in domestic money costs may justify the speculation against the currency. The adverse speculation would itself have justified the adverse speculation.

It is, I think, a great pity that in so much of the present great debate on these issues the case for variable exchange rates has been argued on the grounds that it will reduce the need for official monetary reserves, since private speculators would provide the needed Liquidity. In my view the case for a greater use of exchange-rate variations is not so much that it deals with Liquidity as that it provides a method of long-run Adjustment. I certainly envisage the monetary authorities as still needing much official Liquidity in order to support their currencies from too rapid a depreciation. To repeat the example which I have already used, suppose country B's wage-costs are rising 2 percent per annum relatively to A's. Then in my view it is in the realm of practical politics for B's currency to be depreciated by 2 percent per annum relatively to A's, while it is not in the realm of practical politics for B's government to reduce the rate of rise of money wage-rates in B by 2 percent per annum without abandonment of its policies for full employment and steady growth domestically.

With this in mind the total Adjustment mechanism which I would advocate would be devised on the following lines. National governments would not adjust their policies as regards long-term capital movements, foreign aid, or commercial arrangements on balance-of-payments grounds. They would use their financial policies to expand or contract domestic demand primarily in the interests of domestic full employment and economic growth, though the authorities in deficit countries might well expand demand somewhat less, and the authorities in surplus countries somewhat more, than they would have done on considerations of the domestic situation alone. The methods they would primarily use for long-run balance-of-payments equilibrium would be incomes policy and exchange-rate adjustment.

In so far as they could, the governments of deficit countries would exert a moderating influence over the rate of rise in wage rates, while the governments of surplus countries should encourage a rather more rapid rate of rise of their domestic wage structure. To rely on this is, however, in my view unrealistic. At the very least it would be such an uncertain and slow process that enormous Liquidity would be needed to finance the balance-of-payments deficits which would continue during the process.

A moderate supplementation of this weapon by exchange-rate variations could be devised on the following lines. The authorities in each country, instead of maintaining a fixed gold parity for the national currency, would undertake not to change the parity by more than, say, $\frac{1}{6}$ percent in any one month. Further, within this narrow limit they would undertake to depreciate their currencies if, but only if, they were faced with what appeared to be a continuing balance-of-payments deficit and to appreciate if, but only if, they were faced with what appeared to be a continuing balance-of-payments surplus. If the right to change the parity were exercised every month, the exchange value of the currency would be changed at a maximum rate of 2 percent per annum. This proposal is made as a supplementary method of long-run Adjustment. It would undoubtedly require ample official Liquidity, since a national currency which was under considerable pressure might have to be strongly supported to prevent its falling by more than $\frac{1}{6}$ percent per month.

To operate such a system the monetary authorities would, of course, have to use their short-term interest rate policies for balance-of-payments reasons. Let us take the extreme possible case. Suppose that

A's currency is confidently expected to appreciate at the maximum rate of 2 percent per annum while B's currency is confidently expected to depreciate at the maximum rate of 2 percent per annum. B's currency would then be expected to depreciate in terms of A's currency at the rate of 4 percent per annum. To prevent the wholesale movement of short-term funds from B to A to take the prospective 4 percent profit on the exchange rate the short-term rate of interest would have to be maintained in B 4 points above the level in A—for example, at 6 percent per annum in B and 2 percent in A. This means that to work a system of this kind the national monetary authorities would have to co-operate in setting their short-term interest rates in the interests of preserving balance-of-payments equilibrium. They would have to rely on budgetary policies and—in so far as they can be determined independently of short-term rates—upon long-term rates, but not upon short-term rates, for the control of domestic economic expansion.

If a system of this kind were adopted, it would probably be sensible for the monetary authorities in each country to give a gold guarantee in respect of balances of its own currency which were held as monetary reserves by other monetary authorities. In this case there would develop a structure of more or less uniform short-term interest rates in all the main financial centres for such currency balances as were backed by a gold guarantee, while divergent short-term rates would appear on balances of national currencies not subject to a gold guarantee—the short-term rate being higher in those centres where the exchange rate was expected to depreciate and *vice versa*.

But would these very moderate degrees of exchange-rate variation be sufficient to ensure a proper Adjustment of balances of payments in a world in which (in the main financial centres) goods were freely imported, capital movements were unimpeded, and domestic financial policies were designed primarily for domestic economic expansion? This question brings us back to the problem of Liquidity. The proposed Adjustment mechanism would certainly be slow in its operation and would be feasible only if the deficit countries had ample sources of international liquidity to finance their deficits as long as they persisted. Indeed, the logic of the argument points to a system of unlimited liquidity so long as the countries concerned were in fact applying the agreed Adjustment mechanism. Such a system could be provided by a Keynesian Clearing Union on which deficit countries could draw without limit for payment to surplus countries on the understanding that deficit countries would depreciate the gold value of their currencies by $\frac{1}{6}$ percent per month so long as they were in serious unbalance with the Union and surplus countries would appreciate the gold value of their currencies by $\frac{1}{6}$ percent per month so long as they were in markedly favourable balance with the Union.

Such might be the ultimate logical solution. But for the immediate future one must work for the more limited aim of finding some method of achieving a substantial increase in international Liquidity as soon as the scale of balance-of-payments pressures makes it clear that there is such a need. What forms might such an increase of Liquidity take?

(1) Personally I do not advocate a once-for-all rise in the price of gold. I do not like the idea of helping the present regime in South Africa in this way. The change would favour those national monetary authorities which had chosen to hold gold rather than dollars or sterling. The possibility of its repetition might make people desire still more to hold gold in the future and any substantial move out of dollars and sterling into gold would *pro tanto* reduce Liquidity. But finally I personally dislike anything which perpetuates the silly, irrational, primitive, magical idea that sound money consists in digging gold in one place and burying it in another. Let us go forward to a more rational control over our monetary arrangements, which is a matter for book-keepers and not for mining engineers.

(2) The second method of increasing Liquidity is the method which I will call 'adhoccery'. *Ad hoc* bilateral arrangements can be made between central monetary authorities for swaps of their currencies; or by bankers' clubs and gentlemen's agreements with a greater or smaller degree of precision the central monetary authorities can engage themselves by making appropriate loans or by holding foreign currencies to support each other's exchanges while Adjustment mechanisms are operating. I cannot claim the technical knowledge or practical experience to describe, much less to choose between, all the possibilities of this kind. I certainly do not want to belittle them. If they are adequate in scale and if the commitments are sufficiently firm in fact (however vague they may be in form) then the only criticism one could make is that they are untidy and—dare I say so?—perhaps a little childish. At any rate on aesthetic grounds an ivory-tower stargazer would prefer a more rational, tidy, generalised and permanent international scheme. Moreover I strongly suspect—and I wonder whether the practical bankers and treasury officials would agree with me—that while the immediate solution may well be achieved through 'adhoccery', this can only be a passing phase. If some contrived continuing increase in Liquidity does prove permanently necessary, then these *ad hoc* arrangements are likely to be generalised into some more tidy scheme. What forms could such a tidy arrangement take?

(3) I am sure that any tidying-up operation of this kind should take place through a development of the appropriate existing institution, the International Monetary

Fund. But there are two broad forms which such a development could take depending upon whether, as at present, Fund transactions take place on the asset side of the Fund's account or whether they should be transferred to the liabilities side of the account. Let us consider first possible developments of the present arrangements broadly on the lines proposed by Mr. Bernstein. An adequate increase in Liquidity might be achieved simply by increasing each country's quota and so under present rules its drawing rights in the Fund. Each member would receive a larger right to pay more of its currency into the Fund in order to acquire from the Fund the foreign currencies which it required. If this were the basic method chosen for increasing Liquidity I would also support two further changes which are often associated with this proposal.

First, we do not need large and infrequent once-for-all increases in Liquidity. Rather as the world economy expands we need a gradual and continuing increase. For this reason it would be desirable that the members of the IMF should agree that every country's quota should automatically be increased by a given percentage each year. I am not going to say how large this percentage should be to meet actual requirements—let us for the present be content to call it x percent per annum. But in calculating x one must remember that Fund drawing rights constitute only a moderate part of total world liquidity which includes the gold reserves, dollar and sterling balances, and other readily available funds of national monetary authorities. An increase of x percent in Fund drawing rights represents something much less than a x percent increase in total Liquidity. We must be content to fix initially some perhaps rather arbitrary figure for x, which could and should be subsequently revised from time to time in the light of experience of the developing supply and demand for Liquidity.

Second, it would be most desirable that

central monetary authorities should 'count their unused drawing rights with the IMF as part of their visible monetary reserves and should very readily use these drawing rights not merely as a last resort but as a normal means of making international payments. For this is the way in which the IMF might gradually develop into the main instrument of international Liquidity. But in order that central monetary authorities should treat their drawing rights as being as liquid as actual reserves of gold or dollars or sterling, it is necessary that the controls over the use of drawing rights should be relaxed. Their use should become increasingly one which each member has the right to exercise without question.

But before drawing rights can be treated as being as liquid as gold or dollars or sterling there is one other major snag which must be removed—namely the possibility that the currency of a major surplus country may become scarce in the Fund. Under present arrangements it is, of course, very possible for the Fund to have sold to other members all its holdings of one particular currency which is in strong demand before those other members have themselves exhausted their drawing rights. This means that their drawing rights cannot be counted as good as gold, since gold will always command a scarce currency whereas their drawing rights may not. We need, therefore, to supplement present Fund arrangements with undertakings on the part of members to lend their currencies to the Fund on a scale which is sufficient to prevent any individual currency from becoming scarce. In 1962 an agreement was reached between the Fund and ten of its leading members for the latter to lend their currencies to the Fund in case of need. It is precisely this sort of arrangement which is needed provided that the obligations on the part of members to lend their currencies are sufficiently firm and on a sufficient scale to prevent any main currency becoming scarce in the Fund, so that unused drawing rights can in fact be treated as being as liquid as gold, dollars or sterling.

(4) This difficulty could be wholly avoided by a rather more substantial change in the *modus operandi* of the Fund. Let the transactions of the Fund be carried out on the liabilities side of the account. The members have paid in their currencies which stand on the assets side of the Fund's account. Let the offsetting items on the liabilities side of the IMF's account be called deposits of the members' central monetary authorities with the IMF. When country A's central bank has a net payment to make to country B's central bank let this be done by raising B's and reducing A's deposit with the IMF by this amount. There would then be no scarce currency problem in the Fund, since as long as the deficit countries still owned deposits with the Fund these could be used to make payments to the surplus countries.

The member countries' central banks would be under an obligation to accept from each other deposits with the Fund in lieu of gold or other foreign-exchange reserves. These deposits would be reckoned in gold units of some kind; and any member country which changed the gold parity of its currency (on the lines discussed earlier in this paper), would be under an obligation to adjust the amount of its currency contributed to the assets of the Fund to the extent necessary to keep its gold value constant. With this type of arrangement it would be the national currency and other assets of the Fund which would remain the fixed offsetting item; the deposit liabilities of the Fund would become the active medium for transactions between national monetary authorities. The only really essential alteration which this simple book-keeping change would bring about would be the removal of the fear of a scarcity of any particular currency in the Fund, so that the way would be cleared for the Fund's deposit liabilities to be treated by national monetary authorities as being as liquid as gold.

This arrangement could readily be combined with the proposal which I have already made, namely that the liquidity provided by the Fund should be increased continuously each year by a given percentage which we have called x percent per annum. If the Fund operations took place on the liabilities side of the account, this result could be achieved if each member country each year increased the amount of its currency in the Fund by x percent and had its deposit with the Fund increased by a corresponding amount.

This change may sound revolutionary. But it is in fact very limited; and it is important to realise some of the things which it does not imply. One feature of Professor Triffin's far-reaching proposals is that international payments made through his reformed Fund would be carried out on the liabilities side of the account in terms of some new gold unit of account in which the national central banks' deposits with the Fund would be calculated. The proposals which I have just made share this feature in common with Professor Triffin's proposal; for it is this feature which presents the most straightforward way of getting rid of the 'scarce-currency' possibility and thus of making the liquidity provided by the Fund as good as gold. But there are two most important features of Professor Triffin's plan which my proposals do not involve.

First, I am not proposing that the management of the Fund should have any power to conduct open-market operations in the capital and money markets of the member countries. The national currencies paid in by these members would simply be an inert book-keeping entry on the assets side of the Fund's balance sheet. If it were decided (as I have proposed) that the liquidity provided by the Fund should be increased continuously year by year, this under my proposal would be done automatically by each member paying in the appropriate additional amount of its own currency and receiving in return an equivalent increase in its deposits with the Fund. The management of the Fund would have no task of deciding from day to day either how much additional liquidity it should provide through open-market operations nor what particular national currencies or securities it should acquire for the purpose of controlling world liquidity. The distribution of the new liquidity would be automatically in proportion to the individual member's predetermined quotas.

Second, it is a central part of Professor Triffin's plan that the existing balances of dollars and sterling which are held by other central monetary authorities as part of their monetary reserves should be paid into the Fund, so that these foreign exchange reserves should be replaced by deposits with the Fund. The Fund in turn would itself become the holder of these dollar and sterling balances. This is not a feature of my present proposal which does not involve any immediate increase in the scale of the Fund's liabilities and assets. My proposal is simply to transfer, on its existing scale, the active operations of the Fund from the assets to the liabilities side of its account so as to avoid the scarce-currency problem and make the existing amount of Fund liquidity as good as gold.

Nevertheless, one must recognise the very real dangers of the existing foreign-exchange reserves held in the form of dollar and sterling balances. Any wave of distrust which caused a wholesale movement out of dollars and sterling into gold could cause a frightening liquidity crisis, since the basic feature of the foreign-exchange reserve system is that it builds a lofty pyramid of international liquidity (in the form of dollar and sterling balances) on a very restricted gold basis.

This danger could be seriously increased by the adoption of any Adjustment mechanism which relied upon an unlimited possibility of exchange-rate variations. If the dollar or sterling were expected to depreciate by an unspecified amount, there could develop a really large-scale run on

these reserve currencies. The proposal made earlier in this paper that the gold value of a currency could be changed by a maximum of 2 percent per annum should not be open to these dangers. In the first place, this is a degree of change which could always be offset by an interest-rate differential. If the dollar were expected to depreciate by at the most 2 percent a year, a 2-percent higher short-term interest rate in New York would make it worth while to keep balances in New York and make up on additional interest what one might lose in exchange-rate value. Second, at present large once-for-all exchange rate adjustments of unspecified amount are possible under the rules of the International Monetary Fund for a country which is in fundamental disequilibrium. It is the expectation of one of these once-for-all vast changes which makes it really worth while to move temporarily out of a currency on a vast scale. If the new very limited exchange-rate variation rules reduced the expectation of vast once-for-all changes and if interest-rate differentials were co-operatively used, the possibilities of big runs on reserve currencies should be considerably reduced. Third, as has been suggested above, it would probably be worthwhile for each main national monetary authority to give guarantees of the gold value of the balances of its currency held by other national monetary authorities. In this case such official holdings would not be subject to any speculative drain.

Reliance on dollar and sterling balances as the main expanding source of international liquidity presents yet another problem. For we are faced with a well-known dilemma in so far as future needs for increased liquidity are concerned. If these are to be met by increased dollar and sterling liabilities, then the U.S.A. and the U.K. must have deficits on their balances of payments in order that they should incur the increased dollar and sterling liabilities to other central monetary authorities. But in so far as their balances of payments are in deficit, their currencies may come to be mistrusted and there might start that movement away from dollars and sterling into' gold which could bring the whole edifice down in ruins.

In my view the wisest and most practical way to deal with this is (1) by 'ad-hoccery' in so far as the existing situation is concerned and (2) by providing any future additional needs for liquidity by some alternative measures. Any present threat to the edifice can be met if the main central monetary authorities do agree on *ad hoc* measures of a sufficient scope to ensure that any incipient run on dollars or sterling is countered by the official support for those currencies by the other central banks. But at the same time it would be foolish in the extreme to go on adding to this problem by relying on additions to dollar and sterling balances to provide the additions to international liquidity in the future. By adopting the measures which I have proposed,—that is to say by taking steps which enable Fund liquidity to be treated as being as good as gold and by arranging for a gradual increase in Fund liquidity—the dangers due to the foreign-exchange reserve system can gradually be reduced, as dollar and sterling balances become less important relatively to other forms of liquidity.

In conclusion, it is essential for the health and well-being of the world that the main developed countries of the free world should use their domestic budgetary and monetary policies for domestic economic expansion— for full employment and steady economic growth; that they should buy freely the products of the underdeveloped countries; and that they should plan and encourage a large flow of capital funds and of financial aid into these underdeveloped countries. But they can do these things steadily and without inhibition only if they are not hampered by recurrent balance-of-payments worries.

There are only two ways of banishing these worries.

First, they could simply cease to maintain the exchange values of their currencies at any predetermined level or within any predetermined limits.

Second, they might rely on an international payments mechanism which provides sufficient Liquidity to enable them to go ahead with their basic policies for domestic expansion and for international trade and aid, while their balances of payments were gradually adjusted by some moderate and limited exchange-rate variations.

The second of these alternatives is the best policy; but its feasibility depends upon international co-operation to provide international Liquidity on the necessary— possibly very extensive—scale. If such agreement cannot be reached, it would be far better to let the exchange rates go than that countries like the United States and the United Kingdom should be prevented by balance-of-payments difficulties from pursuing basic policies for domestic expansion and for international trade and aid.*

---

* [With the second edition of this volume, Professor Meade has added the following postscript: Much has happened in the international monetary sphere since this paper was first published in 1964; and these events have underlined the need for the reconsideration of the two problems of *Adjustment* and of *Liquidity* which I outlined in this paper. In so far as the problems of adjustment are concerned (and I still believe these to be the most important), nothing has happened to make me wish to modify the basic analysis in this paper. In so far as liquidity is concerned, important changes have taken place, such as the Special Drawing Rights scheme approved by the International Monetary Fund in 1968 and the isolation of existing Central Bank gold reserves from the outside open market for gold. Let us hope that these will prove to have been the first tentative moves in the direction of relying less and less upon the vagaries of gold supplies and of the accumulation of dollar and sterling balances by surplus countries, and more and more upon an orderly creation of international credit by the International Monetary Fund, as means for meeting the world's growing requirements of international liquidity.—*Ed.*]

Part VIII

INCOME STABILIZATION
AND FORECASTING

29

Potential GNP:
Its Measurement
and Significance*

ARTHUR M. OKUN

POTENTIAL GNP AND POLICY

"How much output can the economy produce under conditions of full employment?" The concept and measurement of potential GNP are addressed to this question. It is a question with policy significance because the pursuit of full employment (or "maximum employment" in the language of the Employment Act) is a goal of policy. And a target of full employment of labor needs to be linked to a corresponding target of full employment output, since policy measures designed to influence employment operate by affecting aggregate

* *

Reprinted from the *Proceedings of the Business and Economic Statistics Section of the American Statistical Association*, 1962, pp. 98–104, by permission of the publisher and author.

Arthur M. Okun is affiliated with the Brookings Institution; he was formerly at Yale University.

* My research in this area was done principally while I served on the Staff of the Council of Economic Advisers, and I had the benefit of many helpful comments and suggestions from members of the Council and the Staff. But the views reported here are my own and do not necessarily reflect those of the Council.

demand and production. How far we stand from the target of full employment output is important information in formulating fiscal and monetary policy. Thus, quantification of potential output offers one of the guides to stabilization policy and one indicator of its success.

The quantification of potential output —and the accompanying measure of the "gap" between actual and potential—is at best an uncertain estimate and not a firm, precise measure. While there are more precise measures of economic performance, they are not fully substitutable for the concept of potential output. To appraise the vigor of an expanding economy, it is important and enlightening to study customary cyclical measures, such as advance over previous peak levels or advance over recession trough levels. But these measures do not tell us how far we have to go to meet our targets, unless we are prepared to assume that each peak is like any other one and all troughs are likewise uniform. The record of the past decade testifies to the dramatic differences among cyclical peaks in levels of resource utilization.

The evaluation of potential output can also help to point up the enormous social cost of idle resources. If programs to lower unemployment from $5\frac{1}{2}$ to 4 percent of the labor are viewed as attempts to raise the economy's "grade" from $94\frac{1}{2}$ to 96, the case for them may not seem compelling. Focus on the "gap" helps to remind policy-makers of the large reward associated with such an improvement.

THE FOUR PERCENT UNEMPLOYMENT RATE

Potential GNP is a supply concept, a measure of productive capacity. But it is not a measure of how much output could be generated by unlimited amounts of aggregate demand. The nation would probably be most productive in the short-run with inflationary pressure pushing the economy. But the social target of maximum production and employment is constrained by a social desire for price stability and free markets. The full employment goal must be understood as striving for maximum production without inflationary pressure; or, more precisely, as aiming for a point of balance between more output and greater stability, with appropriate regard for the social valuation of these two objectives.

It is interesting and perhaps surprising that there seems to be more agreement that a four percent unemployment rate is a reasonable target under existing labor market conditions than on any of the analytical steps needed to justify such a conclusion. Economists have never developed a clear criterion of tolerable price behavior or any quantitative balancing of conflicting objectives which could be invoked either to support or attack the target of a four percent rate. Indeed, I should expect that many economists who agree on the four percent target would disagree in estimating how prices and wages would behave if we were

on target. Nor can the four percent rate be said to meet Beveridge's criterion for full employment—that job vacancies should be equal to the number of unemployed. We simply have no count of job vacancies and could not possibly translate Beveridge's goal into any available measure of unemployment.

Having said what the four percent unemployment rate is not, I shall now state that it is the target rate of labor utilization underlying the calculation of potential GNP in this paper. The statistical and methodological problems would not be altered if a different rate were selected; only the numbers would be changed.

POTENTIAL GNP AS A SHORT-RUN CONCEPT

In estimating potential GNP, most of the facts about the economy are taken as they exist: technological knowledge, the capital stock, natural resources, the skill and education of the labor force are all data, rather than variables. Potential differs from actual only because the potential concept depends on the assumption—normally contrary to fact—that aggregate demand is exactly at the level that yields a rate of unemployment equal to four percent of the civilian labor force. If, in fact, aggregate demand is lower, part of potential GNP is not produced; there is unrealized potential or a "gap" between actual and potential output.

The failure to use one year's potential fully can influence future potential GNP: to the extent that low utilization rates and accompanying low profits and personal incomes hold down investment in plant, equipment, research, housing, and education, the growth of potential GNP will be retarded. Because today's actual output influences tomorrow's productive capacity, success in the stabilization objective promotes more rapid economic growth.

THE MEASUREMENT PROBLEM

As it has been defined above, potential output is observed only when the unemployment rate is four percent, and even then must be viewed as subject to stochastic variation. At any other time, it must be regarded as a hypothetical magnitude. The observed actual measures of labor utilization tell us by a simple arithmetic calculation how much employment would have to increase, given the labor force, to make the unemployment rate four percent. But they do not offer similar direct information on other matters that might make labor input at full employment different from its observed level:

(a) how average hours worked per man would be altered if the level of aggregate demand were consistent with full employment;

(b) how participation rates in the labor force —and hence the size of the labor force— would be affected under conditions of full employment.

Nor do the actual data reveal directly what aggregate labor productivity would be under full employment conditions. There are many reasons why productivity might be altered in the aggregate: the added workers, changed average hours, possible alterations in the sectoral distribution of employment, higher utilization rate of capital, and altered efficiency in the use of employees all could make a difference in productivity at full employment.

THE LEAP FROM UNEMPLOYMENT TO OUTPUT

Ideally, the measurement of potential output would appraise the various possible influences of high employment on labor input and productivity and evaluate the influences step-by-step, developing quantitative estimates for each adjustment to produce the desired measure of potential.

While I shall discuss the steps individually below, the basic technique I am reporting consists of a leap from the unemployment rate to potential output rather than a series of steps involving the several underlying factors. Strictly speaking, the leap requires the assumption that, whatever the influence of slack economic activity on average hours, labor force participation, and manhour productivity, the magnitudes of all these effects are related to the unemployment rate. With this assumption, the unemployment rate can be viewed as a proxy variable for all the ways in which output is affected by idle resources. The measurement of potential output then is simplified into an estimate of how much output is depressed by unemployment in excess of four percent.

STATISTICAL ESTIMATES

The answer I have to offer is simple and direct. In the postwar period, on the average, each extra percentage point in the unemployment rate above four percent has been associated with about a three percent decrement in real GNP. This result emerged from three methods of relating output to the unemployment rate.

1. *First differences*—In one technique, quarterly changes in the unemployment rate (Y), expressed in percentage points, are related to quarterly percentage changes in real GNP (X). This regression equation, fitted to 55 quarterly observations from 1947-II to 1960-IV, yields:

$$Y = .30 - .30X \quad (r = .79)$$

According to this estimate, the unemployment rate will rise by 0.3 points from one quarter to the next if real GNP is unchanged, as secular gains in productivity and growth in the labor force push up the unemployment rate. For each extra one percent of GNP, unemployment is 0.3

points lower. At any point in time, taking previous quarters as given, one percentage point more in the unemployment rate means 3.3 percent less GNP.

2. *Trial gaps*—A second method consists of selecting and testing certain exponential paths of potential output, using alternative assumed growth rates and benchmark levels. The percentage "gaps" implied by these paths are then related to the unemployment rate (U) using a regression equation: $U = a + b$ (gap). The criteria for judging the validity of the assumed potential paths are: 1) goodness of fit; 2) absence of any trend in the residuals; 3) agreement with the principle that potential GNP should equal actual GNP when $U = 4$.

The slope terms in this equation fitted to various paths and different periods consistently ran from .28 up to .38. One such equation was reported in the March 1961 statement of the Council of Economic Advisers to the Joint Economic Committee. It was:

$$U = 3.72 + .36 \text{ gap } (r = .93)$$

where the gap was derived from a $3\frac{1}{2}$ percent trend line through actual real GNP in mid-1955. The equation was fitted to quarterly data for 1953–60. It implies that an increment of unemployment of one percent is associated with an output loss equal to 2.8 percent of potential output— or a somewhat larger percentage of *actual* output when actual is below potential. The estimated unemployment rate associated with a zero gap is 3.72 percent, not too far from the 4.0 percent ideal.

3. *Fitted trend and elasticity*—The first method described above relied on the use of *changes* in GNP and in unemployment. The second method used *levels* but assumed the trend of output-growth at constant unemployment rates. It is also possible to derive the output-unemployment coefficient from data on levels without assuming

a trend. The following model permits such a calculation:

a. There is a constant elasticity relationship in the relevant range between the ratio of actual (A) to potential (P) output, on the one hand, and the "employment rate" ($N = 100 - U$) as a fraction of its potential level (N_F):

$$\frac{N}{N_F} = \left(\frac{A}{P}\right)^a$$

b. There is a constant growth rate (r) of potential output starting from some level P_o such that at any time t:

$$P_t = P_o e^{rt}$$

By substitution and rearrangement:

$$N_t = \frac{A_t^a \cdot N_F}{P_o^a \cdot e^{art}}$$

Logarithmically:

$$\log N_t = \log \frac{N_F}{P_o^a} + a \log A_t - (ar)t$$

The log of the employment rate is here related to a time-trend and to the log of actual real GNP. When a regression equation is fitted to $\log N$ as the dependent variable and $\log A$ and t as independent variables: 1.)—The coefficient of $\log A$ is the "output elasticity of the employment rate"; 2.)—The coefficient of time is the product of that elasticity and the potential growth rate; it therefore yields an estimate of the potential growth rate; and 3.)—The intercept yields the benchmark (P_o) for any given N_F, here taken as 96.

Fitted to varying sample periods, the estimated elasticity coefficient ran .35 to .40, suggesting that each one percentage point reduction in unemployment means slightly less than a 3 percent increment in output (near the potential level). The trend growth rate, fitted to 1947–60 quarterly data, was 3.9 percent, but it was clear that this was not uniform throughout the period. For the post-Korean period, the estimated trend growth in potential was near 3½ percent, while, for the 1947–53 period, it was near 4½ percent.

The uniformity that emerged from these various techniques was the approximate 3-to-1 link between output and the unemployment rate. My own subjectively weighted average of the relevant coefficients is 3.2, yielding the following estimate of potential:

$$P = A[1 + .032(U - 4)]$$

When the unemployment rate is four percent, potential GNP is estimated as equal to actual; at a five percent rate of unemployment, the estimated "gap" is 3.2 percent of GNP. In the periods from which this relationship was obtained the unemployment rate varied from about 3 to 7½ percent; the relation is not meant to be extrapolated outside this range. I have no reason to expect the 3.2 coefficient to apply if unemployment were either 1 or 15 percent of the labor force.

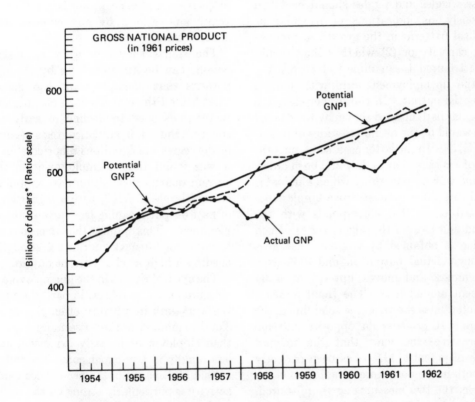

POTENTIAL AND ACTUAL GNP, 1954–1962.

SMOOTHING THE POTENTIAL PATH

The dashed line in the accompanying figure shows the implied time-series of potential GNP derived by applying the 3.2 coefficient to excess unemployment for the period 1954 to date. The result is a curve that wiggles from quarter to quarter, even dipping at times. The dips and small increases in estimated potential are concentrated in advanced stages of expansion—1956–57, 1959, and early 1962. Quarters of rapid rise in estimated potential output occur in early expansion—1955, 1958, 1961.

The question that arises is whether (1) these wiggles and jiggles should be taken seriously, as indications of irregular or cyclical patterns in the growth of productive capacity or (2) whether they should be attributed to an imperfect correlation of the unemployment rate with unused potential output. In the former case, the irregular path upward shown by the dashed line would be the estimated series of potential GNP. In the latter case, some smoothing of that irregular path would be in order.

One way of smoothing which eliminates all the ripples is to substitute a simple exponential curve that corresponds with the trend and level of the wiggly series. Such a line is obtained by a trend that goes through actual output in mid-1955 as a benchmark and moves upward at a $3\frac{1}{2}$ percent annual rate. The trend measure of potential is shown as the solid line in the figure. It presents an opposite extreme alternative—the view that the upward path of potential GNP has been perfectly smooth in the post-Korean period. On the whole, the two measures agree quite well. A trend line with either a 3 or a 4 percent growth rate—or with a markedly different "benchmark" level—would clearly not fit the dashed line equally well. In general, periods of early expansion—like 1955; 1958-II to 1959-I; and 1961-II to 1961-IV —show larger gaps by the unemployment measure than by the trend technique. The

reverse is true for late expansion and recession periods, like 1956-II to 1958-I and 1959-III to 1961-I.

My own inclination is to select the smooth trend measure of potential output for the post-Korean period. I find it difficult to accept the verdict that potential output has actually contracted at times, as the unsmoothed unemployment measure implies. Nor can I believe that the economy's *productive capacity* rises most rapidly in early expansion, even though actual production may be increasing briskly. This is not the period when investment expenditures—much less completed investment projects—are at a peak; nor is it a time of heavy innovations, by any external evidence I know.

The spurts shown in early expansion periods can be accounted for by the hypothesis that unemployment lags somewhat behind the movement of output, and therefore is slow to decline in early recovery. Indeed, in statistical tests of some of the regression equations reported above, it was found that unemployment in the current quarter depends on past as well as current levels of GNP, with a higher level of past output meaning less current unemployment. This implies that decisions on hiring labor for next quarter are strengthened by a high level of current output.

The cyclical ripples in the unemployment measure may also reflect, in part, a lead of the workweek in advance of employment. Total manhours worked rise more rapidly than employment in early expansion and less rapidly in late expansion. The initial impact of a change in the pace of economic activity is particularly strong on the workweek and is later shifted more fully onto employment. Presumably, this lagged effect might be incorporated into the estimate of potential based on the unemployment rate, in such a way as to smooth that potential curve and bring it closer to the trend estimate of potential. But, for the post-Korean period, there is no obvious shift in the trend of potential; and the $3\frac{1}{2}$ percent trend line, while obviously too smooth a time path, fills the assignment rather well.

The trend estimate of potential for the 1954–62 period still rests on the unemployment-output relationship reviewed above, that an excess of 1 point in the unemployment rate means, on the average, a loss of about 3 percent in output. The trend line, however, suggests that the output loss per point of the unemployment rate exceeds 3 percent in late expansion and in recession and is somewhat less than 3 percent in early expansion.

It should be noted that this trend does not fit the earlier postwar years. If one projected the $3\frac{1}{2}$ percent trend back to 1947, the trend-technique would clearly overestimate potential output. The indicated potential growth of the 1947–53 period is nearer to $4\frac{1}{2}$ percent. The lower potential growth rate of the post-Korean period is associated, in part, with less success in making full use of our potential. The "gaps" between potential and actual have held down the size and held up the average age of our capital stock, thereby lowering the growth of potential.

THE STEPS

The findings above assert that a reduction in unemployment, measured as a percentage of the labor force, has a much larger than proportionate effect on output. To appraise and evaluate this finding, it is necessary to inspect the steps which were leaped over in the statistical relationships between output and unemployment. Clearly, the simple addition of one percent of a given labor force to the ranks of the employed would increase employment by only slightly more than one percent: $100/100 - U$ percent to be exact. If the workweek and productivity were unchanged, the increment to output would be only that $1+$ percent. The 3 percent result implies that considerable output

gains in a period of rising utilization rates must stem from some or all of the following: induced increases in the size of the labor force; longer average weekly hours; and greater productivity.

LABOR FORCE

Participation in the labor force as we measure it consists of either having a job or seeking actively to work. The resulting measures of labor force are not pure reflections of supply; they are affected by job availability. In a slack labor market, people without a job may give up when they are convinced that job-hunting is a hopeless pursuit. They then may be viewed as having left the labor force though they stand ready and eager to work. Furthermore, there are secondary or passive members of the labor force who will not actively seek employment but would accept gainful employment if a job came looking for them. This latter group suffers little or no personal hardship in not having work, but the output they would contribute in a fully employed economy is a relevant part of the nation's potential GNP.

There may be induced changes in the labor force in the opposite direction: e.g., the loss of a job by the breadwinner of a family might increase the measured labor force by leading his wife and teen-age children to seek work. The prewar literature debated the probably net effects of these opposing influences on participation rates. However, the postwar record has convincingly delivered the verdict that a weak labor market depresses the size of the labor force. But the magnitude and timing of the effect is not clear.

Even the conceptual problem of defining a potential labor force is difficult—we should not wish to count only the secondary labor force members who would appear for work tomorrow morning; on the other hand, we would not want to include all those who might be attracted by many years of continued job availability. The response of participation rates is likely to be a complicated lagged phenomenon which will not be closely tied to the current unemployment rate. While this aspect of the difference between potential and actual output is hard to quantify, zero is certainly not a satisfactory estimate. At the end of 1960, the Bureau of Labor Statistics estimated the difference between actual and "normal" labor force at 561,000. If this figure is taken as the induced effect of poor opportunities for jobs, it implies that, in those recession conditions, for every 10 people listed as unemployed over and above the 4 percent rate, there were three additional potential workers who were not actively seeking work.

HOURS

Taking into account the normal secular decline in hours worked per man, there is a clear relationship between movements in average hours and in output. When output has been rising rapidly, average hours have expanded—or, at least, have not contracted. On the other hand, periods of low growth or decline in GNP mean more rapid declines in average hours per man. The data point toward the concept of a full employment path of average annual hours. But the concept of full employment hours is hard to quantify: e.g., in a rapid rise of output toward full employment, the amount of overtime might well push the workweek above the level consistent with steady full employment. Furthermore, economy-wide data on average hours are notoriously poor. However, using what evidence is available, we find that each one percent difference in output is associated with a difference of 0.14 percent in hours per man, including both overtime and part-time work.

The figure of 0.14 is obtained by fitting a least-squares regression line to annual data for 1947–59. The data are found in the Bureau of Labor Statistics. Release (USDL-4155) of June 28, 1960. The variables are percent change in manhours of work per person employed (Y) and percent change in private nonagricultural output (X), restricted to private nonagricultural output and employment; establishment figures are the source of the manhour estimates. The fitted line is:

$$Y = 0.843 + .142X \ (r = .85)$$

When this equation is used to compare average hours for different possible outputs at the same point in time, the 0.142 coefficient reflects the percentage difference in hours per man that accompanies a one percent difference in output.

Returning to the finding that a one percentage point reduction in the unemployment rate means 3.2 percent more GNP, the hours-output estimate above indicates that it will also be accompanied by an increase of nearly one half of one percent in hours per man, or an addition of about 0.2 of an hour to the workweek. With an allowance for induced gains in labor force, based illustratively on the 1960 estimate cited above, the reduction of one point in the unemployment rate means perhaps a 1.8 percent increase in total labor input measured in manhours. Then, to get the 3.2 percent increment in output, manhour productivity must rise by about 1.4 percent.

PRODUCTIVITY

The direct checks that could be made on productivity data were consistent with this implication of the output-unemployment relationship. The record clearly shows that manhour productivity is depressed by low levels of utilization, and that periods of movement toward full employment yield considerably above-average productivity gains.

The implications and explanations of this phenomenon are intriguing. Indeed, many *a priori* arguments have been made for the reverse view—that depressed levels of activity will stimulate productivity through pressure on management to cut costs, through a weeding-out of inefficient firms and low quality workers, and through availability of more and higher quality capital per worker for those employees who retain their jobs. If such effects exist, the empirical record demonstrates that they are swamped by other forces working in the opposite direction.

I have little direct evidence to offer on the mechanism by which low levels of utilization depress productivity. I can offer some speculation and try to encourage other researchers to pursue this problem with concrete evidence at a micro-economic level. The positive relationship between output and labor productivity suggests that much of labor input is essentially a fixed cost for fairly substantial periods. Thus high output levels permit the spreading of labor overheads, and low production levels raise unit fixed costs of labor. At times, we may take too seriously our textbook examples which view labor as a variable factor, with only capital costs as fixed. Even the most casual empiricism points to an overhead component in labor costs. There are many reasons why employment may not be easily variable:

1. *Contractual commitments* may tie the hand of management in a downward direction—employees may have guaranteed annual wages, supplementary unemployment compensation, rights to severance pay, etc. as well as actual contracts for a term of employment.

2. *Technological factors*, in a broad sense, may also be important. A firm plans on a division of labor and degree of specialization attuned to "normal" operations. If operations fall below normal, there may be marked indivisibilities which prevent the firm from curtailing its employment of specialists, clerical and sales personnel, and supervisors in parallel with its cutback in output.

3. *Transactions costs* associated with laying off labor and then, in the future, doing new hiring may be another influence retarding the adjustment of labor input to fluctuations in sales and output.

4. *Acquired skills* that existing employees have learned on the job may make them particularly valuable to the firm so that it pays to stockpile underemployed labor rather than run the risk of having to hire untrained men when business conditions improve.

5. *Morale factors* may also make layoffs undesirable.

All of these factors could help explain why slack economic activity is accompanied by "on-the-job underemployment," reflected in depressed levels of manhour productivity. Firms obviously do lay off labor in recession but they do so reluctantly. Their problems may be mitigated, in part, by the presence of voluntary quits which permit a downward adjustment of employment without layoffs. In part, the impact of slack on manhour productivity may be reduced by shortening average hours to spread the work and the wage-bill without a cut in employment. But these appear to be only partial offsets.

To the extent that the productivity losses of recessions are associated with fixity of labor costs, they would not be maintained indefinitely. If the recession was of long duration—or merely was expected to last a long time—firms would adjust their employment more drastically. On this reasoning, in an era when business cycle dips are continually short and mild, one might expect productivity to bear more of the brunt of recession and labor input to be less affected, even relative to the decline in output.

Changes in the level of economic activity are associated with shifts in the composition of employment and output by industry. A slack economy is accompanied by particularly depressed output in durable-goods manufacturing industries, where output per manhour is especially high. My own intuition suggested that this might be an important explanation of the relationship between productivity and the unemployment rate. But calculations on the change in composition from recession to recovery years indicate that, while shifts in industrial composition do influence aggregate productivity in the expected direction, the magnitude of the effect is trivial. There is some significance to the compositional shift between agriculture and nonagricultural industries. Manhour input in agriculture seems to be independent of overall economic activity in the short run, so all variations in labor input can be regarded as occurring in the nonagricultural sector. I assumed illustratively above that a point reduction in the unemployment rate means an increase in total manhours of 1.8 percent. If all of that 1.8 percent goes into nonagriculture, this would add 0.1 percent to economy-wide productivity (for given levels of productivity in each sector). This is still only a minor part of the total productivity gain that accompanies reduced unemployment.

Thus far, I have ignored the dependence of labor productivity on plant and equipment capacity. The entire discussion of potential output in this paper has, in effect, assumed that idle labor is a satisfactory measure of all idle resources. In fact, measures of excess capacity in industrial plant and equipment do show a close relationship to unemployment—idle men are accompanied by idle machines. But the correlation is not perfect and operating rates in industry should be considered along with employment data as an indicator of the gap between potential and actual output. Obviously, if capital were fully employed while there was much unemployed labor, this would hold down the productivity gains that could be obtained through full employment of labor. Robert Solow did use capital stock data together with unemployment data in fitting a production function for 1929 to date (see the *American Economic Review* of May 1962). His estimates of potential output for the post-Korean period agreed remarkably well with those I am reporting.

Still, I shall feel much more satisfied with the estimation of potential output when our data and our analysis have advanced to the point where the estimation can proceed step-by-step and where the capital factor can be explicitly taken into account. Meanwhile, the measure of potential must be used with care. The trend line yields a point-estimate of the "gap," e.g., $31.3 billion for 1962-II. But that specific figure must be understood as the center of a range of plausible estimates. By my personal evaluation of its degree of accuracy, I find potential output useful—and superior to substitute concepts—for many analytical purposes.

30

Multiplier, Accelerator, and Liquidity Preference in the Determination of National Income in the United States*

GREGORY C. CHOW

This paper is an attempt to study statistically the multiplier, the accelerator, and the liquidity preference relations in macroeconomics, and the extent to which they, alone, can explain and predict national income in the United States. Although economists have granted these relationships in theory, they are skeptical in practice.

❋ ❋

Reprinted by permission of the publishers and author from *The Review of Economics and Statistics*, vol. 49 (February 1967), pp. 1–15. Cambridge, Mass.: Harvard University Press, Copyright, 1967, by the President and Fellows of Harvard College.

Gregory C. Chow teaches at Princeton University; he was formerly with the IBM Research Center and Columbia University.

* I would like to thank Gary S. Becker, Edwin Kuh, and Franco Modigliani for valuable suggestions, without implying that they necessarily agree with the views expressed here. This paper is a condensed version of an IBM Research Paper of the same title, number RC-1455 (Aug. 10, 1965), presented before the Econometric Society meetings in New York in December 1965.

Perhaps the recent tendency toward complicated econometric models, at one extreme, and the search for one equation, such as the quantity theory of money, at the other, are sufficient evidence of skepticism. Is such skepticism justified? Although large econometric models are needed to explain the detailed working of a national economy, a statistical study built upon a few major aggregate relations, derived from and specified at the same level of aggregation as macro-economic theory, may help pinpoint the essential sectors and assess the possible gains of disaggregation, thus serving as a complement to the building of econometric models.

This study may be considered as a partial statistical appendix to such classic papers in macro-economics as those by Hicks [7], Modigliani [12], and Samuelson [14]. In section I, the three major relations are formulated. In section II, we discuss the statistical problems involved in confronting the model with annual data for the United States. The empirical results are presented in section III, and the goodness of fit and forecasting ability of the model are examined in section IV. An attempt is made in section V to evaluate the relative importance of the above three relations acting on a private economy, of fiscal policy and of monetary policy, in the determination of national income. The dynamic characteristics of our model will be briefly noted in section VI, and section VII contains some concluding remarks.

I. FORMULATION OF THE MODEL

To test statistically the hypotheses of Keynes' *General Theory* [9], the post-Keynesian formulations, and the acceleration principle, some modifications to the formulations of Hicks [7] and Modigliani [12] are unavoidable since they are essentially static in nature and, as such, they are not identifiable (that is, they fail to include sufficiently different sets of variables in different equations). Fortunately, by introducing simple distributed lags, one can specify an adjustment process toward equilibrium, supply enough distinct variables in different equations to insure identification, and keep the model as close as possible to macro-economic theory.

A. The Consumption Function

The following simple distributed lag consumption function, relating equilibrium consumption $\dot{C}$ to current income Y, is consistent with two major post-Keynesian findings on consumption, that aggregate consumption can be explained, and that its response to current income is small:

$$\dot{C}_t = a_0 + a_1 Y_t. \tag{1}$$

Assuming a fraction β_1 of $(\dot{C}_t - C_{t-1})$ to be realized,

$$C_t - C_{t-1} = \beta_1(\dot{C}_t - C_{t-1})$$
$$= \beta_1(a_0 + a_1 Y_t - C_{t-1}) \tag{2}$$

implying

$$C_t = \beta_1 a_0 + \beta_1 a_1 Y_t + (1 - \beta_1)C_{t-1}. \tag{3}$$

To avoid high serial correlation in (3), we will test

$$\Delta C_t = \beta_1 a_1 \Delta Y_t + (1 - \beta_1)\Delta C_{t-1}. \tag{4}$$

The effect of the stock of money on consumption, M_t in equation (3) or ΔM_t in equation (4), will also be tested.

Concerning the treatment of consumer durables, should the variable C be the stock in existence or the amount purchased? The answer depends partly on our hypothesis about consumer behavior and partly on the choice between statistical approximations. It may be reasonable to hypothesize that (3) or (4) describes consumption (measured by stock in case of durables), rather than consumer expenditures. As a matter of statistical approximation, equations (3) or (4) may be applied to the purchase of new durables if their durability is short. The less durable a commodity is, the better is the approximation in treating it as a perishable. In our model, we choose to deal with an aggregate of consumer durables. Whether this aggregate belongs to equation (4), or behaves more like an investment (flow) equation, to be derived in subsection B below from assumptions about desired stock, is essentially a statistical question.

B. The Investment Function

The investment decision might be complicated, but we will simply modify the static theory of the firm by a stock-flow transformation and by lags. Let the equilibrium demand for a capital good $\dot{K}_t$ be a linear function of the firm's output Y' and the relative price p of its service, and let β_2 be the adjustment coefficient. Analogous to (3), we have

$$K_t = \beta_2 b_0 + \beta_2 b_1 Y'_t + \beta_2 b_2 p_t$$
$$+ (1 - \beta_2)K_{t-1}. \tag{5}$$

A serious statistical difficulty in using equation (5) is the lack of accurate data on capital stock. Taking its first difference, or obtaining an equation for net investment $I_t^n = (K_t - K_{t-1})$, does not avoid this difficulty, but taking the difference $K_t - (1 - d)K_{t-1}$, d being the percentage rate of depreciation, will yield gross investment I_t:

$$I_t = \beta_2 b_1[Y_t' - (1 - d)Y_{t-1}'] \\ + \beta_2 b_2[p_t - (1 - d)p_{t-1}] \\ + (1 - \beta_2)I_{t-1} + \text{constant.} \quad (6)$$

Equation (6) shows the acceleration principle by relating investment to the change in output $[Y_t' - (1 - d)Y_t']$. It implies statistically that if both Y_t' and Y_{t-1}' appear as explanatory variables for gross investment, the coefficient of Y_{t-1}' should be approximately equal to the negative of the coefficient of Y_t'.

The rate of interest, R, affects investment through the price effect, that is, through the relation $p = P(d + R)$, where P is the price of the capital stock. This simple relation implies that the interest elasticity of demand equals a fraction $R/(d + R)$ of the price elasticity of demand, since a one per cent change in R will result in an $R/(d + R)$ per cent change in p:

$$\frac{\partial \log p}{\partial \log R} = \frac{\partial \log (d + R)}{\partial \log R} = \frac{R}{d + R}.$$

If $R = .05$, this fraction will be .20 for $d = .20$. It will be .50 for $d = .05$. Thus, except for the very durable among durable goods, say those with depreciation lower than .10, the interest elasticity is a small fraction, say lower than one-third, of the price elasticity of demand. Our theoretical analysis suggests that the interest elasticity for most durable goods is small (smaller for the less durable), and that the investment functions with interest as an explanatory variable should be classified according to the durabilities of the commodities.

In our macro-economic model, we will ignore the effects of relative prices and assume constant rates of depreciation, leaving R to be the only variable affecting p. In equation (6), p will be replaced by R (without introducing a new symbol for the coefficient b_2). Furthermore, we will use the same national product variable Y in the consumption function for the aggregate product variable Y' in the aggregate gross investment function. Thus,

$$I_t = \beta_2 b_1[Y_t - (1 - d)Y_{t-1}] \\ + \beta_2 b_2[R_t - (1 - d)R_{t-1}] \\ + (1 - \beta_2)I_{t-1} + \text{constant.} \quad (7)$$

Two theoretical complications may arise in our formulation of the investment function (7). First, we have implicitly assumed that the capital market is near enough to being perfect so that the cost to a firm of using the service of a capital good is simply its equivalent rental. In a perfect capital market, the rent would be equal to $p = P(d + R)$. If the capital market is highly imperfect, the firm will find it much more economical to purchase a capital good than to rent it, and the quantity of a capital good that it can purchase will be restricted by the amount of liquid assets available. To some extent, the availability of liquid assets is measured by the rate of interest. However, liquid funds may simply be "unavailable" to the firm, that is, the effective rate of interest on the firm's borrowing may be much higher than any observed rate. This would make the amount of liquid assets available an important constraint on the firm's ability to purchase capital goods. In our empirical investigation, this possibility will be examined by introducing ΔM into equation (7).

Second, the lag structure that has been assumed may be considered too simple for the demand for capital goods. Since K_t denotes the actual quantity of capital goods, and I_t denotes investment actually realized, there is the possibility that the change $K_t - K_{t-1}$ may depend on decisions to fill the gap between desired and actual stocks made more than one period (year) ago. Instead of the simple lag, one might assume, for example,

$$K_t - K_{t-1} = \beta_{21}(\dot{K}_t - K_{t-1}) + \beta_{22}(\dot{K}_{t-1} - K_{t-2}) \quad (8)$$

implying an equation for K_t. Then, $K_t - (1 - d)K_{t-1}$ will be

$$
\begin{aligned}
I_t ={} & \beta_{21}b_1[Y_t - (1 - d)Y_{t-1}] \\
& + \beta_{21}b_2[R_t - (1 - d)R_{t-1}] \\
& + (1 - \beta_{21})I_{t-1} \\
& + \beta_{22}b_1[Y_{t-1} - (1 - d)Y_{t-2}] \\
& + \beta_{22}b_2[R_{t-1} - (1 - d)R_{t-2}] \\
& - \beta_{22}I_{t-2} + \text{constant}. \quad (9)
\end{aligned}
$$

Thus, the lag structure (8) requires, as explanatory variables for investment, one more period of observations on income change, interest change, and lagged investment. In the empirical section, we will first employ the sample structure (7), bearing in mind the possible complication (9).

C.   The Demand for Money

The derivation of our demand function for money will parallel the development of our consumption function, equations (1) through (4), yielding

$$\Delta M_t = \beta_3 e_1 \Delta Y_t + \beta_3 e_2 \Delta R_t + (1 - \beta_3)\Delta M_{t-1} \quad (10)$$

where β_3 is the adjustment coefficient. As in the case of investment, the demand for money may involve more complicated issues than our simple derivation of (10) seems to suggest. Some of these issues have been discussed elsewhere [3]. Without going further into these issues, we merely report that the final form of a demand function consistent with United States annual data from 1897 to 1958 can be first-differenced to yield (10). The rationalization for this final form may be

more involved than is here indicated. However, in view of our present objective of setting forth a macro-economic model, short of embarking on a major project on each equation, we have chosen the simplest and most direct set of assumptions to justify the aggregate equations to be tested.

D.   The Model as a Whole

To build a macro-model from the three major equations (4), (7), and (10), we have to decide what statistical series to use to measure the aggregative variables, and what phenomena in real life to ignore for the purpose of examining the role of the three selected relations alone in determining national income. Consider the identity

$$\text{GNP} = C + I + G + E$$

with consumption, gross investment, government purchases, and net exports over imports as four components. First, we will omit net exports E from our analysis and treat GNP as if it had only three components, $C + I + G$.

It seems reasonable to assume that the income variable appearing in our three demand equations should be net national product $C + I^n + G$ minus government taxes net of transfers T. For the consumption function, such an income variable would differ from the more widely adopted disposable personal income mainly by the inclusion of undistributed corporate profits. Whether undistributed corporate profits should be included in the income variable affecting aggregate demand is an open question. However, the income variable Y which we actually use is $C + I + G - T$, rather than $C + I^n + G - T$. Gross investment is used instead of net investment because the data on capital consumption allowances are admittedly poor, and because the change in the cross-income variable is approximately proportional to the change in the net-income variable.

From the definition of our income variable

$$Y = C + I + G - T \qquad (11)$$

and from our treatment of net exports over imports, undistributed corporate profits, and capital consumption allowances, the strategy of building our model seems apparent. We prefer to combine or to omit certain components of GNP in our equations rather than to introduce additional equations whenever we believe that such aggregation is justified as a first approximation. This strategy differs from the practice of some recent econometric models where we find additional equations introduced for components of GNP without much recourse to theory. The difference in strategy is due partly to our aim of testing macro-economic theory per se, and partly to our unwillingness to introduce equations of which our theoretical knowledge is weak as they may contaminate other equations while using up degrees of freedom.

So far, our model consisting of equations (4), (7), (10) and the identity (11) has not specified the role of government. In our model, government purchases, G, will be treated as exogenous. Taxes minus transfers, T, will be treated as endogenous:[1]

$$T = g(C + I + G) + g_0. \qquad (12)$$

If we denote private aggregate demand

[1] To treat G as exogenous and T as endogenous, rather than $G - T$ as exogenous, is not only a majority view with which I concur, but was supported by a preliminary statistical analysis, where $(G - T)$ showed a negative coefficient in the reduced-form regression of Y. This result can be rationalized by a simplified four-equation model, $C = aY$, $I = bY - bY_{-1}$, (11) and (12), G exogenous. If $g = .2$, then $T = .25Y$. The coefficients in the regression of Y on Y_{-1} and G would be, respectively, negative and positive if $(1 - a - b - .25) > 0$, but the coefficients in the regression of Y on Y_{-1} and $(G - T)$ would be, respectively, positive and negative, as we found (together with other predetermined variables), if $(1 - a - b - .25 - .25) < 0$.

$C + I$ by Y_1, the first difference of the income variable entering into equations (4), (7), and (10) will be

$$\Delta Y = (1 - g)(\Delta Y_1 + \Delta G). \qquad (13)$$

In our statistical investigation, we have occasion to separate the two components, $(1 - g)\Delta Y_1$ and $(1 - g)\Delta G$, of ΔY and study their relative multiplier effects. Since major changes in tax rates occurred during our period of study, in particular in 1943 and 1964, we have to allow for a change in our economic structure in the estimation of its parameters. The same method employed in estimating a changing structure will also be used to assess the effects of the change of tax rates in 1964.

Simple assumptions have been made in order to evaluate the effects of fiscal policies through government expenditures G and the marginal tax rate g. How about monetary policies? Our model is very crude, and possibly too crude, in this regard, since the stock of money, M, will be treated as exogenous. We have made this assumption not so much because a large body of the macro-economic literature has done so, as because we consider the present study as an intermediate step towards an understanding of the role of monetary factors in economic life. If the stock of money is found to be very important, the monetary sector will be investigated in greater detail.

One further issue has to be cleared up before the formulation of our model is complete. This is whether the above equations explaining aggregate consumption and investment expenditures should be interpreted in real terms or in money terms, and, if the former, how are nominal expenditures to be explained. For those who believe that these equations refer to variables in nominal terms, nothing further needs to be said. For them, our model is meant to explain consumption and investment in current dollars, leaving open the decomposition of changes of expenditures into changes in physical units and changes in the price level.

For others, including myself, who believe that considerations in real terms do enter into the behavioral relations specified above, some form of price deflation would be necessary. As our model is not intended to explain relative prices, only the general price level P_t will be used. The relation between a variable, say consumption, in real terms (denoted by C_t^r) and the variable in nominal terms (C) is simply $C_t = P_t C_t^r$, or

$$\Delta C_t \simeq P_t \Delta C_t^r + \Delta P_t C_t^r.$$

Since the second term is small as compared with the first, i.e., the ratio of $\Delta P_t / P_t$ to $\Delta C_t^r / C_t^r$ is small, and since our model does not explain ΔP_t, we will approximate ΔC_t by the first term, and, in fact, by $P_{t-1} \Delta C_t^r$.[2] If our consumption and investment functions are designed for variables in real terms, such as $\Delta C_t^r = \Delta C_t / P_{t-1}$, then equations relating nominal variables can be obtained after multiplication by P_{t-1} and will have the same form as the previous equations except that they will have P_{t-1} as an additional variable. Note that the consumption function as specified by (4) does not include an intercept, but the possibility of a trend would require an intercept. Note also that we purposely did not mention deflation of the demand function for money. The justification, more thoroughly discussed elsewhere [3], is that the income elasticity of demand is unity so that a double-log demand function in nominal variables is valid, and the linear function is considered as an approximation to it. In short, for the consumption and investment functions, we will use a linear deflation device by introducing P_{t-1} as an additional (predetermined) variable.

In summary, our model consists of the

[2] I am indebted to Curry W. Gillmore for a discussion of this point.

following equations (with some simplifications in writing the coefficients):

$$\Delta C_t = a_1 \Delta Y_t + a_2 \Delta C_{t-1} + a_3 \Delta M_t + a_4 P_{t-1} \tag{14}$$

$$\Delta I_t = b_1 \Delta Y_t + b_1' Y_{t-1} + b_2 \Delta R_t + b_2' R_{t-1} + b_3 I_{t-1} + b_4 \Delta M_t + b_5 P_{t-1} \tag{15}$$

$$\Delta M_t = e_1 \Delta Y_t + e_2 \Delta R_t + e_3 \Delta M_{t-1} \tag{16}$$

$$\Delta Y_t = (1 - g)(\Delta Y_{1t} + \Delta G_t) \tag{17}$$

$$\Delta Y_{1t} = \Delta C_t + \Delta I_t. \tag{18}$$

We have chosen to write out the two terms ΔY_t and Y_{t-1}, rather than Y_t and $(1 - d)Y_{t-1}$, in the investment function partly in order to facilitate interpreting the statistical results regarding our formulation of the acceleration hypothesis. According to our formulation, the coefficient of Y_{t-1} should be the rate of depreciation, d, times the coefficient of ΔY_t when these two variables are used. The coefficient of Y_{t-1} is minus $(1 - d)$ times the coefficient of Y_t, as equation (7) was originally written. In equation (15), I_{t-1} has been subtracted from both sides, with ΔI_t replacing I_t as the dependent variable. This would require reinterpretations of the coefficient b_3 and of the multiple correlation coefficient of this equation, the latter being expected to be lower than for I_t. Note also that ΔM_t is included in both equations (14) and (15) just to allow for the possibility that it might affect consumption or investment directly.

Our model of five equations (14) through (18) explains the five dependent variables, ΔC_t, ΔY_t, ΔI_t, ΔR_t, and ΔY_{1t}. Equation (18) is an identity. Equation (17), though not an identity, will be treated as given since g is to be estimated from outside information. We are thus left with three structural equations to estimate. Note, however, that the consumption and investment equations may be broken up according to the durability of the goods concerned, as pointed out in the theoretical discussions above, so that there may be more than three structural equations in our statistical analyses. This and other statistical questions will be discussed in the following section.

II. STATISTICAL CONSIDERATIONS

A. Possible Disaggregation of Consumption and Investment Functions

It has been pointed out that total consumption expenditures might be broken up into two dependent variables, nondurables plus services, and durables. Of course, further disaggregation such as separating services from nondurable goods, and so forth, would be possible, but would not be consistent with the objective of our study. If the behavioral assumptions made in equation (4) apply to consumption expenditures, rather than consumption per se, one may not wish to treat consumer durables separately. If the assumptions made in equation (4) apply to the quantities consumed (i.e., consumption of services from total stock in the case of durables), one can introduce an equation for the expenditures on consumer durables separately. Such an equation can be derived from equation (1), treating C_t as the stock of durables. Instead of taking the difference $C_t - C_{t-1}$ for net investment in consumer durables as in (4), we take the difference $C_t - (1 - d)C_{t-1}$ for gross investment or expenditures on durables as in (7). The resulting function explaining expenditures, denoted by C'_t, will be

$$C'_t = C_t - (1 - d)C_{t-1}$$
$$= \beta_1 a_1 [Y_t - (1 - d)Y_{t-1}]$$
$$+ (1 - \beta_1)C'_{t-1}. \qquad (19)$$

It will have the same form as our gross investment function (7).

Even if we interpret the assumptions about consumer behavior as applying to the amount consumed rather than the amount purchased, equation (4), with C

measuring expenditures, may still be a good approximation to reality. By equation (19), the change in expenditures would be

$$\Delta C'_t = \beta a_1 \Delta Y_t - \beta a_1 (1 - d)\Delta Y_{t-1}$$
$$+ (1 - \beta)\Delta C'_{t-1}. \qquad (20)$$

The only difference between this equation and equation (4) applied to expenditures is the term involving ΔY_{t-1}. The coefficient of ΔY_{t-1} will be small when the rate of depreciation, d, is large. Some consumer durables have annual depreciation rates much smaller than one, for example, approximately .25 for automobiles. However, many consumer durables so classified by the United States Department of Commerce have large annual depreciation rates. It would be a better approximation to group them in equation (4) with a zero coefficient for ΔY_{t-1}, than in equation (20) together with other durables with much smaller rates of depreciation. The ideal treatment of consumer durables, under the constraint that only one equation is introduced, would be to find an optimal grouping of some durables with short lives to be included in equation (4) and other durables with longer lives to be included in equation (19). Short of such a regrouping, it may be as well to treat all consumer expenditures by equation (4). This we will do first, in our statistical analyses, bearing in mind that equation (19) may be introduced for consumer durables separately if the aggregation of all consumer expenditures in (4) fails to be a good approximation.

As far as investment expenditures are concerned, we have pointed out that the interest elasticity varies according to the rate of depreciation. There are three components of gross investment in the Department of Commerce classification, namely, new construction, producers' durable equipment, and change in business inventories. The rate of depreciation for construction is in the neighborhood of the rate of interest, so that $R/(d + R)$ being approximately one-half, the interest elasticity is about half of the price elasticity. Producers' durable equipment is a horse of a very different color. Going through the list of items included in it, one finds very few whose rates of depreciation are as low as .20. Even for $d = .20$, and $R = .05$, the interest elasticity would be about .05/.25, or one-fifth of price elasticity. Therefore, we are led to treat new construction and producer durables separately.

There are three possible treatments for the change in inventories. The first is to combine it with producers' durable equipment, with misgivings partly because it is not a gross concept as gross investment in producer durables, and partly because the statistical entity called change in business inventories is constructed by accounting rather than economic concepts. The second is to treat it separately, thus making a total of three investment equations. If the same functional form as (7) is employed, a similar misgiving as in the first alternative may arise. The third is to exclude inventory change in our definition of GNP (and Y), as net exports E have been excluded. In our statistical analysis, we will first combine inventory changes with producer durables, bearing in mind the other two possibilities if our first attempt fails.

B. Treatment of Change in Tax Rate

During the period of observations used to estimate the parameters of our model, 1929–1963, there was at least one major change in the tax rate, g, occurring in 1943. This change affected the parameters and necessitated a statistical procedure for estimating the changing parameters. Furthermore, to assess the effect of the reduction in g that occurred in 1964, it would also be necessary to evaluate the effect of g on the parameters.

It is quite straightforward to set forth algebraically the dependence of our structural and reduced-form parameters on the tax rate, g. In doing so, we will use a structure of only three behavioral equations, observing that the relations so derived can easily be generalized to deal with possible disaggregation of the consumption or investment functions. When $h(\Delta Y_{1t} + \Delta G_t)$ is substituted for ΔY_t, using equation (17) of section I.D and denoting $(1 - g)$ by h, the three structural equations become

$$\Delta C_t = a_1 h \Delta Y_{1t} + a_1^* h \Delta G_t + a_2 \Delta C_{t-1} \\ + a_3 \Delta M_t + a_4 P_{t-1} \tag{21}$$

$$\Delta I_t = b_1 h \Delta Y_{1t} + b_1^* h \Delta G_t + b_1' Y_{t-1} \\ + b_2 \Delta R_t + b_2' R_{t-1} + b_3 I_{t-1} \\ + b_4 \Delta M_t + b_5 P_{t-1} \tag{22}$$

$$\Delta R_t = c_1 h \Delta Y_{1t} + c_1^* h \Delta G_t + c_2 \Delta M_t \\ + c_3 \Delta M_{t-1} \tag{23}$$

where we have distinguished a_1^*, b_1^*, and c_1^*, from a_1, b_1, and c_1 to allow for the possibility that government expenditures may have different multiplier effects from private expenditures, and we have solved equation (16) in section I.D for the dependent variable ΔR_t, to obtain equation (23). Thus, the proportion of income after tax $h = (1 - g)$ is a multiplicative factor in the coefficients of ΔY_{1t} and ΔG_t in all three structural equations.

The way h enters into the coefficients of the reduced form can also be derived in a straightforward manner. The reduced-form equation for ΔY_{1t} can be obtained by first combining equations (21) and (22), using the identity $\Delta C_t + \Delta I_t = \Delta Y_{1t}$, and then substituting for ΔR_t, using equation (23) and rearranging terms,

$$\Delta Y_{1t} = \frac{1}{1 - h(a_1 + b_1 + b_2 c_1)} [a_2 \Delta C_{t-1} \\ + b_3 I_{t-1} + b_1' Y_{t-1} + b_2' R_{t-1} \\ + h(a_1^* + b_1^* + b_2 c_1^*) \Delta G_t \\ + (a_3 + b_4 + b_2 c_2) \Delta M_t \\ + b_2 c_3 \Delta M_{t-1} + (a_4 + b_5) P_{t-1}]. \tag{24}$$

This reduced-form equation shows that h affects the multiplicative factor $1/[1 -$

$h(a_1 + b_1 + b_2 c_1)$] as applied to all coefficients alike, and, in addition, affects the coefficient of ΔG_t in particular. If (24) is substituted for ΔY_{1t} in the structural equations (21), (22), and (23), reduced-form equations for ΔC_t, ΔI_t, and ΔR_t will result, but they will not be recorded here.

Equation (24) justifies a simple method of estimation using time-series data when tax rate changed from g_1 in period one to g_2 in period two. Let

$$k_1 = \frac{1 - h_1(a_1 + b_1 + b_2 c_1)}{1 - h_2(a_1 + b_1 + b_2 c_1)}$$

To estimate the reduced-form coefficients as of the second (standard) period, we simply multiply the dependent variable ΔY_{1t} by k_1 and one predetermined variable ΔG_t by h_1/h_2 for the first period. The estimated values of the dependent variable for the first period in stage one, of two-stage least squares [15] for example, are estimates of $k_1 \Delta Y_{1t}$. If the coefficients as of the second period are again chosen as standard, structural equations (21), (22), and (23) require that the estimates ΔY_{1t}^* for the first period be multiplied by h_1/h_2. No further changes in the data on ΔG_t are required since it was already multiplied by h_1/h_2. Therefore, *after the reduced form is estimated by changing the data on ΔY_{1t} and ΔG_t as previously indicated, the standard set of structural coefficients can be estimated by multiplying the estimated dependent variable for the first period by the factor $h_1/h_2 k_1$.* The same procedure applies if the method of limited information-maximum likelihood (LIML) is chosen instead of two-stage least squares. The only difference is that, in the second stage, the method of LIML minimizes the sum of squares of residuals of a structural equation in a different direction by treating a linear combination of the dependent variables [2].

In our model, only the reduced-form equation for ΔY_{1t} has to be estimated in the first stage of the method of two-stage least squares. Although another dependent variable, ΔR_t, appears in the investment equation (22), we can estimate the structural equation (23) first to obtain estimated values of ΔR_t, which can then be applied to equation (22) in the second stage. Our method, as described, assumes knowledge of the various factors by which the data on ΔY_{1t} and ΔG_t are multiplied. In practice, we will use extraneous information to estimate the tax rates, g_1 and g_2. Insofar as the factor k_1 depends also on the structural parameters a_1, b_1, b_2, and c_1, we will make some crude estimates of them for insertion into k_1 in order to apply the above estimation procedure. One could iterate until the estimates of these parameters turn out to be close to the values put in for k_1.

Once the reduced-form coefficients in (24) are estimated as of period two, one can obtain a forecasting equation valid for period three, say, when the tax rate is changed to g_3. We multiply the coefficients as of period two by $[1 - h_2(a_1 + b_1 + b_2 c_1)]/[1 - h_3(a_1 + b_1 + b_2 c_1)]$, and the coefficient of ΔG_t, in addition, by h_3/h_2. This case illustrates the point so well discussed by Marschak [11] on the necessity of estimating the parameters of the structural equations even for the purpose of forecasting. It is also an example of the changes in the multipliers resulting from a structural change so much discussed in the literature of macro-economics.

C. A Summary of Statistical Hypotheses

The hypotheses contained in the three-equation model, (21), (22), and (23), that are fairly widely accepted are concerned with:

H1) The signs of various coefficients, except (H4) and (H5) below.

H2) The ratio (depending on the rate of depreciation) of the coefficients of Y_t and of Y_{t-1}, or the ratio of the coefficients of ΔY_t and Y_{t-1}, in the investment function.

H3) Government expenditures having the

same multiplying effects on consumption and investment as private expenditures.

The hypotheses contained in the three-equation model that are somewhat questionable relate to:

H4)   The additional effect of the stock of money on consumption, given income.
H5)   The additional effect of the change in money stock on investment, given the rate of interest.

Other areas which we would like to explore, not necessarily restricted to a three-equation model, include.

H6)   The difference in the interest effects on new construction and on gross investment in producers' durable equipment.
H7)   The possibility of treating expenditures on consumer durables as part of consumer expenditures in one aggregative consumption function.
H8)   The possibility of combining inventory change with investment in producer durables in one equation.
H9)   The extent of money illusion in the aggregate demand functions, and the possibility of applying our model to nominal values of all variables without using the linear deflation device.
H10) The relative importance of the behavioral characteristics of our private economy (including the effect of private expenditures on consumption, the effect of its change on investment, etc.) and of government policies (G_t and M_t) in the determination of national income.
H11) The relative importance of deterministic versus random factors in the explanation of cyclical patterns of national income fluctuations.

The major problems in macro-economics which the present study will not cover include, among others:

1)   The determination of price level.
2)   The mechanism of the supply of money, when money is not treated as exogenous.
3)   The effects on the rate of interest of the demands for other assets than money.

D. Sources of Data

National income data are taken from the United States Department of Commerce. Money data are taken from the *Federal Reserve Bulletin*. In order to make our statistical results reproducible, exact page references will be given. The period of observations on the dependent variables is, annually, from 1931 to 1940, and from 1948 to 1963, providing 26 observations. A list of symbols, their definitions, and sources, is given below.

C_1 Personal consumption expenditures on nondurable goods and services, in millions of current dollars, 1929–1946, from *U.S. Income and Output* (U.S. Department of Commerce, Office of Business Economics, 1958), 118–119; and 1947–1963, from *Survey of Current Business* (July 1964), 8.

C_2 Personal consumption expenditures on durable goods. Source, same as C_1.

C Total personal consumption expenditures, $C_1 + C_2$.

I_{11} Gross private domestic investment in producers' durable equipment, in millions of current dollars. Source, same as C_1.

I_{12} Change in business inventories. Source, same as C_1.

I_1 $I_{11} + I_{12}$.

I_2 New construction. Source, same as C_1.

I Total gross private domestic investment, $I_1 + I_2$.

Y_1 $C + I$.

G Government purchases of goods and services, in millions of current dollars. Source, same as C_1.

$T - G$ Government surplus or deficit ($-$) on income and product account, 1929–1945, from *National Income, 1954 Edition: A Supplement to the Survey of Current Business*, 164–165; 1946–1955, from *U.S. Income and Output*, 188; 1956–1958, equal to federal government surplus, *Survey of Current Business* (July 1962), 16, plus state and local government surplus, *ibid.*, 17; 1959–1963, equal to federal surplus, *Survey of Current Business* (July 1964), 18, plus state and local surplus, *ibid.*, 19.

Y $Y_1 + G - T$.

M Currency and demand deposits adjusted in the middle of the year, in millions of current dollars, 1929–1957, from *Historical Statistics of the United States: Colonial Times to 1957* (U.S. Bureau of the Census, 1960), 646, Series 267; 1958–1963, from *Federal Reserve Bulletin*, various issues.

P GNP deflator (1954 = 100), 1929–1946, from *U.S. Income and Output*, 222; and 1947–1963, from *Survey of Current Business* (July 1964), 10.

R_a Yield of 20-year corporate bonds, 1929–1957, from *Historical Statistics of the United States: Colonial Times to 1957*, 657; 1958–1963, from *Statistical Abstract* (1964), 472, annual percentage rate multiplied by 10,000 in our calculations.

R_b Yield of five-year corporate bonds, source same as R_a.

R_c Bank rate on short-term business loans, 1929–1957, from *Historical Statistics of the United States: Colonial Times to 1957*, 655, Series X-322; 1958–1963, from *Federal Reserve Bulletin*, March issues.

III. EMPIRICAL RESULTS

Graphic method was first used to estimate g_1 and g_2. Annual data on $(C + I + G)$ and on T were plotted on a scatter diagram, for the years 1929 to 1963. Two lines were drawn by free hand to approximate the relationships before and after 1943, respectively. Their slopes are $g_1 = .11$, and

$g_2 = .21$. The ratio h_1/h_2 to be used to adjust the prewar data is therefore $.89/.79$ or 1.12658. After five iterations to estimate the structural coefficients of equations (25) to (28) (see table 1) by the method of two-stage least squares, modified to deal with the tax change, it was found that $a_1 + b_1 + b_2c_1$ is approximately $.88$. The factor k_1 is thus $.711286$. This value will be used for all calculations presented below, without further iterations. If consumption (or investment) is separated into many components, the coefficient a_1 (or b_1) will be the sum of the income effects on these components. In the formula for k_1, this sum will replace a_1. Therefore, the same value of k_1 should be applicable to different versions of our model with varying degrees of disaggregation.

The main set of estimates to be presented belongs to a four-equation model with one consumption function, two investment functions (producer durables combined with inventory change and new construction), and one money demand function, and with no direct effect of money on investment. Eight predetermined variables were used to estimate ΔY_1^* in the first stage. They are ΔC_{t-1}, $I_{1,t-1}$, $I_{2,t-1}$, Y_{t-1}, ΔM_t, ΔM_{t-1}, ΔG_t, and P_{t-1}. Recall that our gross investment function captures the acceleration principle by using ΔY_t and

TABLE 1

COEFFICIENTS OF FOUR STRUCTURAL EQUATIONS

Equation	ΔY_1^*	ΔR_a^*	ΔC_{-1}	$I_{1,-1}$	$I_{2,-1}$	Y_{-1}	ΔM	ΔM_{-1}	ΔG	P_{-1}	Constant	$\dfrac{R^2}{D.W.}$
(25) ΔC	.308 (.094)		.194 (.130)				.408 (.410)		.078 (.159)	87.7 (46.4)	−4797	.850 2.26
(26) ΔI_1	.278 (.084)	.123 (.489)		−.672 (.300)		.010 (.035)			.161 (.192)	152 (193)	−5703	.683 1.87
(27) ΔI_2	.106 (.021)	−.166 (.147)			−.457 (.207)	.033 (.027)			−.061 (.046)	104 (51)	−6060	.773 2.10
(28) ΔR_a	.111 (.062)						−.739 (.305)	.318 (.248)	.187 (.114)		−973	.336 2.54
(29) ΔM	.150	−1.35					.430		.253		−1316	
(30) ΔI_1	.281 (.082)			−.663 (.291)		.009 (.033)			.168 (.186)	159 (187)	−6125	.682 1.91
(31) ΔI_2	.105 (.021)	−.220 (.144)			−.510 (.207)	.041 (.027)				92.8 (51.3)	−5996	.752 2.14

Y_{t-1} as income variables, and ΔR_t and R_{t-1} as interest variables. The coefficients of Y_{t-1} and R_{t-1} are expected to be the rate of depreciation, d, times the coefficients of ΔY_t and ΔR_t, respectively. An explanatory variable, Y_{t-1}, was used in the investment functions to test this formulation of the acceleration principle. R_{t-1} was omitted because its coefficient is a small fraction, d, of the already small coefficient of $\Delta R_t - R_{t-1}$. R_{t-1} had been used in an early stage, but was found to be insignificant. In table 1, the numbers in parentheses denote standard errors of the coefficients, and the last column gives the squared multiple correlation coefficient and the Durbin-Watson statistic [4] for serial correlation, the former above the latter.

Judging equations (25) to (28) against the hypotheses (H1), one must conclude that the signs have all turned out to be as expected, except the coefficient of interest in the investment function (26) which is insignificant anyway (being one-quarter of its standard error). The estimated consumption function shows a marginal propensity (highly significant) of .308 with respect to current income, and an adjustment coefficient (somewhat inaccurate) of $1 - .194$ or .806. A most noteworthy feature of these results is the strong confirmation of our formulation of the acceleration principle (H2). The coefficients of lagged income in both investment functions are small fractions of the coefficients of the change in income, i.e., they are opposite in sign but approximately equal in magnitude to the coefficients of current income. In principle, the ratio of the coefficient of Y_{-1} to the coefficient of ΔY_1^* is an estimate of the annual rate of depreciation, but the point estimates of the coefficients of lagged income in our two investment functions are subject to large errors. The stronger interest effect on construction than on producer durables is in agreement with our hypothesis (H6). In fact, the interest effect on the latter turns out to be

insignificant. The larger adjustment coefficient, .672, for producer durables than the coefficient, .457, for construction appears reasonable, but these estimates contain fairly sizable errors.

In regard to the demand for money, we have found positive effects of income and of lagged money stock, and negative effects of the rate of interest. The estimated equation (28) was solved for ΔM to yield equation (29) for the ease of reading. When equation (29) is compared with a demand for money equation obtained by applying least squares directly to explain the dependent variable M, without using first differences [3, table 2], the coefficients of income and of lagged money stock are found to be similar, but the coefficient of the interest rate, -1.35, turns out to be much larger (in absolute value). This difference can be attributed to the fact that the slope of the regression of M on R is smaller than the slope of the line obtained by regressing R on M. One should note the small squared multiple correlation coefficient, .336, for equation (28). While our demand function for money can explain a large fraction of the variance of money, it can only explain a small fraction of the variance of the rate of interest. As Ralph Turvey [16, p. 460] has reminded us recently,

> If we reverse the demand function for money, we deduce that, ceteris paribus, a change in the quantity of money will alter interest rates. But there are also demand functions for short-term and long-term paper. By the same token, therefore, a change in the quantities of these assets will also alter interest rates. Thus knowledge of the demand function for money, though necessary, is not sufficient to explain interest rates.

The determination of the rate of interest by simply inverting the demand function for money is probably one of the weakest links in macro-economic theory.

The coefficients of P_{-1}, relative to their

standard errors, suggest that, on the question of money illusion (H9), the use of some deflation device is helpful in constructing macro-economic demand relationships. One might disagree on the degree of money illusion, but one should not overlook the possibility that consumption and investment decisions may be made by considerations in physical terms. Our present concern is less with measuring the degree of money illusion than with allowing for the above possibility in testing a set of macro-economic hypotheses.

Concerning the role of government expenditures, it is generally assumed (H3) that G should be added to $C + I$ as a part of aggregate demand. However, our calculations show that this assumption may not be valid. The coefficient of ΔG is smaller than the coefficient of ΔY_1 in all three components of demand (25), (26), and (27), being (insignificantly) negative in the last case. While one might rationalize these coefficients by pointing out the possibly nonpermanent (i.e., undependable for forming future expectations) nature of government expenditures, we are prepared to present our results merely as a vote for skepticism and as a suggestion that G may be given a smaller weight than $C + I$ as a component of effective demand.

The coefficient of money in the consumption function is about the size of its standard error. It is consistent with the hypothesis (H4) that the stock of money has a positive effect on consumption, given income. However, we have found that, via the rate of interest, the effect of money on investment is small. First, there is the weak link between money and interest. Second, the interest effect on durables with relatively short lives is insignificant, and the interest effect on construction is not very strong. This statement remains valid, and so do the other results presented in equations (25) to (28), when interest rates R_b and R_c replace R_a in our calculations. We have also tested the direct effect of

money on investment (H5) by adding ΔM to equations (26) and (27). While the other features of these equations remain about the same, the coefficients of ΔR_a^* and ΔM (and their standard errors) are, respectively, 1.11 (1.67) and .926 (1.494) in the equation for ΔI_1. They are, respectively, $-.070$ (.293) and .095 (.250) in the equation for ΔI_2. These coefficients certainly do not speak for an important effect of money on investment expenditures. An economist whose a priori estimates of the effects of money are high may conclude that our results are consistent with positive (however small) influences of money on consumption and investment. On the other hand, our theoretical discussion has suggested a small interest effect on investment (except for the very durable, perhaps), and the absence of the direct effect of money (except when the capital market is highly imperfect).

There is the possibility, pointed out in section I.B, that the lag structure of investment may be more complicated than that given in equation (7). The more complicated structure (9) was tested. To avoid the problem of multicollinearity, the variables $[Y_t - (1 - d)Y_{t-1}]$, $[R_t - (1 - d)R_{t-1}]$, $[Y_{t-1} - (1 - d)Y_{t-2}]$, and $[R_{t-1} - (1 - d)R_{t-2}]$ in equation (9) were replaced, respectively, by ΔY_t, ΔR_t, ΔY_{t-1}, and ΔR_{t-1}. The variables $I_{1,t-2}$ and $I_{2,t-2}$ were also omitted from the list of predetermined variables used to compute ΔY_i^* in the first stage of two-stage least squares. The nine predetermined variables used in the first stage are ΔC_{t-1}, $I_{1,t-1}$, $I_{2,t-1}$, ΔY_{t-1}, ΔM_t, ΔM_{t-1}, ΔG_t, P_{t-1}, and ΔR_{t-1}. The results are presented in table 2, with the coefficients of both lagged investment variables given in the same column.

First, it can be observed that all major findings from table 1 hold for table 2, including the more significant interest effects on ΔI_2 than on ΔI_1. The t ratios for both the coefficients of ΔR_a^* and $\Delta R_{a,t-1}$ are

TABLE 2

TEST OF AN ALTERNATIVE LAG STRUCTURE FOR INVESTMENT

Equation	ΔY_1*	ΔR_a*	ΔC_{-1}	$\dfrac{I_{1,-1}}{I_{1,-2}}$	$\dfrac{I_{2,-1}}{I_{2,-2}}$	ΔY_{-1}	$\Delta R_{a,-1}$	ΔM	ΔM_{-1}	ΔG	P_{-1}	Constant	R^2 D.W.
(32) ΔC	.308 (.095)		.186 (.130)					.421 (.408)		.078 (.159)	89.7 (46.2)	−4936	.850 2.20
(33) ΔI_1	.298 (.127)	−.074 (.486)		−.433 (.503) −.395 (.229)		−.135 (.157)	−.123 (.332)			.113 (.213)	316 (215)	−13035	.731 1.92
(34) ΔI_2	.110 (.026)	−.244 (.145)			.057 (.182) −.286 (.171)	−.051 (.036)	−.054 (.099)			−.075 (.044)	151 (48)	−7160	.812 2.15
(35) ΔR_a	.128 (.061)							−.786 (.296)	.294 (.242)	.188 (.111)		−1027	.369 2.36

larger (in absolute value) in equation (34) than in equation (33); in fact, they are extremely insignificant in equation (33). Second, the results of table 2 are inconclusive regarding whether the more complicated lag structure (9) is an improvement over the simple structure (7). There are minor improvements in the negative point estimates of the two interest coefficients in equation (33), in the negative coefficients of $I_{1,-2}$ and $I_{2,-2}$ in equations (33) and (34), respectively, as expected. On the other hand, the coefficients (though insignificant) that have wrong signs include the two coefficients of ΔY_{-1} and the coefficient of $I_{2,-1}$ in equation (34). Thus, there is insufficient evidence in favor of choosing the structure (9) in preference to (7).

We have also separated expenditures on consumer durables (H7) according to equation (19), and found expected signs and magnitudes for all coefficients. When inventory change (H8) was separated from I_1, the coefficients also behaved as expected. However, the gains in disaggregation did not justify inclusion of either equation in the model. Space does not permit presentation of results using real (1954) values (omitting P_{t-1}), but they support all stated conclusions.

As an over-all evaluation, one must conclude that the very aggregative model of table 1 has stood up very well against the

data of the United States from the 1930's to the 1960's. Not only have the signs of all coefficients turned out as expected, but the fractions of the variances of annual changes in consumption and investment expenditures that are explained by the respective equations are quite large. Note that I_{t-1} has been subtracted from both sides of the original investment function to yield a function explaining the first difference of investment. The multiple correlations for levels of investment are even higher than the ones shown for changes in investment. Investment expenditures have been found to depend heavily on the changes in income, thus being no more exogenous than consumption expenditures. The Durbin-Watson statistics are all close to two, indicating that most serial correlations in the residuals have been eliminated by taking first differences. When the levels of the variables were used instead, the Durbin-Watson statistics ranged between .5 and 1.2, approximately.

IV. GOODNESS OF FIT AND FORECASTING VALUE OF THE MODEL

For the purposes of explaining and predicting national income, the reduced-form equation for ΔY_1 will be used. This is the restricted reduced-form equation, obtained by solving the estimated structural equations, rather than the unrestricted equation, by regressing ΔY_1 freely on the predetermined variables. Since the coefficient of ΔR_a^* in equation (26) and the coefficient of ΔG in equation (27) both have the wrong sign and are highly insignificant, they are assumed to be zero, and equations (26) and (27) have been recomputed to yield equations (30) and (31) in table 1. Equations (25), (28), (30), and (31) are used to compute the restricted reduced-form equation for ΔY_1.

Following the well-known Hicksian discussion [7], we will first obtain an IS (equation 36) curve relating income, interest, and the predetermined variables by combining equations (25), (30), and (31). The LL (equation 37) curve is simply equation (28), now solved for ΔY_1 as a function of interest and the predetermined variables. These two equations are presented in table 3. Using them to eliminate ΔR, one arrives at the restricted reduced-form equation (38).

When the restricted reduced-form equation (38) is used to explain the actual changes in private expenditures ΔY_1, for the periods 1931–1940, and 1948–1953, the square of the correlation coefficient is .69, and the standard error is approximately eight billion current dollars. Our model thus explains about 70 per cent of the variance of ΔY_1. It is significant to note that a standard error of eight billion dollars in explaining national income is not large even compared with econometric models consisting of many more equations [13].

In table 4, the values of ΔY_1 computed from the restricted reduced form are compared with the actual values (in billions of dollars). For the ten observations of the prewar period, the actual figures shown are $k_1 = .711286$ times ΔY_1, and the predetermined variable for the changes in government expenditures is $h_1/h_2 = 1.12658$ times ΔG, since the standard set of coefficients of equation (38) given in table 3 is valid for the period 1948–1963. The model is able to trace the declines in income during the three depression years and in 1938. For 1949, it shows a downturn, but overestimates the level of income by some 11 billion dollars. It would have predicted practically no increase in income in 1957, while the actual annual figures indicate no change in 1958. In this connection, one must note the limitation of an annual model in explaining the timing of minor recessions.

Besides examining the goodness of fit, it is interesting to evaluate the predictive value of the reduced-form equation for the years 1964, 1965, and 1966, not included in the estimation of its parameters. The data on the predetermined variables for these years are shown in table 3. The figures for 1966 are guesses made after inspecting the data for the first quarter of 1965, which is the last set of data available at the time of writing (July 1965). Using the coefficients of equation (38), and *without adjustments for the change in income tax rates that occurred in 1964*, one obtains the values of estimated ΔY_1 as given in table 4.

TABLE 3

DERIVATION OF REDUCED-FORM EQUATION THROUGH IS AND LL EQUATIONS

Coefficients of			ΔR_a	ΔC_{-1}	$I_{1,-1}$	$I_{2,-1}$	Y_{-1}	ΔM	ΔM_{-1}	ΔG	P_{-1}	Constant
(36)	IS	ΔY_1	−.7171	.6323	−2.162	−1.664	.1631	1.331		.8046	1106	−55195
(37)	LL	ΔY_1	9.017					6.663	−2.866	−1.688		8770
(38)	R	ΔY_1		.5857	−2.002	−1.541	.1511	1.724	−.2112	.6210	1025	−50479
Data												
	1964			18200	35400	46600	457000	6187	4622	6000	118.5	
	1965			24300	38800	48900	487000	6669	6187	5000	120.7	
	1966			28700	45000	51000	524000	7000	6669	6000	122.7	

TABLE 4

GOODNESS OF FIT OF REDUCED-FORM
EQUATION (38)

Year	Actual ΔY_1	Estimated ΔY_1
1931	−10.23	−6.24
1932	−11.83	−9.72
1933	−1.73	−5.81
1934	4.98	3.62
1935	5.54	10.82
1936	6.01	5.91
1937	5.68	.02
1938	−5.48	−7.89
1939	3.97	4.22
1940	5.80	4.94
1948	24.53	20.14
1949	−7.26	4.18
1950	30.80	21.93
1951	21.16	16.68
1952	3.50	14.69
1953	13.35	17.26
1954	3.91	10.61
1955	33.89	24.69
1956	16.50	5.79
1957	14.01	1.41
1958	−1.45	11.29
1959	36.42	36.31
1960	13.72	3.83
1961	6.12	22.05
1962	29.77	26.17
1963	21.08	19.87
1964	30.00	21.43
1965	. . .	21.32
1966	. . .	16.98

By how much should the estimates of ΔY_1 be raised because of the tax reduction? It was indicated in section II.B that the estimate should be multiplied by the factor $[I - h_2(a_1 + b_1 + b_2 c_1)]/[1 - h_3(a_1 + b_1 + b_2 c_1)]$, and that, in addition, the coefficient of ΔG should be multiplied by h_3/h_2. The latter adjustment is minor. We will not go into any elaborate method of estimating the marginal tax rate after 1964 since this can be a project in itself. To get a rough estimate of the effect of the 1964 tax reduction via our model, it is sufficient to try some reasonable guesses on g_3. If g_3 is .18, as compared with $g_2 = .21$, the above factor will be $[1 - .79(.88)]/$

$[1 - .82(.88)] = 1.095$. It will be 1.131 for $g_3 = .17$, and 1.061 for $g = .19$. It seems reasonable to increase the estimates of ΔY_1 given in table 4 by about ten per cent for the years 1964, 1965, and 1966.[3]

Regardless of the accuracy of our guess for g_3, one can reasonably conclude that our forecast for 1964 is quite close. We are also predicting two more prosperous years, 1965 and 1966, with the rate of increase perhaps a little lower in 1966 than in 1965. How good our forecasts for these years are, only time will tell.

V. RELATIVE IMPORTANCE OF VARIOUS FACTORS IN INCOME DETERMINATION

Since the effect of the rate of interest on investment expenditures and the direct effect of money on the same are small, the reduced-form equation (38) in table 3 is nearly the same as the IS (equation 36) curve alone. With ΔY_1 plotted along the y-axis and ΔR along the x-axis, the IS curve is practically flat, and the LL (equation 37) curve nearly vertical.[4] Thus, the expenditure sector is much more important than the monetary sector in the determination of aggregate demand. The multiplier and the accelerator are more important than liquidity preference.

The effect of money amounts to 1.7 dollars of ΔY_1 per dollar of ΔM, and minus 0.2 dollars of ΔY_1, per dollar of ΔM_{t-1}. During the 26 years included in our sam-

[3] These are short-run effects of tax reduction, given the predetermined variables for the current year, and not the (larger) long-run effects of comparative statics. This note is added after conversation with Carl Shoup.

[4] The coefficients in table 3 are point estimates, some subject to sizable errors. The LL curve would be more nearly vertical if money were dropped from the consumption function (25). Without preconceptions, we have no reason to drop money from (25), especially because the coefficient of ΔM in equation (38) is not far from the coefficient in the unrestricted reduced-form equation for ΔY_1. This note is added after a comment from Michael Lovell.

ple, the standard deviation of ΔM was 2.7 billion dollars. To prevent the fall in Y_1 of ten billion dollars in 1931 (in a structure equivalent to the postwar period), it would have taken an increase of 10/1.7 or 5.9 billion in money stock, as compared with its actual figure. Since ΔM was -1.6 in 1931, the net increase required would have been 4.3 billion. The effectiveness of monetary policy depends also on whether such large changes in money stock can be achieved by the government authorities, a question beyond the scope of this paper.

While the coefficient of ΔM in equation (38) is 1.7, the coefficient of ΔG is only .62. Thus, a dollar increase of government expenditures has a much smaller effect on private expenditures than a dollar increase in money stock. (In the unrestricted reduced-form equation for ΔY_1, the coefficient of ΔM is 1.3 and the coefficient of ΔG is .76.) We have pointed out that ΔG has smaller coefficients than $\Delta(C + I)$ in the consumption and investment functions, and that our results question the generally accepted treatment of government expenditures on an equal footing with private expenditures in macro-economics. Our calculations show that, while the multiplier of ΔM is not large, the multiplier of ΔG is even smaller, being slightly over a third of the former. The multiplier is here defined for private expenditures Y_1 only. The multiplier of ΔG for GNP would be one plus .62, similar to the money multiplier.

Having suggested two main qualifications to the "extreme Keynesian" expenditure model, namely, the dependence of investment on income and the small weight given to government expenditures, we wish to emphasize the limitation of using a demand function for money alone for the determination of national income. As the LL curve in table 3 is much less important than the IS curve in the derivation of the reduced-form equation (38), it would be highly misleading to use the demand for

money equation alone to explain or predict ΔY_1. The coefficient of ΔM in this equation is 6.7, but the partial derivative of ΔY_1 with respect to ΔM in equation (38) is only 1.7.

VI. A NOTE ON DYNAMIC CHARACTERISTICS

Space does not permit a thorough discussion of the dynamic properties of our model. By simulation or analytical methods, one can investigate the cyclical patterns of national income fluctuations inherent in our model. Since one of the intellectual stimulants of the present study is Samuelson's classic paper on the interactions of the multiplier and the acceleration principles [14], we will briefly indicate whether the structural equations net of random disturbances and of exogenous forces can generate cyclical fluctuations in the dependent variables.

This task is accomplished [1] by retaining only the lagged dependent variables in the reduced-form equations:

$$Y_{1t} = 1.7368C_{t-1} - .8510I_{1,t-1} - .3898I_{2,t-1} - .5857C_{t-2} \qquad (39)$$

$$C_t = 1.4210C_{t-1} - .5707I_{1,t-1} - .4285I_{2,t-1} - .3744C_{t-2} \qquad (40)$$

$$I_{1t} = .2157C_{t-1} - .1729I_{1,t-1} - .3810I_{2,t-1} - .1643C_{t-2} \qquad (41)$$

$$I_{2t} = .1001C_{t-1} - .1074I_{1,t-1} + .4196I_{2,t-1} - .0470C_{t-2} \qquad (42)$$

$$C_t^* = 1.0000C_{t-1} + .0000I_{1,t-1} + .0000I_{2,t-1} + .0000C_{t-1}^* \qquad (43)$$

The characteristic roots of the matrix of the coefficients of the system (40), (41), (42), and (43) are 1.0003, .49010, and .08878 $\pm$ .12202i. The largest root indicates a very slight element of growth (all exogenous variables including M constant). Since a pair of complex roots exists, there are signs of oscillations in the system.

Although our system is different from Samuelson's simple system [14], especially in the fact that the Samuelson system postulates the dependence of investment on the change in income lagged one period, it is capable of generating cyclical fluctuations.

VII. CONCLUDING REMARKS

A major limitation of this study is that, because annual data are used to cover both the prewar and postwar periods, the precise lag structures of the equations cannot be ascertained. This limitation applies in particular to our test of the more complicated lag structure (9) for investment and to the use of the reduced-form equation (38) for the purpose of forecasting the timing of a recession. Our major finding is that macroeconomics is useful, the multiplier and the accelerator being more important than liquidity preference. The multiplier stems not only from the dependence of consumption expenditures on income, but also from the dependence of investment expenditures on the change in income. Our formulation of the acceleration principle has come out beautifully, supporting the consensus of recent studies of investment on a micro level [5, 8, 10]. While the stock of money is not so important as the advocates of a modern version of the quantity theory of money [e.g., 6] would claim, government expenditures have even a smaller multiplying effect on private expenditures, dollar for dollar, than money stock.

REFERENCES

[1] W. J. Baumol, *Economic Dynamics* (New York: MacMillan, 1959).

[2] G. C. Chow, "A Comparison of Alternative Estimators for Simultaneous Equations," *Econometrica*, 32, No. 4 (1964), 532–553.

[3] G. C. Chow, "On the Long-run and Short-run Demand for Money," *Journal of Political Economy*, 74, No. 2 (1966), 111–131.

[4] J. Durbin and G. S. Watson, "Testing for Serial Correlation in Least Squares Regression II, *Biometrica*, 38 (1951), 159–178.

[5] R. Eisner, "Investment: Fact and Fancy," *American Economic Review*, 53, No. 2 (1963), 237–246.

[6] M. Friedman and D. Meiselman, "The Relative Stability of Monetary Velocity and the Investment Multiplier in the United States," *Stabilization Policies* (Englewood Cliffs, N.J.: Prentice-Hall, 1964).

[7] J. R. Hicks, "Mr. Keynes and the 'Classics'; A Suggested Interpretation," *Econometrica*, 5, No. 2 (1937), 147–159 [reprinted in this volume, Selection 10].

[8] D. W. Jorgenson, "Capital Theory and Investment Behavior," *American Economic Review*, 53, No. 2 (1963), 247–259.

[9] J. M. Keynes, *The General Theory of Employment, Interest and Money* (New York: Harcourt, Brace, 1936).

[10] E. Kuh, "Theory and Institutions in the Study of Investment Behavior," *American Economic Review*, 53, No. 2 (1963), 260–268.

[11] J. Marschak, "Economic Measurements for Policy and Prediction," Chapter I of W. C. Hood and T. C. Koopmans, ed., *Studies in Econometric Method* (New York: John Wiley, 1953).

[12] F. Modigliani, "Liquidity Preference and the Theory of Interest and Money," *Econometrica*, 12, No. 1 (1944), 45–88.

[13] M. Nerlove, "A Tabular Survey of Macro-Econometric Models," Technical Report No. 9 (Institute for Mathematical Studies in the Social Sciences, Stanford University, 1965).

[14] P. A. Samuelson, "Interactions between the Multiplier Analysis and the
Principle of Acceleration," this RE-
VIEW, 21, No. 2 (1939), 75–78 [re-
printed in this volume, Selection 18].

[15] H. Theil, *Economic Forecasts and*
Policy (Amsterdam: North-Holland,
1961).

[16] R. Turvey, "On the Demand for
Money," *Econometrica*, 33, No. 2
(1965), 459–460.

31

Employment, Inflation and Growth*

A. W. PHILLIPS

1. INTRODUCTION

Since the end of the second world war economic policy and controversy in Britain have been directed to ways of attaining a number of related objectives, prominent among which are the maintenance of a high and stable level of employment, reasonable stability of the average level of final product prices, a fairly rapid rate of economic growth, a satisfactory balance of foreign trade and reasonable stability of foreign exchange rates. It can hardly be claimed that there has been complete success in the attainment of these objectives. It is true that employment has been maintained at an extremely high level. The average level of unemployment since 1948 has been little more than 1½ percent of the work force. This is probably a lower level of unemployment than that attained

***

Reprinted from *Economica*, New Series, vol. 29 (February 1962), pp. 1–16, by permission of the publisher and author.

A. W. Phillips teaches at the Australian National University; he was formerly at the London School of Economics.

* Inaugural lecture given at the London School of Economics and Political Science on 28th November, 1961.

in any single year in peace time during the previous century, except perhaps in 1872. Even in the boom years of the pre-war trade cycle the percentage of trade unionists unemployed rarely fell below 2 percent and over the 53 years from 1861 to 1913 it averaged 4½ percent. The actions taken to improve the stability of the system have also had some measure of success. Before the first world war there was a fairly regular trade cycle with an average period of about eight years, during which trade union unemployment fluctuated between about 2 and 10 percent. Since the second world war the cyclical movements in economic activity have become more rapid, with a period of four or five years, but the fluctuations have been smaller. Unemployment, indeed, has only fluctuated between about 1 percent and 2½ percent, that is, over a range of about 1½ percent, but the percentage fluctuations in gross national product about the growth trend have been about five times as large as this,[1] the range of the fluctuations as a percentage of the trend being about 7 or 8 percent. Between 1948 and 1960, gross national

[1] See F. W. Paish, "Output, Inflation and Growth," to be published.

product increased at an average rate of about $2\frac{3}{4}$ percent per annum and productivity per man hour at perhaps $1\frac{3}{4}$ percent per annum. Though these rates of increase probably compare favourably with those in earlier periods of British history they are lower than those of a number of other industrial countries in the same period. The average rate of rise of the retail price index between 1948 and 1960 was 3.7 percent per annum. There would be fairly general agreement that this rate of inflation is undesirable. It has undoubtedly been a major cause of the general weakness of the balance of payments and the foreign reserves, and if continued it would almost certainly make the present rate of exchange untenable.

It is my belief that one of the main reasons for the difficulties that have been experienced in devising and implementing appropriate economic policies is lack of adequate quantitative knowledge and understanding of how the economic system works. Of course, economists do understand, in a general sort of way, quite a lot about the working of the economic system and do now have a mass of quantitative information about important economic variables. But in order to bring this knowledge to bear on the problem of formulating and attaining a consistent set of policy objectives we require also knowledge of the quantitative relations between economic variables. In particular it is necessary to know what quantitative relations hold between those economic variables which are either the objectives of policy or the instruments through which we attempt to attain the objectives. For example, if some relation holds, in given institutional conditions and on average over a period of years, between the level of employment and the speed of inflation, failure to take account of it may lead to the adoption of inconsistent objectives and to a type of schizophrenic behaviour as attempts are made to attain these incon-

sistent aims. Knowledge of the relation would lead either to modification of the objectives to make them consistent or perhaps, since an economic relation is only the result of fairly regular patterns of human behaviour, to some modification of institutions or behaviour which would alter the relation so as to permit some more desirable combinations of consistent aims. Or again, if at a certain time unemployment is felt to be too high and short-term interest rates are lowered in order to raise the demand for goods and so for labour, how large will the effects be and when will they occur; will the higher demand also lead to an increase in fixed investment and if so how large an increase and after what interval of time; will wage rates and prices rise more rapidly as a result of the higher demand; if internal demand and prices rise will imports rise and exports fall, and if so when and by how much? If we are to assess the effects of our attempts to influence the course of economic affairs we need answers, numerical answers, to questions like these. If we do not have this knowledge the policy adjustments will almost certainly be inappropriate in magnitude or timing or both and may well cause, as I believe they have often caused in the past, unnecessary and harmful fluctuations in economic activity.

We may obtain tentative estimates of a quantitative relation in economics by making a preliminary subjective analysis of human motivation and behaviour and then carrying out a statistical analysis of relevant data from past records. We also need to investigate the degree of error that there may be in the estimate, the extent to which the relation in successive short time periods departs from its average over longer periods and whether there is any evidence that the average relation changes in any systematic way through time. On the basis of quantitative estimates of this sort it is possible to set up simplified models of the economic system and by studying the properties of different models with a variety of policy relationships we can form some judgement of the likely effects of alternative types of economic policy. The empirical study of economic relations and the quantitative investigation of the behaviour of models of economic processes are comparatively recent developments in our subject. The knowledge and understanding which have so far been gained are far from being adequate for a firm and detailed appraisal of economic policy. I think they do, however, make possible some attempt at clarification of the problems we face and justify some suggestions for methods of dealing with them.

2. SOME GENERAL PRINCIPLES OF FLUCTUATIONS AND STABILITY

The first policy objective I should like to consider is that of maintaining a stable level of employment; but before proceeding to this it seems desirable to illustrate some general points about equilibrium, stability and fluctuations in the simplest possible way. Let me therefore consider a single commodity which is being continuously produced and consumed and which is traded on a perfectly competitive market. Assume that the rate of production is an increasing function of price, the rate of consumption is a decreasing function of price and that the rate of change of the price is proportional to the excess demand, i.e., to the rate of consumption minus the rate of production. This is the simple text-book example of supply and demand in a single competitive market. It is frequently stated, and has indeed been stated with some emphasis by such eminent economists as Walras, Marshall and Wicksell, that such a system is necessarily stable, i.e., that it always tends to an equilibrium in which the price is such that the rates of production and consumption are equal. The argument is usually very simple. Suppose the system is not in equilibrium; for

example, suppose there is excess demand. Then the price will rise. This will increase production and reduce consumption and so reduce the excess demand. Since the price continues to rise so long as there is any excess demand and any rise in price reduces the excess demand the process will continue until the excess demand is eliminated. In brief; the existence of any discrepancy between production and consumption causes a movement in price which tends to correct the discrepancy. Therefore, the argument runs, the system is stable. This argument is, of course, fallacious except on the assumption that the complete response of the rates of production and consumption to any change in price occurs instantaneously. If there are any time lags in any of the responses the system will usually fluctuate. Whether the fluctuations will die away or whether they will increase in amplitude and tend to some regular and sustained limit cycle depends on the precise forms of the time lags, on the slopes of the supply and demand curves and on the speed at which the price changes when there is a given excess demand.

The competitive model which we have been considering, and other so-called "self-equilibrating" models of economic processes are, in fact, examples of what are known in other fields of study as "negative feed-back control systems." In order to see intuitively why these systems are often oscillatory and may well be unstable (which means in practice that they tend to produce fairly large and regular cyclical movements) let us consider again the competitive market. Assume this time that some factor other than price causes small cyclical changes in production or consumption, so that excess demand is alternately positive and negative (see curve *a* of Figure 1). We shall call this an exogenous movement of excess demand and see what further movements in excess demand would be induced by price changes which depended only on this exogenous movement. In other words we shall find what would usually be called the corrective movements in excess demand which result from the price changes caused by the exogenous movements in excess demand. Since we are assuming that the rate of change of price is proportional to the exogenous movements in excess demand, the rate of change of price would have the same time pattern as the exogenous movement. The price itself, however, would lag behind the rate of change of price by a quarter of a cycle (see curve *b*) since the price would be at its maximum when its rate of change was zero and changing from positive to negative, and would be at a minimum when its rate of change was zero and changing from negative to positive. If the complete response of production and consumption to any change in price was instantaneous, the excess demand induced by the movements of price would be at its minimum when price was at its maximum and vice versa (see curve *c*). Suppose, however, that production and consumption responded to changes in price with a time lag equal to one quarter of the period of the cycle. Then the excess demand induced by the price changes would be exactly in phase with the exogenous movements in excess demand (see curve *d*). Instead of tending to offset or correct the exogenous movement, the induced changes would tend to accentuate or amplify the fluctuations in excess demand caused by the exogenous movement. It is intuitively plausible, and can in fact be proved, that if, in this case, what are usually called the equilibrating or corrective forces are strong enough to make the amplitude of the induced movements in excess demand greater than the amplitude of the exogenous movements, the system will be unstable, that is, the fluctuations will increase and tend towards a regular and sustained limit cycle.

The exogenous movements or disturbances which affect economic activity are

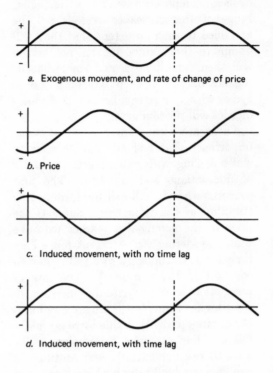

a. Exogenous movement, and rate of change of price

b. Price

c. Induced movement, with no time lag

d. Induced movement, with time lag

Figure 1.

not usually, of course, of the simple type assumed in this example. They are more likely to be of a rather arbitrary or random pattern which can be described only in terms of a statistical or stochastic process. Such processes can, however, be analysed, by a method known as spectral density analysis, into cyclical components with periods ranging over the whole spectrum from zero to infinity. If disturbances of this sort operate on the model we have been considering, any cyclical component whose period is such that the time lag in the response of excess demand to price results in a lag in the neighbourhood of a quarter of the cyclical period will be amplified, while cyclical components whose periods are widely different from this will be reduced in amplitude. If the "correcting forces" are sufficiently strong the cyclical components within a particular range of frequencies or periods will be amplified to such an extent that they will dominate the market movements, which will then exhibit large and somewhat irregular fluctuations, in which, however, cycles with this particular range of periodicities will predominate.

There are two more matters of some importance that I should like to refer to while dealing with the general principles of fluctuations and stability. The first concerns what I shall call the form or distribution of the time lags. Suppose the price in the commodity market we have been considering was constant for a long time and then suddenly rose and remained constant at the new level. The rate of production would eventually increase to some higher value, but there are any number of time paths that this increase might follow. For example, production might start to rise immediately and continue to rise at a gradually diminishing rate, or it might remain constant for a while and then increase gradually, or it might remain constant for a longer time and then increase very suddenly (see curves *a* and *b* and *c* in Figure 2). Now it can be shown, but

by methods which I shall not inflict on you here, that the existence of a time lag of the first form in the corrective process is much less likely to cause fluctuations and instability than a lag of the second form, and a lag of the second form is less likely to cause these troubles than is the third form of lag. An important rule in devising a corrective system is therefore to get the corrective adjustment started immediately the discrepancy it is intended to correct begins to be observed. Provided a fair proportion of the effect of the corrective action is obtained fairly quickly it does not much matter if the remaining effects are delayed; but it does matter very much if the corrective action itself or all of its effects are delayed.

The second matter which I should like to deal with briefly is that of alternative types of corrective action. It is perhaps best introduced by asking what would happen if in the simple commodity model which we considered earlier it was the price rather than the rate of change of price which depended on the excess demand. We see from the curves that the price movements would occur a quarter of a cycle earlier as a result of this modification, and the induced movements in excess demand would no longer be in phase with the exogenous movements, so that the destabilising effects of the induced movements would be reduced or eliminated. Depending on the form of the time lag, it might or might not be possible to find a cycle of higher frequency, that is, of shorter period, for which the lag in the response of excess demand to price was half a cycle instead of a quarter cycle. If so, an exogenous movement of this higher frequency would lead to an induced movement in phase with the exogenous movement and if the amplitude of the induced movement was sufficiently large instability could still occur at the higher frequency. But since most forms of time lag are in effect weighted averages and tend to pro-

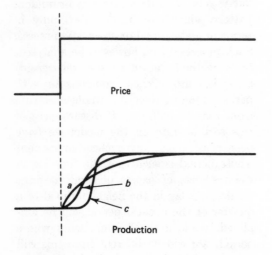

Figure 2.

duce a low amplitude of response to high frequency cycles the likelihood of cyclical instability would be reduced. On the other hand this form of correction, which is called proportional control, could never ensure that production and consumption were brought into equality, since the price would be constant if excess demand were constant, even if it were not zero. However, a combination of proportional control and the type of correction used before, which is called integral control, overcomes this difficulty and gives better performance than integral control alone. We may go further in this direction and consider the effect of adding to the corrective action a component based on the rate of change of excess demand. Since the fluctuations in the rate of change of a cyclical variable lead the fluctuations in the variable itself by a quarter of a cycle, this component of corrective action, known as derivative control, has a somewhat similar effect to that which would be obtained by basing the corrective action on a forecast of excess demand. A derivative component of control is used in combination with proportional and integral components in most negative feed-back control systems. By an appropriate combination of the three components it is usually possible to obtain very good regulating performance of a system, with corrective actions based only on the actual values of the variables and their rates of change in the immediate past, and without any recourse to predicted values or forecasts.

3. FLUCTUATIONS IN EMPLOYMENT AND ECONOMIC ACTIVITY

I hope I have not bored you too much by this rather long and somewhat technical digression on the general principles of fluctuations and stability. But I think some understanding of these principles is helpful in a discussion of the stability of employment and economic activity. For the cor-

rective adjustments which affect employment and activity in the whole economy, whether they be inherent in the working of the economy or applied as deliberate instruments of policy, are again examples of control by negative feed-back. The use of forecasts in policy does not substantially affect this statement, since the forecasts are themselves largely based on observations of the economy and its movements in the recent past. Indeed, given the present state of the art of forecasting I believe that better results might be obtained by basing suitable corrective action directly on observations of the economy and its changes rather than on forecasts which are themselves largely derived, perhaps by dubious processes, from those observations.

Even if there were no special features which might accentuate disturbances and fluctuations in the economy as a whole, it could not be assumed that the existence of corrective adjustments, even quite powerful corrective adjustments, would stabilise an economy. If they operate with long time lags, and especially if there are long delays before they commence to operate, they will cause cyclical fluctuations, and the stronger the corrective forces the more violent will be the fluctuations. But there is fairly general agreement among economists that there are special features of an economic system, in particular the multiplier process and adjustments in inventories and capital equipment, which accentuate disturbances and tend to cause cyclical fluctuations. These features increase the need for deliberate stabilisation policies, but also make it more difficult to devise suitable policies.

The problem is best studied by investigating the properties of a variety of models in which use is made of the limited amount of quantitative knowledge at present available about economic relationships. The work involved in such investigations is greatly reduced and the range of possible models is widened by the use of modern electronic equipment. The results obtained in this way cannot, of course, be conclusive, but from the investigations I have done so far I have considerable confidence in two simple propositions. The first is that corrective action taken in an attempt to reduce the amplitude of the short cycle of four or five years which is typical of the post-war period is not likely to be successful unless it is based on recently observed rates of change of economic activity as well as on the level of activity. The other is that even if the corrective action is appropriate in this respect it will still be unsuccessful unless a fair proportion of its ultimate direct effect on demand, say about a quarter of it, occurs within three or four months of the occurrence of the error it is designed to correct, and at least one half of the full effect within about six months.

Let us examine some of the existing means of influencing demand in the light of these requirements. The response of investment to changes in monetary conditions and interest rates is almost certainly delayed and slow. There is probably a delay of some months before decisions to invest are significantly affected and with most types of investment there is probably a further long time lag between the decisions to invest and the actual production of capital goods. If this is so, fluctuations are likely to be intensified rather than reduced by attempts to correct them through operating on long-term interest rates and investment in fixed capital. This does not mean that interest rate policy is unimportant. I believe it has a vital rôle to play in the slower adjustments required as a result of changes in the desire to save or invest, and thus in influencing the average level of employment and the average rate of change of the price level over fairly long periods.

It is more difficult to judge the effect of operating on short-term credit and short interest rates. Adjustments in these can be made more quickly than in long rates, and to the extent that they affect the desire or ability to hold inventories they might have a significant effect on production within two or three months. But I think much more empirical work will be needed before one can judge with confidence the magnitude, speed and reliability of these effects. I suspect that if fairly large and rapid adjustments in short-term credit conditions were made in response to both the level and the rate of change of economic activity they would help to reduce the amplitude of the short cycle. But there is a difficulty in using adjustments of short-term credit and interest rates for this purpose. Short rates, and perhaps to a lesser extent credit, are closely related to bank rate, and the level of bank rate is often made to depend as much on the state of the foreign reserves as on the internal condition of the economy. To the extent that fluctuations in the foreign reserves are the result of fluctuations in the balance of trade they will tend to lag behind fluctuations in the balance of trade by a quarter of a cycle. Since the balance of trade moves fairly closely with internal activity, fluctuations in the reserves tend to lag behind internal activity, so that changes in bank rate tend to be too late for satisfactory correction of economic fluctuations.

My conclusion concerning monetary policy is thus similar to that of the Radcliffe Committee;[2] ". . . monetary measures cannot alone be relied upon to keep in nice balance an economy subject to major strains from both without and within. Monetary measures can help, but that is all." My reasons for this conclusion are perhaps a little different from those of the

[2] *Report of the Committee on the Working of the Monetary System*, Cmnd. 827 (1959), p. 183.

Committee. I think that changes in interest rates and credit conditions probably do have quite powerful effects on demand, but that their usefulness for correcting short-period fluctuations is seriously limited as a result of the long time lags in the response of investment to changes in interest rates, and in the case of credit as a result of the temptation or need to make the adjustments in response to the state of the foreign reserves rather than at the times appropriate to the correction of fluctuations in internal economic activity. Much more research will have to be done, however, before the last word is said on these matters, and I would heartily endorse the Committee's statement[3] that ". . . it is essential to have much greater and more systematic knowledge of the factors that make up the financial system and of their relative movements."

Turning to fiscal methods of influencing demand, it is clear that adjustments through annual budgets do not meet the requirements I have stated for the correction of short-period cycles. Budget changes have probably played some part, together with monetary policy, in overcoming the more severe and longer cycles of pre-war days, though this may have come about as much through the confidence of business men that the budget could and would be used to avert a severe slump, with the consequent greater stability of their investment plans, as through the actual use of budget changes. The recent introduction of general adjustments of purchase tax as a regulating device is a more promising development. It suffers, however, from two defects; the rather arbitrary and limited range of goods affected, and the fact that when demand is high there might be expectations of an increase in purchase tax which would lead to a further increase in demand and when demand is low there

might be expectations of a decrease in tax which would further diminish demand. Hire purchase controls suffer even more severely from these defects.

None of the fiscal instruments at present in use satisfies the conditions for a satisfactory means of correction. If the purchase tax were changed into a general sales tax and adjusted by small amounts at frequent intervals it would do the job. But a preferable alternative would be the introduction of adjustments of direct taxes. A fairly simple way of adjusting direct taxes would be to calculate every tax to be paid in exactly the same way as is now done and then to add or subtract a certain percentage to the calculated figure as a stabilisation adjustment. In the case of P.A.Y.E., which is calculated on the basis of income and allowances cumulated from the beginning of the tax year, the figure added or subtracted in each pay period as a stabilisation adjustment would be kept separate from the figure for the normal tax and would be neglected in forming the cumulated tax paid. The figure calculated for the normal tax in each pay period would thus not be affected by earlier stabilisation adjustments, and no change would be needed in existing P.A.Y.E. tables or in the method of using them. The percentage to be added or subtracted could be changed if necessary at regular intervals; quarterly intervals might prove to be short enough, though changes at monthly intervals should be possible. In this case those P.A.Y.E. taxes which are paid quarterly should be adjusted by the average of the percentages prevailing in the preceding three months. Similarly all annual assessments for direct tax should be calculated as at present and then the average of the percentage adjustments prevailing over the year applied to this figure. Sufficiently fine adjustment would probably be obtained if the changes in the percentage to be added or subtracted were

[3] *Ibid.*, p. 336.

made in steps of $2\frac{1}{2}$ percent, i.e., sixpence in the pound. The absolute value of the tax adjustment would of course be much larger for a person with a high income than for one with a low income. This has advantages from the point of view both of equity and of efficacy; the larger adjustment is needed to induce the person with the higher income to change his expenditure. There would no doubt be some administrative difficulties in introducing a scheme of this sort, but once it was in operation the additional work involved would not be very great. I believe that the choice lies between accepting the minor inconvenience of such a scheme and accepting the continuation of the fluctuations in employment and economic activity which we have experienced since the war.

4. EMPLOYMENT AND INFLATION

I have so far been discussing fluctuations in employment and economic activity without any reference to the average level about which employment is fluctuating. Consideration of the average level of employment brings us to the question of the relations between employment, or unemployment, and inflation and the rate of growth. In the past few years a number of people have carried out empirical studies of the relation between unemployment, or some other index of the demand for labour, and the rate of change of wage rates or earnings. Somewhat different methods and hypotheses have been used by different people. In my own very crude attempt to study this relation[4] I assumed that changes in the cost of living only affect wage changes in years when prices are rising rapidly, usually as a result of rapidly rising

import prices. Others[5] have assumed that changes in the cost of living have a proportionate effect on wage rates in every year. For the post-war years this is probably nearer the truth than the assumption I used. But we must then recognise that changes in the cost of living are in turn mainly the result of earlier changes in wage rates and to a lesser extent of changes in import prices. If these two behaviour relations are fitted to empirical data we can proceed to eliminate price changes and obtain a single relation expressing wage changes in terms of unemployment and changes in import prices, or alternatively we may eliminate wage changes and express price changes in terms of unemployment and changes in import prices. These new relations are not, of course, behaviour relations, but they are valid relations for prediction purposes, and are indeed in the most useful form for prediction. The relation I obtained is best considered as a prediction relation of this sort. If the other studies are also interpreted in this way there is reasonable agreement in the results obtained. It seems that if the average level of unemployment were kept at a little less than $2\frac{1}{2}$ percent the average rate of increase in wages over a period of years could be expected to be about 2 percent per annum so that with the rate of increase of productivity experienced since the war the average level of prices would be almost constant. Also, in the range between $1\frac{1}{2}$ percent and $2\frac{1}{2}$ percent unemployment, for every 0.1 percent that the average level of unemployment was re-

---

[4] "The Relation Between Unemployment and the Rate of Change of Money Wage Rates in the United Kingdom, 1861–1957," *Economica*, vol. xxv (N.S.) (1958) [reprinted in this volume, Selection 17].

[5] See L. A. Dicks-Mireaux and J. C. R. Dow, "The Determinants of Wage Inflation: United Kingdom, 1946–56," *Journal of the Royal Statistical Society*, vol. 122 (1959); L. R. Klein and R. J. Ball, "Some Econometrics of the Determination of Absolute Prices and Wages," *Economic Journal*, vol. lxix (1959), and R. G. Lipsey, "The Relation Between Unemployment and the Rate of Change of Money Wage Rates in the United Kingdom, 1862–1957: A Further Analysis," *Economica*, vol. xxvii (N.S.) (1960).

duced, wages and prices would rise at about 0.3 percent per year faster. If it is true that such a relation holds we are faced with a difficult choice. Then we can only reduce inflation, for any given rate of increase of productivity, at the cost of higher unemployment. I think such a relation does hold now, and unless it can be changed we shall probably move towards a compromise solution with a rather higher average level of unemployment than in the past few years and a lower, though not zero, speed of inflation; perhaps about 2 percent unemployment with about 1 percent per year rise in prices.

To consider whether the relation can be modified we must know why it is that wages continue to rise while there is significant unemployment. A number of possible causes are often mentioned, in particular lack of mobility of labour and industry, resulting in uneven geographical and occupational distribution of unemployment, competitive bidding by employers for the most suitable labour and trade union pressure.

The mobility of labour and industry would be increased if geographical and occupational movements in relative wages were allowed to take place more freely. If wages in areas and occupations where unemployment is low or excess demand is high rise more than those where unemployment is high or excess demand is low, there will be a greater incentive for labour to move to the areas and occupations in which wages have risen most, and for industry to move to the areas where wages have risen least, and also for industry to adapt its production methods to use more labour in those occupations in which wages have risen least.

Competitive bidding up of wages in a particular occupation and area by employers can easily occur even when some labour in the same occupation and area is unemployed. The basic reason for this is the wide range of ability that exists among different individuals in the same occupation. Some people, even in a single narrow occupational classification, are worth to an employer considerably more than the average rate of pay in the occupation; others through individual defects of character, intelligence or physique, are worth less. A wide awake employer will often find it profitable to pay 5 or 10 percent above the average rate of wages for a particular class of labour in his locality. In this way he can choose the best men and may well finish up with employees whose productivity is 10 or 15 percent above the average. If a large proportion of employers adopt this practice wages may be bid up quite rapidly even when there is a significant amount of unemployment. The best solution would seem to be to allow more flexibility in the wages paid to different individuals in the same occupation.

The fourth possible reason I mentioned for wage rates rising when there is significant unemployment was the power and pressure of trade unions. I have some doubts whether this has been an important factor, but if it has, and if the trade unions fully understand the results of their actions, it can only be countered at the cost of occasional major strikes. But have the results of an irresponsible use of their power been made clear to trade unions by Governments? If it were widely and clearly understood among the members of trade unions that the full use of their power to force up money wages would only lead, at a given level of unemployment, to a faster rate of inflation and that the Government would have no alternative but to check this higher rate of inflation, in part at least, by lowering demand and causing some increase in unemployment, it seems possible that the trade unions might see where their true interests lay.

I am not so naive as to expect that the suggestions I have made for trying to shift the relation between employment and the rate of rise of wage rates in a way which would make it possible to maintain a higher level of employment with any given speed of inflation are likely to meet with an enthusiastic response. They are all suggestions for more flexible arrangements which would allow freer play to the market forces of supply and demand. But for at least a century and a half before the second world war wage-earners frequently had a pretty raw deal from the market forces of supply and demand, for in most of the years of the trade cycle, and especially in the catastrophic inter-war years, there was a deficiency of aggregate demand. The traditions built up over that period still persist and will continue to persist for some years yet. But in due course it may be realised that continuously rising standards of living come only from continuously rising productivity and that provided the Government is not prevented by inflation from maintaining a high aggregate level of demand for labour the market forces are no longer harmful but play a vital part in helping adaptation and progress.

5. EMPLOYMENT AND GROWTH

I have suggested that a slightly higher average level of unemployment than that which we have had in the last few years, perhaps a little over 2 percent, may be accepted as a necessary condition for moderating the speed of inflation. One often hears heated arguments against checking inflation in this way, on the grounds that if the rate of growth of the economy were more rapid prices would not rise so fast, and that the rate of growth will be reduced by operating the economy at a slightly lower level of employment. It is true, of course, that a higher rate of growth with the same rate of change of wages would lead to a lower speed of inflation. It is also true that while unemployment was actually increasing, let us say from $1\frac{1}{2}$ percent to 2 percent, output would be rising less

rapidly than it would have been if unemployment had been kept at $1\frac{1}{2}$ percent. But the argument is often phrased as if the steady rate of growth of the economy with unemployment constant at 2 percent would be less than the steady rate of growth with unemployment constant at $1\frac{1}{2}$ percent. I doubt whether this is true.

During short-period cyclical fluctuations the variations in output as a percentage of the growth trend are about five times as large as the variations in the percentage unemployment. The difference is largely accounted for by variations in short-time and overtime; by some people, mainly married women, moving into and out of the labour force; and by "hoarding" of labour during a recession which is expected to be short. If unemployment were to rise by $\frac{1}{2}$ percent and stay at the new level, the hoarding of labour and some of the initial change in short-time and overtime would be only temporary and when the adjustments were completed the percentage fall in output would be considerably less than five times the increase in the percentage unemployment. If account were taken of the value of leisure the fall in real income would be still smaller, since that part of the fall in output which was due to a reduction in overtime and movement of people out of the labour force would be partly compensated by the value to the people concerned of the extra leisure. If an increase of $\frac{1}{2}$ percent in unemployment caused a decrease of $1\frac{1}{2}$ percent in output, with equal proportional decreases in investment and non-investment expenditures, investment would fall by $1\frac{1}{2}$ percent of its own value, and assuming that the growth rate was proportional to investment the growth rate would also decrease by $1\frac{1}{2}$ percent of its own value, for example, from 2.5 percent to 2.4625 percent; an extremely small decrease. If all the decrease in output resulted from a decrease in non-investment expenditure there would be no change in the rate of growth. The main conclusion from this is that the difference in the steady state rates of growth before and after the transition to the higher unemployment would be extremely small if the growth rates were proportional to investment. Other influences, such as possible extra incentive or compulsion to invest in cost-reducing equipment might easily outweigh any small difference due to the slight change in investment.

It is sometimes argued that the decrease in demand would slow down growth by reducing the desire of firms to invest; but this could always be remedied by reducing interest rates. Indeed since we are assuming that a Government could hold unemployment at the new level, investment in the new steady state, as in the earlier one, would have to be brought into equality with savings. It is on the willingness to save, and the more general influences of educational improvement, research, and so on, that the rate of growth depends in present circumstances. I do not think that very small changes in aggregate demand and unemployment have much effect on these.

6. RATES OF EXCHANGE

The final question I wish to discuss, very briefly, is that of rates of exchange. The other major trading countries have problems of employment, inflation and growth which are similar to those of Britain. The question arises whether all countries are likely to hold that balance of internal objectives which would be consistent with the maintenance of fixed exchange rates.

Professors Samuelson and Solow[6] have considered the relation between unemployment and the rate of change of the consumer price index in the United States. Their tentative conclusion is that assuming

continuation of the conditions of the postwar period the price index might be stable if unemployment were held at 5 to 6 percent, and might rise at about 2 percent per annum if unemployment were 4 percent. Some estimates which I have made lead me to think that the situation in the United States is less favourable than this. I estimate that 7 to 8 percent unemployment would be needed to maintain a stable price level, and that at 4 percent unemployment the price level would rise at about 4 percent per annum. Of course efforts to increase the rate of growth and to reduce structural unemployment may improve the relation between unemployment and price changes; but unless my estimates are badly out or considerable improvements are obtained it seems likely that if unemployment is reduced, as seems to be hoped, to 4 or 5 percent, the United States may well have a rather faster rate of inflation than Britain would have with 2 percent unemployment.

In Germany similar problems are beginning to appear. Unemployment has fallen steadily from about 10 percent in 1950 to 1.2 percent in 1960, and labour costs are now rising rapidly. The growth rate is still high but some special factors which contributed to it, such as reconstruction after the war and the currency difficulties, and availability of skilled labour from unemployed or from refugees, are passing. It may well be that in Germany too the problem of choosing between inflation and unemployment will become acute. These three countries, and others, may perhaps be prepared to adjust their own choices about internal balance in order to make them consistent with a regime of fixed exchanges. But I have some doubts whether they will be prepared to do so, or if they are whether they in fact know the quantitative workings of their own and other economies well enough to choose the appropriate objectives before gradual divergencies in price levels have cumulated to such a degree

[6] P. A. Samuelson and R. M. Solow, "Analytical Aspects of Anti-Inflation Policy," *American Economic Review*, vol. L, no. 2 (1960) [reprinted in this volume, Selection 27].

that they impose a heavy strain on the international monetary system.

If this is so, it might be better to allow a limited flexibility into the exchange system, so that gradual drifts in relative prices, which would probably not be at a rate of more than 1 or at most 2 percent per year, would not produce cumulative disequilibria in balances of trade which might eventually necessitate large and sudden movements of exchange rates and do serious damage to the international monetary system. A limited flexibility could be introduced by an agreement that the par value of any one currency, in terms of gold, could be changed at any time provided the total change in one direction in any period of twelve months did not exceed 1 percent. There would, I think, be much more confidence that a country could in fact work within this rule than that it could for ever succeed in keeping the par value constant, so the fear, or hope, of a sudden large change in the rate, with the tremendous speculative movements it causes, would be greatly diminished. The maximum permissible rate of change of the par rate, 1 percent per year, could easily be offset by short-term interest differentials, so it need not lead to any major transfers of capital. And this limited degree of exchange flexibility would allow each country time to find by trial and error that compromise between its internal objectives which was consistent with its exchange rate policy.

I said at the beginning of this lecture that I believed one of the main difficulties in devising and implementing appropriate economic policies is lack of quantitative knowledge and understanding of how the economic system works. By now I have no doubt amply demonstrated at any rate my own lack of knowledge and understanding, and it only remains to apologise to any of you who may have come here expecting clear and definite answers to the problems I have been discussing. I hope the next person to face the ordeal of giving an inaugural lecture on election to the Tooke Chair will be in a position to explain these matters more clearly.

32

The Role of Economic Forecasting in Income Stabilization

EVERETT E. HAGEN

I. INTRODUCTION

A rising tide of public sentiment has thrust upon the U.S. government responsibility for controlling the level of economic activity. By the Employment Act of 1946 the federal government formally accepted this responsibility. That acceptance, however, was not a solution to the problem of income stabilization but only a mandate for its consideration. The problem of how to stabilize income is yet to be solved.

In seeking to stabilize the economy, there are three possible guides to action.

This is a revised version of a paper which was originally published, under the same title, in *Income Stabilization for a Developing Democracy*, edited by Max F. Millikan (New Haven: Yale University Press, 1953), pp. 169–211. Copyright, 1953, by Yale University Press. Reprinted by permission of the publisher and author.

The revisions, undertaken by the editor of this volume with the author's consent, are of a general nature, including primarily some rearrangement and updating of the original material.

Everett E. Hagen teaches at the Massachusetts Institute of Technology; he was formerly with the Knappen, Tibbetts, and Abbett Engineering Company.

Congress may (1) legislate after unemployment or inflation has occurred, (2) adopt permanent legislation which will provide more or less automatic changes in federal programs whenever conditions warrant them, and (3) accept a forecast of the anticipated changes in economic conditions and then legislate the appropriate changes in policies.

It *seems* clear that when unemployment has increased, or when inflation is under way, Congress should take stock of the situation and legislate measures to counteract the unemployment or the inflationary pressure. However, adopting remedial measures after the event has hazards. The chief of these is that planning and enacting legislation, putting it into effect, and then waiting while it bites into the economic situation may cover such a time period that a measure which was adequate while it was being planned is insufficient or futile by the time it takes effect; or a measure which was appropriate when planned may be positively wrong by the time it takes effect.

The time involved in planning and en-

443

acting legislation is especially long with respect to government spending and tax policies, which in most circumstances are the most direct and powerful tools by which to influence employment and output.[1] After the President has prepared his budget, Congress independently duplicates—or, because of the coordinate position of the two houses, triplicates—much of the process of investigation and analysis followed by him in preparing it. Because Congress guards jealously its "power of the purse," this independent consideration of budgetary matters is followed even when the President and the two houses of Congress are controlled by the same political party. When opposing parties control, the degree of duplicate consideration is intensified.

This time-consuming result of our Constitutional separation of powers requires that the budgetary process begins, in the executive branch, almost a year before the beginning and almost two years before the ending of the fiscal year to which it applies. It is worth noting that, in addition to the traditional bill-by-bill consideration, the budgetary process is prolonged by focusing attention on integrated or over-all Congressional consideration of the economic effects of the federal budget.

These statements apply with particular force to expenditure changes. The length of time required for the preparation of tax legislation is somewhat less; but here too, because of the American legislative structure and because of the conflicts of interest concerning tax legislation which exist, the process is time-consuming, except for emergency action taken without review of the entire tax structure. But emergency action cannot be expected regularly.

On humanitarian and ethical grounds the total time period involved is too long for involuntary unemployment to be endured. In addition, a cumulative downswing may have set in which makes the problem much worse than it need have been if speedier action had been taken. If a goal is set of preventing unemployment in excess of, say, 4 million, then preparing specific measures after a downswing has clearly begun will be inadequate, for the downswing ·may carry unemployment far beyond 4 million before the countermeasures take hold.

And if delay is unfortunate in the case of unemployment, it is equally detrimental in the case of continuing inflation. For during the period of planning and enactment of legislation to check inflation, a cumulative spiral may develop. Never is it more true that lost time is never found again than when fighting inflation.[2]

In some situations action taken after a time-consuming process of planning and enactment will have an even more extreme defect. Not all economic swings are indications of a continuing trend; some reverse themselves. As a result, a measure developed by Congress after a certain situation was faced may come into effect at a time when conditions have changed, so that its effect is perverse.

The only way in which the time involved in legislative and administrative processes can be shortened, if the planning begins after the event to be countered has occurred, is by hasty improvisation. Alternatives to waiting until after the event has occurred must be considered. One such alternative is to have permanently on the law books measures which will counter economic fluctuations whenever they occur.

Such built-in devices to counter fluctua-

---

[1] Monetary policy can be implemented more quickly, but its subsequent impact on the economy is generally much more time-consuming than that of fiscal policy.

[2] This applies to both a demand-pull and cost-push inflation. However, if the latter prevails, then some sort of an "incomes policy" would have to be resorted to, since the available fiscal and monetary tools are not sufficient to assure price stability in a cost-induced inflationary situation.

tions in employment and income are of two kinds, which may be called *passive* and *active*. By passive measures are meant measures which are actually in force at all times, but which have a different effect in prosperity or inflationary boom from that in depression, because they affect the individual consumer or business firm differently at different times, depending on the degree of his prosperity.

Unemployment compensation is an example. An employed worker does not benefit; if unemployed, a worker draws compensation which offsets a part of the decline in his income and keeps his spending from falling as low as it otherwise would. Agricultural price-support measures are another example. If the demand for the farm products covered by the price-support program declines, and the price drops, government loans or purchases set a floor under the fall and check the fall in farm income. If demand and farm prices (and farm income) rise, government support is withdrawn.

Progressive income taxes on individuals are among the most powerful of these passive, built-in stabilizers. The more progressive the tax structure, the greater the stabilizing effect. In times of inflation, measures such as price supports and unemployment compensation exert no positive anti-inflationary effect. At best, they have merely the negative virtue of ceasing to contribute to demand, as employment becomes full and farm prices rise above support level. But as inflation proceeds, a progressive income tax does more. It takes a bigger bite of money income as it rises, thus checking demand and cutting into the inflationary spiral. Indeed, a progressive income tax alone, if well enforced, could stop a demand-induced inflation at some point—provided that the government refrained from spending its swelling receipts. On the downswing, as income falls, income tax liability falls faster, so that the income after taxes of an

individual falls by less than does his income before taxes. Or, put in another way, his buying power falls by less than his income. Thus, demand is partially sustained and the fall in output and employment partially checked—provided that the government does not curtail its expenditures as its revenues fall.

It is because such measures have been in effect that recent swings in economic activity in the United States have not been more extreme than they were. And these devices could be improved, to make them more effective.

It is an important characteristic of these passive devices that they can only *temper*, but never *prevent* or fully counteract, fluctuations in economic conditions. So long as an unemployed person suffers a partial reduction in his income, his expenditures tend to decline and the curtailment in his buying will cause unemployment to spread. The government cannot consider fully sustaining his income, for that would cripple the incentive to work. No responsible person, I think, has seriously proposed automatic income-sustaining measures which would fully maintain a person's income when the market for his services has shrunk and he is not making his normal contribution to production.[3] Nor has anyone seriously proposed that a tax law should take *all* of an inflationary increase in income, for to do this would also cripple incentives.[4]

If automatic devices are to assure a

---

[3] Farm price-support sufficient to prevent any fall whatever in farm prices would completely prevent market prices from exercising their function of turning producers from the production of commodities in lesser demand to those in greater demand. And only this degree of support extended to all commodities and services would prevent any fall in income and employment.

[4] Whereas a progressive tax structure works at least in the right direction during an inflationary boom, it acts as a "fiscal drag" in the early stages of a recovery, when there is still a substantial amount of unemployment in the economy, for by reducing the expansionary forces it retards the move toward full employment.

reasonable degree of income stabilization, then *active* devices are required which provide that *new measures* will automatically go into effect when income or employment falls and will be terminated or reversed when income rises. For example, a tax law might provide that tax *rates* should be reduced, not at any specified date, but automatically (on announcement by the appropriate official) when unemployment rose. Such a measure, by positively increasing private spending power, instead of merely lessening its rate of decline, might check the rise in unemployment completely. Similarly, an automatic rise in tax rates when prices rose by a certain percentage could, if sufficient in amount, positively reduce total demand and thereby check the price rise. The President might be authorized by Congress to set in motion certain preplanned public works projects, if unemployment were to exceed a certain number. Or the Federal Reserve might be granted additional authority to control credit expansion, effective in cases of a specified rise in prices.

Other devices could be cited.[5] It is the opinion of the present writer that such active, automatic measures are necessary for an adequate income stabilization policy. But it should be recognized that they would require the forfeiture by Congress of prerogatives which, both on selfish political grounds and for deep-seated reasons of governmental theory, Congress would not give up under present circumstances. Congress would have to give up, in some degree, the power of the purse. It would have to delegate either to the operation of blind economic forces, or to administrative discretion, the initiation of new expenditure programs or of changes in tax rates. These are radical and far-reaching steps, which

Congress would and perhaps should be loath to take.

Hence it is doubtful that the alternative of active, automatic devices is feasible. It is therefore worthwhile to consider the third alternative—namely, short-term forecasting of economic conditions, in order that measures may be adopted by Congress in anticipation of economic changes and put into effect in time to counter an undesired change.[6] If this is feasible, it would preserve Congressional prerogatives and at the same time make effective action possible.

II. THE PRESENT STATUS OF FORECASTING

A forecast, if known with confidence to be accurate within a fairly narrow range of error, would be a sound basis for a firm set of policy proposals designed to meet the known prospective course of events.[7]

1. Criteria for a Usable Forecasting Method

a. *It Must Possess Great Accuracy.* The forecasting method must have an unusually high degree of accuracy if forecasts are to be used as bases for decisions to inaugurate changes in stabilization measures. In most social sciences a high probability that a forecast a year in advance was correct within 5 percent would be high accuracy indeed. For some business purposes, such as production scheduling, and for some public purposes, such as anticipating the demand for Tennessee Valley Authority

---

[5] For a brief discussion of some devices, see my paper, "The Problem of Timing Fiscal Policy," *American Economic Review, Papers and Proceedings,* vol. 38 (May 1948), pp. 417–429.

[6] For purposes of aggregate policy, attention must be focused on the problem of forecasting *on the average in the United States as a whole.* It is true that, for example, employment and unemployment do not change uniformly throughout the country. Fairly small changes in the national unemployment total may hide larger fluctuations in certain industries, regions or groups of people whose specific problems require solutions that lie outside the scope of this paper.

[7] Insofar as the forecast caused changes in public policies, which alter the course of events, the events forecast would then of course not occur.

power or the number of cases to be presented to a court of law, a forecast which had, say, a 2-to-1 chance of being within 5 percent or even 10 percent of the correct value would be useful. *But this moderate margin of error is too great to permit the forecasts to be used as a basis for the formulation of public policies designed to influence the level of output, income, and employment.*

That unusually great accuracy is needed for this purpose is readily seen from a simple example. Suppose that the forecast which seems most probable is employment of 77 million and unemployment of 5 million, but that it is agreed that there is a considerable probability that the employment forecast may be in error by 5 percent, or about 4 million. There is a significant chance that the correct forecast of unemployment may be either 1 million or 9 million. Unemployment will not literally fall to 1 million; for without a system of rigid price controls, a high demand for goods will not push unemployment down this low. Instead, such a forecast would imply that fairly intense inflationary pressure will exist and prices will rise. On the other hand, unemployment of 9 million indicates that fairly serious deflationary influences and fairly serious unemployment will exist. The policy implications of the two alternative forecasts are diametrically opposed. In such a circumstance the forecast obviously furnishes no basis for a single line of public policy, though it does furnish the useful conclusion that public policy must be prepared to meet either serious inflationary or serious deflationary tendencies, or any condition lying between them.

If the forecast indicates unemployment of 10 million, the consequences of error are, of course, much less serious, for the general nature of public policy is clearly indicated, regardless of where within the probable margin of error the correct forecast lies. In such a circumstance, however,

prospective conditions are probably sufficiently clear to common sense analysis so that the more elaborate forecast is unnecessary as a basis for policy judgments.

b. *Its Accuracy Must Be Demonstrable.* Not only must the forecasting method be highly accurate; it must meet a more exacting test. Its accuracy must be demonstrable at the time the forecast is made.

In the past, most forecasting of economic events has been a product of "informed judgment." Men of experience have first reflected and then expressed their opinions concerning future developments. Each person may have stated explicitly the reasons for his judgments; but the reasoning was subject to dispute. Valuable though such judgments often are, this sort of forecasting will not do as the basis for public policy. Men of experience disagree. The most informed of judgments will err seriously concerning economic prospects, as anyone is well aware who has observed the forecasts before or since the war by government officials, or by professional economists, or by leading business executives. If forecasting is to be based merely on that intangible, informed judgment, then each legislator and each administrator will exercise his own judgment. It will often be difficult to arrive at a consensus, and where a clear majority opinion is reached, the majority will not be certain enough of its own prediction to make major changes in public measures in anticipation of future events. For if the future is clouded, it is less embarrassing to have left matters unchanged than to have acted rashly and been proved wrong. Further, this diffidence will be justified; the majority will frequently be wrong.

Forecasting will, therefore, not be acceptable as a basis for government action if the forecast is merely a consensus of informed opinion or the judgment of any economic authority, no matter how revered. It will be necessary to develop an accurate *objective* method of forecasting—objective in the sense that it is based on verifiable data and is capable of being stated so precisely that any trained worker, starting with a given set of facts and using the method, will arrive at the same forecast of the level of employment at, say, 12 months hence and the same estimate of the margin of error in the forecast. With such a method, the accuracy of the forecasts can be checked, and if accuracy is proven by experience, the forecasts can be used with confidence. Only if such an objective method of proven accuracy is developed can legislators and administrators be expected to accept the responsibility of using it as the basis for adopting economic measures in anticipation of events which have not yet occurred.

2. The Passing of the Barometric Method

Up to the recent past the most popular method among professional forecasters was a "barometric" one. A search was made for an economic series, or a group of them, which in the past had moved up or down in advance of movements in business conditions. If one was found the question was asked whether there was any logical reason why changes in this item should precede changes in business conditions. If the answer was yes, to the satisfaction of the forecaster, such a series was accepted as an indicator of changes in business conditions.

One of the most interesting of such barometers was the price of steel scrap. The logic was as follows: Good times are almost invariably accompanied by business expansion and a high level of industrial construction and equipment purchases. These types of activity use steel, and when they are planned, orders for steel will increase. Increased orders for steel will increase the demand for steel scrap and send up its price in advance of the increase in steel output. Therefore, a rise in the price of steel scrap may be taken as a harbinger of a rise in the level of economic activity. Conversely, a decline in scrap prices heralds a decline in business activity. By and large this logic is reasonable; but unfortunately a sufficient number of other circumstances also affect the price of steel scrap, so that on several crucial occasions its use as an indicator led to grievous error.

Another barometer was stock prices in general or the prices of selected groups of stocks. The logic here was that the smartest observers of business conditions operate on the stock market; when prices of most stocks (or a significant group of stocks, such as industrials) rise or fall, it is as a result of an informed and "smart" consensus which is probably correct.

That the stock market, like other barometers, is an unreliable one is an oft-told tale which need not be restated here. With the repeated failures (mixed with some successes) of the barometric method, there has occurred in recent years a renewal of hope that the basic causes of economic fluctuations are coming to be well enough understood so that forecasts can be based directly upon analysis of the causes at work rather than upon the discovery of some barometer.[8]

3. The Influences Which Determine the Level of Output and Employment

a. *Analysis of Causal Relationships.* It will be useful at this point to review the analysis of national spending and income in order to show its relation to the problem of forecasting. As Mr. Millikan has explained,[9] analysis of the causal factors in

[8] This is not to suggest that the sophisticated statistical work of the National Bureau of Economic Research on leading and lagging business-cycle indicators is not of substantial help in assessing current trends in the economy. See R. A. Gordon, "Alternative Approaches to Forecasting: The Recent Work of the National Bureau," *Review of Economics and Statistics*, vol. 44 (August 1962,) pp. 284–291.

[9] Max F. Millikan (ed.), *Income Stabilization for a Developing Democracy* (New Haven: Yale University Press, 1953), chap. 3.

business fluctuations may begin with consideration of the four great markets for the goods and services produced in the economic system—namely, sales to consumers, to business enterprises for capital purposes, to foreign buyers, and to government (see the table below).

Of all of the goods and services produced in the United States (or any other country), the bulk is purchased by consumers. In addition to purchases of services and goods of various degrees of durability for use currently or in the near future, consumers spend a good deal on purchases of new houses. These housing expenditures are grouped, in the national accounts, with domestic investment.

Business enterprises, in addition to producing or purchasing goods for resale to consumers, also spend money for various types of physical plant and durable equipment and at times to increase their inventories and to build houses for rental. This is a second main source of demand for the output of the economic system.

Foreign buyers create a third source of demand, their net demand being measured by the excess (or deficiency) of their purchases from the United States over their sales to the United States.

Finally, the various units of government —federal, state, and local—not only produce many services with the labor of their own employees but also purchase goods and services from private business enterprises.

Consider further the influences which seem to be the major ones determining how high the level of each of these types of expenditures will be. Tracing even the major influences for forecasting purposes is a fairly complex process, but when it has been completed, some important general conclusions may be drawn.

The largest single category is consumer purchases. The expenditures of all consumers in the United States, combined during any given time period, depend primarily upon consumer or personal "disposable income," that is, the income remaining to consumers after paying income taxes during that same period of time.

These expenditures will, of course, vary somewhat even when disposable income does not, but the relationship between consumer expenditures and disposable income is not nearly as erratic as one might suppose before examining the data. On the contrary, it is rather dependable. It is true that the living habits of the people and their attitudes toward saving and

GROSS NATIONAL PRODUCT OF THE UNITED STATES, 1968

			Billions of Dollars
Personal consumption expenditures (consumer purchases of goods and services)			536.6
Gross private domestic investment			126.3
Nonresidential		88.8	
Structures	29.3		
Producers' durable equipment	59.5		
Residential structures		30.2	
Change in business inventories		7.3	
Net exports of goods and services (the excess of sales to abroad over purchases from abroad)			2.5
Government purchases of goods and services			200.3
Total			865.7

SOURCE: U.S. Department of Commerce, *Survey of Current Business*, July 1969, p. 14.

spending change gradually from generation to generation and even from decade to decade as new products and new possibilities of comfort, health, and pleasure develop. But at any one time those habits are not erratic, and the amount which all consumers in the country will spend at a given level of disposable income, or the amount by which consumer spending will increase or decrease if disposable income goes up or down, can be forecast without too great an error, provided that circumstances other than the level of income do not change so as to interfere with the forecast.

This, however, is an important proviso. For many other influences which do change must be taken into account in forecasting consumer expenditures, and some of these influences are difficult to evaluate.

For example, during a depression the level of consumer expenditures depends not only on the level of income but on the standard of living to which consumers become accustomed during a preceding prosperity period. People spend more out of a given income if they have previously received a higher one and grown accustomed to a higher living standard than if they had not done so. Economists feel, however, that they have learned enough about this trait of human behavior, so that in forecasting consumption they can allow for it without too much error—though unless and until another depression occurs it will not be possible to test whether this confidence is justified.

Aggregate consumer expenditures in the nation are also influenced somewhat by the degree of inequality in the distribution of income among the families and individuals of the country. For several reasons, however, this fact does not cause as great a difficulty in forecasting as was previously believed. In the first place, the degree of inequality in the distribution of income does not vary considerably from year to year. There is a material change

between prosperity and depression, but this can be allowed for. Secondly, a change in the degree of inequality in income distribution does not affect aggregate expenditures out of a given aggregate amount of income, in the country as a whole, as much as was once thought. Finally, the surveys of the spending and saving of families and individuals at various levels of income have furnished a basis for judging the effects on spending of any given amount of change in income inequality.

When we come to making allowance for influences not directly related to income, influences responsible for the "autonomous" changes in consumer spending, the problem becomes more difficult. Consumer expenditures at any given level of income depend upon the amount of cash and assets readily convertible into cash—that is, liquid assets, such as government savings bonds. They also depend upon the accumulated shortages or stocks of consumer durable goods—automobiles, household electrical appliances large and small, and the like. The ownership of cash and other liquid assets influences spending not only because these assets represent purchasing power or can quickly be converted into purchasing power but also because, even if these savings are not spent, their possession makes their owner freer in his spending out of current income. This is known, but too little is known about the precise degree to which ownership of liquid assets affects spending to permit very accurate allowance for it.

It is obvious that if shortages of consumer durables exist, spending for them will increase and that as consumers stock up, their purchases of durables will decline, but too little is known to permit accurate estimate either of when purchasing of such items will taper off or, more important, of the degree to which, as it tapers off, it will reduce total consumer spending on the one hand, or on the other, merely cause a shift of spending to other types of goods and services.

The influence of accumulations of liquid assets and the influence of shortages of consumer durables are apt to be great at the end of a major war. They are among the many circumstances causing extreme difficulty in forecasting at such a time.

The third type of influence affecting consumer expenditures—in addition to those relating to current income and to assets holdings—is expectations concerning future and "permanent" income, future prices, and the availability of goods. It is clear that such expectations are very important at some times. Between the fourth quarter of 1948 and the first of 1949, consumer expenditures fell more sharply than did disposable income, and it has been said that this occurred not only because consumers had satisfied the bulk of their deferred demands for durable goods but also because, anticipating a continuation of the decline in prices which had begun, they were holding off for lower prices. During the third quarter of 1950, following the Communist aggression in Korea and the initiation of a major rearmament program in the United States, purchases by United States consumers rose far more than did income, presumably because of fear of shortages of goods or of price rises or both. To predict such "buying sprees" in anticipation of higher prices and shortages or consumer "strikes" in anticipation of lower prices is extremely difficult. Anticipations are subjective psychological phenomena, and economists and statisticians have as yet developed no precise method of measuring their intensity or their effect upon consumer behavior. Forecasts of the effects of such anticipations upon consumer spending are therefore very crude indeed.

Of course, this list of influences is not complete. Consumer expenditures also depend upon a variety of other influences, such as the relative prices of various types of goods and services, including rents; upon the weather, style changes, and so on; but the influence of these various factors upon *total* consumer spending seems to be either fairly small or very temporary. The dominant influences, typically, are those mentioned in preceding paragraphs.[10]

These paragraphs have discussed the influence upon consumer expenditures of disposable income, consumer asset holdings, and consumer expectations. Of these three types of factors, the most important at most times is the level of disposable income. Changes in disposable income are more often the causal factor in large changes in the level of consumer expenditures than are the other two factors.

But what determines the level of disposable income? It depends in part on the amount of special government payments, such as GI aids, social security payments, farm price supports, and upon the level of personal taxes. It depends also upon corporate dividend payments. However, by far the most important determinant is the volume of production in the country; disposable income goes up and down as production and employment go up and down.

Consider next the four categories of "gross private domestic investment"— residential structures, nonresidential structures, purchases of producers' durable equipment, and increases in business inventories.

Some new houses are built by consumers for their own occupancy, but the great majority of houses and apartments are built by commercial builders for rent or sale. Much the same influences affect both classes of construction, for it is of course the prospect of sale or rental to consumers which determines the volume of housing

[10] Consumer expenditures may also change because of official regulations, such as the tightening up or relaxing of permissible terms of consumer credit and housing loans.

construction by commercial builders. The dominating factor which causes the volume of housing construction by commercial builders to rise or fall is a change in the anticipated profitability of housing ventures. Possession of capital or ability to obtain it is a limiting factor, but since capital becomes available to the house-building industry when profit prospects are attractive (unless competing uses of capital are too lush) and ceases to be available when they are not, expected profitability is the touchstone in this respect also.

Expected profitability in turn depends upon the scarcity or excess supply of existing housing units on the one hand, and construction and financing costs on the other. If housing units (that is, houses plus apartments) are in excess supply, rentals and sale prices will be low, and the amount of construction will be small; if housing units are scarce, rental rates, sale prices, and hence the amount of construction activity will all be high.

The relative scarcity or availability of housing units—the "vacancy ratio"—will be determined by the relationship between the number of families seeking housing units and the number of housing units in existence. This relationship is liable under certain conditions to fairly sudden changes of which the forecaster must beware. For while the number of housing units in existence is a given quantity which needs no forecasting, the number of families is not a biologically determined figure which can be depended on to increase steadily from year to year as the population grows. Instead, economic adversity will cause marriages to be postponed and families to "double up" (forming one family for housing purposes), so that over a period of several years the number of families increases little or even declines, though the population is rising. Then, with improvement in economic conditions, families may undouble and the marriage rate jump, so

that an increase of several million in the number of families seeking separate housing units—an increase which might normally cover six or seven years—may occur in half that time.

An increase of, say, a million in the number of families seeking housing units will cause only a moderate increase in housing construction if there are several million housing units standing idle, but if the number of families has increased enough so that the housing situation is fairly tight (if the ratio of vacant units to the total number has fallen below 5 percent), a further increase of a million families will cause housing scarcities in many places throughout the country and will initiate a housing boom. Thus, it is not merely the absolute increase in the number of families seeking housing but the precise relationship of this to the number of housing units in existence which is important. Once a sufficient number of housing units have been built so that the housing situation is loose again, the housing boom will taper off, though other forces cause high prosperity to continue and the number of families remains large and even continues to grow gradually. The 1920s illustrate these tendencies of housing construction activity. In the early twenties a housing deficit appeared, and housing construction activity soared. Then, because the deficit in housing needs had been more than made good, housing construction declined rapidly after the record years of 1925 and 1926, even though the number of families continued to grow gradually and their income remained high. Following 1929, as the number of families seeking housing units shrank, construction activity fell to only a small fraction of the 1925–1926 level.

The scarcity or excess supply of housing, and the consequent prospects for rental rates and sales prices, constitute only one blade of the scissors which determine the volume of housing construction. How high a housing boom will swell or how low the amount of construction will fall in depression depends also on construction and financing costs.[11] Financing costs depend upon the rate of interest. For many housebuilders this depends directly upon the terms of housing loans or loan insurance furnished by the federal government; for others it depends upon the money market in general, which in turn is controlled by the monetary authorities. Thus, the forecaster must make some assumptions about the future course of interest rates. Housing construction costs depend upon wages in the construction industry and on the prices of building materials. Building materials prices are fairly rigid or "sticky"; that is, they do not vary from prosperity to depression to prosperity as much as do prices of, say, agricultural products. But they do vary and their variation is fairly closely related to the tightness of the economy as a whole. Thus, a forecaster who had a basis for forecasting economic conditions in general would also be able to forecast with some degree of confidence at least the general trend of building materials prices. Much the same situation is true of wages in the construction industry. Construction workers in large cities are almost completely unionized and strongly resist reductions in wage rates; but various bonuses vary considerably from prosperity to depression, and the pressure for increases in wage rates will be effective in a boom but not in depression. Thus, the variation in this element of construction costs is fairly closely associated with the degree of tightness or looseness of economic conditions.

This analysis suggests that aside from the number of houses in existence, which is given by past history, the amount of housing construction depends largely upon general economic conditions, but in a fairly complex way—a high level of demand for housing leading only to a temporary boom.

[11] And for apartment buildings, operating costs.

While the nature of the influences affecting the volume of housing construction suggests that it would be easy for forecasts to err, there is nothing in the nature of these influences to suggest that accurate forecasting is intrinsically impossible.

Other types of private domestic investment will be considered in somewhat more summary fashion.

Expenditures by business firms for new plant and equipment seem to depend to a large extent, though not entirely, upon the prospect for profit from the investment[12] and upon either the possession of liquid assets sufficient to finance the investment or ready access to the capital market. A business enterprise will often undertake a new project, or a project of expansion or modernization, if it has the ready cash, even though in the same circumstances the banking community may not consider the venture safe enough to lend the money.

Economists do not know enough about business behavior to generalize with certainty concerning the bases on which businessmen judge profit prospects. It seems probable that in part they do so simply by an empirical rule-of-thumb consideration of the level of recent profits and the trend in them, but that in greater part they judge the future level of sales in some way (most commonly on the basis of recent trends in sales and any unusual elements in recent sales, such as deferred demand) and compare it with productive capacity. The desirability of added construction and equipment purchases, if this analysis indicates tightness or shortage of capacity, is then considered in the light of construction costs (and financing costs, especially if the money must be borrowed).

These considerations indicate why there

[12] This comment should not be taken as acceptance of the conventional assumption of classical economic theory that economic man is moved solely by the profit motive. Modern psychology has demonstrated clearly that the motivations of human behavior are far more complex than this.

are sometimes temporary spurts of commercial and industrial construction and of equipment purchases, just as there are of housing construction. If somehow our growing economy has entered a period of sustained prosperity, there may be a steady pressure of expanding sales on productive capacity, and plant expansion may continue fairly steadily for, say, a decade or more. But, on the other hand, if the economy has swung up from depression to press hard and fairly suddenly upon productive capacity, there may be a sudden great need for added capacity. This may lead to a temporary rate of plant construction and expansion well in excess of the rate which the economy needs year after year. Such a boom in business construction will end fairly abruptly—construction not ceasing but falling to a more moderate level—when the urgent needs have been met.

Such a burst occurred after World War II. Shortages of productive capacity appeared throughout the economy, and expenditures for plant and equipment soared. The burst of plant expansion was not concentrated into an even shorter period than it was mainly because, while some firms rushed to expand at once, others, thinking the unprecedented level of demand only temporary and hoping that soaring construction costs would turn down, held off. As the boom in demand proved fairly durable, many of these others executed their expansion plans after one or two years of delay, thus prolonging the construction boom.

This brief description, of course, ignores many minor factors affecting business investment. Even assuming that it is a fairly accurate summary of the major factors, it indicates the complexity of the conditions which a forecaster must judge.

Business prospects at any time will of course vary widely from industry to industry. A forecast which considers the factors only in the aggregate, for the economic system as a whole, will presumably suffer from a greater margin of error than one which is able to analyze each major industry group separately—agriculture, mining, public utilities, and so on.

Construction on farms and purchases of equipment by farmers, for example, depend to a much larger degree than other business investment upon the current income and the liquid assets of the person making the investment.

Other nonresidential structures and purchases of durable goods—by hospitals, private schools, and a variety of other nonprofit institutions—seem to depend largely upon the general level of income and business activity in the country as a whole, which affects the income and financial condition of such institutions.

The volume of purchases for adding to business inventories is at times an important temporary factor in a boom. At times, too, reduction in inventories is an important factor in a recession. Waiving inventory speculation for the moment, decisions to expand or contract inventories depend upon *changes* in the level of sales. If sales rise, inventories must be increased or the higher rate of turnover will create repeated shortages. There results not only an increase in orders to match the increased rate of sales but a temporary additional increase in orders to increase inventories. When inventories have been built up, orders will be reduced even though the high level of sales continues. Similarly, if sales decline, orders will temporarily decline even further and will then be increased when inventories have been reduced to the desired level. Inventory cycles may thus exaggerate more basic movements in the level of economic activity.

The sectors of economic activity discussed so far have been analyzed almost wholly in terms of economic causation operating within our economic system. This, however, is not true of the two remaining sectors—the excess or deficiency of exports over imports and government purchases of goods and services. The relationship between imports and exports depends not only upon the level of economic activity in this country but also upon world economic activity and, in times like the present, upon U.S. government policy. This relationship cannot be forecast, therefore, without a judgment concerning both world economic conditions and the non-economic factors affecting future government policy decisions.

Some historians assert that government policies (and therefore taxes and government expenditures) are determined largely or wholly by economic influences—by the economic interests of the dominant class or classes, for example. Although this theory obviously contains a large element of truth, it is equally obviously impossible to state any relationship which will enable one to forecast the tax structure and government expenditures directly from economic conditions.

b. *The Effect of Labor Union Activity.* One other factor which affects business decisions to invest, and to a lesser extent consumer expenditures perhaps, deserves separate mention—the influence of labor union activity. What effect, for instance, did the successive rounds of union demands for wage increases have upon business activity after World War II?

Part of the answer is that union activity affects the general level of wages and prices, and the relationships between various prices, much more than it affects the level of output and employment. Most wage increases are apt to be passed along in price increases, or may prevent a reduction in prices which would otherwise have seemed advantageous. Suppose that widespread union pressure for higher wages results in a price level, say, 4 percent higher than it would otherwise have been. Insofar as through wage increases disposable income in the aggregate has risen with

prices, the physical volume of consumer purchases will be little changed. And if banks have plenty of excess lending capacity, so that it is fairly easy to borrow the added funds needed to cover higher costs of construction and equipment, the level of business structures and equipment purchases may not be greatly affected.

Any individual businessman faced with an aggressive union is apt to get a partial and somewhat distorted impression of this process. The pressure of the union's demands upon his costs and, particularly, the anticipation of future pressure deter him from making expenditures for capital purposes, he is sure. However, an increase in money incomes throughout the economic system increases his market and enables him to charge a higher price, so that this offsets in whole or in part (or may in certain cases more than offset) the direct effect of union activity upon his calculations. The businessman often does not reflect that this increase is a result of the same wave of union activity which increases his costs.

However, collective bargaining in a number of cases certainly does increase wages *at the expense of profits*, rather than at the expense of prices. For the country as a whole, wages may be somewhat higher and profits somewhat lower because of union activity than they would be otherwise. This, together with the psychological effect of the anticipation of perpetual future pressure, would have some net depressing influences on business expenditures for capital purposes, even though they may be less than a businessman is apt to think.

Further, price rises themselves are apt to lessen the aggregate amount of goods and services purchased, even though income also increases. It was noted earlier that the possession of cash or other liquid assets stimulates business expenditures which would not be made if bank loans had been necessary. Insofar as a price rise reduces the purchasing power of liquid asset holdings, it will tend to reduce somewhat the physical volume of structures and equipment expenditures undertaken by business enterprises. Similarly, the reduction in the purchasing power of consumer liquid asset holdings reduces the physical volume of consumer purchases, though such evidence as is available suggests that this effect is not great.[13]

On the other hand, insofar as union activity causes a shift from profits to wages, undistributed corporate profits may be decreased and total disposable income increased, bringing about some reduction in the inequality in the distribution of disposable income (even though wage earners with fairly high wage incomes tend to get the largest increases). Both the increase in disposable income and the change in the distribution of income will tend to increase consumer expenditures. However, as has been noted above, a moderate shift in the distribution of disposable income does not seem to have any marked effect upon total consumer expenditures, so that this effect will not be great.

The net effect of union activity upon the level of business activity is thus difficult to measure. For forecasting purposes, what is important is the effect of any intensification or diminution of union activity.[14] One rough way of measuring this would be to assume that union activity increases with an increase in the percentage of all wage earners who are union members, and to include in one's forecasting system the assumption that as this percentage increases business expenditures for plant and equipment will be adversely affected. This is a very rough and uncertain rule, in view of the other factors which may affect union activity and the difficulty in assessing the likely effects of union activity upon business decisions. However, union activity should be kept in mind as one possible causal factor but one difficult to measure.

c. *Four Generalizations Concerning the Causal Factors.* Out of this brief item-by-item analysis of the major causal factors affecting the level of economic activity, four generalizations of importance to forecasting may be drawn.

One is that the analysis of the influences determining the level of various types of output does not indicate threads of causation leading to one single central focus. There is no one key indicator or barometer which will furnish guidance concerning the whole economy. There is no royal road to forecasting.

In the second place, the analysis suggests that forecasting of most, if not all, sectors of economic activity may be possible on the basis of *objective* relationships. For example, the level of housing construction depends largely upon prospects for profits from the sale or rental of housing, which is a subjective evaluation of the future. But if that evaluation in turn depends primarily on the relationship between the number of families and the number of existing housing units, knowledge of the number of housing units plus an accurate forecast of the number of families may make it possible to pass directly to an accurate forecast of the level of housing construction. Similar *objective* relationships have been suggested above for other sectors of economic activity. If it is possible to estimate from past experience *how great a change* in each sector of economic activity (for example, housing construction) is

---

[13] In the post-1945 period of "overfull" employment and inflationary pressure, this depressing effect of an increase in the price level upon expenditures means that there was somewhat less inflationary pressure remaining, after wage increases had raised the price level, than there would have been at the lower price level. Indeed, the inflationary pressure at the lower price level would have tended to raise prices even if wage increases had not led the way, so that much, though probably not all, of the price increase which was popularly associated with wage increases would have taken place even if unions had not existed.

[14] Since a forecast will be concerned with forces causing *change* in total expenditures "next year," compared with "this year."

caused by a given change in some objective causal factor (for example, number of families, relative to number of housing units), then it should be possible to develop a purely objective method of forecasting.

The third general statement is that, to an impressive degree, all sectors of economic activity other than government activity and foreign trade depend either upon conditions inherited from the past (productive capacity, the existing number of housing units, and so on) or upon the general level of economic activity and changes in it. But since the general level of economic activity is simply the sum of economic activity in all of these sectors combined, this statement means that all sectors of economic activity *depend upon each other*. This mutual interdependence of the various sectors of economic activity is the most striking single fact developed by modern students of econometrics. The level of output and employment almost anywhere in the economic system depends in major degree upon the level of activity elsewhere in the system, because all parts of the system are interconnected by income flows, mutual demand for productive resources, and price relationships. It is of little use to try to forecast output and employment by examining six or eight or any other number of economic sectors separately, forecasting the level of each in turn, and then adding the results. *No sector, it seems, can be forecast until the other sectors have been forecast first.* What this indicates is that it is necessary to make quantitative forecasts of activity in all sectors of the economy *simultaneously, taking account of the interrelationships between them.* This is the keystone of modern forecasting.

Finally, it is clear that government activity and foreign trade have mainsprings which lie outside the field of United States economic activity, so that in these sectors at least purely objective methods of forecasting are impossible. The would-be forecaster must not only enter some degree of judgment about world conditions; he must also go outside the realm of economics entirely into analysis of the considerations which govern public affairs.

4. The Econometric Method of Forecasting

a. *Mutual Interdependence and the Need for Precise Statistical Relationships.* The fact of mutual interdependence between various sectors of economic activity does not imply a lifting-oneself-by-one's-bootstraps effect, so that any level of economic activity will sustain itself. Instead, there is one level of economic activity, and only one, which will tend to be brought about by the interrelationships within the economic system. This can be made clear by a grossly simplified example. Suppose that after surveying economic conditions a forecaster had tentatively decided at the end of 1967 that the average level of output in the United States during the coming 12 months would be as follows:

	Billions of Dollars
Consumer purchases	526
Residential structures	30
Nonresidential structures	29
Business purchases of equipment	59
Increase in inventories	7
Net exports	5
Government purchases (including payrolls)	193
Total gross national product	849

The tentative forecast of gross national product is $849 billion. However, the forecaster might have noted, after the necessary calculations, that this level of output would yield consumers an aggregate income, after paying income taxes (and after including any special government payments to consumers) of $580 billion; and that out of that level of income, judging by recent experience, consumers would spend not the $526 billion initially estimated but $2 billion more. The estimate of consumer purchases would therefore have to be revised upward. But this increase in consumer purchases would increase total output, which would increase disposable income, causing a further increase in the estimate of consumer purchases. After a succession of adjustments the forecast of consumer expenditures might therefore be increased to $530 billion; of gross national product to $853 billion; and of disposable income to $583 billion.

But the forecaster might have decided that at this higher level of purchases inventories would not be adequate. He might then have increased the estimate of change in inventories from $7 billion to $7.5 billion and increased the estimate of gross national product accordingly. But this increase in output would increase disposable income, consumer expenditures, and total output somewhat further.

With demand estimated at this higher level the forecaster might have felt that a moderate upward movement in prices which he had not anticipated would appear. He would then have to decide how this would affect expenditures. Further, at this higher level of income, is the estimate of residential structures too low? What about business structures and equipment purchases? If the estimates of these are revised, the total changes and a whole round of secondary adjustments must again be made. So the process would go, with each change in any one item setting off a series of necessary changes throughout the entire area of the forecast.

The important point is that the process of repeated adjustments could finally result in a forecast, every sector of which was consistent with every other sector—in which, for example, total output, disposable income, consumer expenditures, prices, inventory changes, net exports, and business expenditures for structures and equipment would all be "in line with each other." It is reasonable to believe that

there is some one level of each and under any given circumstances, only one level, which the interrelationships between the various sectors will in fact bring about.[15]

However, though there is some one level, the forecaster has no reason to be sure that he has correctly forecast it. His final forecast was the product of a series of tinkerings, and as the process is sketched above the judgments involved are sufficiently imprecise so that the forecast might be considerably different from what it would be if some other student of economic affairs had done the tinkering—and both might be considerably different from the course of events which the future will in fact bring about.

At least two difficulties cause this possible discrepancy:

(1) In making the various adjustments it is necessary not only to have analyzed the causal relationships correctly but also to estimate *by how much* a change in each causal factor will influence spending. This necessity has been referred to above. If disposable income decreases by $10 billion, by how much will this tend to decrease consumer spending? If liquid asset holdings of consumers increase over a period of time by $50 billion, by how much will this tend to increase consumer spending? If total sales of business enterprises decline by $10 billion, by how much will profits fall? If profits fall by a given amount, by how much will this reduce expenditures for new plant and equipment? If interest

[15] The thinking of some readers concerning the influences which determine the level of output and employment is probably couched in terms of the multiplier analysis via the relationship between savings and investment. These readers may wonder why this relationship has been largely ignored in the above discussion. The answer is that the level of output which the interrelationships between the various factors at work will bring about is a level at which savings equal investment, in the ordinary sense of those words. Analysis like that above is an alternative to the "savings-investment" analysis. But to analyze the effect of the various factors upon aggregate expenditures is simpler than, and in fact theoretically preferable to, analyzing their effect upon savings and investment.

rates fall by $\frac{1}{4}$ percent, as a result of some anticipated change in monetary conditions, by how much will this affect expenditures for new plant and equipment, if at all? And so on. Informed analysts may differ considerably concerning the precise numerical relationships involved.

(2) Even if some precise estimate of every relevant relationship were arrived at, the piecemeal adjustment of each item throws the estimates of other items out of line, and it is extremely difficult to get the forecasts of all of the items entirely consistent with each other so that there is a basis for confidence that a reasonable overall estimate has been arrived at. So many relationships are involved that the human mind has difficulty in coping with all of them at one time.

Mathematical and statistical techniques can give aid in solving these problems.

b. *Determining the Statistical Relationships.* The only way in which objective estimates of the quantitative relationships can be arrived at is by analysis of past data.[16] In the past, what change in profits was associated with a given change in the volume of sales? What change in plant and equipment expenditures was associated with given changes in profits, in the relationship between sales and productive capacity, in interest rates, and so on?

Obviously, the first step is to obtain data for each factor involved for as many years as possible. Some factors cannot be taken into account for lack of information; for example, no known data will furnish a reliable clue to the quantitative effect of consumer anticipations concerning price or income changes on consumer expenditures. Even when as many as possible of the desired data have been gathered or estimated, analysis of the relationships is difficult simply because many changes occurred at once. If business expenditures for new plant and equipment increased

from $13.5 billion in one past year to $15.4 billion in the next, and at the same time total sales in the economic system were up by $6 billion; profits were up $1.6 billion; capacity was up by $5 billion as a result of last year's plant and equipment expenditures; construction costs fell by 3 percent; and interest rates fell by $\frac{1}{8}$ percent—if these various things occurred, how much of the change in business expenditures for plant and equipment is attributable to each? Suppose that each of the five causal factors—sales, profits, capacity, construction costs, and interest rates—is expected to change in a future year, by varying amounts. How much weight should be given to each in forecasting the plant and equipment expenditures which will result?

The analysis of such relationships is one branch of econometrics. The analysis should be made, of course, not only for one year but for all years for which there are data. Conclusions based merely on one year may be badly in error because of some unusual development in that year or perhaps because some of the data for that year are somewhat in error.

The analysis should be made, for all years, for each of the sectors of output. What influences are the causes, and in what amounts, of the observed changes in consumer expenditures? residential structures? business expenditures in various industries for plant and equipment? changes in inventories? What change in disposable income will result from a given change in gross national product? in special government payments? What influences are the causes, and in what amounts, of the observed changes in interest rates? corporate profits? residential rental rates? changes in the price level? And so on. Until recently it was thought that changes in any one item could be explained by relating the data for that item, over a period of years, to the data for items believed to exert an influence on it, by the

---

[16] Unless surveys, such as those of consumer intentions to buy or of the investment plans of business enterprises, are regarded as objective estimates.

statistical technique of multiple correlation. For example, the change in consumer expenditures caused by given amounts of change in disposable income, in liquid assets held by consumers, and by the previous level of expenditures to which consumers had grown accustomed, were analyzed in this way. Statisticians now know, however, that because of interrelationships between all of the items in the economic system, treating one dependent item and the causal influences which affect it separately from the remaining dependent items and the causal factors affecting them will give inaccurate estimates of the relationships. *The relationships between every dependent variable and its group of causal factors must be estimated simultaneously.* The very complex statistical procedure by which this can be done is known as the "method of maximum likelihood." [17]

When the analysis has been completed, a statement will be obtained (in the form of a mathematical equation) for each sector of economic activity—consumer expenditures, residential structures, and so on. The statement will indicate by how much activity in the given sector will rise (or fall) with a given change in each causal factor. To cite a simple hypothetical example, the analysis may indicate that the volume of inventories held by all business firms in the United States, combined, will be increased (or decreased) by $1 billion for each $7 billion of increase (or decrease) in the volume of goods sold; that they will be increased by a given small amount for every .1 percent fall in short-term interest rates; and that there are changes in inventory holdings (presumably due to swings

in business expectations concerning the future) which are not accounted for by changes in sales or in interest rates and which it does not seem possible to account for objectively.

It should be observed that the change in inventories depends upon the change in the level of sales, while the change in the level of sales depends in part upon the change in inventory holdings (for additions to inventories require purchases of the goods held, that is, *sales* by some other firm). Hence, neither the level of sales nor the change in inventories can be forecast before the other. The two must be forecast simultaneously.

One important limitation should be noted. No known statistical technique will insure that the forecaster has analyzed the true causal factors affecting each sector. The results may indeed give some suggestions concerning this. If there are large or apparently systematic changes in the activity being analyzed (for example, additions to inventories) which are not explained by the causal factors used in the analysis, this may suggest to the forecaster that he should seek other causes; and if changes in some presumed causal factors seem to cause only slight changes in the activity being analyzed, this may raise the question of whether there is a true causal relationship. But these indications are by no means infallible; in the main the forecaster must depend upon economics rather than statistics for the selection of the proper causal factors.

The two sectors of the economy which cannot be analyzed in this way are, as was mentioned previously, net exports (or imports) and government expenditures. Though neither can be estimated merely on the basis of economic relationships within the United States, their past data entered *as causal factors* into the explanation of changes in the level of other sectors.

The volume of net exports depends in part upon world conditions, including both

[17] It has been shown by statisticians that this method also has a bias of its own. No known procedure will give entirely accurate estimates of the true relationships. For a discussion of the problems and various alternative methods of estimation in simultaneous-equation models, see E. Malinvaud, *Statistical Methods of Econometrics* (Amsterdam: North-Holland Publishing Company, 1966), especially chaps. 19 and 20.

the level of economic activity abroad and the international policies of our own and other governments (such as the foreign aid program). It also depends in part upon the level of output and income in the United States (which affects one side of the picture, our imports). Therefore, the volume of net exports cannot be forecast in advance of the general forecast of gross national product in the United States; the two must be forecast simultaneously. For simplicity, however, an approximate estimate of the probable level of gross national product can first be made and a forecast of net exports based on this. This forecast can then be used in the final forecast of gross national product.

Tax revenues can be forecast on the basis of the past relationship between tax revenues and the level of economic activity, adjusted for changes in tax laws. In addition, a political forecast must be made of any change in tax laws which may be in effect during the period to which the forecast applies. And with respect to those government expenditures which vary automatically with changes in economic conditions, such as unemployment compensation and farm price supports, the relevant relationship can also be derived. But, as in the case of taxes, allowance must be made for changes in laws concerning these expenditures which have altered the relationship in the past, and a forecast must be made of further changes in these laws which will affect future expenditures. Other government expenditures, which are determined from year to year by Presidential recommendations and Congressional action, must be forecast on the basis of judgment concerning that action.

c. *Making the Forecast.* When the procedures just described have been completed, the necessary ingredients for a forecast are at hand. Assume for convenience that the forecast is for a one-year period in the immediate future. The ingredients are:

(1)   Knowledge of varying degrees of precision of the stocks of consumer and capital goods (automobiles and other consumer durables, number of housing units in existence, stocks of inventories, productive capacity in various industries) on hand as the year begins; and of the cash and liquid assets in existence. These stocks of goods, productive facilities, and liquid assets are among the factors which will determine the level of economic activity during the coming year.

(2)   A forecast of net exports and of tax revenues and government expenditures.

(3)   Specific estimates in mathematical form of the network of quantitative cause-and-effect relationships between all of the major factors affecting the level of economic activity.

With (1) and (2) determined, there is only one level of gross national product and its components and of the incomes derived from it which the set of relationships included under (3) solves mathematically.

This procedure thus meets one test suggested earlier in this paper for a forecasting method. Any forecaster using a given set of relationships is bound to arrive at the same forecast. But the method is still subjective in the sense that the set of causal relationships used depends upon economic analysis concerning the appropriateness of which economists may and probably will disagree. The proof of the method must be in its results. It must meet the other test—namely, accuracy. What can be known about the accuracy of a forecast derived by such a method?

d. *Sources of Error.* It is evident that there will be some errors, for the forecasting method described cannot take all causal factors into account.

(1)   Some factors must be omitted because even though the forecaster knows or believes that they have an influence, he cannot derive any quantitative measure of them or of their effect. This is conspicuously true of some types of expectations about the future. Swings in business

sentiment concerning the future of prices certainly cause bursts of accumulation or decumulation of inventories—commonly referred to as speculative. Yet it is extremely difficult to state objective changes in economic conditions, which can be forecast, causing these speculative inventory movements. There probably are similar elements of anticipation concerning the future which influence the level of consumer expenditures or of business plant and equipment expenditures, which slip through the meshes of the forecaster's objective analysis and cause changes in the level of output and employment which he has not forecast.

There may be other known omissions. In the complexity of life, minor forces must be ignored to obtain a clearer statement of the important ones. Some factors thought to be minor must be excluded to keep the statistical analysis within manageable bounds.

(2) But there may also be sins of omission or commission of which the forecaster is not aware. The basic analysis of cause-and-effect relationships may be faulty. The modern study of economics is only two centuries old; the concept of a general equilibrium of mutually interacting forces which determines economic conditions at any given time, about three generations; the intensive study of *quantitative* economic relationships, not yet two generations; and the specific development of a system of econometric relationships designed to explain the level of output and employment, hardly one generation. Under these circumstances it will not be strange if the system of cause-and-effect relationships embodied in recent econometric models is found to be at fault. Some lines of causation may be incorrectly stated, simply because of the inadequacy of analysis to date in this field, and some important causal factors may have been excluded because of deficiency in the analysis.

The omission of influences, which turns out in fact to be important, results not merely in making the analysis incomplete; it may render inaccurate the statistical analysis of the factors which are considered. If one important causal factor is in fact omitted, the result may be to associate with one or more of the others a larger share of the causation than is actually the case, thus leading to an erroneous forecast of the effect when that causal item varies.

(3) There may be errors in the past data from which the quantitative relationships between components were estimated. Many of our economic data for past years are estimates rather than precise measurements. In witness of this, note the magnitude of many of the revisions in data made by the Department of Commerce in its various National Income supplements. Insofar as the data used are in error, the relationships estimated from them may be inaccurate and the forecasts based upon them in error.[18]

(4) It is possible that the economic system may have changed, so that causal relationships which held true in the past will no longer do so. The forecasting method sketched here is based on the assumption that human reactions to economic circumstances will, in general, be the same in the future as in the past—or, that if those reactions were gradually changing, that gradual change will continue.

Surely in general these assumptions are correct. Folkways are deeply rooted; human behavior changes only gradually. But there may be exceptions. Perhaps the war gave many persons glimpses of new standards of living, so that a higher per-

[18] Even if the relationships have been correctly estimated, inaccurate current data upon which the projections are based would lead to erroneous forecasts. For an attempt to measure the forecast error resulting from data error, see Rosanne Cole "Data Errors and Forecasting Accuracy," in Jacob Mincer (ed.), *Economic Forecasts and Expectations* (New York: National Bureau of Economic Research, 1969), chap. 2.

centage of each added dollar of income will be spent. Perhaps the enactment of broader social security legislation, such as health insurance or the adoption of a public housing program, will further change spending habits. Perhaps the gradual increase in the wage earner's share of the production dollar was associated with a growth in the strength of labor unions' bargaining position, which has now been checked. In any of these cases a forecast based on the assumption that the future can be judged by the past will prove in error.

The method of forecasting discussed here can be adapted to changed relationships. Whenever it is felt that a changed relationship has entered into economic behavior, the new relationship can be introduced into the forecasting process. But by virtue of the fact that the new relationship *is* new, its estimation is hazardous. The greater the number of relationships derived from past experience which must be altered because it is felt that human behavior has changed, the greater the risk of error.

(5) Finally, the forecasts of net exports and government expenditures—the two forecasts made not as a part of the general analysis but separately, as special cases— may be in error. If so, the error will be reflected in the over-all forecast.

e. *Reliability.* The existence of some errors in forecasts will not necessarily invalidate their use as a basis for action by Congress or the executive branch. The basic question is how great the margin of error is apt to be. The remarkable degree of precision necessary in such forecasts, if they are to be used as the basis for social action, has previously been noted.

The proof of the pudding is in the eating, and it may be thought that the reliability of a forecasting model can be ascertained only by making forecasts year by year for a considerable period of time and seeing how they turn out. Fortunately, this is not necessary in order to evaluate the only recently developed econometric models. For, unlike informed judgment, which is typically correct, by its own appraisal, in explaining retrospectively events which have already occurred, the econometric method can be checked against the past. Using the system of relationships which has been derived, and using actual data for net exports and government revenues and expenditures for a given past year, a "hindcast" of gross national product, employment, the price level, and so on, can be made for that year. When similar hindcasts have been made for a series of past years—presumably for all years whose data were used in estimating the relationships—the estimates of gross national product (or of any component in which there is especial interest) can be compared with the actual past data and the error in each estimate noted. From this series of results a statistical estimate can be made of the probability that *any* such hindcast taken at random will be within any given margin of the correct figure. Since for several reasons forecasts may have a greater error than these hindcasts, this procedure will furnish only a minimum estimate of the probable error of a forecast.

Up to now the forecasting performance of econometric models has turned out to be no more accurate than that of the better business forecasts (which lack objective rigor).[19] The minimum probable margin of error in present forecasting methods is much greater than the permissible margin, and hence in its present stage of development economic forecasting is much too inaccurate to be used as the

---

[19] Victor Zarnowitz, *An Appraisal of Short-Term Economic Forecasts* (New York: National Bureau of Economic Research, 1967), p. 135. See also H. O. Stekler, "Forecasting with Econometric Models: An Evaluation," *Econometrica*, vol. 36 (July–October 1968), pp. 437–463, where an examination of several recent quarterly econometric models revealed some rather mixed results.

basis for changes in stabilization measures.[20]

This fact should not lead to undue pessimism. The work of Lawrence Klein, Henri Theil, and many others in universities, research institutions, and government agencies (in the United States and abroad) has grown significantly in recent years, and no one can say that great improvements in results may not be achieved in the future. But for the time being, at least, no objective method of forecasting (and no other method) is sufficiently accurate to be used confidently as the basis for public action.

At this point some reader may object that this conclusion could have been reached much earlier. The much-publicized forecasts of depression during the reconversion period after World War II—to one of which the writer was a party—were so greatly in error as to leave no question concerning the possibility of accurate economic forecasting. In answer to this objection, it should be noted first that the reconversion period was a very special situation, not typical of that faced in peacetime forecasting, and second that the reconversion forecasts were made by very crude methods. Techniques have developed considerably since that time. The experience of the reconversion period is of little relevance in evaluating the accuracy of forecasting today.

III. STEPS TOWARD MORE ACCURATE FORECASTING

If greater accuracy is to be achieved, what is the path toward this goal? This section suggests possible steps forward.

1. More Work Needed

The basic prescription for lessening the margin of forecasting error is simple—*continued work on the problem.*

This work must take the form not merely of the application of thought by an informed expert sitting at a desk—a form of research whose value should not be underestimated—but also of statistical research and work "in the field." On the one hand, there is needed the accumulation and refinement of data, the improvement of statistical techniques, and the statistical testing of tentative hypotheses;[21] and on the other, surveys by competent analysts of the procedures by which business decisions are actually made and the motives which influence them, and of the influences which motivate consumer behavior. If, for example, business executives typically act not so much to maximize profits as to maintain or improve the relative position of their firm in the industry (and whether this is true remains to be determined), this fact has relevance to an explanation of the forces which determine the rate of business plant and equipment purchases. If spending by the typical consumer is importantly influenced not only by the amount of his disposable income and the other influences mentioned earlier in this paper, but also by the level of his income *relative to other incomes in the community* in which he lives, this fact affects the behavior of consumers when the level of income changes. These and other plausible hypotheses concerning economic behavior which have been advanced in recent years must be further explored.

Research must take the form of cross-fertilization between theory and empirical study. If some new explanation of the

---

[20] This statement should not be taken to imply that the forecasting now being done by various private economic consultants is necessarily too inaccurate to be useful for some other purposes.

[21] Fortunately, technological developments of high-speed electronic computers make it possible now to cope with some very complex mathematical computations.

motives affecting business decisions seems plausible, how can it be tested statistically? If the statistical testing furnishes partial verification, but suggests certain peculiarities in the data for some years, what new hypotheses are suggested or what questions arise which may be resolved by further field work? The combination of inductive and deductive reasoning is as essential in this field of analysis as in any other science.

a. *"Quantifying the Nonquantifiable."* A principle fondly asserted repeatedly by one of the early students of educational psychology is that "whatever exists, exists in some amount, which is subject to measurement." In a certain limited sense this is true, and one of the possible paths of improvement in economic forecasting is to devise ways of measuring certain phenomena and their causes which at present seem nonquantifiable.

The most conspicuous class of such nonquantifiable factors is anticipations (both of businessmen and of consumers) concerning the future. Are there swings in such anticipations, not based upon objective factors in any way which is now understood and therefore not allowed for in the forecasting apparatus, which play an important part in bringing about changes in output and employment?

The fact that such nonquantifiable influences may exist should not necessarily lead one to the conclusion that their importance is great. In the past, references to such influences have often been a mask for ignorance, just as savages attributed storms to the anger of the gods out of ignorance of the true causes. If one does not know why a certain change has occurred, it is often convenient to attribute it to "speculation," or to "bearish business sentiment due to foreign political developments." This is the kind of game which financial-page writers play in analyzing the previous day's stock market activity,

and, of course, the explanations may at times have substance, but they need not be accepted without critical examination by social scientists. It may well be that, as understanding of economic relationships grows and as mathematical analysis of them becomes more refined, the area of variation which it seems appropriate to attribute to such influences will steadily shrink. For example, there have been numerous periods of accumulation and later unloading of business inventories in the United States during the 1920s and 1930s. Thirty years ago it was fashionable to attribute them in the main to speculation; now, on the basis of improved data and analysis, it seems more reasonable to attribute most of them simply to lags in the adjustment of inventories to changes in the level of sales.

Yet, whatever degree of debunking of "psychological" factors may be appropriate, it remains true that an unsolved problem exists here.

Concerning consumer anticipations, survey techniques which attempt to measure attitudes are now in use.[22] But to date they have made little progress in measuring the quantitative significance of attitudes, and it can only be said that they may hold promise of improving understanding in this field.

b. *The Use of Surveys of Projected Business Plant and Equipment Expenditures.* Possibly the best way of dealing with business attitudes and intentions is to short-circuit the entire problem by the use of surveys which obtain information concerning business plans for near-future expenditures for plant and equipment, without attempting to identify the causes which affect those plans. These are ex-

[22] Such as those conducted by the Survey Research Center at the University of Michigan which periodically provide information on consumer buying plans as well as on attitudes about the general state of the economy.

penditures for which in the main (though not in all cases) fairly definite plans are made by business enterprises in advance— by large enterprises, some considerable time in advance. This being so, it is the most obvious common sense to suggest that the process of economic forecasting should include direct surveys of business enterprises in which they are asked their plans concerning expenditures for plant and equipment. There is a considerable margin of error in forecasts of such expenditures based upon past data for business profits, sales volume, plant capacity, and so on, and if forecasts of the level of these expenditures could be made on the basis of surveys of business plans, this one stroke would do much to improve the accuracy of economic forecasting.

Several such surveys, dealing with a one-year or shorter time period, are now made. Following the lead of the Department of Commerce and the Securities and Exchange Commission, surveys of investment anticipations are periodically undertaken by *Fortune*, the McGraw-Hill Publishing Company (whose results appear in *Business Week*), and others. The survey conducted jointly by the Department of Commerce and the Securities and Exchange Commission provides annual as well as quarterly data on anticipated business fixed investment and is perhaps the most promising for forecasting purposes.[23] Since its initiation at the end of World War II, the usefulness of this survey has been increased by the supplementary information, which is now obtained quarterly, concerning manufacturers' sales and inventory expectations. With these additional data, adjustment of the probable expenditures for plant and equipment can be made if the final forecast indicates that the level of sales or inventories will be

higher or lower than businessmen anticipated when they made their present plans.

Even with this information, using such a survey effectively is a very difficult matter. It should not be assumed that reported plans for plant and equipment expenditures can be either taken at face value or used after merely a *simple* adjustment for change in sales and inventories from that anticipated. There will be a discrepancy between present plans to spend and future expenditures which will actually be made, even if sales and inventories develop precisely as expected. Some plant and equipment expenditures, which were not visualized at the beginning of the year, will be made during the year as needs become clearer; some which were not planned for lack of funds will become possible because funds are more freely available than was anticipated; new firms not included in the survey will make expenditures; and some firms included in the survey will be unable for a variety of reasons to make expenditures they had anticipated.

The results of the Commerce Department-SEC survey show that large firms have estimated fairly accurately their plant and equipment expenditures, whereas smaller firms have not. This may be because smaller firms plan less far in advance, or because large firms are sophisticated enough to add an allowance for "expenditures not yet planned," while smaller firms are not, or for some other reasons. The change in a firm's plans, as sales or inventory expectations change, probably depends upon this firm's liquidity, on what is happening to this firm's sales relative to those of the entire industry, and possibly on other factors. Accurate forecasts of plant and equipment expenditures probably cannot be made until enough experience has been gained to adjust the survey results on the basis of these factors.

Yet, in spite of these necessary adjust-

[23] See Arthur M. Okun, "The Predictive Value of Surveys of Business Intentions," *American Economic Review, Papers and Proceedings*, vol. 52 (May 1962), pp. 218–225.

ments, it is easy to exaggerate the degree of error which will necessarily be involved in the forecasts. And it must be remembered that even if the margin of error is at first fairly great, that margin may be reduced as experience increases. If the funds can be acquired and the necessary ingenuity and technical competence applied to the task, and if the cooperation of the business community can be obtained through creating an understanding of the importance of the project, development of an improved survey of business investment intentions would probably afford a greater advance within a short period of time in the accuracy of economic forecasts than any other step which could be taken in the near future.

c. *The Need for Better Data.* A more pedestrian method of making possible a certain degree of improvement in forecasting would be to improve economic data. Improvement both in the speed with which data become available and in their accuracy would be helpful. Greater timeliness of data would be useful to all forecasters but of greatest advantage for very short-run forecasting. For many types of economic data, reasonably reliable estimates (few data are complete, most are estimates) are not available except after a lapse of many weeks, so that data for a three- or six-month period just ended, which are basic to a forecast of the near future, are themselves based on incomplete information. Reduction in this time lag for many economic series is possible without exorbitant increase in cost, though any speed-up in collection or processing of data is apt to involve some increase in expense.[24]

Further, even after enough time has elapsed for the process of data collection to be complete, some types of data are less accurate than is desirable. Though the United States undoubtedly has the best economic statistics of any major country, even United States data are subject to inaccuracies which may appreciably weaken the forecasts based upon the data.

Since almost all important economic data originate in the federal government, these observations apply especially to federal statistics. The improvements suggested here cannot be obtained by exhortation nor, in general, by improvement in administration. Data collection is an expensive operation, and by and large an essential step is that Congress be persuaded to appropriate more generously for these unspectacular statistical activities.

For the purpose of improving the data currently collected and advancing the time of their availability, more funds are needed for the Office of Statistical Policy in the Bureau of the Budget, for the Bureau of the Census and the Office of Business Economics in the Department of Commerce, for the Bureau of Labor Statistics, and for units in other federal agencies which exercise parallel data-gathering and estimating functions. More money must be appropriated both for basic censuses and for the current operations of statistical agencies. Frequent complete censuses of industry and trade and frequent sample censuses of consumer income and expenditures are needed to furnish the bench marks to which intervening current estimates can be tied. Inadequately prepared surveys have to be redesigned, and additional monthly and even weekly series of important economic data need to be obtained and published promptly to permit

---

[24] To expedite the release of economic data, the Bureau of the Budget recently set up guidelines which lay down that the compilation of the principal monthly and quarterly series should be completed within 20 working days after the reference period, and that these figures should be released within the following 2 days. On this and other efforts which are currently being undertaken to

improve official statistics, see Julius Shiskin, "Strengthening Federal Statistics," *American Statistician*, vol. 24 (February 1970), pp. 15–20.

a more accurate appraisal of the current state of the economy. To refuse to finance these necessary improvements is a penny-wise and dollar-foolish policy.

2. Are There Ultimate Limitations on the Accuracy of Forecasting?

The general philosophic question remains to be asked whether, when all possible improvements in analysis and techniques have been made, the nature of human economic life sets ultimate limits to the possible accuracy of forecasting. To a believer in a mechanistic universe the answer is, "Absolute accuracy is conceptually possible." If cause begets effect, and if every effect is totally determined by antecedent causes, then our ability to precisely forecast the future is limited only by our understanding of the past and the present.

But some developments in the physical sciences place this rigid mechanistic theory in question. Heisenberg's principle of the indeterminacy of certain aspects of the behavior of physical matter is no longer useful in the physical sciences (if it ever was); but the theory which suggests that light consists neither of impulses of matter nor of ethereal waves, but of "wavicles," particles whose movement in space is in the nature of a "probability distribution" —this same theory may by extension suggest that even with omniscience a forecast of human action cannot be unqualified but instead can only be a statement of the degree of *probability* that human behavior (either of one individual or of a large number) will be within specified distances of a certain value. If the "probabilistic" rather than mechanical nature of scientific truth be granted, the ultimate limitations of forecasting need further philosophic analysis. But even if such conceptual limitations exist economic forecasting has not begun to approach them.

3. The "Feedback" Effect

One last difficulty which economic forecasting may encounter perhaps deserves discussion—the feedback effect.

In the early days of radio reception, when countless high-school boys were constructing their own receiving sets, an improved hookup, known (if my uncertain memory is correct) as a regenerative hookup, came into vogue. The electrical impulse coming from an amplifying tube was fed back into the tube so that the impulse was reamplified. One result of this feedback, however, was that if the set was tuned ever so slightly above or below the frequency of the broadcasting station being received, instead of being precisely on it, electrical impulses raced crazily through the circuit so as to produce a squeal or howl in the earphones, and in addition broadcast impulses which interfered with reception for blocks around.

Some persons fear similar effects from the feedback of economic forecasts into the economic system. Even if forecasting is otherwise entirely accurate, what will happen when consumers and business executives react to the forecast?

It should be noted that this effect will be of no concern when the millennium is reached—when the accuracy of forecasts is accepted by everyone, including legislators and administrators, and when corrective measures are at hand. For a forecast of an increase in unemployment of 5 million will then not be an unqualified forecast but a statement that unemployment will increase unless the government takes corrective action. And if corrective action is expected, and is expected to be effective, the forecast will not interfere with the public's expectation that prosperity will continue.

It is the effects of forecasting at a time when the announcement of a forecast does not bring the accompanying expectation that government can and will take effective stabilizing action which deserve consideration.

First, it should be noted that a forecast of prosperity cannot of itself sustain the prosperity. That is, if underlying economic conditions, correctly analyzed, indicate a recession, announcement that prosperity will continue will not preserve the prosperity even though the announcement is believed. A nation cannot normally "talk itself into prosperity." On the contrary, when depressions have occurred, it has typically been true that even though everyone had anticipated the continuance of prosperity there would not have been enough expenditures, in the aggregate, to sustain the prosperity.[25] Thus, the feedback effect is not in itself a cure for economic ills.

Nor is a correct forecast of depression apt to cause the depression to be deeper than if the forecast had not been made. If an unheralded recession occurs, and after a time the fall reaches a bottom and conditions level off at a depressed level, this implies that, at that level, aggregate output and aggregate demand are in balance. If instead of being unheralded the recession were announced in advance, such an announcement would be apt to do little more than cause the adjustments to the lower level of output to be made more promptly than would otherwise be the case.[26] The announcement, if the reaction to it were panicky, might of course cause the drop in activity to overshoot the mark and to bobble up and down before settling at the depression level.

[25] Admittedly, it is difficult to summon historical evidence to prove conclusively such an "iffy" statement, but I think almost all economists would agree that it is true.

[26] Whether such an acceleration of the onset of a depression would make its total duration longer than otherwise, or whether recovery as well as the recession would be advanced correspondingly, is a question too complex to be discussed here.

Whether or not an *incorrect* forecast of a depression could of itself cause one is a more difficult question. It is an economic axiom that a decline in output and income will ordinarily result in a smaller decline in expenditures. Therefore, if the underlying economic circumstances are such as to sustain prosperity, and if a $30 billion cut in output and income occurs because of an incorrect forecast that a recession is in prospect, aggregate demand will fall by less than $30 billion. As a result, at the lower level of output producers will find that demand is high enough to make an increase in output advantageous and the economy could spiral back up to full employment.

However, this is not necessarily always the case. For some of the expenditures which are sustaining prosperity may be due to plant expansion which is occurring because productive capacity is too small to serve the prosperity market. But if a bearish forecast causes a reduction in demand, this may cause cancellation of the plans for plant expansion and this, combined with the fall in consumer spending, may be sufficient to keep aggregate income and expenditures in the economic system at the depression level until such time as some fortuitous circumstance or some measure of public policy caused employment and output to rise again and thus caused the revival of the plans for expansion.

Though these undesirable feedback effects are possible, the possibility should not be given too much weight; the effect would occur only if the forecast were rather generally believed and in that case a strong demand for counteracting public action would immediately arise. This fact, however, indicates an opposite danger. An incorrect but generally believed forecast of depression, if it caused expansionary public action, could cause inflation; and an incorrect but generally believed forecast of inflation, it it caused the government to take deflationary (that is, counterinflationary) measures, could cause a depression.

The moral, of course, is that forecasting cannot be the basis for changes in stabilization measures, unless and until it attains an assured high degree of accuracy. If forecasting gains a *moderate* degree of accuracy, it may become the basis for a strong request by the President to the Congress for "stand-by powers," by which to throw measures into operation if the contingency which seems probable should arise. This seems a likely middle ground before forecasting gains a firmer status.

IV. CONCLUSION

So long as economic forecasting remains a highly imperfect instrument (and it may always remain so), no public body charged with the responsibility for forecasting can appropriately do more than make conditional statements about the future. Such statements might, for example, note potential demand in certain sectors of the economy and comment that under certain conditions this demand might come onto the market and cause inflation. Or under other circumstances the forces which are sustaining high employment might be indicated, and the probability noted that if certain of these forces decline serious unemployment will appear, unless public policies are formulated to meet the situation.

At certain junctures such a forecast might be a warning light, focusing the attention of the nation on critical problems. In the present stage of economic knowledge, however, the forecast would typically be so hedged about with qualifications that it would amount to little more than an analysis of the factors which affect economic activity and would partake only slightly of the nature of a prediction.

Perhaps, therefore, the main beneficial effect of well-informed conditional forecasts is to give legislators, administrators, business executives, and the public generally a better understanding of the operation of the economic system and therefore of the way in which economic circumstances may be controlled or influenced by public or private policies. An examination of leading business publications indicates how greatly that understanding has improved over the past three decades—but it also indicates how stubbornly certain ancient beliefs and prejudices die.

The annual *Economic Report of the President* to the Congress and the appended report by the Council of Economic Advisers to the President play an important part in this educational process. Besides their conditional forecasts, issued at the beginning of the calendar year, they provide a knowledgeable appraisal of the state of the economy and bring together a convenient collection of statistical data. If these reports receive the attention they deserve, their continued presentation will steadily improve the economic understanding of community leaders throughout the country.

Index of Names

(Italicized number indicates starting page of author's paper included in this volume)